PRAISE FOR *THE LIFE OF CHRIST*

Since all sanctification and perfection are contained in the life of the God-Man, Jesus Christ Our Lord, the better we get to know His life, the closer we will be to the sublime goal God had in mind when He created us. Ludolph's *Life of Christ* is a priceless companion to the Gospels and leads to that goal.

—DOM PIUS MARY NOONAN, OSB, Prior of Notre Dame Priory, Tasmania, author of *Fig Leaves Are Not Enough, Whilst It Is Day, The Grace to Desire It* and *Divine Providence and Human Freedom* (Cana Press)

This spiritual classic is addressed to all. It aims to be practical, rather than speculative, Wilmart, the famous Benedictine scholar, said, "It is no exaggeration to say that it is one of the most beautiful and learned works to have come to us from the Middle Ages... almost the whole of Patristic literature is included in it." Its holy Carthusian author—never canonised, because the Carthusians don't bother to keep a score of their saints—offers an historical vision of salvation, from Christ's going out from the Father to his final glory. Its popularity and influence is shown by the fact that by the late 19th century, it had already gone through something like sixty complete editions. May this translation continue the good work!

—FR. GILES GONACHER, OSB, Pluscarden Abbey

The Carthusian Ludolph's *Life of Christ* is not so much a biography of the Lord as a compendium of contemplative Christology. Saying even this does not do it justice. Influential across centuries, it was foundational in St. Ignatius of Loyola's conversion of life, and a strong influence on Ignatian spirituality, especially its particular method of meditation. The influence it could have in our day resides in those who would take time to read this fine modern edition of a classic of Christian spirituality.

—FR. HUGH SOMERVILLE KNAPMAN, OSB, author of *Ecumenism of Blood: Heavenly Hope for Earthly Communion* (Paulist Press)

I am thrilled that Ludolph the Carthusian's masterpiece *The Life of Christ* is available in this convenient Reader's Edition. *The Life of Christ* marked a breakthrough in pious imagination, zooming in on the details of the Gospel and bringing them to life. Ludolph claims no mystical insight but simply draws from the Fathers and Doctors of the Church to inform his reading of the sacred text. And by doing so, he went on to influence later saints such as Ignatius of Loyola, Teresa of Ávila, and Francis de Sales. Thanks to these two affordable volumes, he can influence us as well.

—MICHAEL P. FOLEY, Professor of Patristics at Baylor University and author of *Lost in Translation: Meditating on the Orations of the Traditional Roman Rite* (Angelico Press, 2023)

THE LIFE OF CHRIST

THE LIFE of CHRIST

VITA IESU CHRISTI

VOLUME 2 ❊ *READER'S EDITION*

LUDOLPH THE CARTHUSIAN

TRANSLATED BY VICTOR CAUCHI

AROUCA PRESS

Source material for Volume 2: Chapters I to XXX in this volume, now chapters 44 to 91 of this book, including an interlude of 18 sections about the Passion of Jesus, are culled and renumbered from Volume 3 of the translation into Spanish of *The Life of Our Adorable Redeemer Jesus*, by Ludolph of Saxony. Edition translated and supplemented by Fr. Antonio Rosello y Sureda. Imprenta de Juan R. Navarro, Editor, Calle de Chiquis, num 6, 1853.

Copyright © Arouca Press 2025
Translation © Victor Cauchi 2025

All rights reserved.
No part of this book may be reproduced or transmitted, in any form or by any means, without permission.

ISBN: 978-1-998492-14-5 (pbk)
ISBN: 978-1-998492-15-2 (hc)

Arouca Press
PO Box 55003
Bridgeport PO
Waterloo, ON N2J 0A5
Canada
www.aroucapress.com
Send inquiries to info@aroucapress.com

*To Marie Therese
and Rebekah*

CONTENTS

🙰 *Chapters 44 to 91 in this volume are culled from Volume 3 of the translation into Spanish of the Latin version of* The Life of Our Adorable Redeemer Jesus, *written by Ludolph of Saxony, a Carthusian monk. The edition has been considerably supplemented by Fr. Antonio Rosello y Sureda, an apostolic missionary priest, and illustrated with several notes by Juan Dadreo, Doctor of Theology at the university of Paris.*

CHAPTERS

44 JESUS CHRIST TALKS TO THE JEWS ABOUT HIS DIVINE MISSION, HIS ETERNITY, AND OTHER TRUTHS, AND THEY WANT TO STONE HIM (JN 8:12-29; 46-59). 3

45 JESUS HEALS A BLIND MAN FROM BIRTH, IS EXAMINED BY THE SCRIBES AND PHARISEES, AND THE SAVIOUR REBUKES THEM FOR THEIR INFIDELITY AND HARDNESS OF HEART (JN 9:1-41) 32

46 JESUS EXPLAINS TO THE SCRIBES AND PHARISEES WITH A PARABLE THE NATURE AND CHARACTERISTICS OF A GOOD SHEPHERD, AND SHOWS THE DIFFERENCE BETWEEN HIM AND THE DAY LABOURER (JN 10:1-16) 48

47 JESUS ATTENDS THE FEAST OF THE RENEWAL OR OF THE DEDICATION OF THE TEMPLE: HE DECLARES TO THE JEWS WHO HE IS AND THEY WANT AGAIN TO STONE HIM (JN 10:22-38) 61

48 THE SAVIOUR DEFENDS HIS DISCIPLES FROM THE SLANDER OF THE SCRIBES AND PHARISEES, AND CONDEMNS HUMAN TRADITIONS AND SUPERSTITIOUS PRACTICES WHICH DO NOT CONFORM WITH THE PRECEPTS OF RELIGION (MT 15:1-20) 71

49 THE LORD HEALS THE CANAANITE, A DEAF AND MUTE, AND WITH SEVEN LOAVES AND A FEW FISH FEEDS FOUR THOUSAND (MT 15:21-28; MK 7:31-37; 8:1-9) 83

50 JESUS COMMANDS HIS DISCIPLES TO BEWARE OF THE BAD YEAST; HE GIVES SIGHT TO A BLIND MAN ON THE ROAD TO BETHSAIDA; AND ARRIVING AT CAESAREA PHILIPPI, HE PRAISES AND REWARDS THE FAITH OF SAINT PETER AND ENCOURAGES HIS DISCIPLES TO FOLLOW HIM AND IMITATE THE EXAMPLES OF HIS PASSION (MT 16:13-19; 24-28). 101

51 THE TRANSFIGURATION OF JESUS ON MOUNT TABOR, IN WHICH HE SHOWS HIMSELF IN FULL GLORY TO THREE OF HIS DISCIPLES, AND THE NEXT DAY COMING DOWN FROM THE MOUNTAIN, HE HEALS A LUNATIC AND POSSESSED PERSON WHO THEY HAD NOT BEEN ABLE TO CURE SINCE THEY LACKED FAITH (MT 17:1-9; MK 9:16-28). 127

52 AS JESUS PASSED THROUGH GALILEE HE MAKES A CLEAR ANNOUNCEMENT TO HIS DISCIPLES ABOUT HIS PASSION, DEATH AND RESURRECTION: ON REACHING CAPERNAUM HE COMMANDED PETER TO PAY THE TAX OF TWO DRACHMAS, AND DEALS WITH THE DISPUTE OVER PRIMACY (MT 18:1–5) 153

53 JESUS FORBIDS HIS DISCIPLES FROM OPPOSING A MAN WHO WAS EXPELLING THE DEMONS IN HIS NAME, EVEN THOUGH HE WAS NOT ONE OF THEM; HE GIVES THEM LESSONS ON MODESTY AND HUMILITY AND COMMANDS THEM NOT TO SCANDALISE OR DESPISE THE LITTLE ONES, THREATENING WITH DREADFUL PUNISHMENT THOSE WHO DO SO; AND ENDS WITH SHOWING TO ALL HIS INFINITE MERCY WITH THE THREE PARABLES OF THE LOST SHEEP AND DRACHMA, AND OF THE PRODIGAL SON (MT 18:1–11; LK 15:1–32) . . 164

54 JESUS CHRIST TEACHES HOW TO CARRY OUT FRATERNAL CORRECTION: HE STATES ONE IS BOUND TO FORGIVE INSULTS UP TO SEVENTY FOR SEVEN TIMES, AND TELLS THE PARABLE OF THE KING WHO WANTED TO SETTLE ACCOUNTS WITH HIS SERVANTS (MT 18:15–25) 189

55 JESUS FULLY REPLIES TO THE TRICKY QUESTION PUT TO HIM BY THE PHARISEES WHEN ASKED ABOUT THE REASONS FOR REPUDIATION; PEOPLE PUT BEFORE HIM SOME LITTLE ONES TO BLESS THEM, AND HE TELLS ALL TO LET THEM COME CLOSE TO HIM; AFTER WHICH HE ANSWERS A YOUNG MAN'S QUESTION, HE TELLS WHAT POVERTY REALLY MEANS (MT 19:3–21) 205

56 ON THE TWELVE EVANGELICAL COUNCILS: ABOUT THE DIFFICULTY AND IMPOSSIBILITY OF THE RICH ENTERING THE KINGDOM OF HEAVEN, AND OF THE REWARD FOR THOSE WHO LEAVE EVERYTHING TO FOLLOW CHRIST (MT 19:27–29) 223

57 THE LANDOWNER TENDS TO HIS VINEYARD, AND GIVES EVERYONE AN EQUAL PAY; A RICH MAN ASKS FOR ACCOUNTS FROM HIS STEWARD, AND THE EVIL RICH MAN IS BURIED IN HELL, WHILE THE BEGGAR LAZARUS IS PLACED AMONG GOD'S FRIENDS (MT 20:1–16; LK 16:1–9; 19–31) 235

58 THE LORD RAISES LAZARUS FROM THE DEAD; THE TEMPLE PRIESTS AND PHARISEES CONSPIRE AGAINST HIM, AND CAIAPHAS MULLS OVER HIS DEATH (JN 11:1–45; 47–54) . . 271

59 THE LORD HEALS TEN LEPERS: THE SAMARITANS REFUSE TO RECEIVE HIM (LK 17:11–19) 291

60 JESUS RESPONDS TO A REQUEST MADE BY THE MOTHER OF ZEBEDEE'S CHILDREN; HE GIVES SIGHT TO A BLIND MAN BEFORE ENTERING JERICHO; HE THEN CALLS ZACCHAEUS, AND AS HE DEPARTS THE CITY HE GIVES SIGHT TO TWO OTHER BLIND MEN (MT 20:1; LK 18:1; LK 19:1) 299

61 JESUS IS RECEIVED BY MARTHA AND MARY IN THE FORTRESS TOWN OF BETHANY; AND BEING INVITED TO EAT AT THE HOUSE OF LAZARUS, THEIR BROTHER, MARY POURS OINTMENT OVER HIS HEAD (JN 12:1–12) 315

62 JESUS ENTERS TRIUMPHANTLY INTO JERUSALEM SITTING ON A DONKEY, AND ALTHOUGH WELL RECEIVED, HE THEN WEEPS OVER THE CITY, FOREBODING ITS RUIN (MT 21:1–9; LK 21:41–44) 324

63 JESUS HITS HARD FOR A SECOND TIME THOSE WHO BUY AND SELL IN THE TEMPLE ATRIUM: THE WIDOW THROWS TWO COPPER COINS INTO THE TEMPLE COLLECTION BOX, AND HE EXPLAINS THE PARABLE OF THE PHARISEE AND THE PUBLICAN (LK 19:45–47; LK 18:9–14; MT 21:10–17) 341

64 THE LORD CURSES A FIG TREE IN WHICH HE DOES NOT FIND ANY FRUIT; PARABLE OF THE GRAIN OF WHEAT, AND OF THE DETHRONING OF THE PRINCE OF THIS WORLD (JN 12:10–36) 354

65 DESCRIPTION OF JERUSALEM 368

66 JESUS CONFOUNDS THE SCRIBES AND PHARISEES ON ALL QUESTIONS THEY ASK HIM, AND TELLS THEM THE PARABLE OF THE LANDOWNER WHO PLANTED HIS VINE AND RENTED IT TO TENANT FARMERS WHO THEN KILLED THE LEGITIMATE HEIR (MT 21:33–46) 378

67 A RICH MAN INVITES SEVERAL PERSONS TO HIS SON'S WEDDING; SOME EXCUSE THEMSELVES AND MANY OTHERS REFUSE GOING TO THE WEDDING FEAST; A PERSON WHO SHOWS UP WITHOUT A WEDDING DRESS IS THROWN OUT; JESUS THEN SATISFACTORILY ANSWERS THE QUESTION PUT TO HIM ABOUT PAYING TAXES, AND ABOUT THE WOMAN WHO HAD SEVEN HUSBANDS, AND REPLIES TO THE PHAR-ISEE WHO WISHED TO KNOW WHICH WAS THE FIRST AND GREATEST COMMANDMENT OF THE LAW (LK 14:16–24; MT 22:1–21; 35–46). 392

68 JESUS CHRIST SAYS THAT ALTHOUGH THE DOCTRINE TEACH-INGS OF THE SCRIBES AND PHARISEES MUST BE ADHERED TO, THEIR WORKS SHOULD NOT BE IMITATED, AND WHO WILL RECEIVE JUDGMENT OF ETERNAL DAMNATION (MT 23:1–12; 34–39). 415

69 THE LORD FORETELLS THE SIGNS THAT WILL PRECEDE HIS LAST COMING AND THE PERSECUTION OF THE CENTURY: HE DECLARES THE COMING INTO THE WORLD AND THE PERSECUTION OF THE ANTICHRIST BY TELLING SEVERAL PAR-ABLES: HE WARNS HIS APOSTLES TO BE FOREWARNED, AND THEN ANNOUNCES TO THEM HIS APPEARANCE AS A JUDGE OF THE LIVING AND THE DEAD, AND WHAT WILL HAPPEN NEXT (MT 24:15–35; 3–13; 42–47; 1–13; MT 25:14–23; 31–46; LK 21:9–19; 25–33). 427

THE PASSION OF JESUS CHRIST BEGINS

70 A COUNCIL IS HELD IN JERUSALEM AGAINST JESUS CHRIST, AND IT IS DECIDED TO SEIZE HIM AND KILL HIM . . . 461

71 HE EATS IN BETHANY AT SIMON THE LEPER'S HOUSE, AND A WOMAN SPILLS OVER HIS HEAD A MOST FRAGRANT BALM 465

72 JUDAS AGREES WITH THE SCRIBES AND PHARISEES ON A SET PRICE WITH WHICH TO SELL HIS MASTER 468

73 JESUS CHRIST SENDS TWO OF HIS DISCIPLES TO JERUSALEM TO PREPARE ALL THAT IS NECESSARY TO CELEBRATE THE PASSOVER 471

74 HE SITS FOR THE CUSTOMARY DINNER WITH HIS APOSTLES, AND DECLARES THAT ONE OF THEM WAS ABOUT TO SELL HIM AND HAND HIM OVER 474

75 HE WASHES THE FEET OF HIS APOSTLES 478

76 EUCHARISTIC SUPPER, OR INSTITUTION OF THE BLESSED SACRAMENT OF THE EUCHARIST 482

77 CHRIST MAKES SEVERAL IMPORTANT THINGS CLEAR, AND MAKES FERVENT SUPPLICATIONS TO HIS ETERNAL FATHER 489

78 HE DEPARTS FROM THE CENACLE AND GOES TO THE GARDEN OF GETHSEMANE OR OF OLIVES 513

79 JESUS CHRIST IS CAUGHT IN THE GARDEN AND TAKEN TO PRISON 517

80 JESUS CHRIST IS PRESENTED TO ANNAS 526

81 JESUS CHRIST AT THE HOUSE OF CAIAPHAS, AND BEFORE THE COUNCIL OF THE ELDERS, SAINT PETER'S DENIAL . . . 530

82 JESUS CHRIST IS TAKEN TO PILATE, AND PILATE SENDS HIM TO HEROD. JUDAS REPENTS HIS ACTION AND HANGS HIMSELF 537

83 HEROD SENDS BACK THE SAVIOUR TO PILATE, WHO MAKES SOME EFFORTS, EVEN IF WEAK ONES, TO SAVE HIM. HE UNDERGOES A NEW INTERROGATION; IS WHIPPED, CROWNED WITH THORNS, DRESSED IN A PURPLE CLOAK AND RIDICULED, CONFRONTED WITH BARABBAS, AND FINALLY CONDEMNED TO A DISGRACEFUL DEATH ON THE CROSS 546

84 JESUS CHRIST IS LED OUT OF JERUSALEM CARRYING THE CROSS ON HIS BACK: WHILE CLIMBING TO CALVARY HE PROPHESIES THE RUIN OF THE UNGRATEFUL CITY, AND AFTER HE ARRIVES AT THE PLACE OF SUFFERING HE IS CRUCIFIED BETWEEN TWO THIEVES WHO ACCOMPANIED HIM 559

85 THE SAVIOUR IS NAILED TO THE CROSS, MOCKED AND INSULTED BY HIS ENEMIES; FROM THERE HE UTTERS SEVEN MYSTERIOUS WORDS, AFTER WHICH HE GIVES UP HIS SPIRIT INTO THE HANDS OF HIS ETERNAL FATHER 565

86 EXTRAORDINARY EVENTS WHICH OCCURRED ON THE DEATH OF JESUS CHRIST; JOSEPH ASKS PILATE FOR THE SAVIOUR'S BODY, WHICH LOWERED FROM THE CROSS IS DEPOSITED IN THE ARMS OF HIS MOST BLESSED MOTHER, AND THEN BURIED 580

87 THE SOUL JESUS CHRIST'S DESCENDS INTO THE DEPTHS TO COMFORT THAT OF THE RIGHTEOUS WHO AWAITED HIS HOLY ARRIVAL. 589

88 JESUS CHRIST RISES FROM THE DEAD, AND THE GUARDS OF THE TOMB FLEE FULL OF FEAR AND DREAD: HE APPEARS THE SAME DAY, FIRST TO HIS MOTHER, THEN TO MARY MAGDA- LENE, THEN TO THE PIOUS WOMEN, AND FINALLY TO THE DISCIPLES WHO WALKED ALL THE WAY FROM JERUSALEM TO EMMAUS (MT 28:1-7; MK 16:1-7; LK 24:13-35; JN 20:1-9; 11-18) 595

89 ON THE SAME DAY OF HIS TRIUMPHANT RESURRECTION THE SAVIOUR APPEARS TO HIS APOSTLES AFTER DUSK AS THEY WERE LOCKED IN THE CENACLE, BUT THOMAS WAS ABSENT: THE SAME THING HAPPENED EIGHT DAYS LATER AT THE SAME PLACE WHEN AGAIN THE DOORS WERE CLOSED, AS THOMAS WAS THERE WITH THEM (LK 24:36-47; JN 20:19-31) . . . 615

90 THE DISCIPLES GATHERED ON THE MOUNT DOING AS COM- MANDED BY JESUS CHRIST, AND THERE HE APPEARS TO THEM; AND THEN HE APPEARS AGAIN BEFORE THEM ON THE SHORES OF THE SEA OF TIBERIAS OR LAKE GENEZARETH (MT 28:16-20; JN 21:1-24) 624

91 JESUS CHRIST ALLOWS ALL HIS APOSTLES AND DISCIPLES TO SEE HIM FOR THE LAST TIME IN JERUSALEM, AND AFTER HAV- ING CONVERSED AND EATEN WITH THEM HE LEADS THEM TO BETHANY, WHERE BLESSING THEM HE ROSE MAJESTICALLY IN THEIR SIGHT AND WENT UP TO THE HEAVENS WITH HIS OWN VIRTUE AND POWER (MT 16:14-20). 638

ABOUT THE TRANSLATOR 653

THE LIFE of CHRIST

VITA IESU CHRISTI

VOLUME 2 ❖ *READER'S EDITION*

CHAPTER 44
JESUS CHRIST TALKS TO THE JEWS ABOUT HIS DIVINE MISSION, HIS ETERNITY, AND OTHER TRUTHS, AND THEY WANT TO STONE HIM (JN 8:12-29; 46-59)

HE Saviour had publicly confounded the accusers of the adulteress with an act of mercy which can only be found in divinity. This tallied fully with the very important mission given to him, namely the making out of a sinful woman a penitent woman, for which she was ever ready to make known the mercy of the Lord who had so admirably freed her. Several and countless were the intentions by which the treacherous Pharisees, who were unable to doubt Jesus Christ's divinity, had however expressed ungrateful surprise at the free bounty with which he forgave persons their sins, wondering among themselves, *Who is this who assumes the power to forgive sins?* And since on this occasion he had not only forgiven a sin within the inner self of conscience, but had in a way pardoned a criminal woman from a penalty sanctioned by law, it so had to be that the mortified pride of the scribes would raise its head with renewed fury against him, and that the attack they directed against him had to be much bolder and more violent in proportion to their great mortification and the bigger the crowd that followed Jesus Christ. The Pharisees' intention was to cause loss to the innocent, that of Jesus Christ was to save the guilty, so that in his eagerness to ensure their eternal happiness he continued teaching them.

It was very comforting for the Saviour to be always surrounded by people who wished to be taught the eternal truths which came out of his mouth, which Jesus Christ opened and said: *I am the light of the world.* It was as if he expressly wanted to tell them: "Do not believe that I am a light only for Judea, I am so for all the world; I have not come here to enlighten a single people or nation, but for all mankind coming into the world (Jn 1:9). I am the light that teaches what should be believed and what should be done; whoever follows me does not walk in the dark, but will have the light of life, the light of faith and of grace, which will lead him to the light of grace and eternal life; but whoever turns away from me does not see the light and walks towards eternal fire which gives no light."

Jesus Christ called himself light according to one and the other nature. In terms of divine nature he enlightens the soul; according to the human nature, he sheds light on the body and completely reforms it *with his miracles, with his preaching and with his examples.* The first belongs to *almightiness*, the second to *wisdom*, the third to *goodness*. It is him alone who is light by essence, while the others which appear to be light are only illuminated by it. As *Logos* or the *Word* he issues forth from the Father, like light comes out of light. He is the light of the world which comes out of the Father and is covered with the veil of the flesh; and it is thus that through this flesh divinity reaches mankind. Enlightening this light remains wholesome by drops of faith, for we are all born blind as children of Adam; so that whoever follows him obeying both his words and his examples, must believe, love and imitate one and the other, so as not to walk in the darkness of ignorance, for he is the truth; nor in that of guilt, for he is the way; nor in eternal condemnation, because he is life and has the light of eternal life because he has Christ, who is the wisdom of God, the unceasing and inextinguishable light, possessing him here by faith, and in paradise by the beatific vision. This difference is perfectly marked in the expressions uttered by the Saviour himself. He said, *whoever follows me*, and indicated all those belonging by merit, *will have the light of life*, and mentioned the prize. Thus he proved without shadow of doubt that he was the Messiah prefigured and announced a thousand times by the prophets with the metaphor of light, and that he was not only to convert Jacob and Israel, but that he had to be the light of all peoples.

Among the various characters with which Isaiah had announced the liberator of Israel, one of the most outstanding was that he would be the light of nations (Is 42:6). "I am the Lord, he said, I have called you for the love of righteousness, taken you by the hand and kept you; I have given you as a covenant to the people, *and a light to the nations*....

CHAPTER 44   5

It is little for you to serve me to restore the tribes of Jacob and convert the despised remains of Israel: behold, I have destined you to be a light to the nations, that my salvation may reach to the end of the earth (Is 49:6)." David had recounted to Israel the immense goodness of God and had told them: *In you is the fountain of life, and in your light do we see light*; that is, we will be enlightened by you and see the light of your divine face (Ps 35:10). The wise Solomon assured that the uncreated wisdom, which is the same Son of God, was like *a pure breathing of his glory and almighty clarity; so that nothing defiled enters it, for she is a reflection of eternal light, a spotless mirror of the Majesty of God and an image of his goodness* (Ws 7:25-26). Daniel, enlightened by God to dispel the mysterious dream to Nebuchadnezzar, had also said: *To Him belong wisdom and strength.... He changes times and seasons, removes kings and affirms them; gives wisdom to the wise and knowledge to those who have understanding; reveals deep and mysterious things, and knows those in the midst of darkness, for the light dwells with Him* (Dn 2:20-22). And finally, when Micah foretold the desolation of Jerusalem and the pride of Babylon for its triumph, he said to the latter in the name of the Holy City: "Do not rejoice or be arrogant over my ruins, I will rise again; and when I sit in darkness, the Lord shall be a light to me (Mi 7:8)."

The scribes and Pharisees, being wise and well versed in the knowledge of the Scriptures, could not ignore the many testimonies as were found in these writings; and while appearing on this occasion to be very ignorant, although among all listeners they were the most attentive since they were the most rigid censors, they interrupted the Lord from the very first words he uttered to argue with him and ask him to explain to them what they thought necessary. *You bear witness to yourself*, they told him, *and your testimony is not true*. They listened to the Saviour, but not to approve of his doctrine; they wanted to hear him, but not to taste and imbibe the eternal truths, but to find a chance to condemn his doctrine and person; for this reason Jesus Christ clothed himself with the authority given to him by his divine mission and by his holy and true doctrine, and he replied to them: *Although I bear witness to myself, my testimony is sufficient and true.* They knew well that it was only the obligation and need to instruct required Jesus Christ to speak about himself the way he spoke; that modesty and humility stood out and shone amid the splendour of his miracles; and comparing his actions with his words, one could see the truth of his actions supported by the holiness of his words, both being the cause for similar edification, since true virtues have their firm and determined character distinguishing them from hypocrisy, which is always lukewarm and irresolute when they require to be imitated. And he defends them with truth, justice and dignity from slanderous envy only when he is censored.

The assertion made by Jesus Christ could not be answered, but it was pronounced with such imposing authority that, after the scribes and Pharisees had been left out of breath to come out of the astonishment which had overwhelmed them, the Saviour continued his speech without waiting for their answer. "*I know very well to what I witness and others witness about me. I know where I come from and I where I am going.* I know that I am the Son of God and sent by my Father to teach and save the world, and I know that I will perform the great and important work of redemption. *Yet you do not know where I come from or where I am going*: you cannot know these things unless I tell you. Although I talk about things that belong to me, I am not for that any less worthy of faith, and the very place I come from must assure you that I am far from lying to you and much farther from self-flattery. It is true that men are very often deceived and that they deceive others servile to self-love, to whom they present things according to their taste; but I also know that at the place from where I come and to which I will go, no person exists who is subject to this miserable passion."

To make them aware how far was his thoughts were from their way of thinking, the Lord desired that after this teaching they came to know of the mysteries of the passion they were preparing for him and which until now they did not understand very clearly. For this reason I must tell you, that as God, he came down from heaven, that is, from the bosom of the Divine One, in whose mind was seated his heavenly and eternal origin, and that as a man, whose holy human nature he had joined in time to the Word of God, would go after his death and resurrection to sit at the right hand of God his Father, since this was the end of his mission. For this is what he referred to and truly meant when he said to them, *When you will raise*, lifting on the cross the Son of Man, that is, the Son of the Virgin according to the flesh, for according to her he must suffer, *then you will know*, that is, some of yours will know by faith, that *I am the true Christ*; that I am the hidden God under the veil of the flesh. I will postpone and lengthen your time of becoming aware so that my passion may be fulfilled. And Saint Augustine says that "It was agreed that it would be accomplished by the hands of those who were later due to believe. The Lord wanted this to happen in this manner so that no one may despair in finding oneself in the midst of wickedness or crime, great as it may be, when contemplating that the murder committed by those who took the life of Christ himself is generously forgiven."

There are three ways how we offend God and subdue and humiliate Him when we follow them, namely. They are evil thoughts, evil speech and evil deeds. When we repent and confess them and set them fully aside, we will then breed Him in the bosom of our hearts and in our souls by loving Him above all things, and we will know Him by adoring Him above all else. So if you want, dear Christian, to know and confess to God raising Him above all else, breed him by means of contrition against evil thoughts, by confession against evil speech, and by moral compensation, penance and mortification against bad deeds.

About certain Jews who then seemed to believe in him, he said very clearly: "*If you keep and remain in my words*, that is, if you will endure in faith to the end, without ever separating from my doctrines, so that through them I would have started to take a seat in your heart, then *you will truly be my disciples*." He said this because some of them believed falsely in him, and these were not true disciples. "Then you will know the truth which is right now covered with a veil of flesh and hidden from you; or otherwise, you will know the truth of the doctrine that I now teach and of the faith you are beginning to have. And the knowledge of this truth will make you perfectly free, because it will free you from the bondage of guilt as from this world, giving you the freedom of grace, which is the point where true freedom begins. In the coming century it will free you from enslavement, misery and eternal misfortune, and it will give you the freedom of glory where peace and the joy of true freedom are consummated and perfected."

Yet some, full of presumption and arrogance and the pride of fools, answered him saying, *We are descendants of Abraham, and we have never been anybody's slaves*; as if to say that they were free and were not in need of the holy freedom which the Lord offered them, pretending not to understand what he was teaching them clearly. They manifestly lacked the truth, since they had first suffered a dreadful slavery in Egypt, which they then suffered in Babylon, and in their own country too when they served the king of the Assyrians and under other nations, and lastly the Romans, to whom they paid a great amount of taxes. The Lord was not however speaking to them of the bodily slavery about which they understood, but he was telling them of another more dreadful and horrible one. So he told them: *I truly say to you that anyone who commits an offence and sin*, whatever his condition might be, whether he is a nobleman or a commoner, Greek or Jew, rich or poor, emperor or beggar, he is *the true slave of sin*. With reference to this Saint Chrysostom says: "Anyone following the will of the devil is his true slave, even if he is free. However he who obeys and serves God is the truly free man, even if he is a slave. Spiritual freedom is not enslaved with bodily enslavement, nor is spiritual slavery undone by bodily freedom, given that this slavery was only brought about by rebellion and poor aptitude of human will. Man was created free, but he soon became a slave." And St Augustine concludes: "The good man, even if he is a slave, is free; the bad man, even if he is king, is a slave; and not only of one man, but of as many men as are the vices that dominate them." And St Gregory adds: "He who stands by the witness of his own conscience is free in the midst of a crowd of accusers."

The Lord could not then tell them more clearly that he was the Son of God, that he was the true free One, and that in use of this sovereign and eternal freedom, which he had as the Son of God, he came to give his life for the true freedom of men, so that from slaves of sin they would become free children of God, bought and redeemed with the infinite price of his blood, from the eternal and dreadful slavery to which they were condemned as children of sin. And for this reason he adds: "You judge according to the passions of the flesh and according to what appears to the senses; but I do not judge anyone this way; and if I judge, my judgment is true, just, and not subject to being rejected; because I am not alone, but the Father who sent me is with me. This does not mean that presently I want to judge anybody, but if I did, know that my judgments would be led by justice and truth. The Father who has sent me cannot be rejected as a witness and my words, supported by his authority, deserve to be believed. The Father passed on to me his infinite power, his wisdom and eternal knowledge, and from the very first instant of my conception all the gifts of His grace were deposited in me, and so I am in my Father and He is with me. And if according to your law two or three witnesses are enough to believe a truth, my testimony and that of my Father must be accepted. I am the One who bears witness to myself, with my innocent life, my divine preaching and my miraculous works; and the Father who has sent me will bear witness to me in many ways." This was like telling them: "Examine your law since you consider yourselves its teachers and doctors, and see what it says about such an interesting point. It teaches you that a declaration is authentic and is received as conclusive proof when supported by the constant testimony of two or three witnesses. So be convinced and cease opposing the strength of my testimony. What I give of myself is true; but my Father who has sent me has also spoken for himself, and has authorised my testimony by his eternal authority. What else do you want?"

The Pharisees could no longer suppress and prevent the spirit of fury and vengeance which was filling them. On a thousand other occasions they had heard the Saviour say clearly and distinctly, that the Father about whom he was speaking to them was his Heavenly Father, God and Creator of all things; but just then, pretending to be ignoring him, they replied full of malice and said: *Where is your father?* Being perverse to the extreme, replete with imagination and duplicity, they wanted to force him to explain himself more clearly so that they might cull reasons from his reply, even though only apparent ones, for new slander. But as the Lord read what was in their hearts, he left them to be confused and mocked in all their malice and foolish hopes, answering them with a stern rebuke which they did not expect, and saying to them: "You neither know me nor do you know my Father. *If you knew me, you would have also known my Father*, assuming that I am in His image unless anyone is prevented by some evil passion like you to see me. So that, if you recognise me, insofar as you are able to do so, after the trials with which I have confirmed my testimony that I am Christ and sent by God as announced by his prophets, I would lead you easily to confess that God is my Father and that I am the Only Son of God. I would show you that one is a consequence of the other. But as long as you are stubborn about contesting my mission and contradicting my right to be believed, it would be useless for me to answer the question you are asking me. So it is necessary that you believe, first by virtue of the miracles made by me and on the witness of Scripture which foretells me and says that I am the Christ promised to your fathers, and in that case it may be that believe and I would let you know of my origin and my true greatness."

There is no doubt that on this occasion Jesus Christ manifested the incomparable greatness of his heart, since being pursued by an astounding crowd of listeners, most of whom were powerful and stubborn enemies, he rebuked them with a very extensive and holy freedom which could only conform with his sacred person. And although the Pharisees did not understand the method and order the Lord wanted to keep in his teaching, they did not desist from their wicked plans; for while the Saviour's teachings were full of moderation and peace, those of his people were full of sedition and struggle. Jesus Christ was respected and loved by the people for his mercy and justice, and yet the Pharisees could not destroy with a popular commotion the peaceful path which the Lord had taken. And so, they saw with disrespect and sorrow how the crowd of listeners followed him, at least if not to know perfectly what the revelation was all about, to place their full confidence in him who was the only One who had the authority to reveal it to them. For that reason they withdrew from before Jesus Christ with great rudeness, and interrupted and ended abruptly the important discussion he was having with them.

It is worth noting the place where this memorable event occurred. The Evangelist tells us: That Jesus Christ spoke these words in the Temple Treasury, or the collection box, *while teaching in the temple*; that is, at the front of a long gallery where the treasure was kept, which was located in the exterior foyer of the house of God, and this was very propitious due to its space, as it could hold a large crowd. Jesus Christ was the priceless and infinite treasure that all creatures should seek, and the Creator, who also knew the inestimable value of their souls and had come to buy and redeem them all with the precious and inestimable treasure of his blood. He spoke to the mob in the main hallway of earthly treasures, to make them know that these were most loathsome in comparison to heavenly treasures. Although they were Jesus Christ's main and vengeful enemies, none of them dared lay their hands on him; and though they did not love him, they respected him and feared his fiery zeal; his time had not come and so he lived among them with the same certainty as if he was living among his greatest friends and dear ones.

Majesty and greatness were inseparable from the Saviour's person, and they shone in all his actions and words. The debauchery of the Pharisees was stopped at his sight, the revulsion of the priests was silenced, the decisions of the scribes were put on hold, and, in short, all the fury of human passions were kept suspended and chained at the sight of the imposing attitude of him before whom all the powers of heaven and earth had to bend their knee, and all the beasts of the abyss were taken over by terror and dread; so that Jesus Christ walked away from the sight of his enemies, leaving them full of dread and fear. With the same majestic and grave attitude he let himself be also seen in the temple the next morning, and this was the last time he did this during his journey. It was Saturday and people went to the temple more than on other days. They gathered around those who were in that holy place, most of whom were Jews residing in Jerusalem, after the Galileans and other foreigners had already left, on Thursday and Friday after the Feast of the Tabernacles had ended. Witty as they had always been, but then more than ever, the scribes and Pharisees did not dare to appear in public to be acting openly against Jesus Christ; so they entrusted their attempts to a band of wicked men capable of fanning a tumult, by walking among the crowd and keeping him in their view waiting for the time when they could seize the chance.

Their ferocious pride had made them conceive of the idea that their presence hindered Jesus Christ from expressing himself with that frankness which very often causes vulgar men to forcefully slip into falls worthy of rebuke and perhaps even punishment; and this was another reason why in this case they hold back from going public. How deceived they were! Eternal wisdom had foreseen everything and nothing was hidden from his foresight of all that was going on in the hearts of those wicked men. As a result it is seen that several times during which Jesus Christ was going to preach, although the crowd was for the most part composed of simple people who were always willing to receive holy instruction, it did not lack a large number of spies, turbulent spirits and unruly persons who were ever ready to provoke a fuss against Jesus Christ, and at most with the purpose of keeping it going. Having made this important thing clear, it is easier now to understand the wonderful order of these speeches Jesus Christ made and why he apparently addressed these circumstances with such bitterness.

"I know all your intentions," the Saviour could have told them, "and nothing is hidden from me of all that you are plotting; but though I keep all this within me, I have discovered that I knew everything when I bluntly told them, *I am going away, and you will look for me, and you will die in your sin.* I am leaving, because the time is drawing near; I am the One who chose you, and all your efforts will be in vain before this time comes, you who long for it so much and which is much more desired by me. You consent to hear me, not to learn, or to be edified or to believe in me, but to have a chance to seize my life. But you should know that I walk to death by my own free will. I will die, not when you like, but when the time set by my Father comes. Stop looking for vague pretexts why I should die. In that hour I will go out to meet death. Then I will leave you and you will experience the sad effects of my absence. Then you will seek me, not out of love, but out of hate, not to find me and have me with you but to erase me from the memory of the living. But as much as you seek me, you will not find me. I will be far from you and you will die in your sin."

Saint Chrysostom and Saint Theophylact carefully seek the cause why Jesus Christ spoke to the Jews so often of his coming from heaven and of his returning there to the bosom of his Father, and they agreed that it was to instil fear in them since he knew of all the stubbornness and hardness of heart with which they were imbued. So that when he portrayed his Second Coming he said to them, "After the tribulation of those days, the sun would darken, the moon would not light up, and the stars will fall from the sky, and the powers of heaven will be shaken: then the sign of the Son of Man will appear coming on the clouds of heaven, at whose sight all the peoples of the earth will break out in tears. *And you will see the Son of Man come upon the clouds of heaven with great power and highness.* (Mt 24:29-30)." And then, when asked by the high priest and adjured by the living God to tell him if he was the Christ, the Son of God, he said, *You have said so, I am*, and he added, *I tell you, hereafter you will see the Son of Man seated at the right hand of the Majesty of God, coming on the clouds of heaven* (Mt 26:63-64). And we are already assured through Saint John that shortly before he had said to the Jews, "I will still be with you a short while, and then I go to the One who sent me. You will look for me and you will not find me, and where I shall go you cannot come." (Jn 8:20-21) Above all, Saint Augustine says: "Woe to the man who seeks Christ but dies in his sin, for how do you presume to attain salvation, if you detest the only One who could give it to you? The sinner today flees from Christ, and says: Tomorrow I will repent. So he today calls you and you say tomorrow? Who promises you that other day? Are you assured by the grace you presume to have in him? Christ does not threaten those who are attracted by him, even those who seek him when he does not want to be found. When does he want to let himself be found by you, only when he calls you? And if you do not take any notice of him when he calls, do you trust he will heed you when you look for him?"

He spoke clearly to them, if they understood him, that he went to heaven, and that they were not going there because they would die a stubborn death in their sin. Note that he did not tell them that *you will die in your sins*, but in your sin which was one, that of *infidelity*, and for which he rebuked them more terribly and harshly. What he had said to his disciples on another occasion, announcing to them a delay in giving them the reward he had promised them and which he was preparing for them in his Father's house, was a prophecy for the Jews of their eternal condemnation. They closed their way to go to the Father, which means having true faith in Jesus Christ. If they lost this faith, no other way was open to them; but they despised what the Lord was saying to them, closed their eyes not to see light, and became ever more worthy of their righteousness and vengeance. Christ came to be the way of men, leading all to the promised glory through the narrow path which he had trailed for himself and for all. And what is this path if not the escape of delight, hatred for the world and the denial of one's will? He who does not deny himself never walks with Christ nor goes to him.

These threats were undoubtedly cruel, appalling and terrible; but they were the punishment for malice, envy, and the ambition and harshness of Judaism. The inhabitants of Jerusalem, who were not involved in the conspiracy plotted by the Pharisees against Jesus Christ, and whose heart was not yet perverted by their cunning and malice, almost understood nothing of the words uttered by the Saviour. So they asked each other and said: *By chance, has he thought of the idea of killing himself, because he is saying: where I shall go you cannot come?* Oh! that we certainly do not want to take his life, let alone wish him any harm. But the majority of spies, of bribed persons and sceptics who are present, could not give the same witness as for themselves, and clearly knew that their conspiracy had been uncovered. Yet still wanting to appear very simple and faithful, like credulous people, some of them repeated the same question with refined and cunning hypocrisy; being unaware that if as wise men and experts they interpreted the Lord's words attributing them to the temporal death in which others simply believed, they too could go wherever the Saviour went, for if his words were to mean, or truly meant in their real sense, suicide they too could make them work for their own benefit. The author of life, he who had come to give it up for all, and who to justify what was important and holy in his mission raised the dead in the sight of such a huge crowd and restored their bodily life to them, he who cast demons out of men's bodies and forgave sins giving spiritual life to souls, could neither speak nor commit a crime as horrendous as suicide. And so it was that to promptly reject and demolish the idea of simple persons and the concurrence of the wicked, he continued his fervent speech telling them: *You are from here below, I am from above*. Which was the same like telling them: You spoke as what you are, like living and earthly persons with no wings to fly to heaven nor taste to savour the invisible delicacy.

Knowing of the proud and haughty character of the Pharisees, they certainly did not admire Jesus Christ who was seeking to humiliate them with such forceful condemnation. Yet they, who never suspected that he was reading their mind, proceeded with their wicked thoughts, disregarding the Saviour's loving words. So that, looking at them with compassionate eyes and truly wishing to get them out of the infidelity and error in which they were, he continued his speech saying to them: "I have already told you with full awareness that you will die in your sin; for if you do not believe in my words when I say to you and prove to you who I am, death will surprise you in your stubbornness. And following wrong and opposite sayings to what I am telling you such as those of the world, you must definitely be unrepentant. For this disbelief, which is the origin of the atrocious crimes you pondered upon, cannot be but followed by lack of repentance, and consequently an unhappy death. Yet if it were replaced by belief and faith, its consequence would be blissful penance, and its crown would be heaven, where I keep my treasure, and as a reward a kingdom of eternal happiness and bliss."

Little or nothing did Jesus Christ's threat, or the hope of the reward he had just promised, move the hardened heart of the Pharisees, but showing themselves seemingly colder and more undecided than ever before, they asked him: *Who are you?* And Jesus Christ answered them, "*I am the beginning who is speaking to you*; that is, the beginning of all justice. I am the aim and author of the perfect cult announced and promised from the beginning of the world. I am the author of a new century, of which all the past centuries have done none other but prepare for its birth and to proclaim and figure out its wonders. I am the firstborn of all the dead and the prince of all the kings of the earth. I am equal to the Father in divinity and less than that in humanity. If I were in the Father, as I was from the beginning, and I would not have taken flesh to speak to men, how would the weak believe in me, in whose heart faith enters by hearing? No man will be pleasing to God until he unites with me, as a member of the same body, under one head, from which all receive action, life, and movement. I am therefore what I have told you since I began to speak to you or from the beginning of my preaching: I am your Messiah, the promised Christ, the Anointed One of the Lord."

In truth, from the beginning of his preaching this had been Jesus Christ's constant doctrine, having been confirmed with a thousand signs and miracles, and wanting to be received and known with this same character. So that being content with discovering their great blindness and persistence in not believing what he taught them, even though they had great help and not a few reasons to give him credit, he did not repeat to them anything else but what he had heard from Him who had sent him. And for this reason he added: "*Many things I still have to tell you and in many things I still have to judge you.* In this judgment you will be resented by the same truth at which you now look with so much dislike. In this judgment you will be judged and condemned without you being able to repeat anything, because there judgment is not based on uncertain speculation: He who has sent me to you is faithful and truthful. He cannot be unfaithful to me, and speaking about what I heard, I cannot lie. I do not say anything to anyone, other than what I have heard so that I always teach the truth." But since the Saviour was talking to disbelievers and stubborn persons, he knew that they closed their eyes and ears willingly so that they might not be aware of who he was.

We have already said here before that the Lord, in order to justify all that he had told them and to prove that he had been sent by God his Father, he told them that when they would lift or raise the Son of Man from the ground nailed to the wood of the cross, then the same disbelievers would know who he was. And indeed, scarcely had the Crucified One given his last breath upon this theatre of horror and disgrace, when those who had led him to it, with loud voices and seditious cries, started beating their breasts, crying and saying in admiration: *Truly that this man was the Son of God.* Only Jesus Christ was entitled to attract signs of this nature. For men the torture of death will come to an end, like all the honour they acquired in the world; but for the Son of God and his disciples they will find in it the beginning and end of their glory.

They did not understand Jesus Christ's language, for so terrible a judgment is voluntary blindness! Yet even if the most stubborn did not understand at that very point what the Saviour was telling them, and that being raised on the cross would cause him the deepest dejection, for many it was also a true illustration of his greatness. Yet comparing some of those who heard his doctrine and wisdom, they were so impressed with his holiness and miracles that they believed in him. Although they confessed their faith, it was still weak and small, and Jesus Christ, who knew their weakness well, was foreseeing their scandal. So, adding links to the chain he was forming, he told those in whom he recognised these passing actions of piety and zeal: "If you firmly persevere in the doctrine I preach to you, you will truly be my disciples, and little by little you will be able to receive more perfect teaching. Mysteries will become even more clear for you, and you will become more and more aware that nothing I have told is untruthful. The which you accept will make you come out of slavery and you will admire the freedom you enjoy."

We have also said that Jesus Christ spoke on this occasion of the freedom of the soul enslaved by sin whose chains, together with the observance of the Law, rupture faith in the Son of God. The Jews, however, who had ill feelings towards the Lord and listened to him with evil intent, explained his words in a detestable manner and in their scheming succeeded to create some sparks whose fire was instantly kindled throughout the rest of the conversation. And so they answered back the Lord, that as children of Abraham they enjoyed perfect freedom, not wanting to understand that all humans, both Jews and Gentiles, are servants of sin and death when they persevere and live in sin. But Jesus Christ made them see that an opposing concept existed between his Father and that of the Jews, and the clarity with which he told them that his works were not worthy of the children of Abraham aroused such a violent tumult among his listeners that even if the Lord had not vested him with his omnipotence, matters could have become dangerous for his person. So that soon enough he further told them: *"If you are Abraham's children, do works worthy of your father.* All your effort reduces itself to desiring to kill me, even though I preach to you nothing but the truth I have learned from God. Abraham, of whom you rejoice being his descendants, never thought like you. He firmly believed in God's promises, and I teach his children to believe them for only in this way would they be the chosen children of his people, the children of God, and His eternal legacy."

They shuddered on hearing these truths and they were very hard to believe the real and true difference between Abraham's sons, according to the spirit, and those who were only according to the flesh. They could not understand that the sons of the spirit could ever take the place of those who were sons of the flesh, despite the privilege of the Law. And for this reason they were neither prepared to receive, with the intimacy of their Father's faith, the freedom given by the grace of the mediator, nor the new cult he had come to establish on earth. They figured out their greatest glory to be found in calling themselves sons of Abraham and Moses, that is, *sons of God*, while they despised God's envoy when he taught them the important truths. So this is what forced the Lord to say to them: "*If God were your Father, you would certainly love me; for from God I proceed and from him I come; He sent me and on his behalf I speak to you*. So where does it come from that you do not approve my words and that your eyes cannot bear my light? With your stubbornness my voice undoubtedly falls on deaf ears. Such stubbornness cannot come from elsewhere but the devil, with whom you have no problem to declare him your brother, following his wicked designs. He is the first liar and the first murderer, for he made men die by giving death to the first of them all. By his evil and bloody suggestions the first death in the world was brought about. He grew up in the light of faith, but preferred the lie to the truth; so that we must not be surprised when he tells lies, for this is his job; to be the father of lies, deceit and sin, causing death." Saint Augustine says about this: "Do not believe that you do not commit a murder when you give bad advice to your brother and induce him to commit guilt and sin; and that you may know well that you kill him, hear you what the Psalmist (Ps 56:5) has to say: Spears and arrows are the teeth of the sons of men, and their tongue sharp swords, ready to give death."

The devil did not remain in truth or in the works of righteousness, for he denied obedience to God; and he who does not obey is neither truthful nor faithful. As God is the Father and author of the truth, so the devil is the father and author of lies and of death; for before he existed neither one nor the other existed, and for him every man is a liar. He did not tell anything to the first man that was not a grave lie: *You will be like gods, you will know good and evil, you will not die*: man gave him credit and put more faith in him than in God, and for this he became miserable, condemned himself to death and to all the misfortunes and hardships of life. He became no less an imitator than the son of the devil, and justified himself as being in irreconcilable enmity in confessing the truths which the Lord teaches him. This allowed for a time and place when the Saviour could terribly challenge the scribes and Pharisees, so that as if to justify himself he said to them: *Who among you can convince me of the slightest offence!* What he was in truth telling them: "You want to kill me; then justify a sin that makes me worthy and deserving of death, and if you cannot find it in me, do know that your righteousness would be seen through clearly, as you seek to condemn me although I am innocent."

It deserves to be contemplated, St Gregory says, and to examine well the meekness of the Son of God who had come into the world to forgive the sins of man. And yet he did not dismiss by showing with reasons and arguments that he is not a sinner, but that there dwelt in him the virtue of divinity to justify sinners. What amazement! He carried upon himself the pains and troubles of a miserable human condition; he chose poverty and he did not absolve himself from the opinion and appearance of ignorance in which he was held by some; but he did not want to suffer the imputation of being a sinner with which he was being accused. They charged him with breaking the Sabbath and he was accused of being a wine bibber; and on hearing such slander, he publicly challenged his evil accusers and invited them to convince him of only one of the crimes with which they were dishonouring him. Yet who could convince them of the slightest fault! And seeing that everyone at his first onslaught had been reduced to a shameful silence, he further said to them, "*If I speak to you of the truth*; if you do not really find in me anything to rebuke; if equally my works and laws could not be condemned, and if with the most convincing witness, and with miracles that you cannot deny I show you to be true as I preach and teach you, why do you not believe what I say to you, namely, that I am not a sinner like others and that I am the Son of God? If you had ever convinced me of being a liar or that you had caught me in some fault, I would apologise to you for your distrust in me; but it is not so, your disbelief is not concealed. Oh! You really prove well what you are. What right or title can you give yourselves to be believed!"

The truth had always been, undoubtedly, the maxim of the prophets sent by God to His people, and each time Judah's hapless sons were more stubborn than ever, not wanting to believe them and being pleased to insult, stone and kill them. For this reason it seems that the Saviour wanted to summarise in this dialogue all that had once been told to them through the mouth of Jeremiah (Jer 26:15), "'Only know for certain that if you put me to death, you will bring innocent blood upon yourselves and upon this city and its inhabitants, for *in truth* the Lord sent me to you to speak all these words in your ears.' And again in Jn 14:6 'I am that *infallible truth* which makes the servants free,' the only One who can deliver them from deception and error. For only the Son of God is the One who can break the chain with which the devil's children are tied up. However, you do not hear this truth because you are not of God; you do not have the divine Spirit as a teacher. For swollen with your pride and being corrupt with your customs, you do not take care of things other than those of the earth, and this is the clear and manifest sign that you are not his sons. He who is a son of God not only by nature but by faith, not by confession of the mouth which is many times sterile, but by the love and conformity of the will; that is, he who hears the words of God, not only with the ears of the body but with those of the soul, hears them freely and gladly. He bows to them and carries around love, and each one hears with pleasure the doctrines of Him to whom he confesses fondness, for hearing of these words then becomes very conforming and natural. He who has neither faith nor love, like the Jews, could not hear the words of God."

With these words and doctrine of Jesus Christ, everyone can know and test his conscience to see whether he is a son of God or not. Whoever hears with pleasure God's voice commanding him to sigh for the eternal and blissful homeland, ought not to covet that which does not belong to him, but distribute his property to the poor, despise worldly glories, work incessantly to attain what is eternal, and perform such other good deeds. Whosoever not only hears all this, but fulfils it with joy, is undoubtedly a son of God. But he who is stubborn and hard of heart despises hearing the word of God, or hears it only with the ears of the body, and in no way does he obey or fulfil what he is commanded to do, and so he is not a son of God. And these were the persons against whom the Lord said that those who do not listen or want to hear, give the most ample public sign that they are not of God. This is the devil's suggestion and it is accomplished by man's own ill will. We are sons of the devil, not by creation, but because we imitate him. And this is what St Augustine had to say about this: "You are not of God, you do not walk in the path of nature, but in that of vice, because the sons of God move by the way of nature, and not by the vice of ill inclination and warped affections."

It was one of the most heinous insults for the Jews to be told that they were not sons of God. It was like hurting them with a double edged sword, and in the most sensitive and delicate part they could have. It was like hurting them in what was most precious in their honour, for they attributed themselves this glorious title to the exclusion of all the peoples of the world. Their vanity and pride was so high in this regard, that they boasted that other nations had none other but sons of men. They confronted all of them, while vainly listing the benefits God had granted them from the instant He segregated them from the other peoples of the earth, calling only them to be His people. They were complacent in remembering how the Lord had freed them from the land of Egypt among hundreds of signs and miracles, until they entered the land which they now inhabited. And above all, they were filled with vanity and pride when they reminded the Gentiles of the humiliations and misfortunes, the blood, horrors and deaths with which God had punished those who were opposed to their onward march to occupy that land, which He had promised by oath to their forefathers. For this reason, when they heard that the Lord told them that they were sons of God, they wanted to rise violently against Jesus Christ saying to him: "It is not without reason that we declare ourselves openly against you, firmly convinced that you are a true Samaritan, that is, *an apostate of the Law of Moses*. This is exactly what you are, and it is undeniable that you are possessed by the devil, for well enough now there has never been such a declared enemy of the Jews who dared to contest their title of sons of God."

They called him a Samaritan out of contempt for his person, and devilish to discredit his doctrine, adding that they were not treating him in such manner out of spite or envy, but out of sheer love for the truth. It is frenzy of the stubborn heart to pay with insults and slander the zeal of he who wanted to cure them, and much more when this is done unhesitatingly or with no remorse of conscience, if the sick man believes that the blindness and error lay with the doctor.

The Jews were satisfied with Jesus Christ's doctrines that they were not sons of God or Abraham according to the spirit, but rather of the devil; and not being able to contradict these true assertions with true works and doctrines, they contradicted them with insults and took cover in slander, since they could not protect their chests with the shield of truth. Contradicting the Lord, they called him a Samaritan and being possessed by the devil, even though they knew well that Jesus Christ was a Jew and not a Samaritan. They gave him this title because the Samaritans were the Jews' most cruel enemies, and as such most hated by them. According to their reckoning, the Samaritans observed a part of the Law of Moses and broke it in another; and since the Jews constantly accused Jesus Christ of breaking the Sabbath law, they did not for this reason refuse to call him a Samaritan. As the Jews saw matters the Samaritans were public sinners, and as they watched the frequency and familiarity with which the Saviour ate and conversed with the publicans and sinners, this was another reason why they fundamentally believed that they could call him a Samaritan. Such a miserable state leads men to hatred, ill will and lack of reason when those who ought to respect and venerate their neighbour strive most to belittle him!

Jesus Christ answered the Jews quietly, without sting and remorse, and said, *I am not possessed of the devil*. It was like telling them: "It is not his language that I speak to you, nor his works those which I perform. You do not understand the care and gentleness with which I speak to you, despite the hardness of your heart. And if I ever speak to you with a more ardent zeal than you desire, you should know that this is not the fury of an evil spirit, but an effect of the living desire with which I seek your salvation. I honour my Father, something which neither the devil nor those who are ruled by him do; but as for you, since I honour my Father, who wants from now on all men to follow a spiritual cult founded on the person of his Son, since I preach a Gospel which makes no temporal distinction between you and the nations, you have dishonoured me in the sight of all the sons of Israel. I do not complain about your injustices, I do not seek my glory; I abandon all in the hands of my Father who judges your opinions and avenges your contempt." What an admirable example of patience and suffering we must imitate, that which the sweet Jesus Christ gave us on this occasion. As Saint Augustine exclaims: "From patience we learn patience, and since nothing does man desire as much as power, Christ has to be that same power; we should the more imitate his patience to come to his power. He disregarded personal slander, which was undetermined and vague, and only tried to disprove the insult which would discredit his mission. For this reason he abandons his glory in the hands of his Father, for He alone is the One who can glorify him, with that glory he had in the bosom of his own Father before the world was made." The Lord expressly condemned on this occasion all those who seek their own glory before that of God, and who place in it all their future hopes, forgetting eternal glory and happiness.

To manifest that this was one of the truest and most important subjects with which he was dealing in the lesson he was giving to the Jews, he told them further: *In truth I tell you, whoever keeps my doctrine will never see death.* Which really meant telling them: Your true interests are the ones I seek, and it depends on you to achieve them. You can still be happy, I assure you again and again, that *Whoever hears my word and obeys my precepts at the right time will not die eternally.* It seems that the Saviour wanted to calm down and soften with this pleasant promise the terrible threats he had previously made to them. But the Jews, who although being instructed that true righteousness freed them from eternal death, despised this as an effect of the actual perversity of their heart, and while also mocking the Saviour's promises and threats, they twisted them in a rude sense, interpreted them as meaning bodily death, and retorted to the point saying: *Now we know better than ever that you are possessed by the devil. Abraham died, so did the prophets; and you dare say that whoever keeps your commandments will never die? Are you by any chance more holy and more powerful than our father Abraham, and better than all the prophets, whom God did not free from death?* If you have overcome all these, do tell us for the sake of your life, by whose power have you done this?

It was only the treacherous Jews who treated as proud he who is meek and humble in heart, and who has told us that he wants us to learn from him this meekness and humility. They blamed him in the face that he boasted being what he was not or much more than he really was. This question was undoubtedly a mysterious one, even if the same people making it did not know the mystery; they had reason to ask him who he was seeing him so dejected, so humble and so despised of all. He was a king, and an immortal king of the centuries; prince of all kings on earth; strength, power, and wisdom of the Father; and yet so much greatness and power, so much grandeur and glory were hidden under the veil of our mortality. They had reason to ask him who he was, for the idea that they had formed of Christ on Abraham's faith and on the portrait he drew of the prophets, placed him in a much higher position than he had to be seen among men and above all the holiness with which the prophets had flourished. Yet since their intention was to force Jesus Christ to say that he was the Son of God and equal to God, to take an opportunity of scandal and a cause for persecution from his answer although he did not answer them with the same words, he explained himself in the same sense and clearly manifested his origin from the Father, and that he and his Father were the same person, that they knew each other, and that he not only gloried in confessing it, but also in fulfilling all his decisions. And so he told them: "*If I glorify myself*, that is precisely as a man, if I stand before men to deserve such human glory from them, I would pretend very little consideration for a certain thing and my glory would not be worth anything. My Father is the One who gives me glory, and He is the same One whom you call your God. You say that he is your God and you have never known Him perfectly: it is good to know, because neither to me has he revealed nor to any other person the secrets hidden intimately within the heart of the Divinity. You do not want to hear or understand what He wants to reveal to you through His Son." St Augustine says that "This is why Christ calls Him his Father, him whom the Jews called their God but did not know Him, for if they knew him they would have received and believed in his Son." This pitiful blindness has been inherited from the Jews by all those who falsely boast of knowing God, while not knowing the Father of our Lord and Redeemer Jesus Christ.

"*But I know him. And if I said I do not know him, I would be a liar like you.* I know my Father and he has revealed all his plans to me. I know his will and I could neither exaggerate nor hide anything. I know God and I am the first to know Him the way He wants me to make Him known to you, and I do not leave out anything from His most holy will." What a sublime witness! He comes to know of this confession and does not fear to seem boastful for not falling into the ploy of being a liar. Council comes about this from Saint Augustine, whom we mentioned before, namely *That the truth should not be abandoned for fear of arrogance to which his confession is exposed.*

Jesus Christ's doctrine about the new worship which patriarchs and prophets had foreseen, about the divine revelation to be introduced into the world by the promised Messiah, was extended beyond what the Pharisees wanted. The nation, which day by day grew ever ruder, substituted for this cult the restoration of the Law to its former perfect state, along with a temporal prosperity and an extension of control far superior to the prerogatives in the same line that had distinguished their elders. On this influential point the sons degenerated from the belief of their parents. It was not possible to attract them to it, and the Gentiles, made true sons of Abraham by imitating their faith, replaced the sons of that patriarch according to the flesh. And so he continued telling them, *Your father Abraham eagerly wished to see my day; he saw it and he rejoiced.* This was a noble witness given about Abraham by Jesus Christ who was his descendant and was bred in his faith. That patriarch believed in the promise of the Lord and led a life eagerly waiting for the joyful day, ever hopeful of universal redemption. With faith he saw this day, not only when Isaac, who was the son of the promise, was born to him but even to the day when in his sacrifice he saw a vivid image of the Saviour's death. The faith also showed him that other day, without either end or beginning, which is uncovered with ineffable light before the eyes of the heart of the eternal Word of uncreated wisdom, the light from light, the arm of God determined to unite with human nature without departing from the Father's sight. With all this it seems that Jesus Christ wanted to tell the Jews: "All your trust lies in your seed of Abraham; but this great patriarch does not recognise you, but rather denies that you are his sons. I ardently desire to see the day of my coming into this world and establishing my reign. He actually saw it and was filled with joy. You have the same joy and do not take advantage of it."

The instant Jesus Christ had just pronounced these words. not believing that Abraham could have seen a man who was born so many centuries after him, and on the other hand not actually knowing the Saviour's age for his work and fasts made him look older than he was, they said to him as if to mock what they had just heard: *You are not yet fifty years old and you want to make us believe that you have seen Abraham?* Such was the blind disbelief of the Pharisees of the clear and express truth which the Saviour had just spoken. But this unjust counterclaim was entirely dispelled by Jesus Christ's humble response. What he had told them referred to his person's divinity, while they understood he was speaking about age related to time reckoned from birth. Yet it should be noted that Christ did not tell them that he had seen Abraham, but was referring this to him; and not that he saw him, but that he wished to see him; and not him, but his day. All this early vision fit into Abraham's prophetic spirit, to whom by public testimony of Scripture, God must have promised him very clearly that the Messiah was to be born from his seed, in whom all the nations of the earth would be blessed. And the Lord continued saying, *Truly I say unto you that I existed before Abraham came into the world*, for he was God from eternity. Speaking as he did, no prerogative had been attributed that was not linked to the eternal pre-existence of his divine person; which ought not to have been ignored by the scribes, as was written by their father David in the Book of Psalms (Ps 89:2): "Lord, you have been our dwelling place in all generations! Before you made the mountains or the earth and the world were formed, from an everlasting age to all eternity you were and will be God." However, when they heard that he had existed before Abraham and the world, they were so enraged, and their anger grew to such an extent believing this assertion to be a great blasphemy, that they took stones to pelt the Saviour.

If on a thousand occasions the blind fury of Judaism was also uncovered very clearly, this was one of them. For the more convenient it was for them to show that they were well grounded in the knowledge of Holy Scripture and that they did not miss anything written therein concerning the coming of the Messiah and all the characteristics of his person, the more did they show, with their conduct and sayings, that they ignored him and did not acknowledge him. Their obsession was ultimately so great that nobody knew the work and strength of the same words uttered by Jesus Christ. He did not tell them I was created before Abraham, but *it is me*, since in the beginning, that is in eternity, *he was the Word*, by which all things were made. Here he bears a new testimony of his divinity, according to what he said to them before, *From the beginning it is me*. The same thing from whose mouth Moses had heard before: "I am who I am. Although you see me made the last of all men because of the discouragement to which your envy and evil nature reduce me, I am the first because of the union of my human nature with the person of the Word, and also because all that which has been created depends on me." For he is the beginning of God's ways, the aim and fulfilment of all his designs (Apoc. 22:13). "My words, my works, all that is seen in me is making it known that I am the Only Son of God, the Word of the Father, the eternal beginning of all things. Woe to whoever does not know me, either as to myself or to my doctrine!" Thus spoke the man who works in eternal truth, so those who could not resist the wisdom of which he spoke fetched stones with which to pelt him. As they could not rationally contradict him with words, those with the hardest heart of all turned to hard and insensitive stones to contradict him, wanting to wound and chase him physically. Those who could not oppress him with reason wanted to ill-treat him with stones. The hardness of the arms on which they laid their hands was a clear indication of the hardness of their heart, and was in perfect harmony with what on another thousand occasions they had shown. Perhaps it was to predict this same hardness that the Lord had given them his commandments written on stone tablets.

Saint Augustine is astonished at the sight of such stubbornness and hardness, and asks where were the Jews going and heading, other than to show to all the world who were the ones who resembled most and were like stones. Yet the Lord, who just with one word could overcome and take revenge on them, did not in any way want to do so, having come to suffer and seeking to tame and defeat his enemies, not with power, but with humility. It is for this reason that he went into hiding as a man and as a humble person, and left the temple while handing over to his own and teaching patience to all in this manner, without using any power at all. He went into hiding, not because he feared death or due to lack of power to resist, but to yield and let his persecutors' fury pass, until the time of his passion arrived; teaching us to flee for some time and avoid the fury of enemies, and so he *left the temple* indicating that he abandoned the Jews, and passed on or over to the Gentiles.

It should be noted that sometimes the Lord fled, at others he went to meet his enemies, and still at others he went into hiding. He fled when they prepared honours for him, when they cried out and celebrated him, as it happened when they wanted to proclaim him king. He went to meet his persecutors, as it happened when those who spoke of crucifying him were capturing him in the Garden of Olives. And went into hiding from the enraged Jews, as it happened, when they wanted to push him down from the top of the mountain and on that occasion wanted to stone him. With these three examples the Lord gives us three most helpful pieces of evidence. Namely, that we should flee from all success and honours which the world affords us; that we should desire to suffer affliction and anguish for he who suffered so much for us; and that we should flee and avoid all litigation and strife in which we would naturally lose patience and charity. Let us now consider, as Saint Gregory tells us, about Jesus Christ's meekness and humility, who, although being able through his omnipotent power to annihilate with sudden death all his persecutors, hid himself away with fear and humility from their presence. He did this to give us three other important and noble teachings. Namely, that the time of his passion and death had not yet come; that he had not chosen that kind of death to which his enemies condemned him by sedition; and that we may learn to flee persecutions when they are of a personal nature, according to what he himself had said on another occasion to his apostles and disciples: "When they persecute you in a city, flee to the other." But when the persecution is not personal, it is unlawful for the prelate to flee, as the Lord manifested in the parable of the hireling and the shepherd. He hid from their physical eyes, for they neither deserved seeing him with those of the spirit. The truth is hidden from unbelievers since they detested following his advice and principles; because truth always runs away and hides from the heart that does not seek it humbly and embrace it fondly. As a man he flees from stones: but woe to those from whom God runs away because they have a heart of stone! He hides not as a shy man in a corner of the temple, nor behind the temple wall, nor does he take refuge in any room, but rather by covering himself with his heavenly and divine power, he becomes sensitive and invisible to his enemies and passes through them vested with all the greatness suiting his divinity. And in spite of this his disciples watched him and followed him without any anxiety or weariness.

Finally, by this example the Saviour taught us that even though we can resist the anger and vengeance of those who are arrogant against us, let us keep away from it with patience and charity. Say no to yourself, what is that which man should do when threatened by his neighbour, when the Son of God flees and hides? No one may return slander for slander to his neighbour, curse for curse, or insult for insult. He will acquire more glory by defeating his enemy with silence and escape than if he confronts him with a frightening response. Many show little attention to mitigate the hardness of their hearts, even if they rebuke that of the Jews. Many have to hate and condemn this because they did not want to hear the preaching of the Son of God, and they are so hard in themselves to do good as those who were so hard to embrace the faith that the Lord preached to them. They hear God's precepts, they know his miracles, but they resist converting from their evil doings. This is what Saint Gregory said.

Have a good look at Jesus Christ, oh Christian, and know how much it is in your interest to act according to his advice and examples; hide yourself by giving in to the fury of the unjust persecution of the Jewish people; for the immense good things he did to them, he gathered none but bitter fruits. Keep a good look at him when he flees, though covered with the cloak of his divinity. Observe the apostles and disciples who follow him brimming with sadness and with their heads bowed, and this flight and sad posture will also move you to compassion.

CHAPTER 45
JESUS HEALS A BLIND MAN FROM BIRTH, IS EXAMINED BY THE SCRIBES AND PHARISEES, AND THE SAVIOUR REBUKES THEM FOR THEIR INFIDELITY AND HARDNESS OF HEART (JN 9:1–41)

HERE is nothing more difficult in the world, and making for a bad impression, than the heart of a powerful rival, brimming with ambition and envy, when it feels no admiration, interest or respect for a seemingly poor and humble adversary. This vice, which is not easily subdued by the opulent and rich, or as better called that petty passion which depraves and degrades man, is never seen to be in any way restrained when those dominated by it are people who obtain command and authority. Being overcome by its power, they give it all possible leeway, rather than repressing and moderating it. Even if we did not have in history, both sacred and profane, thousands of examples that justify this terrible doctrine, suffice it to be considered as a dogma. It is mentioned by Saint John and elaborated by Jesus Christ on leaving the temple of Jerusalem shortly after the dispute mentioned before with the scribes and Pharisees. Had this happened anywhere else or had there been any others who witnessed it, unlike the false, ambitious and proud doctors who had control over the ungrateful city, they would have been disappointed and converted. At most they would have been concerned and, if falsely warned, they would have submitted themselves to suspending their concern. They would then have dedicated themselves to seeking and knowing the truth, and would have adopted it without retort, well satisfied with what they had found.

Jesus Christ came out of the temple without being followed by his fierce enemies. For, however heinous and unjust were the persecutions which he suffered, they could neither quench nor weaken the fire of his charity; so that even if he saw reversals, he immediately stretched out his hand to give help as a benefactor. A poor blind man from birth sat begging alms from those who entered his Father's house, and the Lord fixed upon him his merciful eyes with great attention, as Saint Chrysostom observes, as if he wanted to ask him something or to do him some miracle. He also did this as if to call his disciples' attention causing them to ask him to do something for him.

Indeed, the apostles being also moved in compassion, asked Jesus Christ eagerly, *Master, why was this man been born blind? Is it through his fault or that of his parents?* They were convinced that there was no discomfort or illness that was not punishment for sin. This blind man was a figure of the human lineage, born deprived of the light of faith, and inheriting voluntary blindness from the primeval liar. In passing near where the blind man was sitting, the Saviour shows us the need for grace for the spiritual healing of man, and of the promptness and fidelity with which we must take advantage of divine mercy. The Pharisees always attributed the calamities and works of the creatures to their own sins or to those of their elders. They believed that most often they were punished by God in advance for the sins He knew they would be later committing. And because most of the Jews believed in the transmigration of souls, and that personal sins were possible in children even before they were born, although his disciples believed none of this, the Lord still wanted to completely dispel any idea which the Jews held, as almost always universal concerns influenced their minds. And so he instantly answered their question and said: It is not for the sins of this man or those of his fathers that he was born blind. As if he would say: "It is true that diseases, setbacks and death have not entered this world other than as consequences of sin; but God who, when He pleases, makes them serve as punishment for sinners, often uses them for the perfection of the righteous and to show his glory. And this is only what God has set out to reveal in the sickness of this man, and it is my duty to tend to him with my ministry."

The glory of God is the main purpose proposed in all His councils, and so in all that happens to men. Since we do not have a living faith of this truth, we are greatly broken down by calamities and misfortunes, and we are afflicted and saddened on many occasions almost to despair, for we do not trust in His mercy as we should. The Lord's mercies are many, Jeremiah says (Lam 3:22), and it is due to them that we have not been totally consumed, for his mercifulness has never been lacking. Great is the Lord's honour in choosing us so that in giving witness with our patience the showing of his mercy may shine brighter. He was not born blind in punishment for his sin, but this is a blindness of dispensation, that the glory of God may be manifested in the wonderful enlightenment to be made by His Son in the person of this blind man. So that with his divine virtue being so declared, men may be more firmly edified and confirmed in faith.

This idea, which reaches its peak in this wonderful healing, is even more discovered and confirmed with what the Saviour himself immediately said: "It is appropriate that I work the works of Him who has sent me for as long as the day lasts." Being a faithful envoy of his Father, he sought in all his works the greatest glory of Him who sent him. This was one of the purposes of his mission, and for this reason he did not give up working all the time of his life, and much more at the time of his passion and death. For this reason he said, "Night comes," namely death is coming, "and in coming, none can do works of merit before God and worthy of His eternal reward. The day is for work and the night for rest: and as the night follows day and at dusk man ceases from work, so that I can say that being with you I enlighten the world, because I am its light, but I will not always be among men. In a short time you will not see me anymore. Then, as night follows day, I will not do all the things that you now see and cause in you so much admiration; and the world, covered in darkness, will feel the absence of the light in which it diminished itself, and which could have served it very well for its eternal happiness." It is of course clear that Jesus Christ spoke of the short time which he still had to live on earth, during which he had to work without respite with new additional merit in making known, in the Only Son, the greatness of the Father. After this time, God demands from his Son neither work, nor sorrows or torments, relying on the Father to glorify and reward his merits. Further to all this Saint Augustine says: "Is it possible that night had so much strength that not even you, Lord, could act in it, being as you were the servant of the night? What night is this that when it comes no man can work in it? Listen to what day is and then you will at once understand what night is. *While I am in the world*, says the Lord, *I am the light of the world*. It is therefore during the day when faith can work for charity; night is the time for outer darkness, when the mouth of eternal light utters to the wicked: *Go into eternal fire*."

These words of the Saviour have another meaning or interpretation, which are no less important, since they showed the feeling of his heart about the loathing and contempt with which the Pharisees treated him. They preferred the darkness of worry, ignorance and error in which they were wrapped, to the bright light of truth which he presented to them to clear up the air, not only with his words and doctrine, but also with his examples and miracles. Chrysostom apparently wanted to refer to this when he said: "Leaving the temple he came carefully to the place where he had to work the demonstrative miracle, not only of his divine omnipotence, but of his charity and eternal love. He himself saw the blind man, and it was not the blind man who approached him. So indeed, charity nor falters or crumbles, nor does it go out of its way. Leaving the temple he healed the blind man wishing to mitigate the unjust fury with which the Jews persecuted him, so that by working the miracle the hardness of those hearts would soften and this would truly confirm the doctrine he was teaching them."

Having said this the Lord spit on the ground and made mud with saliva from his mouth, filled the blind man's eyes with mud, and said to him, Go and wash in the pool or bathing pond of Siloam. It is clear and evident that mud covers the eyes and causes blindness; but in the hands of the omnipotence of the Son of God it becomes an instrument for giving sight.

The lordship of Christ shines here over the laws of nature as well as the piety with which he dealt; not so much in healing the blind man as in practising his obedience and faith. With the mud made with his saliva he smeared the eyes of the blind man, to prove that the same thing happened when out of mud he had formed the first man, and to make known that blind as he was with the sin of pride, nothing had more effect in healing him than by bearing in mind humility, or rather the despicable vileness of the matter out of which he was formed. Saliva mixed with earth was the image of the union of the divine nature with the human person of the Word; and in order to show the sovereignty and omnipotence residing in the Son of God made man, he commanded him to go and wash himself in the *bathing pond or Pool of Siloam*. The meaning of this name is another point of view from which the virtue and power of Christ can be clearly seen. Siloam is a Hebrew name meaning *the Envoy*, or *he who has been sent*. this is one of the names by which the *promised Messiah* is proclaimed in Holy Scripture as the Redeemer and Saviour of mankind, for all of whom he is the light. The *Sent One* therefore enlightens men, and he sends the blind man from birth to wash in the bathing pond of the *Envoy*. And it is not strange that there he receives the light. We rightly admire the virtue which on this occasion the Saviour linked with Siloam's bathing place. Oh, how worthy of tears is the cold blindness with which those of us, blinded by sin, view the washing away obtained by penance and the neglect with which we sometimes approach it! How deserving are we of punishment when we ungratefully despise so great a gift for which He so liberally invites us!

The miracle was rowdy and made in public. It could not less than arouse general admiration on the one hand and jealousy, ambition and persecution on the other, much more since it was done on a Sabbath day. For which reason the hypocrisy of the Pharisees reproached and condemned him, never wanting to persuade themselves that these miraculous healings, always performed by the eternal charity of the Son to seek in everything and make publicly seen the glory of his Father, could be lawfully worked on the Sabbath without breaking the precept of the sanctified dedication of the holy day. Saint Augustine very opportunely says for this purpose: "He who has no sin is the One who keeps most strictly the Sabbath day. To observe and keep the Sabbath spiritually is to have no sin; this made them clearly understand God himself when he said: *You shall not on that day engage in any servile work.* Which miracle was no servile work, so did the Lord declare it when he said: *Anyone who commits sin is a servant of sin.* The Pharisees kept the Sabbath in the flesh, but broke it spiritually." Agitated, therefore, and moved by the presumed breaking of the Sabbath and having seen that the miracle was so public and rowdy, they wanted to examine it in a most severe and scrupulous manner. Nothing would have made the examination any stranger had it been so strictly conducted with a righteous intent, and on confirming its certainty it would have produced change and repentance in the hearts of those judging. But when the angry and proud ones went back to their rash business, how eccentric were they? So it happened that the evidence of their questioning produced in the village an undesired effect which went entirely against the wishes of the scribes and Pharisees.

One cannot express the admiration this miracle caused in the neighbours and relatives of the hitherto blind man, and more particularly in those who had before seen him ask for alms and helped him in his misfortune. His fame spread through all the quarters of the city, and whoever came to know of the event ran to the house of the healed man to see for themselves that the miracle had happened. And full of wonder they said to each other: *Is not this the blind man who sat begging alms?* Although the fact did not admit of any doubt, they thought it was in their imagination and they distrusted its certainty even when they saw and felt it. A few said he was the same person, others claimed he was not but rather a person who quite resembled him; but this doubt could not last long. The fact was undeniable: the healed person was but one and the same; thousands of witnesses witnessed to the truth, and among so many voices there emerged the very sound of the man who was no longer blind, saying: "Yes, it is me who was blind from birth, and now you can all see well that I am not." A laudable confession that at once cut off all arguments and disagreement, and forced the most stubborn to confess and believe. Yet it was also laudable gratitude that he did not remain silent, said nothing or was confused, threatened as he was by angry and violent persecutors. A manly and zealous man defended, as a constant and fervent athlete would do, the truth of a fact which was admired by all. And to the scorn and sorrow of the mob's uproar he confessed the benefit he had obtained not to incur punishment for being ungrateful. He proclaims evangelic grace and freely confesses the truth to seek the greatest glory and praise of God. Saint Chrysostom says about him: "There goes the town crier of truth; see how he announces how much he has heard from the beginning and how much he has suffered by word and by deed. He is not ashamed to say that he had been blind, nor does he fear the outcry of the commoners, or refuse to stand out or expose himself to proclaim and make public the merciful liberality of the benefactor. Do also know, oh man, that these things are written that we may imitate them."

From the certainty expressed by the blind man it appears clearly what the truth is, and how strong and irresistible is its command. If it succeeds in taking hold of the heart of a poor and despicable man, it then makes him generous, forgiving and enlightened. And it also shows how great the weakness and utter foolishness of the liar is, for the braver and more generous he wants to show himself, the more he is credited with being an idiot and a coward. Having cleared up matters by factual truth, they no longer yielded to doubt and lying; thus, the Pharisees no longer dealt with the matter but to know how it had worked out. Since the healed man was faithful and truthful, the only and best way how to know was to ask the man himself; so that when he was called by the scribes and magistrates he underwent the most thorough questioning. So they asked him: "How were your eyes opened?" And he answered them: *A man, who is called Jesus, spat on the ground, made mud with his saliva, anointed my eyes with it, and said to me: Go and wash in the pond baths of Siloam. I went, I washed, I was blind and now I see.* In so many words he gave them utmost satisfaction, and this clear and glorious testimony resulted in many becoming enthusiastic followers of the Saviour. The congratulations of recognition and gratitude were inscribed on the face of all the simple and well meaning men, who certainly were the least. There were many, however, who were possessed of rage, swearing in their hearts once more that they wanted to take his life promptly. Ever so eager to find in his words a legal motive to cover up their retribution, they again asked him: "Where can we find the man who on the Sabbath dared give you such orders?" As the blind man took them to the pool, Jesus Christ left the place and did not appear there again; so that the blind man who had been healed could not tell them anything but "I do not know." At the same time, many other eyewitnesses were also examined; and when in the same manner the blind man's statement was corroborated by them in person, they were all led before the Pharisees. Being questioned again, they reproduced his first statement and asked him to speak of what he felt feelings about that wonder and the man who had performed it.

Since all their thoughts and desires were vicious, they would probably have gladly left the pursuit of a task which would not affect them in accomplishing anything advantageous to them, and all they did was with regard to a man whom they wished to annihilate and get out of the way. His fame was widespread, his reputation was great, his doctrine holy and comforting, his miracles public and notorious; therefore, all the odds of advantage were in favour of this mystery man. So as all this compromised the honour of the magistrates and Pharisees, they needed to veneer their false zeal with a layer of justice which they could do by seeking against innocence equally wicked and passionate accusers. They all agreed to despise the miracle, or at least to prevent its consequences; but they did not agree about how to disapprove of him.

Two actions had occurred as were revealed by the blind man in his repeated clarifications, namely that *the mud formed with dust and saliva,* and that *the blind man who wanted to be healed was sent to the pool of Siloam.* And although neither of these two went against the letter, let alone against the spirit of the Law, this notwithstanding those men of doom assumed they could use them to accuse the Lord of having often been in breach of the Law. The populace, being a faithful spectator of the wonder, uniting their affectionate feelings of gratitude with those of the man healed of his blindness, blessed and praised God, and venerated Jesus

Christ as a unique person sent by Him, as a universal remedy for all miserable persons. Nevertheless, the enemies were filled with wrath and fury and they cried: "He is not a man of God, for he neither keeps His laws nor observes the Sabbath." Others said that as a sinner he could not work great miracles, accusing him of deceiving his brethren and blaspheming against God. So that it is seen that the supreme arbitrator who always used to choose the weak and the feeble to confuse the proud and the haughty, made use of these different opinions and councils to destroy the wicked thoughts which the evildoers had conceived. For since they were not able to agree or to concur among themselves, they upset everyone's spirits and could not but choose to make the same blind man who had been healed the arbiter of their differences. The good Jews, who were firmly convinced that with sensitive miracles, such as those they had just seen, along with the fulfilment of prophesies was the manner in which the promised Christ had to be made known, claimed that he was the One who worked so many portents and miracles. And so those scribes and Pharisees, who held otherwise, asked the blind man a new question, although an untimely one and out of subject, which was most suited to fill them with confusion.

"How do you judge," they told him, "and claim that is the man who opened your eyes?" While the righteous One confesses, the non-believer is consumed with rage. The Pharisees did not see in their hearts the same things which the blind man already showed on his countenance. For this reason, when one had confessed the truth faithfully, the others denied it, or at least intended to obscure the miracle as jealous evildoers. Some intended finding serious guilt in the same miracle according to the circumstance of the day, while others denied him obstinately due to the bad impression they had of the author. Yet what breach could be brought forward against him who was holy in essence and by nature, and the eternal origin and source of justice and holiness? In truth, there was no sin or weakness in the Lord. They turn to the blind man himself, who had received the gift of sight, to speak. What a strange decision! After seeing the light, what could he speak but the truth? So this is what he answered them, he could not doubt he was a man sent from God, a saint, a prophet. The thoughts of all those who pondered evildoing missed out in this occasion, for as David said elsewhere: *Man draws near to a benevolent and generous heart, and God is exalted.* The malice of the Pharisees had led them to believe that this poor beggar man, either since he was overwhelmed with fear, or else to flatter the whims of the moguls, would express something which would arouse pique and envy. Yet his heart, which was already full of charity and steadfast in true faith, did not hesitate to confess the truth before his greatest enemies, and this confession raised him to the peak of saintly knowledge and to merit the true and ineffable promises of God.

The scribes and Pharisees could not disguise the irritation caused to them by the grateful man's naive words. So they turned against him, treated him as an imposter because he spoke well of the One whom they abhorred and wanted to eliminate, with their brutal fury reaching to such an extent that they wanted to persuade and make others believe that he had never been blind, and that his healing had been a sham. Supported by a considerable number of unbelievers from their sect, they managed for a few instants to stir the people and make them suspend what they were contemplating. But knowing that their word on its own would not be believed against the evidence of the blind man himself, and the assertion of so many that had known him to be completely blind, they were convinced that the parents of the miserable man, in whom they assumed they could not find the same gratitude and recognition of their son, would not dare, out of respect for the advice of the magistrates, to sustain in their presence that he was their son or that he had been born blind. And so they sent for them to come before them and they asked them: "Is this your son? Is it true he was born blind, as everyone says? What do you say? And if he is your son who was blind, how is it that he now sees? Who could have opened his eyes?" What excuses would a presiding iniquity not use from its seats of power to outlaw and banish the truth, when his confession is undeniable proof of the injustice committed by those in power! Their investigation had gone too far, and they had laid more snares than enough against the poor to discourage and destroy them; but these knew their ways and were wise enough by then to avoid it. If the miserable man's parents were to publicly confess the divinity of the benefactor who had healed their son, they were threatened with a kind of excommunication or banishment, since the Jewish leaders had already decided in a council that whoever dared accept Jesus Christ as the Messiah and say anything in his praise was to be separated from their assembly and banished from their Synagogue. And so the parents contented themselves just saying: "We know very well that this is our son; that he was blind from birth; that until today he could not see. As to why he now sees, we do not know, nor who is the man who has opened his eyes and made him see. Ask him about that; here he stands before you. He is enough of age to account for himself; ask him, and have no doubt that he will answer you."

The reply given by the blind man's parents shows a pitiful mix which is noteworthy. They knew all the truth concerning the fact, and although they did not say all they knew, the authenticity of the miracle could, however, be seen since they expressly spoke of the disease. Being in any case fearful of the persecution of the Jews, they did not have the full courage to face up to it; and shaking off all the heaviness of the burden, they exposed their son to the cruelty of the Pharisees, while keeping themselves safe. How few are those who venture the honour and interests of the world to bear witness to the truth! But the son, who contains the proof within himself, the conviction and benefit of the miracle, did not suppress or weaken his witness to the truth out of human respect. The reply given by the parents caused the scribes and Pharisees to turn again their wickedness to the son. And simulating a show of religion, they implied that he should have great regard for what he was about to do, and to fear the presence of the sovereign judge who was listening to him. "Give glory to God," they told him, "we are sure that the man you are talking about is a sinner." This can be called a completion of the treachery of Judaism, and rank it as a certification of its hardness and blindness. It had been resolved in the council of hell to prevent faith in the Messiah from entering into the world; but all their thoughts of wickedness were smashed against the decrees of the Lord's providence. To give glory to God they called for a denial of His multiple mercies, his gifts and his graces; but whoever is determined to divulge them as a gift of the glory of God never lacks the prudence and the strength which are necessary to confess them.

These graceful gifts of the Lord were seen to shine admirably in the blind man, and so it was that, with an astonishing freedom the Pharisees were not expecting, he replied: "If that man is a sinner, that is not something I can dispute with you, nor has it been dealt with here. What I know, what I have to say you, and what I cannot deny is *that I was born blind and that now I see*." The answer was clear and definitive, he did not admit to any distortion or doubt and yet again, as if they had never heard how the Saviour had worked the miracle, the Pharisees urged him on and said: "Then what was the remedy which gave you sight?" "I told you," the blind man replied; "and you may well have understood it from the first time. Why do you want me to repeat it to you once more if I have nothing new to add? What is all this inquiry and examination for? You must have some hidden purpose. Or do you want by chance to increase the number of his disciples?" Having said all this with the candour and natural simplicity with which truth is pronounced, raised the tempers of the Pharisees to the extreme; and considering him to have rudely insulted them they burst into offensive words and atrocious curses against him. "Get out of the way," they told him, "because you are wretched and cursed. Go and be counted among his disciples, for we do not want any other master than Moses, to whom we know God speaks. But as to this man we neither know from where he comes nor on whose behalf."

Saint Augustine examines this curse which the scribes and Pharisees cast against the blind man, and says: "*Be you his disciple*. Let us and our children fall on this curse. It is indeed a curse if you look at the hearts of those who pronounce it; but it is not if you tend to the true meaning of the words. And it will be much less so if you tend to what others said, *But we are disciples of Moses*. This augured prosperity, fertility and worldly riches to those who keep his Law. That is why he has more disciples than Jesus Christ, who preaches poverty, humility and other similar virtues to those who follow Him and which he proclaimed to them. The true follower of the law of Christ confidently awaits the fulfilment of his promises, and neither crumbles nor loses heart when he is mistreated because he seeks the glory of his Lord. It is this portent, which really happened, which was seen to be renewed in this new person confessing Jesus Christ. The Lord provided him with new strength to sustain the attacks of his adversaries, and put in his mouth admirable answers, with which he truly shamed and confused them. I see there, he told them, a new wonder which you understand less than you do the miracle of which I am a living and perpetual witness. You esteem yourselves to be wise men and you become our doctors, yet you do not know from where this man, who had the power to open my eyes and give me sight, comes. But since you seem to ignore this, you must at least agree that you, me and all know, and about which there is and cannot be any question, and it is that God does not listen to sinners nor does He perform miracles to authorise the false piety of hypocrites. This is what you teach, and we and you believe it to be so, just as we also believe that He listens kindly to the pleas of those who serve him. It has never been heard that anyone restored sight to a blind man from birth, you know that well. So tell us, could a man who did not come from God do such a great miracle?"

The doctors could not swallow such a wise and healthy reflection, because they were sure that no one would ever dare remind them in as many apparently harsh and strong words. For this reason they filled up with their resentment, being accustomed as they were to the fact that the populace always bowed their heads before their authority. And to uphold it, believing the matter to be greatly worn out, they turned to insults, affronts and contempt. Filled with that pride, which was their own distinctive character, they told him: "You are a despicable sinner born in sins and hardened in them; you, who have not deserved to see the light of day; you, miserable and most vile of all men, do you dare teach us and give lessons to the doctors? Get out of our sight, get away from here, and let us never see you here again." Which was in a way declaring him excommunicated, unworthy to enter the temple, and forever excluded from congregating with his brethren. For the Jews this was the greatest opprobrium, as with excommunication among Christians now and among peoples where faith reigns.

For having confessed the truth and remained consistently united to Jesus Christ, he was cast out of the temple by the Jews. For not despising God he was despised by men; woe to those who despise God not to displease men! Having been cast out by the Jews, he did not lose anything neither before God nor before men, and wounded by the anathema of the court of injustice, which was that of Jesus Christ's enemies, he was not deprived of the fruits of mercy, nor did it take long for him to be visibly and considerably comforted by the persecution that his gratitude and mercy had brought him. The injustice with which the poor blind man had been treated was not hidden from Jesus Christ who so looked for him immediately and compassionately, and having found him he told him: "Do you believe in the Son of God, that is, do you believe that it is him who has given you the use of your eyes which nature denied you?" "And who is he, Lord," answered the healed blind man. "Let me know him that I may believe in him." Which was like saying: "Show me where he who gave me sight abides, so that I will go and look for him, thank him and adore him." "You have seen him," the Saviour replied, "and you see him, for he is the same person who speaks to you." He had barely heard this word when he said, "I believe in the Son of God," at the same time prostrating at the feet of his benefactor and adoring him as his Lord and God. With his words he converted to the Lord and with his works he justified the faith of his word, because he humbled himself in Jesus Christ's presence. "I believe in him and confess him to be true God and true man." It is not strange that he whom the Jews repel was received by Christ; for inasmuch as man may be despised by God, the more is he sought, received, and comforted by God. Chrysostom says of this: "Those who, by confessing Jesus Christ's faith and divinity, are oppressed with injustice by men, are the most honoured by God, the same thing as occurred with the blind man from birth. The Jews threw him out of the temple and he found the Lord of the temple, and he received him as an athlete who fought for a long time until he finally won and was crowned by Jesus Christ. He had entirely healed him, giving sight to his eyes on his physical body, and enlightening his inner heart within. It was so that the Lord, a most docile lamb sent to take away the sins of the world, washed and at the same time enlightened the eyes of the body and those of the heart for that miserable man. And he confessed him, not only as the Son of Man, but also as Son of God. This confession was all the more praiseworthy, as it was made not only before a great crowd, but also in the presence of many Pharisees. There is no doubt that if it was great joy for the blind man to regain bodily sight, much more was it for him to be healed from the spiritual blindness which prevented him from knowing God. Nothing was lost by being thrown out of the Synagogue of the wicked, and he won by being admitted to the communion of saints. It is glorious for man to be treated as a dissident for the world, and greater glory it is to be still inscribed in the catalogue of God's faithful lovers and constant worshippers. The banishment which the world imposes upon us when it throws us out for being an enemy of its precepts and doctrines is the crown with which it unknowingly honours us and makes us worthy of the Lord's mercies and solace."

After delivering the blind man from birth from his physical blindness, Jesus Christ took occasion and had reason to speak to the scribes and Pharisees of the spirituality of the soul, which he also wished to heal for them. As this became more and more incurable, instantly believing in the stubbornness of their hearts, Jesus Christ said to them: "I came to this world to do a just judgment so that those who do not see might see, those too who see or presume to see although blinded by their pride." Which was the same as telling them: "My feeling is for the occasion of the most severe condemnation of this rebellious world. So look at this ungrateful city which I have come to visit, so that those who do not see may regain their sight, enlightened by faith and knowledge of truth as long as they are simple and humble of heart, and those who see, namely the teachers of the Law and the proud sages who boast that they can see, and so do not care about seeking the doctor who can give them their sight, become increasingly blind, remain in blindness and harden their hearts by infidelity." There was no doubt that Jesus Christ was prophesying about the Jews and Gentiles. The darkness in which nations were submerged opposed the nearby light which was attempting to penetrate it, as well as the lights being now offered to the stubbornly blind sages of the Synagogue where their extreme hardness would soon end. Without being embarrassing, the present Pharisees asked him whether by chance he was saying this because he counted them among the number of blind persons. And Jesus Christ answered them: "You would be blessed if you were, for you would not have the sin which is in you; but because you say, we see, and judge yourself to be very well instructed, this is why your sin persists in you. This means that it will grow greater and will so be more severely punished. You are the doctors and teachers of the Law. You boast of being enlightened and of having knowledge, which other nations do not have; and these are the ones that will condemn you, for the sin of those who know the Law but do not observe it is much greater than that committed by those who do not know the Law. For this reason the penalty is much greater in those who act in this manner. So that it is written that the servant who knows the will of his Master but does not fulfil it will be punished with much greater scourging." A terrible threat indeed, but which will irreversibly one day be accomplished!

CHAPTER 46
JESUS EXPLAINS TO THE SCRIBES AND PHARISEES WITH A PARABLE THE NATURE AND CHARACTERISTICS OF A GOOD SHEPHERD, AND SHOWS THE DIFFERENCE BETWEEN HIM AND THE DAY LABOURER (JN 10:1–16)

N a furious frenzy turning against the doctor who wants to heal them, the scribes and Pharisees turned against the most meek Jesus Christ, who wanted to heal them from their spiritual sickness and the voluntary blindness from which they suffered. This was the reason why, although brimming with wonders, they could not deny or diminish them, and refusing to confess them they became like distracted or misunderstanding persons, wondering with each other from where that man claiming to be the Messiah had come. Being blind and unbelievers, they refused to draw near to the light of Christ, who was the way, the truth and the life. They did not want to enter the sheep's fold to be counted among the Lord's number. They gloried in seeing and knowing the truth without Jesus Christ, and for this reason they despised him. So it was that, having begun to speak mildly of their pride and boastfulness, Jesus Christ toughened his speech once more and proposed to them the parable of the humility of the sheepfold and the door through which they entered. Through that gate only the meek and truly humble entered, and so he said to them: "Truly, truly I say to you, that whoever does not enter through the door in the sheepfold, but climbs or scales up in some other manner, is a thief and a robber, but whoever enters through the door is the true shepherd of the flock. The doorman opens the door to them and the sheep know his voice. If you want to enter through this door in the humble sheepfold, you must humble yourselves too and not think so proudly of yourselves." He told them this parable, not only to hint humility to them, but also to show them by which door to enter the fold, thereby teaching the different condition of the sheep's thief and of their shepherd.

The thief does not enter through the door, because he does not seek the good of the flock; indeed he looks for ruin and doom, or what is similar, destruction and slaughter; and for this reason he seeks a false and treacherous entrance. But the good shepherd who seeks the good of the flock, who wants them to graze in an abundant and delicious pasture, knocks on the door and the doorman opens to him, because he is sure of his kind intentions, as he is the true shepherd. He calls each sheep by its own name, takes them out of the fold and leads them to the pasture land. He calls them, because he knows them all by name, otherwise unknown to anyone who is not a true shepherd. He takes them out of the fold and walks in front of them, and they follow him. For they know the sound of his voice, having passed through and knowing from experience that he leads them to lush land and pleasant pastures, where they can eat calmly and in rest. But they do not follow the hireling shepherd for they are not used to hearing strange voices; so they flee away from him, believing him to be a fake shepherd and maybe even a thief.

The Pharisees did not believe they could understand this parable, nor could they imagine it was addressed to them. Being replete with wise men, they believed knowing all that the Lord wanted to say and mean, peeling off only the crust without understanding any of the mysteries enclosed within. Recounting it Jesus Christ wanted to show them that neither wisdom, nor observance of the Law, nor living well, nor anything else however good it seemed to be to them or actually was, none was worth but the merits of Christ, and that it was impossible for them to get anywhere without him to know the truth and God their Father who had sent him. He who does not enter through the door, namely through Jesus Christ, in the sheepfold, namely in feeling with the Church and in the congregation of the faithful, is a raptor and thief as are all unbelievers and bad Christians. Saint Augustine says that he who enters through Christ enters through the door, and he who knows the humility of Christ. But he who enters through this door, that is through faith and humility of Christ, and who imitates all the other virtues which shine in him, enters to graze the sheep with the spirit of truth and can be reputed to be a good shepherd. It is not believed, however, that anyone who enters through the doorway is the true shepherd, for through it also sheep enter. However, the Church is only one, and it is universal, and this universal unity within it is discovered and known perfectly well in the unity of the one and true pasture given daily to the sheep grazing in its bosom. The good shepherd who leads them towards this pasture, is revealed by the Holy Spirit, namely, he is anointed and consecrated, thus showing that he is anointed with the Spirit of intelligence, wisdom and understanding, and consecrated with the gift of understanding, council and strength, so that he may feed the flock and the sheep hear his voice, that is, his doctrine, and receive it. He calls them by their own name, to imply the familiar deference he has with each one of them, and that this familiarity emboldens them to approach him with confidence. By teaching them he passes them from the darkness of error to the light of truth, and from the sadness of servitude to the kingdom of freedom. And when he has brought them out of the darkness of ignorance to the light of life, and from the prison of guilt to the freedom of grace, he walks before them giving an example of good deeds and a holy life. And they follow in his footsteps by imitating his good examples, by the righteousness of their intentions and with the saintliness of their works, because they know his voice and delight in hearing it.

This does not happen when whoever enters the sheepfold is a stranger and does not enter through the door. Sheep are unaware of his voice and life. They do not follow him because they neither receive his doctrine nor imitate his examples, for his words bring about error and his examples evil. They flee from him the same as from a thief and an enemy, for they are unaware of his voice, being that of a stranger who speaks nice things about truth. And they run away from him, that is from his doctrine, also because they do not know it.

If all this doctrine is compared with the manner in which the Pharisees had treated the blind man from birth, and the Saviour himself for having healed him, casting the blind man out of the Synagogue because he confessed that Jesus

Christ was the Messiah, and blaspheming against Jesus Christ and treating him as a seducer and false prophet, it would be seen that with this mysterious parable the Lord wanted to throw in their face all their injustice and wickedness. For it is very noteworthy that when Jesus Christ wants to announce anything, he calls in a particular manner the attention of the crowd around him by saying, *Truly, truly, I tell you.* By means of this he shows the great need for this doctrine and the strong resistance with which not only the scribes and Pharisees, but the whole world, were to oppose him and the small number of followers of his holy doctrine.

Jesus Christ also wanted to make them know that in his quality as God's envoy, of whom Moses and all Scripture had given testimony and prepared the way, he had entered into the sheepfold through the true door. He was not come to be revealed until after having established with indisputable evidence his legitimate right over the flock, in whose thought it was very easy to know the great difference between Jesus Christ and the Pharisees. So that he had three years to justify his mission, not only with the holiness of his doctrines and with that of all his steps and actions, but by confirming it with miracles which were so awesome and great that they drew the admiration of all the people. But to be seen in the leaders of the scribes and Pharisees, and in all of their doctrines, were only the fortune and vanity of intruding usurpers who diminished the herd and gave them poisonous and deadly pasture land.

The common fold of all sheep is the Catholic Church under the head and direction of a single, supreme and true shepherd, who is Jesus Christ. Yet in this Church there are also several particular congregations comprising herds of true sheep, such as convents of male and female religious, and gatherings of convent and parish churches, where God calmly rests his sheep, which are faithful, simple, meek and humble. Whoever does not enter through this door who is Jesus Christ, that is, who does not enter by the confession of the principles of the Christian religion and by that of the truth handed down in Jesus Christ's Gospel, is a heretic. He who does not come by confessing the principles of grace by which God calls creatures, and distributes them and communicates their gifts, is guilty of simony. He who does not come to enter through this door with full and perpetual freedom, but enters with force, or is impelled and dragged by necessity, is an intruder. He who does not enter through this door with the simplicity of the dove, that is, with the candour and innocence of a true son of God, is a deceiver. All these enter through an abandoned place. Some bring a ladder to enter from the top; these are the ambitious ones like Lucifer and like Korah's sons, the disgraceful Dathan and Abiram, whom for their ambition the earth split apart and swallowed them up (Num 16). Others have to enter expecting to break the walls and corrupt hearts; these are the greedy ones like Simon Magus. And finally others must enter undermining the foundations to destroy the whole building; and these are heretics like Arius. They are all thieves and raptors, differing only in the culpable means they use to enter. The raptor is the one who takes advantage of nightfall and the darkness of the night, namely of men's ignorance, to snatch rich items disregarding their owner, and the thief is the one who steals and usurps rich things with utmost forced entry and violence also in disregard of their owner. Jesus Christ wanted to show a difference between the raptor and the thief. With these two words, the raptor dejectedly erodes and undermines the foundations of the sheepfold to sneak in and usurp not only the old ones from the Lord, but anything useful they produce; and he is a hidden and cunning deceiver, a hypocrite and heretic, because he intends to steal and destroy the herd and all it uses. The thief is the one who still commits theft with violence, and is like all those who feel strengthened with their force of authority and power, invade the preserve of the Church and cut down, destroy and steal all its beauty, splendour, magnificence and glory.

To enter through the door of the fold of the Church through exercises of Christian and Catholic life, and to raise to the summit the dignity of a true shepherd of his sheep, is to enter through the path of truth, freedom, graceful goodness and holy simplicity. Entering through the door of truth by Catholic confession, by liberality, by the higher vocation with which God calls each one of us and by graceful goodness, is not entering through temporal promises; but by the door of holy simplicity when there is no simulation or deception at the entrance. Christ is therefore each and every one of these doors; and if anyone dare enter by any other, the supreme and true Pastor can tell him very well: *How did you get in here without wearing the wedding dress?* And he could be the daring person who is thrown out of the fold and cast into outer darkness. But to him who enters through the true door which is Christ, it would be he himself, who is equally the true doorman, who opens it to him and introduces him. And after that by a thousand means and ways he tries his faithfulness and faith, he grants him a position of dignity and honour, and lifts him up to the high hierarchy of pastor and doorman. Then he could open the door for the worthy and close it for the unworthy, and feed those who entered after grazing the pasture of the divine word, which is the grass of life and salvation. So that he closes and opens, as he sees suitable and just, and forgives and retains guilt and sin, with his authority and power reaching so high that he opens and closes the gates of heaven.

The Pharisees did not understand the meaning of this very interesting and instructive parable, and they would have remained in their ignorance had the Saviour not abided by the kindness, as he usually did, to make evident to them the mysterious meaning it held within it. He then opened his divine lips and told them: *"Truly, I say unto you, that I am the door of the sheepfold where my Father's flock is enclosed.* I am the gate by doctrine and example; through me the sheep come to their true shepherd. All those who have come before me and have made themselves herders and grazers, have been intruders in the job and they have become thieves and bandits whom the real sheep did not want to hear. I am the door of the fold: those who enter and believe in me, which means, constantly follow my doctrines and examples, walk along the proper path, and happily reach the port of salvation, since they find everywhere good pastures and receive the food of a revitalising and healthy doctrine, which will produce peace in their souls and be their final and complete joy. Whether it is the heat of the day or the darkness of the night, I will be their shadow and their light.

I will cover them with the mantle of my providence, lead them with the inextinguishable light of my providence, and deliver them from the fury of all voracious and harmful beasts. They will not have to fear the burning heat of the sun, for they would rest in the mellow shadow of my protection. Nor will they feel the intensity of thirst, for I will quench it with the inexhaustible source of my mercies and in the lasting torrent of my graces."

Saint Augustine says about this passage: "Within the fold of the militant Church the candid and simple sheep will find the pasture of doctrine and grace, and within the triumphant Church they will be satisfied with the pasture of joy and glory. Although there is no lack of healthy pastures in this fold, although thorns and thistle are often also found, it will not be lacking for those who take refuge in a pasture where they can be completely satisfied, where he goes out to feed the timid sheep and where all the hopes and desires of his heart are filled, the same as it was not lacking for the one to whom it was said: *Today you will be with me in Paradise.*"

"The robbers and thieves also engage in herding flock; but they do not do so other than with the harmful intentions of stealing, destroying, slitting and carrying away as much sheep as they can. On the contrary, I have come so that all men may have, through faith and by observing the commandments, a life of grace, which I want them to have abundantly in all kinds of merits. Namely, I want you, as far as you who have lived in the shadow of the Law of Moses and passed a distressed and anxious life, under the purest and most perfect law of the Gospel, to enjoy a greater abundance of good things in eternal life. I am the Shepherd, and it only belongs to me to lead them where it suits them best, and so they must recognise me and follow me, because the good shepherd offers his soul for his sheep. And so it is that as the shepherd does as he wants and by his work grazes the fold, so it is that all the faithful are governed by Jesus Christ, our Redeemer, and maintained with the spiritual banquet of his body and blood." And to make known the difference between the inner soul of the good shepherd and the thief, he further says: "Who is a good shepherd, not only in nature and grace, but also in his office and pastoral care, performs well the work and pastoral care of the good shepherd." About which Chrysostom says: "The Saviour is called Pastor, and the door equally so, without any difference. Knock on the door, because it leads us to the Father, and shepherd, because he acquires our lives and gives it to us. If this is therefore the sign of the good shepherd, much is to be feared for the lack of good shepherds today. If your neighbour's animal falls in a pit, many will help to lift it out; if the soul of a righteous man falls then there is no one among his friends who guides him or helps him to lift it up, but the truth is that everyone has a great obligation to love his brother's soul, which is his own body. But how can I risk my body for a person, if I do not want to give that which is temporary to free that person from sin? Surely then, if so I would not be performing the office of a good shepherd."

With a view of further stating what was the office and obligations of the good shepherd, Jesus Christ said: "The mercenary and he who is not a shepherd, those whose sheep are not their own, sees the wolf coming, and leaves the sheep, and flees; since he is a mercenary and does not care about looking after them." The shepherd is a mercenary or day hirer and leads the flock hoping to receive the agreed payment; so that whoever is not a shepherd does not look forward to the prize and trophy of heavenly glory, but has all his sights set on worldly interests and profit. According to Saint Gregory, he rightly loses the glorious name of shepherd, for he loves his gain more than the healing of his sheep; and this is what the Saviour wanted expressly to imply when he said: *Those whose sheep are not their own.* He gives proof of this when he sees the wolf, who is the devil, coming to snatch the sheep, or when he sees the heretic coming to deceive them and the tyrant to put them in bodily suffering and torture. And fearing some harm might come to him, or tripping over his own feet, he abandons them and runs away quietly, neither putting up any resistance nor providing them with proper help, and since he seeks alone the gains of this life, he betrays his soul by neglecting several different evils. He is here condemning the shepherd's negligence and carelessness, since with regard to these things he neither seeks a remedy, nor is he aroused with true zeal, or cares or involves himself with any fervour of true charity. This indolent mercenary is a day hireling, since he only cares about worldly interests, and indeed caring for the sheepfold does not seem to bother him at all since he neither commits himself to them nor does he work for them. Saint Augustine says: "In his sheep he does not love Jesus Christ, our Lord, to whom they belong, but only covets their milk and wool."

Jesus Christ said: "And while the mercenary lives a careless life and wastes his life in laziness, the wolf arrives, snatches and scatters the sheep, putting them at risk of various evils and turning them away from the uniting bond of charity and the Church, making them suffer. But the good shepherd gives his life to face these dangers, resists enemy intruders, rebukes vices, fights the falsehood of heretics, preaches Catholic truths, and faces up to the cruel persecutions of the wicked, praying and beseeching God to defend the sheep and help them. The good shepherd ever seeks the good of the sheep; but the evil mercenary seeks only his gain." In the words of Zechariah (11:17) God rebuked the little zeal, neglect and carelessness of a worthless shepherd saying *Woe to my insincere shepherd, who deserts the flock*, as if to say that you are no shepherd at all, but only one who resembles him. The good shepherd does not seek his own good, but that of those pertaining to Jesus Christ. That is why he watches with utmost care over his flock, thinking every day of the account he has to render to God about the sheep entrusted to him. So that Saint Augustine, speaking to his listeners, says: "You know well that you fall under our decisions when we give witness about your good behaviour and motives, and for this reason I always say to God in my prayer, 'You well know, Oh Lord, that I love you; You know well that I do not cease asking; You know well with how much fervour of the heart I said what I had to say; You know well that I cried when I said these things relating to my pastoral office and was not heard, and all this, I think, is the whole account and motives I have to give you.'"

After this Jesus Christ continued with this most interesting speech, proving with true signs to the scribes and Pharisees that he was the good Shepherd, telling them: "*I am the good Shepherd because I know my sheep*, not only by the universal tidings by which all things are evident in my sight, but by the good news of approval and love, according to which I know those who are worthy of the eternal life promised to them." Jesus Christ also knows his sheep through the image and likeness they have in resembling him and which he imbues in them. He knows them through the weapons and attire of the virtues with which he pervaded the faithful, and with the signs of the good works with which he fortified them for his doctrine; and especially for the charity with which he filled and justified them all, so that all these qualities are found in them. More than this, he also gave another second sign by which his sheep may know him. So he said, *And mine know me*. Those who are Catholic and faithful know Jesus Christ by knowledge and work, and are aware of his blessings by virtue of charity, and for this reason they cannot be deceived. The loving awareness therefore between the good shepherd and the sheep is both equal and mutual. For the good shepherd sees his herd many times, and so knows them well by name and is aware of all their doings and conditions, and he loves them. The sheep too, owing to their constant memory of the benefits he bestows on them, look at him, know him and love him with a special familiarity of love; this is what exactly happens between Jesus Christ and true Catholics, by means of which it is clearly inferred that he is their true Shepherd.

Finally, the most obvious, proper and characteristic sign of the good shepherd is the love which he shows and has for his sheep, which cannot be greater than to willingly expose himself to death for them. This is what the Saviour did for his faithful in saying *I lay my life for my sheep*. Which apparently means that it is only the sheep of Our Redeemer Jesus Christ which benefit from his passion. See then how by virtue of the good shepherd's love he lays his life for his sheep. True love considers nothing to be so hard, bitter or grievous, and what appears to be the more deadly he considers to be the least dangerous. There are no spears or darts, arrows or slingshots, nor any death which can overcome perfect love. Love is an impenetrable shield, it resists all shots, mocks all dangers, and scoffs and triumphs over death itself. And as there are three things which endanger man, namely property, relatives and one's own self, all three must be given up with great difficulty and danger, even unto death, for the sheep to be healed. These three things Jesus Christ gave up for the healing of his sheep, about which he said, through Jeremiah (Jer 12:7), "I have forsaken my house, I have abandoned my heritage; I have given the beloved of my soul into the hands of her enemies."

The true shepherd leads all the sheep to the sheepfold. In order for us to understand that Jesus Christ, Our Redeemer, would die for each and every one, he said: "And I have other sheep that are of the line of the Gentiles, those who in terms of the secret of predestination should believe in me, And it would suit those who are not descendants of Israel but of other nations, to be gathered in a congregation, one faith and one Church with the people of Israel." And according to Saint Chrysostom: "This phrase, *it is required* or *it suits me*, which the Lord utters, confirms another phrase of his when he said that he would save all his sheep. And he said, 'They hear my voice, and they will come to the faith,' so proving that the Gentiles would receive faith through the apostles' preaching, and they would form a sheepfold, namely, a gathering and a Church of the Jews and Gentiles and a shepherd, who in heaven is our Lord Christ, who is our peace." As the Apostle says, he made out of the two nations one sheepfold and one Church. This shepherd on earth is the supreme pontiff, vicar of Jesus Christ, Our Redeemer. He is bound to feed the flock, as this obligation was imposed on him by the Sovereign Shepherd when Saint Peter was instituted his vicar on earth and pastor of the Church. Jesus Christ then told him, *Feed my sheep*. The good shepherd is also compelled to love his flock, and for this very reason Jesus Christ himself tested Saint Peter about his love and charity in asking him whether he loved him. And finally, he must keep and defend his flock from the wolf, which Jesus Christ implied in telling Saint Peter himself, *And as for you, when you convert some time soon you will then confirm your brethren.* All that which Jesus Christ himself fulfilled very appropriately, had to serve as an example and perfect model for all shepherds and for the prince of them all.

How great was the care of this pious Shepherd and his paternal concern for the lost sheep, This is shown by the parable of the shepherd and the lost sheep, one of a hundred, which he sought with the greatest care, and later carrying it with the greatest joy on his shoulders to rejoin the company of the other sheep. Indeed! And how well did the Prince and model of all shepherds say that *the good shepherd lays his life for his sheep*. This prophetic saying which he had uttered was truly and mainly fulfilled in himself. In order to feed his sheep good grass and cover them safely from all storms and tempests, not only did he suffer much labour, tiredness, poverty and hunger, besides great and various dangers, passing through cities and castle towns while evangelizing the kingdom of God his Father, spending many nights in prayer without rest or sleep. Yet such was his generosity and mercy that he sought out the publicans and ate with them, exhorted them with affectionate charity to win them over and save them, while despising the murmuring and scandals of the Pharisees, affirming it was for the sick and sinners that he had come into the world. So that finally, he sought the penitents and reserved for them such special love, that so in order for them not to be led astray again, he always kept open for them the unfathomable bosom of God's mercy. When the shepherds hear this, and look in the mirror presented to them, they learn what they have to do to please the Lord.

These holy and deep reflections compelled the honey-tongued Bernard to say: "In all his deeds or words may the servant of God never seek anything which is his own, but in everything seek the glory of the Lord, the healing of his neighbour or anything of benefit pertaining to him. Yet no one can ask for the glory of God and benefit for his neighbour, unless he scorns what belongs most directly to him. Oh indeed! How great it would be for man if he despises all his works to direct himself only to his spiritual advantage! For in truth, what advantage is there for him to win over and conquer the whole world, if he later suffers in his soul an eternal downfall into everlasting condemnation? If the measure of love of one's neighbour is the measure of self-love, no one will know how to love his neighbour unless he knows how to love himself." So that there are two things which, after having committed an offence and sin, restore peace and tranquillity to a good conscience, and they are, repentance from past evils and abstinence from committing new faults which, as Saint Gregory says, means to weep for the sins committed and not to commit others again for which you will be weeping afterwards. The heart which knows that it is well accustomed to these two virtues and clothed in them, can well abandon itself and dedicate itself to all that which it knows to be able to win over others.

May the shepherds keep watch not to scandalise their congregation and not to be the scandal stones where they stumble, for those who give scandal to little ones shall be visited with pain and eternal lamentation. As many deaths are those of worthy church dignitaries, so as many are the evil examples they give to their faithful. As Saint Augustine says: "Those who inflame souls to sin and turn them away from God, commit much more sin than those who crucified the flesh of Jesus Christ, Our Redeemer." Do not believe, however, those faithful who say that the cause of the great punishments with which God often punishes them is to be found in prelates, also because many times it is to be found in them. The shepherds' defects and neglect only follow the sheep's perversity, because those who are evil do not deserve to have good shepherds. When Saint Gregory was once asked a question by a shepherd, he was prompted to write this, among other things, to the clergy of Milan: "However I intend it to be, he told them, and it has always been an ancient custom, not to make anyone carry or receive a heavy burden of pastoral care. So now pursue the election to office with prayers, that the Almighty shall give strength to such shepherd as in his tongue and customs pastures of divine preaching can be found. Yet since it is according to the merits of the people that usually, by judgment of the Most High, the faithful are provided with their shepherds, do seek spiritual matters and love heavenly things. Despise worldly and fragile things, and be very certain that you will receive a shepherd who lives according to the will of God, Our Lord, if in your deeds you seek carefully to please God."

CHAPTER 47
JESUS ATTENDS THE FEAST OF THE RENEWAL OR OF THE DEDICATION OF THE TEMPLE: HE DECLARES TO THE JEWS WHO HE IS AND THEY WANT AGAIN TO STONE HIM (JN 10:22–38)

EVERAL authors have interspersed, between the parable of the Good Shepherd and the celebration of the Feast of Dedication, the question of traditions, the healing of the Canaanite woman, that of a deaf and mute man and the miracle of the multiplication of the seven loaves and some fish to feed four thousand men. Saint John, however, does not intersperse any of these between that parable and the narration of this very important event which he refers to in the tenth chapter of his Gospel. However, all those who have written in some way Jesus Christ's life commonly recount that a few days passed after having made known to the Pharisees that he was the good Shepherd, before he let himself to be seen again in the house of God, at the start of the celebration of the Feast of Dedication in Jerusalem.

The feast is also called *Encenia*, from the Greek word meaning renewal; therefore, the feast of Dedication was intended to be in memory of the day when the temple, which had been desecrated by Antiochus, was purified and re-consecrated by the religious zeal of the brave Maccabeus. This feast lasted eight whole days like the great solemnities of the Pasch, Pentecost and Tabernacles. It started on 25 Kislev, the ninth month of the Mosaic year, which was also the thirty-second year of age of Jesus Christ, when he was already entering the thirty-third year of age, the last of his life on earth. It is worth knowing that we read in Scripture that three dedications were made of the temple of Jerusalem. The first was held by Solomon taking place every year on 10 September, which was the same day when the temple had been dedicated and consecrated to the Lord, until it was destroyed by the Babylonians. The second was celebrated every year on 12 March, in memory of the event on the same day when it had been restored and re-consecrated by Ezra, Nehemiah and Zerubbabel, after the return from the Babylonian captivity. And the third is that which we have mentioned before.

It is not so very important whether the Lord let himself be seen in the temple on the first day of the solemnity, or if it was only on the eighth day which was celebrated like the first; for there are well-founded reasons to believe that he did not stop in Jerusalem but for one day, since the record only mentions one conversation he then had with the Jews. We see him then immediately disappear from the capital, staying away from it for about three months, up to the time he is again observed to return for the last time to fulfil the last orders from his Eternal Father for the good of the whole world.

In the place where he had previously been in the same temple during the Feast of Tabernacles, he had witnessed to the truth of his mission and given such decisive evidence of the divinity of his person that one and all stood in jealous observation of the role acted out by the scribes and Pharisees in view of such an extraordinary man. The public spoke very well about him and although Jesus Christ publicly wrought so many wonderful miracles on their behalf, yet his imitators and detractors still spoke great evil about him.

No wonder that, in expectation of this general commotion, temple attendance was greater than ever when the word later spread that Jesus Christ had let himself be seen in that place. As it was early winter, contributions were commonly collected at the place called the *Portico*, or Solomon's Porch. This was the great hall which, at the time when Zerubbabel restored the temple, had been given Solomon's name in memory of the first founder of the house of God. It was there that Jesus Christ entered and walked, when he was suddenly surrounded by scribes, Priests, Pharisees and all the chieftains of the nation. Wanting to shed light on certain doubts they had about his previous speeches, they said to him: "For how long will you keep us in suspended animation, continuous perplexity and wavering between doubts and difficulties? For how long will you hold us in distrust? Speak frankly to us, see that we want to know who you are. If you are the Messiah and the promised Christ, tell us openly and we will believe in you." Undoubtedly, after what had been seen publicly for three long years in all parts of Palestine, and very recently inside the capital itself, nobody could assume the least degree of good faith in such a question. It was put to Jesus Christ without any degree of modesty or remorse by rather learned people who were even more aware of all that happened being men and teachers at the Synagogue. So Jesus Christ answered them: "*I have told you and you do not believe. Yet even if I had not told you, the works I do on behalf of my Father bear witness to me and clearly show who I am.* But you do not believe because you are not of my sheepfold, namely of those who, being faithful to the voice of my Father, sincerely seek the truth and become docile to the imprints of grace. Your worries blind you and your envy hardens you. My sheep hear my voice, I know them, I love them, and they follow me. I am the One who rewards them with eternal life when they persist in faith and remain constant in keeping my commandments."

The scribes and Pharisees did not believe that the Lord would answer so forcefully the much apparent flattery with which they had spoken to him, pretending that they wished to know the truth from his very mouth. "*If you are Christ,*" they told him, which means *King and anointed*, "tell us clearly, since we not only ought to know the truth, but also to proclaim it." Oh, how evil! Oh, what cunningness! Never has such great deception or treachery been seen! This was the same thing as saying to Christ: "We sin if you are the promised One according to the Law and the Anointed One to be sent by God, and we do not believe you, but we do not want to sin." They asked him a question and demanded from him a closing answer to accuse him later of being Caesar's enemy. They would say that he made himself king and so have occasion and reason to deliver him to Roman ministers, so that he might be condemned to death. They did not rack their brains about the truth, but were only preparing their slander; and since they spoke with deception and treachery, the Lord softened the manner of his answer and said to them: "*I told you so, and you did not believe*; my works bear me witness. And if they are so eloquent and persuasive for you, as are all the amazing miracles, and yet you still do not believe, how will you believe my words?" Thus, he did not say in so many words that he was Christ, which was the answer for which the Jews were looking, but he said something to the same effect or rather greater. Still, this was not quite enough to satisfy the wishes of the scribes, although it was enough to answer truthfully and exclude any motive of insult or slander.

There is one thing in Jesus Christ's sheepfold which the herd can fear as to its salvation and eternal perishment, and it is precisely its inconstancy and light heartedness. As long as the herd remained intimately attached to its shepherd, who leads and guides it, no one will have the power to snatch it out of his hands. This is indeed what Jesus Christ himself meant when He continued saying to the scribes: "The Father who gave them to me is far above all and greater than all things. This is what I have received from Him, namely a power which is equal to His over my flock, and you know well that no one can take anything out of my Father's hand." Saint Augustine has this to say: "My Father gave them to me that I am his only begotten Son, his *Logos* or Word, and I who am His light. And no one can take them away forcefully or violently from my Father's hand, for his power is infinite. And so nor can they be taken out of my hand, which holds, guides and keeps them. *My Father and I are the same thing*, as much in virtue and power as in divinity and essence. Note, however, that from the Saviour's word that *My Father and I are the same thing*, there are two incompatible mistakes contrary to faith in the Holy Trinity. Sabellius placed in God a unity of persons, as well as a unity of essence; this error is wiped out with the same words uttered by Jesus Christ, *I and my Father are the same thing*. If it were so that the Son is the same person with the Father, I would say *is*, in the singular, rather than *are*, in the plural. Arius, on the other hand, established the diversity of essences, as well as the diversity of persons, and this is excluded by saying, *we are one or one same thing*, in neutral terms. For if the Father and the Son had different essences, I would not speak the eternal Truth that *we are one or the same thing* to express the distinction and equality of persons and the unity of essence. In this manner the Lord addresses both statements when he says *One or the same thing*, and this delivers you from Arianism; and when he says we *are*, this frees you from the errors of Sabellius."

Because of the consequences of his speech, it would be easy to know the attitude of the Jews as they cornered Jesus Christ to clearly explain his role of Messiah. Infidelity and disbelief had always been the emblem of the scribes and Pharisees, as it still is with all those who do not belong to Jesus Christ's flock. God, rich in mercy, pours out certain graces and gifts upon disbelievers and bad Christians who, however, abuse of them because of their wickedness. What Saint Paul says is a dogma of faith (Rom 2:4,5): "God's kindness is meant to lead you to repentance, each and every one of you whose hardness of heart is storing up anger for the day of wrath." Do not say "I am evil, God looks at me with hate." for these words come from hell. The Church, being a teacher of truth ruled and governed by the Spirit of God, who is full of truth and charity, tells you that you will be saved if you hear Jesus Christ, if you open your heart to the law of fear and love, if you obediently believe the light and inspiration coming from heaven, which is the sign of Christ's sheep. What can the wolf do against these sheep, Saint Augustine asks, what can the thief do? The Good Shepherd has counted his sheep, because they are his and he knows this, they have been earmarked, called and sanctified by him for his glory. These sheep are neither carried away by the wolf nor stolen or killed by the thief, for hell holds no power against them. The Father, who is greater than all, gave them to the Son; the Son, who is equal to the Father, and is therefore called *the strength of God and his arm*, feeds or grazes them, leads them and defends them. Who can have any power against them? This is the foundation of the Catholic religion, the basis of Christian hope, a compelling force of the love we owe to God and witness of the unity to which we are called in this life. It is a perfect model of accomplishing this unity which will make us blessed in the next. Had the Jews been obedient to the voice of truth, they would have come to acknowledge the Saviour's divinity with only these words, and that since he was God the same as the Father, he does all things with him, not only by conforming to his works, but by virtue of a single operation; and that the Father and his Son, Jesus Christ, eternally hold together the same virtue, the same majesty, the same power and the same will. Encouraged by this faith, they would have given him the most humble thanks, because being eternally the same essence with the Father, he was also worthy to become our brother for our eternal salvation.

The scribes and Pharisees were outraged against Jesus Christ, after hearing the answer he gave them, and they took stones to throw at him, as they had done on other occasions. The first time they attempted such outrage, the Lord escaped from their clutches, which they could not prevent and had to withdraw from the confrontation: but he remained there in their midst. His posture was serene, and his imposing, majestic and steady bearing left them disarmed. And continuing his speech with such severity and firmness as were proper to his character, all so divine and imposing, he said to them: "I have wrought many good works before you, and I have also worked many wonders for your sake. For which one of them do you want to stone me?" Which was like telling them, "You arm yourselves with stones and thirst for my blood. Tell me, I beg you, what is the reason for all this rage? I have made you see many admirable works which I executed for you, with the blessing of my Father to do this. Which of these works of charity and mercy raises your loathing, that you want to stone me for them? Is it by chance when I cured the paralytic who was sick for thirty-eight years? Or is it for the healing of the blind man from birth that arouses your anger?" They found it hard to pose a sound motive to such an undeniable and effective apology; and in any case it could be seen that such an outstanding person, who had done so many good things, was risking to lose his life in the hands of those same persons who had witnessed the wonders he was claiming.

There is much to be learnt by men comparing the scribes and Pharisees' criminal conduct to Jesus Christ's blameless person. They sought to stone him as they would a blasphemer, rather moved by the poison of envy than by the love of justice. They were upset inwardly not with any order or express command of the Law, but wanted to stone him because they were hard of heart and blind in understanding, and could not grasp the depth of the Lord's words. For this reason, looking for hard stones, they ran to them and armed themselves against the God of wisdom and bounty. About which it would be right to know that there are some who are always ready to pay back men with evil for some evil they would have received from them, forgetting that this is highly forbidden since it is God who reserves for himself revenge for the evils men commit against their neighbours. Others must constantly return their neighbours with good deeds for the good they received from them; but they must be warned that this is a natural and not a debt deserving merit, with which the publicans comply, and many a time also animals themselves. There are others who fall short of returning good for evil although this shows what perfect charity is like and how to be a true child of God. This is what Jesus Christ did and practised, also teaching his apostles and disciples to practise it. Yet those who horrify and make one shudder most are those who return evil for the good done to them, which is somewhat cruel and evil; and this is precisely what the Jews put into practice against Jesus Christ. For this reason he challenged them by asking them for which of the good deeds he had done them they wanted to stone him.

The Saviour's humble response somewhat soothed the violent resolve that grew within them, and so it was, that those who apparently seemed to be calmest among them answered him: "We are not seeking to stone you for your good works, but for your blasphemy. Being a man like us, you made yourself the Son of God, and stoning is the penalty which the Law lays down for blasphemers." You have no reason to complain or treat me as a blasphemer because I said I am the Son of God. Open your scriptures, and in them you will find written, in very expressive and formal words, *I have told you, you are gods.* If Scripture calls sinful men and unjust magistrates with the name of gods rebuking their iniquities, if it honours those who should represent men on earth precisely with this great name for having a slight share in God's authority, and if for this reason the prophet's saying can be verified and is actually verified, why dare you say that I am a blasphemer when I call myself Son of God?" They saw him as a man and considered it impossible that he was also God.

This doctrine of God's union with man, of the humility of the Word made flesh, of the charity with which the flesh is raised highly to the glory of God and to the adoption of sons, was a horrible blasphemy for the Jews. They were not aware of a higher elevation of man than that caused by pride, nor could they comprehend any humiliation in God, who should neither degrade his dignity nor diminish his glory. So they mocked the Lord when he told them he was the Messiah who had been promised by his Father, and the expected One in his day; that he was the Christ or the Anointed One, namely, Son of God, man and God, and equal to God in all things; and above all, that he was the One whom his Father had sanctified and sent into the world to establish perpetual worship.

To prove that he was God and Son of God, he contrasted the meekness of the divine character that shone in him, with infidelity and slander. He also went out with the forceful and decisive language of Scripture to justify that he was not uttering any blasphemy. And what other more conclusive test could Jesus Christ claim in his favour than the powerful restraint with which he had cut down his great and relentless enemies, when speaking to them, to shameful silence? Any other teacher of religion should have spoken in such case with the strength of truth to contain the devastation caused by error and slander. But Jesus Christ knew, being true God, that the mystery of the Divinity should not be made public to the world before the time intended by eternal council, and so he defended himself on this occasion against slander, not with public and extraordinary displays of his omnipotence, but simply by referring to the holiness of his life and the truth of his mission.

"If I do not do the works of my Father," the Lord said, "you do not want to believe me; but if I do them and you do not want to believe me, believe my works, and you will know and believe that my Father is in me and I in my Father." It was just like saying to them: "You do not want to believe me only by my witness when I announce to you that I am the Son of God. I certainly excuse you from believing me if I do not do the works of my Father and if I do not make evidently credible the hidden truths which I reveal to you. If I did not confirm the divinity of my mission with the witness of my miracles, how could I tell you, *My Father and I are the same thing?* But if I testify to you and confirm the truth of my doctrine with works that can only be attributed to God my Father, how can you fail to recognise without sin that the Father is in me and I in him?" Jesus Christ explained himself in this manner on this occasion, since all his defence against blasphemy was reduced to clearly confessing what he had just said; but the Jews were not even satisfied with this. In all this their insanity, or rather hardness of heart, was remarkable. They wanted to know if he really was Christ; and because he showed this with deeds and words, they wanted to stone him. For they were inclined to believe in him neither with deeds nor with words, but being stubborn, all their eagerness was in their intention to catch him and the more so to kill him. But Jesus Christ wanted to persuade them in a natural manner and not forcefully, that is to say, not wanting them to become disappointed for not understanding him. Since he also wanted their will to be inclined towards submissiveness, respect and obedience, he did not want to give them any other explanations than those he had already given them. By these he had clearly and conclusively told them all about whom he was, which was what they wanted to know.

The Saviour's answers increased his disciples' belief in him, while his enemies became even more stubborn in not believing that he was the Son of God, as he claimed. So by desisting from the thought of stoning him, they resolved to capture him to judge him and condemn him to death. Poor people! How much better it would have been for them to approach him and beg forgiveness, to worship him with deeds, and to embrace him close to their heart! They wanted to catch him, but not for to hold him, but to get rid of him by death. Do find him if you know him by faith, hug him close to your breast and hide him in your bosom so as never to let go of him, and do possess him forever so that nothing happens to you like those ungrateful Jews. The Saviour walked away from them, freeing himself from their clutches, but also gaining a large number of proselytes. For many of the Jews themselves resolved to believe in him in spite and regardless of the persecution of the scribes, the rhetoric of the Pharisees, the lack of self restraint of the priests and the declared violence of the nation's chieftains. Jesus Christ for his part remained for some time in the most adapt place to gather the new disciples whom he had just won for the Gospel, and to confirm in faith all those sent to him by his Father. With all this in mind he chose to retire to the district of Bethany; not the town so near to Jerusalem where Lazarus lived with his family, but the other Bethany, or Bethabara, beyond and east of the Jordan river. There the Baptist had once dwelled, instructing, teaching and baptising all who came to him and joined his school, before he felt the need to retreat to Galilee, hounded by the unjust persecutions of the scribes and Pharisees.

CHAPTER 48
THE SAVIOUR DEFENDS HIS DISCIPLES FROM THE SLANDER OF THE SCRIBES AND PHARISEES, AND CONDEMNS HUMAN TRADITIONS AND SUPERSTITIOUS PRACTICES WHICH DO NOT CONFORM WITH THE PRECEPTS OF RELIGION (MT 15:1-20)

HE Lord moved out of the way of the clutches of his relentless enemies, the scribes and the Pharisees, and of those who constantly moved against him. They were unable to cause him any harm, despite the hatred with which they spoke against him and having already gone through all this on several other and various occasions. Rather, with more courage than ever, they were determined to capture and get rid of him as soon as possible. So they followed him everywhere in groups to find him in Galilee, which was the ordinary place where he resided, determined as they were to aim a new shot at his habits and doctrine. It is very likely that the scribes and Pharisees who on this occasion dared combat Jesus Christ, were Galileans who, having suffered with others in Jerusalem the defeats we have seen in the previous chapters in the same temple of the Lord where they had attended for the celebration of their solemnities, retreated full of remorse and sorrow for not being able to satisfy the thirst for vengeance which devoured them. Still they were neither discouraged nor did they falter, firmly believing in what they could achieve in making him out as a suspect of religion and disobedience to the Law of Moses. For them this was the only remaining manner to draw away from him the people's support and remove from them their good opinion of his holiness.

As there was nothing in his habits of which they could accuse him and rebuke him, they got hold of a very little thing, one of minor importance, which showed very clearly that it was not the zeal of their discipline or observance of the Law which encouraged them, but the fire consuming them with a most evil envy. For even if they saw him with the eyes of a rude faction, no direct charge could be laid against him, but against his disciples. They were no longer accused of breaking a precept of the Law, but of introducing a ceremony in the midst of legal tradition, under the pretext that they were thus more in conformity with the Law. Having distorted the Law with false interpretations, they had to sustain it with superstitious supports, that their feigned spirit and truth might somehow show. This custom was to clean very thoroughly the table ware and utensils, although they took little care to keep their souls clean of the revolting vices with which they were stained.

According to this practice or principle, they dared not sit at table without having washed their hands and arms many times up to the elbow, on returning from the market or public squares, where they could hardly have not come near an uncircumcised person, with great scruple not to touch food unless having previously gone through some sort of bath or any of their ritual washings. They even subjected themselves to a myriad of other annoying practices, such as frequently purifying the cups, jars, copper cups, and even the brazier tables or couches, on which they were to eat or over which they reclined during the meal. There is no doubt that all these customs were a superstitious extension of the misunderstood ordinances of Moses which, with their inclusion, make the observance of legal ceremonies, which were already onerous of themselves, become an almost intolerable yoke. And the Pharisees, who sought to acquire a great reputation and credit for holiness, preferred observing these superstitious traditions rather than the Laws of God, even the most essential ones. So that, in order to give a new facet to the new persecution they were pondering against Jesus Christ and his disciples, saying that they were shocked to see that some of them sat at table without washing their hands, they had the audacity to publicly reproach the Lord who tolerated this abuse which he should have been seeing as a horrible sin. "Why did you suffer," they tell him, "that your disciples violate with impunity a tradition bequeathed to us by our parents, and which is none else but a sign of the purity of customs?" It is very likely and plausible that the Galileans, in particular those who practise some industrial trade, were not as scrupulous as they wished in these overbearing practices, and did not see any offence in dispensing with them. But as Jesus Christ's apostles formed a school contrary to what the Pharisees taught, the latter asked for rigorous observance in all that they called perfection of the Law. And in seeing fault in this, they accused their Master of being an enemy of Moses, that he had ambitious sights, and that he was trying to rise against the nation's giver of the Law.

This was not the only time that slander and envious superstition sought to cover up with the cloak of observant zeal for the Law of God. But much as they did try, the poisonous arrow they wanted to shoot was soon uncovered, since they are entirely opposed to the practice and language of envy and virtue. The good and virtuous man tends to be corrected by others, but the envious hypocrite only looks at his own honour. He insults and confounds his neighbour, only to look like having a holy and virtuous spirit, calling the other a sinner but himself an innocent person. A haughty person poisons even the purest works; he hits back furiously, suffers with bitterness, rebukes with hatred; he becomes a judge without authority, an accuser without truth, a witness without knowing facts. All this happened exactly in such manner in the unjust reprimand with which the scribes and Pharisees were addressing Jesus Christ. In their self-conceit with their vain wisdom and with the pretentious virtue under which they took cover, they strapped latches around Jesus Christ and made a case out of the guilt of the disciples. What awful stubbornness it is to scold the Son of God, for not keeping the traditions of men! The Venerable Bede says of this: "They took in the flesh the spiritual words of the prophets concerning advice about the cleansing of the heart and reforming deeds in saying, *Wash yourself, be clean, and wash and cleanse all you who raise the holy vessels consecrated to the Lord.* They understood it only as referring to the external washing or cleansing of the body. So that the superstitious tradition of men more often took hold of the external ablutions and washing only for eating bread; so that it is even more necessary that those who wish to partake and eat the bread that comes down from heaven, should wash and be prepared, by giving alms more often, with tears and other works and fruits of justice, to purify themselves from the evil works they did."

God does not disapprove of the habit of washing one's hands before eating, of having nothing in one's heart against His law so that one can turn to His glory. What He condemns is the superstition with which it is done and other external practices of cleaning and grooming, or that what only matters is having good learning only as practised by those false teachers of justice. They were the type of those who are more jealous of transgressing human traditions than keeping divine precepts; more of breaching decrees than keeping the Gospel; and more of observing customs than making spiritual gains. Due to these pressing needs of exterior cleansing and little of introspection, the hypocrites are full of pretence and treachery to incriminate others by the commission of very slight faults, even if it is them who bear the weight of very serious faults, and who see the straw in the others' eye and do not see the beam in theirs. Yet Jesus Christ's disciples, who did not resemble them in anything, ate without washing their hands, because they knew well that this did not pertain to true virtue, which is the beautiful inner adornment of the soul. "Jesus Christ's disciples did not wash their hands before eating," Chrysostom says, "for they already looked with contempt at all superfluous things, tending only to those that were truly necessary. And not finding anything about this washing written in the Law as a precept, they sometimes washed but at others they did not, as circumstances required, for why should those, who by following Christ as a rule discard the necessary food, care about washing?

In plenty of arguing and boasting about this fault alleged by the scribes, it can never be seen to be in their favour owing to their false web of indiscreet zeal, but only as a lack of good education and political acumen. Yet it will always be more of a source of praise for the apostles than an accusation, for they preferred being called tactless rather than superstitious, and so all rebuke and punishment had to fall on the unjust censors who condemned what deserved praise and unduly praised what only their greed could allow.

The Lord could not pass through a disturbance, and wished that they would understand how much God disliked their malice. So, laying aside in a certain manner his normal gentleness, he gave them a stern rebuke, saying: "How dare you, hypocrites, condemn the innocent, you who commit such great abuses. who destroy true piety with such abominable practices and who, in poisoned hearts. hide your passions under a false appearance of zeal to serve God?" He did not excuse the apostles, but he confounded his accusers. And indeed, what is ablution of the Law compared to what Christ wants? Chrysologus says that Christ provided us with a bath in which to wash us, not our body to look decent in this life, but our soul for eternal salvation. Even the heart should draw near to the water of grace, in which the water enters to purify man from the filth of sin. The Pharisees were far from understanding this; that is why they did not embody true sanctification, since by ignoring the righteousness which has its source in God, they tried to establish a different one which they forged for themselves. Indeed, how fearsome is the false zeal of those who neither study the spirit of religion nor adhere to the Church's doctrine and prudence! Perversion is not to enliven with the spirit of God the external practices of piety, or only to put in them full acceptance of their spiritual sense without caring about charity, which is the first and supreme law, or rather the summation of the Law itself and of all laws.

The eternal Legislator presented the false doctors an argument which they could not contest, for as Saint Bernard says he was twisting a nail with another nail: *And how is it that you break God's commandment to fulfil your traditions?* Which means, if you break God's commandments to comply with your traditions, why do you argue that my disciples break men's commandments to fulfil God's precepts? Nothing is pleasing to God, whatever it was that you offered Him, if it despises what you are bound to fulfil.

"How well did the prophet Isaiah prophesy about you," the Lord continued, "when he wrote in your fathers' time: *This people honour me with their lips, and their hearts are far from me* (Is 29:13). The honour you give me is a vain ritual where precaution and whim are more important than motive. It will happen to you scribes and Pharisees, as to those in whom a sad prediction occurs to the letter. For you abandon the Law of God and keep with great care the vaunted tradition of your fathers. You resort to frequent washing and ablutions of your cups and jars, and I see you fully occupied with such small practices. In view of all this, if you do prefer the performance of works more than duty requires for God's precepts, you may already be excused. But by overdoing and upgrading precepts, you degrade and annihilate others, which are incomparably more essential and of utmost importance. Suffice to quote just one example, and this one is enough to confound you, since you pride yourself in being the most jealous observers of the Law of Moses."

"Whatever your way of thinking," Jesus Christ continued, "you cannot doubt that the Law God, given to you by the hand of Moses and written in the hearts of men with the finger of God and that of nature, prescribes children's obligations towards their parents. So here, see the terms in which it is written that *You shall honour your father and your mother*. This honour entails respecting them, obeying and maintaining them, if necessary, and to assist them in their needs. And the Law further states that *Whoever curses his father or his mother, will be committed to death*. This really means anyone who outrages them by word, or makes signs of contempt against them or abandons them with insult in their need. The divine precept commanding us to honour and maintain parents is very clear. Yet you treat all this in a despicable manner, teaching that the son's offering pleases God more than helping his father in his needs. This is an insult to God's law and makes a sham of it, which due to the perverted aims of our passions demotes it to the whims and dreams of corrupted thinking. He kills his father whoever, under cover of very great perfection, abandons his parents when they are in need. Whoever takes away from them what he owes them by justice and gratitude, commits a sacrilege even if he does it to give to another person with pious and holy intention. Where have you seen or could ever see mercy unless it is related with charity? And where do you have, or have you ever seen, charity without the order established in it by natural and divine law? And what charity would that be of whoever was supported by his father or mother to help him in his needs, or to relieve him in later years, to answer them that the gifts which I present to God in his temple shall make the Lord favourable and providential towards you; this is all the relief I can offer you? Do you think that with this response he would have already satisfied the Law, and that the son was relieved of all obligation? Do you forbid your children from going any farther, and want parents in their need and destitution to be content with the harsh words that they are not breaking God's commandment?" Jesus Christ did not speak but of this precept, when he could have also mentioned all others and embarrassed them with the changes he had brought about in them.

In truth, the hearts of those evil men were far from God, for which reason they unjustly rebuked and accused those who with the greatest scrupulous faith fulfilled his commandments. They also dishonoured the patriarchs and prophets by making themselves authors of the harmful novelties which they introduced, and with this false devotion and religion under which they appeared and inspired simple gullible people, they not only showed contempt for the most dignified and holy truths, but also for the true traditions which they had received from their parents. Certainly, it was praiseworthy that the Saviour chose to shut the mouth of his malicious and false accusers, since the abuse to which abandoned parents were continually exposed was of special interest to one and all. With all that, he did not judge anything he had exposed to be sufficient to silence the malice. So he also wanted to warn the crowd with a brief parable against the virtue and holiness which were all so apparent in the flesh of those false doctors and with which they embattled the spirit of the Law. They persuaded their disciples to be slavishly subject to the letter of human traditions, and unaccustomed to meditate on the spirit of the Law, that greater perfection only consisted in the choice of food or in the preparation of animal bodies to be eaten. For the flesh of animals entering the stomach was pure of itself otherwise it would stain one's conscience; this Jesus Christ told them without giving them to understand that obedience to the Law or its violation, was what made good or bad before God the use of certain foods, and as to that which was prohibited, it did not matter much on this subject.

Then in order to combat this ideal of justice held by the Pharisees, Jesus Christ called all the attending crowd close to him and told them: "Listen to me and understand well what I am about to tell you. Although the Lord has never allowed men to eat indistinctively from all kinds of food, and since there are some men who have wanted to abstain at certain times, it is not the food that enters through the mouth which makes man unclean. The consumption of exquisite food, or of whatever kind, does not on its own make any difference, for it is only disobedience that makes it sinful. But it is what comes out of man's mouth which is sometimes of such nature that it stains the soul. All that comes from outside and enters man cannot make him a sinner, but what comes out from his inner self is often bad and can justly accuse him of sin. Look here what I have to tell you. Blessed are those to whom God has given the grace to understand it." It was easy to know that Jesus Christ spoke of the spiritual stain, which is not precisely contracted by food and drink, but by intemperance and gluttony, by disobedience to God's laws, and by lack of charity in consuming fine food. Yet beware, for undoubtedly it gives us what is hidden in our hearts, rather than the unknown things coming from outside. For this reason the Lord left it for those who had heard him to consider and inquire into the mysterious meaning around the parable he had just told them. The mobs drew away from Jesus Christ, glad to have heard the Saviour's justification, while strongly resenting the scribes for the humiliating effrontery they had just received. They had exposed themselves very often to such humiliations, since being proud and overly passionate to their doctrines, they entertained great vanity. And as they were bribed to speak of their gifts, they made a very poor choice of subjects to create slander against the Saviour, so that no matter how little did Jesus Christ answer them, they could not leave from before his presence but full of confusion. It would surely not have happened to them, if those who boasted being wise men had based their wisdom on the fear of God and knowledge of the Holy Scripture, for they would have found written in it that his father David had relentlessly prayed the Lord (Ps 141:3-4) to guard his mouth and keep watch over the door of his lips, so that his heart would not incline to utter evil words.

Being shy and weak, even Jesus Christ's disciples were frightened to hear the scribes and Pharisees speak with such strength and courage. Approaching Jesus Christ they said to him, "Do you know, Lord, that the Pharisees have been greatly shocked and offended by the words you have just spoken?" "Do not worry about this," the Saviour replied to his disciples with the same energy and firmness that he had previously spoken to the others. "Do not take notice of the ill will of these people. Every plant that is not set by my Heavenly Father will be uprooted, as none of them should grow in my Church, which is the ground I have come to cultivate, and all who belong to another ground die hopelessly." Such are these scribes and Pharisees, sowing busily among people principles which go against true piety. "Or more clearly," as Saint Gregory says, "every plantation of human traditions, namely, of man-made doctrines, which do not conform with God's law, and so are not plantations of my Heavenly Father but rather of the coldness of the flesh, will be uprooted by reproach together with those who planted them from the field of my Church, whose foundation is Jesus Christ himself. They will be uprooted from among the faithful, by separation, and from the land of the living by deprivation, for they do not retain a solid foundation and firm roots. The time will come when they will be exterminated; let them wither away, since they are unwilling to enter the right way. Let them move on to the beginning of their eternal damnation, and as for you avoid their doctrine, for they are none else but a bunch of thorns who do not let the grains of the Gospel bear fruit in the earth of man's heart. The heavenly Worker who came to plant this, will not allow the bad seed to overtake the good seed. Leave them, the Lord repeated, for they are the blind who lead other blind ones; and you know that when a blind man leads another, both of them fall off the cliff. They are blind because they lack true understanding of the Law, and they lead other blind persons, because they blind them with their errors and walk them off the cliff."

Elsewhere, Saint Gregory himself says: "When a shepherd walks on the cliff edge of vices, it is most likely that the flock falls into the precipice." And Saint Bernard adds: "It is ridiculous, and I rather say very dangerous, to have a blind leader, an ignorant doctor, a lame forerunner, a negligent prelate, a mute town crier. Yet alas! There are many lame persons who want to show the way and many childish and foolish persons who want to preside. Many people are willingly blind because they abhor the light, and close their eyes not to see what the light really shows them. Others who have the light of knowledge muddle along and are blinded by the smoke of vanity. There is also that person who holds high the light for others to see but stays in the dark himself. Owing to his blindness we must flee, and how much more than the blindness of the first. What love can a soul embrace in the hands of a blind man? It is great misery to fall into the hands of a director who lacks the light needed to guide souls through the narrow path."

It seems that after Jesus Christ gave this explanation, he returned to his hometown and life in Nazareth, followed by his apostles and sending people to their homes. As soon as Saint Peter found himself alone with Jesus Christ and his other companions, he took the liberty of asking him on behalf of all for a clearer explanation of the parable he had just told them, as it seemed to them more mysterious than it actually was. So Jesus Christ told them: "Are you still in such a state of need and imprudence, when after being with my way of teaching for so long, you find yourself with great lack of understanding and speechless? Do you not understand that what enters man from outside cannot stain or corrupt him? Do you still fail to consider that nothing consumed through the mouth enters the heart but goes to the entrails, and exits with all the bodily waste and is thrown into the sewer? But it is not the same with what comes out of man's mouth, for the heart comes and goes, and this is what pollutes him and makes him unclean and sinful. It is from man's heart and inner self from where evil thoughts come; that is where adultery, murders, all other dishonesty, thefts, greed, false witness, fraud, lust, envy, blasphemy, pride, foolishness, recklessness and ill temper grow. All these evils and many others come from within. The mouth does not give them to light before being first conceived by the heart." See here what stains man in God's eyes. Yet food which is eaten without washing one's hands does not stain a man, nor does it make him guilty of sin in the eyes of the Lord.

Let them therefore learn, those who neglect the custodian of their heart, this important doctrine that the sovereign Master knew in a very timely manner how to turn for the benefit of his apostles, making this and everything else done in his preaching, a means to perfect them in the apostolate, while instructing them how to react to their enemies' insults. Let them learn those who always keep the windows of the spirits open, through which slavery, corruption and death enter into the soul, for by despising all the flattery of the world and the lust of the flesh, they will know how to confuse the holy doctors even if they wage against them a more cruel and terrible war than the persecution of tyrants. After all this Jesus Christ also showed with his speeches and examples that the apostles ought not to be deceived, even with the pretext of their neighbours' spiritual needs according to the flesh. And that if they can for some time assist and treat their neighbours very carefully, they must be involved with less reserve to strangers, being ever more willing to take heed of the work of a Gospel minister than that of their household and relatives. Above all, it is what Saint Augustine says: "It is necessary for men to understand that our evil intentions are not always aroused by the devil, but are often aroused by the activity of our free will; yet good thoughts always come from God. Understand and learn from the council I give you about the manner of omitting them from your will. Never argue with evil thoughts or with the wicked inclinations of the will, and when they annoy you and engage in battle with you, distract yourself and occupy your thoughts and will with some useful and fruitful consideration. And so, fight hard until you can make a thought vanish away as soon as possible, for there is nothing that destroys a bad thought and bad inclination more than another which goes against the first.

To this end it seems that the Apostle said in a timely manner when writing to those of Galatia: "Proceed according to the Spirit of God and you will not satisfy the appetites of the flesh. For the flesh has desires contrary to those of the Spirit, and the spirit has them contrary to those of the flesh, as they are opposite things to each other, for which reason you do not do all that you want. But if you are led by the Spirit, you are not subject to the Law. Well manifest are the works of the flesh, they are: adultery, fornication, dishonesty, insults, enmities, lawsuits, quarrels, dissensions, heresies, envy, murders and other similar ones. On the contrary, the fruits of the Spirit are: charity, joy, peace, patience, kindness, goodness, faithfulness, meekness, faith, modesty, continence, and chastity." (Gal 5:16-23) The principle and root of those vices, which blind the eyes of reason and perfect knowledge because they come out of the bottom of a corrupted heart, are easily extinguished by the exercise of these virtues. Union with God is another more purposeful remedy which makes man see the light, which is always surrounded by the dreadful darkness which hell casts around it, because this union is the healthiest remedy in every temptation. And this is what Saint Augustine said: "When I became one with you, O Lord, I unburdened myself of an unbearable weight, and I do not suffer anymore from labour or pain." And who is unaware that such union is our first obligation? Who can think himself to be so strong that he can carry such a heavy burden? Who can rely so much on his own forces that he believes he does not need the help of God's grace, when at the bottom of his heart he carries his strongest and most formidable enemies? Who hears this and does not tremble, and does not examine himself, and does not attempt to seriously begin reforming his customs, with an entire change of heart, from where come the stains that make man abominable in the divine presence? So guard your heart, oh man, lock it with the seal of God's fear, so that there may the roots of vices dry out, and only His holy and true love may be born in him.

CHAPTER 49
THE LORD HEALS THE CANAANITE, A DEAF AND MUTE, AND WITH SEVEN LOAVES AND A FEW FISH FEEDS FOUR THOUSAND
(MT 15:21-28; MK 7:31-37; 8:1-9)

ALL the journeys Jesus Christ made after the narration in the previous chapter were away from Jerusalem, and his plans after going to Nazareth all point very clearly to the end of the race in which he ran and to the terrible moment of his sacrifice. Two and a half years had passed from when, having dedicated himself to the preaching of the Gospel, he worked incessantly in establishing the kingdom of God, being seen in almost all the places of Palestine where his mission spread. It was from almost all villages, large and small, that crowds had gone to visit him while he was at Capernaum. They were both ordinary and simple folk, besides men of culture and princes, centurions and Pharisees, doctors and publicans. For his charity reached all, and he did not withhold his lessons and solace from anyone. However, there were some areas where he was not seen, and others where he had only been seen in passing; and yet he did not want any of the sons of Israel and Judah to say he had forgotten them. Although the cities of Tyre and Sidon were located within the confines of the land of Canaan, within the limits of the province of Syria in Phoenicia, Jesus Christ did not want to stop visiting them since they belonged to the tribe of Asher. Indeed this is very much like the neighbouring peoples of Naphtali, Zebulun and Manasseh, who did not destroy, as ordered by God, all the idol worshippers who possessed the land they had to occupy; yet they were still kept at the centre of the Saviour's attention, so much so that after the return from the Assyrian captivity, the Jews residing in those places were confused with the Canaanites, who were known by the name of Phoenicians and Syro-Phoenicians. It was to these, who formed part of the field which he himself was to cultivate by his own hand, that he went to offer them

the light, although they were surrounded by pagans and sunken in the darkness of idolatry.

Undoubtedly, the shabbiness of the valleys surrounding Lebanon and the vicinity of the seas were one of the reasons why the sons of Israel were not able to expel or exterminate the Gentiles entirely from the Promised Land. So that when the cult of false gods was introduced among them, and ever farther away from the safeguards provided by the Holy City to its brethren, they were due to receive more specific attention by the Son of God. We do not know for how long the Lord worked and remained in these countries because it seems they were not dealt with by sacred historians, other than to let us know that no section of God's people was despised by the Messiah, and perhaps also to contrast a foreign woman's faith with the unfaithfulness of Abraham's children.

When Jesus Christ left Nazareth, he went on to the periphery of Tyre and Sidon. Having entered a house to rest from the day's travel, a Canaanite woman sought him secretly. She was a Gentile and a Syro-Phoenician by birth, and had a daughter who was possessed with an unclean spirit. On finding Jesus Christ she called out to him telling him, *Lord, Son of David, have mercy on me; my daughter is severely possessed by a demon*. But Jesus Christ did not say a word to her. It is important to note here the expressions with which the Evangelists introduced this new miracle, and by means of which the coming of the Universal Benefactor spread throughout that country. The reasons why the Saviour leaves one land to go to another are hidden in God's council. By this we learn faith even more who the Lord is through his gifts, and that he gives them and distributes them to whoever he wants as he does not owe us anything. As Jesus Christ leaves one land to go to another, so does the woman from the periphery of Gentile and sinful lands go in search of him. He so wants to teach and make us understand that the sinful soul must leave its shell, or its sins, on a path of penance to find the Saviour; for it is not enough that man turns away from sins unless he leaves their borders, being the occasions and causes of sin. According to the Gospel text, it seems that Jesus Christ had not yet manifested himself to the Gentiles and kept away from having anything to do with them; but as a special favour he wanted to make himself known to a single Canaanite woman, to show his great mercy. It was so then that, showing greater wisdom, she looked for him at his abode, or that being inspired she knew the way through which he would pass. True to say, however, that after she saw him she was crying behind him, and that the apostles, who surrounded their Master and believed they knew his intentions, would not allow her to approach him. She had heard of the fame of the miracles Jesus Christ had wrought and firmly believed he could heal her daughter; so this kept her shouting to draw his attention, greeting him as Son of David, that he might show compassion for her and her daughter. And could he desist from caring for her, being the One who with infinite kindness went all out to meet those who did not seek him? Him who without being requested goes out to the region of the Gentiles to haul them out from darkness to light and to fill them all with his gifts? To seek Jesus Christ the foreign woman left the confines of her land; meaning that for the human heart to find him, it must be despoiled of earthly affections and give up itself to mortification and penance. The wisdom of those who achieve salvation does not encompass earthly gifts and delights. Abraham had to leave his native land to be blessed by God; Lot had to leave Sodom not to perish among the fires; and the sons of Israel would have never entered the Promised Land had they not left Egypt. No wonder, then, that this woman left the borders of Sidon to meet Christ. When she found him she cried out to him. Her discovery is part of the prize for her faith, and the healing she later obtained for her daughter fulfils that prize; for her plea was accompanied by humility and sealed by hope.

The Saviour's disciples put up every obstacle for her not to come close to him, but this was none else than a prelude of much more she had yet to encounter in following him, pleading to him with such great trust; for surely, until then the Lord had not made anyone wish so ardently for his mercies and graces. This fervent woman being unable to get any closer to Jesus Christ, she raised her voice even more did and cried more strenuously to be heard: *Lord, Son of David, have mercy on me; my daughter is cruelly tormented by the devil; I beseech your help.* Although she was an afflicted mother stricken with pain in seeing her daughter possessed by a demon, the Lord still did not answer even a word; he wanted to avoid the people's slander right then in seeing him preach to the Gentiles. At the same time he also wanted the beseeching woman's faith to shine even brighter by keeping himself unknown. In the apparent harshness with which God often treats us, there is hidden true mercy with which he also prepares his gifts for us. Blessed is he who does not faint or falter in these trials but further enlivens his faith with new groans, being grateful for the healthy thrusts of mercy. As Jesus Christ showed no sign of responding to the pleas of the Canaanite woman, nor of turning his eyes to her, the more did she raise her clamour so much so that the apostles, being worn out and moved by her constant perseverance in crying and imploring, interceded for her. They drew near to Jesus Christ and said to him: "May we pray you, Lord, that you send her away and grant her favour. Grant her what she asks, also for her not to bother us any longer, for she has been screaming behind us." Which was like telling him, "We well know that you have come here to teach the sons of Jacob; but this does not prevent you from hearing in passing the pleas of a foreign woman who shows so much confidence in you; at least give in to her pestering." But the Lord answered: "I have not been sent other than for the lost sheep of the house of Israel."

The answer Jesus Christ gave seemed very harsh and hard, and did not seem like promising anything favourable to the Canaanite woman. Nothing apparently stopped the Lord, but walking even faster he entered the house where he wanted to stay hidden until the next morning. But the woman, constant in her faith and encouraged by hope, followed Jesus Christ, entered the house, and threw herself at his foot adoring him and saying *Help me, Lord*, beseeching him to cast out the devil from her daughter. It can be clearly seen here how much God wants to be prayed fervently, with ardent faith, deep humility and trusting hope, even for that same thing which He already wishes to give. And it is also known how pleased He is that, by distrusting ourselves, we appoint his saints to intercede for us and the pure chosen ones to pray for us. The apostles did not bother about the cry of faith, but they longed to see it awarded, and so they mediated for her with their prayer. The Lord was silent to the Canaanite woman's cries and pleas which she addressed by herself, but when the apostles joined in her plea, he disposed of his goodness. It seems as if the doors of gentleness were closed for this Gentile woman, but since faith makes children of Abraham out of those who are not of his descent according to the flesh, the Canaanite woman, who was made faithful by the gift of Christ, was not excluded from the salvation he brought to the world. And so it was that to protect this same faith, as soon as she could approach the Lord, she prostrated herself before him and adored him. To the unexpected prayer she added worship, faith brought her closer to God, humility prostrated her in His presence, and trust gave encouraged her to persevere. No one can steal trust from spiritual fervour, so that there is nothing that gets in the way of prayer. But Jesus Christ, who still wanted to further purify the good mother's faith, answered her: *It is not right to take the bread of the children and throw it to the dogs*. In spite of their disloyalty the Lord treated the Jews as children. Who is not moved by Jesus Christ's meekness? Who will have the courage to pay back evil for evil? Surely that as much as we discover Jesus Christ's apparent resistance in comforting the woman, just as much does this unfortunate woman's faith shine out and is exalted.

The answer given by Jesus Christ appears to be more mysterious than harsh. It is like the touchstone with which the carats of the most precious metals are assayed and known, since with it all that this magnificent and singular woman values as faith is also recognised. She does not complain about the manner with which Jesus Christ treated her, but she rises to the occasion of giving further shine and force to her prayer. This is a flair of humility, and this is her eloquence: to deject and humble herself the more so when the Saviour reproaches and mortifies her most. "I am not complaining, my Jesus Christ, just because you are treating me like a bitch. On the contrary, I confess to you that I am more disgusting than dogs. But you know well, *that even dogs eat from crumbs that fall from their masters' table*." As to the sinner who truly seeks God and desires to be saved, it is no wonder that he is treated with the holy severity that forms part of penance. Everything seems sweet and bearable when he remembers that he deserves hell; his eagerness is to approve of this severity to draw himself away ever farther from guilt. He would joyfully subject himself to the laws and spirit of the Church; appreciate the humiliation which makes him worthy of forgiveness; and consider it as very desirable to hold on to Gospel precepts to deserve in this manner that God looks at him with mercy. He does not seek the safety of forgiveness in a quick confession, but in perseverant prayer, which is what strengthens the soul in goodness and roots it in holy purpose. And this is what this faithful and pestering woman showed in the heroic perseverance with which she insistently pleaded the Saviour. Saint Jerome said about this woman: "In the Canaanite woman, the faith, patience and humility of the Church are wonderfully discovered. Faith, because she believed that her daughter could be healed; patience, because although she was often despised, she persevered in her prayers; and humility, in comparing herself not to dogs but to puppies."

Chrysostom also contemplates on the humility of this woman, and cannot fail to exclaim: "Oh truly admirable patience and humility! God calls the Jews children, and she calls them lords; nor does she resent the Lord when he praises his enemies, nor is she angry at the embarrassment and contempt she suffers, but rather the more so humbles herself." Jesus Christ calls the Gentiles dogs to, while she compares herself to puppies which apparently resist being given bread, but she only asks to be allowed to eat from the crumbs that fall from the table, Which was the same thing like saying to the Lord: "I know well that I do not deserve the sons' bread, and that I do not deserve to eat food with them or to sit at the table with the Father, yet I am happy with the morsels that are thrown at the puppies." Or it was rather like saying to him: "You pour out abundant favours on Abraham's descendants; I do not expect but the least of graces which you very prodigiously shower on them." We can here see clearly three requests being made by the Canaanite woman, In the first she asks for freedom, saying *Have mercy on me, Lord, Son of David.* In the second she asks for God's help, because she knows her weakness, and so adds *Lord, help me*. And in the third she seeks being satisfied in some manner, and so ends her plea saying *Because puppies eat from the crumbs that fall from their masters' table*. In the first she confesses being a servant, in the second being a sick woman, and in the third a petitioner. So this is the order: man first becomes a slave by sin, then powerless to come out of such an unhappy state by himself, and finally he becomes a beggar since he cannot relieve himself of the evils with which he is afflicted. These three requests mean and represent the effects of grace: in the first, the grace of remission as pertaining to justifying grace; in the second, that of good works as found in operative grace; and in the third, that of consolation, corresponding to perfect grace.

Before mentioning the honourable faith which Jesus Christ showed towards this unfortunate woman, it is worth mentioning, even if only in summary form, the reasons why he had to proceed in such rough manner with her. In Jesus Christ's time, the Jews were extremely proud and no less concerned, believing that Almighty God was only their God, and neither God of the Canaanites, or of the Egyptians or of any other strangers. They also believed that the promise of the Messiah, of salvation, the kingdom and happiness was a grace and a benefit which were exclusively bestowed upon their nation. Owing to this mindset they looked upon the Gentiles and foreigners as filthy animals, damned and unworthy of God's care, and of His providence and love. This is how the Jews conceived the Gentiles, and this concern was the origin of their stubborn resistance to the Gospel. During the Saviour's long dialogue with the Canaanite woman, he speaks of this very absurd opinion and other than confirming it, he indirectly rejects it by stating facts. And if he immediately refuses to grant the Canaanite woman the grace for which she was asking him, it was to test her faith and call the attention of those present, implying that he had many chosen ones both among Jews and Gentiles, with the Gentiles always having more faith and submissiveness than the Jews. And while he says that he has come to shepherd the lost sheep in the house of Israel, he also ensures that he came to save all men and to preach the Gospel, first to the Jews and then to the Gentiles, and that there will be nothing but one flock and one shepherd for all men. God wants to save all men and that they might become aware of the truth.

When Jesus Christ heard the humble and patient response of the Canaanite woman, he answered her saying: "Oh woman, great is your faith; let it be done with you as you wish. Since you have asked humbly and persevered consistently, you have been heard. Go back to your house and you will find your daughter free of the demon. Right now as I speak to you, the evil spirit has abandoned her." From that woman's charity the greatness of her faith was born. Christ let himself to be affected by the force of love. And how could he stop hearing the prayers of love, he who for love's sake came down from heaven and died on a cross? Jesus Christ allowed such repeated pleas so that the admirable faith of the woman may shine brighter, and so that the liberality with which he rewards acts of love may be equally found to shine with him. So he healed the daughter of the Canaanite woman for he absolutely had no doubt about the mother who asked for it. She ran back home and found her daughter actually free, and for ever, from the clutches of her persecutor. "Oh, woman!" Chrysostom exclaims. "Great is your faith; you did not see a man being resurrected from the dead, nor a leper suddenly made clean, nor did you hear the prophets, nor did you ponder the holy law of the Lord, nor did you see how the sea parted and was divided. None of this could you see or contemplate, and being nevertheless despised and intimidated by me, you did not retreat, but persevered in your asking. And since your faith has been so great, this is why the grace that has been poured upon you has also been the more abundant; be comforted because your daughter has already been healed."

Let us therefore pray with great and fervent petition to God our Lord that He may free our souls and heal them from all sin, since because of them our souls are badly tormented by the devil. Let us cry unto the Lord with humility and perseverance, saying together with the Canaanite woman: "Have mercy on me, Lord, Son of David; and Lord, help me. My soul is very tormented by the devil, for it continues to sin and perseveres in offences; should it convert and not

CHAPTER 49

despair of the Lord's mercy, it will be told by the most merciful Jesus Christ: Let it be done as you wish; and it will become immediately healthy; for at any time when the sinner converts and mourns his faults and sins, *he will live and not die.*" So do not despair or cease begging, for if you ask with a pure and faithful heart, persevering in prayer and humbling yourself in the presence of the Lord, considering yourself unworthy of his blessings, do firmly believe that you will obtain anything you ask. And just as the apostles prayed for the Canaanite woman, the angel of the Lord will pray for you, and your petition will be well and promptly dealt with.

After Jesus Christ had worked this miracle which was, so to say, drawn from his compassion in not being able to do otherwise, he departed from the neighbourhood of Tyre and passed through Sidon to the Sea of Galilee. He took a great turn along the borders of the ten cities near the Jordan River, such that their waters flow on either side and soak them with their currents, and visited all the places occupied by native Jews, preaching everywhere the coming of the kingdom of God. When he arrived at the western shore of the Sea of Tiberiades, where he was not very eager to stop for a long time, a deaf and mute person was brought to him, who prayed him to place his hand on him. He was not deaf or mute since birth, nor due to any illness that had come upon him, but he was precisely so since the devil had deprived him of hearing and speaking. This happened so that when he was healed three miracles occurred; he regained his hearing, and his speech, and he was freed from the devil. They asked the Saviour to place his hand upon him, being the Almighty One and having created everything. For indeed, the Lord holds in his hand a great virtue to heal and save, for he is salvation and life, doctor and medicine, and heals whatever he touches, and gives salvation to all who look upon him. So the Lord took the miserable man and drew him apart from the others' company, wet his fingers with his own spit, and put them in the man's ears while also touching his tongue. Although the Lord had taken the deaf and mute man apart and a short distance away, he acted in such manner that all his actions could be seen and all his words heard. He raise his eyes to heaven to address his prayers to his Father, an inexhaustible source of all good things. Then he lowered his eyes and fixed his gaze on the miserable man he wanted to heal, sighing over his misfortune and crying with a loud voice *Ephetha*, which in Syrian means *Be opened*. When this word was uttered the man's ears became unblocked and his tongue was loosened, and he understood what was being said and spoke easily and fluently in a perfect manner.

There is no doubt, as the Holy Gospel states very well, that *wherever the Lord passed through he did good to all, and freed and healed all those who were oppressed by the devil*. This travel from one people to another shows the extent of the Saviour's zeal, and teaches a lesson about the measure with which charity proceeds even in the relief of spiritual needs. The praise which the mobs gave him did not cause Jesus Christ to stop in any one place, nor did it take away from him the envy or slander of the Pharisees; in everything he does he continues according to the ends of his mission, giving proof of it and always accomplishing, wherever it might be, his Father's will. When the Lord is so incessantly engaged in these events in doing good, it is no wonder to note what Saint Matthew says: "Great crowds gathered around Jesus Christ, bringing with them from their neighbourhood a large number of dumb, blind, lame, paralyzed and sick from all kinds of ailments, whom they put at his divine feet and he healed them all (Mt 15:30)."

Jesus Christ worked the miracle of healing this deaf and mute man with all the good will he had and was characteristic of him, in accordance with the designs of his charity and eternal love for man. Yet it is worth noting that before performing it he set his eyes on heaven, sighed with compassion, and in seeking the favour and help of his Father's hand he showed that he was truly a man. But by performing the miracle, speaking with command and authority, he attested that he was truly God. The deaf and the mute are in human lineage the fathers and doctors of the Church who never heard either the warnings or the doctrine of eternal salvation, and so failed to praise God our Lord. It is for him that the Patriarchs and Prophets had prayed, expecting the Incarnation of Christ our Redeemer, that he might place on them the hand of mercy that heals man through his coming in the flesh. Blind is man when he looks at things which are not to be seen, and deaf is he when he hears those things which are not to be heard. This man is maimed, when he reaches out to touch prohibited things; he is crippled, when he rises himself ever higher by pride; ailing with dropsy, when he lusts for evil; full of leprosy, when he is stripped of virtues; and finally dead, when he defends stubbornly and harshly his evil doings.

The Venerable Bede says that "In these actions of Christ his two natures, divine and human, were well demonstrated. Sighing and begging his Father showed that he was truly a man; and healing with one word the deaf, mute and possessed man, gave him credit as being omnipotent and almighty. The Lord unblocks every day and opens the ears of the sick to hear and to speak, when so justified by the grace of he who is Most High on earth and in heaven, and unhesitatingly obeying the holy warnings and praising with tongue and heart the giver of all goods, we constitute here on earth a choir with the heavenly spirits, and we bless and praise with them the living for ever and ever." It was also with his sigh and groan that Jesus Christ instructed us about the great diligence we must put into action each day in the Service of God and by holy obedience to Him, for all sinners while praying ceaselessly for them; and this ought to be done in the same manner as those who brought the deaf mute before the Saviour and also prayed wholeheartedly for him so much that Jesus Christ deigned to heal him. Saint Gregory observes about this same passage that "Having opened the deaf mute's ears and loosened his tongue, the man *spoke fluently and says...*" This makes us understand that we must proclaim and preach to others the mercies and graces we receive from the hand of the Lord, for this being a heroic confession is also a wonderful manifestation of our gratitude; its opposite would be to keep always one's ears closed and the tongue tied, about which the Lord complained in Isaiah's words saying: "When I called, you did not answer; when I spoke, you did not listen." (Is 65:12) Which means that, the disobedient person is deaf, and he who ceases to give God due thanks and sing his praises is mute. Finally, it is also worth noting that the deaf mute is free from the devil in the presence of the ten cities, namely the ten commandments, which if we observe we are free from the power of hell.

From his first prodigy with the deaf and mute man, the Saviour forbade those who had witnessed it to say what they had seen. It happened to be a Saturday, but no one thought himself to be bound by obedience as the general awe, joy and gratitude made this impossible. This is not a command with a precept of obligation, but only to teach men that they should humble themselves taking his example. However great and wonderful the good deeds Jesus Christ did, they were still to hold this prohibition at all times when he performed these most extraordinary signs. Saint Augustine particularly points to two reasons as being of great importance, why Jesus Christ gave this prohibition. The first was to teach us that no one should boast about virtues and wonders, other than about the cross and his dejection and contempt. The second, that in all the mercies and benefits we bestow on others, we should never seek our own praise in them. But inasmuch as those who receive such benefits should always praise their benefactors, so has the Lord permitted that the more he commanded them to keep silent in proof of his great humility, the more would circumstances arise to make public the magnificence, greatness and mercy of such a singular Benefactor, saying loudly, "He did everything well, giving hearing to the deaf and speech to the dumb." All the good things God wanted to make known to exalt his glory, will not be hidden or forgotten by the humility of the person on whom he would have wrought them.

With remarkable intellect Saint Jerome writes that the evangelist said, *the Lord did everything well*, so that we might understand that it is not enough for man to do good things unless they are done well. They are done well when in doing them we ask for our Lord's help, and when we oust the vainglory we may be seeking in them. If we were by chance to do anything good that is praiseworthy, we must not eulogise or preach about it, waiting for the people's applaud; on the contrary, we are bound to cover it up humbly. Saint Augustine says about this: "He who has virtues should seek to keep them by fleeing away from vainglory, for being in contempt of them is considered to be very laudable in God's eyes. He who belittles the praises of flatterers which are held in esteem by the Lord and his saints, and also those who are wise in the world according to God, brag about them and magnify them." And Saint Chrysostom concludes that: "Vainglory, though highly coveted, is a perverse thing. It is a vice that shows deep ignorance, and it is difficult for those who are possessed by it to open their eyes since they love themselves and their things very much. This vice cuts off a man and departs him from heaven, nailing down to earth the wretched hearts which are already held captive without letting them see the true light. This vice begets greed, causes envy, accusations and outrages. This vice arms and provokes those who have not received any evil or harm, against those who never did them any wrong. It neither recognises loyalty nor friendship, and whoever falls into this filthy illness loses all shame, dismissing from his heart all that which can cause him to be humble, becoming a miserable man with no friends, for all mock him. They will never tell him the truth, but only shower on him praise and flattery while feeling in their heart much the opposite of what they say."

It is precisely so that whoever wants to live according to the holy law of the Lord, should constantly watch over himself to receive and preserve in his heart the priceless virtue of humility, fleeing from the flatterers who mock him and sneer at him. Man should only expect to be praised by God in heaven, in the presence of all the saints, for which it is compulsory that he is despised on earth. The true honour that is enjoyed before God is to despise that which belongs to this world and not to take any account of the vanities of this earth, and to conform wholly with the will of Him who with utmost scrupulous diligence examines all intentions and scrutinizes all hearts. Let man be praised by God and by the inhabitants of the heavenly homeland, from which all good must come, and from whose hand he must receive all mercies; and this will certainly ensure his steadfast and eternal happiness and glory.

Jesus Christ performed these works of charity over three days, during which the mobs attended without fail to hear him, attracted by the softness and sweetness of his words, and as if enchanted and carried away in contemplation by his goodness and mercy. So many miracles as the Lord did came, however, to be sealed with an even more general and greater One. Jesus Christ called the apostles, who were then mixing with the mob, around him. Fixing his eyes on the crowd, he said to the apostles: "I truly pity this great people. You see that for three whole days they have been determined to follow me and not to depart from me. They have eaten all they had while some have come from very far away. Were I to send them away in this state they will lack the strength to walk along the way. I cannot solve this and you have to feed them." Only a few are those, and hopefully not many, who in their eagerness to seek and follow Christ forget their own comfort and their life's needs. In the eyes of human wisdom these people were reckless, exposing themselves to starvation in order not to abandon the interior food of the spirit. So that in the eyes of religion it was very sensible and worthy to be rewarded with one of the Saviour's great wonders. What an important lesson did Jesus Christ give to everyone on this occasion! Let those who first and foremost seek the reign of God and his righteousness not fear being abandoned by Providence, since nothing required for their spiritual growth would be lacking.

Jesus Christ called his disciples before performing the miracle, as if to speak and consult them. And, according to Saint Jerome, he did this, to give example to teachers not to feel belittled in consulting younger persons and asking for their advice at some times and occasions, even if the pupils are minors and their masters are their seniors and much wiser. And it was so for the apostles to understand at the same time the great wonder of consulting them about what he was going to do and of his magnificent mercy. The Lord talks to his disciples about it being necessary to compel the poor to come to him, and to teach the rich, who have received their goods from him, to be compassionate with the poor. Jesus Christ's words are clear evidence of his mercy. *I am sorry for these people*, he said. Oh, how sweet and affectionate this word *sorry* is! It alone penetrates entrails and heart, for there is no other Lord who has similar compassion for our miseries and needs as our Maker, whose mercy is above all his works. As a true man he sympathies with us; and as true God he feeds us and keeps us well. The Saviour gives two reasons in favour of the multitude: The first was the long patience the people had, following him for three days. The second was their need, for as he said, they did not have anything to eat. Jesus Christ pointed out to the apostles that if he sent them away without eating, they could faint along the way and perish. Yet how could they faint or perish, if they were with the Saviour of the world and were walking along the way with his blessing! How poorly imitated is the Saviour of the opulent and of the rich who sends away fasting from his house the hungry and does not reach out to help them! These do not have the benign entrails of the Saviour, who feared the mobs fainting along the way. Yet some want money to be used only to satisfy their own greed, rather than to help the needs of others. By not extending their hand to their treasure chests, they would have preferred starving to death those whom Christ fed at the cost of a miracle.

Christ said that they had come following him from afar. Great faith! Heroic hope! Amazing charity! They had come from afar, yet still carrying all kinds of sick people because they firmly believed that the Lord had the power to restore salvation to them, hoping to receive out of his mercy the benefit they wished. The Lord could therefore not be insensitive to this great show of faith, hope, and charity. From afar comes to God he who cries out to Him from the depths of his sin; from afar comes he who has run for a long time down the path of doom, who is hardened in vices, and rushes hurriedly to the Lord to heal him or to unload the heavy burden of his guilt. Oh what comfort for those who come from afar, to know that infinite mercy awaits them, precisely to feed them, absolve them and help them! From this mercy he gave proof with his words before doing the works. If they are left fasting and worn out with journeying and hunger, they will slump along the way, and so it was necessary to give them to eat. It should be noted that the virtue of the Creator is so great as is the need which the creature has of Him, that if a single thing were to be left out, then all would fail.

The faith of Jesus Christ's disciples was still weak, their hope somewhat frail, They did not understand what to expect, not knowing their Master's full virtue, nor how far his power could go or remember his first miracles. Astonished as they were and as if out of themselves, they said to him: "How could anyone feed them, or from where can they be fed in this wilderness?" Short is the power of man and his provisions are scarce, undoubtedly, even for the most common needs for life. How many times would we have perished, had we only depended on what another man could give us! This full void of human weakness is supplemented by the living faith, taking us along with God so that we may implore his help in life's needs. Those who look for God in the wilderness of this world have never feared starving. So in order to inspire his disciples of such a living faith, he asked them: "How many loaves do you have?" He was asking not because he did not know what they had, but because the miracle would be more evident by their own answer. He did not ask rhetorically, not to be told, but to make them know their need and to compel them to confess it. They would have better answered: "If you will, Lord, you can easily solve anything. Only by willing it, you can turn all the stones of this desert into bread." This was what the Bethsaida event must have naturally suggested to them when they witnessed it a few months earlier. The way Jesus Christ showed his sympathy with a hungry and exhausted crowd made them understand well his willingness to make them look forward to a new miraculous multiplication. "We have seven loaves, Lord, the disciples retorted, and some small fish." It is well seen that all this was very little for such a crowd of persons, in which we discover the self-restraint and abstinence the Saviour and his disciples kept in food and drink. They did not eat meat but fish, and then not a big fish but a few little ones.

Jesus Christ then checked about the disciples' supply and commanded the crowd to sit on the ground. It is worth noting here that when on another occasion he gave the mob to eat in the wilderness, the Evangelist warns that there was plenty of hay in that place. But now the pasture was already missing, since according to Origen and several other authors, this miracle was performed in winter. Some still believe that it was on the very day of the Epiphany of the Lord, since many other miracles were performed by him on the same day. It is very plausible to keep the same order on this second occasion as in the first, so that while the disciples were busy dividing by class or family unit those present, the divine Redeemer took the seven loaves and blessed them, thanking his Heavenly Father for the power He had given him. He also took the fish and blessed them. Then came the apostles, and in his presence broke the bread and divided the fish, commanding them to share out everything among the crowd. They all ate of this miraculous bread and of the fish the Lord had blessed, as much as they wanted. And when the apostles collected the leftovers, they filled seven baskets with these remains, four thousand men being the number of those who had been fed, not counting among them women or children.

The difference between the first and second nourishment is remarkable. In that performed with the multiplication of five loaves, there was figured the Old Testament doctrine contained in the Pentateuch or the Five Books of Moses. Here the Law of the New Testament is revealed, in which the truth is most broadly manifested and the grace of the seven gifts of the Holy Spirit is given, and the seven sacraments and the seven virtues, three theological and four cardinal, are foreshadowed. In the first nourishment the loaves were of barley bread but in this they were wheat loaves, thus showing how much more delightful, clear and tasty is the New Testament doctrine than that of the old Law. In the first nourishment they sat the crowds on the green hay and in the second on the ground, to show that in the Old Testament earthly things were promised to the children of Israel, while Christians are taught in the law of Grace to despise all, including riches and delights. And what more, that they ought to renounce and despise themselves to find God more easily and follow Him with greater freedom. Finally, it should be noted that five thousand men were fed in the first nourishment, according to the number of bread loaves and that of bodily senses, to which the masters of the Old Testament attributed sensuality. In this second feeding there were but four thousand, symbolising the holy men sanctified by the perfection of the four Gospels or by the exercise of the four cardinal virtues, with which virtuous men live their spiritual life without defect. However, what

Jesus Christ wanted to make us understand was not only the great difference between the two Testaments, but that it was for us to also realise that in setting our sights on everlasting life, and in duly loathing of all that which is earthly, we must likewise distribute the surplus of all our goods to the poor as such liberality and generosity lengthens our temporal life and assures us of a spiritual one.

When the Saviour saw that all the sick had been healed and the crowds fed, and so had garnered enough strength to undertake their journey, he dismissed that great gathering with his holy blessing. It must be believed that after so many visible benefits the people would undergo a painful and sensitive moment to be separated from the Lord, but it was very necessary that they come down to reality; and to escape from those who still wanted to stop him, Jesus Christ embarked on a boat together with his apostles. He ordered them to set course for *Dalmanutha*, a place or village located on the territory of *Magadan*, on the same coast as Capernaum, but much farther north towards the source of the Jordan river. This neighbourhood, like Phoenicia, was inhabited by Jews and Gentiles, each being separated into separate settlements which barely traded with each other than for indispensable goods. By these journeys Jesus Christ made it is shown that his plan was to proclaim his Father's kingdom in all the places where the Jews were settled. Yet it is also clear that wherever he went the Pharisees came out to meet him, and that whatever his miracles and doctrines were, they always stood as his unjust detractors and most relentless enemies. Whenever the Lord visited and passed through the plains of *Magdala* or *Mageda*, east of the Sea of Galilee, in the midst of the tribe of Manasseh, several scribes and Pharisees would stand before him, rather to tempt him or tire him with their questions, putting his patience to the test of their evil nature rather than greeting him. They carried along with them a growing number of wicked and unbelieving Sadducees, whose doctrines went fully against the Law of Moses. Yet the Lord confounded and reproached them on all occasions and continued to preach to the faithful and simple ones about the coming of the Messiah into the world and the founding of his Father's kingdom.

CHAPTER 50

JESUS COMMANDS HIS DISCIPLES TO BEWARE OF THE BAD YEAST; HE GIVES SIGHT TO A BLIND MAN ON THE ROAD TO BETHSAIDA; AND ARRIVING AT CAESAREA PHILIPPI, HE PRAISES AND REWARDS THE FAITH OF SAINT PETER AND ENCOURAGES HIS DISCIPLES TO FOLLOW HIM AND IMITATE THE EXAMPLES OF HIS PASSION (*MT 16:13–19; 24–28*)

E have said at the end of the previous chapter that when the Lord arrived at the plain of Magdala or Mageda, a band of Pharisees and Sadducees came out to him to tempt him, asking him, as they had done on other occasions, to make them see some new sign or signal from heaven. It should be noted that the Sadducees, as we have already said, were a generation of disbelievers fully against the Law of Moses. They were one of the four main sects among the Jews, taking little or no notice at all of the ancients' traditions which were so much to the heart of the Pharisees, and like the *Karaites* they kept to the letter of Scripture. They denied the immortality of the soul, the resurrection of our bodies and the existence of spirits. Since they believed that all the reward for good consisted in the good name and wishes they enjoyed on earth, while despising all that which they had heard the Lord preach about the joys of eternal bliss and themselves teaching with all true certainty the doctrine they professed, they said to him trying to convince him of being an impostor if he resisted to their demands: "Your miracles and all the great cures we have seen you do here are not sufficient witness to the title you assign to yourself and the rights you repute for yourself. It is exactly so that you must shut your mouth to slander and curse, and to work portents and miracles in another sphere more appropriate to Divinity. Make us see a wonder in heaven, and in that case we will not only believe in you, but we will also teach our disciples and command them to believe in you and hold you as a man coming from heaven." It was not zeal for the

glory and greatness of the Lord that encouraged these men, but their desire to discredit and dishonour him saying that his power did not match that of ancient prophets.

It should be noted that many of the scribes and Pharisees, forgetting the study of the Law and the Prophets, which was what interested them most to govern and instruct the people well, were engaged in astrology. And so it is that to this day many great astrologers are seen among the Jews, and mostly in the class of rabbis, who by examining and reckoning stars they desire to come to know how laws and sects started. They also seek to see whether by this means they can arrive at knowing the time of Christ's coming and the commencement of a new law. But this is absolutely impossible, since this does not happen due to stars or by their influence, even if it is true that they may cause the future regulation of times, such as rain, snow, blizzard, heat or cold to affect other similar matters. And to know above all and with certainty whether he was the Christ promised in the Law, they asked him for a sign from heaven to show his majesty and almightiness, such as rain, rays or sparks, or to cause manna to fall for some time from on high as in the time of Moses, or to make the sun stop in the midst of its orbit as in the time of Joshua, or to make it move backwards in its orbit as in the time of Isaiah, or ultimately to make fire descend from on high as Elijah did. But the Lord not being able to hear this request without bitterly moaning about the source of this disbelief, said to them: "You, who think yourselves to be fortune tellers and are so skilful in speculation, why do you now come to me to ask for new proof about my mission? You, who on seeing a red sky in the afternoon can tell that the next day will be fine, and that red clouds in the morning will give way to a tempest during the day, you hypocrites who can only judge by the colour of the sky the weather, can you not know from the clear signs that you see every day, that you are in the fullness of time and that the Messiah has already come? Great is your ignorance and greater still your malice. You become the blind and the deaf for not receiving he who with his gifts compels everyone, and you commit a kind of adultery, excluding the legitimate spouse from your house and company to engage with others and so breach the faith which is due to him. Indeed, your actions are those of a wicked and perverse generation, the enemy of truth. You beg in vain and complain in vain, for you will be given no other sign than that shown in the person of the prophet Jonah. Delve, if you will, into this ancient wonder, and you will see at once the manner how you are behaving with me, the reason why you are today asking of me to see these miracles in heavens.

The Pharisees were greatly offended by Jesus Christ's response. The Saviour, however, wanted to show them even to the greatest extent the bad faith of their demand. So he hastily walked away from their sight and as he had already done in this neighbourhood as his mission required, he took again to the sea with his apostles and landed on the banks of the eastern coast of Tiberiades. As the order for boarding was given very hastily, the disciples forgot to take the necessary provisions with them, so that on disembarking they found that they only had one loaf of bread on board. They did not hide this from Jesus Christ, but his disciples were only concerned with the bother of the visit he had just made and wished to free him from it, and so forgot all about their own food. And as if to warn them of their carelessness, on disembarking Jesus Christ said to them: "As soon as you can and it would be possible for you to do so, beware, my disciples, watch out and be warned against the yeast of the Pharisees, Herodians, and Sadducees." The disciples, who were not yet straightforward and quite crude understood yeast in a material sense rather than in terms of their Master's intention, and thought of none else but the bread they had forgotten to bring along with them. The Saviour wanted to instruct them about keeping three species of yeast which were very harmful to their eternal salvation. They were hypocrisy and greed, as that of the Pharisees; false doctrine, typical of the Sadducees; and ambition and pride, as that of Herod and his court. But they did not understand the figurative and moral sense of those words, and taking them in their usual and ordinary sense as in the case of yeast, they remembered that they had forgotten to take bread with them. So they said between themselves: "What shall we do in this country if we do not have any bread to feed us, if the Master does not want us to buy it from any of the parties living here?" This carelessness of theirs made them rather uneasy, and the predicament in which they found themselves presented them not only with an embarrassing situation, but with an almost impossible one.

The Saviour, who was firmly aware of the unease in which they were and penetrated their most hidden thoughts with the kindness that was his hallmark, though mixed with some air of discontent, said to them: "What is this sadness about you since you lack bread? For what reason have the few words I spoke to you induced such restlessness and unease within you? Where is your faith? It seems that you neither have understanding nor knowledge, no memory to remember things, no logic with which to reason. As irrational men you let yourselves to be guided by your senses; though you have eyes you do not see, and having ears you do not hear anything, so that you imply that after so long that the light has dawned on you, you are still in darkness. Do you not realise that in your presence I multiplied one day in such manner five loaves, which were enough to feed five thousand persons? Say then, how many baskets did you pick up from leftovers! And when recently five thousand men have eaten of seven loaves, how many baskets have you collected?" And having answered him they collected seven baskets, he went on to say to them: "How do you fail to understand the sense in which I speak to you? Do you think my business has to do with the ordinary bread that serves to feed the body? Know, then, that this will not be lacking while I am with you. I speak to you, my disciples, of a yeast that corrupts the spirit and ravages the heart; which means, that I want you to guard yourself against the yeast of the Pharisees, Sadducees and others, for it is a deadly poison."   It was necessary for him to reduce the conversation to these terms in order to open the eyes of his apostles. In spite of such a long time they passed in familiar conversation with the Lord, they had however not yet learned how to distinguish between a common and familiar style in their talk, and the meaning of certain words which, having been uttered after some great event, contained a supernatural and divine doctrine. So by this they understood that the sovereign Master was not throwing in their face anything about the carelessness they had shown in failing to bring along with them the bread they needed for their journey, or that he was forbidding them from eating leavened bread as they had at first believed, but rather that his whole plan was to draw them away them from the damaging doctrine and harmful principles with which those sects were infecting the whole of Judea.

The fathers and doctors of the Church state with well-founded motives, that by divine disposition there could be many reasons why the apostles forgot to take on board any food supplies with them. The first was that the Lord did not want them to be too much concerned about tomorrow. Secondly, in order to seek the fathers' help in collecting the seven baskets of leftovers. And thirdly, because the Lord wanted them to put their trust fully in him, since having seen the miracles he had worked, they ought to have been firmly persuaded that they would never lack anything. The Venerable Bede adds a fourth reason, which is that Jesus Christ wanted them to taste the inner sweetness that lay in his heart that the only true bread was to be found in his company. It contained, gathered and conserved within it the taste and delight of all delicacies, so that being attracted by its softness and sweetness they would be less drawn to the outer visible crust. So Bede adds: "The only loaf to be found on the boat meant mystically our Saviour Lord himself, the bread of eternal life, with whose love, ever finding inner strength in their hearts, they were less drawn to the earthly bread they used to feed their bodies. With this he showed the apostles' zeal and desire for the heavenly doctrine and their contempt for the world's delights, so evident was the little care they had for life's essentials. The same can also be seen from how inseparably they lived together with Jesus Christ, how much they delighted in his loving presence, and how much they felt they could not part from him even for an instant. For at the simple bidding of his voice they entered the small boat, forgetting all about taking provisions with them for the journey." And Saint John Chrysostom adds: "So captivated were they with love for their Master, that they did not desire to turn away from him for a single moment. So far away did they keep themselves from the world's delights and appetites, that all despised them for always being with him, without whose help human fickleness could not survive. In possessing Jesus Christ, who is the true joy and perfect possession of all virtues, no urge or ambition could afflict them, or sorrow sadden them, nor could anything destroy the inner joy which they felt." And since the Pharisees, Sadducees and Herodians were unable to enjoy this inner peace and joy, due to the many disgraceful vices that dominated them, the Saviour told his disciples to beware of their yeast, whose sourness enters and ferments the whole mass.

The apostles, accompanied by Jesus Christ, went along their journey across the sea while they were being given this most worthy instruction, until advancing farther on they reached their port of call Bethsaida. The Lord had already preached in this city another time and there worked different miracles, for which reason he only wanted to pass by the port. But while walking through with his apostles, he was recognised and stopped by the crowd, gathering around him as if wanting Jesus Christ to work a new miracle there. And not doubting that he could do it, they took a blind man before him, with the simple request that he should only touch him, being firmly convinced that this event would come to the happy ending they were seeking. The poor man was a non-resident beggar making the rounds in the neighbourhood and from time to time going around to beg the Jews for alms. So that it is very plausible that he was a Gentile, as the Saviour did not want to heal him in the presence of those who had prayed for him, for persistent as they were in the natural pride of their nation, they would have been shocked to see Jesus Christ attend to a man who was not of Jacob's line.

The Lord took great care as to how he bestowed his mercies, not only to the sons of Israel, but also to all Gentiles, for he had come into the world to save both Jews and Gentiles. They did not think it would take much to comfort the poor man they had brought to him, although he did not expect at all to acquire the sight which he lacked. And so, taking him by the hand out of the crowd, he smeared his eyes with spit and then asked him whether he was seeing anything and whether he could tell objects apart. The blind man opened his eyes, and widening his sight as much as he could, he said he was seeing men walk, but they looked like trees, owing to the weakness of his pupils, so that he could only make out with great difficulty the movement of passers-by. Jesus Christ did not doubt the physical state of the healed person, yet he did not want to cure him but little by little. It was either that the Lord wanted to test the sick man's trust, since he had not gone on his own to seek salvation, or so that his gladness would be increased gradually, such that his unexpected cure would not significantly harm his salvation due to his excessive joy. But the merciful Doctor did not want to leave half-done the cure of that miserable man; so he put his divine hand again on his eyes and he started seeing very clearly and distinctly, not only people but even the smallest objects. Then the Lord said to him: "Go to your house by the most direct way; and if ever you want to re-enter Bethsaida, do not tell anyone what I have just done for you." This command from Jesus Christ to the cured blind man gives us enough reason to speculate since the man neither resided in the city nor was he descended from Jacob. The Gospel does not say whether the man obeyed Jesus Christ on this occasion, or whether the same happened as many other times before when thankfulness depended more on affection due to the gift received than on his Benefactor's orders.

After Jesus Christ had shown his amazing charity with that miserable person, he kept going on his way and went to visit the places, villages and fortresses of the dependencies of Caesarea Philippi. Their layout was located within the borders of Judea towards the foothills of Lebanon, not far from the source of the River Jordan, where it flowed and separated the land of Judea from that of the Gentiles. This was the ancient city of *Paneas*, which had been given to Caesar, and for which reason it was called *Caesarea*, in honour of the Roman emperor; the term was then added to *Philippi* in honour of Herod's brother, tetrarch of Iturea and Trachonitis. At the summit of this city, and on the slope of Mount Lebanon, is the source of the two gorgeous springs of *Yor* and *Dan*, meeting downhill and forming the Jordan River, which after taking long detours enters the Sea of Galilee running very close to the city of Corazaim. This Caesarea was known as of

Philippi, to distinguish it from another Caesarea of Palestine, where the centurion Cornelius reputedly lived, and another Caesarea, metropolis *of Cappadocia*, which is nestled in the region of Turkey. Caesarea Philippi and the land within its confines was peopled by Gentiles. And as Christ also wanted to reveal the mystery of his Incarnation in this place, he also shows by this that another one of the Church foundations is founded on the faith of the Gentiles. Finally, in this city, which borders to the north with the region of the Gentile Phoenicians and the outer limits of Judea, where all taxes were taken as to a provincial capital, and where it is said that the universal description of the whole world applied in the time of Caesar Augustus, the Lord wanted to pay the tribute of faith to the king of kings and lord of lords, since it was also there that the census was taken or material tribute paid to the emperor of the earth.

There is no doubt that for all these reasons Caesarea Philippi was famous, yet it lacked the title that it was to be given by the most renowned person. So, as the Lord drew near to the city, he withdrew to a secret place, only taking with him his apostles, even leaving them apart to pray on his own, It was his habit, which he always observed, not to accomplish anything great and decisive in his ministry, before passing a long time in intimate communication with his Heavenly Father. The people who had reached him along the way waited for him in the countryside, while his disciples who were always around him, watched him with respectful silence. Saint Mark observes (Mk 8:8) that Jesus Christ did not speak to his disciples within the city walls, but in the middle of a field, where there is ample space and no limits, undoubtedly to show that Peter's confession in that place was not to be constrained or limited to a single people like the Old Testament, but that it was to extend to all kingdoms and nations to the ends of the earth.

When the Lord finished his prayer, he went back to his disciples and walking slowly with them, he asked them by way of conversation, what were the people saying about him? As if he was saying to them: "People talk more freely with you than they would do with me; you could hear what they say as they open up with you about the Master you follow.

Tell me then: How do the mobs who follow the Son of Man view him? What do the Jews and Gentiles say about me?" He who is infinitely wise was not asking to learn, but to be better informed; The Lord thereby gives to all a practical lesson of the prudent care we must have in keeping our good name, not by getting upset against those who speak petty things about us, but by seeking to live in a way that does not bother us. This is why the Apostle Paul said that he sought to live well, not only in the Lord's sight, but also in the sight of men (2 Cor 8:21). And while elsewhere he seems not to take notice of the world's judgments, being content with the witness of good conscience, he does not support in all this those who do not care about what people say. For although they should not take notice of any criticism when conscience bears witness that they are performing their duties well and that it is not lawful to omit doing anything, this will be counted as not giving reason to be judged without cause (1 Cor 4:3). This is one of the main reasons Saint Gregory had in saying: "One must fear and be reverent to the judgments of good persons, for they are members of God and do not rebuke on earth but what God condemns in heaven." The slander of evil persons is an approval of our lives, because then there seems to be something good about us when our lives displease those who are not pleasing to God.

Notice that Jesus Christ asked the Apostles who were the people saying is the Son of Man, and he does not say, who were they saying is the Son of God. He did it to confuse the pride of those who, when they want to make themselves known, break out using titles of high dignity, despising those of humility which are the titles that most uplift man. According to Saint Jerome, he does not say who do people say I am, to run away from every thought of vanity and boasting, since that worldly pride which he had come to condemn was not something that his disciples believed that he kept in his heart. Saint Chrysostom adds: He says the Son of Man, because he wants this to be believed in the divine economy of the mystery of the Incarnation, wanting to induce his disciples to confess it. So with their characteristic simplicity they answered Jesus Christ: "Some say that you are *John the Baptist*, others that you are *Elijah*, others *Jeremiah*, and others finally, that you are one of the prophets." All these beliefs showed fear among the Jews about giving him their support. Some, believing in the error of the Pythagoreans that souls migrated from one body to another, believed that John the Baptist whom Herod had ordered his throat to be slit was resurrected, and now presented himself with the name and in the person of Jesus Christ. Others, noting his zeal for the Law, said it was Elijah. And still others who had seen him weep over the city of Jerusalem prophesying its desolation and destruction, thought he was Jeremiah. This is what the populace thought of Jesus Christ's person, confusing him with other prophets, who though holy, were ultimately none else but pure creatures.

However Jesus Christ, who wanted to hear and know from his apostles their particular opinion of him, said to them: "And as for *you*, what side do you take among so many different opinions? Who do you say I am?" This was the main question; other previous ones were only by way of introduction to it. Peter, who like at the remarkable meeting in Capernaum on Christ's divinity and the Eucharist was always first to speak, took it upon himself to answer. So now too he stepped forward and with respectful submission Jesus Christ answered and said to him: *You are the Christ of God, you are the promised Messiah, you are the Son of the living God.* It was an admirable confession of faith, deserving the most beautiful praise, and followed by the most magnificent awards. Jesus Christ asked but did not stop at the erroneous judgment of the world's ignorant persons, but sought the resolve from wise and good persons such as the apostles. He had made them very aware of his attributes and shown them great mercy. This is why he was asking them for an exceptional confession of his divinity, for it is his normal way of behaviour to ask much from anyone to whom he has given much; and since he had given them much light and knowledge, it was a more sincere and over-powering confession that he demanded from them. *You are Christ*, Peter answered; which is to say the *Anointed One*, of which David says that it had to be with the anointing of joy on all those partaking with him, and so he confessed his humanity, doing so by anointing others with the holy oil of grace. "You are the Son of the living God, not an adoptive son like others, but natural and eternal, equal in all with His Father"; which was like saying: "You are the Messiah expected and yearned for throughout so many centuries, which you took in human nature, was to be anointed with spiritual anointing as a priest king according to the custom of the Old Testament. And this name of Son of God comes from birth and lineage, for you were born with and in Him; and to be called the same as He who begot you, you need not beg or take anything from anyone (Ph 2:6)." For he did not become Son of God when he became Son of the Virgin, or at the same time that he was born from her virginal womb to give light to the world. He was the Son of God since eternity, before the sun was created or shone, when centuries had not yet begun. It is what Saint Paul later said writing to the Hebrews (Heb 1:4-5): "Having become as much superior to angels as the name he has obtained is more excellent than theirs. For to what angel did God ever say, Thou art my Son, today I have begotten thee?"

"Blessed art thou, Simon, son of John," Jesus Christ continued, "for it is neither flesh nor blood that has revealed these sublime truths to you, but my Heavenly Father who is in heaven." Which was like telling him: "Your conviction and profession of believing that I am the Son of God is not the work of a natural inclination and of purely human attachment, but the fruit of the light you have received from my Heavenly Father: He is the One who has made you know me, and the One who gives you fervour and encouragement to make it known." For faith is rewarded by the vision of God, the Lord wanting that whoever by his authority believes what he does not see, is rewarded by seeing what he believes. And so it was that Peter not having inherited knowledge of the Son of God from his father John, nor having received it by human means, it was revealed to him by Jesus Christ who had received it from his Heavenly Father. His manifestation made him see clearly what he had already believed, that Jesus Christ was the true person of the Son of God and his Divine Master.

Peter's singular confession was followed by Jesus Christ's most excellent praise of him. Peter taught the apostles who

Jesus Christ was, and Jesus Christ taught Peter who he was, what he was destined to do, and those who should be his successors to represent him. Peter said to Jesus Christ: "You are the Son of God," and the Lord answered him, "That you may be convinced that I am indeed the One you have declared and confessed, I say to you, *Thou art Peter, and upon this stone I shall build my Church, and the gates of hell shall not prevail against it.*" On another occasion, when Jesus Christ saw Saint Peter for the first time, then called Simon, he had already told him that his name would be *Cephas*, the Syrian word for stone. But on this occasion he declared the very significant meaning contained in that word, showing that he had chosen him as the foundation stone of his Church, and this was a certain sign, fitting this noble dignity, which instilled in the depths of his soul a gift of firmness, love and faith for Christ. This was a mysterious name, involving the prerogative of Architect and Supreme Pastor of his Church. The Church is the great house of God; Jesus Christ built it when He founded it, and it is built by the apostles and prophets, the evangelists and his other ministers when new members join or feed and govern those already incorporated within it with the bread of holy doctrine (Eph 4:11–12). Only the Church built on Peter is the Christian, Catholic, visible one possessing the *seat of unity, the doctrine of truth and the life of charity*. It does not match idolatry which destroys unity, nor heresy which goes against truth, or even schism which fights charity. Only those who belong to this house are God's building (1 Cor 3:9). That which is not founded on its base, will be ripped off by the hurricane of error, or swept away by the rains and terrible pathways of schism. Whoever does not look up to Peter as Christ's vicar and as the visible head of this body on earth, does not want to partake in the mystical body of Christ.

This name was like a sign of Peter's zeal and fearlessness to get ahead in all that seemed to touch his Master's honour and relief. It was an unmistakable indication of the firmness of love which he imbibed from loving his Master, in response to which the Supreme Shepherd ordered him to feed his sheep. And it was finally the granting of the exclusive privilege that, when his Master was gone, would be the cornerstone upon which he would lay the great building. Jesus Christ himself would at the same time be the *cornerstone, first foundation and divine Architect* of this building. Every stone which did not conform with the foundation, laid by Jesus Christ's own hand, would be left apart in the construction of this building and would not be included in his providence. And the work and inseparable union of all parts with this main stone would result in the building's solidity, receiving eternal durability, for the firmness of Christ's Church is forever. The science of those who pursue truth is foolishness and it weakens the power of those who imprison, burn and dismember its defenders. That which is guarded and protected by God's mighty arm cannot be destroyed until the passing of all centuries. The fortress does not waver, neither does truth err, nor does holiness sin: the Church is embattled, but it is not overcome.

After this magnificent and comforting promise, which gives us such a relevant idea of Peter's person, the Lord passes to another no less majestic comparison. He however declares what his power will be in the government of the Church itself, seen as a society and congregation of the faithful subject to his government and guiding principles. "I will give you," he said, *"the keys of the kingdom of heaven. All that you bind on earth will also be bound in heaven; and all that you unbind on earth, will also be unbound in heaven."* When he mentioned the foundation stone of his Church, and said that all the power of hell would not prevail against it, he was referring to the weakness of all the enemies of the Church who had no power against the faith of true believers. So that by *the gates of hell* Saint Epiphanius understands the heretics, Saint Ambrose vices, Origen both one and the other, and Theophylact the persecutors of the Church itself. At the same time Jesus Christ also wanted to show that this house, or rather impregnable bulwark which the most skilful architect founded not on quicksand but on the unshakable rock of faith, would not be overthrown either by the flood of vices, nor by the downpour of heresies, or the whirlwinds of persecutions, even if all the joint forces of hell were to gather against it. But in being given such broad and extensive power to bind and unbind on earth and in heaven, this is undoubtedly also given to the Church over all the gathered forces of hell.

Before starting to examine the great distinction which Jesus Christ bestowed on Saint Peter for these particular and distinguished considerations, we should not forget that before the mystery of our redemption was performed by the divine Saviour, the kingdom of heaven was closed, so being due to the unconquerable door that God placed as a result of the guilt of the first transgressor. The angels were locked up there, and they only came into the world when the Lord sent them in connection with some particular mystery; but that path was hidden and not trodden by anyone of Adam's sons. As holy as anyone was found in his death, his soul was lowered into *limbo*, which was the place of deposit where one should wait until the Saviour's coming, who was then to bring these souls out of there. But with heaven being opened with his death, and having raised up the spiritual building of this new Church, he wanted to vest in Peter and his successors the power to open and close the doors of this kingdom, to forgive and withhold forgiveness, to bind and unbind. He wanted to authorise them to impose on sinners the penalties corresponding to their faults, and to keep them away from the sacraments and subject them to long penances, and if necessary also to separate them from among the other faithful, because the Church binds no one nor can it bind anyone through guilt, but with punishments serving as a remedy or as a restraint for guilt with which its bad children were constrained. For sure, a most praiseworthy declaration of the ecclesiastical power over the militant Church was indicated by the name kingdom of heaven. With these keys the eternal kingdom closed by sin is opened, and the gates of hell which are open are thereby closed.

From this exalted and lofty power, which agrees with God's power, no one can use anything contrary to Jesus Christ's intention, who gives it, or of the Church to which he gives it. Saint Paul calls this power the ministry of reconciliation; for this reason Saint Peter and all his successors had, have and will have all the power necessary to form, guide, extend and govern Jesus Christ's Church by the means which he himself used in establishing, founding and acquiring it with the price of his blood. This promise which Christ made to Saint Peter was fulfilled in its time in an exact manner equivalent to the vehemence of the expressions in which it was conceived when Peter, already head of the apostolic college, after Jesus Christ's death and ascent, became father of fathers and shepherd of shepherds, as well as of all sheep. Because on that occasion when Peter confessed Jesus Christ to be the Son of the living God, he was only promised but not yet given the keys for if they had he would not have committed the error of denial as he later did at the time of the passion. In this regard the Venerable Bede, grasping the opportunity, said: "The keys were then promised to him, but they were not given to him, for they had not yet been forged on the sweet anvil of the cross, nor had they been tempered with the blood of the Saviour, He kept these keys reserved for when they can be first used and exercised. Even if they had apparently not yet been perfected, they were still put in the very heated furnace of the passion when the Lord had first to open with them the gates of heaven to the robber and assassin, so that you might later open them after his example also to publicans and prostitutes. You will exercise judgment on those who confessed their guilt and waited with resignation and patience for their punishment and shame. For this reason you will have an ordinary jurisdiction and the power to judge, about which you need to know two things: the authority to know and ponder on guilt, and the power to judge and to acquit or condemn it. And these two things you will be given in due course with the name, use and exercise of these keys which I now promise you."

The power of these keys is that of judging in the inner forum of conscience, but not on bodies, This power consists of two things, namely that of discerning or knowing in the examination and investigation of the case, and that of defining and determining by condemning or absolving. The first power is called a discipline, not as a branch of knowledge, but as an authority and power to discern and judge knowingly before having and acquiring that field. The second is called the power to admit or exclude from the kingdom, according to the true judgment which is formed, by which the unworthy should be excluded and the deserving admitted. As Saint Bernard said: "Peter received the keys within the knowledge and power given to him from above, and these are the power to open and to close, and the discretion to discern among those who must be admitted or left out. This power was also given by the Lord to the other apostles, and also to the other bishops and priests, and in them to the whole Church. It is well understood, however, that what is the power of authority lies in God alone, who bestows it through the infusion of grace: the power of excellence lies in Jesus Christ, which opens through the merits of his passion, and the ministerial power is in the prelates of the Church, which they open through the ministry of the sacraments. But in this manner Peter received the power of the keys and of the principality of judicial power so that all believers who are scattered and disseminated all over the world may understand, that all those who willingly separate themselves from the unity of faith and society and from the communion of the Church, that in no way can they be unbound from the bindings of sins, nor can they enter through the door of the kingdom of heaven."

Hear this so that the bishops and prelates of the Church, and if they rejoice and enjoy their dignity, do not become arrogant in their power. If they bind like Peter and unbind as he does, what they bind will be bound and what they unbind will be unbound. So let them imitate him in discretion and justice those who want to imitate him in his power to bind and unbind. It was only to him that this was told by Jesus Christ so that others would look at him as in a mirror, and so live, and so bind and unbind, that peace and harmony may never depart. From what Saint Gregory said: "Let the pastors of the Church bind and unbind with great restraint; but even if the pastor is justly or unjustly forced to do so, his sentence must always be feared and respected by the flock. Let the pastor fear absolving or binding indiscriminately, and let him who is in his custody be afraid of being bound, nor should he recklessly rebuke in the depths of his heart the shepherd's judgment, for even if he was unjustly bound it would not be something that owing to his inflaming pride it would then result for him in a new fault which he did not have before."

The apostles were cheerful and extremely pleased at the great news they received about the person of their Master, and they would have been willing to reveal it had Jesus Christ not forbidden them all generally and severely from telling it to anyone that he was Christ sent by God and His Only Son. He wanted to make them understand that although he did not want to hold the truth captive, yet his will was to be known and believed by all the world. He did not as yet know his Father's designs of adorable Providence or the wealth of evangelical preaching with which he would later instruct them, and so he told them that it was only him who was to proclaim the sublime mysteries of the divinity of the Father's Only Son. He would then establish this revelation with miracles, and seal it with all his blood, but that they were to wait for the mystery of his Resurrection and for the Holy Spirit to be poured out upon their heart. Although he still had a short time to live, yet he would pass that still left to him to bear the last testimony of the truth which his Father had made known to them and to which Peter had just confessed. That is what they would then propose to the universe as a truth, which faith would be the beginning of all righteousness and the foundation of all worship pleasing to God. See, then, that this prohibition was a temporary one and for a very short instant, because if this important dogma had been disclosed before Jesus Christ's passion, faith in the hearts of those who believed in the future scandal of the passion would have been vexed, as it actually happened in spite of all this to the same apostles who cowardly abandoned the Saviour.

Passion time was a time of ignominy during which there appeared men's sickness and weakness, but after the resurrection, when perfect victory over death was already achieved, it was the time for Jesus Christ's glory to be shown. It was the time when the cause, namely the scandal of the passion, ceased and so did the prohibition. Chrysostom said: "If he had manifestly been known to be the Son of God, no one would have dared to lay his hand on him, and he would not have been crucified, nor would he have risen from the dead; consequently the kingdom of hell would be on earth and the devil would dominate over the whole universe." And

Saint Ambrose adds: "For many reasons the Lord ordered his disciples to keep silent on this occasion, to deceive the prince of darkness, to flee vainglory, to teach humility and not to oppress the rough yet imperfect disciples with the heavy burden of deeper and more interesting preaching. He forbade them to start evangelizing about the Son of God, to speak about him crucified later. This is the glory of faith, although it has to be understood as the cross of Christ. These truths are so great, sublime, and truly divine. Their fulfilment is today our joy and our glory. It is because of them that we are true worshippers and God is honoured by men as He rightly deserves. But it is also necessary to confess that these sad predictions were announced resolutely at a time when hearts were not yet ready to receive them, or they would have fully scandalised the faithful, or maybe delayed them from believing."

Jesus Christ, who understood well how far the resistance of the apostles themselves could go even after just having very explicitly manifested his divinity, wanted to give a great example to the world, together with them, by putting to the test their submissiveness and the profession of their faith. While warning them at the same time to keep silent, he ordered them to let him act according to the designs of his Father's providence, and at most to be only content to announce what they had done until then by his order. Namely they were to proclaim that the kingdom of God was near at hand, that the time announced by the prophets had come, and that to bear fruit it was appropriate to do penance. This would be the order of events they would soon see passing before their eyes, and he did not want to hide anything from them as it was appropriate to keep them away from scandals, by which he knew they would get carried away easily.

After warning them to take these precautions, the Lord continued showing them the future, but being really on the lookout for close events he said to them: "You should know, my disciples, that my Father has resolved that I should go to Jerusalem, and that although I am his Only Son and firstborn of men, I must there suffer greatly from the scribes, chiefs, priests and elders of the people. That after I have passed through all shame and humiliation, and suffered all the torments that can be imagined and contrived, I will be reproached by them and committed to death with ignominy, and that on the third day I will rise again to a new life. And you should know finally that up to the time these forebodings are fulfilled, you will neither preach nor announce publicly what you have now confessed secretly." This story seemed both bitter and sweet to these men who were tenderly addicted to their good Master. And Peter, who loved him more than his other fellow disciples, was not only surprised but appeared to be very restless and offended. So Peter, holding the Lord by the hand and pulling him apart from the others to avoid that what he said would be reputed as a reprimand, and also being possessed with true love and the most ardent pain, said to him: "No, my Lord and Master, this will not happen to you so. None of these misfortunes you mention will fall upon you. Such unworthy ill-treatment cannot be reserved for someone who is as merciful to men as you."

Peter's love and his scant understanding of God's doings seem to be able to hide his daring. Yet he undoubtedly did not want to give scandal, and so to keep Jesus Christ away from all fatal consequences he could not do anything less than treat him roughly and severely. Jesus Christ began by looking with a severe face at each of the apostles, to give them to understand that what Peter was going to say also applied to each one of them, if they all thought like him. And then he said to him: "Get away from my sight, Satan; your thoughts scandalise me, and I can only hear them with horror. You speak as a man of flesh who knows nothing good or great but earthly things, and with no taste for those coming from God.

Only someone, who was penetrated by Peter's fiery zeal and encouraged by his most lively desire to please Jesus Christ, could form a certain judgment of the terrible impression which a displeasure had made in his spirit with such harsh expressions. At least the loving Saviour was kind enough to do without the guilt of public rebuke. The great Origen points it out in a way worth considering and says: "*March behind me.* Namely, by conformity of the will. *Come back*, and not against me. *Satan*, that is, the adversary and rival, because you contradict and speak things which go against my will and the path which I must take to attain the universal salvation of men. Do not try impeding my passion; on the contrary, follow me and try to imitate my steps. Blessed is he whom Christ converts to him and looks at him, even if he casts his eyes upon him with the intention of correcting him." And the Lord added: "You are a scandal unto me, for you give me occasion of an affront; and you offend me in what you are saying and doing, because you give credit to not understanding the things that are of God, He who has resolved about my passion, but you appreciate and prefer the things that are of men, loving me only with purely human affection." It is very noteworthy that the Saviour now calls Satan the person whom he had such a short time before ennobled and raised above all others, him who had precisely because of human considerations gone over to dissuade him from his passion and hindering him from undergoing it. Then it is clear that in order not to incur Jesus Christ's rebukes we must not love human things, but divine ones; not matters of the flesh, but spiritual ones; not earthly affairs, but heavenly ones.

Moreover, it is extremely noticeable that Peter loved the Saviour with a most burning love As one reads in Saint Clement's *Itinerary*: "So fervently did Peter love Jesus Christ, that after his glorious ascension to heaven, he recalled many a time his sweet presence in a very amiable company and tender fellowship. So many times did rivers of copious and ardent tears flow from his eyes, that his cheeks seemed like burnt by their ardour. So that it is inferred that owing to the zeal and love he professed towards his Master, he wanted to impede his passion. But since this zeal was indiscreet, he was for this reason harshly rebuked." With this example we must also understand that by alleviating the temporal sorrows we should deserve for sins, we must not abandon doing spiritual exercises, by means of which we must deserve the great and ineffable comforts of our souls.

After this important speech encompassing such great evidence, the mobs that were waiting for the Saviour went to join him to proceed along the road to the neighbourhood of Caesarea. In so doing he instructed the people who were moving along with him, so that the apostles themselves knew that this was a continuation of what he had told them up till then. Addressing the mobs in general, he said to them: "If any of you want to be counted among my disciples and come after me, deny yourself, take up your cross and follow me." It is one thing to go to Christ or to walk towards Christ, and another is to go after Christ. All seek the first one: there is no Christian who does not want to go to Christ and see him where he reigns on the right hand of his Father. Yet few are those who really want to go after Christ. For the path Christ takes is full of tasks and sorrows, which easy-going worldly persons would resent taking. It is strewn with thistles which hurt delicate feet, and is like a tough climb for the lazy, a narrow path for those who are wide open to their heart's affections. And since most persons can be classified as such, it so results that there are very few who walk after Christ. Yet he is not much concerned that these are few, as much as that there may be someone hoping to reach Christ but not walking along Christ's way. For he is the reason for the way and the path itself: reason in the beginning and middle of the race towards eternal salvation. For which reason, and paying attention to it, whoever wants to reach Christ but does not go after him on the path which His Divine Majesty planned for him, is fully out of course. Saint Chrysostom says: "Since the Saviour is holy and most kind, he does not want to have any servants who are deceived or forced, but who are free and willing, and who thank him for admitting them to his service." Thus, without violently or forcing anyone out of necessity, but convincing and doing good to all, he attracts towards him those who want to serve him. For if anyone gave great amounts of gold or distributed all their treasures to those who followed them, there would not be anyone who would not run after them. How much more then do you have to run after Christ to attain the treasures that are in heaven?

Self-denial of one's own will and self-contempt are like the early basics of Christ's school, to which they are united with sturdy links, that each one take up his cross and follows Christ; since Christian perfection consists very much of these three things. As for the former, the apostle Peter

(1 Pt 2:11) tells us *that we lived as aliens and exiles*, that is like people who being unaware of worldly customs could be deceived easily. We were always forewarned about these things, to abstain from the desires of the flesh which are in constant battle with the soul. Which is as if to say that you must know that on the path to heaven, where you walk like pilgrims, there is an army of soldiers to make war on your soul and snatch it on its way. These hardened soldiers are the appetites of your flesh, those which hide themselves as in ambush wanting to surprise you, not letting you use the weapons of reason to defeat you and drag you to their side, forcing you as captives to all they order you to do. In feeling then some carnal appetite that asks for something against the law of the spirit, let one be aware that this is the soldier who is advancing to cut off your path to heaven.

According to this wholesome doctrine there are three things from which man must deny himself so that he may truly and freely follow Christ. First, he must deny and renounce what he owns; for it is written in Lk 14 that *Whoever does not renounce all that he possesses cannot be my disciple*. Secondly, he must renounce those he calls his own, as we also read in the Gospel: "If anyone comes to me and does not hate his own father and mother, and even his own self, he cannot be my disciple (Lk 14)." And thirdly he must deny himself, shedding off the old man with all his deeds and passions, and putting on anew Jesus Christ, so that he may cease to be who he was and start being who he was not. For what would it take him to give up his possessions and his own, if he did not deny or renounce his own will, which is what always drags man and loses him? Jesus Christ wanted to give us all this great example as an admirable One, telling us, *That he should come down from heaven, not to do his own will, but that of his Father who sent him*. Saint Chrysostom expresses with a precious comparison about what denying oneself means: "Consider," he says, "what it is to deny something to another person, and that way you will understand what it means to deny yourself. He who neglects giving care to another person whom he sees injured, cast in jail, punished, or is committed to do anything, and he does not bow down to his prayers or feel any compassion for his misfortune, because he behaves with him like a person whom he does not know or is out of his circle of friends, neither cares about his own matters nor give a whit to his good or bad fortune." According to him then, it is he who denies himself, who does not care for his body in what he asks for it against reason and justice, more like as if he did not know about it. If they despise him he does not do much about it, if they hurt or otherwise harm him, he does not stand in his own defence, and if he suffers cold or heat or any other discomfort he does not care about it and lets himself suffer. Finally, he does not care much about himself as if he did not know himself. This is denying oneself and acting as Christ did, who shed his majesty and greatness, took the form of a slave and the body of man, and wearing the sack of our mortality, suffered all torments and shame in his painful passion and disgraceful death on the Cross."

Yet the Saviour added that whoever wanted to follow him must take his cross, that is, *his own* cross, for in it was the price of our redemption and the weight of our sins. So that whoever is his disciple must always be willing to suffer for his love, as he was to suffer for us, without ceasing or faltering by worldly tasks, however great they may be. Not by carrying the cross by force or as if dragging it, but by receiving it and taking it with joy, doing it all for profit and enjoying oneself in doing it as the apostles enjoyed themselves when leaving the courts, having been worthy to suffer for the name of Christ (Acts 5:41). It was this consoling thought for all who are persecuted and troubled in this life that prompted Saint Hilary to give us this sublime writing: "Christ must also be followed by taking the cross of his passion, that which if it did not affect us with fortune, must be sought with good will, and it must be embraced with good will in order to follow the Redeemer. Saint Paul lived so fully in self-denial to following Jesus Christ, that he said to the faithful of Galatia (Gal 6), *For me the world is already crucified and I am crucified for him*; following which he did not hesitate to affirm when he wrote to the Colossians, *That he lived, but it was not him who lived, but that it was Jesus Christ who lived in him* (Col 3). Excellent proof, indeed, of the self-denial to carry with full confidence and love the cross of Jesus, our Saviour and Redeemer, and to follow him with a very ardent desire to be crucified for him."

This endeavour was hard and very strenuous, a seemingly scary advice but no less one to be followed. "Anyone," he told them further, "wanting to save his soul, that is to preserve his life at the expense of his faith or to seek comfort on earth, renouncing his belief or practice of the Gospel, will lose his soul forever. On the contrary, however, so it is that whoever loses his soul or exposes his life, or goes all the way to lose it by confessing the truths which I have announced, will find his life and save his soul for ever. Fleeing from death he will find his death, and seeking to preserve his life, he will lose his life. Fleeing from temporal death, he will find eternal perdition, and wishing to preserve temporary life he will also lose eternal life." Jesus Christ was foreseeing a time of persecution, knowing how harsh it would be and wanted to prevent it. The struggle would be terrible, but necessary; victory would be difficult, and more than enough to win or lose all. And what good will it be for a man, adds the Lord, to gain all the treasures of the world, if this gain comes at a cost or one's salvation or life? Nothing in the world is precious enough to pay for a man's life if he passes from temporal to eternal life, because there is nothing in this world which can be compared to blissful and everlasting yearning, for which he will greatly rejoice in losing one to gain the latter. Be a king of the world, enjoy its pleasures for many years, do not lack desiring anything on earth. Even for this very happy man, who is yet to be found, what advantage would he take of such great temporal happiness if he were to lose eternal bliss?

"And what good would it serve man," Jesus Christ continued, "were he to win over all the world, if nothing can recompense the irreparable loss of his own soul?" Who is so crazy as to dare choosing temporary enjoyment, whose only purpose is that of eternal damnation? Buying a damaged good at a value which is less than another greater one, even if both are temporary and perishable, it is always considered a loss; What is it like to acquire a temporary good at the expense of an eternal one? To save our souls, everything has to be ventured without moaning on the cost to be paid for it, inasmuch as we close our eyes when need arises, or cut off our feet and hands in the spiritual sense which Jesus Christ orders us to do, and to leave father and mother, wife, children and estates, and also to offer up bodily life if necessary. Man will not achieve anything from this world when he dies to carry along with him, except his virtues and his sins; he will leave behind all that is worldly and as a matter of fact will only carry that which is immortal. Since the soul is thus immortal and incorruptible, it must be put before and preferred to all that is mortal and transient. Especially foolish and greedy, and even worse than the devil, is he who loves worldly riches and treasures more than his own soul or the souls of others, because the devil esteems more just one soul than the whole universe. So much so that the devil dared telling Jesus Christ, thinking he would deceive him: *I will give you all this*, and he showed him all the world, *if you prostrate before me and worship me*. Following which the great Origen does not hesitate to write: "This proposes two things to us, that we better choose losing the world and winning our soul, than to lose our soul to win the world." And Saint Chrysostom concludes with this very familiar example: "If you are in need and you find yourself on the brink of misery, you see your servants spending recklessly all they have, what are you gaining in being their master? So what will your soul gain if your body squanders all in sensual delights? Even if you had Solomon's wisdom, Absalom's handsomeness, Samson's strength, Enoch's longevity, Croesus' riches, and all the power of the Jews, of what advantage would all this be to you if in the end your soul was to be delivered to the demons to be tormented endlessly, and your body was to become grass on which worms graze?"

Jesus Christ, the humblest of all creatures, wanted to teach everyone by his words and example that the glory of his true disciples consisted in giving up that of the world, for if anyone were ever ashamed to confess him in the presence of men, there is no doubt that he would disown him before his angels and saints. Anyone who felt ashamed to profess his teachings and imitate his examples would be confounded on the day of his triumph, In short, if anyone had difficulty believing and following his teaching, which was so contrary to that of the world, causing scandal to those who follow him and love him, he would condemn them before the whole universe, when, accompanied by his angels, he would come from heaven with all the majesty of his glory and that of his Eternal Father to judge men and to punish or reward each one, according to one's works. There he would not look at people's faces but at their merits, without any cutback. To the righteous he will give the prize, to experience the glory of soul and body; and to wrongdoers, the suffering of both. This is the place of deserving one and the other, of freeing and saving the soul, and to receive from there according to merits. Walk then right here while you still have light, that is, while you live, for it is not worth the darkness of death catching you unprepared. Receive death over here so that you may then receive immortal life. Do not fear, for after life's sorrows heavenly glories and joys follow. If you fear death, fix your gaze on the glory of he who triumphs; if you are shameful of the cross, be aware of the angels' ministries. Listen and know with caution Saint Bernard's words: "Do you want to know what you owe Jesus Christ? You owe him your life, because he gave his for you."

As the apostles were still close-minded and were apt to fall into doubt as to whether the Lord would come in the manner he announced to them, that they might not falter while expecting him, he said to them: "Know that some of those who are here present and are listening to me will not see death until they have seen him whom you now see as being in all manner like other men, clad in majesty, full of radiance, adorned with power and beauty, and before feeling an unspeakable joy, which will be the anticipated effect of the joys of his heavenly kingdom. In mortal flesh I express to you, not your immortality, but an openness in all that is similar to the true light of future immortality. And I make you this gracious promise, which I will fulfil for you with the greatest faithfulness and promptness, so that you may see the future glory of the resurrection and the contemplation of the steadfast joy you will enjoy in that place, you will suffer with greater resignation and constancy the passing labours and tribulations of the world."

CHAPTER 51
THE TRANSFIGURATION OF JESUS ON MOUNT TABOR, IN WHICH HE SHOWS HIMSELF IN FULL GLORY TO THREE OF HIS DISCIPLES, AND THE NEXT DAY COMING DOWN FROM THE MOUNTAIN, HE HEALS A LUNATIC AND POSSESSED PERSON WHO THEY HAD NOT BEEN ABLE TO CURE SINCE THEY LACKED FAITH (MT 17:1-9; MK 9:16-28)

S Jesus Christ was determined to make known very clearly to his apostles that the time of his passion was drawing near, he spoke to them of none else than his approaching departure, of the insults, outrages, torments and sufferings, of the cross and his death. He showed them Jerusalem as the theatre staging the bloodiest and most inhumane of all tragedies ever seen in centuries, with its impious inhabitants making God made man victim of their own infidelity. He did not think of anything but of gloomy thoughts, speaking to his best friends of sad and heartbreaking reflections. All this was happening at a time when to liven them up, even though while telling them of plots and characters, he made them a great and comforting promise which had to be made before his death. The fatal term drew nearer, and the Sovereign Master was in a great hurry to finish the great work of instructing all the children of Israel within the different neighbourhoods of Palestine, as this had to be done before the sacrifice was consumed. A few days were enough to make himself known throughout the neighbourhood of Caesarea Philippi, in the locality of the tribe of Naphtali, bordering to the south with Mount Tabor and the tribe of Zabulon in the middle of Galilee. This area comprised from almost the headwaters of the River Jordan to the outskirts of Mount Lebanon. As soon as his arrival was announced in one part, people ran from all neighbourhoods to hear him speak of the kingdom of God.

Only Jesus Christ, from whom nothing was hidden, knew quite well that this was the last of his journeys in Judea and Galilee, that which like a long day would slowly lead him to Calvary, whose weights were all measured in the eternal decrees of God's wisdom. And as the bloody scene of Golgotha was to be the true triumph of hell and death, the Lord wanted to herald it with a glorious performance, whose magnificence foretold the cross and seemed solely destined to remove in advance the scandal this would cause. Six whole days passed, as Saint Matthew and Saint Mark say, not counting the first and last day, or the eighth, as Saint Luke says, but also counting the first and last day, namely that on which Jesus Christ made his last sermon, and during which the memorable event we are about to narrate occurred. Jesus Christ was then with his apostles on the lower slopes of a high mountain surrounded by a large crowd, to whom he had explained, as he normally did, his health-giving truths. And though it should not have caused any wonder to see him withdraw at the end of the day to spend the night in prayer, as was usual with him, it was surprising to see him taking with him his three most intimate friends, Peter, John and James, the latter two being brothers and sons of Zebedee, while the others remained on the plain along with the people who had followed them.

Relying on certain authors about what was said by some travellers, who were often less religious than they were taken to be, and about various planes of Palestine, whose accuracy is rather doubtful; and above all given that the sacred Evangelists do not name the mountain on which such great wonders occurred; the criticism of the unjust Gospel detractors preclude us from believing that the event took place on Mount Tabor, as according to what they said, that mountain was situated on the border between Galilee and Samaria, far from Banias and the Jordan headwaters. Assuming that Lebanon was where this wonder took place, which was much higher than Tabor and closer to Caesarea Philippi; yet it being equally undeniable that the Tabor is only four miles from Nazareth, and that Jesus Christ was then travelling through that country in the direction of Galilee; it is not hard to believe that this was the mountain where the wonder occurred; and all doubt disappears when those contrary to this opinion do not prove that in the whole of Palestine there was another mountain that bore the same name; and in the very ancient Persian version the title to Matthew's Chapter XVII reads: TRANSFIGURATION OF CHRIST ON MOUNT TABOR.

Yet still hidden in the bosom of divine Providence are the reasons why Jesus Christ would have to show this particular act of kindness to only three beloved apostles and not to all others. There can be no doubt that the Lord really had a good reason for this, among which it seems that Jesus Christ wanted the matter to remain very secret until after his resurrection. For those same three to whom he revealed a part of the magnificence of his glory were also to witness the opposite end to this in his agony in the Garden of Olives on the evening before his death. So that in compensating the glories of Tabor with the opprobrium of Calvary, the cross would not be a cause of real scandal for those who believed in the Lord.

Saint Jerome very wisely resolves any doubt that might arise, about Matthew and Mark counting only six days from Jesus Christ's last discourse, or rather from Peter's confession to the transfiguration, while Luke counts eight, saying: "All this suits the present mystery very well, because just as Christ and after the seventh in which he had rested in the tomb, on the eighth day he was risen, the same with us after six days in the world, symbolizing man's life, in which we work and suffer for the Lord, then after the seventh, which means rest for the souls, we will be resurrected on the eighth and rest eternally in the kingdom of heavenly bliss."

He only took along three with him, to show that the saying of three witnesses is sufficient to bear witness to the truth, while at the same time wanting to declare that all who steadfastly preserved in their life faith in the most dignified mystery of the Holy Trinity, would later rejoice in the eternal vision of God, Triune and One. He took along with him Peter, James and John, to teach us that anyone wanting to see the glory of God, should necessarily know Him by faith like Peter; by leaving behind all earthly business like James, and by having the grace of doing good deeds like John; because the full merit of a creature consists in believing the truth, to turn away from evil and to do good deeds. Likewise he also chose these three to represent all states, because as to Peter it means that they represent married persons and prelates; as to James, penitents and all those who in the holy mystery are dedicated to active life; and as to John, all the virgins consecrated to the Lord. And at the right time, in the end, he took the disciples to a very high place to show them the glory of the resurrection, to make us understand that if we want to share in that glory, we must keep away from evildoers and live far apart from the riots and fuss of epochs. By this we might know that we should not seek joy, happiness and glory in the deep valley of this world, but in the kingdom of bliss high above. The Lord recounts his death to all his disciples, but it was to only three that he manifested his glory. He appeared to many more disfigured on Calvary than transfigured on Tabor. So he chose the three whom he had called to be apostles before all others: Peter, who was destined to become the cornerstone of his Church; James, who was the first to bear witness to the truth with his blood before the other apostles; and John, who was to stand with him at the foot of the cross. This distinction was made among those who were close to him, by him who is absolute Lord of his gifts, and who in distributing them does not care for the dignity of whoever receives them, but sees to the mercy with which he bestows them and through them he prepares their hearts for the distribution and reception of even greater ones.

He took them up alone on a very high mountain. As a gift to his friends the Lord chooses to keep them away from the hustle and bustle of the world, lifting their soul high upon the solitude of a mountain. When Moses went up on the mountain, no people were allowed some distance away from its borders (Ex 19:12,24), and when Jacob struggled with the angel, he walked away from the sheepfold not to be disturbed by their noise (Gen 32:23). There is much to be seen through faith in that most of its important mysteries occurred on mountains. Isaac was due to be sacrificed on a mountain, on another Moses received the Law, the Saviour was transfigured on a mountain, and on another he was crucified. The Lord thus sanctifies the concepts of meaning to help form the spiritual man. Faith lifts the heart of earthly beings, prayer deprives of carnal passion, charity unites man with the highness of his divinity. Man does not climb any of these mountains without Christ; but nor does a man who appears to follow Jesus Christ climb, if he wants to carry along with him other things that condemn and reject Christ's law and teaching. While Jesus Christ kept prayerful watch and his disciples slept, he transformed his whole outer appearance as sovereign Lord, and the glory of his blessed soul suddenly and presently shone out. His divine face, ever solemn and serious, became as resplendent as the sun; his plain and simple tunic appeared shining and as white as snow. He showed them for an instant what was to be forever after the day of his ascension. "This is the kingdom or the royal city," as Pope Saint Leo says, "in that shortly before the Lord had promised some of his disciples that he would show himself to them. So he showed his glory before chosen witnesses, and that body of his, equal in human nature to that of other men, illuminates and brightens him up with the lights of his eternal candidness."

"What the sun is for the eyes of the body," says Saint Augustine, "that is Christ for the eyes of the soul; what that is for the flesh, this is for the hearts. Christ's garments are the Church. She will shed her clothes if she is not supported by the One who covers himself with her. In this weave Paul came to be the last trim, with himself saying that he was the last among the apostles (1 Cor 15:9); and just like the woman who suffered from a serious health issue just by touching the trim of Christ's clothes, so the Church coming from the Gentiles is saved by Paul's preaching. How strange it is that white garments mean the Church, when God promises through Isaiah (Is 1:18) to bleach like snow what was red like scarlet? Christ, resplendent on the Tabor, denotes the state of clarity with which he must forever reward the momentary tribulation of his elect." And Saint Augustine adds: "The whiteness of their garments, came from the glare of his face; and this was a real change in the face, not in the dress. He does not depart from the true substance of the flesh, nor does he destroy or separate the truth from his body, but he added candidness and radiance to it. Clothed therefore with our mortal flesh, he manifested to us how he wanted the light of immortality and of his glory, to give us greater certainty of that same glory which he preached to us."

This so glorious transfiguration was like a pledge of the future bliss we expect, and as a certain and sure proclamation of his Second Coming, in which Christ himself and his saints shone with a candidness much brighter than that of the sun; and so it was that I do not take on that occasion the dowry of candidness, but the likeness of that dowry. For as Pope Saint Leo himself continues saying: "With the apostles being still clothed in the sack of mortal flesh, in no manner could they see the ineffable and inaccessible light of divinity, which is reserved in eternal life for those with a clean heart. The glare on Jesus Christ's face means the candidness of his divinity, and that of his garments, that of his hallowed humanity."

Ultimately, we must contemplate three things about this surprising and glorious transfiguration; namely that he takes up with him his most beloved disciples, that he went up the mountain, and that he anticipated the event with prayer to show that no one comes to glory unless accompanied by virtue, leads a life detached from all earthly things, and is given to prayer and engages fervently in it. Happy is he who always carries with him such excellent support.

At the same time Moses and Elijah appeared to them talking to him. Moses had died many years before, but it must be presumed that for this passing his soul came out of Abraham's bosom and united with his body, being preserved for this purpose incorrupt in the tomb given to him by the angel of the Lord overlooking Mount Peor, or Phogor. So Moses looks at Elijah, who had been snatched alive in a chariot of fire, departed from the resting place of his body, where he had been waiting for more than nine hundred years for the orders of the Messiah. One carried the tablets of the Law in his arms, the other was dressed in his camel-skinned garb, girdled with a leather belt. Filled with light and being participants of the glory of God made man, they needed to show their characteristic symbols to be recognised by the apostles, such as indeed could not be mistaken. They spoke to Jesus Christ, but we do not know for how long the conversation lasted, and we would have ignored its subject, unless after the disciples were awakened they had seen the two ministers of God talking to their Master, and had not heard them speak among themselves of the cruel death which he had to suffer very soon in Jerusalem. Moses and Elijah, the Law and the Prophets, are of little avail until they speak with Christ. "Who would read the Law," says Saint Augustine, "who would read the Prophets unless they bear witness to Christ? Moses and the prophets spoke and wrote; yet they were full with Christ when he poured out himself. They were the vessels, Christ was the source; they were the servants, Christ was the Lord. Steadfast is the truth made public by the trumpet of the Old and New Testament, as confirmed by the Gospel aided by prophecies. One and the other Testament complemented each other. He who was under the prohibition of ancient mysteries had promised the figures of that Law; he now reveals the glare of glory, and the promised and announced Christ is fully discovered and revealed."

To what could Jesus Christ's enemies of religion object in this most public and superb revelation? The religion promised before the Law is not new, locked in the Law, attested to by itself, announced by the prophets, discovered, bound and glorified by him who was white among all prophets, and where next to Tabor the harmony could be seen between the Law and Prophets, and between the Gospel and the apostles. The Law was given by Moses; grace is the work of Christ; in it he fulfils the promise of prophetic figures and the observance of legal precepts. He taught by his presence the truth of prophecies, and by his grace the opportunity given by the commandments. The Law was given to alert, warn and enlighten the sinner and to make known the need for grace, and this was given to fulfil the Law with charity; the truth to dispel the darkness of idolaters, the shadows of the Jews and the hypocrisy of erring Christians. The Law figures, prophesizes and promises grace, and gives truth effect and fulfilment in the Law, which is Jesus Christ and charity. The servant Moses could not do anything more than publish the Law and declare the will of his Lord. Only Jesus Christ, God and Redeemer of souls, could become their

Lord by his grace, make them love according to his will, and fulfil in them the truth of his promises, transforming stones into Abraham's children. All this was said in a very few words by the Apostle in Rom 3:20-21. Through the Law, he says, comes knowledge of sin; but now, other than by the Law, God's righteousness has been manifested *which is only* borne witness to by the Law and the Prophets, *who make it radiant*.

Moses and Elijah spoke to Jesus Christ about his passion, not to tell him anything unknown to him, but to worship him for coming into the world in mortal flesh, and also since they already saw the mystery of the passion which he himself had predicted and announced drawing very close to its accomplishment, and also because they saw the time of their redemption and that of all the human race approaching. However, he sympathised with Christ, for that glorious and shining face was to be disfigured, spat upon and mocked, and his holy and immaculate person was to be handed over for envy, to be judged and crucified. Nor is there any doubt that among the apostles and prophets there was very great joy and happiness, not only for Jesus Christ's transfiguration, but also for the mutual and reciprocal vision, for the princes of both Testaments came together with God of Abraham. There, Moses, leader and prince of the Jews, and Peter, prince of Christians, were seen together. Elijah and John, the virgin, were also seen there, and both praised James, the one among the apostles who was to be the first martyr. However, it seems that the three apostles did not give much notice and attention to the subject matter of the conversation, until they came to their senses even more full of admiration and surprise caused to them by such novelty. They were so moved and dazzled by the greatness and radiance of the marvellous sight that Peter, being attracted by the revelation of this great mystery, despising all love of the world and annoyed by earthly afflictions, seized by the desire for eternity and possessed of the most intense joy which that unexpected vision caused him, dared to interrupt their conversation to say to Jesus Christ, *Lord, it is good for us to be here*. He desired to remain with Jesus Christ in that place where he enjoyed the vision of his glory. This desire was a disorderly one, seeking rest before work and a crown before glory; and he did not deserve Christ's answer to it. Such desire is requested by whoever now seeks peace in patience, while comforting himself in the tasks the Lord sends him. Whoever suffers for Christ's love is with him, and will be with Christ if he remains so. Anguished peace is rewarded with glorious peace.

How good we feel, Lord, to be here flooded with joy in contemplating your glory and sweetness, those which once felt, all of earth's tastes and enjoyments are already regarded to be vile and contemptible. And so it is not strange that Peter kept on saying to his Master, *If you wish, let us raise three tents here, one for you, one for Moses, and one for Elijah.* They are not the tents for glorious bodies, already freed from committed injuries. Who would not fear worrying and deceiving himself in God's way, when the prince of the apostles, surprised and astonished with that vision, upsets God's order and deals with heavenly order as an earthly one? Peter did not speak or think of putting up a dwelling for himself and his companions, since he assumed that as disciples they would all remain gathered within their Master's abode. The manner how Peter prayed his Master expressed his wish to stay up on the mountain to partake a little in the taste of the future glory which he saw in him, so that we may learn that nothing must seem difficult for us to suffer for Christ to climb the mountain of eternal bliss with him. With regard to this the Venerable Bede says: "Oh how very blissful will it be to be perpetually among the angels, in the sight of the divinity, if only the transfiguration of Christ's humanity, accompanied by only two saints, was so delightful that Peter so eagerly desired not to depart from his presence! And how much greater will be the softness and sweetness of seeing the Supreme King seated on the throne of his majesty and glory, and in being in the midst of the choirs of all the angels and saints in heaven? Peter was then mistaken and did not know what he was saying in asking his Master for such things: even because, just as a passer-by in the world and banished in it, he sought within a valley of tears his true homeland, or because he judged to be true glory that which was only an image and shadow of the future, forgetting that the kingdom of God has not been promised to saints on earth, but to those in heaven." This made Saint Augustine exclaim and forced him to say: "What are you saying, oh blessed Peter? Is the world coming to an end, and are you seeking in the world a place where to retreat? Are you seeing so many people getting together and meeting, and you seek calm and rest? Are you seeing so much darkness in the middle of the world, and you want to hide the light that is to cast it out? It would not suit you, oh Peter, that Christ stays up on the mountain, for if he stayed there, the promise he made to you would never be fulfilled, nor would you ever have held the keys to the kingdom of heaven, nor would the tyranny of hell and death have ever been repressed."

Peter was still talking when a glowing cloud dazzled them. What was being undoubtedly shown to him was that no tents were needed on earth for such persons who had them in heaven. This cloud also served as a shadow to dim the light that had dazzled the apostles, and marked the presence of the Father, whose voice, coming out of its darkness, bore witness to the divinity of the Son. And the cloud was an unmistakable indication of the great difference between the Old Testament and the Gospel. In the Old Testament the Lord appeared in a dismal and dark cloud, which denoted the shadow of the Law and the spirit of terror with which even the children of holy people were filled. This is the glowing cloud which denotes the truth of the New Testament and its spirit, which is charity. It is not thunder and lightning which come out of this cloud, but the voice of the Father declaring the divinity of the Messiah. As the cloud gave shade to all and in a way served them as a tent, a voice came out of it proclaiming: *This is my beloved Son in whom I am well been pleased.*

This voice of Majesty and grandeur is the same one which was previously heard over the Jordan waters. It was there, during Jesus Christ's baptism, that the whole Trinity appeared, the Father in the voice, the Holy Spirit in the dove, and the Son in the waters. So too is the Father now manifested in the voice, the Son on the mountain, and the Holy Spirit in the cloud. This cloud had shadowed the Virgin, so that without defiling her purity she could conceive the Son of righteousness, and temper within us and extinguish the flames and carnal desires, in order that the spirit may prevail in the flesh. Moses and Elijah were there; and it was not said for them that these are my beloved children, for the Only Begotten Son is one thing and adoptive sons are another. The One about whom the Law and the Prophets had boasted was now being recommended. Thus when the Father said, "This is my beloved Son," it was as if to say, "This is the Son, who from eternity is with me and is born of me, for neither the Father is before the Son, nor the Son is after the Father. They are not separated from each other by divinity, nor are they divided by power, and they are not distinguished by eternity: in the Father is the Son and in the Son there is me." The Son did not usurp from anyone the equality he has with the Father, but remaining in His glory to fulfil his eternal council and that of the Father for the eternal reparation of men, he lowered his unchanging divinity to the form of a servant. When the three disciples Peter, James and John, who until then had shown some strength, heard the Father, they fell down in a faint and were as if taken by a strong trembling fit. Hitting the ground with their face, they were so frightened that no one even dared raise his eyes to look.

Saint Ambrose makes it clear that when the voice of the Father pointing to his Son was heard, Moses and Elijah disappeared, so that the apostles might not run away and that they might know for certain whom they ought to hear and follow. Because of this it was also said *In him I am well pleased*, which means "In him I am determined to fulfil my consent for the redemption of the world." Or as Saint Chrysostom adds: "This is my very beloved Son in whom I delight, in whom I rest, and whom I accept. For he fulfils all things that are of the Father with the utmost diligence and accuracy. One is his will and that of the Father, and in both there is only one will. So *Listen to him*, more than to Moses and Elijah for Christ is the end of the Law and of the prophets. *Listen to him* as the Supreme and only Master who will teach you all things necessary to achieve eternal salvation and salvation. *Listen to him*, because he is the truth.

Look for him, because he is the life. Follow him, for he is the only path which leads to eternal life." Or as if one also wanted to say in other words, that the legal shadows and all the enigmatic types of prophets will disappear, and only the new light of the Gospel, which you must follow, will shine. The apostles were happy then, because they did not only deserve to see the brightness of the Lord, but also to hear the Father's voice. Nor shall we be estranged from this bliss if we believe the One whom they believed, and just as they lived loving him, so shall we, like them, live by loving him with all the strength of our hearts.

Another thing is even more worthy of attention, namely that just as human fragility remains impressed in Jesus Christ's presence with the greatness and glory of God, so did the disciples when they heard the omnipotent voice of the Father. They fell on their faces, and this was a sign of the righteousness and holiness with which they were adorned, because falling back is typical of cruel and wicked persons. The righteous bow and fall on their faces, sometimes out of fear as was the case on this occasion, sometimes out of humility as when the magi adored Jesus Christ in the cave of Bethlehem, and sometimes by way of thanksgiving like the elders before the throne of the Lamb. And *they feared greatly*, for they knew that they had erred in the appearance of the shining cloud which enlightens all that which is mysterious and hidden in the darkness, and reveals the hearts' secrets. Also because the voice of the Father was like a dreadful thunder which threw everyone to the ground, so did it happen that the prophets fled, and the apostles fell, and even the earth trembled under their feet. But those who were drowned by their human frailty were promptly comforted by the sweetness and kindness of the omnipotent and charitable Master. For getting closer to them he mildly touched all three and told them, *Arise and fear not*. They were weakened, and Jesus Christ's touch persuaded them and confirmed their belief in the mystery they had just witnessed. Blessed are those whom Jesus Christ touches. Blessed are those whom salvation and life touch them. They rise from their fall and feel fearlessly safe. May his merciful right hand deem fit to touch us and wake us from our dream, astonishment and ignorance, opening our eyes that we may see him! A sweet friend is our good Jesus Christ, since he comforts us and helps us as the Almighty One.

Touched by Jesus Christ, encouraged and strengthened by him, the apostles returned to their senses and found themselves alone with their Master. After the whole remarkable vision had disappeared, had Moses and Elijah remained, not only would the voice of the Father seem uncertain but it could also have been doubted who it was that gave witness. The two disappeared so that it could be seen that the fatherly voice was not referring to them, but that it only pointed to Jesus Christ. If Peter had been then carried away for a few moments, he felt deceived and did not conceive the events foretold by this manifestation. His error did not last long, however, for it soon wore off; at the latest when the Messiah, having been received in the chair of his glory, communicated his Spirit to his disciples and shed upon them the fullness of his light. It was then Peter himself who tenderly and thankfully recalled the special gift with which Jesus Christ had honoured him. He gladly referred it to the first Christians when, as a father and shepherd, he instructed them on the greatness of the Lord and Master whom he had had the joy of serving, saying to them (2 Pt 1:16-18): "My dear children, we did not make known to you the power and coming of our Lord Jesus Christ following clearly devised myths, but as eyewitnesses to his greatness. For in receiving from God the Father that glorious testimony when from the cloud in which the glory of God appeared with such brilliance, a voice came down which said to him, *This is my beloved Son in whom I am well pleased, listen to him*, we also heard this voice coming from heaven and saw his glory being with him on the holy mountain." Notwithstanding that Peter wrote this to the first children of the Church with a full outpouring of his soul, he was not free to be able to say it in secret to the other apostles who were his colleagues, because when Jesus Christ came down from the mountain, he expressly forbade the three of them from telling anyone, while he was still living, what they had seen up there. A time would come for them when they could speak freely about him, pausing only until the Son of Man had risen from the dead to sit at the right hand of his Father. And Jesus Christ was promptly obeyed on this matter.

We would close this recount, of so many interesting points as this mystery presents to us, possibly by silently referring to some very timely and essential observations of the eminent doctors Leo the Great and Augustine. When the Eternal Father declares to us from the cloud that Jesus Christ is his Beloved Son, He is not content in making this most important declaration, until he later gives it to us as the sovereign Master who knows about salvation, and for this reason He tells us to listen to him. Because he is the One who with his blood redeems the world, who ties the devil and takes away his spoils, tearing up sinful writings and treatises of cursed perversion of justice. He is the One who opens and paves the way of heaven, preparing for us the ladder by which we climb towards the kingdom in the ordeal of the cross. When he commands them to listen to him, he asks not only for attention, but for faith and obedience, a desire and love of truth, and a plea and prompt action in putting it to work. Listening not through the ears but the heart, in the sense which Saint John calls *blessed*, are those who read and hear the words of his prophecy and together keep what is written in it (Apoc. 1:3). Life within us is a sign of faith. Living faith is obedient, and he who is not with Christ does not hear Christ as the Father commands him to do. If we want to be God's beloved children, let us listen to His Beloved Son. The Gospel is the cloud from which Jesus Christ speaks to us. One voice recommends another voice: the Father's voice commends the Son's word. The Son of God precedes us in tolerating adversity and in the fulfilment of the divine will. Let us not boast of loving God if we do not listen to Christ, for keeping the law is the test of love, but love is the principle of keeping the law. No one hears Christ unless love opens the heart's doors to receive his word. Let us listen to Christ, let us do what he commands, let us wait for what he promises.

Encouraged by such holy and heroic hope, let us not tremble or faint when we hear the Lord's voice speaking to us. David wanted to hear it, because he said it would speak of peace and what was suiting for the peace of his heart.

The voice of love is soft, sweet and charming, whereas that of justice is majestic and terrible. It moves deserts, shakes mountains and valleys, and fells the sturdiest cedars of Lebanon, and it is the voice of virtue and grandeur. Man is unable not to hear it without being moved when it sounds from the top of the heavens and exits from a cloud's entrails. It is not strange that the apostles bow down upon hearing it, this indeed being an important lesson which should not go unnoticed. Yet it is important that we learn even more from the principle of this debility. Their weakness was the cause in them, inasmuch as respect and love in us; and the awareness and confession of our indignity will preserve us from a dreadful fall and make us worthy of God's mercies.

The Lord's infinite mercy, whose action with regard to man is as old as man himself, was on this occasion shown to the apostles clearly and sensitively. Jesus Christ communicated his power with his presence, his sacrifice with his contact, and his spirit with his word. He chased away from them the fear of the flesh and armed them with the constancy of faith. It is not right, he says, that you now fear in my passion those who by my gift you will not fear later in your own. For the disciples' falling to the ground meant their bodily death; when Christ tells them to rise, this expresses resurrection. And since after the resurrection the Law or prophecies no longer serve any purpose, so when they rise they will no longer see Moses or Elijah, for the Word remains to be all in all. There will be Moses, but not the Law; Elijah will be seen there, but not the prophecies. Everything will then cease, science disciplines will disappear, there will neither exist Church ministries any longer, nor languages or writings. He will no longer see the Church other than Jesus Christ in God, and God in Jesus Christ. The eternal bond will then shine of the members' love among themselves and with Jesus Christ. Charity will consummate bodily head and members in God and with Jesus Christ, who is our true law and the sign of our life, so that whoever with simple heart now holds within him the faith he received in baptism and believes and confesses it later in the light of the eternal vision, will openly contemplate all that he would have previously believed and confessed.

The circumstances which would involve Jesus Christ in a few days time were sad and distressing, just as those of his passion could not be any less so. And since the Jews' wickedness turned everything into poison, and the imperfect even crude apostles did not have due taste for the things of God, they could not understand what he was telling them about his forthcoming resurrection. So they kept wondering among themselves, "What does he mean to say in commanded us not to reveal this wonder to anyone, until the Son of Man rises from the dead?" "Actually," Saint Jerome says, "it seems rather incredible that while enjoying such glory today he will be hanging on a cross tomorrow." Nor did the Lord want the other disciples to be sad in having lost that wonder and to envy them, and as he was used to do he commanded them to remain silent; yet from then on there arose much greater doubts in the minds of his trusted disciples. They had just seen Elijah accompanied by Moses, conversing familiarly with Jesus Christ, and could not understand that Jesus Christ was the end of the Law and completion of prophecies, because the time had not yet come for them to discuss matters of faith so adeptly. Elijah's transitory sight was rather hard for them, leading to their intelligence to be opposed to the truths announced to them. And they did not disdain from saying this to Jesus Christ with holy simplicity.

"Master," they said to him, "about what you are teaching us about your faith and establishing your kingdom, will it be very soon as it looks like you want to have us understand? And if matters are so close at hand, how can one explain what the scribes and Pharisees say when they publicly teach that before all events it would so happen that Elijah returns and preaches to us? And that after him Christ will come to take possession of his kingdom (Mk 9:10)." This was undoubtedly something hard for ignorant men to understand and interpret the Scripture. The Lord, in order to instruct them fully and to bring them out of their ignorance, explained to them the passage in Malachi (4:5), in which the scribes and Pharisees supported his doctrine. Then he told them further: "It is true that Elijah must come first (Mk 9:11); that it is prophesied of him that when he comes he would work to renew the early righteousness of customs in the people, by attracting sons to the piety of their fathers, and to restore the practising of virtues. But do not imagine that he will do this without being despised by men, without undergoing many insults and without exposing himself to many bad treatments. A person who is destined to preach the ways of Christ must experience and have a destiny like his own. Such is this Elijah, who must come before me, and prepare the children of Israel for the setting up of my kingdom. However, do not be fooled by this prediction. Elijah has already come and fulfilled his ministry. Your scribes and Pharisees did not want to know him. They have made him suffer as many indignities as they could have invented for the purpose, to remove him from his works and discredit his person and his word. They do not lack anything any longer unless it is to treat the Master as they have treated the disciple, and the Messiah as they treated his Forerunner. I warn you, they are not far from putting the last straw on their malice; they will lose themselves in wanting to verify all the prophecies referring to the Son of Man at such cost. Upon hearing this explanation, the disciples clearly knew that the Elijah, who was to precede the reign of Christ, had already come and that he was John the Baptist.

It is easy to presume that with such instructive and pleasant conversation the three apostles would not feel having been any favoured on their way down the mountain, and that they would soon find themselves with the crowd they had left on the plain. But as he approached the plain, the Lord observed something that offended his divine eyes and forced him to express his displeasure, even though we do not know the motive for it and can only conjecture about it. He drew near to his nine apostles to comfort them after his short absence but finding them surrounded by a large crowd, he heard them in a shouting match with the scribes. They were shocked and overtaken by fear on seeing him as they did not expect him back so soon, but even so they greeted him respectfully and were joyful of his early return. No one, however, sighed more for the Saviour's return than a grieving and bereaved father who had not found in Jesus Christ's disciples all the promised comfort. Jesus Christ arrived at the place of the dispute and asked what were they fighting over so hotly? And suddenly throwing himself at his feet the father begged his mercy telling him: "Master, I have brought with me my son hoping that you will show him your love. For he is possessed by a demon which drives him mute, and this is only the lesser of all evils which make him suffer. At the beginning of each month it causes him some very tedious accidents. Anywhere he gets the fit, it causes him to fall, knocks him down and drags him over the ground, shaking him with fury. The poor boy gives many cries without being able to articulate a word, foams and grinds his teeth, is consumed and shatters. Many times he throws himself into the fire, at others he jumps into the water, and the demon never departs from him without first redoubling its fury, so that it seems like shattering him to pieces. It is a real wonder how this unfortunate boy has been able to resist for so long. So then, Lord, have mercy on me and my son, for he is the only One I have. Use your virtue to free him. I have taken him to your disciples, I have begged them persistently to throw out this demon from him, but none of them was able to make him obey them."

Jesus Christ went down from the mountain so that with his Father he would deal intimately with the most interesting work of human health and salvation. No less than ever before, could he ignore the fervent plea which had just been made to him and so, as if he wanted to teach us that after retreat and the gift of prayer we ought to return with new fervour and spirit to the exercise of our ministry, he made us see the fruit of retreating to pray away from the eagerness of the crowd which was seeking salvation and doctrine from him. The possessed son who is presented to him is an obvious proof of the original guilt, since it was due to the first man's sin that all his descendants deserved to fall under the devil's domination and tyranny. He is also a figure of the lordship which the devil has over the heart through man's passions. The mute spirit dominates and possesses all those lazy spirits whose mouths are shut in shyness and worldly respects so that they do not defend the Gospel, being traitors to God and to their conscience. And the evildoings about which the hard pressed father spoke to Jesus Christ, through which the devil would pass his son, are precisely the image of the anger and fury with which the devil treats those whom he dominates by sin. The devil takes advantage of the mood, passions and various other causes to hide himself in bodily possession no less than in spiritual temptation. For indeed, the intervals between one sin and another in a hardened sinner are rare and brief! Oh, if you only felt so vividly this misery in your soul and the devil's spiritual illusions the same as the father felt those of his own sick son! Your son is your heart, your only son, whose salvation matters to you more than being king of the whole earth. Watch how edgy he is about his passions, how he crashes into his own anger, how enraged he is with pure pride, how arid his envy keeps him. Take pity on yourself and run to Jesus Christ to seek your remedy.

If it is surprising that Jesus Christ's disciples could not cast out the devil from that body for a whole night, this should not cause us great wonder in view of his baffling judgments. The Lord often permits that his ministers do not actually heal many souls, either owing to a just judgment on the souls themselves, or else to teach the ministers that they are ever so inadequate to do anything good on their own. For they should expect everything from Jesus Christ and it is to him that they should attribute the happy success of his zeal and charity. The Lord also allows some sinners to fight at some point against their bad habits, so that they may better understand what sin is and its slavery. The sinner's first efforts seen in his prayer, are not useless even if they seem so, for with them grows the desire for freedom and awareness that Jesus Christ is the Saviour. The depiction of evil and the plea for relief, while breathing all the tenderness of an overly moved father, also justify the impelling desire animating him to see his son fully freed, and that he was expecting to receive this benefit from Jesus Christ's own hand. Jesus Christ undoubtedly pitied the unfortunate child; but his mercy could not be shown before he had expressed his indignation. "Oh incredulous and wicked race," he exclaimed "how much longer will I be with you? And how long should I suffer and tolerate you?" It cannot be denied that these words, coming from the mouth of the most meek Jesus Christ, were a living and ardent rebuke to whoever they were addressed. Some say they were directed at the scribes, others at the father of the unfortunate child, and others at the apostles. Yet it seems most certain that all understood and that the common disbelief, even if greater in some more than the others, brought a general rebuke to the fore. He understood the child's father, who did not enjoy due confidence in Jesus Christ's disciples, looking at them as apprentices and inexperienced persons in the art of curing the sick and working miracles. He understood the disciples who were dazed and fainted on meeting the devil's resistance, the rumours surrounding them, and the insults and denigrations of the false doctors. And also the doctors themselves who from the disciples' inaction concluded they were weak and ensnared by their Master and the falsehood of the doctrine he preached. And it would somehow be a manner how to disprove the sincerity of Jesus Christ's disciples, wanting to exempt them from such weakness which they themselves did not deny. When we read what they said in private conversation with Jesus Christ on this subject, we will fully know how necessary this was from time to time for them that their faith might be encouraged and their trust affirmed.

The kindness Jesus Christ had for all did not undergo any delay when it came to freeing creatures from the devil's power. So Jesus Christ uttered in a loud, though very gentle voice, *Bring him to me.* So they led the boy before him, but seeing Jesus Christ the spirit began stirring within him, and falling suddenly to the ground the boy rolled over foaming at the mouth. These were the last efforts of an enemy's rage who felt his victor drawing near. Whoever considers himself useless in forcing out captivating sin from souls, may still lead these souls to Jesus Christ, praying to him fervently for them or to direct them to others who are filled with his spirit. Inasmuch as the sinner moves closer to penance, the devil redoubles his efforts and increases the obstacles to prevent it. Yet nothing should ravage those who truly wish to be saved or those who are charged with directing souls, for among the greatest dangers all must walk fearlessly. When souls look for directors and directors for souls, they must always keep Christ's plan in mind, which is to save them all. "How long has it been," the Lord asked the boy's father, "that your son has suffered similar events?" "From his childhood," the father answered him adding, "I have already told you, Lord, how much it makes me suffer. Ah! if you can do anything, help us; for you must have never seen two grief-stricken persons more worthy of compassion." The father's petitions were great indeed; but neither the liveliness of his faith nor the firmness of his trust matched his desires. He truly represented the feigning faithful persons of our days who run after all of earth's remedies before turning with faith towards heavenly ones; so that they do not turn to God unless forced to do so after despairing of human remedies, and pining with passion to be heard they can hardly wait for the time when they will be heard. Temples are full of these shy supplicants, none less common than the father's invocations. What should those who doubt that God can and wants to help them expect from Him? Yet it would be much better to ask them. What does it matter that baptism freed them in childhood from the bondage of sin, if very early they let the devil back into their hearts to take them over again? Many years of serving passions inflate and weaken the will, making it impossible to break the chains of sin. So dreadful is the influence that the devil takes over the soul he seizes and this becomes like a vile slave. Every single time it is harassed and humiliated by the ferocity and tyranny of the lord which enslaves it. Who will set it free if not the mercy of God and the love of the Church which incessantly prays for the conversion of sinners?

One thing arises, however, on this occasion and which is very worthy of observation. Without any regard to the Pharisees or to the crowd of people who were watching, this father implores the Saviour's piety and help for his son to teach us that we must go to Jesus Christ with eagerness, a sorrowful spirit, and confessing our needs, poverty and misery. In so going we ought to be aware of his power and not to pay attention to the obstacles which the world, the devil and the flesh present us to deny us healing from our faults. For this reason this merciful Liberator who had come to earth to deliver everyone from the devil's power and who had given salvation and freedom to several others with his living faith before, wanted the son's health to depend on his father's faith, and so he said to him: *Do you believe I can do what you are asking of me? If you can, then do believe since all things are possible for anyone who believes, as there is no miracle which is above my power.* "Ah! Yes, Lord," the father replied, shedding ample tears dropping from his eyes as a vestige of doubt and suspicion, yet showing clearly that he felt being reprimanded. "Yes, Lord, I believe; but if you see also see misfortune in my soul in any disbelief that offends you, heal the father by delivering the son, and do two miracles at the same time." Who does not love the most precious gift of faith, for which he does not refuse anything? Who does not want to see such a rich treasure grow in himself? Who is he who sleeps, rests or desists for one instant without searching in Christ's entrails? He who gives everything and wants to give us everything is the one who told us, "Ask and you shall receive," but it is necessary to ask in faith. The father was asking with faith, despite confessing he was sceptical. This is a trait of heroic humility for which the Saviour judged the father worthy to receive the food of faith which he missed, and the grace of his son's healing for which he was so truly imploring.

It was already late in the day and the mobs were still searching for Jesus Christ. Their very great numbers took with them many sick to be healed, being determined to see them healed. The poor boy meanwhile kept on struggling and being furiously tormented so that Jesus Christ, being eager to instruct the crowd around him, clothed himself with that authority distinguishing the Master from his disciples and with an air of majesty, which hell respected and feared about him, he severely threatened the devil telling it in a loud voice, *Unclean spirit, deaf and dumb* (that is causing men to become deaf and dumb) *I am the One who commands you; get out of this boy, and dare not ever enter into him again.*" The devil obeyed even in his spite and with sorrow, but obeyed for its very being, with fury, vengeance and spite. It obeyed, bellowing with courage and forcing the unfortunate boy to give dreadful cries, shaking him with such violence and fury, that he was left lying for some time on the ground, not moving at all and as if dead, as all those around him dared saying loudly in Jesus Christ's presence. The Saviour, however, who in the midst of the turmoil and confusion that reigned around him retained the same composure of omnipotence and highness that belonged to him, took the boy by the hand, helped him rise and stand on his feet, and immediately turning his eyes to the boy's father said to him: *Take your son, he is already free from the devil, and do know that he is forever.* This young man was the image of the sinner's hardness steeped in evil, who cannot be healed by ordinary means, for it is necessary that Jesus Christ commands him, threatens him and terrifies him with his almighty word. How is it possible that those who are possessed by this deaf and mute spirit, those not wanting to speak of God, nor hear anyone speak about Him, are otherwise healed? Or those who never confess or even acknowledge their faults, or those who become deaf to the threats of God's wrath and judgment, to eternal truths, to divine inspirations, to corrections and exhortations by the Lord's ministers? Wretched are all those, and so will they be eternally, who are deaf and dumb of their own will, for they stubbornly ignore the voice of the Lord who calls them. Yet the day will come when they will cry out to the Lord, and Jesus Christ too will turn a deaf ear to them. For man will not receive anything in his death which he has not sown in his life.

It seems normal that the healing of the father's unbelief followed this praiseworthy sign, because the remedy was very effective and had been worked on him by the most skilful and clever hand in the universe. And if one and the other were not confirmed in faith, so that they would never waver in it, it was necessary for both of them to have a heart as hard as that of the evil spirit itself which had tormented the son and cruelly afflicted the father for such a long time. They had to believe in order to be grateful, and to deny the devil entry into their hearts for ever, since Jesus Christ had commanded it never to enter again into the son. But since salvation is often short-lived even in many who know how difficult it is to recover it, one might fear that the door could be willingly reopened to this spirit and that the final stages would be much more miserable. Yet among the many sorrowful and bitter thoughts assaulting the heart of a man's brother, and considering his misery and natural fragility, there are also other comforting thoughts which come to console him. Blessed is the man whom the Lord will raise up and hold, indeed blessed is him whoever the Lord will raise up and hold. And here Jesus Christ was teaching the father as he lifted up and sustained his son. Blessed is he who, festered by the devil's attacks, in the midst of obstacles to his conversion from his passions, the inclination to evil and the power of custom, finds the beneficent hand of the Lord's zealous minister who, being moved and strengthened by the most beloved Saviour himself, helps him to rise up, breathes into him the spirit to undertake the path that leads to God and instructs him about the devil's tricks so that he will not be overcome or seduced by it.

The weakness of human frailty today apparently demands miracles from God to believe, as might have been demanded in Jesus Christ's time by unbelieving Judaism, and man would not believe until he sees that his pleas are heard. But if he does not see this, he first falls into discouragement, then into indifference and instantly into disbelief, without realizing that today miracles are not so necessary as they were when the Saviour came to preach the Gospel and to found his new Church. Then, the Messiah had to prove his divinity and his mission with the actual amount of miracles he worked, both for us who later had to believe, and for those who were witnesses of his doctrines and wonders. Now that ancient miracles assure our faith, we must assume that when God does not work on our behalf the miracle we beg Him to do for us, it is either because we do not ask Him in faith, or it does not lead to His greater glory, or it would not be to our benefit. However, if we look at ourselves, if we contemplate the nature and the march of events and continual occurrences, how many public and very evident miracles are there which we do not notice? A fervent Christian is easily persuaded that for him great miracles in the order of grace are performed every day when he contemplates the inner comforts with which God visits him, the graces with which He provides him and the mercies which sustain him, and he is happy with such marked signs of benevolence and love.

Father and son returned, thankful and appreciative, and the people blessed God in admiration and celebration of the wonders He worked through the ministry of whom he had sent to be the light and comfort of all Israel. But the nine apostles felt much remorse in not being able to work a miracle themselves, with so much glory which would have resulted from it. However, either out of shame for having seemed so powerless against such an evil spirit, or for fear of not being able to cast out other spirits from now on, they did not want to publicly declare to Jesus Christ the sorrow and apathy they felt for not having done a good job, and so they hoped that the Saviour would return home before speaking to him about it all. So they came to the matter, with their hearts pierced by the affront they had received in the presence of the scribes whom they saw as their greatest enemies, privately reached their Master and said to him: "How is it, Lord, that being your disciples and having given us power over all unclean spirits, we could not make that evil spirit obey us, even if we send it to you in your name?"

Jesus Christ mainly gave them two reasons: the first was their lack of belief for as he told them, "If you had a living faith with as much proper strength as a mustard seed of all seeds, you would move mountains from one place to another. All things would be possible to you and nothing would resist your virtue. But your faith is lean and nothing of the sort found in God's pure and specially favoured souls. This heroic faith is the one that which can do everything, that which commands nature, has power over evil spirits, obtains from heaven whatever it wants, yet to which your faith cannot however be compared." The second reason was their little fondness and taste for prayer and fasting, which are the spiritual weapons we always need to overcome our spiritual enemies and which Jesus Christ himself always used to overcome them. After coming down from the mountain, where he had prayed and fasted, he was more justified in telling them there were certain evil spirits which were ever more determined not to leave human bodies, and that it was impossible to cast them out without the help of prayer and fasting. This power was left by Christ to his Church, undoubtedly, but it is not exempt from turning to prayer, fasting, vigils and to the other practices with which it seeks the saintliness of its children. To cast out evil habits from man, it is necessary to humble the spirit by prayer and to tame the flesh by penance. Otherwise the material nature of certain outward practices is futile, although they are always used with fruit when they are accompanied by faith, hope and charity, together with penance and prayer.

We should believe with good reason that this was the last conversation Jesus Christ had with his disciples in the surroundings of Caesarea where he ended his mission with the two important miracles that have just been narrated. The arduous crossing from one end of Palestine to the other, from Tyre and Sidon to the headwaters of the Jordan and slopes of Lebanon, fully brought to an end the mission of the Messiah, who was especially sent to the wayward sheep of the house of Israel. He was obliged to undertake this mission for the salvation of the inhabitants of those most distant precincts from Jerusalem, as a consequence of which nothing prevented him from approaching the sacrilegious city to enter it on the precise day he had foretold. This was the end he had proposed to reach within a few days, proceeding on his way to bring to an end God's work, which had been almost carried out to perfection.

CHAPTER 52
AS JESUS PASSED THROUGH GALILEE HE MAKES A CLEAR ANNOUNCEMENT TO HIS DISCIPLES ABOUT HIS PASSION, DEATH AND RESURRECTION: ON REACHING CAPERNAUM HE COMMANDED PETER TO PAY THE TAX OF TWO DRACHMAS, AND DEALS WITH THE DISPUTE OVER PRIMACY (MT 18:1-5)

IF Jesus Christ had not been God like his Father, and like Him infinitely wise, and thus ignored the sufferings, insults and the cross that awaited him in the midst of the ungrateful city, the name of Jerusalem itself could not fail to cause him but annoyance and horror for the insults which the scribes and Pharisees had already made him suffer. He called the city as being the will of his Father and, being most obedient and resigned, he did not hesitate to go there, in spite of all the aversion his human nature might arouse in him. Saint Mark says (Mk 9:30): "They went on from there and passed through Galilee; and he would not have any one know about it. He trod along outlying paths to arrive at Capernaum and took great care to avoid people who knew him and wanted to stop him anywhere he was seen. With so many precautions he managed to hide his movements, not occupying himself about it all the time but thinking of his passion, about which he spoke frequently with his disciples. He was more concerned about teaching and instructing them on such an essential issue than to seek their own comfort. "He did not flee Jerusalem," Saint Augustine says, "for he would have abandoned his almightiness, but to comfort and encourage our misery by healing he was forced to hide due to the unjust persecutions of our adversaries, and to teach us that the members of the body could not regard what happens to the head as an outrage."

In Galilee, where he had been conceived and raised, he spoke freely with his disciples and instructed them in all that was related to his passion. In being already accustomed to hear what was about to occur, he did not want them to be shocked when it happened. Along with his death he also foretold his resurrection, so that they were not bound to be dismayed at the time of his passion. So he said to them: "Keep all these predictions in your heart, since remembering them will be very useful to you. *The Son of Man will be delivered*; by the Father, through His immense and eternal love, by the Son, through his own obedience, by which his will complies with that of the Father. He will be delivered by the suggestions of the devil, by the great greed of Judas, by the deceitful envy of the Jews and by Pilate's undue timidity. And he shall be *in the hands of men*, because of the Jews and Gentiles, and of the many and various states of persons, and because of the soldiers, kings, princes, priests and all the peoples of the earth, *and they will kill him*." A great, horrible, dreadful and unheard of cruelty for men to kill their own Saviour and so, that this terrible news would not kill them and fill them with sadness, he further told them, *And I would rise on the third day*. This notwithstanding, the apostles who listened to the prediction did not understand it. For them their Master's violent death and resurrection was an inexplicable and incomprehensible enigma. They knew of his power but could not fathom why he would not use it to defend himself against his enemies. As far as he looked forward to his resurrection, they seemed no less confused. They did not grasp whether Jesus Christ was speaking to them in the proper sense of a bodily and physical resurrection, or if it was a metaphor with which he wanted to give them to understand that after his death he would restore the kingdom of Israel to its ancient splendour from heaven above. They did not agree on anything among themselves, and did not dare ask their Master for a more specific explanation, fearing that their concerns would be confirmed, their hopes shattered and their hopes rebuked for having so low pretensions. They tenderly loved Jesus Christ and could not hear anything with patience humiliating and distressing about him. So they were deeply saddened, and neither being told of the resurrection nor hearing the voice of the Father, or any flattering idea, were enough to wrest from their hearts the sadness that had overwhelmed them.

Yet among all the ideas of melancholy which oppressed them, they were hounded by a most obsessive thought, namely that they were told of this as something happening soon, which was for them an unbearable martyrdom. And although being otherwise pleased that in whatever way they understood the resurrection this would be at the end of servitude in their home on earth, they did not however wish that their Master would in any way pass through all he was talking about. And as they apparently looked at him absorbed in deep meditation on the designs of his heavenly Father, of which he had just spoken, they let him walk on his own while they went on conversing between them until they reached the gates of Capernaum. Fearing they might be overheard, it is known that their conversation must have been little agreeable with the lessons they had received for so long in the Saviour's school. Yet it was in vain that they tried to hide even their slightest thoughts from him, for Jesus Christ knew and involved himself in everything; more than once they had had occasion to make sure for themselves, that Jesus Christ sensed even the most hidden human inclinations.

Saint Jerome spoke at length on the apostles' indecision, conspiracy and doubts saying: "Sadness is always goes along with prosperous affairs, so that when Jesus Christ comes, even if he does not all of a sudden find himself in the midst of the apostles, yet their spirits still move calmly as if the events for which they had already been prepared are occurring now. If he tells them that he was to be crucified, they should also be glad to hear that on the third day he will rise again. For if only sad things were to happen, who could withstand them? And if you prosper, who will despise you? But they ignored the mystery of the passion, for the Lord wanted to keep it covered in plain sight as with a veil, so that it would not be an ongoing torment for them." The Venerable Bede further says: "Jesus Christ hid the mystery of the cross from his disciples due to the great love he had for them. For they were still rough and carnal, not being able to understand his spiritual superior qualities and greatness. And knowing him to be true God they could not believe that he had to die, let alone to be persuaded how this could happen to a person, dying and yet not dying, to die as a man and not to die as God."

As the Saviour thought out things with foresight, prudence and infinite wisdom, he moved to Peter's house where he usually abode. The disciples, engrossed in their conversation, followed him in the distance, emotionally arguing among themselves and Peter walking in front. As he was the best known of all, he was stopped by the commander in charge of collecting the two drachmas which were then paid as tax to Herod Tetrarch throughout all Galilee. This tax had been imposed on all families, and so it was also demanded from Jesus Christ as the head of a company composed of twelve persons, which was like a fairly large family and was considered as such for the scope of public affairs. The tax collectors did not dare approach Jesus Christ, whom they respected by virtue of his great miracles, and let him pass without uttering a single word. But they turned to Saint Peter and told him: "Does not your Master pay the tax of two drachmas for himself and his disciples?" It is most common for Saint Peter to defer any answer until consulting about it, especially since dealing with the tax problem was like explicitly recognising Caesar's imperial rule throughout the Jewish kingdom. And since the Saviour had been raised in Nazareth, which was a city of Galilee subject to Capernaum, the tax was demanded in that place. Capernaum is interpreted as *the village of consolation and the field of fatness*, and it is there that the tax is demanded from the Lord who fills all with comforts and gifts. The Saviour wanted to pay like all others, and his Church not having yet been established or Jesus Christ recognised by the people and less so by the prince, he did not want to be exempted from public charges. Astonished as he was, Saint Peter entered his house to ask Jesus Christ what he should do, so that foreboding his question Jesus Christ came out to meet him without giving him a chance to ask the question himself.

"Peter," Jesus Christ addressed him, "What do you think? From whom do the earthly kings of the land demand and receive taxes? Is it from their sons or from strangers?" Peter unhesitatingly replied and said: "Only from his subjects who are strangers: the princes' sons do not count among this number." "You are speaking well," Jesus Christ replied. "So the sons are free persons." This was like telling him: "You know that I am the Son of David by birth and the legitimate heir to his throne. Knowing this you can well say that I owe Herod no tax. But we must avoid any doubt and cause for scandal. Let us not give these people any pretext to tell us that we despise the authority of the established powers. Even so you should not rush to pay. I will tell you from where to get the money without touching anything of that given for our provisions. Go running to the sea shore, throw the hook and open the mouth of the first fish you catch. There you will find a *stater* (which is a coin of four drachmas), take it, pay the collectors with it and tell them that *you are paying for me and for you."* The Lord wanted it to be understood that after him, Peter was the head of the apostolic family, and that some day as shown by the Holy Spirit, he would be the head of the whole Christian school. This would not only be composed of disciples embracing the Gospel, but also of teachers and doctors who by their state and character would be in charge of teaching and instructing it. An excellent arrangement of God's providence and justice, wanting to show by this miracle the respect and veneration owed to those who in His name ruled the world.

Jesus Christ clearly and openly manifested his divinity by foretelling this marvel which happened very promptly. Saint Jerome contemplates it and says: "I do not know what comes first and is most worthy of admiration; whether the stater in the mouth of the fish, or the magnificence and greatness of God's virtue, by whose order that coin was immediately created in the mouth of the wetland fish. The meaning of all these things is mysterious. The fish represents Christ, the sea the world, the hook death, the stater found in the mouth of the fish, the price of our redemption foretold by Jesus Christ himself: and so the tax was paid and we were free. The Lord paid the tax, not because he should have paid it, since both according to his divine nature and according to his human nature he was the son of a king, and thus he was free from paying tax. But he did this because of his humanity, becoming a little child, and paying what was not due by him, to give us an example of humility and to teach us that they should never give us scandals. The two drachmas that the stater had, symbolised the hardships of the body and those of the soul. The first are hunger, thirst, cold and the like, and the second are fear, sadness and others that afflict and torment. Anyone is obliged to suffer paying this tax of two drachmas to the Supreme Emperor for his own sin and that of our first parents. Even though Jesus Christ has no sin whatsoever, he still endured the tax for the sins of all, for he took flesh like the sinner although he did not take sin, and gave his body and soul as the price of our redemption, so paying the tax of two drachmas to his Eternal Father for the sins of men." Finally, this was not the first fish Peter caught obeying his Master, also showing us the merit of obedience and how God rewards it even in this life. Happy with this new marvel, the disciple ran to the tax collectors' house and there paid for his Master and himself, in terms of what he had been ordered to do. He then returned to look for Jesus Christ at the house itself, where he was waiting for him with the rest of the apostles.

Just as the enemies of the fledgling Church insisted on ridiculing and infamously slandering it, the new sophists, deceitful and unbelieving like them, have sought in these times to denigrate and debase it by concluding from this passage that Jesus Christ dispensed Christians from paying taxes to the sovereign princes and to the civil authorities. They say that the sovereign determination of Church ministers to refuse to fulfil the sacred duties pertaining to every good citizen, and their obstinacy in defending their real and personal immunities, emerge from there. Fortunately, however, the whole world has seen this to be a gross slander, and still more a worse commentary, the most violent and evil that can be made of the Saviour's doctrine, and a reckless and foolish judgment of the ideas and opinions of Christians and sanctuary ministers.

Whatever their class and category Church pastors and ministers always considered themselves members of society and never forgot their duty and obligation to respect the laws of the country and to contribute as much as possible to the preservation of order and to the prosperity of the state. "No, we refuse," said Saint Ambrose, "to pay tribute to Caesar; the Church estates and fields promptly satisfy the burdens and levies by which they are affected. Give to Caesar what belongs to Caesar, namely as Saint Jerome puts it, currency, tax, money; and to God what belongs to God, namely tithes, first fruits, obligations, victims." We must follow Christ's example, who paid the two census coins as tax for himself and for Peter. Although it cannot be denied that some Christians, either out of ignorance or for an irremediable fanaticism as found in all states, have shown disgust in paying taxes, believing themselves free of all real and personal burdens, it is not that this is less true than leaving aside perhaps even the most just, holy and indisputable rights. They have matched at all times and occasions the calls made to them by kings and states, for it was the priests who first gave to all this great and admirable example of generosity and detachment. Catholic clergy have never tried to exempt themselves from these most sacred duties for sanctuary ministers were always convinced that when faced with government's public needs and hardships they should be the first to set an example of zeal and adherence to both sovereign and public affairs, and to concur with all their might to increase public funds. These feelings of the clergy are authentically proven by their conduct, and it can be assured that there is no body in the state from whom princes have taken so much advantage, nor in whom they have found more resources than in the Church. Who can count in figures what the clergy, in addition to the burdens common to each owner and subject, has contributed to the benefit of the state? Of course it may be that Jesus Christ and his disciples had departed from there and continued their onward journey to Judea, then the Messiah's main aim where to fulfil his ministry. But he did not want to set out on his way without first giving them important lessons about his conduct, as provided to them by those facts and events they had just passed through. Jesus Christ had not forgotten the ardent conversation they had with each other while returning from Caesarea to Capernaum. Wanting, however, to know it from their own mouth, he asked them by way of conversation or instruction, what was troubling them in that long journey after he had just given them news of his passion, death and resurrection which so suited his Father's glory and the healing of the world. They fell mute and looked at each other, not daring to answer him. They significantly conceived misgivings that their conversation would have displeased him, for although he had not overheard it, he had every reason to presume that nothing was to be hidden from him.

We should not be astounded by the apostles' silence on this occasion, for their conversation and dispute had been on a matter of vanity and ambition, and this was quite embarrassing for them to confess. They were born without any pretension in this world, and more than two years before they were educated in the school of humility; so they could not avoid blushing or being confused in doing the confession that was being asked of them. But in spite of all, they did it and even dared to question the Master to be the arbiter of their dispute, ignoring the new shame that would come with the solution Jesus Christ would give to their quarrel. So they approached him and asked him, *Whom do you consider the greatest in the kingdom of heaven?* Peter had in his favour more than one statement from his Master about present and future superiority. In many things he had given him the first place; he had allowed himself to be treated with great familiarity which he reciprocated; he had already told him he would give him the keys to the kingdom of heaven, called him blessed, and also lately making him pay the tax for both of them with the money he found in the mouth of the fish. Andrew could aspire to share this authority with Peter, since both were brothers. John, son of Zebedee, was known to his colleagues as being Jesus Christ's Benjamin. And there were others too who had the joy of being his relatives according to the flesh, so that in short each one thought he had ample support on which to found his pretensions. They all let themselves be carried away by human passions and were determined to speak to their Master.

If our hearts were healthy and our understanding were not preoccupied with the illusions and fantasies of this deceiving world, what an effective example would not the behaviour of the apostles offer us to open our eyes and convince us of our pettiness and misery? For men could be foolish and rude in never lacking pretexts to acquire honours and preferences, or at least to pretend them, even in the holiest things. The apostles were faithful and righteous for in following Christ they had given up all they had, and with it also the hope of having more. Yet in the midst of this temporal contempt, the care for another higher place in Christ's kingdom found its place in them. But being better educated some time later about the nature and dignities of Christ's kingdom, they fully altered their affections, thoughts and language. And one would judge them unfavourably in attending only to their old frailties without realizing the righteousness of their soul in the confessions they made of themselves to honour the Master's patience in bearing them and the power of divine grace in curing them of these weaknesses.

To cure this affection in his apostles and to uproot it, he sought a means which was as equally light as effective. First he said to them that whoever wanted to be first among his own, had to find himself in the last place and to be pleased with it (Mk 9:34-37). He was to serve others, and none was greater than he who was regarded as least of all. After that he called a child who was there present and holding his hand he hugged him and put him in their midst, telling them: "I can tell you nothing better to satisfy your question and to open your eyes, than to assure you, that if you do not change your life and do not hold as a habit of virtue a low feeling of yourselves and the innocence, sincerity and simplicity which nature and the tenderness of age grants to children, you will have no place or part in the kingdom which I have founded and established on earth, which is the foundation of that of heaven. See it this way: children are the model of humility, frankness and simplicity which must shine in all those who want to be raised to the high honour of being my apostles and ministers." "For children do not know how to be envious," Saint Chrysostom says, "neither setting their eyes on outward honour, nor desiring the first places and dignities. But they possess this most high virtue of humility and true simplicity. Whether affronted or punished they do not detest anyone, being praised and honoured they do not get angry. Their tender age exempts them from all arrogance, from the fury of vainglory, from mad envy, from all strife, and from other such affections. Rather, in being fortified with humility and simplicity, they are not angered either by one thing or another; they possess these qualities and none attributes anything to himself. Know then that the principal manner of being extolled by me is to be low-spirited and humiliated, and *that no one will be held or taken as great if one does not become little as I am.* I love these young ones; but the humble take the affections which through a wise simplicity willingly lowers them to the state of a holy childhood."

Be warned, and it is well worth remembering, what Jesus Christ commands us in this Gospel, do not believe those fools who command us to do impossible things. He does not order us to return to the age of childhood, but to innocence so that what they have because of their age we may achieve by means of virtue. That is why the Lord did not tell us *if you were not children*, but *as children*, which means, meek, benign, humble, scorners of the things the world esteems the same as children despise them. Nor did the Saviour want us to be like children in everything, for those who become children are rebuked by the Wise saying to them: "How long, oh simple ones, do you desire to live your childhood? (Prv 1:22)" "Do not be children either in your thinking, and it is good to be babes when facing evil, but on things regarding your salvation be mature" as the Apostle says (1 Cor 14:20). The One who by not having evil was like a child, took out the demons from his cellars. As Saint Jerome sees them, these demons are the asps which the babe in arms had to pluck from their hideout. And as to this, aid surely came from Peter, the prince of all, who referred to all peoples saying: "So put away all malice and deceit, and pretence and envy, and all slander: like newborn babes, long for the pure spiritual milk of the holy doctrine, that by it you may grow up to salvation (1 Pt 2:1-2)." So just as prudence and a spotless life transforms an old man into a youth and makes him into such a man as is praised in Scripture (Ws 8:8-9), so do sincerity and humility make the old become like children, and it is the Saviour himself who as such recommends it here.

In truth, Jesus Christ's holy doctrine had more to do with the edification of their souls than they could imagine, and it was much stricter than what they could perhaps still not grasp well. It was because of this that they were told: "If you do not amend your affections, if you do not change your conduct until you become like children who disregard all affections, truly I say unto you, that far from being the first in the heavenly kingdom, you will not reach it or even make it to the last seat. *Whoever humbles himself like this little child, he is the greatest in the kingdom of heaven.*" That is, whoever does not understand comparisons, nor feeds the heart with preferences, who judges his equals favourably and sleeps without harbouring any sorrow which overwhelms him, this is the one who will be truly great among my disciples. The more one perfects this character in oneself and strives to enter into the smallness of childhood, the greater and more redirected will he be in a realm where elevation and greatness will not be measured by class exaltation, but by the humility of the hearts. Exultation, which is the prize of humility, grows with a person and beats its frequency in everything; so that a man becomes worthy of the highest degree of honour if he humbly knew how to place himself on the lowest step. The passion to dominate is very difficult to heal. The imitation which had been introduced in the apostles, was not yet appeased with such effective lessons, for we will still see it sprout more than once, and a remedy will often have to be applied. And this did not come to heal perfectly, until the heavenly fire that fell on the apostles consumed the relics of the old man in their hearts and made them new men. Thus Saint Paul particularly recommends the very effective exercise and practice of this precious virtue of humility saying, "Love one another with brotherly affection (Rom 12:10)," and as for us let us choose inferiority and subjection. I do not know whether it is smoke or a vestige of pride in those who think to find someone in the sky who says to them: *Go up higher.* He highly recommends humility he who said that *without it no one can be saved, and that is what gives seniority in God's kingdom.*

CHAPTER 53

JESUS FORBIDS HIS DISCIPLES FROM OPPOSING A MAN WHO WAS EXPELLING THE DEMONS IN HIS NAME, EVEN THOUGH HE WAS NOT ONE OF THEM; HE GIVES THEM LESSONS ON MODESTY AND HUMILITY AND COMMANDS THEM NOT TO SCANDALISE OR DESPISE THE LITTLE ONES, THREATENING WITH DREADFUL PUNISHMENT THOSE WHO DO SO; AND ENDS WITH SHOWING TO ALL HIS INFINITE MERCY WITH THE THREE PARABLES OF THE LOST SHEEP AND DRACHMA, AND OF THE PRODIGAL SON (MT 18:1–11; LK 15:1–32)

SO underhanded is envy and it works so cautiously on a thousand occasions, that when the most modest and prudent virtue and the most ardent and fervent zeal appear in all of them, it introduces its perverting and deadly poison in a creature's heart. Surely wretched is the man in whose heart it seeks to enter! It will be a cruel executioner which harasses him; and it will make him certainly feel even when he sees a single good work done by his neighbour, encouraged by the desire to prevent it. Oh, how many and how great evils has envy brought into the world! Pride and envy run in pairs; and if hell is populated by demons and men do not dwell in paradise, these two hellish monsters have depopulated hell and filled earthly paradise.

The Saviour had just condemned in his disciples the abominable monster of envy that had produced the argument over seniority in the kingdom of heaven, teaching them that this vice was detestable, not only in them but in all men, when Jesus Christ's very doctrines offer John, son of Zebedee, a rather well-founded scruple, from which he certainly wanted to depart. He told the Lord with very modest zeal of the doubt which afflicted him, without being able to convey the slightest hint of that detestable plague. "Master," he said to him, "you command that all those who believe in you are to be received and treated as yourself. With all that, see there what I have done together with other disciples of yours. We found a man who cast the demons out of the bodies and delivered the possessed by calling your name, and we have very expressly forbidden him to use this office from now on and to abstain from such work, as he is not one of yours. You have not received him in your company, and you have not passed on to him the power to perform miracles as you have done to us. Have we done well in this?"

It is undeniable that in John's innocent enquiry envy does not seem to play a hand, nor does any other deranged passion. But he could not hide the fact that at least there was in his action a great influence, a zeal that was largely impolite and deplorable. Since it is also true that the disciples sinned more out of ignorance than malice, the Saviour did not openly rebuke the man's zeal for intervention and indiscretion, and he was content saying clearly to them: "Do not oppose this man or prevent him from exercising himself in such a beneficial task. The freedom taken cannot but produce some good, for it is almost incredible that he should speak evil of me after having cast out demons in my name. And if that principle saying that whoever is for us as long as he does not declare himself to be against us is true, this cannot be verified truer on any other occasion than this, in that whoever acts in this manner cannot be considered to be impartial, and you must consider him as a friend whoever does not act in any manner against you as an enemy, but rather does the same thing that you do and uses the means which you use to reach the same end. Are his actions by any chance culpable before God? If they are not, why do you disapprove of them and condemn them? You should have treated this man as I want you to be treated. Know well that I have determined in your favour that whoever seeks any help from you, even if it is nothing more than a glass of cold water, so long as he does it because you are my disciples, will not lose his prize. So also believe that the works of charity this man does will be paid back in this life and in afterlife, even though right now he does not have the joy of being with us.

It is a beautiful and marvellous comparison that Jesus Christ put together in this speech, giving his disciples one of the great instructions to solidly establish his Gospel full of love and peace, and to extend it to the ends of the earth. For this was the meaning of telling them: "If I think so favourably of those who honour and console you, in view of the close relationship that I want you to have with me, what should I do with a person who, without being one of my apostles, does not cease to respect me, to invoke my name, and to spread my glory? But there is even another point in this same matter that must be done, which is to see things rightly. The person about whom you are speaking to me and you have prohibited, as being a usurper in exercising a power which you imagine belongs only to you, is one of those little ones to whom the simplicity of their faith inspires confidence and who perform miracles in my name, for they do not have their mind set on self-glory." So that he implied to them that these were the men he wanted them to resemble and to whom they should fear giving scandal. Above all, this is what Saint Ambrose duly said: "The apostles should be convinced that whoever receives a follower of Christ receives Christ himself, and he who receives the image of God receives God Himself. Jesus Christ's rebuke was rather a very timely instruction; for John worked for the great love he had for his Master, and so believed that no one should exercise the power they had if he did not enjoy the dignity of apostle or the gift of following Christ. But Jesus Christ wanted to instruct him in a very interesting matter, which was that he was God of both the strong and the weak, of the healthy and the sick; and that if he rewarded the strong and healthy who followed him, he did not exclude the disadvantaged and the weak from the prize, for no one should be set apart from the strength of goodness of which he formed part. On the contrary, he was to be encouraged and aroused to approach him confidently and to partake with him."

Nor on this occasion was the Venerable Bede any less eloquent and fruitful in saying: "Instructed with this doctrine the great Apostle of the Gentiles, Saint Paul, did not hesitate saying: "I know that many of my brethren in the

Lord have been made confident because of my imprisonment, and with greater encouragement dare preach without fear the word of God. It is true that there are some who preach Christ out of a spirit of envy and rivalry, while others do so with good intention. The latter do it out of love, knowing that I am put here for the defence of the Gospel. Others, on the contrary, do so out of jealousy and fear against me, not sincerely but thinking to afflict me in my imprisonment. But what does it matter? Provided that in any case Christ is proclaimed, whether in pretence or by true zeal, in this I rejoice over and over again (Phil 1:14-18)." About which he added: "We are forbidden from detesting all those who do not follow Christ, since he taught us for all and commanded us to pray for all, for one day they will become like Paul and become so many preachers of the Gospel and announcers of Jesus Christ's glories." If the wicked do some good deed, they are not to be forbidden from doing it, even if it has no merit because it is not done out of love, for at least it works to amend life. Oh! How many invitations does the Lord make to us that we may enter the path of humility, this being the most characteristic virtue of Christians; and yet we resist reaching it, always postponing it, and living in pride, even if by pride we become worse than the demons!

In addition to that the Lord let them know that just as there is no good work without reward, so there is no evil without punishment; and that the laws which order penalties for minor offences, prescribe more rigorous ones for greater crimes, such as public offences which can be of a scandal to weak souls. For as Saint Chrysostom says: "Just as those who honour and edify little ones for God will receive remuneration, so will those who dishonour and scandalise them suffer the ultimate vengeance. He is somewhat of a scandal whoever with a word or with a less righteous fact causes ruin to anyone, making him commit guilt and sin, and by his words and examples induces him or impels him to it. And he warns them first and foremost to avoid active scandal, that is the scandal that is given to others; and then passive scandal, that is one's own." By this doctrine the Saviour meant: "You, my disciples, do not alter or dispute the primacy of honour, for there can result from this dispute a scandal to little ones, not of age, but of faith, because recently they were born for Jesus Christ and converted to him. And if you scandalise them you will lose them forever. Call these little ones because they have willingly deigned to descend from a proud worldly height to humble themselves before God, entering the guild of faith. These newly regenerated persons are indeed weak and sickly, and in no way should they be scandalised, for they are more easily scandalised than those who are already robust and strong."

In this sense we must also understand what the Saviour meant when he said that happy was the man who welcomed all the little ones who believed in Jesus Christ and who sought to favour them. And on the contrary, he said clearly that anyone who discards them and gives them cause to turn back, with the contempt which he shows for the virtue they have conceived and to which they have devoted themselves, will be wretched and unhappy, and that *it would be better for anyone who was so scandalous, to tie a millstone around his neck and throw himself into the depths of the sea.* Just as the first promise attracts us to contribute to the spiritual good of simple ones, so does the present threat keeps us away from being an occasion to sin. The same God, who greatly rewards beneficial things made by his own, so does he take it upon Himself to avenge insults, these being much more those of a spiritual order, which are scandals, and of which Scripture is replete. So that it is seen how wrong are those who with great calmness of conscience oppress or trod upon the poor and helpless, and even more those who do not care to be a cause for the simple and humble to offend God, for whom Jesus Christ first greatly cared and then gave his life. But among all these the Saviour appears to make a direct threat to those who with their words and persuasions, or by any other means, corrupt the spirits of simple people and introduce a school of evil, by opening their eyes that they keep moving forward with the sincerity of their good life. For Jesus Christ did not see in his fellow men anything but virtuous actions or incentives for virtue.

Alas, for the world because of scandals! the Saviour added. Jesus Christ's expressions are harsh and dreadful, and in a very particular manner fell on the doctors, on the priests and on the big ones of Jerusalem, who set apart the people from the faith of the Messiah and were considered under the general name of "the world." Miserable is the world because of scandals; and Jesus Christ strongly repeats his *alas!* to indicate the gravity of the offence, the awfulness of the curse and the dread of the condemnation hurled against those committing it, later confirmed by the words of Jesus Christ himself, that it would be much better for *whoever gives them* to drown himself violently in the sea. And how many, without perceiving it, are considered to be under the weight of this *alas!* which so many utter, but whose meaning not everyone knows? *Alas!* to those who invent new ways of offending God and go around scheming as to who they will tomorrow make fall having today found him firm in virtue! These have particular punishments set for them, such as that all faults for which they are responsible will be attributed to them, and that the same anger which God has for sin will always keep them awake against whoever invented it. So that Saint Augustine did not hesitate to affirm that Arius does not even undergo in hell all the punishment he deserves, nor will he have it until the end of the world; for you then did not know all the evil caused by the very bad seed sown in them. Alas for those deceitful prophets who, as Saint Peter says "are false teachers who will secretly bring in destructive heresies, even denying the Master who bought them freedom, bringing upon themselves swift destruction. Many will follow their debauched behaviour, and because of them the way of truth will be reviled. In their greed they will exploit you with false words. From long ago their condemnation has not been idle, and the destruction awaiting them has never been asleep! (2 Pet 2:1-3)" Alas for the licentious and dazzling philosophers, who being false teachers invent a new expanse in God's path, which is not born of charity but of the relief of passions, a disastrous consequence of that very much preferred debauchery which with so much excess they preach and sustain! *Alas! alas! alas!*

But despite this *alas!* he also said that *scandal will come, for it must come; but unhappy and wretched is he through whom it will come.* The Lord planted his Church in a world ingested with evil, which is the tares mingled with the good grain which the great Landowner planted in this field which is His. It is inevitable that there will be scandals on the part of the wicked who are always on the wrong side of virtue and the virtuous. But with this prophecy of Christ, just as he does not need the wicked to be so, likewise it does in no manner excuse those who by their falls and scandals cast blame on God and argue with Him saying that for those that must necessarily come they have no arms to willingly oppose them. It is then against them that Jesus Christ thunders furiously when he says, *But alas of that man through whom scandal comes.* Saint Paul used this same language, who even though he said that he agreed there were heresies in the Church (1 Cor 9:19), yet he was careful to warn elsewhere that those who disturb the simple people and hinder those who run to obey the truth, whatever they may be, will pass through a very narrow gate. This inflamed his spirit in such manner when he contemplated the gravity of this sin, that his zeal would make him utter grave exhortations to preserve the Church from it, saying that there was no reason for those of us who are brothers in Jesus Christ to put a stumbling block in the way of a brother (Rom 14:13). For we ought to follow all that is done unto peace and for the edification of one another; that no one should take leave which serves to stumble upon the weak; that even in what is lawful we walk with feet of lead, and that we keep ourselves away from anything which causes scandal (1 Cor 10:23-24). So that aiming in everything we do at the good and benefit of our brothers, we do not give scandal to anyone, be he Jew or idol worshipper, being a motive for edification in everything and to all.

Jesus Christ was very prudent to judge on this occasion not to spare his apostles the warnings and comparisons which could further encourage and impress them, and so he said to them: "There are friends in the world, who are deemed essential to do without them willingly, the same as the hands are necessary for the body to work with them and the feet to walk. But if you have a true love for yourselves, it is necessary to break this friendliness when it hinders you from fulfilling your duty; it is necessary to cut off this hand and throw it far away from you when it leads to evil. For it is better that you enter the kingdom of heaven with one hand, than be thrown into hell with both hands to suffer eternal torments, where the worm that gnaws the soul and the body never dies, and the fire that burns the two is never extinguished. And if you must not have anything to do but to give these false friends any attention, even if their friendship seems to you as necessary as one of your hands when God's honour is involved, you should be ready by the same fate to separate yourself from those whose familiarity is harmful to your souls, even if they seem to you as necessary as one of your feet. Do not forgive the foot which so harmfully leads you to the precipice; cut it off, indeed, and throw it away from you. The greatest evil that can happen to you is to be lame without it; but how much greater evil is it to go down with both feet to hell to be tormented there up to the end of time? And what could be more precious than one of your eyes? With all that, if an eye is free to look where it wants and is a cause for you to offend God and put your souls in manifest danger of perishing, have enough courage to cast it out; to be without an eye is undoubtedly bad, but it should be reputed as of great benefit when by that means it serves to reach heaven where the blessed are exempt from all pain and sorrow. It is better for you to lose your eyesight if it is harmful to you, than to hold on to it and both you and your eye will walk directly and more swiftly to hell."

"Do not miss, my disciples," Jesus Christ went on, "the hardness of these councils. It is necessary to be violent to reach the kingdom of heaven, and so it is also to break and separate from those friends whose familiarity and examples are cause of scandal, to leave them before you condemn yourself in their company. I do not doubt that you will find it difficult and it will cost you some sorrow in breaking with this kind of affection, but if the Law wants victims to pass through fire and that there is salt in all sacrifices (Lv 2:14), it is also necessary that the righteous, as living hosts that are consumed in God's service, be tried by fire, that they may add to the holy burnings of divine love the painful salt of mortification. This prodigious salt preserves the soul from the corruption of sin. But let it be understood that the best salt, once its quality has been dissolved and worn out, is not fit for any purpose, and it would not be possible to have its original properties and strength restored. So provide well for this spiritual salt, and see to it that it does not waste away. See then as to how to keep the peace which I desire to reign among you, and which will achieve for your souls the respect of other virtues."

The Saviour often resorts to talking to his disciples making use of the simile of salt by applying it to different matters, since there are different kinds of salts, and even the same one serves for very different uses. For bodies condemned to hell there is the salt of inextinguishable fire; for victims, a salt which consecrates them; for food, a salt which seasons it; for conduct, a salt of wisdom and prudence which directs and sanctifies it. "This is what I speak to you under the figure of common salt when I said to you: *Good is salt;* keep in you the salt of prudence and discretion; make use of it to avoid with prudent precautions that which may for others be the cause of fall and scandal; for if those who scandalise themselves by not doing a painful, but necessary, severance from the cause of their ruin, they are severely punished and handed over to the deathless worm, how do you think," says the Lord, "that men will be treated, who either have no qualms or are so proud, that they do not fear giving scandal to little ones who believe in me?" "No greater penalty," says Saint Ambrose, "than the rodent worm of consciousness that always gnaws inwardly. By chance, is not this running away more of a torment than death, than all the wastefulness and banishment? Not even the hellfire that burns the body from the outside is extinguished or consumed, because it is a fire of distress and not a consuming one, and its nature will last forever, as there is no adverse element which can extinguish or destroy it." And the Venerable Beda adds: "Just as the worm is an inner pain which always accuses, so fire is an outward sorrow which is a martyrdom in itself."

Jesus Christ presented his apostles with other considerations, of no less weight, to remind them of their responsibility not to scandalise the little ones and of the regard in which they had to keep them. *Look, he told them, do not despise any of these little ones who believe in me, for I tell you that their angels in heaven always see the face of my Father who is there.* Which was like telling them: "The angels, who are their guardians and to whom they are entrusted, have their abode in heaven, and so do they present themselves incessantly before the throne of my Father to give Him all of their authority and doings, and to ask him to punish those unbecoming and proud men who do not care to lose out with their speech or examples to those whose healing is entrusted to the vigilance of the heavenly spirits."

In this whole speech, the causes of the reverence and compliance, with which we faithful must look at each other, shine admirably. For Christ did not say that we should respect those who are rich, others because they are wise, and others still because they are noble or deprived of some temporary lord, or due to some other external title of those who amaze and stupefy the world, but because they are children of God. It was because for them that the Only Begotten Son of the Highest was crucified and the Heavenly Father has them under His protection, without whose power no one can tear away just one hair from his head. And lastly, since by His guardianship and protection, He has destined the nobility of His heavenly abode and the burning spirit of His love, He does not seek other than how He can please them in everything and make them reach the aim of their desire, them being absorbed without ever tiring to look at Him and contemplating Him. Jesus Christ wants us to look for these things in our brethren, and only if we obeyed him in this would many evils and sins afflicting the Church be severed from their root. It is worth listening to Saint Jerome on this detail as the highest among doctors: "Afterwards, he says, that he also taught us to avoid contempt, as it is the root of the same scandal, and although to avoid this he commanded us to flee all carnal affections, I do not go so far as to despise those of whose salvation we can have founded hope and for which we must for the same reason hope. It so gives us a special reason, not only not to despise them, but to honour them, for the servant should not despise those whom the Lord honours so much. We must seek their salvation, because the Saviour sought that of all." Saint Bernard adds: "The groom's friend is faithful, knowing what mutual love is, but not being envious he does not seek his own glory but that of his Lord. Wandering between God and the holy soul, who are both lovers and loved, and to one offering vows and affections of love, and to the other bringing gifts, he counsels him to inspire fervour in him, and appeases him so that he may not be angry. And as he is an insider and known in the palace of heaven, he is not afraid to be repelled and repulsed when he performs missions from one place to another, and he always has the joy of seeing the semblance of the Father, to whom he incessantly prays for the soul entrusted to him."

Finally, the discreet Saint Anselm affirms that, "Thousands of thousands of angelic spirits fly incessantly between heaven and earth, running incessantly from one place to another like hovering bees in the midst of meadows and flowers. They solve all things very gently and promptly, like messengers in whom there is no room for deception, obeying with utmost punctual obedience. So look at how faithfully our angels serve us, and how caring they are with us. Do nothing in their presence that might displease them. If anger incites you to return evil for evil to your neighbour, do not look at the one who is less than you, or who is older than you, or in authority, or in wealth, but stop and think that you deliver the shots of vengeance against one who has God as his father, and Christ as his brother, and the heavenly spirits as his guardians. Of them the Lord has said that whoever touches the faithful, touches the apple of my eyes (Zech 2:8). Walk in everything with caution, for everywhere and in all places and occasions, your angel is present, and all those of God are ready to fulfil His orders, be they of mercy or justice, and do not dare doing in your angel's presence that which you do not do in men's sight."

It was after this that Jesus Christ imparted his instructions, teaching by example what he had explained with his speeches and doctrines. He explained that not only were they not to despise the little ones, but that they had to seek to attract them to the faith and confirm them in it. But his enemies noticed deceitfully that those who most often accompanied him in his tours spreading the Gospel, besides the poor and the sick who did not leave him, were publicans and sinners. Thus, moved by the desire to have their faults forgiven and full of true compunction, they came to hear from his mouth and learn the way to eternal salvation, preparing themselves to receive the Gospel faith. Although they were ashamed of their disorders, they were not abashed to seek the remedy. Jesus Christ attracted them to his school, received them with charity, helped them grow with care, and was pleased to have them in his company. This was the lost sheep from the House of Israel which he sought with eagerness and fervour and led it back into the fold.

It is worthy, much worthy to look at Jesus Christ's conduct from all points of view: but under the figure and name of shepherd there lies the most exemplary model which all pastors must seek to give to their flock. For it seems that nowadays much of this figure of charity, compassion and sweetness have already been forgotten, By only a little or for nothing are the ancient ideas of religion altered and moved, and it seems wrong for the disciples to resemble their Master. An austere air, harsher manners, extreme principles, scorn and contempt are many a time, and most unfortunately, those things which appear in public. And for those who see these things, it is what people usually admire and what it does in the eyes of the ignorant and those who are little educated by the grand security guards of the Law and the learned guides of the spirit of the Gospel. It amounts to none else but settling to the taste of the Jews, re-establishing the practices of the scribes and introducing the customs of the Pharisees. Alas! And who could erase, not only with tears from his eyes, but with the same blood from his veins, certain outrages of some men, having nothing to do with the character of a true shepherd! What Jesus Christ did, full of humility, meekness and disdain, exceedingly offended his enemies, whose arrogance and harshness he condemned. They expected a man who stood as the Messiah and presented himself as the nation's healer, should take a different course of action. They surmised that his only company should be that of the righteous and the wise, for it was greatly unseemly and indecent for him to be seen always surrounded by the least trusted and most loathsome persons of all. This man, they say publicly, and once in his own presence, shows a singular taste for sinners, receives them with preference to others, and often chooses their houses to eat and stay. It was a wicked and terrible accusation which greatly offended Jesus Christ's meekness, his mercy and leniency, and disfigured him in the eyes of Israel so that he would not be recognised as the promised Messiah, and the Redeeming God and Saviour of his people.

A single word that Jesus Christ had spoken would have been more than enough to confound the haughty pride of his unjust detractors. He could very well have told them that in it they contained a sin which was much more difficult to heal than those which reprimand the publicans. And although from time to time the interest of the truth led them to confuse him in this aspect, on this occasion he wanted to stick solely to the accusation as considered in its most culminating and essential point of view. It supposes its people as a certain number of faithful men who are observants of the Law of Moses as to its natural precepts and legal observances, and are as virtuous and innocent in their state as much as with the help of heaven any weak and fragile human being can be. On the other hand Jesus Christ looked at a crowd of sinners who, without abandoning their faith in the midst of their vicious habits, allowed themselves to be dominated by their passions. He let himself be seen and presented himself as having been sent to both one and the other, as a minister destined to prepare all hearts for the Gospel. But in the exercise of his ministry he manifested himself to prefer sinners to righteous persons. It was about this that they were accusing him, and to this end it is worth considering his apology. This is reduced to some simple but effective parables that he proposed to some critical and wicked men, who from the greatness of his mercy took occasion to censure him.

There are three things which particularly induce man to have mercy and compassion for his neighbour, and they are *simplicity, kinship, and need*; and these three things also induce God to use mercy with us. The first, which is our simplicity, appears in the parable of the wayward sheep, because man is very unassuming and simple with respect to the devil, a very cunning and shrewd enemy. For this reason David cried out and said, *I have gone astray, Lord, like a lost sheep; so seek your servant, who has not yet forgotten to keep your commandments* (Ps 158). The second, which is the kinship we have with Jesus Christ, is symbolised in the second parable, which is that of the lost drachma, since the drachma shows the king's effigy and an inscription of his name, the same as with man who is formed in the image and likeness of God and bears Christ's inscription for it is from the name of Christ that he is called a Christian. So that Jesus Christ also has compassion for us, as the Apostle says, as no man ever hates his own flesh (Eph 5:29). And the third is our need and poverty represented in the prodigal son who returns to his father's house, remembering that there abide many servants who eat bread, while he perishes of hunger in a foreign land. Jesus Christ uses these three mysterious and significant parables to condemn the evil treachery of the Pharisees, who were proud and envied the applause which Jesus Christ rightly received from the people when he showed them mercy and compassion. Being even more ignorant of God's ways and believing that holiness consists in never dealing with sinners or approaching them, they could not suffer the benevolent welcome which all found in Jesus Christ, and so he said to them: "Who is it among you that having a flock of about a hundred sheep, when he loses one of them, does not leave the ninety-nine alone in the countryside to seek with all due care the one which was lost? And after it has been found, who will it be that does not show such joy, that carrying it on his back takes it as if in triumph to his house, invites his neighbours to congratulate and rejoice with him that he has found the sheep which he had already deemed lost? It is not only that this excess of joy should not be condemned, but it should rather be praised in a shepherd who tenderly loves his sheepfold."

From this parable Jesus Christ then drew a corollary which made the scribes and Pharisees shudder, for it significantly justified his conduct relating to the kindness he showed to sinners. "See in it," he told them, "a portrait of your Heavenly Father. See in it an image of what happens in heaven when a sinner converts. It is a new joy for the whole court of the kingdom of wickedness when a man lost in the ways of evil turns to penance. Joy would be much greater and lively than that for the ninety-nine sheep which keep on the right path by not straying away from the faith and do not need penance." From which it follows that whoever works for the conversion of sinners, far from being profane and sinful like them, performs a very pleasant task in the eyes of God and of angels. Origen said of this: "We give cause of joy to the angels in heaven, when walking on earth and turning sinners away from sin, making them incline their heads to penance, we also have our conversion in heaven."

This model of charity that the good shepherd proposes to the bishops of his flock, is a very narrow law which does not allow them to abandon their sheep when they stray from the good path. In this case they are the new worries, making for the greatest concern and most tender love to walk in search of them without ever tiring or giving their eyes sleep until they return them to the fold. It upsets the order of pastoral obligations and disregards Christ's example when the pastor dedicates himself entirely to only oversee those souls which serve God, whose direction is gentle and flowing, while fleeing from those souls which are lost, whose conversion and guidance costs greater worries and labours, groans and tears. Few shepherds think of the binding obligation they have in certain cases to flee from the persons who seek them and to show them unnecessary attachment, to be able to run after those who flee from them and whose perdition will either be imputed to their laziness, the disorder of their charity or the indiscretion of their zeal. The good shepherd extends his own penance to others' sins; the souls he leads to God are of no burden to him, since nothing is burdensome for charity nor is there anything hard for whoever loves others' souls for God's sake and knows what Jesus Christ did and suffered for him and for all. Great, indeed and undoubtedly, very great must be the joy that is in heaven for a sinner who does penance.

The Saviour at once moves on to tell them another parable, almost without giving them time to reflect on the first one. "Imagine," he tells them, "a poor woman, who having saved ten drachmas loses one of them because she strays from the place where she put them. She turns on a light at the spot, examines every corner, turns the whole house upside down, and finds no respite until she finds it. And then when she finds it, she feels great joy. Unhesitatingly she calls her neighbours, tells them she has found it and asks them to make merry and celebrate her joy with her, since she found what had been lost." "Such is the rejoicing there shall be," the Lord says again, "by the angels of God in heaven if they see a single sinner who once more by penance turns to the grace of the Heavenly Father." Is this because the retrieved drachma has a greater value and is worth more because it was lost? Is the sheep back in the fold more cared for now, after having gone wayward for a long time? Is the penitent sinner more worthy of heaven's favours, because he deserved his most severe punishments? Certainly not; it is undoubtedly because the joy of anything recovered must be measured in proportion to the pain caused by its loss. The righteous who perseveres, harvests an unvarying and joyful yield of a similar self-satisfaction. A converted sinner brings pain and feelings to an end, wipes out the tears, and revives the joy and happiness which seemed to have been lost forever. So that if the lost coin has no value when compared to the soul marked with the same image of God, how great and appealing to the Lord's presence should the petition and zeal be of those entrusted with seeking lost souls, even if it comes at the cost of cravings, fatigue and humiliations? How great would his joy be for a single soul which he is lucky enough to find? "How strange is it that the wisdom of God," as Saint Augustine says, "in order to find this wealth which belongs to Him, takes his torch which is Christ's flesh ignited with eternal light, which is the divinity of the Word?" It is for two main reasons that Jesus Christ rejoices in a sinner's conversion: first, because conversion soothes his righteousness; and secondly, because the price of blood is not spoiled in that soul. It is so much to the Jesus Christ's taste, and it causes him so much joy, to see a sinner converting, that if the passion and death he suffered did not suffice for him to bring about conversions, he would once more go through the suffering and even die again. Just listen to what Saint Dionysius the Areopagite wrote to the renowned Demophilus: "When a certain faithless man caused the faithful Carpus, who was known to be a very holy man, to turn away from the faith, he took it so badly that he beseeched God that both would be burned alive. Jesus Christ appeared to him at midnight as suspended in mid-air and accompanied by an immense multitude of angels. On the ground below, however, there appeared a burning furnace full of snakes, to which those two unfortunate persons were led. When Carpus begged that they both be thrown into the fiery furnace, taking it very badly if his wishes were not immediately carried out, Jesus Christ at this instance descended to the ground, and stretching out his arms, he snatched both men from the mouth of the furnace into which they were about to be cast. He turned to Carpus with raised hands, and told him, *Wound me once more with the spear, for I am determined to suffer and die again to save men.*" "Let us then conclude," Saint Bernard says, "that no matter how small a person is, should anyone be despised, the Lord will always take particular care of him, for by faith and by grace he is the adopted son of God."

Another third parable was told by the Lord to clarify the true meaning of the two preceding ones. He also told it to give greater expression and liveliness and to show better the ardent love of his heart to win over ours even more by filling them with greater confidence and solace. To understand it well it is advisable not to lose sight of what triggered the discussion between Jesus Christ and the Pharisees. It was again about the Synagogue's righteous men, which the Lord was apparently postponing, preferring sinners although he is chided as being bountiful in his care and tenderness to them. Jesus Christ is not opposed to the justice and innocence attributed to some, and plainly and sincerely agrees with the bad state of conscience of others. It is assumed that he wants the Pharisees to listen more to what he is going to say, and to see whether they will do him justice.

"A man," Jesus Christ tells them, "had two sons, and the youngest of them said to his father, 'Give me, dear father,

CHAPTER 53   181

the portion of your goods due to me to increase it as it suits me.' 'It is all very well,' the father replied, and so dividing them into two parts, he gave to each one of them his due. A young man with too many goods in hand and too much freedom always takes great risks and this unfortunate young man soon had a taste of it. He knew that in his father's house, and even elsewhere in his own country, he was always being kept back by a beneficial slowdown on his passions, so he decided to travel to a foreign country where there was no one who could notice his faults and correct them. There he gave in to all kinds of excesses and fickleness, and in a short time he wasted all his money in debauchery. But at the peak of his misfortunes, when he had nothing left of his substantial assets, a terrible famine ensued unexpectedly and it devastated the country. Then, feeling all kinds of needs and deprivations, he took to the only thing he could do, which was to become a servant. He had left a good father and had to look for a master who so happened to be most cruel, one who did not allow him to live in the city and banished him to a farmhouse, charging him to take care of a herd of pigs. Even so, who can believe it. not even at the cost of such humiliation could he find enough food to eat. He envied what the pigs ate, but still he was not allowed to take from the filthy food they ate."

"In this state of such extreme misery," Jesus Christ continued, "how many would be the bitter reflections made? How many regrets to grieve about? Such a violent and precarious situation must necessarily cause despair in a less confident heart. Fortunately, the feelings of goodness and mercy that were so natural in his father had not yet been erased from this young man's heart; and recalling them, and that this was his father and that he was his son, looking first of all at his own unworthiness, knowing that he has no right to demand his affections again, but not doubting his kindness and mercy but now full of trust he decides to return to him. To seek more courage as to his holy and heroic resolve, he felt the urge to say: 'How many servants and housekeepers currently live in my father's house, where they have plenty of bread, and I am here starving! Ah! So I shall then leave, and go and seek my father and tell him, 'I have sinned, oh father, against heaven and against you: I am not worthy nor do I deserve the high honour of calling myself your son; but at least, sir, do not deny me the grace to be admitted among the number of your servants. To your sight, my father, I will every day mourn my straying away from the straight and narrow path, and my tears will make me as each day passes more worthy of you. You and heaven will witness my repentance, and I hope you will still one day bless me for having returned repentant before you.' And he did as he vowed."

A person cannot portray more accurately the sinner who strays away from God by his disordered love for his own freedom, and who, while deviating and living to extremes, wastes away the natural gifts and casts out from him what is supernatural, bartering wisdom for foolishness, truth for lies, richness for poverty, and keeping unswerving and eternal goodness for instant pleasure. The hunger which the prodigal son suffered in the country where he went shows the misery of the heart which is not fed with the bread of heaven. Having set out to serve denotes the devil's bondage of whoever subjects himself to it by casting out Christ's sweet yoke. To send him to care for pigs is a figure of the foul deeds to which man casts down himself for the love of the flesh and of the world. His desire to eat acorn represents the hunger for temporal pleasures and goods. It is a perpetual hunger because it never fills and renders a most unhappy person he who always wants more and achieves what he wants, since he finishes off the goods of fortune and grace, those of good fame and honour, and those of vitality and salvation, weakening, degrading and demeaning himself until he reaches a worse condition than a mule's or a horse's which are not aware of anything.

Being inspired by the liveliness of his son's truly filial affections, the father felt all love's tenderness beat in his chest. He later coupled it with the fire of penance through the repentance which broke him down, transforming him from a wicked into a good man, and from a slave to sin into son of God, so that he did not reject the united action of grace with which the Lord helped him and uplifted his efforts. When the sinner finds himself in a state of being enlightened with the light he first despised, he begins to see the dark chasm where sin had cast him with a great fall, While feeling the lack of lost goods, he envies the true wealth of those serving God, saying like the prodigal son: *How many day labourers in my father's house have bread to spare, while I am here starving!* He recognizes where he was, because when he was in sin he grieved; where he will be, because he had to undergo judgment and he feared; what he can do, because he is miserable and groaning; and what he cannot do, because he lacks glory and that is why he sighs. For this reason he returns to himself exceedingly hurt by his offences. Already disgruntled with the mockery of the world, frightened by the misery of his passions, and being resolved to give up sin and the occasion of sin, he says: "*I will rise up and go to my father.* With my desires that are the feet of my heart, I will seek the One who is my father and who loves me as a father, walking towards him with steps of love until I prostrate myself at his feet and confess my guilt to him saying: *I have sinned, father, against heaven and against you.* I turned away from you by giving up loving and by miserably loving what is infinitely less than you. I became a slave of my passions so as not to be overtaken by love. I was ungrateful to your love, I have conspired against you by opening the doors of my heart to lust's tyranny. I did not keep for you the fruits of love; I have lost the right to call you father, and *I no longer deserve to be called your son.* Oh father! I am not worthy of your grace and of your mercy. Oh father! How great has my ingratitude been towards you!"

"Where are your affections?" he would continue saying. "What have you done, dear father, with the affections which you once showed me and caressed me with them? You held me close to your chest, and your fiery mouth imprinted upon me the sweet seal of your love. My heart was pounding, and I felt the beats of yours leaping for pleasure every time you looked at me. Ah! Then I did not feel worthless in being your son. So now leave your affections and tenderness of a father for your good children, for the innocent, for those who in mud pleased you and did your will. But though I am not one of these, my father, *treat me even as one of your day labourers,* admit me into your house, and in it I will lead a painful and harsh life of penance, subjecting myself entirely to your service to compensate with tears and with the effort of the spirit for the offences committed against your Majesty."

As a thousand contradictory ideas struggled in that son's heart, so do they also combat a penitent man's heart. The knowledge of faults produces humility, that of the father's goodness begets confidence; with humility man prostrates himself in the presence of God, with trust he rises up and runs to Him. He was still well away from his father's house, when his good father sensed his arrival. Rags and misery never so distort a son that they make him unknown to the father who gave him life. His bowels were moved and his heart shook at the sight of his son. So he ran to meet him, threw his arms around his neck and embraced him tenderly. It is so that the young man fulfils his vows, and before his lips pronounce a single word, his tears become faithful interpreters of a repentant heart, telling clearly of the sorrow eating him up within. He breaks the silence filling the air with sighs, and his lips utter the words which were the prelude to his conversion: *"Father, I have sinned against heaven and against you; I am not worthy to call myself your son.* I have no excuse but to plead in your presence, nothing can spare me the just punishment I deserve." He does not deny him the sweet name of father, but he confesses that he has despised the dignity of being son. He does not stop running to his father's house, but he asks for the last place, which is that of the day labourers. He confesses his guilt and seeks out him who has been offended. He recognizes the tenderness of the father, and harbours no doubt hunger will ever kill him. Although he tries to find himself, trust must prevail over fear, for it is important that these two affections are never separated from inner humiliation, without which penance does not yield fruit. Pity the man who sins and does not live constantly humiliated, because he knows for certain that he has lost his grace and is unaware whether he has recovered it. This uncertainty, while not going against trust in God, compels the sinner to be humble and at least to subordinate himself to the innocent.

The father was so beside himself with joy that without answering his son and without allowing him to finish what he had to say, he called his servants and said to them: "Come on, quick! Bring my son's best robe and clothe him before me; put a ring on his finger and let him wear new sandals. But all this is very little; run out to my herd, bring a fattened bull calf, kill it and lay the table for a great banquet. Let us eat together and rejoice, for my son had already been dead for me, but now see him here resurrected. I had judged him lost and I have now found him." And so when the table was laid, they sat at it and resounded the hall with musical tunes, letting themselves to be given to joy and mirth. Yet above all is what Saint Chrysostom said: "The father was aware of repentance and penance, and he did not expect hearing any words of the confession. So he prevented and anticipated the concessions by acting mercifully." And the Venerable Bede adds: "The father goes out to meet him, for he sees him coming and happily foretells his repentance. But not being content with granting him little things, he prepares to grant him greater ones. And passing without delay from one extreme to the other, he restores to him a son's original dignity, no longer dealing with him with a day labourer's wage but with a son's inheritance."

In spite of all this and after a man is admitted to God's grace, will he by chance be allowed to submit himself, seek rest and calm down in his life that he may from now on live as if he had never sinned? Although penance is true and fervent, that does not mean that the sinner must give himself over to the use and exercise of those things which, though being allowed to the innocent, do not suit penitents. The Holy Spirit assures us that even forgiven faults ought to be feared. And how can man fear his sin if his memory does not humiliate him? And what humiliation is it to believe oneself entitled to worldly honours and to strive for temporal goods and not to flee pleasures, and in the end to proceed in everything as if there were no sins about which to satisfy God, and to believe oneself unworthy of His providence and His mercy? This true humiliation of the penitents is a stimulus of God's kindness as seen in the eagerness with which this father ran in search of his repentant son and threw his arms around his neck. The spendthrift son begged him to take him back as a servant, but the father does not scorn calling him a son. He was not put off by his poverty, nor did he discard his nudity, nor did he hesitate to give him his blessing. But he went out to meet him, and clothed him in very good clothes, and killed his hunger with a solemn and copious banquet. The music and dance which found expression in him denote the joy of the Church when a sinner converts, and shows shepherds and spiritual directors the gentleness of love with which they must treat newly converted persons. For without the smoothing balm and restorer of this most high virtue, sins' wounds would remain open for a long time, without a man feeling the slightest calm in his heart. While the party went on and the father showed all kinds of joy, the first-born son returned from the fields. And when he heard the sound of musical instruments and the singers' voices he was overcome with admiration and, as if not believing his own ears, he called one of the servants to find out what was going on. The servant told him of his brother's return, and that his father was so glad to see him well that he had immediately sent to kill the fattest calf to share it with his friends. The servant spoke only of corporal health, but the father had greater esteem for spiritual health which, as he saw it, had greater value. This news caused extraordinary bitterness and sorrow in the brother's heart, so that while the father made known to all and sundry his rejoicing, the brother could not disguise his sorrow and spite. The father invited all with the satisfaction he enjoyed; and the eldest son condemned all that excess of joy and, far from taking part in it, he implied his sadness and jealousy caused by the joyous way his brother was received.

The envy between two brothers is such a common vice that the eldest brother's outrage should not be any news. He resolved not to enter the house and not to disturb the party, as he was persuaded in his anger that it would be superfluous. When the loving father was told of his eldest son's sorrow, he was aware that he had two sons whom he loved equally, but each one according to his condition. He went out to search his eldest son, and meeting him he said to him, more as a friend than as a father: "What is all this about, my son! Enter the house I beg you, and share in my joy and delight for it would not be polite at all if you offend me." "And how do you want me to be seen?" the envious son suddenly retorted. "After so many years constantly serving you, tell me if I have by chance at any time failed to follow your wishes and do your will. This notwithstanding, has it ever crossed your mind to offer me a kidskin to give to my friends? Has your son, who they are saying has come back, done any better than me? He has wasted all he had, and has spent it living a depraved life. But he now returns ruined and a beggar and you open your heart to him. You command a fattened calf to be killed and you cannot feast him any better." "My son," the father replied not showing any anger for his bad mood, "you are always with me and all my goods are yours. I let you dispose of them as you will, and you are at home as much as a master as myself. Have you considered well how much these benefits are worth? What does a short lived party mean in comparison to such a free and constant love and friendship, which I am bound to host in such a unique occasion? I was bound to lay an extraordinary banquet and to give something for the full joy of my household, because your brother was dead and he has risen; he was lost, and we have had the joy of finding him again."

The elder brother's resentment and complaints denote the prying jealousy that imperfect people usually have of the sensitive sweetness which God gives to new penitents. The father's response is a warning to whoever ignores God's ways in the conversion of lost persons. It was also a sign of the wisdom with which he helps weak persons at the beginning of their new life, and the strong away from the gifts of his house while he exposes them to heat and cold and the hurricane of temptations. He is aware that with the eyes of faith and the providence of God's mercy, he is now further away from falling into one of the ordinary temptations through which good servants pass. The memory of good works is like cobwebs of holiness when years of service are counted to demand a prize of temporary benefits. Never compare yourself to the one who has just converted, nor should you say that he comes *today* to serve God, while you were here for some twenty or more years working at his household. But think that in so many years you may not have had a single moment of fervour, and that each one of your merits is a debt contracted with God, which unless you humble yourself will not be satisfied. For God, whose grace is sufficient, only awards and grants it to the little ones and the humble. And in contemplating the elder brother's affront and anger, Saint Augustine says: "Nothing proves better the will and the heart of the spiritual man, as the healing and remission of an external sin if, by meditating on the freedom which the miserable person achieves and the help of the divine grace with which he is freed, he gives thanks to God for the greater glory due to Him, and rejoices in this and in the salvation of his brother." And in the same sense and concept Saint Dionysius the Areopagite has also said: "Indeed, the divine Jesus Christ is good, very good, and of the utmost goodness above all, showing himself kind to those who return to him; ever going out to meet those who draw close to him; and lovingly embracing them all, he greets them with love. And as soon as he sees them having departed from error, he carries them on his shoulders without remembering the faults they had previously committed. When they return, he celebrates a feast with his friends, and then there is common joy to all, where even the angels themselves are invited."

There is no doubt that the three parables we have just referred to are just as much awesome as instructive, in the same order as Jesus Christ had presented them and told. They provide men with a thousand tender and affectionate reflections to comfort penitent sinners, and to confuse hypocrite and overconfident righteous persons. It would be impossible to attempt implying them to all, and since everyone understands what he wants, we will leave their scrutiny to the good judgment of true believers, and now follow Jesus Christ in the last lessons which he will be giving us before coming to his passion.

CHAPTER 54

JESUS CHRIST TEACHES HOW TO CARRY OUT FRATERNAL CORRECTION: HE STATES ONE IS BOUND TO FORGIVE INSULTS UP TO SEVENTY FOR SEVEN TIMES, AND TELLS THE PARABLE OF THE KING WHO WANTED TO SETTLE ACCOUNTS WITH HIS SERVANTS (MT 18:15–25)

GREAT as the pleasure is which the angels enjoy in heaven for a sinner who converts, equally so is the joy they feel when a human strives as hard as possible to lead back the sheep which were led astray from the path of salvation. The apostles understood this truth well when Jesus Christ showed them his love and zeal as a gift from the little ones who believed in him. So much desiring to please him as it was expected, they asked him about how to behave when anyone of their brothers wanted to get lost because of his malice. And Jesus Christ obliged to instruct them as they wished, telling them: *If your brother sins against you, go and reproach him, you and him alone.* Which was like telling them: "Do not believe, my disciples, that I want that if any of your brothers were vicious and so misguided that he would offend and greatly offend his fellow men with his deranged behaviour, he would be left without proper correction, nor that you would let scandals persist with a lazy and cowardly kindness. Go and find the deceiver and rebuke him alone, tempering the fortitude which you ought to observe with the softness and sweetness which I want you to have, and be your character trait and that of those who boast that they follow me. On the one hand you must see to preserving the guilty person's honour, and, on the other the innocent person's good name. So do correct him privately. No one flatters his neighbour' vices, no one conceals them, and no one asks whether he is his brother's keeper?" The silence of whoever can rebuke him is a tacit consent to sin. "If he sins against you," Chrysologus says, "forgive him as a brother, but reproach him as a judge." It binds forgiveness with correction, one work of mercy with another. Your brother's rage is his illness; look after the sick and help him regain salvation. Correct him to heal him, forgive him that you may not get sick yourself.

It is necessary, however, that you are very well aware of this imposed commitment thrust upon you, since if you fail to correct him, it is you who will be sinning. What shall we say of whoever clasps his hands and is unable to comply with this law? Such are those who do not change their customs, those who live dominated by their passions and animated by the spirit of the world. None of these can be in a state to correct others. Who could be aware of this sin? Whoever does not live with a certain moderation and does not give such a good odour of virtue to anything he does, infringes the common charity of all Christians if he is in a position to help someone by fraternal correction, and to set right bad customs, but does not do it. Seek how to correct a person while keeping in mind his honour. Even this secrecy contributes to correction; because if shame is lost with fame, it would be easier for the sinner to harden in his guilt. "So correct him," Saint Augustine says, "but do not praise him with flattery. Do not kill him with threats and insults, do not call for shame, do not despise him for laziness, do not disguise fearful threats, enmities or temporary damage, nor help him finally by siding with servile and vigilant persons. Listen if you want to be helpful. If you tolerate and suffer your friends' vices, you make them your own. You will be sinning twice if you bestow platitudes on whoever sins."

If he hears you with docility, if he submits to your advice, if he stops sinning because of your reprimands, you will have the consolation of having won over your brother who was lost, without having either excessively humiliated or ashamed him. You will have earned his soul by preserving his good name, and his reputation and honour, and you will have achieved for yourself a great spiritual gain, because in seeking the salvation of others, Saint Jerome says, we would also be securing ours. What greater praise could be given than that of correction, after the first and foremost was uttered by Jesus Christ himself, than that which the Great Doctor had earlier spoken about? You have had a

CHAPTER 54

part in the work of another person's salvation, and you have laboured with great usefulness in your own. For whom have you won over your brother? For Christ, who has died for him and for you, and who has snatched you and him from the power of the devil. If you win him over, trust that you will not be lost, for God has mercy on whoever uses it with his neighbour.

If on the contrary he abuses you in all you do and in caring for him, if he refuses to listen to you, even then take with you one or two prudent witnesses, knowing as you do of the other person's sin which afflicts you, and rebuke the sinner in their presence, so that being convinced together with them that it is equally impossible to deny the fact which is causing scandal, you would make it clear to him that you have warned him enough and that you have corrected him prudently. For the one who does not stop sinning after being corrected, shame and fear will be the restoring medicine for him. So these witnesses ought to help in the primary aim of correcting and amending the ways of the sinner. If sin were, however, entirely hidden, so would all kind of correction also be hidden; but if it were public, so would correction also have to be public; for then it would not only be necessary that it be amended, but also that those who are scandalised with his guilt are edified by his punishment, and through his example to fear all and to turn away from evil. But if he were to adopt none of the proposed ways, the Lord added, there is another third way, commanding that sinner and sin are condemned by the Church by public denouncement and accusation, so that whoever was before only a charitable and friendly corrector because of his stubbornness, now becomes a public accuser. And the one who did not want to make amends by fraternal correction, being convicted by the judgment of witnesses, will see his malice publicly rebuked. You, my disciples, are judges and shepherds, and you must not ignore that it is in the flock's interest that it is set apart from contagious sheep. Tell the Church, so that he may receive his public rebuke from it deserving of his scandal. These means just as well conform with evangelical charity. The canonical penalties and the public severity which in certain cases the Church uses frighten other sinners; and although they do not change their hearts, they hold them back from accomplishing their wicked plans.

It does not seem normal to correct publicly a miserable sinner who ceases to repent and make amends. But if his audacity were such that he would go ahead with his shamelessness and obstinacy, and despise the means of conversion which you offer him in persistent confusion, in such case you will forbid your brethren to treat and communicate with him, you will abandon him to his hardened spirit and he will be separated from meetings of the faithful, in the same manner as the Jews do not admit communion of worship and religious exercise to ethnics and publicans. You will eliminate him as a plague-ridden person which every good government cuts off from society not to infect healthy persons. The Church retains this dreadful punishment of excommunication for such sinners, by which a Christian loses the right he has to call God his Father, and Jesus Christ his Saviour, and the Church his Mother, and the members of this mystical body his brothers. Let us beware of those who in their behaviour and in their talk show that they do not listen to the Church. For truly I say unto you, the Lord adds, who was given all the power in heaven and on earth? Truly I say to you who are my apostles, and in your person to all your successors or to those who associate themselves with you in governing the Church, that whatever you bind on earth will be bound in heaven, and whatever you will loosen on earth will be loosened in heaven. Such wonderful power Christ gave to the Church about how to remit sins and how to impose canonical penalties. Who does not fear and respect this terrible judgment? In order to forgive and retain sins in penance, the confessor should be informed of the penitent's aptitude. This is a very clear requirement for sacramental confession. Let those of us who are ministers of Christ arm ourselves with the spirit of God to make good use of this power, and let us be aware of the range which the Church entrusts in our hands to use it.

The first tier of this scale is love, the second is fear, the third is shame, because where love does not reach fear may reach, and where this does not arrive shame may enter. And so it is that even to make the preceding doctrine worth more, and so that they might better accomplish such severe acts of the jurisdiction bequeathed to them, the Lord wanted them not to sit in court to pronounce their sentences without first having invoked God's help with fervent prayer, and thereafter, feeling safe with divine protection, they could talk with someone and handle him full of confidence. All that was like telling them: If in a judgment of the kind we are relating, *two of you*, having entrusted their reasoning to God, agree here on earth what is shown clearly to you that should be granted or denied, allowed or forbidden, and my Father Who is in heaven will give you the necessary help to judge well. For wherever it might happen that two or three gather in my name to exercise a public ministry with which I entrust you, I will be with them and in their midst to suggest to them the resolutions that should be taken.

Already in his time the great scholar Origen said on this matter: "The reason why God does not hear us many times when we gather to pray, is because those of us gathered do not agree on the same thing on earth. Just as in music, if there is no tonality or consistency of voices there is no harmony or delight for the listener, so in the Church if there is no agreement among those who request in prayer, God does not delight in it nor does He hear the voices of those beseeching Him." And Saint Jerome adds: "We can understand this spiritually, because if the spirit or the soul and the body do not agree with each other, but are in conflict and open war on the same thing, as if in man there were two wills, of course their request will never reach the Father; because when good things are requested, the body would want that which the soul desires. What will those who despise and contradict common prayer say to this? Peter was delivered by prayer, and so did Paul ask for it from the faithful. What does love of meekness not obtain from God? He is holy and merciful; he always looks at his children as little ones and takes pleasure when he sees them being humiliated in his presence and begging him with fervour. They cannot be deceived by him who told them, *Ask and you shall receive*."

In a matter of such consequence, responsibility and the significance of what was asked by Peter, as prince of the apostles, were sure proof of the expanse of authority and power which he received, this is how he replied to Jesus Christ saying: "If this is what we ought to do as shepherds of your flock; if these are our rules when we ought to act as fathers and judges, clothed in your authority and assured of your help, what should we do as individuals, and how should any little disciple of yours behave in this respect? How many times will you convince me to forgive any of my brothers who had offended me? Was it enough for me to forgive him up to seven times?" Saint Chrysostom says that Peter believes he has exceeded this number. It seems like being enough to forgive your enemy only once. Who concedes to a second offence? Self-love keeps its status very rigorously; it has to be offended only once to be humiliated by love, so that it keeps watching and stays on guard not to be outdone a second time. It is consequently and above all necessary that man arms himself with the spirit of God against this primitive traitor, for he is at constant risk of infringing love at the least expected hour. He must not rely on the great victories which he might have been able to achieve. It is what we say to a celibate person, never to be sure of himself, because he is always carrying with him his enemy, this being what we must also say to a person who for many years forgives his enemies with all his heart. This always goes against our pride, namely, that root which is always alive within us, and whose offshoots can only be cut with the knife of prayer and contempt for worldly honour. Oh, how few are those with enough virtue and courage to do these trimmings, however sweet the knife with which they must be cut!

However Jesus Christ promptly replied to Peter and told him: *It is not enough to forgive your brothers up to seven times, but pardon them up to seventy times seven times;* which is like saying as many times as such occasion arises, not being vengeful to personal insults, because the expression *seventy times seven times* is an indefinite number that extends to all times and ties up the predicament of the obligation to forgive insults. No one can put up fences or walls to inner love, where the forgiveness of ill doings and love of the enemy belong. Your neighbour insults you a hundred times, a thousand times, ten thousand times, perhaps a million, yet just as many times you have to forgive him. You are insane if you refuse to forgive your brother while you need God to have mercy on you; why forget this mercy while you live the world? Do you need God's infinite mercy, while you limit your own? Whatever you are for your brother, so will God be to you. Just as the piety which God uses with us is law and a specimen of what we owe others, so does our hardness to others become the law and the model of what He will do to us. Of what use is the balm if the dart is still in the wound? Satisfaction and prayer will be just as useless for you as long as you hold the grudge in your spirit. So that you must never forget saying to God every day: *Forgive me, Lord, as I forgive*. This should be your plea and your precept: it is up to you to decide about absolution or eternal damnation.

To explain better to his disciples what he had hitherto said to them, and with the intention that it would be better imprinted on their heart, Jesus Christ continued imparting his stiff instructions, wishing to tell them another no less instructive and interesting parable: "There will happen in my Church," he told them, "which I call the kingdom of heaven, something similar to that usually happening between an earthly king and his vassals when he wants to adjust accounts, and asks them about the asset management of what had been entrusted to them."

"The first to show up and give an account," he continues, "is a steward who owes him ten thousand talents, which no way could he pay." Before getting into the meaning of this parable, we should note that the first thing the Saviour wanted to imply in it was the severity of his judgment, in which he will ask of us a brief account of all our works, words, thoughts, affections and desires. We are all servants of this great King, being so called not to do our will but His. We fear nothing which we call our own; everything belongs to Jesus Christ who receives it from his Eternal Father and delivers us from the hands of the devil, rescuing us with his own blood. His gifts are our existence, salvation and all other gifts with which we are enriched. Of these goods he is the only Lord, us being custodians and distributors. What sort of payback would he give God if he did not use His original gifts according to His will, squandering and channelling them to devious purposes and other people's plans for his own glory? Even faithful servants will be there settled, accused, judged about the way they would have used their natural talents and supernatural gifts, skill, time, wealth and authority; of the use made or not made of Jesus Christ's words, his graces, his mysteries, the Sacraments and other sustenance of religion. What will become of those who in the use of natural and supernatural talents have proceeded as absolute lords, rather usurpers of God's goods? Who works in the affairs of his eternal healing without forgetting that he is a servant or losing sight of the account his Lord will ask of him? By chance, does he who goes against God's commands think of this? For if this does not attract our attention, where is our faith in the last judgment? And if we do not believe in it, what religion do we profess?

There is no doubt that all this advice suffices to make man walk with righteousness and purity in all of his life's acts, since otherwise we will owe more than ten thousand talents on the day of the account to the sovereign and most righteous Judge. These would relate both to the goods which He gives us without meriting them, and to the misfortune we deserve if we persist in evildoing. This is the sole and infallible rule by which we ought to measure our debts with God. And who can reduce them to a simple figure or to a fixed amount, mostly if we consider that nothing in us makes us worthy of a single gift of his mercy, or can be just enough for a single sin? The earth would be burned in God's love if we were to reflect with living faith on the sins which He has washed away from us with the blood of His Son, and on the countless ones from which He keeps us away, transforming us with his grace into new creatures. Whoever believes he owes less to God because he has sinned less, neither knows what sin is nor the mercy that keeps him away from it, nor even the grave errors and offences he would commit without such mercy and in being abandoned to his own misery.

The talents are our debt to God with the penances by which we do not pay back for the offences we continually commit, which in turn aggravate our doubt and keep on increasing it. The talents are our multiplication of vain and useless thoughts growing within us, putting us off from thinking about God and dealing only with His work. The talents are the hours, days and whole years we spend without doing a single good thing, using them in fake breaks and hobbies perhaps a thousand times worse than just being idle. Well, what should we say if we were to examine God's benefits, for which we hardly show gratitude! And with regard to Him the abuse of His gifts, of His Sacraments, of His truth and of the very clever means by means of which He communicates with us? And finally, in forgetting to resort to him in our works, and in being disrespectful and with our aptitude, provoking His anger with our lukewarm prayers, paying little attention to the private and public calamities He sends us to pay our debts? If we meditated on all this with living faith, we would be scared away by the patience with which God endures us and not only would we be aware of the holy obligation we have of being grateful to Him, but we would see that our debt to Him is not of ten thousand talents, but of immense and infinite value as is Himself.

He spoke of his debt with the steward, and being unable to pay it back, the king ordered that he should be seized and sold, together with his wife and children, profiting from his labour to have the debit paid back to the royal treasury. On hearing the sentence, the unfortunate man threw himself at the king's feet, and with an abundant flow of tears he cried out in distress and said: *Do, sir, have a little patience with me and give me some respite, and I promise paying you back the amount I owe you.* None of man's riches can satisfy God if a person is judged without mercy and respect in reparation and to Christ's merit. The seraphic Theresa of Jesus says about this, that when we say to the Lord *forgive us our debts*, we would be saying it in the company of Christ our Lord, by virtue of which we must hope that forgiveness will be well accomplished, for so did the Son of God himself fulfil it for men. What reconciliation can one promise God if he only counts on his own righteousness to obtain it? How can one who is shorn of all assets pay his own and other persons' debts? And under what title did he present himself to satisfy God for his own debt? Then no one can price his own works according to their value, but in union with Jesus Christ's merits. The Saviour appeared humble before the throne of God his Father to pray for sinners and pay back for all their sins; and likewise did the debtor steward also present himself humbly to ask his king for forgiveness, or at least that he might cut his great debt for him. He confessed being a straightforward debtor and poor, and so having lost hope of being able to pay back for himself, he implored his lord's mercy. This was unnecessary to move the master to compassion for he had more mercy and showed his servant greater pity than a faithful one deserved. Not simply counting on freeing him, he also forgave him all his debt. Saint Chrysostom says about this: "Look at the mercy of God. The servant only asked for some time to pay back his debt, and he received forgiveness for it all."

One may not be called presumptuous if, being unable to pay the debts of divine Justice, he becomes self-reliant by resting on his own merits and their fulfilment, but not on God's patience and Christ's merits. For these are infinitely priced riches, from which the Christian's penance assumes its full value; and if we add to it the humility of prayer, why should the fervent supplication of a contrite and humiliated heart not reach God? It is written that God will not despise him. God's pity for sins is the love with which he looks at the sinner, and this love is the source of grace. This grace then is God's almighty hand at work, which cannot be hindered or delayed by anything, not because it infringes the will, but because it animates it to want and freely choose the good that commands it. The effect of this work is to let it loose from the chains of the devil, so that when the writing which enslaved it by sinning is wiped off and nailed to the cross, it may serve its legitimate Lord, of whom it was unaware. And being grateful to him who with his blood paid back its debt, it may consecrate itself to imitating his virtues and to obey his commandments.

"When the steward relinquished his ties with sin," Chrysostom continues, "and was freed of his debt, he was not totally free from becoming a servant of iniquity." Having soon forgotten the mercy he had been shown, he found one of his servants, namely of the sinners who like him were also servants of God, who owed him the small sum of *one hundred denarii*, hardly one-sixtieth of a talent and a small amount indeed compared to what he had just been forgiven. He suddenly threw himself at this unfortunate man, grabbed him by the neck, and almost smothering him cried out and said: *Pay me back what you owe me.* Then the poor debtor fell down on his knees and asked him for more time to pay him back his debt. *Be patient,* he told him, *you will not lose anything with me.*

Yet the ungrateful steward mercilessly urged against his debtor and had him taken to jail where he ordered that he be kept until he paid his last coin. Humanity shuddered at seeing this servant almost in the same humble and submissive incident as he had been with his creditor now so harsh and relentless with his debtor. But what can be said of this if not that it is a vivid portrait of his real self? How can a person be seen grateful to God if he does not justify being his neighbour? If you are converted show the fruits of this holy change, and these are an acknowledged love for God and mercy for one's brother. In the debtor who humbles himself before you to beg time, be aware of your position with respect to God. Just as he kneels at your feet awaiting the result of his humiliation, so will you someday see yourself at Christ's feet waiting for that sentence which will decide your eternal destiny. How do you not anticipate the term of God's justice by asking him for a spirit of penance to pay the eternal debt you have contracted? What will become of you if the Lord discards your lukewarm supplications, your imperfect humiliation, and your forced and weak penance? Truly, your fate would be a very unfortunate one.

Just as there is none more loving than God, so there is no earthly creature harsher and more prideful than man. It is most horrible to compare God's love with man's hardness. He was not aware that the cruelty with which he treated his brother was a process of condemnation for himself; that with it he closed God's ears forever to his pleas and opened the gates of hell, throwing himself on top of that divine Justice that forgives nothing and punishes everything. It is not simply the law's council proposed to us by God to imitate his mercy in this, assuming that he commands it to us as a requisite to achieve it. There is nothing else worth doing than to forgive your neighbour, while what you owe God is infinite. There is very little what all can do against you and still more, having deserved as much harm and bad treatment as you can receive from men. Although they would be sinning in harming you, their sin does not consist in what they make you suffer, but in the right which they usurp from God. But no matter how you look at whatever you do against God, it is always infinitely unjust and if you measure your greatness with that of God, you will find in every sin an infinite injustice. For however advantageous this affair might be to you, why do you not resolve to forgive? It is much like losing the heavenly kingdom for whoever, while keeping in his heart ingratitude and vengeance, forgets that he must face God as his judge and opponent.

The other servants, much as they were outraged, viewed the steward's inhumanity, him who the master and lord had just so generously forgiven. And being extremely saddened they then went to tell the master about the cruel action they had just witnessed with their own eyes. Such sadness of those faithful servants, accompanied by holy outrage borne out of love, was fired by a zeal for unity. It was much like the anger and sadness aroused in Christ himself by his followers' blindness. How horribly cruel it is to sadden our neighbour by committing offences, when we even grieve him by not feeling sympathy towards him for his weakness in not doing that which is lawful. Saint Paul condemns this as a crime against love (Rom 14:15). These do not only make the righteous grieve, but the spirit of God who dwells in them too. For which reason it is incumbent on Christian piety to defend the slandered, oppressed and persecuted neighbours, to intercede for them and to make known their uprightness or their needs to whoever can protect or help them. When man's help does not serve, recourse can always be had to divine piety, which we must implore with humble supplications.

When the king heard the terrible news given to him by his servants, he ordered the steward about whom they had told him such atrocious things to appear before him. When he saw him, he was full of wrath and said to him: *Wicked servant, perverse attendant, you know well that at a simple request of yours, and when you first told me, I yielded to my rights and forgave you all debt. Remember that it was ever increasing to a great amount. Was it so not reasonable that for such a smaller amount you should have had mercy on your friend who asked mercy of you, as I had of you who am you lord?* Debt has to do with justice, and this charity relates to one's neighbour to whom God transfers in a certain manner the right which He has over us through the mercy with which He has forgiven us our debts. In dealing with this important idea Saint Chrysostom analyses the vileness of the steward's ingratitude, and says: "How much did he owe to his master? Ten thousand talents. However, he did not insult him then or call him a wicked servant, other than at the time when he fell into the bad habit of such hideous ingratitude, that is when he said angrily to him *wicked servant*. Because on that occasion he proved to be worse than he had been before." And Saint Gregory adds: "Just as good persons who are insulted and despised become better persons, so do always evil persons when receiving benefits become worse. By chance then, does it not suit you, oh ungrateful servant, to sympathise with your attendant, forgiving him a small amount just as I had forgiven you so much, without being paid back anything, only because you begged me? You asked me for a longer term to repay the debt, and I forgave you everything. How could it be that such great grace did not move you to also forgive the debt which as you were begged to do? Well it is clear that you are ungrateful. How can you condemn him for the amount of debt if you were at the least unwilling to grant a longer term? If this seemed like serious harm to you, amending your ways should be the biggest profit you can make. If this precept seems serious and unbearable to you, consider how big the prize is. If it seems to be serious and painful to forgive those who beg you, it is more serious and painful to fall into eternal fire. The Gospel does not relate of any answer which this servant gave to his master; which shows that after this life, and soon enough on judgment day, the sinner can make no more excuses."

Nor could this wicked servant be excused for any reason before his king and master, who being fairly angry, ordered him to be handed over to the court marshals until he had paid his last penny. Apparently there was nothing fairer that could be done than this terrible decree. What mercy can one expect if with harshness towards his neighbours he breaks the covenant of his reconciliation with God, denies the sacred condition of Christian prayer and usurps the supreme Judge's rights which he has reserved for Himself avenging and paying back our insults. This is a sign of what God will do on the day of His fury to avenge the holiness of this merciful covenant violated by our wrath. These marshals stand for the tools God uses to punish the wicked, in a manner worthy of His righteousness, which is holy, infinite and eternal.

The most exemplary model of eternal charity concluded his mysterious parable with a terrible exclamation to the scribes and Pharisees who were present, saying to them: "My Heavenly Father will deal with you in the same manner, if each of you does not forgive his brother from his heart." "It is worth noting," as Chrysostom himself notes, "that Jesus Christ did not tell them *your Father*, but my Father; for it is neither worthy nor respectable that such men as the Pharisees called God their Father, bearing so much hatred and resentment against His Only Begotten Son." And Saint Jerome exclaimed: "This is a terrific sentence uttered by God, it is necessary that we understand it. We will not be forgiven for the great offences we committed against God, unless we forgive the small offences we received from our neighbour."

The charity residing within the heart not only excludes from man, like the justice of the Pharisees, the outer displays of anger, but also the most hidden hatreds and resentments. What does the crust of the Law serve you without knowing its purpose, which is love born out of a pure heart (1 Tm 1:5)? We have as judge of our conduct Him who does not let Himself be deceived by any external and hypocritical keeping of His commandments, but who judges by what the heart feels, and is obvious and clear in His eyes. So do not forget that every man is indebted to God and has his brothers as debtors. For this reason God justly gave us a rule so that we might know how to work with our debtors, for in the way we act with them, so will He behave with us. Understanding well all these things and meditating on the enormous debt of ten thousand talents, we cannot help but hasten to forgive our neighbours their small and negligible things. Let us flee from lack of mercy and cruelty, understanding that we should not do to others what we do not want done to ourselves. When we are willing to recall the evil which we have received from others to justify ourselves not to forgive them, let us also remember that we are then binding our own sins and not our neighbour's. We assault our brother; let us thank God for the injustice he committed against us, and so doing we glorify God our Father and obtain infinite mercy; and if we pray God for him, we will become like God Himself. Little is truly what we can lose and give, and much is what we can expect and receive. How much we give for God and forgive our neighbours, all is perishable and obsolete, but what we can hope for and receive, all is infinite and eternal. Give for God and wait for God, not doubting that he will pay you back and be your prize. Above all hear what the great Saint Gregory had to say in a very timely manner: "From the certain hope we ought to have in God that he would forgive us our debts, we must neither set aside their quality nor their quantity; for if one man on his own had committed the sins of all men, and would have despaired like Cain and Judas; if it were possible for that wretched man to repent and ask God for forgiveness, surely the Lord, who is infinitely good and merciful, would not deny him forgiveness. We must wait for a long time for Jesus Christ's merits, without which we could not save ourselves. All our merits are rooted in them and derive from them, both as for the restitution of punishment, and for the merits of eternal life."

Let us conclude then with Saint Bernard: "It is the creature that must mainly trust in the infinite merits of Christ's passion, as it gives very special solace to the wretched. Your passion, Lord, is the last refuge. If the creature lacks wisdom, he must know that the most essential remedy is not to discharge justice, nor to be capable of holiness while missing all merits, as these alone defray and suffice for everything. I will not despair about my sins, for I have been given in the sacred refuge of your wounds the safe place where to do penance, even if the day of my death is uncertain. You forgave, Mary Magdalene, Peter and the thief, Lord, as a sign that you will also forgive all kinds of sinners and all kinds of sins." And then turning to his brethren, he said to them: "Let us, my brethren, have faith in the mercy of God our creator, and let us turn with tears to the most merciful Judge who is waiting for us. Then as just as it can be, he would not seek to cease forgiving us; let us consider that he is infinitely merciful and holy, and let us not despair. He is our Father and our God, he wants us to come closer to his heart so that we may taste the joys and sweetness of his love."

CHAPTER 55
JESUS FULLY REPLIES TO THE TRICKY QUESTION PUT TO HIM BY THE PHARISEES WHEN ASKED ABOUT THE REASONS FOR REPUDIATION; PEOPLE PUT BEFORE HIM SOME LITTLE ONES TO BLESS THEM, AND HE TELLS ALL TO LET THEM COME CLOSE TO HIM; AFTER WHICH HE ANSWERS A YOUNG MAN'S QUESTION, HE TELLS WHAT POVERTY REALLY MEANS (MT 19:3-21)

AFTER with these great and precious parables Jesus Christ had given his apostles and disciples, the most interesting and awe-inspiring examples, he passed from Galilee to the ends of Judea and the other side of the river Jordan. It is worth knowing that generally speaking Judea consisted of all the land occupied by the Jews, to the exclusion of other nations; it is the whole area of the country facing south, inhabited by the tribes of Judah and Benjamin. It was the area properly and specially called Judea, unlike other regions found in the same province, such as Samaria, Galilee, Decapolis and others. When the Lord left Galilee he then withdrew to this land which is truly called a province of Judea. And not to lose the fruits of his zeal, seeing that his life's end was nearing, he wanted to reach the climax of the most important work of redemption entrusted to him by his Father. But after having preached several times at Jerusalem the adorable mysteries that would be the object of faith and veneration of all the faithful, he also preached them while travelling across that land, making countless converts even though on this occasion his speeches were not accompanied by wonderful miracles.

Many Jews, being moved by the gentleness and effect of his appeals, so resolved to believe in Jesus Christ, in spite of the general excesses of priests and magistrates and the outright violence of the country's heads. The Saviour for his part remained where he could gather the disciples who had been just won over to the Gospel, and to confirm in the faith all those sent to him by his Father. With this in mind he chose the small town of Bethany where he could retire. It was not the place with the same name neighbouring Jerusalem where Lazarus dwelt with his family, but it was another Bethany, situated to the east of the Jordan, where the Baptist, cast out by the scribes of the deserts which he first sanctified with his preaching, went to baptise and teach, before new insults forced him to retreat to Galilee.

Although the time of his sacrifice was not far away, Jesus Christ remained in this place expecting it with holy patience and in conformity with his Father's will, He pass this time, almost of three months, fighting the doctrines of the Pharisees and Herodians, and comforting the faithful. It is not hard to believe that the first to seek him at the place of his asylum were for the most part John the Baptist's disciples, those who being enlightened by the holy forerunner's preaching and doctrines, justly reasoned out on sound principle among themselves as follows: "John the Baptist did not do any miracle, and this notwithstanding we did not cease believing in his word. His virtues and the austerity of his life, the effect and wisdom of his speeches, compelled us to see him as a great prophet. Today we already know from experience the truth of all that he had told us about Jesus Christ, whom our princes persecute unjustly. Now that we ourselves see Jesus Christ himself, who confirms everything he preaches with wonders which can only come from God, why should we not believe in him? We could not be excused before God if we were to be influenced by the many enemies he has and refuse to believe him." Convinced as they were of their correct reasoning, they went to seek the most loving Saviour who received them with special signs of goodwill and love. The critics and nonetheless scathing censors of the Gospel, fill in the interval made by the sacred Evangelists of the important narrative which Jesus Christ made following his departure from Jerusalem for the Feast of Tabernacles. They resume with that story after his second trip to the capital, letting himself be seen for just one day on the Solemnity of the Dedication. They inferred things from this lack of uniformity between one event and the other, as narrated with some difference by the Evangelists, and without wanting to notice that Jesus Christ's aims were the same everywhere. At times he confirmed his teaching with miracles, at others preaching but not doing any, with his works being always directed to the same end. It was to prepare the people of Israel for the setting up of God's kingdom, always and everywhere keeping the same method in all he did and taught.

His ruthless enemies could not but shudder seeing the huge crowd which followed him. To make him lose his standing and fame, while forcing him to give answers which caused scandal among the crowd, they asked him some well thought questions which they thought would make him fall into the subtle net they had laid for him. But as always, it was them who were confounded. More than once the Lord had explained himself with utmost clarity and frankness about the indissolubility of marriage. This was the most delicate matter, since Moses, whose disciples they were, had appeased about the severity of the Law which Jesus Christ wanted to restore to its pristine purity. And not doubting that the Giver of the New Testament had to oppose the Old Testament in something or another, the Pharisees made use of this occurrence to address some tricky questions to him to make him fall into the snare. So they said to him: *Master, is it lawful for a husband to repudiate his wife for any reason or excuse?* To which Jesus Christ answers them: *Have you not read that when God made man in the beginning of the world, did he not create definitely but a man for a woman and a woman for a man?* For which reason he told them: "Let the man leave his father and his mother and be closely united with his wife, so that both are one flesh and one body."

To understand well the Pharisees' question, and the simple shrewdness of Jesus Christ's answer, it is useful to know that there were in Jerusalem and throughout Judea two very influential families. There were those who belonged to one party were called the *house of Samay*, and those pertaining to the other were of the *house of Hilel*. Between these factions or parties there was a chasm in adhering to certain principles, one of which was about the causes of divorce. Those of the house of *Samay* claimed that the mere suspicion of adultery was a sufficient cause to allow divorce. For the house of *Hilel* any other cause, no matter how small, was enough for this. And there was even another third opinion which came closer to the house of *Samay*, although it was also divided into several precepts. So the Pharisees, pretending to have a keen desire to get out of these doubts, addressed their question to Jesus Christ, so that by declaring themselves in favour of any one of these precepts, they would make others appear to be hateful. But as the Saviour was aware of all the cunning of his enemies, he sought to baffle their plans with some very clear precept from Holy Scripture, which no one could challenge or argue about without a tinge of faithlessness.

With this thought in mind Jesus Christ did not declare himself to hold any of the opinions about which those families disagreed on this very essential issue, and he confined himself to spelling out clearly the will of God with regard to marriage. It was advisable and God's resolve that a lawfully contracted marriage is not dissolved, because nothing can be divided without being detrimental to its unity. This was the existence and nature of marriage established by God, which should always remain so. For although by man's malice this was degenerating from its own existence and virtue by tolerances and bad habits which are much removed from such perfection, it should be known that there is no rule of limitation for God's decrees.

According to the intentions of the universal Creator, marriage is the seedbed of the human race by the union of the two sexes in the state of marriage. It is the begetting and conservative principle of rational entities, the germ of the multiplication and reproduction of men, the basis of civil society and of public prosperity and a very important doing that in all times and ages called the attention of legislators of different political societies, moralists, philosophers and sages. They all saw to inscribe this natural teaching in laws and to perfect it according to the designs of the Supreme legislator. However, old jurisprudence did not come to understand quite clearly this part of natural law and by dividing moralists and philosophers in their opinions, a few sowed a thousand errors in this contract and demoted it to a lesser status. Others, though more prudent and wise, could not hold back the torrent of vices, abuses and mess with which people desecrated it. Yet in the midst of darkness light dawned, and Jesus Christ, the author of grace and truth, has taught us how much we care to know about this matter. By putting before our eyes, and declaring the primitive lessons which Adam the common father of mankind was given by his Maker, he restored marriage to its primitive dignity and original holiness.

God created one man to be the trunk and root of the whole human race. He gave him a companion who was extracted from the substance and flesh of man himself, by means of which God showed that he wanted man to see woman as part of himself, and that woman would recognise man as her original principle of existence. When man saw this creature he exclaimed: *See there a bone of my bones and flesh of my flesh, for which man shall leave his father and mother, and remain so closely united with his wife, that both may come to be one flesh and as two souls in one body.* The Lord blessed them, and with his blessing he gave them the fruitfulness and virtue of reproducing themselves: *Grow and multiply, he said to them, and fill the earth; which means bear fruit and procreate.* See then how Divine Wisdom shines impressively in the institution of the marriage bond. By making the bond between man and woman permanent and indissoluble, God has effectively provided for the perpetuity, prosperity and perfection of the human race.

"So that it is certain," Jesus Christ continued, "that according to what God has instituted, man and woman, once united with the bond of marriage, are not two but one and the same flesh. This being so, no man may separate what God has bound together." From which it follows that so united the two must remain together for life, attending to the education of the children that God wants to give them, and receiving reciprocally from each other the comfort and relief brought about by a society which does not blame them. So that the strength of that contract could not be expressed so beautifully by any other words than that such bond signifies an intimate union, sweet friendship, blind love, mutual trust and inviolable fidelity which spouses owe to each other. These are their duties according to natural law, which is none else than the very will of the Creator, from which it results that man cannot depart without violating his own nature, nor contract another bond without attacking the divine institution. Jesus Christ has done more than restoring it and reproaching all that goes contrary to this primitive right, such as adultery, repudiation, simultaneous polygamy, concubinage, the simple desire for infidelity in husbands and all that can foster evil passions. And he also added a new bond which raised marriage to the dignity of a sacrament. Yet the Pharisees, who did not regard it as such nor did they understand well the exalted dignity of the union instituted by God between man and woman, and allowed themselves to be too much carried away with the violent passions born in the depths of their perverted heart, replied to Jesus Christ and said to him: *Why has Moses not explained it this way and commanded the disgruntled husband to give libel of repudiation and leave his wife?* This was where they wanted to get and about which they boasted that Jesus Christ would be caught off his guard, But he answered them: "And what does Moses tell you on this matter?"

They could not help but be surprised to hear the Saviour's rebuttal and question. But facing up to having to answer him they said to him: "Moses has allowed the disgruntled husband to write a libel of repudiation and to dismiss his wife, freeing the two separated persons." Which was just as saying that had Moses understood the Law as strictly as yourself, he would not have issued this ordinance. "You are deceived," Jesus Christ said. "It is neither an ordinance nor a law but only a mere tolerance by Moses, that is, he has not commanded you to repudiate your wives, although he has allowed you to repudiate them. And he felt he should act with such kindness since he was aware of the hardness of your hearts and feared that if he did not change things a little, you will let yourself be carried away by greater abuse. But at first it was not so, that is, in the times when men remembered the first institution of marriage by God, this was not so. All upright persons in faith regarded this custom as an innovation and tolerance. As far as I am concerned, I definitely tell you that I will not allow it in my Church and that I will restore things to their original purity. So see here that the regulations and laws are kept in this regard for it shall not be lawful for a man to leave his wife other than because of fornication and infidelity. He who has left his wife and marries another while his wife is still living is guilty of adultery and concubinage. A man who marries the repudiated woman while her husband is still alive commits the same offence. The law looks to women just as it does to men, so that a woman who entrusts herself to a second husband, even while the first is still living, is dishonest and adulterous."

The Lord did not condemn Moses, for he knew well what he would have done if he had found better disposed hearts and more compliant spirits. With this deep wisdom and prudence the Saviour would restore the old laws on the indissolubility of marriage, doing this without touching the reputation of the holy lawgiver, while humiliating those who abused his name.

In this manner Jesus Christ prudently freed himself from the scribes' malice, although the harshness of his morality rather frightened his apostles. They had to care for whoever chose to practise this awe-inspiring morality, and to prevent those difficulties as the perversity in man's heart, which always repeats itself, could imitate in the future. So as they entered together with their Master into the house where they were staying, they again spoke to him about the same matter. But the Lord answered them, without removing or adding anything to the principles he had uttered a short while before, and so that they would never depart from them, he would repeat them again to the last word. The disciples were intimidated with the new retort and repetition Jesus Christ gave them, so they said to him: *If man has such an obligation towards his wife, that he can never leave her to marry another woman, it would be better to renounce to marriage.* To which Jesus Christ replied: *Not all can understand this except those to whom it is granted*; it benefits one to be aware of the grace to understand and practise it. Which was like telling them: "It is not in everyone's interest or ability to resolve so generously; so that I do not command it or lay it down by law to be abided with. That will be the privilege of some chosen souls whom God calls and invites with a state of perpetual continence and corresponding to the calling. You may encourage my disciples to it, but not exact it from them. There are eunuchs who were born so from their mother's womb; there are others who have suffered this injury from men, and there are even others who have made themselves eunuchs for the kingdom of heaven. These are those men who, moved by the advantages of continence and its merit, impose on themselves the law of keeping it for life. Whoever feels strong enough to adhere, with the grace of God, to such a glorious and difficult obligation, consenting to embrace it, will surely receive the prize of such a heroic resolve. Everything can be done with God's help, and anyone desiring and wanting to do this, may decide upon taking such a holy state. I only give advice, without establishing any precept, and this is what you should teach."

The apostles faithfully followed the plan drawn up by Jesus Christ, preaching his doctrine with utter strictness. The Church and all the Christian nations have attributed the most respectful veneration to Jesus Christ's teachings and have sought to give due importance to the sacrament of marriage, seeing to its being celebrated in public, with all possible entourage and solemnity, and in the eyes and presence of God, with certain ceremonies and formalities. Religion presides over these acts, confirms the contract, and with the blessing uttered by the church ministers, marriage acquires the dignified character of holiness and grace. The contracting parties, tying this knot before the altars, undertake to respect and regard each other's promises as sacred and inviolable. The ceremonies retain the dogma, and this ensures the endlessness of civil rights with regard to the contract. Civil laws and public rights, in conformity with Jesus Christ's teachings and church discipline, have greatly improved marriage for the husband-and-wife relationship is now nowhere better regulated or as happy as among Christians.

The sophistry used by modern unbelievers and so called reformers of public and private morality, do not deserve to receive from among Catholics the honours of such a wide falsity, just as stretched out are the speeches of impiety with which they seek to destroy the holy and uplifting doctrine of the Gospel. Such sophistry would be enough to bring everything to nothingness saying that people cry with blood tears to see divorce, polygamy, extramarital sex and widespread cohabitation being accepted between them, all of which reduce, destroy and annihilate the population, putting their faith in the ideas and ancient opinions of the Epicureans and pleasure-loving immoral persons who made marriage detestable and hateful among them, so that they were engulfed in all the horrors of a real and dreadful anarchy. And suffice it to say that ancient lawmakers of civilised Rome and Athens went into the detail of appealing to legal regulation to compel citizens to marry, and to attract them to marriage with the lure of honour, and with prizes and rewards.

Marriage, instituted to be the primary and strongest bond of society, could not produce this effect were not this link between spouses indissoluble and everlasting. A fleeting and temporary union would be similar to that of animals, and it would neither form a more perfect society, nor would there be lasting relations between spouses, between parents and children, or a constant and continuous education, or any mutual aid, or would they have among themselves other contacts and children than those they could have when they unexpectedly depart from earth like trees and plants. When instituting marriage God did not only want to perpetuate the human race and promote the happiness of spouses, but also the wellness of children and the advantages for domestic society and that of the whole human race. Divorce goes against all these ends. Great as the drawbacks of marriage indissolubility may seem, so can it be well assured that they are much smaller than those that would result from repudiation. And although to cover up this scandalous and unpleasant picture, decency and modesty compels anyone to retain thoughts and feelings of order, usefulness and virtue, it must be said that indefinite divorce, and even that limited to certain cases, would very soon degenerate into debauchery and breakup, as it happened in Rome. Juvenal says he knew of a woman who in the space of five years had eight husbands. And Saint Jerome claims having seen another buried in Rome who in her life had had twenty-two husbands.

What would the fate of spouses, children, family life and the state of public and private customs be among such disastrous dissolution? Adultery and causes of infidelity would multiply every day. Scandalous accusations would regenerate at every moment and the unfaithful party would stir up trouble for the other. An unproven accusation would inflame an eternal hatred, as is presently the case in separation cases. The healing of children, public decency and the interest of society would be unworthily sacrificed to the inconstancy and perversity of either spouse. It is indeed true that when corrupt customs infest marriages, life falls into a wretched state and most sad abyss; yet breaking the sacred bonds because of corrupt customs, is like widening and opening the sore instead of closing it. It is a grave error to attribute anything resulting from disordered passions to the state of marriage, which is holy and perfect in its own right.

As we have seen, Jesus Christ neither recommends nor authorizes mutilations, much less such a harmful operation as castration. The barbaric custom of making eunuchs, which was so common in Persia, Egypt and eastern countries, is rooted in polygamy. The Jews, however, never adopted this usage, and Moses outlawed such cruelty by punishing with disgrace anyone who consented to being castrated. The eunuch will not enter the Church (Dt 23:1-2), will not be acknowledged as an Israelite, and cannot enjoy all the rights and privileges of a citizen. Nor will the illegitimate child, namely whoever is born of a prostitute woman, enjoy them, nor will he be able to enter the Church of the Lord up to the tenth generation. This is what the Book of Deuteronomy says. What Jesus Christ said about those who became eunuchs for the kingdom of heaven should not be understood in a material sense, as Origen mistakenly did, and follow immediately after those of his disciples: *If this is how marriage is, it is not advisable to marry.* On this occasion he recommends and finds praise in making an overstatement, that of a most unselfish resolve of whoever not only renounces to sexual pleasures, but also to marriage itself, although it is holy and good.

The Apostle most beautifully unwrapped Jesus Christ's mysterious doctrine when he said, *Now concerning the matters about which you wrote and consulted me, I say unto you: That as far as the unmarried are concerned, I have received no command or precept of the Lord.* And he further added in a long chapter on the subject (1 Cor 7): "The state of continence, the virginity of celibacy, are not prescribed by divine law, but I give my opinion and council as one who by the Lord's mercy is trustworthy. If a either man or woman is unmarried it would be good for him or her not to seek marriage, but to remain celibate. Virginity and celibacy are advantageous. I think that in view of the impending distress it would be good for either man or woman to remain as he or she is. Yet those who marry will have worldly troubles, and I would spare you that. So I say to the celibate, to the unmarried and widowed, that it would be better for them to stay like me, because I wish and want you to live without worry and free from worldly affairs. The unmarried is anxious about the affairs of the Lord and only thinks about pleasing God. The woman who is truly widowed and lives alone, hopes in God and duly passes day and night in prayers and petitions. However, he who is married cares for the things of the world and how to please his wife and is distracted, while it is that the single woman and the maiden meditates on the things of the Lord to make herself holy in body and spirit; the married woman lives a distracted life and understands worldly affairs and how to please her husband. However, I say this to you for your own benefit and not to lay any restraint on you. I say it to promote good order and to secure your undivided devotion in serving the Lord. So that I do not intend pointing fingers at anyone or that anyone should be forced to do more than one can do. Everyone is free to choose what he understands will be most useful to him, according to the gift and grace he has received from the Lord."

I do not disapprove of marriage: the state of marriage is a good and holy one. Let marriage be held in honour among all (Heb 13:4), and the marriage bed an unstained pure bed. Give a daughter in marriage, but give her to a man of understanding, says the Wise One (Sir 7:25), and you will have finished a great task. So that writing to Timothy, Saint Paul added (1 Tm 5:14): "I would have younger widows to marry, raise children, be mothers to the family and to rule their homes. And not only is marriage good and holy, but it is also very much needed. So I say to the unmarried and widowers that if they do not have the gift of continence, let them marry, for it is better to marry than to burn. And in order to avoid incontinence and the sins of the flesh, let each man have his wife and each woman have her husband."

"In this manner," Chrysostom says, "Jesus Christ was guiding his apostles and disciples towards desiring and choosing virginity, by showing them that this very high virtue was possible and very easy to bear, making men live the life of angels and giving purpose to such sublime and worthy reasoning. For although he showed them on the one hand his great highness and grandeur, he taught them mercy on the other, which he did not want to include as requiring any law, meaning that it was very possible to fulfil on one's own, so that the desire to embrace it might ever grow in them."

With extraordinary attention and pleasure Jesus Christ's disciples heard this lofty and interesting speech which was, however, suddenly interrupted. The house where they had retired was full of parents who had come to present their little children to the Saviour, and to ask him put his blessed hands on them, say some prayer for them and deign to touch them. These parents were persuaded that such ceremony would not be useless for the innocent little ones; they rather believed that it would be of a heavenly blessing for them. While the apostles dedicated themselves to meditating and being enraptured by the lessons imparted to them by their Master, they still did not have engraved on their chest any of the feelings of goodness with which Jesus Christ was replete. So, thinking that the Saviour was not happy with the drove around him and that they were doing a service to him, they pushed aside the little ones roughly and insisted on clearing the mob. Jesus Christ, however, was not angry with the crowd around him but rather disapproved of the disciples' conduct. Being greatly displeased and seemingly resenting their behaviour, he called them close around him joined by all those children who, in spite of all, did not turn away but rather felt wronged and were in tears. Turning to his disciples Jesus Christ said to them, "*Leave the little ones, and mind you never prevent them coming close to me. Truly I say* unto you, that unless a man submits himself to the kingdom of God, that is to my Church and to my Gospel, with the simplicity of a little child, shall not enter that kingdom or be admitted for its purpose among the number of my disciples." Which was like saying: "Blessed are those who imitate the frankness, ingenuity and innocence of children, for my Church, which is God's kingdom on earth, will only be filled by persons who resemble them." About which the great Origen said: "This is the Saviour's doctrine to which we must attend, not being one of preferring greater wisdom and spiritual adaptation, so that we despise the little ones as big ones of the Church, forbidding them from coming and drawing near to Jesus Christ."

The little ones can also mean the poor and those on the lowest scale of the ladder of society, and the disciples preventing them from drawing close to Christ could mean the Churches' princes or prelates and rectors, who owing to poverty or the low class from which the former come, repel them and keep them away from being promoted to and receiving ecclesiastical orders and dignities, although being fit and worthy of them. So that, those who dare hold them back are angrily rebuked by Jesus Christ's own words, who says to them just as he did to the apostles: "*Let the little ones come to me*, since I accept all, *and do not in any way forbid them from drawing near to me*, nor terrify them with threats or molest them with bad examples, because these are the form and figure of truly humble persons, whose familiarity and companionship is what I seek and like." And Saint Chrysostom adds: "Why do you forbid the little ones to come near me? If they are to be saints, why do you keep back the children from drawing near to their Father? If they want to be sinners, why do you condemn them before seeing their guilt? What they are now, is up to me; what they will be later, they will see to that for themselves. So respect what is mine, and pity them for what they might be." Then adding that *Of such persons is the kingdom of heaven* he did not say of these, but of such persons, to recommend humility and innocence. He did not say of all, but *of such*, which is like saying of all those who by their care and position have such virtues, as little ones have by humility and innocence.

About which Saint Ambrose smartly concludes: "It is not some age which is preferred to another, because otherwise it would be an obstacle to grow older if you want to reach the kingdom of heaven. Why is it then that he says that only the little ones can enter the kingdom of heaven? Perhaps because not knowing any malice they do not know how to deceive, they do not dare fake things, they fail to scrutinise anything which does not suit them, and they do not covet riches and honours. Virtue is not found in ignoring what is wrong, but in despising it. Nor is being unable to sin a virtue, but it is not to want to do so."

It was clear from all that had been said that Jesus Christ is very pleased with the virtues of innocence and humility, as Jesus Christ did not miss a single chance of praising them, ever recommending them as belonging to his Gospel. We are ungrateful to Jesus Christ in turning away from him when we need to worship him even more. He commands us to be as simple as children, and we stuff up ourselves with the arrogance of philosophers, ceasing to be simple and transient to prove that we are a critical and understanding lot.

The Saviour, who could not keep deep in his heart the tenderness apparently aroused in him by the innocence of those infants, drew all the children presented to him by their parents close to him. Embracing them all, one after the other, he laid his hands on them and sent them off, replete with blessings. They were the children of the faithful, and he had already adopted them in his adorable thoughts among the number of his members. This ministry, which may be regarded as the institution and beginning of the sacrament of confirmation, was later passed on by the Lord to the apostles and so on to others. So that in the administration of this sacrament those who are being confirmed are marked on their forehead, with the sacred chrism and by the hand of the bishops who in the Church of God take the apostles' stead. And by the imposition of the bishop's hands the confirmants receive the Holy Spirit and are confirmed in faith.

As soon as Jesus Christ performed this loving action with the little ones, which was very much to his loving heart, he left his abode accompanied by his apostles and went to preach at some other neighbourhood of the same quarter where he had not yet let himself to be seen. Barely had he started on his way when a young man, who was very distinguished and virtuous in the country and truly desired salvation, drew near to him and with the utmost modesty and humility told him, *Good teacher, I pray that you may have the goodness to instruct me on what it is best for me to do to attain eternal life.* Saint Mark tells us that this man knelt before Jesus Christ in making this plea (Mk 10:17). So holy a question could not but be answered with a very wise reply. "You ask me about the good that should be done," Jesus Christ answered him, "and at the same time you call me good." Which was like saying to him: "Do you know that giving me this name, as you do, you definitely give me a name that only belongs to God? There is no one who is good but God, who is good by virtue of His excellence and nature. No one but He can call Himself a Good Master, for only He can teach men what true goodness is, for which heaven is the prize. Other men are only good by way of sharing, doing so for God and in God." Saint Chrysostom says that "God does not exclude them from sharing in His goodness, by which they are good, or can be called as such if they believe in Him and faithfully fulfil His precepts." And the Venerable Bede adds that this was the same as if Jesus Christ had said to him: "Understand well that by accepting the name you give me of Good Master, I instruct you in the infinite distinction you should make between me and the other doctors whom you might consult. And as you have been brought up in this truth, you should know that in order to achieve the eternal life you want, you must fulfil the commandments of the Law, and you will surely attain it in this manner."

The young man was enthralled to hear the Sovereign Master's answer and so he immediately replied: "And would you be so good, Lord, as to tell me which commandments I must observe?" He was not asking why he should be ignoring the precepts of the Law, but only that he wanted to know from Jesus Christ's own mouth whether what he was referring to were the same commandments as those which he had actually kept. And so the Lord said to him, *Thou shalt not kill, nor commit adultery, thou shalt not steal, thou shalt not give false witness, thou shalt not commit fraud and tricks, thou shalt honour your father and your mother, and love your neighbour as yourself.* The young Israelite, not failing to be filled with joy, looked at Jesus Christ and said to him: "I have practised all this, Lord, since when I was young, and I can tell you and assure you that there is nothing right now which might stir my conscience. So show me now what else there is for me to do." The Saviour looked at him lovingly, implying that he was satisfied with his conduct and wished to raise him to better perfection, and so he further said: "Although you have done all this, there is still something else for you to do: *if you want to reach a higher degree of perfection, go therefore, sell what you have, and give its price to the poor, and you will have a treasure in heaven which will never be lost, nor decreased, nor can thieves take it away from you, and take up your cross, and come after me, and follow me.*" This uplifting evangelical council was later practised by many of the Lord's disciples and Church history is strewn with examples of such generous and heroic resolution. The Acts of the Apostles narrates (Acts 2:44-45) that all those who believed, were united fully together, so much so that they were all of one heart and one soul: no one claimed anything he possessed as being his, but all things were held in common. And selling their possessions, houses and estates, they brought the price of the thing sold and deposited it at the foot of the apostles. so that all was distributed among all, as anyone had need, and no one among them was lacking.

In the Saviour's doctrine precept and council can be seen and distinguished clearly, so that by Jesus Christ's answer it is shown that it is a very fatal error to confuse wisdom sayings and the lessons of perfection with the commandments and precepts of obligation. Those are not always practicable or convenient other than for certain and specific persons; but these comprise all. It is absurd to demand from general morality sayings an accuracy and precision such as that of a geometry problem. Its application depends on the circumstances of time, place, person and of a thousand other things which do not allow us to form an exact calculation and a universal rule. The law insists on prohibiting crime and to order that which is just to be done. Yet advice and moral precepts extend further and are like a bulwark surrounding the law which defends them and ensures their fulfilment.

The ancient philosophers recognised this great difference, and would describe as reckless anyone who criticised their precepts as so many other harsh laws. So that the distinction between advice and precepts is not only founded on the moral and political order of human society, but also on the very nature of things. This is not a fleeting nicety invented by theologians to overcome very serious difficulties raised by evangelical morality, as some have dreadfully thought. Jesus Christ himself has said it was he who made and recognised this distinction in the answers he gave to the young man who was asking him questions. As to the first one he pronounced precepts, as to the second he gave him advice. The precept of observing the law is a general requirement to achieve eternal life; and the council to renounce goods and riches to follow Jesus Christ, binds only those who by reason of their status and office have a duty to aspire to perfection like the apostles.

When the young Israelite heard Jesus Christ utter his doctrines and lessons, he was very distressed and frightened. He left the scene extremely sad because he enjoyed many possessions, and his spirit could not decide whether he should abandon them. He seemed very fervent at first, but barely had he heard of voluntary poverty when he lost courage and judged it very difficult to walk the path of perfection which had been laid out before him. So that although he had gone out to consult Jesus Christ full of joy and happiness, on hearing his precepts and councils he withdrew sad and heartbroken. He humbled himself when he saw his weakness, but did not consider himself a criminal. He left determined to serve God for the rest of his days in an innocent though less perfect state than that which he was endowed by Providence, yet still thinking of making good use of that property from which he was not bold enough to cut off himself. This is the noble thought, observing the manner in which Jesus Christ spoke to him, which Origen noted when he said: "Notice the words with which the Saviour expresses himself: Tell him, *if you want* this, if you are willing, because you are in full and perfect freedom to do it. Do you want to rise to a state of perfection greater than that which ordinary men observe? Go then, sell your goods, and by doing this you will be showing your contempt for all earthly riches: share your yields with the poor and become poor yourself to come and follow me; as it is even me, though being infinitely rich, have also for your sake become poor. Follow me, and you will have a treasure in heaven."

Saint Chrysostom adds: "The Lord spoke very well and at the right time, not making any mention of eternal life but of the treasure he would have in heaven, since the discourse was then about riches and the renunciation of them all. The Lord spoke of riches, but of those in heaven; of those that being infinitely greater than the whole world were the signs of the greatest and most abundant recompense he was offering him if he were to renounce the world's rewards. And *follow me* by walking in my footsteps and walk as I walk; for true perfection consists in Christ's teachings or in following his charitable works." The principle of that perfection lies in the renunciation of goods and in the voluntary poverty which is embraced and is consequent to such relinquishment, for it relieves from the care for temporary things those which separate the spirit from the love of God and charity towards one's neighbour. Passing on from the young man's sadness and his decision, Jesus Christ began another speech to give his apostles other greater and more elevated lessons on detachment from worldly riches and the acceptance of voluntary poverty, that they might follow him with greater faithfulness and for all those who followed him to attain the promised kingdom of heaven.

CHAPTER 56
ON THE TWELVE EVANGELICAL COUNCILS: ABOUT THE DIFFICULTY AND IMPOSSIBILITY OF THE RICH ENTERING THE KINGDOM OF HEAVEN, AND OF THE REWARD FOR THOSE WHO LEAVE EVERYTHING TO FOLLOW CHRIST (MT 19:27–29)

THERE is a very obvious difference between precepts and evangelical councils; precepts are necessary to achieve healing and eternal life, councils are however necessary to achieve the greatest perfection. We are bound to observe the precepts, but not the councils, although undoubtedly their observance is very conducive not to keep back from following the precepts. Twelve are the so called proper and truly evangelical councils: the first aims at poverty, the second obedience, the third chastity, the fourth charity, the fifth meekness, the sixth mercy, the seventh verbal simplicity, the eighth fleeing sinful occasions, the ninth correctness of intentions, the tenth conformity of works with words, the eleventh avoiding life's solicitations, and the twelfth fraternal correction. As to some of them it can also be said that precepts exist if such circumstances as persons, times and places are taken into account.

In the preceding chapter we have just confirmed very explicitly the council of poverty in the answer which Jesus Christ gave the young man who asked him what he should do to be perfect. Well, we have already seen what the Saviour told him: "If you want to be perfect, go, sell all your possessions, and give them to the poor, and come and follow me." And Saint Luke had earlier also told us that the Lord had clearly told his disciples that whoever did not renounce all he possessed could not be his disciple. These doctrines clearly show that this love of poverty, generosity and detachment are a mere council to which the greatest perfection is precisely linked. In those other councils, confirmed in Saint Matthew, in which Jesus Christ told us that whoever wanted to walk after him should likewise deny himself;

and that the scribes and Pharisees had sat on the chair of Moses, advising the mobs to obey what they taught, but not to act as they did; the advice of obedience most clearly shines out. For what else can denying oneself, sacrificing the desires of one's will and having no self-will, mean other than to obey with a most prompt and blind obedience? Or what else does it mean to obey the doctrines of the scribes and Pharisees sitting on the chair of Moses? They were inclined to evil, they schemed advice of impropriety, they were inflated with courage and rage against Jesus Christ, they were tireless in plotting pretexts and means to get rid of him; yet Jesus Christ advises them to hear them and obey when they speak from the chair on which the legislator sat, that had once been given to him to lead them to the Promised Land. And the third council, that of chastity, also shines out as we saw in the preceding chapter, when Jesus Christ told the Pharisees that there were eunuchs who had made themselves so to obtain the kingdom of heaven. As a precept he had commanded abstention from fornication, telling us again elsewhere in the Gospel of Saint Matthew that looking at someone else's woman and desiring her was already breaking the precept in one's heart; whereby it is seen that the advice was very important to be able to better observe the precept.

These three councils are special for those who desire to attain true religious perfection, since all those who observe them are kept away from evil, not only in terms of guilt but also as to its cause. As a matter of fact, all evil is born from three roots, namely from of the flesh, from lust of the eyes and from the pride of life; and these three roots are fully cut off by chastity, obedience and poverty.

The fourth council, which is founded on charity, does not cease to be a council, although it seems to have the force of a precept. Here the council and the precept can be united in the same root, and sprouting from it they can open up in two branches. The precept is to love our enemies, but it is also an important and uplifting council: it gives advice about *affection*, and it is council as to *effect*. Seek peace with the enemy, grace and glory, all are really needed; but also, to render charitable works in his favour and to give him proof of goodwill, is a word of advice and perfection. The fifth council is intimately linked to that we have just explained. Meekness is so intimately linked to charity that one cannot be truly meek unless one is truly charitable. So that in giving us this council of meekness the Saviour said to us in Matthew's Gospel: *If anyone hurts you on one cheek, offer him the other*, which was as much as saying: "I wish your patience to reach such an extreme limit, that after being slapped one time you are willing to being slapped a second time." This council of patience and meekness talks only about injury or harm to the body, because as for the damage of the soul he also told us we must be determined to suffer all worldly agonies rather than consent to harm being done to our soul. To this same council and as if to confirm this same doctrine, Jesus Christ himself added: "If anyone intends to litigate with you in court to take your robe, give him also your cloak." The sixth is to have mercy and distribute freely what we have, as he told us in Saint Luke's Gospel: "Give to anyone who might ask of you, not only for the sake of giving to whoever is begging you but also to open up the sphere of the common good." Giving what is superfluous to a person in extreme need is a duty of justice; giving what we need for ourselves when God so asks us to do is council. Indeed, the practice of this council underscores the greatness of mercy, and the spirit kindled with God's love is inflamed. It is therefore necessary to give in order to receive; and to give for God to receive from God. There is nothing to fear about ever lacking anything which we give for God, even if we needed it for ourselves. Give, and you will be given a good, brimful, overflowing measure, and God's goodness will be poured out into your bosom.

As the Lord wants the good creature to be, that is poor, obedient, chaste, charitable, meek and merciful, so does he also want him to speak simple words, and this is the seventh council. "Let your words be," he tells us, "yes, yes, and no, no, simple and unpretentious, always affirming the truth, and contradicting and denying anything which is a lie. Let the tongue be a faithful interpreter of the heart's feelings, and in the same manner let affirmation and denial be in the mouth just as in the heart. For you have heard what was said in old times: *Do not commit perjury.* But I say unto you: Do not swear in any manner." The eighth council, which directs us to flee sinful occasions, was well expressed by the Saviour when he said: *If your eye gives you scandal, pluck it out and throw it away from you.* Saint Augustine says about this: "Do not heed to the letter of this council, for the Lord does not command you to cut off or tear away any limb, but to avoid and flee sinful occasions. Do all your works with a righteous intention and with a healthy and pure purpose, which is the ninth council which he himself gives you: see that you do not work your righteousness before men, just to be seen and praised by them. Do it, yes, so that it may be seen by God and be pleasing to Him, so that men may then praise the Lord and glorify Him. This is what he later confirmed saying: so *may your light be seen before men, that by seeing your good works they may glorify your Father who is in heaven.* Man would have little merit in his good works, if he only sought in them his own benefit and profit, forgetting to give glory in them to Him who gave him his grace to work." Yet since it is spelt out that deeds and words have to fully conform with each other, so that the Lord's virtue and grace may shine upon them, Jesus Christ gave us this tenth important council: *Whoever does or practices good works, and teaches men how to practise them, he will be great in the kingdom of heaven.* It is not enough doing only one of the two things, both must be practised together, as otherwise you would stumble upon that obstacle which was the hallmark of the Pharisees, and which is recorded in the Gospel of Saint Matthew by these words: "They tie heavy and unbearable burdens on men's shoulders, but do not want themselves to put out a single finger of their hand to help them carry it." They are men who talk but do not act; this is why the Lord says that whoever acts and teaches will be the greatest in the kingdom of heaven. And in the Acts of the Apostles we read that Jesus Christ himself practised this great council: *I start, Jesus says, by acting and teaching.*

No less important is the eleventh council, by which Jesus Christ taught us to put all our hope in our Heavenly Father, saying to us: "Do not wish or care about what you have to eat and drink, and about your footwear and clothes, for these things are sought after avidly and eagerly by all those who have their hearts attached to the world. Your Heavenly Father knows that you need all these things, and He will not allow you to be let down your hopes. If anything, look at the beautiful feathers with which the birds flying in the air are covered. They do not work, spin or gather grains in the barns and yet your Heavenly Father cares for them. See the beauty and gallantry vesting the beautiful lilies of the valleys. Truly, I tell you, not even Solomon with all his glory ever boasted as much magnificence as any one of them. If the hay of the field, which God dresses with such splendour, grows today and is burned tomorrow in the oven, how much more will He take care of each one of you? So do not worry, for the hairs of your head are counted and not even one of them will fall without your Father's will, for each one of you is more valuable before Him than all the birds flying in the sky."

The final and twelfth council is that of fraternal correction. Little have we talked about it; however, let us say, that at times it is a mere council and at others a formal precept. When a brother is corrected about slight or venial faults, and such correction is given coming out from the depths of that charity which ought to be commonly shared with one's neighbour, then it is council; but when it is given about a mortal sin, then it is a precept, and a precept which is always binding, though not for ever, but as relating to situations of place and time, and when it is believed that correction will be useful. This precept binds high dignitaries and government officials, and all those who should care, and it is incumbent on them to do so, for their subordinates. And by observing and keeping the same proportions, the council may be practised, for it is always a good thing to practise charitable works.

When all these doctrines were so linked and intimately related with the evangelical poverty advised and practised by Jesus Christ, he became aware that the young man whom he had advised was losing heart; besides this had also touched the heart of his apostles. So he looked at the young man very attentively and said to him: "Truly, it is very difficult for those who have many riches and who love them, to enter in the kingdom of God." And as they were more frightened by his words, he said to them again: "Sons, how difficult it is for those who put their trust in their riches to enter the kingdom of God! It is easier for a camel to pass through the needle's eye, than for a rich man to enter into the kingdom of heaven." Origen quotes Celsus the philosopher as saying that Christ had taken this sentence from Plato's works, having written that: "It is impossible to reconcile virtue with greed, or that there cannot be a holy man who excels in goodness and is at the same time excessively rich, as if Eternal Wisdom had to beg from Gentiles the sublime principle of divine goodness." Jesus Christ rebukes and condemns greed, and the excessive love and abuse of riches; but according to his principles heroic virtue is not always irreconcilable or incompatible with them. The proverb which Jesus Christ used to express his thought was a common and familiar way of saying things between Hebrews and other eastern peoples; with it he did not mean anything but that it involved lots of hard work or that it was almost impossible for misers and great lovers of wealth to gain salvation. Yet, terrified as they were, the apostles then replied by an overindulgence of admiration in which they found themselves by the terrifying simile they had just heard, and said to him: "Where can we find anyone not ridden with love for worldly goods?" But Jesus Christ, always a wise and sweet Master, looked at them with compassion in his eyes and said to comfort them: "It is true that man cannot be saved only by his human efforts. It is also true that the rich are not saved without extraordinary grace. But what is impossible for the creature is not impossible for the Creator, for He holds such effective graces in his treasury that, without taking away men's freedom, they raise up to heaven those who find it most difficult to detach themselves from the world."

Jesus Christ did not want his apostles to become demoralised, fall out of spirits, and lose heart. So to encourage them to walk on the new path he had laid for them, he hinted at himself with that same sweetness with which he knew how to stoke their faintest hopes. He assured them that no matter how impracticable his doctrine seemed to them, he would have the happiest success in the task with which he had entrusted them; which was like telling them: "My spirit has not yet been poured out on earth, do not despair, for when I shall send Him from the height of my glory, you will admire his power. On your part do that which depends on your preaching and the examples you give; my spirit will finish what is missing. In spite of the greed that reigns in the world, you will see the rich despise their riches, make good use of them or renounce them, and mingle with the poor to embrace my Gospel and practise its perfection."

The Prince of the apostles was encouraged by this speech, and knowing that he and his companions were extremely happy to have embraced evangelic poverty, he spoke on behalf of all and said to Jesus Christ: "Well, you see Lord, we have left everything with the aim of following you and of living always in your company, on the path your examples. So what will our reward be? What will become of us?"

After hearing so many of Jesus Christ's doctrines on the virtue of poverty, and such great and healthy council, the apostles wanted to know what prize was awaiting them. But since Jesus Christ was pleased to repeat to them such useful and comforting lessons as he had given to all those who thought of the joy of imitating them, he was pleased to be asked that question. So he replied: "In truth I say to you, that your reward will be so great that you can hardly think of it or expect it to be the same. When things are renewed and I will sit on the throne of Majesty, you will sit on twelve thrones to judge the twelve tribes of Israel. You will be judges of all the nations of the earth, of which I will form from now on a single Church that will be my people and my inheritance, as those tribes have been until now. You will exercise this judgment on the day of the general resurrection, when the souls of all the deceased will be united with their bodies. And then you will see this man whom you now see in everything like you, sitting on the throne of his glory, presiding over all men and judging their good or bad deeds to award them their corresponding prize or punishment."

Many Church Fathers and sacred writers want Jesus Christ to speak here of the renewal of the world by baptism, as if the Lord were to say: "When things are renewed, when my Church is born by baptism, which will be the character of my subjects, and what will happen when the Son of Man after his death and resurrection will sit at the right hand of his Father, is that you will also take your place on twelve thrones. From there you will exercise the spiritual authority which I give you absolutely over the twelve tribes of Israel, those who must first take care of you, and after that over the whole world; for the empire of the Church, which I have come to found, will extend from one pole to the other and all the nations of the world will receive the soft yoke of my law."

Saint Bernard, who for God's sake had renounced the world and all its things and retreated to the solitude of his beloved Clairvaux, says: *So see, Lord, that we have renounced all things and we follow you.* These are the enchanting words which have indeed persuaded men all over the world to abandon and belittle earthly life, counselling them of voluntary poverty. These are the words which fill the cloisters with monks and the deserts with anchorites. These are the words which strip Egypt of its power and rip off its most precious jars and jewels. This is the living and effective word of God which converts souls with joyful imitation of holiness and with the faithful promise of truth. And indeed, I would say very well, we have renounced all things, not only our possessions, but also the very desire to possess, and most specifically those things that affect and hurt the heart, more than owing to worldly lust but due to the marrow or core they hold. This is the main reason why they have to voluntarily renounce all things, for there are hardly any of them that are not founded on a disorderly fondness, and not conceived by worldly lust. Our nature is very prone to cling and lean, frequently and with lots of violence, to the things of the world; so it is necessary that we keep our nature at bay, contain it and tame it. So seek you, being ready to give up all things of the world to count yourself among the number of those who renounce to all, and if you intend to follow him who stripped himself of everything for you and took the form of a slave, also to strip yourself of your heart's affections. First and foremost, seek to renounce even to your own desires so that, not being their slave, you will arrive to Jesus Christ's true discipleship. Shed off and throw away forever from you that very grievous burden which oppresses and annoys you. Abandon those five pairs of oxen which you have foolishly bought, because being oppressed with the fatal inclinations, together with carnal lust, to which these five senses drag you, you would not be able to come to the feast of spiritual weddings for which the Spouse is calling and inviting you.

The Lord answered his apostles, and showed them three prizes acquired by those who give up everything to follow him and walk along the same path as himself. The first is, that they will be judges with the supreme judge when he comes to judge the living and the dead. And he told them this about it: "You who, in giving up all things, have followed me by imitating my way of life *in the regeneration*, that is in the judgment or at the time of the regeneration of mankind, not in the first one when souls are regenerated by water and the Holy Spirit in baptism, but in the second one, when the bodies are regenerated in the universal resurrection, then you will sit on twelve seats to judge the whole world. You shall sit next to the Son of Man, since just as he was judged in the form of man, so will he also come to judge in human form, and just as you have followed him in human form, so also when he will sit on the throne where he will show his power, you will sit next to him when he comes to judge with highness and greatness." The twelve apostles represent the universality of all saints who, having renounced everything for Jesus Christ, will accompany him in his court on judgment day; and the twelve tribes also represent the universality of all the good and bad who must be judged. Happy are those, Oh Jesus Christ, who embrace voluntary poverty and leave everything to follow you! Happy indeed and so assured will your chosen ones be on the day of such a resounding conflagration of the elements, of such a tremendous scrutiny of merits, and of such great and terrible variance in judgments. On that day there will not be just one judgment, but many judgments. There will be the judgment of the chief authority in which the Hallowed Trinity will judge. There will be the proclaiming judgment, by which Jesus Christ, true God and true man, will pronounce the sentence. And there will be the judgment of the accessory divinity, which is the judgment by which the apostles and other saints, sitting as advisers to the supreme Judge, will give their assent and approval to the sentence uttered by the Saviour, not by their own authority, but through the assent and union of will they have with the Redeemer's will. The Venerable Bede says about this: "It is in truth a fair and worthy retribution for those who gave up everything and despised the glory of the world for the love of Christ, to be associated with him on judgment day and to assist him as councillors when the world and all its doings will be judged by eternal fire; for while they lived in the world they certainly did not want, for the love of Christ, in any way or respect to separate themselves from him, so also reaching with him the peak of the power to judge.

The second prize due to whoever leaves everything to follow Jesus Christ, will be the overabundance they will receive in comparison to the little which is all they left, because they will receive one hundred for one, that is, one hundred times of the spiritual consolation and abundance of virtues, a hundredfold value of gifts and of graces, or one hundred thousand times greater than all the delights and riches of the land they would leave. They gave up a house in the world, and reached an eternal palace in glory. They left an earthly father and acquired a heavenly and divine One. They left earthly human brethren, and they shall have for their brother Christ and all the angels and saints in heaven, whose joys, compared to others, shall be had by those receiving a greater advantage of a hundredfold. Finally, they will receive the third prize consisting in God's joy, His glory and eternal blissful beatitudes, with which nothing in the world can in the least compare. In the world everything is hard and perishable; in heaven everything is permanent and eternal. In the world there is man with all the lust and sins that surround him, in heaven there is God with all the majesty and greatness belonging to Him and with His beauty and splendour filling everything with happiness and joy. On earth there are sin, miseries and misfortunes, sighs and tears, and then death. In glory there are no sorrows, no sufferings, no tears, no sighs, no death, but eternal living and joy, a perpetual peace and a most substantial and complete benefit.

Most appropriately Saint Augustine writes about these prizes, and says: "Because men like living on earth, they are promised life; and because they fear very much dying, eternal life is offered to them. It seems that it should have been enough for real comfort of human weakness that you were told you would have eternal life. It seems it would suffice to allay human frailty to be told that you would have eternal life. Let us love it then, and by loving it we will know how much we must work to achieve it, seeing that the men who love present, temporary and finite life, when overwhelmed with the fear of death, work as much as they can, not to remove it but to delay it. Truly it can be said that this voluntary poverty, which receives a hundredfold in reward right now, and eternal rewards in future, is truly blissful. To barter for such a great prize a person can well leave his father and mother, brothers and sisters, wife and children, fields and inheritance, to practice more perfectly and preach the Gospel with more freedom. He will receive a hundredfold in this life and eternal life thereafter. There is no comparison between the spiritual goods enriching his soul and the temporal ones he leaves behind; so that the gifts he receives on earth and the joys he encounters in heaven may not be considered as bartering, but always as extremely gainful prizes. And even the persecutions done by the Lord's enemies, which Jesus Christ says that despite all this cannot be missed by those who follow him, will serve only as an increase in the affection shown by the faithful, being those who will vigilantly attend to their needs and act as father, mother, brothers and sisters. So that after being so well paid in this world for their sacrifice, they will enjoy eternal bliss in future times, as the Lord concludes."

What the Saviour says here briefly is confirmed with long experience by the joys felt even in this life by those who have voluntarily renounced themselves and their goods for Christ. And these consolations supersede by so much those promising the abundance of temporal life, that no one in the world can have so much satisfaction and joy in his delights as much as that had by a poor man following Christ in being hungry and thirsty, in walking naked and being cold, and in suffering all discomforts for him. This variance in joy is born from the difference between the goods relinquished for Christ and those found with Christ. For Jesus Christ's servant leaves undone and false goods, and finds real and true goods; he leaves movable goods that change with time and do not pass beyond this life, and finds goods far superior to them, which with death are perfected and exchanged with other greater ones; he leaves goods of the body, and finds goods of the soul; he leaves false honours, and finds true honour; he leaves delights, or vicious ones, or that can easily self-corrupt, and in their stead finds delights not having, and which cannot have, a mixture of filth in them, accompanied by the pure and lasting joy which penetrates and fills the heart and raises him above himself, sighing for the day of eternal life.

Consider well this recompense, be happy and thank God for predisposing so favourable a deal of earning right here from earth a hundredfold for one, while yet after providing you with eternal life. Take this holy thought into account frequently, which you can easily do with prayer. Be ashamed of yourself that so much stupidity and madness are found in you, that you dare discard a hundredfold for just one, and eternal life for worldly life. And seeking to make yourself like the apostles in everything, forsake all that you possess to follow Christ. Do not forget that the Christians of the early Church sold everything they had to embrace the law of the Crucified Christ, and laid their gold and silver at the foot of the apostles themselves. In this one thing they did they contemplated two other more gainful and worthy actions. Since these early faithful abhor gold and silver, they put it at the feet of the apostles, and since they equally despise it they do not receive it, nor do they touch it with their hands; indeed they accept it, but only to share it among the Lord's poor ones. You are Christ's steward; give out gladly and joyfully all your extras to the poor, and you will deserve eternal life.

CHAPTER 57

THE LANDOWNER TENDS TO HIS VINE- YARD, AND GIVES EVERYONE AN EQUAL PAY; A RICH MAN ASKS FOR ACCOUNTS FROM HIS STEWARD, AND THE EVIL RICH MAN IS BURIED IN HELL, WHILE THE BEGGAR LAZARUS IS PLACED AMONG GOD'S FRIENDS (MT 20:1-16; LK 16:1-9; 19-31)

UNFATHOMABLE are the treasures of the Lord's mercy and grace, ever incomprehen- sible and worshipful are the designs of His Providence; so much so that whoever wants to examine and probe them will perish immersed in the immense ocean of His greatness. So that it is necessary for us to worship and follow constantly all inspirations of grace and pleas for mercy. It is known that the Saviour entered right through the hearts of the Jews when he offered them prizes as great as those which we have just seen in the previous chapter. He desired to encourage them to follow him and to love him sincerely, much more than temporal riches, always so full of dangers for those who seek eternal salvation; and those who were infatuated by concerns and cares, to substitute the time of present life with an unalterable tranquillity founded on the cares of Divine Providence; and an eternal kingdom after death in the abode of the blessed. Yet Jesus Christ, foreseeing with his infinite wisdom that these men, blind with their love for riches and hardened with their greed, would yield inestimable advantages to the nations, and that the Gentiles would make their own what they despised, concluded his interesting instruction with this very sad prophecy for the Jews, namely that *Many of the first will be the last, and the last will be the first*, that is many of the Jews who have been among the first to be called will be the last in my Church, which is the kingdom of God on earth. They will be so few, that they could barely be counted for anything. On the con- trary the Gentiles, who will be the last to be called up, will come in great numbers to give their name in my kingdom, and the congregation of my faithful disciples, being spread all over the world, will be called the Church of the nations.

In truth, Jesus Christ had demanded from the apostles an effective renunciation of all things, of all temporal business, of temporal requests, of goods and wealth, and even of their own family and kinship, to entrust them with the preaching of the Gospel. And this was very much required and necessary for only in this way could the conversion of the world be realised and the foundation of the Church consolidated. But Jesus Christ, infinitely wise and far-sighted, knew well the sinister meaning some of his enemies would give to these and other verbal statements he made and were to be uttered shortly after by his disciples. And so that they might be able to understand his preaching to them, or at least to put them in a position of duly understanding it when they saw it being fulfilled, he exposed it with a more individual meaning in a mysterious parable. *The kingdom of heaven,* he said to them, *is like a Landowner who went out at dawn to rent day labourers for his vineyard.* The kingdom of heaven here means, according to Jesus Christ himself, that part of the Church which militates on the ground, whose members, knowing and worshipping, fearing and loving the true God, prepare to unite with the other part, which enjoys him in the homeland. God, who has been the great Landowner of the world since it started, who existed in its creation, was choosing people in every age to cultivate this vineyard. It did not need material hands to till and cultivate until it bore fruit. He may well have done it himself, but he wanted to honour his creatures by allowing them to take part in other people's work of sanctification, which is something greater than having created heaven and earth. His vineyard is also our soul, planted with his preaching, surrounded by his law, watered with his blood, guarded by his angels, cultivated by his apostles and ministers, and finally entrusted to all creatures to work in it and not let the beasts of passions cut it down and steal its loveliness and beauty of its fruit. He chose the day labourers and proposed to each one of them the prize of his daily wage, which was to be a denarius coin, and having set the price and entered the contract he sent them to work in his vineyard.

A covenant implies rigorous righteousness and a sacred duty of man, to contribute with a full day's work to God his Lord and Supreme Maker; to give him the works and affections of his whole life, for which God promises him heaven in repayment for them all. When God sets this unison with his vineyard, he would be giving value to our works, subjecting them to a fabric superseding their own, making them worthy by his grace of what they could not be worthy on their own. Who might not be encouraged to work on his salvation when he sees this public writing, by which God binds Himself to repay Christian works with heavenly recompense? The Lord is faithful and He will fulfil the covenant. He has put us in this world to work and not to rest, to work on our salvation and not to hoard wealth. All the work of life, whether short or long, is none else but a day's labour, after which we will receive our reward. God calls us and seeks us for this work from dawn to dusk; that is, from the beginning to the end of our life. He calls us with inspirations through angels, preachers and confessors, good books and good examples, and also through success and misfortune. He constantly rebukes our laziness and the little care we put into matters concerning our salvation, telling us day and night: Go and work in my vineyard and I will give you your wages.

How could it be that you do not work in a vineyard to make it fertile? It is tied, pruned and manured. The vine implores when it is pruned, and if it were possible it would complain that it was feeling bad; but the labourer's reply would be that this was necessary for its own good, because otherwise it would not bear fruit, it would be cut and thrown into the fire. We weep and grieve when God takes away our goods, our health or that which we love most, and without reason we complain about God; sure, if He did not act likewise with us, we would not bear any fruit. It is therefore necessary that each one takes here the pruning shears and cut in his heart all that which he finds redundant, for there is but one remedy, and that is, either suffer here the iron or hereafter the fire. This is what God himself meant to us when in the book of God's purest loves with our soul He says (Sg 2:15): *Catch us the foxes, the little foxes, that spoil our vineyards, for our vineyards are in blossom.* He wants us to have great care, not only in cultivating, but in safeguarding our soul's vineyard; so that He complained through David's mouth that His fence had been destroyed, for it was so exposed for the picking of all passers-by, saying further that: *The wild boar from the forest ravages it, and all that move in the field feeds on it* (Ps 79:13).

This vineyard also means, in a most particular manner, the Holy Church which Jesus Christ has planted and watered with his blood. The workers are the apostolic holy men who have been called to cultivate it, and who will be after their death abundantly rewarded if they worked in it dutifully and properly, for it is for this that they are sent. Blessed are those who work for the salvation of souls! Theirs is indeed a laborious task, they need take the brunt of the day and of the heat to go with it. As Saint Paul said to Timothy: *Work on everything and fulfil your ministry. Work as a good soldier of Christ.* Oh, of what glory and benefit this work is for man! How noble, how holy, useful and of great merit it is! How do they strive to work night and day in the devil's vineyard, and how few care to work in Christ's vineyard! Whoever fails to give good example and causes scandals, leading others to sin, can say in all truth that he is Satan's minister and that he works in his vineyard, whose bunches are full of asps' venom and the gall of dragons, and which will later serve to drug him in hell. Only he who builds up his neighbour and works on him with his speeches and good examples, can truly say that he works with God for the salvation of others. Oh my vineyard, the Lord says, which I have picked out of all trees! The vineyard which I have planted with my hands and watered with my blood. Why have you yielded to me a bitter fruit and such a rough wine? Have I not cultivated you enough? I will sing to my beloved One the song of my cousin to his vineyard. My beloved One had a vineyard which he had planted in fertile and abundant soil. He fenced it around, built a tower in its midst and built a winery. He hoped it would produce good fruit for him, but it did not produce anything but wild fruit. So that now, you inhabitants of Jerusalem and men of Judah, judge between me and the vineyard. What should have I done that I did not do? Was I right in hoping it would give me good grapes and not sour fruit? So now I will show you what I will do with my vineyard. I will remove its fence and let it be exposed to thieves; I will tear down its defending walls, and it will be in everyone's way. What will those who have so cynically, presumptuously and scandalously put their devastating sickle to the most pleasant vineyard of the Church say to this? This is the most dreadful sentence uttered from the mouth of the supreme vineyard grower. He will put those wretches to a miserable death, and let out the vineyard to other farmers who will give him the fruits in their season (Mt 21:41).

It can also be understood that this vineyard is Jesus Christ's passion, which he had to bear with torments to extract from it the wine of his precious blood. We ought to work in this vineyard by constantly meditating on all that. This vineyard could also be understood as the sacred Eucharist. In holy communion we unite ourselves with Jesus Christ's body, like a shoot to its vine, from which it receives its sap, its spirit, its juice and its fruit. "I am the vine," Saint John recounts (Jn 15:5) "and you are the shoots; so who is united with me and I with him, will bear much fruit, for apart from me you can do nothing. Whoever does not remain in me will be cast out like the useless shoot, and he will dry, and they will get hold of him and throw him into the fire where he will burn. I am the true vine and my Father the labourer; he will trim all shoots bearing no fruit in me, and he will prune all those bearing fruit that they may yield more; abide in me, that I will abide in you. Just as the shoot cannot yield any fruit if it is not united with the vine, neither can you if you are not in me." Are you a green shoot by chance? Are you a useless shoot? Even so, you have not yet been cut from the vine; but be afraid, as you might be.

At the third hour, that is, at about nine in the morning, the Landowner returned again to the town square, where he found many standing and with nothing to do, and he said to them: "You too, go to work in my vineyard, that I will give you your due reward." Approving of such an advantageous offer, they went to the vineyard and settled down to work along with the others. How many spend their childhood and youth in the awful leisure of their vices! What do you live for if you do not serve God? It is pitiful indeed that although we were bought at a high price we do not even want to give to God that heart which we give to the world in vain. However, to know the kindness of the Landowner, it should be noted that he did not blame them for their offences and ignorance in which they showed themselves to be deeply rooted, but rather that he provided them with the prize of virtue with which he invited them. The Lord shows great compassion in going out to look for day labourers, yet knowing that unless there is a wage in view he cannot take them to work in his vineyard. Blessed are those who serve God only to please Him; but He does not omit those who only work if prompted with a wage. Such concern is good, since with it God moves into idle people's lives, but let us use it to proceed in serving God, without thinking of the prize which charity certainly has in store. We should also note that these day labourers went along without saying anything and gladly accepted the work they were given. They did not resist their calling, for which they received the promised reward in good time.

At the sixth and ninth hours, that is, around noon and three in the afternoon, the Landowner went out again in the town square, and finding other unemployed men he also sent them to his vineyard. These day labourers had not been in the town square when the Lord first went out, for we must believe that had he seen them he would also have sent them to work. It does not lie in anyone's hands to go to the place arranged for their salvation if God does not take them there. Man's footsteps belong to the Lord, only he can set them right driving them in the right direction. Who led the eunuch to the place where he was to be taught in faith and baptised? Who led the Samaritan woman to the well where she was to fetch heavenly water? Who sent the other sinner to the banquet where her sainthood was awaiting her? It is most certain that God speaks to us in the heart after having led us into solitude.

At the eleventh hour, which was the last before sunset, he saw again in the town square several idle men standing there, and he said to them: "What do you think about all day standing idly without doing anything?" "It was," they replied, "because no one gave them work to do." To which the Father replied: "Go also you to my vineyard, and work with those who are already there working." This was a hopeless time indeed at sunset: who would ever hope finding at that time of the day anyone who gives him a day's wage? What might we clearly state here but that there is no age, occasion or time that would not suit anyone to work on the task of eternal salvation? How many times does God go out in his Church seeking out those who have lost the best part of their life, without remembering him or providing good works for eternity? At the time when man is sought by God, whether young or old, he must begin to serve him. The remedy lies in prompt and fervent penance for the ongoing abuse of God's gifts and the stubborn hardness of all his life.

Undoubtedly, the Landowner's reply was addressed well and it contained a terrible rebuke against the idleness of those who, because of it, complained they had not until then found anyone who would give them work. What do you expect to hear from him who at the dawn of your life called you to faith and who is all the time calling you to do penance? Do you presume to justify that hopeless idleness of your vices without finding anything that excuses you? What do those persons think who have unfortunately lived in laziness for years without having worked for a single day, neither in the care of their soul, nor in the Church of God, or in being of any use to others? Are they perhaps waiting to be told: "Go ye also to work in my vineyard before death arrives?" The endless life of evil should be condemned by youth if they want to live it well in their prime. There will be terrible judgment for those who live badly and idly for some sixty or seventy years. Cry bitterly over the days and years which you cannot bring back, passing the last hour that you have left in cultivating the vineyard. For God is giving it to you, so put your hand to the hoe; being weak at your age restores the fervour of desire and humility in you. The desire to return to early years to live the time you did not give to God will somewhat serve to absolve you. Think well, in letting yourself go you are lost if God does not seek you. Any work you do without His word, and His mission and His help, will become known as idleness; it will serve you nothing for eternal life.

It should be noted that although he rebuked the idle men, he did not dismiss them but rather invited them with the same reward, to be acquired at the same cost and with less work. It is unfortunately all too true that old persons who spent their lives idly tend to fall out and even surrender to despair when they see themselves already so near to death. But who could it be that, no matter how many days he has lived without doing anything good, on hearing such news of mercy, will despair of God's remedy? Trust God for a single moment of your life, adopt Him in your life and go to Him. For it takes very little time for charity to make up for what passion has destroyed and failed to gain. Saint Chrysostom observes that on this occasion the Evangelist says that the Landowner found others idle *at the meeting place* and notes that by meeting place we must understand the world, where slander, insults and strife, on various deals and money matters, are always hindrances which move a person and cause turbulent upheavals in him; in this place the souls of men are also presented as being mercenary. This *place* or *big market* represents two traders or buyers, namely God and the devil. Some are so blind as to sell their soul to the devil for a very vile price; they sell it for a small delight of temporal life, such as the lustful and gluttons do. There are others who sell it for worldly honours and glory, and these are the proud and the vain. And there are yet others who sell it for riches and temporal benefits, and these are the thieves and the misers. Let us flee from doing deals with the devil for it is inevitable that we lose out; instead we should sell our souls to Jesus Christ who will buy them with the infinite price of his precious blood.

Idleness is failing to do the works which ought to be given to Jesus Christ by right; so that sinners should be regarded as dead persons, and not idle ones. He who serves the devil is dead; he who fails to do the works of God is idle. He who steals the stranger, is dead; he who does not give up his own things, is idle. So while you cultivate the works of mercy and exercise yourself in them, you may well say that you worked in the Lord's vineyard; and beware, and never forget the words uttered by the great Landowner to the idle: "How is it," he said to them, "*that you are over here*, that is, in such a dangerous place, so transitory, foul-smelling, full of abomination and scandals, such that it would suit you better to depart from it? Do you not know that life is short, the road is long, the strength of your virtue is weak, to stay all day long in such an open place? Now that you have the chance of a favourable time and security of wage, not just any wage but a good wage, it is an unforgivable offence that you remain for so long in idleness without caring to take advantage for your own salvation." And although they replied that no one had hired them until then, he did not really believe their answer such as to excuse them from guilt, so that he told them further: "Get going to work in the vineyard you too, believing in your mind, confessing with your mouth and practising with your works all that I command you to believe, confess and practise." The Lord's work must certainly be done, so that Chrysostom himself continues: "*Whoever does not work in this age, that is, in this world, will not eat or rest in the future age, that is in heaven.* This day or this age, are the day and age of works; the one that follows, if one works well here and to one's benefit, will be a day of rest, and it will ultimately be a day and age of glory. So that it is clear that, at any time and being of any age, God calls men to grace and glory, for there are always some who on hearing the Lord's voice obey him and are rewarded for doing so. If penance were sincere, it would never be too late.

Not only does the Lord reward those he called to work very early, but he also rewards and pays those he calls in the evening. And so when his procurator arrives he tells him to call the workers. He had a procurator, and it was not because of this that the Landowner believed he was free from caring for the day labourers and being only present when they were paid their wages. What lesson is so important for all those who neglect matters relating to their salvation, entrusting others to pray for them, fast or make other mortifications? God is Lord of all and his Only Son Jesus Christ can be called His procurator, for in his hands the Father deposited the important business of calling the Gentiles, as well as the Jews and all the nations of the universe, to the bosom of the new vineyard, the Holy Church, which he had come to plant. And he can believe, without risk of being misunderstood, as Saint Augustine says, that it is to him to whom his Eternal Father says: "Call the workers before the court and give them their due wage," which is their eternal pay. And take note that he does not say "call out the idle", for he wants to grant rest to those he calls, which is only found after work. He wants to give them joy, which is only found after sadness; he wants to give them peace, which is not achieved until after struggle; he wants to give them the crown, which is not achieved until after triumph. This is why he does not tell him to call the idle, but those who have worked; and all men are condemned to work, whatever their condition and status. The great and mighty easily cast on strangers' shoulders the burden which God placed on their own. They demand honour and profit from their office and dignities, burdening others with work and bother. Who can list the evils arising out of this fateful principle? The evening is the end of life, in which everyone is to be given the reward for his works, and until then whoever wants reward and not punishment must persevere in working faithfully. This work includes not only the keeping of God's commandments, but also the commands laid down by the particular laws and obligations of one's class, profession and state.

The Lord called upon all to pay workers their wage on the same day of work, not wanting to defer such payment for another day, for he was well aware of that awesome sentence of the Holy Spirit (Sir 34:22), *To take away a neighbour's living is to murder him; to deprive a worker of his wages is to shed blood.* He paid everyone with the utmost punctuality, starting with the last and finishing with the first. In such doing he wanted to put the Gentiles on the same level as the Jews in giving his reward for the faith to which he had called them. God does not let time pass to reward merit. Only a few moments of fervour were needed to convert the thief from the ordeal of offences to the seat of the righteous. There is therefore no reason to ask God for a long life, but for fervent charity. Those who had gone at the eleventh hour walked in and each received a denarius coin, and the same was paid to those who had been sent to work in the first hour of the day. They assumed that having laboured more than others, and made a greater fortune, they would also receive a much higher wage; so when they drew near bearing this self-confidence, and just received one denarius like all others, they took it but still murmured against the Landowner. There is little point in overcoming greed, taming the flesh and exercising long years of penance, if these virtues yield fruit of pride, of considering ourselves better than others and of being more worthy of reward. In the first ones the Lord rewarded the humility by which they believed themselves to be inferior to others, and punished in them the pride by which they believed themselves to be greater. Humility puts the lesser ones on a par with the greater ones in the award, and it is almost always a cause which the Lord anticipates. We are all servants of God, our health and life belong to Him, so do our wisdom and time He grants us belong to Him. They always and in all belong to Him, for we have received everything from him: so that we act very badly when we do not pay Him back anything, and it would be rather us who should be seen as useless persons. By what right do we dare bother God because He gives us less graces than others? And when he gives us more, how dare we expect Him to give us what we are entitled to?

"This would serve the creature, properly speaking, to seek glory in his works and not to receive good thoughts, desires and works as God's gifts making him deserve heaven. How could you ever grumble against God knowing that you are not worth anything in His presence, and that the rewards you await are only gifts of the Lord's liberal bounty? He first paid the last ones," Saint Augustine continues saying, "although it would certainly be afterwards given to them all. Yet those who receive it after only working for one or a few hours, receive it before those who worked much more and then received it." And Saint Chrysostom adds: "Justice consisted but to give first to all; but giving first to the latter labourers did not go against righteousness, but only a way of showing mercy, since the others were also paid, and the Lord's mercy did not order otherwise for its distribution, but according to his own will, which always looks first at the heart of the labourer to know what it deserves, rather than the time spent in work." This is why those who do not understand this method of Providence, unjustly complain about God when they envy the preference with which his grace treats humble persons. With the same injustice they grumble against the Lord and point fingers at his way of doing justice, so that it would be themselves who close the door to mercy, and instead of gifts after receive only punishment. They muttered their grumblings against the Landowner and said: "The latter have only worked for only an hour and you have put them on par with us who have carried the brunt of the day and of heat." God greatly abhors these comparisons with which man dares saying how He ought to distribute His graces, without noting that the reward does not match just the good works taken on their own but rather the grace from where they proceed. If this is greater, although involving less work, it has a greater reward; for what God expects from men and rewards is faithfulness, humility, perseverance, purity of intention and the other virtues that crown their works. Those labourers did not portray their work to extol grace and mercy, but to increase their reward. Wretched are all those who complain like those ill-boding workers. It is for this reason that even Saint Paul said: *For I have worked harder than any of the others*, he did not forget to say before and after, *so that what I was and what I do is by the grace of God.* (1 Cor 15:10). It is God's grace that distinguishes us; yet humility is what preserves His gifts.

The Landowner did not lose his natural composure, in spite of the labourer's unjust grumbling, and it so happened that he told him: *Friend, I have done you no injustice nor any wrong. Did you not agree with me on a denarius coin for a day's wage? Take your due, and walk on in peace. As far as I am concerned, I want to give the latter labourers the same wage as you. Why can I not do whatever I want? Should you consider things to be wrong just because I am good, or cannot I be open-handed without you being envious?* There is no doubt that this chiding is vigorous, severe and forceful, even if it is so meek and moderate; human pride really deserves to be sanctioned in being forceful and proudly aspires to inquire about God's judgments, daring to condemn with righteousness what it fails to understand. Where there is no debt and everything is given by grace, there can be no offence. How can you complain about God's Providence? Why do you say, God gives that person so many goods and nothing to me? Is he healthy and me sick? Who are you to argue with God? Humble yourself before Him, worship His judgments, and use the time you spend commiserating to beg for His mercy. Thank Him for fulfilling all His promises in you, without any merit of yours. He could not call you, yet He calls you, adding to His call the covenant of the reward and giving it to you with the utmost faithfulness. Therefore be happy with what the Lord gives you, and never move your lips to complain and grumble, but to thank, praise, and sing eternally the mercies which the Lord used with you. If you received more, do not despise your brother, and if you received less, do not despair, since it shows that the heart is damaged by whoever turns God's goodness into inciting envy, taking scandal of the good He does to sinners.

This is how the Saviour concluded: *It will be that the last will be the first, and the first will be the last; for many are called and few are chosen.* Whoever hears this and has the spirit to prefer anyone, however small and despicable he may be? Let us always fear and humiliate ourselves; let no one trust himself, even if he has been doing penance for a hundred years. But no man distrusts God, even if he has not done anything good in all his life. Do not presume anything, even if you have Peter's faith, nor throw yourself like Judas into the chaos of desperation, even if you are a traitor like him. Whoever might be far from God today may tomorrow receive an extraordinary grace from Him, and with it the glory allotted to it. And whoever now is a very holy person, may tomorrow lose weight and unfortunately commit some offence.

Many are called but only a few chosen. The deluge floods the world, and only eight persons are found in the ark who are saved. Six hundred thousand soldiers left Egypt and only two entered the Promised Land. A wide field is sown, and only a quarter of it bears fruit, and then maybe even less than the amount of grain sown in it. There are only two doors to enter eternity, a big one and a small one. Passing through the big door man enters into eternity without joy, yet the small door leads to a blissful eternity. And there are only two paths leading to the next world, a wide path and a narrow one: the wide path leads to hell, the narrow one to paradise. The wider path is more worn out than the narrow one; so although there are many who are called, only few are chosen. For more prefer taking the wider road sown with roses than the narrower one sown with thorns. For man to be chosen he must essentially walk along the narrow path, stepping on the thorns and mortifying the senses, restraining passions, struggling continuously against nature, suppressing it so to speak and depriving it, not only of illicit pleasures, but also of many other lawful ones. It also takes carving out what is superfluous, leaving only what is necessary, and finally to make man observe all the commandments, and sometimes also the councils, however hard and difficult they may be. How many times should man fear, and what is that greater danger which constantly threatens his salvation? Why does not destiny query whether in being on the wide road, should I not be treading the least worn out and narrow road? Do I lead the life of worldly persons, an easy life full of pleasures, or am I doing penance and mortifying my flesh? It would do man good to delve deep into his soul and dialogue with it, ever repeating to himself: "Many are called and few are chosen. If I want to be one of the chosen, I must walk the narrow path of penance that leads to eternal salvation, and flee from the comfortable and wide one leading to ruin."

"Enter through the narrow door, for the door is wide and the way that leads to destruction is easy," Jesus Christ himself says according to Saint Matthew, "and many are those who enter through it" (Mt 7:13). How narrow is the gate and tight the path leading to life, and few are those who conform with it! And according to Saint Luke, Jesus Christ also said to those who followed him: *"Strive to enter through the narrow gate"* (Lk 13:24). David, who did not have these paths hidden from him, and from whom those of God's mercy and goodness were not hidden either, often told the Lord: "Make me to know your ways, oh Lord, teach me your paths" (Ps 24:4). And elsewhere he repeated: "See if there is any wicked way in me," that is if I walk some evil path, "and lead me through the one taking to eternal life" (Ps 138:24), drawing me away from that leading to ruin. This is what the wise one knew perfectly well; and in order to teach us he wrote in the Book of Proverbs: "There is a way which seems right to a man, but its end is the way to death" (Prv 14:12).

God wants all men to be saved; He brightly shines his light on all who come into the world: He does not deny his grace to anyone; He gave up his Son unto death to save all sinners. He never abandons man unless it is man who departs of his own accord. How is it then, that so few are saved? It all starts from the perversion of nature and a strong inclination to evil. It finds its origin in the little violence which causes man to live by the Jesus Christ's sayings, which are so contrary to those of the world. It starts off by not thinking of God or listening to His divine word. And finally it originates in the contempt with which we treat God in our life, without wanting to take into account that God despises in death those who despised Him in life. Rarely does the devil release in death the prey he held in his hands for a lifetime; they all carry to the tomb the vices of their early years, they sink deep into the marrow of their bones, and they sleep with them in the tomb's ashes. Do we read in the learned Book of Job (2:11). How strange it is that this is so, that so many are condemned and so few are saved? Nor is it any less that, speaking through Hosea, God said to an ungrateful Israel: "If you are lost, oh Israel, it will be your fault; if you are saved, it will be by my grace and mercy; in me is your help, and this has never been lacking in anyone (Hos 13:9)".

Finally, it should also be noted that the loathsome sin of envy was clearly visible in the labourers who grumbled against the Landowner, for paying the same wage to the latter as to the first ones. If men knew well how horrible and savage this passion was, which so often took hold of them, surely they would flee away from it with all their strength. Envy is a dark and devilish passion which carves its hell out of the paradise of the blessed, and its paradise from the hell of the condemned. There is a stray passion which constantly seeks out the light and yet cannot endure it; which always looks at virtue and yet cannot sustain its splendour. It is an unjust and ironic passion which abhors man because he is good, and incriminates him because he is happy and innocent; who would ever wish to muddle the source of all goodness and break the unity which holds the tassel between nature, grace and glory. It is a reckless passion which dares censure Divine Providence, and conspires to obliterate world leadership because it honours and favours virtue. It is a hellish passion whose penalty for causing pain is the happiness of others, of which the envious is deprived, and the penalty of the senses is a burning fire and the worm that gnaws at it. It is an evil passion which fights against the Holy Spirit, taking offence because it does good to men, and pouring out its poison on all the graces which make them worthy of being loved, it denigrates and despises them. It is finally a desperate passion and an evil which does not seek any cure, because it stops the wellspring of the graces of which the envious are deprived, and does not find its remedy but in destroying innocence.

It is simple to understand how grievous was the envy of the day labourers who grumbled against the Landowner as this sin, like all others, has its greatest or lesser level of gravity, according to the greater or lesser evil being wished for one's neighbour, or according to the greater or lesser benefit of which wanting to see him deprived. They would have grieved over the prosperity of their neighbour, and they would have been glad had not even a quarter part of a denarius coin been given to them. This seems to be the first degree of envy. Feeling sorry about the spiritual goods received from God by one's neighbour, is the second. And to be displeased about those received from God himself in the order of supernatural goods, such as those of grace, virtue, perfection and holiness, is the third degree. Satan's sin is in all these degrees found in the envious, and so they must suffer the same ordeal as it. The Book Wisdom says: "Through the devil's envy death entered the world (Ws 2:24)"; so that we should not be taken so much by surprise when we see envy reign to such an extent. Men wage such a deadly and disastrous war against each other that it would be preferable either that they bury themselves forever in solitude fleeing hastily from the world, or avoid all means of communication and contact with everyone, or die in the truth with God's kiss and peace instead of witnessing so many evils and misfortunes as happen continually in the world due to envy.

The conclusion of the Lord's mysterious parable provides us with a preamble showing us his utmost shrewdness; in it all we only see a lengthy comparison between Jews and Gentiles. Those who were the first called to Jesus Christ's Church were excluded from it because of their envy against the nations. And the Gentiles, who were last to be called, took the place of the Jews and preceded them in the kingdom of God, being the most noble and forming the greater part thereof. If we re-examine in parts the whole parable as explained, we will even understand it further; and it does not contain a single word which does not necessarily enter into its whole context to form a complete whole. Finally, if we were to clearly uncover the Jews' unbearable grumblings against the Gentiles, or rather one would say against God, when they saw that the Saviour no longer made that great and exceedingly honourable distinction which had been made for so many centuries to the children of Abraham, considering themselves being the beloved portion of the Lord's inheritance and his unique people. They looked to the reign of the Messiah as the prize owed to them for keeping the Law, promising themselves the restoration of their former superiority by virtue of it. So that they could not endure the nations being received into the Church of Christ without first subjecting them to Judaic laws; that is to circumcision and its obligations, the requirement to offer their sacrifices in the ancient temple, and the obligation to recognise Jerusalem as the seat of Israel's reign and centre of public worship. No one is unaware through apostolic traditions, and more so through the one who was Apostle of the nations, that this was for the Jews the great scandal, and that this equality, together with the abolition of the Law, was the most invincible obstacle they always encountered for the conversion of the sons of Jacob. Saint Paul's great disputes with the guards in the Synagogue revolved very particularly on this free and general calling of all men to the Gospel and to Christ's Church, without distinction of Jew, Greek, Scythian or Hebrew, those yet to be circumcised or the circumcised.

It is also known and I notice that Saint Paul not only responded but constantly crushed the Jews' unjust complaints and grumblings, even showing them the evidence that God did not do any injustice to them; that He had not promised them to keep the Law, which was only in preparation for the Gospel; that Jesus Christ had set them apart by entrusting them with was said by their prophets, causing their nation's Messiah to be born, and starting with them, if they so wished, in founding their new cult. "You did not deserve it," he told them. "God wants to bring strangers into His Church, those who do not deserve it like yourselves. He wants to give to the Gentiles who, like the faithful Jews, believed in the virtue of being sons and heirs of his kingdom, co-heirs with his Son Jesus Christ. Nothing is taken away from you, but it is a law without justification," he further told them. The same thing is given freely to others as to you. What reason do you have then to grumble, and what dare you complain about?

Despite such clear explanations, little did Saint Paul and the other apostles garner in relation to the Jews' wounded spirits. Judea always resisted, and Jerusalem was particularly renowned for its excesses. It is from here that it derives that the Jews constantly looked at the Gospel as a stumbling block to their glory and turned away from it, while the Gentiles on the contrary looked at it as a blissful ending to their blindness. For this reason they were received into the kingdom of God in ever growing numbers; not because the Jews had not been the first to be called and in large numbers, but because few of them responded to the calling and wished to form part and associate with the Messiah's disciples. So this was the sin of the Jews, and as Jesus Christ said, the first called would be the last, and the last would come to be the first. This is not the only foreboding made by Jesus Christ in which he speaks to the unbelieving Jews of their harshness and misery. Jesus Christ kept on talking making sure that fear was aroused in them by speaking to them under different figures of speech which ever made more clear the meaning of what had just been explained, and that both one and the other would help to achieve greatest clarity. For both this and the other parables that follow all indicate that the nearer the Saviour drew to his end, the further did he reiterate his warnings and threatened to bring into the fold the wayward sheep of the House of Israel. He had personally shown painful care for them and so, knowing with his infinite wisdom that the twelfth and last hour of the day had arrived, he did not want to waste a single moment in advancing the salvation of this unbending people, although they made use and profited from everything to cause the most distressing ordeal to their God and Redeemer.

The Lord was followed by his apostles and disciples, and by a fairly large crowd of people, who were joined by many Pharisees, a greedy, stiff-necked and opportunist bunch. Since his aim was to attempt inspiring humility, meekness and poverty to those who followed him and would become like the seed and plant of his new people, he then proposed telling them two well known parables on the use of riches. In one he wanted to teach them the use to be made of goods, distributing them by way of abundant alms, mainly when there might be some suspicion of injustice in acquiring or possessing them, and their real owner is known. In the other he announces, in a manner no less strong than sensitive, the severe punishment that was reserved in eternity for those rich persons who lack compassion. But since the Pharisees were then offended, and greed is an evil with roots which can only be plucked with difficulty and which can easily sprout even in the holiest of states and conditions, the Lord wanted to avoid his disciples shyness and ingratitude so he turned to them and said: *A rich man had a steward whom he entrusted to administer his property on the field, and about which he was charged before him as being a spendthrift, and that he was giving them away behind his master's back. On receiving this news, he sent for him and told him: What is this they are telling me and of which I hear about you? Give me an account of your stewardship, for I have made up my mind to stop employing you as a stewardship, for I am determined not to employ you any more to take care and administer my property.*

All men are God's stewards of his goods: they are wit, health, life, wealth and other gifts, all belonging to the Lord. They are handed to us in order to use them, not according to our whims and impulse, but according to His will and His laws, while still being Lord of all and with the right to withhold them from us or to ask for an account of them whenever and howsoever he wishes. Everything has been given to us by Jesus Christ, God and our Lord, the only, supreme and absolute distributor, so that we may make good use of His gifts; that is, that we may praise Him, glorify Him, love Him and see that He is loved, so that we may help our neighbour in his bodily and spiritual needs, allowing him to share in our goods and comforts.

In the manner how God distributes His gifts, and how we ought to distribute those which we receive, we see clearly the extreme and universal poverty, even of the richest who are in need of everything and are always dependent on God, to whom all the goods they possess belong as does the right to order their use. Who would dare waste others' money, knowing that he will be asked to account for it at the end of the month or of the year? Oh, how few would misuse wealth, time and other natural gifts were they to consider that this property belonged to another master, who decided about how his stewards were to distribute them! Much will be recalled from those who would have received much, and if from the Lord we have received all we possess, we must well believe that he will request back from us everything. We have to give detailed accounts of how we made use of our soul's vigour and the strength of our bodily senses: we must give very detailed accounts of the goods of fortune, of nature and of grace, of our credit and authority, and we must give them to the One who is their only Lord and ours, He who placing us and weighing us on the scales of His justice, will judge with severity whether we have distributed them according to His will: what will sinfulness respond to offended holiness then? It is vanity we now hear; the day will come when speaking truth to us He will say: "What is it that I see in you? What I have given you to help you in your need you have used to incite into your pleasures: you have greedily stopped ordering surplus goods to be sent to the poor. What have you made out of health, wit, power and authority? And finally what have you made out of illness, poverty, persecution and the other works with which I sought to enrich you in virtue? I made you a steward of all this and you rose with it; tell me now what is the amount of this wealth, and of the gain or loss you have made out of it. This accountability will be universal, just and accurate, so that nothing will be hidden from God's knowledge. It will be essential to give an account also of words, thoughts and desires. What harshness!

Soon enough the steward grasped the misfortune he was facing, and seeking his best interests he said to himself: What will I do were my lord to take away my stewardship? I am in a tight corner and my needs are most urgent. I no longer have the strength to work, and I will find it very hard to beg. So I know what I will do and it would be convenient for him to absolve me, so that besides keeping my job people will not fail receiving me in their homes. Who is the spendthrift of God's goods, except a proud poor man who can have no recourse other than to despair and death? If he is weak in doing good, he does not see that he could pray to be attractive or easy, nor would he resolve and desire to do penance. Yet few or none are those who would say to themselves: What have I done? What will I do when it is my time to stand before God? Are my accounts settled well? Are my interests arranged well? Am I speaking haphazardly about being able to appear before the court of Divine Justice? And if I am not, why should not I prepare myself and settle my own accounts now to give them later to God? Saint Chrysostom says: "Present life requires abiding by the commandments, future life will find consolation in having practised them. If you have not done anything here, it is in vain that you expect a prize or reward in future life. That is why the steward said: 'I know what I will do: I will reduce and forgive the debts to my master's debtors, and I will deliver their own riches to them, so that when

I am thrown out of my job they will receive me in their homes.' Just as we cannot imitate this steward's wastefulness, neither can we continue to approve the malice with which he reduced his master's creditors' debts."

So he asked the first one: How much do you owe my master? One hundred measures of oil, the debtor replied. Quite an amount, the steward continued; there goes your obligation, tear it up, sit down and write another receipt stating only fifty measures, and you take the other fifty. A second debtor followed the first one, and owing the master a hundred bushels of wheat, he tore up his obligation and only bound him to pay eighty. All this hurry seen in the steward because of his misdeeds, should serve as a lesson to take timely measures and hold back our anger on our life's last day, because it will arrive, and no one will know when. Saint John says that "Night will come, when no one can work" (Jn 9:4). Fearing this same thing, David said: "Tell me, Lord, the short number of my days, and do not call me to my abode in the middle of them" (Ps 101:4). Saint Paul formed a sort of epilogue or collation about all this doctrine, and continued writing about it in some of his letters. Writing to the Corinthians, he said: "For we must all appear before the judgment seat of Christ, so that each one may receive good or evil according to what he has done" (2 Cor 5:10). And he added writing to Timothy: "Those who desire to become rich, fall into temptation, into the devil's snare, and into many senseless and hurtful desires that plunge men into death and perdition. As for the rich in this world, charge them not to be haughty, not to set their hopes on uncertain riches but on the living God, who abundantly provides us with everything to enjoy; that they do good and become rich in good deeds" (1 Tim 6:9,17).

When the master was informed of his steward's conduct, he could not fail to praise the expertise of a man who, with more prudence than mere skill, laid the way for a plan when the time came for him to lose his management. He did not approve of evil, but he only knew too well how to save his head. So that he is not proposing to us a model of his disloyalty but of his prudence, wherein he states that today's children know better how to run their business, that is to say persons busy with the assets of present-day life, and can apply themselves better and are more skilled in preserving them than the children of light about the benefits of heaven, not ignoring that a dwelling place must be prepared during this life for all eternity. They strive too much and reveal a miser, an ambitious or sultry person reaching the vilest pursuits of his passion, more than a Christian seeking to save himself. The wrongdoer makes the most of everything, using well his assets and paving the way for everything; he runs over everything, and puts right neither sinful ways nor reckless plans. Whim or debauchery render anything useless useful, the weak strong, and it turns all men into tools of their own ruin. What is similar to this in the lukewarm who serve God? They lack light, penance tires them, repetition annoys them and the will falters; so that as time passes it happens that the children of light become children of darkness and anger, due to their own tepidity and paying in death for abusing faith in their lives.

"I am the One who tells you," the Lord concludes. "Imitate these last traits of the steward's prudence if you have done what he did in his primary injustices. If by anything in the administration of public funds, which is a dangerous profession even if profits are made out of it and it is sought after, or in business, where the expected yield is very often obtained with fraud, you would have enriched yourselves at the expense of your brothers without even knowing who these prejudiced persons are, as is often the case with publicans and businessmen despoiled of wrongful riches, let them pass into the hands of the poor. Thus, when you will be called to God's judgment for committing errors, the saints you have nourished and relieved on earth will receive you in eternal abodes, where they would have taken their seat before you." But in order to understand this doctrine perfectly and to close one's mouth to the criminal curse of unjust detractors of the Gospel, it would still be necessary to be well aware of what Jesus Christ said immediately after:

"He who is faithful in small and unimportant things will also be faithful in greater things; and he who is unfaithful and unjust in small matters, will equally be so in big ones. For if in false riches you have not been faithful, who will entrust you with the true ones? And if in others' things, which are not yours, you were unfaithful, who will give you what is yours? It is frightening to see the serenity with which men of the world live in the midst of life's turmoil, which just like the waves of stormy seas beat the fragile boat of human life, and the discomforts, fatigues and labours to which mortals are exposed and suffer to enrich themselves. Everything seems to them easy, soft and bearable to barter insofar as they increase their treasures, wealth and fortune. They do not repent using any means or resources, or omitting vile worship, falsehood and trickery; more often than not they sacrifice justice, virtue and truth to bribery, injustice and treachery, to collect wealth like this steward; or at least to secure their livelihood and fortune by means opposed to all divine and human laws. And they do it in such manner that, seeing the Gospel's relentless enemies with whom Jesus Christ told the mobs to make friends, they keep them close with benefits and win them over to their side with unfairly gained alms, so that after their death they might be received into the eternal abodes." They were scandalised by what he said since, in their opinion, it went very much against reason, fairness and all rights; however these presumed wise men erred about the wisdom of what the Saviour said, interpreted it ominously, and were feeble too when presenting it to the public very inaccurately and much against its original meaning. "Make almsgiving," the Lord says, "not from unjustly acquired riches and goods, but from *the wealth of unfairness.*" This expression clearly meant futile riches, even though they were otherwise lawful and rightfully earned; false, perishable and temporal goods, as commonly referred to in Holy Scripture, as opposed to heavenly ones and to true and eternal riches. This is the force behind Jesus Christ's expressions addressed to the Pharisees on this occasion: "Having unworthily abused earthly riches and employed them so badly, how do you expect God to entrust you with spiritual goods? If you have used these false and outdated riches to further promote your greed and all kinds of vice, how will the Lord make you aware of heavenly things, of evangelical doctrine, of the mysteries and dogmas of religion, of the vocation to Christianity and the predestination to glory, being the true riches and goods which are infinitely more precious than all those of the world?"

Here is the true and literal meaning of the sentence spoken by Jesus Christ, fitting in all the style and wisdom of the holy language. *Immoral riches* is a figure of speech common among eastern languages, like Chaldean, Syriac and Arabic; it is *mammon* according to the Syrians, and *matmon* in Hebrew is taken from the root, *to hide, to conceal,* and it retains a very wide meaning in those languages, like *treasure*; and it applies to gold, silver and other metals; for the fruits of the earth, estates, good personal property and origins, and finally, for all that is understood in the term wealth or goods. The word *mammon* indistinctly stands for the concept of injustice and sinfulness, of falsehood, of vanity or outward appearance, and is so used in many passages of the Old and New Testament, to denote vain, fragile and outdated riches. Earthly riches too, although justly and lawfully acquired, are mentioned in the Gospel using the term immoral riches, as they commonly cause regret and turn their possessors into insensitive, arrogant, greedy, effeminate, negligent and careless persons in the important task of their salvation. For which reason it results that worldly-minded philosophers lack precise information to clearly know, explain and apply the Gospel's sayings and words with principles of wholesome and holy morality. It also results that the whole doctrine of this passage revolves around the core idea of mutual human generosity and charity; on the great positive precept of brotherly love, and on the negative one of not wishing or doing harm to anyone, either in his honour, or in his person or goods and properties. No one can ignore how sacred, according to the Jews' Lawgiver, is the right to property and the harshness with which those who robbed or defrauded their brothers in their property were dealt. It was an injustice which was then only put right, like now, by restitution or full compensation. Elsewhere we shall have occasion to see what this prescribes.

Preaching these doctrines which are so just, fair and holy, it seems that Jesus Christ wanted to say to his disciples, to the mobs that followed him and, more particularly, to the scribes and Pharisees: "I speak to you of the justice by which you must abide in acquiring worldly goods, in the detachment to be kept in their use, of the need to get rid of unlawfully acquired things, and of the obligation to distribute them to the poor, if these cannot be returned to whom they belong. This is not a New Testament; you despise the old one, and I lay it down again." Then he added: "Of the goods which lawfully belong to you, you are bound to give part of them to persons in need, and anyone setting aside this precept will be eternally condemned. Will you perhaps say that in this too I am going against Moses and the prophets? What was it then as to temporal goods that the whole law had not promised on God's part as long as you were naturally fair with your brethren and more charitable with the poor? So listen about this to the parable that I am about to tell you. It deals with what should be believed and practised in terms of the Gospel, and you will not find anything different from what you must believe and practise under the Law."

A rich man lived among your people; he was clothed in purple and fine linen, and was served with all goods splendidly and magnificently at the table. This is a portrait of Babylonian citizenry, namely, that of lovers of the world who fix their lives to worldly goods, neglecting God's love, ever forgetful and ungrateful, entirely separated from the spirit of mortification and penance regarding His gifts. No fault lies with God-given wealth, but in its fostering of pride and the delight of owning it. The goods are given by God, so that by deriving from them the demands arising out of necessity and a well understood decency, we distribute the surplus to the poor according to the laws and purposes of Providence. God is Lord of all goods; man is but their keeper and administrator; and God would be robbed of His privileges were we to use this deposit against His intention. It is not bad to dress in deep red and linen and to use other clothes and precious furniture when this is required as a status symbol, times or some other just cause. But to spend on this unnecessarily, out of pure vanity or for other devious ends, makes one the poor man's wealthy robber. For according to God all that appears to be wholesome and done with a right mind belongs to the poor man, and the rich man does not need it for his morality of truth. This is how all those crazy and costly expenses which could maintain entire poor houses for many years will be measured, and those persons can in no manner be admitted as righteous ones before God's judgment seat. And these are the original types found in the rich man of this Gospel part, himself being none else than a true copy of the Pharisees. Misers and worldly minded persons despised Jesus Christ and his doctrines, saying in public and without excusing themselves that he advised and commanded things which went fully against the Law and the Prophets. For them very rich persons had been very pleasant and acceptable to God and considered to abide by the Law which promised them temporal goods. For they were not astounded that as the Law had been given to worldly men, they were offered less; and since the Gospel was given to people who were to renounce the flesh and live according to the laws of the spirit, they were promised greater things; so that it was the difference in equality between the promises made to the observers of the Law and those of the Gospel, just as equally distant were the precepts imposed upon them. It was said in the Law that *If you love me and listen to me, you will eat from the goods of the earth*; while in the Gospel it is said that *Blessed are the poor of spirit, for theirs is the kingdom of heaven*. The Pharisees' outrage lay in misunderstanding the first proposition, as the Law did not promise temporal goods to be the main reward for a virtuous act which was put to practice. But what he promised them was that in his proposition they might understand the spiritual and eternal goods, which were mainly specified in them.

The Gospel says that the rich man held a daily sumptuous banquet. Good food brings together admiration and worldly fame; but many a time the people's outrage and revenge are also avoided when they become aware that the superfluous cost of banquets feeding those who do not need it, is the result of the theft made of the fruit of their sweat and labours. Feasts do not suit Christians if they do not glow with charity, but only concern flavoured food and refinement, table manners, an exquisite taste and all that which satisfies the flesh and stokes its fires. Despise the big vices arising from these tables, yet those serving them are respected as benefactors of society. The world does not even notice this inconsistency; religion knows it, hates it and condemns it, and prompts plain and easy means of preventing it. God, from whom nothing is hidden, knows well man's heart and uncovers all the evildoing locked inside it; thus, he publicly condemned with this parable what was completely filling the heart of the Pharisees. Saint Gregory notes that it so happens that he does not reveal the rich man's identity by his own name, as he does in the case of Lazarus who begged at the rich man's door. A poor man joined the rich man, as if counterpoising each other; the rich man temporally stands out better than the poor man, and the poor man spiritually better than the rich man. For this reason Saint Chrysostom said: "While the rich man sustains the poor man, he is also sustained by the poor man himself. The poor man's name should be mentioned since he was known and approved by God; so that the poor man is told to *Be glad and rejoice, for your names are written in heaven.* Lazarus, a poor and humble man, deserves being named in the Gospel, but the rich man does not have this honour. The names of the poor who serve God with humility and patience are written in His Kingdom's book; the names of the rich who insult and despise the poor, and misuse their little wealth, are listed in the devil's book. There is a great difference between the lay laws of the world and the benign laws of God! The rich are renowned in the world by their names; those of the poor are hidden, and are not known in the world. And this is why in the Gospel the name of the rich is silenced while that of the poor is mentioned.

It is by God's provision that as soon as a rich man is found in the world, there sits a Lazarus at his doors. By seeing the others' misery, God wants to soften the bronze entrails of the haughty and proud rich man. If he were to compare the luxury of his house with the scarcity of things in that poor family which lives with him, he could not but help notice the horrible disparity taking shape in the eyes of God between the quantity and fineness of his clothes and the poor man's naked state. The rich man's excesses are the hunger of the grief-stricken, and his delights the beggars' needs. It is not strange that on this occasion, on contemplating the rich man's hardness and the misery of Lazarus, Saint Chrysostom exclaims: "Oh you, most miserable of men, no matter how blissful you presume yourself to be, in entering and leaving through the door of your house and seeing the unfortunate Lazarus lying on the doorstep full of wounds, covered by rags and starving to death, you do not consider the death that awaits you and move to show mercy! If you do not consider the precepts of God, nor fear his threats, at least sympathise within your own self by contemplating your mortal condition, and fear that you will not very soon be found like him by a terrible judgment of the Most High. It would have greatly benefited Lazarus and been a very singular consolation of him to be able to take the crumbs that fell from the rich man's laden table; but in the house of men having neither compassion nor mercy, the servants soon learn of the hardness of their masters. The servants themselves despised poor Lazarus, and none of them thought giving him any of the most insignificant leftovers. They threw everything to the dogs and after they went to lick his sores. As the poor man knew of the rich man's hardness, he was pleased to desire the leftovers of his table, and yet did not dare ask for them. The hunger of the poor cries out to heaven against the forgetfulness of those who could satiate it. All that Lazarus wished for was that he could meagrely get the help he needed; the rich man could not think of anything but how to pile up his treasure. A poor man's wish is almost always of no avail, for the rich man's greed is always insatiable. There is no misery or poverty greater than that of the miser; the waste and trash left over after he gives away his flesh and having his vanity satisfied, are still needed to satisfy his greed. He has greater mercy for his vices than for others' misery. What greater proof is there that the miser is the public enemy of society? The poor man's condition is a rather sad one in the eyes of the world; one person robs him, another persecutes him, yet another insults him, and the majority despise him; yet what would the poor man come to if he were not comforted by the hope of an eternal reward, which God promises to anyone making good use of poverty?"

It was not the voice of Lazarus that cried out to heaven, but the hunger that showed on his face; but even this cry for a basic need served little to distract the miser and tear his heart out of the closets where it was locked up and imprisoned. God put sores on the body of Lazarus to open the heart of the rich man with open wounds, but all was in vain. The hapless end of the perverse rich man proves that he made a treasure-trove on earth and not in heaven. The beasts were more human to the poor man than to their own master. He fattened his own dogs and denied his table's leftovers to the beggar. Ah, it seems that the backdrop in the rich man's house looks much like those of many present-time scenes! Now and then barking dogs are heard inside, while the hungry poor cry outside without being given any attention? Saint Chrysostom spoke out very well and opportunely when he said that dogs and horses ought to appear in God's court as prosecutors and accusers of many rich men. Neither Lazarus could get rid of the dogs himself, nor was anyone charged to drive them away; so that even if he had got bitten, there was no one who would care to defend him.

Lazarus carried on patiently his works and later died. His soul was carried by the angels into Abraham's bosom, and he was received among the good and pious Jews in the place of rest and sweet hope of ultimate happiness. True to say that man's happiness cannot be measured by what happens in the present life. One need wait a little. Death will soon tell between contemptible and happy persons. Being detached from earthly wealth, the poor keep their heart far away from the world and are more willing to unite with the One who conquered the world with his death. Lazarus died, and as a beggar he achieved richness. An angel was not enough to carry a poor man, and so many were sent to form a joyous chorus. Each one of the angels was glad to hold such a holy burden; it was pleasant to carry him because they received great joy in taking men to heaven. The rich man also died and hell was his burial place. Condemned never to leave there again and suffering all the harshness of eternal torments, he raised his eyes and could see in the distance his father Abraham, in whose bosom Lazarus rested.

This passing from the soft bed and from the opulence of the world's rewards to eternal fire and at best to the inconsolable groan of misery and ignominy, and then not for a day or a year but for ever, is something which, only to imagine, would shake the strongest heart, let alone were a man to see it for himself? What would become of our faith if we do not prevent this bitter drink now that we can erase our guilt with penance and redeem it with almsgiving? This rich man was taken as a parishioner of the devil to hell's cemetery by its demons, and there he was buried without prayers, without incense, without holy water, in the way that irrational animals are buried in the ground, according to what Jeremiah says (Jer 22:19), speaking of the damned: *With the burial of an ass he shall be buried.* They are skinned after death, their skin is given to their owner, their meats are eaten by dogs, birds of prey and beasts, and their bones are given to be consumed by the rains, hail and the sun's scorching rays. It also happens when an evil man dies and his heirs become owners of his goods, the worms consume his flesh and hellish torments torture his soul which, being immortal, could still be represented in a certain manner in the bones which are hard to consume.

"Torment has opened eyes which had previously been closed by guilt. Later, whoever always had his eyes fixed to the ground would raise his eyes to heaven," Peter Chrysologus says. "Those eyes of yours, oh rich man, accuse you. Is it now that you look at the reward for virtue? Why did you not look at it when you could still aspire for it? The Judge is now annoyed by those very eyes with which you should have appeased him. He opened them for you, but for your greater torment. He fixed them on Abraham, whose son he was, and had been his companion in riches, but not in charity; for this reason his eyes accused his harshness, made his ungodliness known, witnessed to his cruelty, and saw in his bosom the same beggar he had despised. Although the place that was called Abraham's womb was a far-removed place from hell, it was not a place of complete darkness, but of light, owing to the hope of a future brightness which those who were there detained would enjoy. Then, those who were there did not feel or suffer any material sorrow and they had to remain there until Jesus Christ descended to the underworld: due to this calm, and as to the relief they enjoyed there, which was called the bosom, just as in the bosom of the sea the stormy anxiety which breaks on its surface, caused by the fury of the wind, is not tested. And he was called Abraham, because he was the first father of believers, and the one who first publicly preached faith in one God. Job called this region a place of darkness, with respect to the divine vision, because there was darkness, compared to the light of the Lamb that shines over the eternal spaces of glory."

The sight of Abraham and Lazarus greatly added to the heaviness of the ill-fated rich man, who started crying out: "Abraham, my father, have mercy on me; send Lazarus to help me. Let him wet his fingertip with water and cool my tongue, because I am suffering cruel pain in this flame." This cry marks the torments' forcefulness. It would be in vain for those on the other side to cry out if they had cast aside all fears on earth. Did you mock here the voice of the Lord with your contempt? Your groaning will be of no use in hell. Forgiveness no longer exists for whoever falls into the hands of eternal justice. How can you have courage to call the Father whom you now despise in His poor? It would be in vain asking for mercy which you have yourself refused when you denied it to the poor. You now confess to being miserable. What have the riches in which you put your trust done for you? You will not be free from eternal misery, because you wanted to add to instant joy by throwing your entrails at another's begging. Now you can see for yourself, that when you omitted Lazarus' sighs you closed your Father's ears so that He would not hear yours. Do not expect Abraham, oh rich man, to send to the place of torment the poor man whom you did not want to feed with the crumbs of your table. Are you rich and you ask for a drop of water? That is what makes you cruel; that is what having been denied by you, dried up the palate of Lazarus, since to refresh that poor man a drop of water and a left-over crumb of bread from your table would have been enough. You would not be thirsty now had you quenched the thirsty man with that single drop you ask for now. It is only that little bit of crust, on which hangs the food and life of the poor, which accuses your humanity. About which Saint Basil says: "Let us flee as far as we can from the world's delights and the abundance of food, let us not become like flesh tormented in flames seeking a drop of water and getting no consolation. It looks like this rich man was full of vices; greed dwelt in his heart, not because he had riches, but because he greedily held on to them and made use of them in a thousand illicit ways. It is there that vainglory abound, which shows in the prettiness of the dresses he wore. He neither lacked gluttony for a short while, because he ate daily with splendour. And to him was above all ascribed lack of charity and mercy, because he did not show any towards Lazarus, covered with sores and a beggar.

Abraham could not help but reply to the rich man's cry: *Remember, son; that you have received good things in your lifetime, and Lazarus had none but evils.* He calls him "son" that he might be aware of the Father's goodness he had lost, and the righteousness with which he was being punished. How miserable it is for man who receives from God good for evil, pays Him back evil for good. Whoever uses temporal goods well returns them to God, sharing them out with Christian prudence, according to the laws of charity and justice. One sign is usually that of condemning temporary prosperity in wicked men. The wicked inherit eagerly accumulated riches, loved with attachment and spent in what encourages vices. Lazarus received evils in life, because this is the inheritance of the chosen ones. For the poor God reserved poverty, disease and shame; blessed is the man who patiently knows how to suffer them all. The lots were turned and it was seen that the reward given to temporary calamity suffered with patience was very different from that which fell on the heart of whoever had possessed temporal goods and was attached to them. Saint Augustine says: "Let all those worldly people and wretches who are presently blinded by the dust of the earth hear this, for otherwise they would have to hear it later in the midst of atrocious torture which their senses would suffer. Let the rich, who do not want to be merciful, hear these things; let them listen to the sorrows and torments which the man on earth who does not want to help the poor carries to hell. Hear him when he rejoices, hear the other when he suffers unspeakable torments in the midst of scorching flames. Compare some things with others: for riches, torments are given, for poverty, comforts are given; for purple robes, flames are given, for being naked, the garment of glory; and the penalties received are in full proportion to the joys they had."

Not only did Abraham excuse himself for not sending Lazarus to the rich man, telling him to remember that he had received benefits in his life, and also evils, but he said further: "In addition to this, there is great chaos between you and us, a terrible and daunting chasm." Truly, this chasm is inaccessible, because the doors of mercy are closed forever to whoever is condemned to live in the lower parts. And this chasm cannot be bridged, because the sentence cannot be changed: there is no longer any time or place where to obtain merit, nor any hope that the heart will reach the aim for which it was created. If you want, then, oh man, to reign with Christ, choose poverty for yourself, and rest with Lazarus the beggar. No one can live the ways of the world and reign with the Lord. Whoever wants to be a glutton with the rich, let him prepare to later suffer hellfire, and because of instant joy to suffer in perpetual fire.

As the rich man lost hope of ever obtaining for himself the solace he needed, he pleaded with Abraham for his five brothers, telling him: "So I beg you, Father, that you send him to my Father's house, as I have five brothers, and I wish you to let them know how much I suffer here, lest they also come to this place of torments and be punished like me for the hardness of their hearts, and their sufferings will increase mine." He did not desire the good of his brothers out of charity, nor even out of the natural love aroused by kinsmen, but to avoid the new torment that would result from being in the company in hellfire of whoever imitated his vices and were heirs of the wealth by means of which they arrived at them. He wrongly presumes to attain penance for others, something which was so cruel for himself to do. And what mark will he leave in you brothers with his words if he did not soften you up with his wounds? "They hold on to Moses and to the prophets," Abraham told him. "Let them listen to them if they want." But if they despised the heavenly writs given by God through the prophets, if they dismissed the wonders God worked through Moses, what would they do about a poor man, tattered and covered with sores? The rich man is blamed for having despised Moses and the prophets; what do you expect after having despised Christ and his apostles? Nor was this condemnation enough to silence the remorse and desperate cries of the condemned rich man, and so he returned to press him on, saying: "No, Father Abraham. Were any dead man to go to them, they will do penance." This is how the wicked run to that place of sorrows after having mocked on earth the credulity of those having faith; but Abraham, who did not think the same way as the rich evil man, answered him for the last time, disillusioned him and said: "No, the help you ask for your brothers will not put them in any advantage, for those who neither believe in Moses nor in the prophets would not even give credence to a man who would rise again and return to the world. All those who do not repent are like this rich man. They look like they would turn to God were they to be given some special notice, and in the meantime they despise the Law which they just keep in view. What would you do about a convict, if you do not fear whoever condemned him? What does it matter that you do not see hell if you have faith in Divine Justice? How do you pretend to ignore what religion teaches you? If you do not believe him who came down from heaven, how would you believe whoever came from hell?" This prophecy of Abraham was fulfilled with the Jews, who were not moved by Moses' miracles, nor by the dead raised by Elijah and Elisha, or Lazarus of Bethany whom Christ himself called out of the tomb, or even the deceased who appeared in the Holy City at the time of his passion; and what is even more, neither by the most clear and indisputable resurrection of Christ himself, or the wonderful wonders which caused it. Hesitant Christians are very good at saying they do not believe; but they disregard the obvious evidence confirming the truth which condones their vices. It is all a mystery how they would like to sin without feeling the remorse which makes their guilt bitter. Whoever loves the Law does not seek proof about its fairness; whoever seeks God in everything easily trusts His word.

It is well seen that the dialogue between Abraham and the greedy rich man, which the Lord interspersed in this parable, are a clear, upright and eloquent exposition of the feelings and inner affections which the souls of saints and those of the damned really have, but which they do not communicate to each other. The tight obligation of rich persons to give alms to the poor, and to draw from them their own benefits, and even on what they willingly call necessary expenses, as well as to succour them in their true needs, are equally known; the same as is hell's inevitable punishment which awaits hardened and unmerciful rich persons. The real and eternal fire which burns condemned souls, and ultimately, God's immense goodness in being ever ready to reward those who believe and hope, are the many other dogmas which Jesus Christ assertively repeated to the Pharisees. By them Jesus Christ dared show them that in the Gospel he renews, overstressed or maligns the Law; above all, that which unbelievers leave unanswered, preferring a shameful silence to the naïve confession of their engaging and abjuring errors; and so, to undergo inward combat with their shameful passions rather than to submit to the most light yoke of the new faith and of the New Testament announced to them by the Saviour.

CHAPTER 58
THE LORD RAISES LAZARUS FROM THE DEAD; THE TEMPLE PRIESTS AND PHARISEES CONSPIRE AGAINST HIM, AND CAIAPHAS MULLS OVER HIS DEATH (JN 11:1-45; 47-54)

AFTER Jesus Christ had given to the scribes and Pharisees, by means of these sublime and instructive parables, the greatest and most wholesome evidence, he departed with his apostles and arrived near Bethany, a village distant from Jerusalem about fifteen stadia, adding up to nearly a league, or to some three miles. Not all sacred commentators hold this opinion; some say he first went to Jericho, and that after healing the blind man sitting on the side of the road, and after resolving the request made by Zebedee's mother and dining with Zacchaeus, he went to this place. From there he departed to resurrect Lazarus, although he had received news of his illness at a distance of some six or seven hours of walking time on the way to the neighbourhood of Jericho. Without entering into this detail we now say the same thing as the Gospel, namely that Jesus Christ received the news of his friend's illness from the messenger his two sisters had sent him, worried as they were of the danger facing Lazarus while being assured of the friendship Jesus Christ had with the sick man. Trust and discretion shine outstandingly in the short words with which Martha and Mary informed the Saviour of their brother's illness, and they can be seen as the most eloquent of all pleadings. *Lord*, they told him, *him whom you love is sick*. For anyone who loves truly it would be enough to know that the loved one is in need, because whoever abandons his neighbour in need and does not help him, is neither friend nor does he love him. So as Saint Augustine warns, they did not tell him to come and heal him. They did not dare tell him either, to command his health to be restored from this very place where he was, but they were content to say: *Him whom you love is unwell*, for they were firmly persuaded in their hearts of his love and believed

it was enough to give him news of their brother's illness knowing that he would certainly heal him, be it from the place where he was or by attending personally to visit him.

Saint Chrysostom said about this very place: "The sisters did not go to see Christ, since they extremely trusted him and were held back by crying; for this reason they were content to send him a messenger with the sad news of their brother's illness, not doubting at all that this was indeed sufficient to have him come, and they were quite right. Jesus Christ loved Lazarus, and these two sisters of his were very dear to the Lord owing to their faith, zeal, tenderness and respectful subjection to him. Their souls and their hearts were a beautiful model of virtue; yet the Lord wanted to try them on this occasion with a very hard trial." The messenger fulfilled his charge, and in very few words the Saviour answered him: *Go and tell those who have sent you on my behalf, that their brother's sickness about which they are giving me news, does not lead to death*; which means that God has not sent it to him to take him out of this world, but only so that His glory might shine and glorify his Son. By this Jesus Christ was already clearly showing them that this event would have great consequences, even if they could not yet comprehend them. His brother had died a few hours after the messenger had departed; and since the Sabbath was due to begin in the afternoon of the same day, which was a Friday, they had to bury him and put him in the tomb before the end of the day.

The Lord's love for Lazarus denotes the zeal of charity with which he came into the world in search of lost souls, for if he did not love sinners, he would not have come down from heaven to earth. Here we see how greatly the Lord's goodness is offended by those who in tribulation, temptation and even in falling in guilt, lose hope in it. Have you sinned? Lift your eyes to heaven and say to the Lord, in faith and with humility: *Him whom you love is unwell*. What else shall I say to you, Lord? For you do love me and it is enough that you know my great misery. Do not run away from the body if it really looks for you.

The plea of the two sisters implies that God grants conversion to sinners when the Church, and her children, pray for them. Such example must stoke confidence and enthusiasm in us to implore the remedy of all the mean things buried in great vices in the very bosom of the Church. Our little faith is such that it does not allow us to attain from God the conversion of great sinners. We have no courage to ask God for this highest mercy, because we see it as impossible or we ask for it in a lukewarm manner, for we do not conceive that we should make use of the power of grace; we have enough misery! We fear making ordinary requests, because we do not believe matters to be worthy of God if they do not fall within men's proportions of thoughts.

The sovereign Master was not unaware of the goings-on in Bethany, although he delayed his consoling response to his two fervent disciples. It is to the most beloved souls that God destines great afflictions, since He prepares the great favours for them. Jesus Christ remained for two whole days in the same place where he had been after receiving news of his friend's illness, and having come to know of his death he resolved to resurrect Lazarus. With so wonderful a prodigy being done at the gates of Jerusalem, this would confound the Synagogue's unbelief if they did not want to open their eyes and convince themselves otherwise. He wanted that more than just disease and death, there should also be rot and corruption in the tomb. Lazarus was laid inside it for three days, and Jesus Christ wanted to raise him to the fourth. On his way there, he had said a word to his disciples of his friend's illness; but he had not told them of his death or of the designs he had for this event. Yet he told them, "Let us go once more to Judea." And they replied to him: "Lord, was it not that two months ago the Jews were seeking you to stone you, and now you are resolved to return to a place where bigheads are staunchly against you?" But Jesus Christ answered them: "The day has twelve hours; while a person walks during this time he can avoid taking bad steps, because he sees the light of this world. On the contrary, if a wanderer keeps on walking at night, he stumbles and runs the risk of falling, because there is no sunlight and he walks in darkness." Which was like telling them: "You should know well that insofar as I am concerned, there is no wavering between light and darkness. I know and I see at every instant what will happen to me. The knowledge I have of present and future, marks within me the times of the day, and directs all my steps and decisions. The Jews cannot do anything against me which I have not foreseen. You should follow me with trust. Let us continue on our way without anxiety, and let us not depart from it. Our friend Lazarus sleeps and I am not going to wake him." To which his apostles replied: "If he is sleeping, he undoubtedly has a better time and maybe this is already a good thing."

"He stayed for two days," says Saint Augustine, "at the place where he was after he received the news, so that in delaying to go and restore his health he could later better resurrect him. He expected greater certainty and evidence of the miracle, and after four whole days the resurrection would be more wonderful and glorious. 'As I could raise him up,' the Lord said, 'since he slept.' For those who did not have this power he was truly dead; for it is easier for Christ to raise a dead man who was decomposing in the tomb than it is for anyone else to arouse him from his sleep when he is lying in his bed." This word sleep or dormition has many meanings in Holy Scripture; it is at times taken to mean natural sleep, as Job is said to *sleep safely* (Jb 11:19). In others it is taken for the dream of death, as when Saint Paul says: "We do not want to leave you in ignorance, brethren, concerning those who are asleep, that you many not grieve as others usually do who have no hope of eternal life" (1 Thes 4:13). Others, finally, are taken to mean due to negligence or carelessness in doing something, as when David says: *He who watches over and defends Israel will neither slumber nor sleep.* Jesus Christ spoke of Lazarus' death as a dream. This figurative way of speaking, especially with regard to someone who had died recently, suited Lazarus even better, whose passing death was to be overcome with a glorious resurrection, explained with the expression of waking up. Jesus Christ's spirit was very different from that of his apostles; and so they understood nothing, neither with regard to Lazarus nor with regard to the rebuke of having somehow to return to Jerusalem contrary to his belief and judgment. So that he said to them: "You do not understand what I wanted to show you; so, I tell you in no uncertain manner that Lazarus is dead, and this death is what I call his dream. And I am glad for you that I was not there so that you might believe, but let us go to him." Which was like telling them: "You know quite well that I loved this faithful son of Israel; yet although I am his friend, I am content I was not in Bethany during his illness, and of not having averted the consequences, as you would have begged me to do. And you must know that it is for you that I am happy that this has happened, for you will believe with more certainty that I am Christ and Son of God. Let us go to Bethany, so that there you may be witnesses of your Master's glory."

Saint Chrysostom says that Jesus Christ spoke in this manner with his apostles so that they may start wondering why he was saying Lazarus was dead, when he had neither seen him die nor had he been told of his death by anyone. He also wanted them to see that nothing was hidden from him, and so they would have greater faith and more trust in him. One of the twelve called *Thomas* according to his Hebrew name, but also known by the Greeks as *Didymus* or the Twin, could not restrain himself when he heard Jesus Christ. So turning to his fellow disciples he said to them: "Our Master is rushing to his death, let us not leave him alone. Let us go and die with him." Thomas was at that instant reasoning matters with great courage and resolve, exhorting the others to follow him and going all out to unite himself with the willingness of Jesus Christ's heart and his spirit of sacrifice. Yet he soon found out that he was not as fearless as much as he bragged to be. Jesus Christ and his disciples continued on their way to Jerusalem, and a crowd of faithful joined them on the way, eager to hear him speaking and to witness his miracles, until they finally reached the place where he was to work one, which would be the most special and extraordinary he had ever worked.

It is undeniable that had the Jews been less unbelieving and caring in Jesus Christ's regard, this occasion would have been most favourable for them to believe in him. Yet Jerusalem was ruled by ambitious men. Sage men were worried, priests were interested and envious, and the people were spoilt. So that the great miracle would irritate them even more, move all their passions and compel the mob to ask with more commotion for Jesus Christ's death.

The castle of Bethany was on the other hand flooded with people who came from Jerusalem to visit Mary and Martha, since people held them in great regard in the city; so they had to offer gifts and condole with them about their brother's death. But this through and fro of visits and paying of regards were very sad and ineffective concerns with respect to what they were seeking in Jesus Christ when showing some of their fears. At the same time that the bewildered sisters came to know that the true comforter was drawing near, Martha rose with utmost haste without waiting for the house to fill with Jerusalem's most learned persons and, ran to look for Jesus Christ. Upon seeing him she threw herself at his feet and falling dejected in a sea of tears said to him: "*Ah, Lord!* what a misfortune for us that you were not here during my brother's illness! You would have restored his health even with just one word of yours. You would not have allowed him to die in our sight. What would it have taken you to cast loving looks on him and heal him. What were you doing then? And how have you failed us in such a great need? Yet just seeing you now I find comfort. I know what you can do for I have not forgotten the reply you sent us." God does not deny you anything you may ask Him. Saint Chrysostom notices that when Martha went to Jesus Christ this time she did not take her sister Mary with her as she wanted to speak to her in person and tell her all that had happened. But feeling greater hope in her heart after she first met her, she then went and called her sister Mary furtively and told her: *The Master has arrived and he is calling you*. And Saint Augustine notes that when Martha called her sister Mary silently, she did it that the Jews who had gone from Jerusalem to the garrison town of Bethany would not rush to the place and have occasion to witness the miracle.

What Martha had said to Mary was enough for her to rise up immediately and to go searching for Jesus Christ. When those who were following her saw this happen, they were firmly convinced that she was going to her brother's tomb where she would be moaning his loss. Their admiration, however, and their surprise grew even more when they saw her throwing herself at her Divine Master's feet. Jesus Christ had not taken a single step forward with his disciples, but had remained in the same place where Martha had spoken to him for he did not want to enter the sisters' abode until after he had resurrected his friend. And Mary, who knew that Jesus Christ was the true comforter of souls, throwing herself at his feet spoke to him almost in the same terms as Martha had expressed herself. The Lord answered both of them with a general truth, by which although hinting at his intention, he did not want to fully reveal. "Your brother will be resurrected," he said to Martha; and she answered him, "I know that he will be resurrected on the newest of all days, that is at the time of the general resurrection of all the dead." She thought so, as all Israel believed. "And you must also know," Jesus Christ continued, "I am the resurrection and the life. Anyone who believes in me, even though passing through temporary death on earth, will live forever in heaven. Anyone who lives and believes in me will pass through death, yet I will resurrect him and he will live eternally in glory. Do you believe this?" the Lord asked Martha. "Yes, Lord," she answered. "I believe it, and I also believe that you are the Christ, the Son of the living God who has come into the world."

It seems very natural that these were the terms with which Martha and Mary consoled themselves after their brother's death in Jesus Christ's absence, as what they told the Saviour seemed to be dictated by the same spirit. But since both lived by faith, they had no need to collude and agree to express themselves in the same terms. Yet it is necessary to confess that Mary's character was somewhat more lively and tender, that her heart was undoubtedly more sensitive, and that the grace which acted naturally within her had been perfected without destroying her. She shed tears while Jesus Christ mentioned her brother's name, so that soon enough she was drenched in them, and the Jews who had followed her could not help but also weep. Jesus Christ's heart was greatly moved to see Mary's tenderness and the inner feelings of all those who were present, although he knew well that it was useless to perform in the sight of the multitude of those hardened men the greatest of miracles he had ever worked until then. Jesus Christ was not unaware that although right up till then they seemed to be very attentive and civil as to his doings, they would look at his adorable person as the object of insults and contempt after witnessing such an unprecedented miracle. It was undoubtedly for this reason that the Lord was greatly moved when he saw this, breathed out a strong sigh coming from the bottom of his heart and gave an unusual sign of bewilderment, which he wanted to be noticed in his countenance. After a few moments he was seen calming down himself from the distress which he did not want to suppress, and said to those present, with a modest yet equally imposing and calm composure: *Show me the place where you buried him.* "Come, Lord, and you will see," they answered him. But when Jesus Christ arrived near the tomb, he let some tears flow from his divine pupils. He teaches us an important lesson here that if we are permitted to be submissive and accept the death of friends, we are not forbidden from shedding tears.

Jesus Christ's tears could be seen, so that they could not go unnoticed by some men who undoubtedly had the best part in them, although they did not think so for they did not know their motive or their price, and attributing these tears to a purely human love, they said to one another: *See there how much he loved him.* Being possessed with a spirit of blasphemy and implacable hatred of which they should be ashamed, they said among themselves with unbridled sarcasm: "Could not this man who works so many miracles and who opened the eyes of a man born blind, have prevented his friend from dying?" As if they were saying, "He deceived us in the first miracle, but if it is not so tell us where he comes from, seeing that he lacks the strength to work a miracle which is presently needed." This talk of the Jews may seem full of humility, but it is undeniable that they atrociously reviled Jesus Christ's omnipotence and goodness, and so they again aroused his bewilderment. He sighed again, this time in apparent anger, seeing himself close to working a great and extraordinary miracle, but one which would make little or no dent in those unbelievers' hearts. He walked towards the tomb, which was closed with a huge stone, still burdened with that terrible sentiment that was afflicting him, and coming to the proper site he stopped and ordered the tomb to be opened. Martha, the eldest of the sisters, being overcome with deep sorrow and shedding abundant tears, threw herself at the feet of the Saviour and said to him: "Ah! Lord, what are you going to do? My brother died four days ago, and the stench of his body must be unbearable." Jesus Christ neither dismissed nor did he severely condemn Martha's holy intention; yet he rebuked her little faith and said to her: "Do you not remember what I told you, that if you have faith you will see how God will be glorified?"

This loving rebuke could not but inflame Martha's heart, forcing her to the greatest impulse to carry out the Saviour's orders more promptly. As soon as the stone sealing the tomb was removed, Jesus Christ also lifted his eyes and his heart to heaven, and uttered loudly before all this tender plea to his Eternal Father to grant graces, saying: *My Father, I thank you because you have heard me and granted what I have begged you in the secret of my heart. I know that you hear me whenever I address you and request to be heard; yet I do not desire it except to conform to your will; and since this people who are going to witness your power and my power are not sufficiently instructed, I want to teach them that you are the One who has heard my petition, so that they may know that you are the One who has sent me, and that being your Son and God, like you, you deny nothing to his desires.*

Majesty and greatness shone in the friendly tone and firmness of voice with which Jesus Christ spoke. His divinity was depicted and shone out from his face. When the tomb was opened the corpse, which had been buried in it for four days, was seen wrapped in linen and it gave off a deadly stench. Possessed of a frightening terror and overwhelmed by a secret horror, those present dared not even breathe at all. It was only the disciples, who were accustomed to seeing miracles, who thought they would be undoubtedly seeing in a short while the greatest miracle they had ever seen. Martha and Mary, astonished as they were, waited for him in all faith to see him act; and Jesus Christ's enemies were watching him and tempting him. The Son of God gave a command and the tomb was opened instantly. Jesus Christ raised his voice, and with the tone and command of omnipotence which only suited Jesus Christ on earth, pronounced clearly and distinctly these three words: *Lazarus, come forth.* The dead man's feet and hands were tied with ribbons, his face was covered with a shroud, and his whole body was wrapped in a sheet. In this state Lazarus rose, obedient to the voice of his God and Lord, and let himself be seen full of life and health. He who in the days of creation poured his divine breath, opened his eternal mouth and said and did all that had to be done; and as he commanded, all was created; so that he could at the command of his voice just as well revive the rotten earth and make it recover new breaths of life. God's majesty and greatness shine in heaven and on earth in the creation of the world and in the resurrection of Lazarus, and with such works the Lord testifies to his omnipotence and power. "Untie him," Jesus Christ said, "and set him free that he might walk." The Saviour was obeyed, and Lazarus joined the company and walked back to his house in Bethany.

When the sacred Evangelists cover with the veil of silence the enlightened pages of this admirable event, and do not tell us anything of the affections and feelings of the risen dead man, of the two sisters' joy and happiness, of their emotions and behaviour when they came to see him, and of the apostles' heartfelt feelings of faith. Such feelings were also in the hearts of those Jews who were present, so that it would also be right for us to submit ourselves to the designs of Providence and not to start querying about what the Saviour wanted to leave as very natural to the reflection and consideration of all those who were present; and of all those who would eventually hear of the miracle that had been worked. Since he was aiming at many of the Jews who had gone to Bethany to comfort Martha and Mary, there is no doubt that it was a very precious favour for them to have been chosen by the Lord to witness such an important and decisive event. Many of them immediately surrendered to the imprint made by grace, believing Jesus Christ to be the One sent by God and His Son as announced by the prophets. Some of them even believing that now they held a powerful weapon to overcome the most stubborn unbelief, ran to seek the Pharisees and referred to them in detail the circumstances of what they had just witnessed and seen. "We have seen," they would say, "what Jesus of Nazareth has just done, him whom you persecute. He has given life to Lazarus, who had been dead for four days, locked and corrupting in a tomb. Such a great miracle dismisses any question about the divinity of his person; we now count ourselves among the number of his disciples, and we now boast that we believe in Jesus Christ."

Such judicious reflections based on such a glorious recent and public fact, would have undoubtedly convinced unbelievers to believe, as long as they retained some good faith, abstained from subjecting themselves to reason and did not refuse to believe the real motives presented as a means of justification. They only managed to irritate more and more envious men, determined by interest and passion not to believe some conclusive evidence in favour of a rival whom they wanted to reject. So it happened that when the sovereign priests were instructed of the miracle which made them frightful of its consequences, they convened a great council of themselves together with the Pharisees and all the heads of Judaism, which was presided over by Caiaphas, who was their chief priest. What did it matter that they had nothing directly against the person of the Saviour, if they were attached to the love of the way things were going and the desire to keep them? This alone was enough for them to persecute Christ. Whoever prefers to love current and visible things so as not to risk on hope or possess these things, forgets invisible benefits, such as truth, justice and spiritual affairs, and despises the fear of the coming evils with which God threatens him. Even the worldly tend to show their faces for Christ, but only do it when it is convenient for the achievement of their desires or when it matches their passions.

It was in this council or Sanhedrin where Christ's death was resolved, and listen to the terms with which the conference moderator expressed himself: "We are still and calm, and we look indifferently at the object most worthy of our precautions, while what one asks most would be attention and vigilance. What should we do and why are we delaying our making a resolution as circumstances demand? This man called Jesus Christ, whom we have uselessly tried so long to discredit, is every day enjoying greater esteem in people's minds. He performs innumerable miracles, we do not hear of anything else, and now he has recently resurrected a man who had been dead four days. What shall we do?" Out of contempt they look up to a man whose works only showed he was also God. They do not say, we believe, but *what shall we do?* They confessed the resurrection of Lazarus, but armed themselves with it to carry out the wicked project which they had conjured against its author. They saw well that such wonders could only be worked by those who had God's approval on their side and were driven by piety, truth and justice; but the righteous One who so acted, the Son of God, true God and true man, brought condemnation against himself for having stood against the worldly laws governing the very members of that council. How strange it is that he will be internally judged, not by the righteousness of God's law, but by self-interest, by the odium of jealousy and envy? Even if the council's preamble were to be naturally heeded, there could not come out of it anything but a peaceful and very honourable conclusion for the Son of God; yet the opposite actually happened.

When injustice, revenge and hatred rule over people's councils and deliberations, they cannot but be foolish and bloodthirsty, usually covering themselves with the cloak of freedom and the zeal for public good. They would reason things out saying that if we allow this man his freedom and life any time longer, all the world will believe in him the same way as many of our fellow citizens who have seen the resurrection of Lazarus have just done; and the people will rally in making Jesus of Nazareth their king; and it will so happen that the outraged Romans will come in big armies and destroy our city; they will take our fortunes, depopulate the country of its former inhabitants and execute us; and Palestine will no longer be the land of God's people. Other greater and even more lasting evils made them fearful of protecting Christ; but these evils were neither visible nor present, and so they did not match the human fear of anyone who fears only the present misfortunes and calamities which he sees, only holding in esteem dated and temporary goods and delights. But what can man do not according to God's council? Would man want to kill Jesus Christ so that no one would believe in him, just so that his death would plant faith on earth? Does not man see what is written in Isaiah: When he makes himself an offering for sin, he shall see his offspring and he shall prolong his days" (Is 53:10)? What posterity is this, but the offspring of the true Abraham, the father of spiritual believers? Being raised on the cross where man wants him to be nailed, he will draw all things towards him. That will be a mercy seat for the wretched, a source of all blessings, an instrument of redemption, a tree of life. It is from that seat that the world which you favour will be judged, and its prince of whom you are ministers will be dethroned.

They feared, as they said among themselves, the Romans would come because once the people had made up their mind to proclaim him king, they would have violated the mandate which they had of not being able to name anyone king without Rome's intervention, giving rise more to fear than to respect of contradicting Caesar. Blinded with these thoughts they did not understand that the time foretold by the prophets had arrived. If they had awe for Caesar and respected him as emperor and king, and he was to appoint whoever was to rule them, *where had the power of Judea gone, and where was the sceptre of the house of Judah?* They feared that were all to believe in Christ there would not be enough people left to defend the city and the temple against the power of the Romans, since they saw Christ and his doctrines as going against the Law of Moses and those of their nation and country. They were fearful and consulted among themselves, but then David's words were fulfilled: *There have they trembled for fear, where there was no fear* (Ps 53:5). If they had believed in Christ and had not killed him, they would neither have lost their place nor their people; but since they were not afraid to kill him, they lost everything. The Romans did not take away their dominion until Jesus Christ's passion, death and glorification. They feared losing temporal things but failed to take care of eternal ones, and so they lost both one and the other. Vain was the fear of the Pharisees, and wholly unlikely, and they confessed it themselves saying: *If we leave things like that everyone will believe in him.* The fear was therefore about those who believed in Jesus Christ. Senseless thinking! They were unaware that whoever gave sight to the blind, life to the dead and grace to so many of his people to believe in him and to follow him, could he not also attract the Romans towards him and make them believe? And is this the greatly feared devastation that, believing in him and not in you Pharisees, keeps that miserable reputation of yours which breeds in you, tightly gripped with hypocrisy? Little did the unbelievers know well until thereafter the illogicality of their reasoning and the truth of the ill forebodings made to them by Jesus Christ. It was not because they recognised their true king but for being unaware that they were hard put to all the evils which they feared.

Then one of them called Caiaphas, who was chief priest at that time, started speaking, and by reason and use of his authority said to them: *You neither know anything nor think it to be convenient that a man dies for the people, rather than for all the nation to perish.* A fatal prophecy and most disastrous principle, which has given rise thousands of times to the innocent and just, who are normally always the underdogs, to perish in the hands of the perverse and unjust, who ordinarily always have the upper hand. The common good, they say, is preferable to anything particular, so it matters little that one perishes to save the community. Envy and fury against Jesus Christ upset their judgment and reason, as in no circumstance is it lawful to kill the innocent and just. For in doing this, far from procuring the common good, the means of destroying are sought, so that that same evil they thought they would avert with the death of Christ, rebound against them that they might have a taste of it. As a consequence of this sin the Romans entered Jerusalem forty-two years after Christ's passion, and completely destroyed the Synagogue, the city and the temple. For Caiaphas it was a serious offence which merited strong doubts and deliberations about the case. In his heart of hearts he took greater account of personal interest and inner feelings, than the causes of justice and the weight of truth; or the uncertain fear of temporal ruin, rather than the solid and well-founded fear God's judgment. And so he treated as fools those who would try to resolve the important question which he had presented before them. Cunning and shrewd like malicious politicians and men of bad faith, he gilded his preferences, resentments and personal hatreds under the pretexts of public order, state serenity and the nation's progress. As if it were not possible that even those who attend to the common good were not exposed to prefer material and personal interests to the laws of truth and justice, as it is very easy for men in authority to go over the law of God without any scruples, while still being bold enough to be thanked for it.

Proud of his conception of his hellish plan, Caiaphas believed he would fulfil the duties of honour and justice, were he to sacrifice innocence, holiness and the justice of his true Deliverer to the people's imaginary happiness. Whether he is just or not, he said, whether he is a prophet or not, whether he is the Christ promised in the Law or not, nothing matters. Believing in Jesus Christ may displease the Romans, this is what matters, so we too do not believe in him. For flesh and blood people, it was far more terrible to displease an idolatrous nation than the true God. Much greater evil comes with the loss of temporal goods than eternal happiness. For moving in everything according to the interest of feelings and by the love for present things, they do not care about God's law or the spiritual reasons inspired by faith about eternal matters. But when Caiaphas uttered these words, which were said to condemn the holiest of men to death, he pronounced them without understanding he was uttering a prophetic mystery, which he would have never uttered had he known it. God spoke through that sacrilegious mouth as through the mouth of one of his ministers who, while being unworthy of his dignity, had prophesied and said the truth solely by virtue of the office he held. He spoke well but thought badly; his understanding was blind and his heart was passionate; yet the Sovereign Lord still kept mastery and control over his tongue. And because the bad priest had clothed himself with pontifical dignity, it was up to him to utter such sayings, so that he became a prophet without wanting to be one, and even without knowing that he was one. He and all those on his council feared the desolation of their country rather than the loss of their souls. At least the false fear, or truth, was the pretext on which they decided among themselves from that very day that it was necessary that Jesus Christ should die.

Saint Augustine says that prophecy is not always a manifest sign of holiness, as witnessed in Caiaphas. God honours in this evil chief priest the highness of his dignity, while using his unjust judgment to announce through his mouth the sacrifice of the Son of Man, and the fruit of that death which was to convert a great number of Jews and add the Gentiles to the unity, holiness and universality of the faith. Holy is the priesthood even of those who desecrate it with their evil doings; respectable and creditworthy is the truth even in the mouth of those who persecute it. According to him it was convenient that Jesus Christ should die for his nation, and not only for his nation, as the sacred historian noted, unless he gathered all of God's children from the dispersion to unite them in his Church, bought with the price of his blood, and to bring all nations into the same fold and to be led by the same Shepherd. This was the meaning of Caiaphas's words, as he prophesied, which were distant from his heart. Annas, his father-in-law and colleague as chief priest, did not have the gift of prophecy like him. Not because he was not elevated to the same dignity as his father-in-law, and because this dignity was not perpetual, but because he did not exercise its main functions during that year, which according to the most likely opinion was the thirty-third and last year of Christ's life.

It was not an ordinance or legal order that there were two chief priests who alternated for years in the main functions of the priesthood, This was an effect of the ambition of the Jews and the greed of the Romans, for according to custom there should be but one high priest, and this for his lifetime. But since the Romans had appropriated the right to name him, they named one, two or more, depending on the number of suitors and the amount they paid to obtain that supreme dignity. Annas and Caiaphas took it in turns, a year each, in exercising the right; the one who entered the Holy of Holies on the feast of the Atonement, were the chief priests for the current year, so that they saw each other as alternating chief priests, not so much in terms of dignity, which they never lost, but as to the functions they exercised in their turn. The prediction of Caiaphas aroused everyone's anger and indignation, and the death sentence was pronounced against Jesus Christ, it being much worth noting that there sat on that council men of most high esteem, science, wisdom and of greater virtue than apparently anyone else had in Jerusalem.

These presumably wise men all of a sudden lost memory of a growing number of prophecies and of a great number of miracles which had been worked every day in their sight, and which for that same reason could not be contradicted; and the impious resolution was made to cause the greatest Prophet the nation had ever seen to die unjustly. They forgot that this man was called Christ, that he had appeared with all his miracles, and at the right time when he was expected, and they supported the resolution with all ulterior and respectable motives, saying he was being worshipped as the Son of God. How much so then that human anger and resolutions should not be feared, when passion, worries and self-interest take the place of justice, reason and the rules of conduct which religion suggests they should have in their hearts, so that virtue and innocence may never be trampled upon unreasonably by injustice! People are corrupted by the influence of authority and it should be assumed that, without having to examine whether justice is in its rightful place, they are easily misguided by the depraved advice of those on whom it is incumbent to lead and govern them. This was one, and perhaps the firmest support for executing evil, planned long before. The Pharisees had deep in their hearts the desire to put an end to Jesus Christ; the senate threatened anyone who believed he was the Messiah with severe penalties; the priests and doctors of law had bound him a thousand times over to remove him from state and religion; and although until then nothing had been resolved out of fear of their subjects, with their tempers inflamed by the prophecy of Caiaphas, their hearts all suddenly changed. What was once only a plan or a wish to kill Jesus Christ now became an absolute resolution they naturally attempted to perform. Indeed, what great influence does a leader's scandal often have on his people's mind and that of subordinate magistrates, due to his bad advice and beliefs! It is not strange that Saint Augustine exclaims in contemplation: "Oh abhorrent advice! Oh appalling town chiefs! Oh most perverse councillors! How miserable of you! What extraordinary anger agitates you? What can this so atrocious order be? What kind of resolution and purpose? What cause ultimately moves you to plot such a dreadful conspiracy against Jesus Christ? Is he not himself by chance in your midst, even though you know him, he who understands all your words and searches all your most hidden thoughts? It will indeed happen as you decided, yet not because of your thoughtful discussion, but because the time has come, and the Father will deliver him into your hands."

In fact, many centuries before the Spirit of God had entrusted to Scripture the circumstantial prediction of the gross errors of this court, which had to be incompetent about the future Messiah. According to what the prophets had said, it suited all to believe that Jesus Christ would be unknown to his people's leaders, and that he would be condemned to death to heal his nation. The violent proceedings which took place in the Synagogue against its true king, predicted and announced as one of the signs with which they should recognise him, did not constitute any permissible prescription against their lawful claims, but formed a clear condemnation by those who conceived them. In the absence of a tribunal's authority, which would make clearly known who was the sent Messiah, completely authorising his doctrines, portents and the miracles he wrought, it was God who had to make his Son's mission so evidently credible, so that people of contrite heart and good will would not entertain any doubt or suspicion. To the Jews who were aware and knew the time appointed for the coming of Christ, it was necessary to study and consider Jesus Christ well; he publicly presented himself as the announced Messiah and the promised Lawgiver. Jesus Christ was more than thirty-two years old when he came into the world at the precise time when the Messiah was expected. He was the son of a Virgin; his birth had been announced to Jews and Gentiles; he had made himself known in the midst of idolatrous nations, and in all his life he had not done anything but made perfect in his person the whole portrait of Christ, with his doctrine, holiness, miracles and the actual fulfilment of all the prophecies indicating that figure. Believing and simple souls, men of good faith, and all those who kept in their hearts the spirit of the Law, did not deny him public faith. Nevertheless, it was not that all had been accomplished, and the resurrection after four days of a dead man who had been dead and corrupted in the tomb raised all that Jesus Christ had done to the highest degree of witness, that he might be recognised as the Messiah. Yet the last decisive blow was the death of Christ on a cross, ordered by the Synagogue and suffered under the hand of foreign peoples, along with other prophesied events and followed, after three days, by his glorious resurrection and crowning with the ascension at the right hand of his Father. This was punctually the sign of the prophet Jonas, who had incessantly called out to the spirits that were considered strong in his time, and to his nation's unbelievers, so that when the sign was confirmed, there remained no doubt that this was the Messiah for whom Jonas' parents had sighed so much.

Although this hour and time were drawing very near, they had not yet arrived; and it was agreed to show that precautions had been taken to avoid any persecution of the Jews. After the resurrection of Lazarus, Jesus Christ left Jerusalem's surroundings, where no one thought he was safe against the surprises and violence of such a widespread alliance. He left the house where he had wrought that most interesting and remarkable miracle, and while resolving to return after a few days, he moved on to a place called the Judean deserts, where the small town of Ephraim in the Wilderness was located, some eight hours' walk away from the capital. Earthly Adam wanted to hide from God; heavenly Adam hides from men. The first showed in his escape the horror and fear which his disobedience had caused him; the second conceals himself with infinite power in abeyance of the time chosen by the Father for the sacrifice. The defenders of the truth found great comfort in seeing the Truth himself being concealed, fleeing, being blasphemed and persecuted with death. This has been the joy of the martyrs, this is the gift of those who confess Christ, this is now and will always be the confidence of those who by following him, risk suffering hatred and persecution from the world which is their enemy. The city welcoming the persecuted Christ should, however, be envied. It imitates zealous Christians who defend God's cause against the sarcasm of the freethinkers who can make their way so well around the world. That is a frightening judgment; Christ passed from the fertile fields of Judea to the dry and barren land of the Gentiles, where he would pour out the fruitfulness of grace which the Synagogue did not deserve. Alas, what hatred and ill-will against the truth! Such gigantic feelings are a great sin, which God usually punishes with blindness and penal harshness, much like a message of lack of repentance at death. If the man whose heart is lost and willingly denies the truth or repudiates it and abandons it after he had the joy of knowing it, would be able to understand the whole dreadfulness of this frightening threat, he would surely abandon his error and return with great desire to seek Jesus Christ and be in close unity with him. Those who abandon him in harsh times do not belong to the Saviour's school, and do not unite more intimately with him when the anger and fury of his enemies rage and rise. Our example was Christ's turning away to solitude in the days before his death. How do we promise to die as Christians if we do not prepare ourselves with Christ and do as Christ did? A small seed can grow into a large tree; this is how we must always advance and grow. A son must resemble his father, be an image to his original, an effect to its cause, a disciple to his master, a soldier to his captain. Be perfect, as your Father is perfect; do as you see me do, says our great Captain; listen to my words and imitate my examples. Whoever did not take advantage in Jesus Christ's school does not deserve to be his disciple. Man must work hard to achieve perfection and enjoy the tranquillity of the spirit. God pursues happiness without any movement or labours; but man does not receive his without much endeavour. You will never be happy unless you use great violence. Jesus Christ flees and apparently hides before entering into a struggle with death. Prepare yourself by fleeing the world for the time when that hour arrives, and victory will be yours.

CHAPTER 59
THE LORD HEALS TEN LEPERS: THE SAMARITANS REFUSE TO RECEIVE HIM (LK 17:11-19)

HE days ran very quickly, and the events in Jesus Christ's life also multiplied with utmost fastness. For he wanted to leave the work entrusted to him by his Father perfectly con- summated, by making himself known to Jews and Gentiles, pagans and idol worshippers, and to all the nations of the earth, and in whatever darkness and gloom they lived. We do not know how far Jesus Christ would be from Jerusalem when he worked another of the most unique wonders to which he was used for the benefit of ten hapless people. His acts of charity and beneficence were the only relief he granted in his travel fatigues, while he unceasingly instructed by way of a gift those who accompanied and followed him. Jesus Christ had crossed along Samaria to Galilee where, on arriving at a certain district, ten lepers came forward to meet him. Being lepers they did not draw near to him as the Law forbade it, but raising their voices in high pitch they shouted, *Jesus, Master and doctor of Israel, have mercy on us.*

According to Saint Luke's narrative, it seems that not all embraced the same faith, although they were united in common misery, and their desire to recover did not prevent them from eagerly looking for the only One who could restore their health to them. There was neither business nor other relationship between Jews and Samaritans, but Jesus Christ had passed through the midst of both cities and as always the fame of his miracles was the clarion call that went before him; so one and all needy persons who had been blessed by the same suffering came to him. We marvel at seeing this multitude of lepers, while not being frightened by the greater number of sinners whom they represented. How many of them are one in their affec- tions and wrong doings, yet how very few of them call for help and ask for a remedy! If leprosy is so disdainful to human eyes, what reputation would sin cause in us if we only knew how to think about it in good faith? And who can suffer the presence of so many people who live in mortal sin, were we to remove the veil of all appearances which dazzle the human eye, and show the spiritual leprosy making our heart so shabby and disfigured? The Law prescribed that no relationship should be had with lepers, and that they were to be expelled from towns. As sad as their status was, it was as distressing as that of the deceased. Indeed, it was like a live image of a Christian who sins, is cast out of the true Jerusalem, his homeland, and detracts from the name of son of God. He no longer belongs to those who harbour within them the Spirit of God, being His grace, but rather to the dead who shelter within them the spirit of the world. What shall we say about the One who, keeping within himself and perhaps loving the leprosy of sin, wants to make company with the clean and take part in the holy mysteries? It is not strange at all that, when cast out of the city, those lepers who represented these other worldly persons, cried out to the Saviour in a loud voice; for the mean-spirited person can resort to no other option but to seek mercy coming from elsewhere.

Their pleas were heard, and the Saviour, who spoke highly of comforting whoever came to him, did not take more than an instant to bestow them with what they asked of him, and he said to them: *Go, show yourselves to the priests*. This happened at the time when the Saviour, because of what Judas had done, had already begun concealing his power to work miracles. For the same reason, without letting them come to him, he was contented to tell them in a loud voice to present themselves to the priests, who only had the right to judge the healing of leprosy and restore lepers to civil society following atonement being made through sacrifice. So that it seemed likely that the order Jesus Christ gave meant that they had been already healed. Actually they were not, but the high esteem they had of the power and wisdom of the Doctor whose help they had implored, made them think that they would be healed even before they came to him. This judgement did not deceive them because while walking bearing this confidence in mind, and while still being on the road, their leprosy disappeared.

The Evangelist says no more than that Jesus Christ looked at them and healed them. This is the gaze of infinite mercy which humbles the heart and leaves it pierced with pain and converted. When they saw Jesus Christ fix his sight on them, the healing came to pass; yet it should be noted that this was preceded by supplication, or prayer. It was heard and well attended to for it was accompanied by submission and followed by prompt obedience; which teaches us that prayer is vain if it is not accompanied by humility; and that penance which is not subject to the laws and order established by the Church is sterile and fruitless. The miracle of healing did not prevent them from obeying the order they had received. They presented themselves to the priests and sought to have them authenticate their healing, later going their separate ways. One of them, seeing that he was clean, returned glorifying God in the presence of all those accompanying the Saviour, thanking him in a loud voice. How many open their mouths to ask favours from God, but so few to thank Him! The spirit of gratitude very rarely abides within the faithful; we pray for our needs, but without attributing glory to God for the many dues we owe Him. Nothing is more proper than for man to pray when finding himself in trouble; but nothing is more just than to give thanks in being cared for, and to try not to detract from the mercy of Him who rewards exceedingly on seeing gratitude and perseverance.

The grateful person returned, praising God along the way. His was not a vain praise and a sham gratitude, for arriving in the presence of his benefactor he prostrated himself at his feet, slammed his face against the ground, and showed his utmost gratitude. How good does it seem to be for the man who, at the feet of his benefactor, confesses his unworthiness and exalts the goodness he has received! If gratitude is not complete, it is not accompanied by humility. What shall we say about those who, living in sin, judge themselves to be creditors of God's grace and keep it in mind to the end of their lives? Yet what is most admirable and worthy of criticism is that the healed man who expressed such gratitude *was a Samaritan*, namely, one of those men who treated the Jews as foreigners and schismatics. Though descendants of Jacob too, they had emancipated themselves from Judea's rule, and they did not recognise the obligation imposed on all Jews to worship God and offer Him sacrifices in His temple in Jerusalem. It is not that educated persons or professionals consecrated to God for many years have always been more grateful and humble before Him. The other nine Jews who disbelieved the occurrence were ungrateful, since being deceived by the priests to whom they had presented themselves, they did not attribute their healing to the miracle that Jesus Christ had wrought on them, but to their having observed the Law by presenting themselves to the priests.

When Jesus Christ only saw at his feet a Samaritan, he was astonished by this eventful occurrence and said: "Were they not ten that I have cleansed of leprosy? Where are the other nine?" The Lord does not ask as if he does not care, but talks in such manner as to indicate being hurt by the ingratitude shown by the ungrateful, and in looking for them he implies that they are unknown to him, like condemned persons. Just as the ungrateful is unaware of the benefit received from God, so the Lord does not recognise the ungrateful one who despises him and acts as if being forgetful of the benefit received. Who is it that does not lack faith and embodies the excessive pride from which this hardness of the Jews was born? Due to their lack of faith the Jews were unaware of the value of God's gifts, and did not care about being thankful for them as they ought to have been. The faithful, grateful and humble Samaritan condemns the proud, foreign and ungrateful Jews. For this reason, when Jesus Christ saw the submissive Samaritan at his feet, he said to him: "Arise and return to your house; your faith has saved you." The leper obeyed and if, as told by the omnipotent Physician, he owed the miracle to his faith and to his trust in him, we have to presume that henceforth he still deserved greater favours by virtue of his gratitude, and that this turned him into one of the most faithful disciples of his Deliverer.

As Jesus Christ many times desired to walk along the roads and to enter most cities being disregarded and unknown, there were others where it seems he preferred entering them in full view of their inhabitants. And so it came to pass that wanting to pass for the last time through the city of Samaria so as to give the Samaritans other great and important lessons, he sent two of his apostles, namely James and John, to find him a place where to lodge. Of this city, once so brimming with people, there are hardly any trace or remains today. Not a single house stands stone on stone over the wide area on which it once stood, and only two small churches are found in the district. One church stands on the prominence of a mountain in the same place where its kings' palace previously stood, while the other is that built in honour of Saint John the Baptist, where the holy precursor was buried between the corpses of the prophets Obadiah and Elisha. The Samaritans envied the glories of the temple of Jerusalem, and were enemies of all those who went there to worship God. They hated Jesus Christ, not only because they were aware of the great respect he held with awe for the Holy City and the temple, but because they saw that he was about to go there to celebrate his last Passover; and for this reason they did not want to receive him in their city or to afford him any lodging. About which Saint Jerome says: "There was a great division of opinion between the Samaritans and the Jews about the place where they ought to offer cult and worship to God. The Samaritans preferred Mount *Garizim* to Jerusalem, and seeing that Jesus Christ was walking towards this city, which they saw as their rival and enemy, they were unwilling to receive him, though it seems likely here there might have been some other shrewd thinking about this. It can be said that it was the will of the Lord God, his Father, that the Samaritans failed to receive him; for since he was proceeding to Jerusalem where he was to suffer and shed his blood, he should not have got involved with the reception afforded to him by the Samaritans and to busy himself teaching in that place; for by doing so he would have differed the day of the passion which he had come to suffer for mankind. So, when Jesus Christ proceeded to Jerusalem, and was resisted by the Samaritans, you ought also consider that if you want to direct your steps to heaven, you will face quarrels on earth, hatred and discord that will put you in conflict; yet do not lose heart and as soon as you can try to be useful for your own sake.

The Saviour's most docile heart was not altered by this repulsion, but it retained a full presence of great tranquillity as an example that, however great is the tribulation which the world raises against us, we must come to him who is our joy and salvation, encouraging us with his example to endure and suffer with the greatest good will and joy. The proof lies in a peaceful and truly resigned heart conforming to the will of God, by feeling pity when the world throws it our way with joy, and by rejoicing with whatever sorrows and troubles might afflict us. The way to sweeten our sorrows is to unite them with those of Christ; and since these are always infinitely greater than those that may happen suddenly to us, if we unite ours with Christ's, they will always seem very sweet to us.

The two apostles, James and John, were extremely enraged; and seeing the Samaritans' ingratitude towards their Master, they spoke to him so, saying: "Lord, do you want us to call fire to come down from heaven and consume these who did not want to receive you?" Oh, how much and how great was their faith in Jesus Christ, for they believed that just by asking for this permission it would have been enough for their desire to be granted! But Jesus Christ thought very differently from them; and if before it was with this in mind that he had praised Elijah's zeal, his apostles were now highly disapproving of it with plenty of zeal. Their zeal was not addressed either to charity, love for true correction, or the desire to see the malice of that people come to an end, but rather to impatience, indiscretion and a desire for revenge. For this reason, looking at them angrily, Jesus Christ said to them: "You do not know to which spirit you belong. The Son of Man whose example of meekness and leniency you ought to imitate, has not come to lose men, but to save them." By which he wanted to tell them that zeal is always inappropriate unless tempered by a discreet will. And the

Venerable Bede, expounding on this section, says: "The Lord said to them: 'Do you not know to which spirit you belong? For you belong to the Holy Spirit, who is good and gentle; and since you are not well aware that you are marked with this Spirit of love and peace, you wish to take revenge with a spirit of hatred, which is in no way lawful for the servants of God'. And he further said to them: 'The Son of Man has not come to lose souls with the harshness of his justice, by imposing on them an absolute death penalty as you wish to do, but he has come to save them by mercy and by relieving their punishment.' This is what suits the mean-spirited best, for they are sooner saved by love than by harshness." And Saint John Chrysostom concludes: "Let us never call out revenge against another person, for we ourselves sharpen the sword and open a greater wound in the bosom of our own heart. If someone hurt us and caused us harm and we want to take revenge on him, let us not take revenge. The best revenge is not to take any revenge even though we can. If you do not take revenge, you make God an enemy of whoever offended you, and you will be avenged in due time. For God said to his people: 'Vengeance is mine and I will repay. In due time their foot will slip: their day of disaster is near and their doom rushes upon them. See how I am the One and only God, and how there is no god besides me. I put to death and I bring to life; I have wounded, and I will heal, and no one can deliver out of my hand. For I lift up my hand to heaven and say: As I live forever, if I sharpen my glittering sword, and my hand takes hold on justice, I will take vengeance on my adversaries, and will pay back those who hate me. Praise his people, oh you nations; for the Lord avenges the blood of his servants, and takes vengeance on his adversaries, and pours out his mercy on the land of his people' (Dt 32:36-43)."

The Lord then, who very clearly announces that every creature yields at his sight, is the One who speaks in this manner and says this. If you then hate the one who sinned against you and want to avenge him, why are you not aware that in doing this you are sinning too and falling into the same shame you condemn? So if you were to be insulted, you should not insult anyone; if you were to be wounded, you should not hurt anyone; if you see yourself upset and grief-stricken, you should not distress or annoy anyone, for if you act differently, this will bring you no advantage, but you would be rather doing everything like the person you condemn. Never has it been that one evil healed another evil; all evils are cured with their opposite actions. The opposite of revenge is charity, which is always meek, humble and kind.

CHAPTER 60

JESUS RESPONDS TO A REQUEST MADE BY THE MOTHER OF ZEBEDEE'S CHILDREN; HE GIVES SIGHT TO A BLIND MAN BEFORE ENTERING JERICHO; HE THEN CALLS ZAC- CHAEUS, AND AS HE DEPARTS THE CITY HE GIVES SIGHT TO TWO OTHER BLIND MEN (MT 20:1; LK 18:1; LK 19:1)

O this day, it so happens in the world that those who go out mostly to be seen and to be considered by men, the more obscure and unrealistic they seem before them; although they are admired on the one hand, they are absurd or at least seem to be so; and in being gazed at, on the other, they do not offer anything more for human thought than reasons for scepticism. One case was the passion of the Son of God, which he himself had foretold so many times to his apostles with such meticulous details that it is incomprehensible how they could doubt what he was saying for a single moment; for they were seeing that Jesus Christ had authorised and affirmed his doctrines with the most obvious miracles, and with his predictions already appearing so close to being fulfilled. Despite all this they still had their doubts, or better still, they did not understand anything of what Jesus Christ told them. The sight of so many horrors was for them an inexplicable enigma. They imagined that the Lord's words could have some mysterious meaning, and they thought that time and circumstances would make things clear for them. It was in this manner they always interpreted what he sometimes told them about the insults he would receive, the whipping, his death and the cross. Since they had not yet learned to love all this, they did not like to hear about it. And because they loved honour, they very often thought of taking front positions and being worth more than others; and because on the other hand self-love is so ingenious, just as it knows how to show differently what threatens it, so does it also know how to hold in high esteem what flatters it; they were firmly persuaded that so however things occurred and were interpreted, they were already very close to the instant when they would see the kingdom of Israel being restored to its former splendour. So they were greatly disappointed by these ideas during Jesus Christ's life.

Being well steeped, John and James, the two sons of Zebedee, one day spoke to their mother that she would request the Saviour on their behalf for something which distinctly showed their inclination to reign. As told to do by her sons, this woman presented herself to the Saviour, respectfully adored him, and begged him to grant her the grace she was about to request. Jesus Christ acquiesced to her plea, and also showed his pleasure at what she was asking of him. Encouraged by this offer, and the more persuaded not only because of kinship, but also because she was one of those devoted women who ordinarily followed him and his disciples, both to hear the Saviour's doctrines and to serve them in any need they might have as itinerants who were always on the move with no fixed dwelling on earth, she said to him: *Grant, Lord, that my sons whom you are seeing, have the first two seats in your kingdom, and that when you attain your glory, one sits on your right hand and the other on your left.* She said it so that none of the other disciples would be allowed to claim any preference over them. It may well have been that the figure of the twelve thrones about which Jesus Christ had spoken shortly before, where his apostles would sit after his resurrection to judge the twelve tribes of Israel, inspired the sons' pretension and the mother's request. The Saviour, listening patiently to Salome's plea who undoubtedly was unaware of the reign which he came to establish or what kind of seats he had prepared in it for his apostles, much less the steep and fragrant path through which they were to climb to them, while not snubbing the mother directed his answer to the sons. By it he did not treat them in the manner which their ambition deserved, but with utmost kindness and tenderness, making them see how inopportune their way of thinking was. So he said to them: *You do not know what you are asking for.* He so gave them well to understand that they had failed absolutely to grasp what was his great kingdom, what its first positions were, and by what means one rises to them; and so he further told them: *Will you have the spirit to drink the cup which I am going to drink? Or to be baptised with the baptism with which I am about to be baptised?* Recalling baptism the Saviour meant that of the blood he was to shed, and by the cup he spelt out his death on the cross. The two disciples knew well that the Lord wanted to give proof of his generosity, and so both promptly answered him: *Lord, we can.* He showed them the way to get there, not to the seats they were requesting, but to those that suited them; which was like telling them: "If you want to get to where I am going, you must walk along the path along which I walk. I am a Son of God and I walk along the path of humility. I came down from above, and humiliated I will proceed to that place. To reach the mountain one must climb from the depth of the valley. If you aspire to the seat of glory, you must first drink the cup of humility."

In spite of this we cannot but admire the apostles' reply in saying to Jesus Christ that they could drink a cup like the bitter one of his passion and death. According to Saint Augustine's thought, this answer was like the promise which Peter had made to Christ, that he would not depart from him until death; this promise was really broken by two words a poor woman told him, although it seems that Peter's answer had its source in charity not in ambition. They presumed to achieve what they wanted, but they were not aware of the weakness they had to reach to get what they had foolishly asked. Ambition blinded them so that they were unable to see their weakness; he lessened their fear, and gave them heart by promising them what they could not fulfil for themselves. Yet, Jesus Christ's answer asserted to a certain extent the strength of his heart, for he said to them, *Surely you shall drink my cup.* He did not say your cup, but mine. And it was as if to say: "You will suffer and die for me, for sorrow is not the martyr's lot, but its cause is." The Saviour's answer can be considered as another new revelation of his passion and death, particularly made to those closest to him. As to which Saint Chrysostom says: "It was proper for the Lord to reveal this mystery to his closest friends, for the glory of God and men's healing are condensed in Christ's passion and death.

There is nothing more rightly pertaining to men than the death of their Redeemer; nor is there anything else for which we must be more thankful to God than the death of his Son.

Nor is it strange that he would like to make this most important revelation to his dearest friends in this particular manner, for great deeds should only be revealed to great friends. This disclosure was very necessary, as it was opportune that the apostles should be perfectly aware of what was about to happen, that they might know that he would suffer voluntarily, and so would not doubt that he was to be resurrected. Due of the fear of the passion, so often foretold and announced by Jesus Christ, the disciples undoubtedly resisted that their Master should go up to the holy and high city. But the Lord went there with all of his heart's affections, and even when still far off he proceeded to the beloved city undertaking the most tender and ardent discussions. He had come to work for the healing of the whole universe, as told in the Scripture, and Jerusalem is situated in the centre of the earth. Just as from a centre point rays of light radiate and rivers of blood flow, so does it illuminate and water the whole earth. Arabia is located to the east of Jerusalem, and in the time of the children of Israel it consisted of a vast wilderness and an almost trackless desert; through this desert God had stopped his people's sons for forty years, raining manna from heaven over them, and making water flow from the rock. This Arabia is separated from Judea by the Dead Sea. Egypt lies to the south of Jerusalem, with all its vast regions; for this reason, when God brought the children of Israel out of the slavery of that city, and directed them along the path of that desert of Arabia, He made them take a very scary detour. To the west it is surrounded by the Great Sea, and to the north by Syria and the Sea of Cyprus, so that one can conclude that the Holy City is sited in the middle of the earth. And as any presiding and commanding person occupies a prominent place, sited in middle or centre place, it is for this reason that the Sovereign Ruler of the whole earth suffered in its midst. The apostles, who were to preach the Gospel throughout the world, were to start off from the centre point and move towards the periphery, bearing the banner of the cross and the sign of redemption to the ends of the earth; and suffering everywhere persecution and martyrdom for the faith of their Saviour, they were to sit on his right and on his left hand, drinking the bitter cup of his passion. But delving into the mysterious secret of Jesus Christ's answer to his apostles, we get to know to a greater extent this most interesting thought contained within it. He told them: "That you be seated to my right or to my left, it is not up to me to grant it to you, but it is for those to whom it is prepared by my Father." According to Saint Chrysostom this means that the Lord did not want to have honours and crowns with them besides him, but agonies, sweat and death. It is as if he told them that it was not the time to talk about prizes, but about struggles, dangers and death; for no one can reign with Christ without first suffering with Christ. God resolved that no one should come to His kingdom unless he deserves it and is worthy of it. As he does not accept persons unless they deserve it, he does not give salvation and eternal life to anyone who is undeserving, because the equality of love, as Saint Augustine says, does not allow the approval of persons. And the Venerable Bede adds: "Jesus Christ says: 'It is not up to me to grant it to you, for I cannot grant it to the proud, and you are acting like proud right now.' They could reply: 'We will be humble,' and Christ could repeat to them, 'But then you will no longer be yourselves.' Christ does not reward blood, but virtue. Those who do not know this philosophy are unaware of Christ. They are unfaithful and traitors since, being imbued with it, they lack courage to put it into action.

Having been so tormented, the two apostles did not insist any longer; yet this was not enough to appease the outrage of the other ten who were present and understood what they were asking for; so they began to murmur, until they called the Lord who, in an admiring manner, reasoned out things with them and calmed them down completely. He gathered them around himself, and as a loving Master said to them: *You know well how the princes and kings of nations behave: they govern with iron rule, they lord over their subjects, and sometimes they treat them like slaves.* Which was like telling them: "Is this what you have perhaps learned in my school?

Is this the model which you should adopt? This should not be your conduct; rather, anyone among you who wants to be any greater in the eyes of God, must be the smallest and serve all others; for it is not in commanding but in serving one's brethren that persons can obtain first places in my kingdom. Keep this example in your sight: *The Son of Man has not come to be served but to serve and to give his life for the redemption of many.*"

Jesus Christ, whom the need to instruct his apostles had been somewhat of a stumbling block to many, continued going along his way with the same diligence as before, and soon he arrived near a very wide plain extending on either side of the Jordan. Jericho, a city of unforgettable memories for the sons of Judah, was sited in that place. Just as he drew nearer to the city, the countrymen went out to meet Jesus Christ, and he was soon surrounded by a large procession of inhabitants. Jericho was two leagues away from the Jordan and seven from Jerusalem, but although it had once been a famous city, it is now razed to the ground. Yet it still preserves the house of *Raab* in testimony and as a sign of her faith, but now only its walls remain covered with some roofing. A precious fountain is also preserved close to this; its waters were bitter to drink, and made the irrigated land infertile; yet Elisha turned its waters into drinking water, and made the soil irrigable and the land fertile. This fountain flows down Mount *Quarantania*, which rises some miles away from the city. As the Lord was heading towards it for a healing mission, as Saint Jerome says, many sick people had gone there before him. While still on the way he saw a poor blind man begging passers-by for alms. From the shuffle and haste shown by these passers-by, he was aware that not far away from him some great event had happened; and on enquiring about it, he was told that Jesus of Nazareth was passing through the plain of Jericho, followed by a great multitude. Jesus Christ was known throughout the country, and those from other lands, as this blind man could have been, knew that Jesus Christ was the son or heir of David, promised to his nation as its Christ and king. The poor and the afflicted knew even better the compassion he had for them, so that no one doubted his power.

Great are the mysteries that begin to be discovered anew, as Jericho represents the world, and the blind man the spiritual darkness of humans. Let us grieve that we lack eyes to see the personal matters which lose our souls, and that we do not even feel that we lack spiritual eyes to know ourselves, to see the truth and make out our way to salvation. Blindness of the heart causes man to settle comfortably in the ways of the world, which ways lead to eternal perdition. And after, who will take us out of them? Could it by chance be other blind persons who also walk along these ways? Ah! These will fasten us down in greater misery, and make our blindness more enduring and permanent. Only he, who passes by Jericho, will save us and take us to Jerusalem.

Nor is it strange that the blind man asked for alms, since misery and spiritual blindness always go hand in hand. The great misery of man does not consist so much in having nothing and to be in need of everything, inasmuch as in not having eyes to see one's own poverty and seeking with great pride the treasures of divine mercy. The blind man's curiosity was also a gift from Christ. Many things seem casual in life, and the order of grace powerfully helps our sanctification. Blessed was the temporal disaster for the blind man as it served him as an occasion to seek and know Christ, and to experiment within himself his great mercy. Filled with confidence, he began to cry out with all strength and to say: *Jesus, Son of David, have mercy on me.*

The loving Saviour heard the cries of the blind man very well, but did not seem to be moved by them; so that the poor man shouted ceaselessly even more forcefully. Those walking at the front of the party, believing that the Lord was apparently walking without taking any notice of him, rebuked him and ordered him to be quiet. A person who knows his disease, who desires to have his health restored and is sure of the doctor's skill and goodness, cries out to be cured. The cry of faith is most vivid when it rises from the bowels of humility. This cry is the beginning of healing and the garment of perfect restoration; and since the devil is aware that by prayerful sighs he loses his kingdom in us and his dominion over us, he thus causes the cries of our spirit to be suffocated by suggestions and temptations, making it impossible for us to cry out to God. As the blind man became deaf to all the reasons and threats of those who wanted to prevent him from sighing, we must also become deaf to hell's threats and suggestions, crying out to God with all the more fervour the greater the temptation is with which Satan threatens and belabours us. The Lord was more pleased with the blind man than what he visibly showed. And yes, having arrived in front of the humble supplicant, who had raised increasingly his voice and cried out with more faith, Jesus Christ stopped and ordered the blind man to be brought to him. The humble and constant prayer moved by faith, uttered with hope, and shining with the fire of charity or love, stopped Christ from moving forward; for he has a deep-seated feeling of mercy for all those who invoke him with a spirit of truth. Christ's commandment was a statement of saintliness brought about by the blind man's faith, and his resolve to be brought before him was his first inkling that in order to follow Christ he had first to renounce the world. And it was well that he could and should do so, for Christ attended to him when the world was rebuking his cry. The world is always opposed to those who seek Christ!

After the Saviour had the poor blind man brought near him, he said to him: *What do you want me to do to you?* And the blind man replied, *Lord, in such state as I am in, what can I want, if not to make me see?* He did not ask for any riches or worldly honours, but eyes to see. Jesus Christ was moved by his desire to have his health restored, and so he had then asked him what it was he wanted. It is a work of grace for man to give his consent to being healed from his vices What does the whole world serve anyone who does not see his own slavery and the need for ransom? Yet the world is filled with blind people who do not wish to see, who love blindness and abhor light. Christ desires more eagerly to give us the eyes of the heart than those other eyes of the body; but because we love vices and desire to still abide in them, we do not want the light which makes us see their ugliness and narrows our view in seeking Christ.

As the blind man was enlivened by faith, Jesus Christ told him that his desires were the same as his, so he told him: *I also want you to see; open your eyes and see; it is your faith which has given you sight.* The miracle was worked in an instant. Christ rewards a gift with another gift, faith with sight. Grace creates faith, faith invokes and attracts mercy and associates it with almightiness. The same Word which brought the world out of nowhere, creates in man a new heart, transforms his darkness into light, and gives the slave true freedom. Why does God enlighten you, if not to see and fulfil your religious duties, that you may know him and love him? That you may fortify faith with works, and in every place and time have Jesus Christ before your eyes, obeying his law and imitating his work? For this reason as soon as the blind man found that he could see clearly, he did not keep back from being full of thankfulness. He followed the Saviour, exalting the greatness of God. The large group accompanying Jesus Christ, being moved after seeing such a great wonder, publicly gave thanks to the Lord in the same place where he had wrought it; for a grateful heart always follows the eyes illuminated with the light of Christ. What good does the day serve for the wayfarer unless he walks while the sun shines? What does it matter that faith lights up your eyes, if your feet are not moved by love? Nor how would it be known that the soul's blindness was cast out, unless Christ is followed? To follow him it is necessary to give him glory, and it is given to him by whosoever with his works confirms the sanctity of his law and extols the greatness of his mercy. Those who love the world deny Christ's glory and bestow it upon the world they love. No glory is given to God because His works are not perfectly contemplated. Those who were amazed by the sight received by the blind man, contemplated the marvellous work they had just seen, and could not help but burst into the Lord's praises.

The Lord did not go much farther that day, retiring for the night to Jericho's neighbourhood, He spent three days going around in that country, spreading as usual wherever he went a unique and unequivocal proof of his goodness. Finally on the third day he entered the city accompanied by a large crowd of people. A rich man who had long wanted to see Jesus Christ and considered him the great Prophet of

Israel, was told that he was passing by and so went out to meet and see him. This man was one of the main publicans of the country, a rich man, as publicans of his ilk usually were; but he was a very short man, and so he remained as if locked up in prison in the midst of the crowd, and all he did to see the Saviour was useless. How true it is that the noise and crowd of worldly affairs is a certain and almost insurmountable impediment to seeing and knowing Christ! Zacchaeus' stature is an image of man's inadequacy to do, desire and think of anything that will lead him to know Christ. So when Zacchaeus saw himself in this state, an opportunity befell him as to climb to the top of a *sycamore tree*, near which Jesus Christ had to pass, to have the pleasure of seeing him. He had the joy of seeing and of being seen by the Saviour, for grace anticipates nature and gives it feet to run in search of a remedy and lifts it above itself. So that by overcoming the impediments of human corruption, he may get to know him who was to give him his healing; and in order for him to know that he was not only being looked upon, but also called by the Saviour by his own name; Jesus Christ called him to come down promptly and told him very pleasantly that, in order that he might have full joy and also enjoy his presence without a hurry, he wanted to stay in his house that day for so it suited him.

According to Saint Ambrose, it was through the Jews that the Saviour made his way to the Gentiles. And as it happened with all peoples, by doing good to all, preparing men for the adoption of the Son of God, who was to work in them by dying, Jericho was not to be a city abandoned by the Lord, although there he did not give unequivocal signs of his natural mercy, being so close to his death. Zacchaeus was the publican, the new fruit of the new epoch, in which what was written in the Canticle of Canticles he was to be mysteriously fulfilled: *The fig tree produced its figs* (Sg 2:13). For the *sycamore* was a kind of fig tree, and Christ came to the inheritance of the world so that the trees might produce men and not fruit, as Saint Ambrose himself assures us. Nathanael saw Christ under the fig tree, because he was still on the outer side of the Law (Jn 1:48); Zacchaeus was however on top of the fig tree, because he was already above the Law. Zacchaeus was for Christ an accomplished defender, Nathanael was a public preacher. Zacchaeus even sought Christ in the Law, while Nathanael, being above the Law, left his kinsmen and followed the Lord.

Since Zacchaeus did not aspire to such high bliss, such as having Christ lodge in his house, although he knew how awesome and advantageous the goodness and worthiness of the divine Saviour was for him, he hastily came down from the tree, being full of joy as a sign that he accepted Jesus Christ's proposal, and led him at once to his house and treated him with utmost appreciation and veneration. Grace being prompt, it does not suffer any delay and obeys with joy, a humble person only desires to climb the tree of faith to advance in the knowledge and love of Christ, and later to exercise himself in mercy.

It is always fickle and unsteady persons, who are just as ready to appreciate as to despise; just as ready to admire and applaud, as to murmur and criticize; and it rarely ceases to be so, that what today may be for them a reason for appreciation, can very soon become a reason for insult and contempt; and so did it also happen and in good time on this occasion. All those who saw the reward and singular favour Jesus Christ bestowed on Zacchaeus, soon began to murmur because he was going to be a guest in a publican's house; as if this fact were a public approval for his sins. This was a very rude slander even to merit a refutation by Jesus Christ. Zacchaeus responded triumphantly to this slander with grandiose and admirable deeds, while justifying the Saviour's actions at the same time, showing that he had come to visit him in an attempt to convert him. The wisdom of the flesh always judges by what it sees: and since it cannot probe the inner depths of the spirit or understand the secrets or mysteries of God's providence and wisdom, it can very easily transform the ideas of what it can only see; and so it was deceived by the thought it had formed when seeing the Saviour visiting the publican's house. After Zacchaeus had listened with the greatest attention to Jesus Christ's sweet counter-claims, much to the confusion of the mutterers, he said to him: "Lord, I confess before those who are here present and know that I am a great sinner. I have nothing to claim in my defence, and God does not want me to increase the number of my sins, while wanting to forgive them. If until now I have been somewhat of a scandal to the public, I would like you to know my resolutions from now on. *Of all that I have I apportion half of it for the poor: I will settle my accounts, and after examination I will give four times more than I may have taken from anyone whom I have defrauded.*" In truth, only the hand of God can work in man's heart such an immense and sudden change, by replacing in him such heroic and sublime desires and resolutions, having had in his life no other thought but to amass riches. What Zacchaeus was thinking could not but be approved by Jesus Christ, then condemning with his approval the hardness of some rich men, in the same manner as he had one day condemned with his judgment and justice. Such men not only resist giving to the poor of the surplus they have in their houses, but also to restore what had been acquired in a wrong manner. Jesus Christ did not want to defer the remedy when the sin was confessed, and he also wanted the satisfaction to be the much greater. So it was the Saviour Himself who testified before the whole world how satisfied he was with that repentant sinner, saying *that was a day of happiness for the house of Zacchaeus;* that this tax collector was a true son of Abraham; and that he had entered his house to deliver him from his wrongful state.

Here the Saviour condemned the Pharisees' reckless murmuring, and rewarded the tax collector's obedient and humble faith by counting him among the children of the Promise. But those murmurers did not understand the mystery of Christian grace, which adds the families of Gentiles to the Abraham's race, and makes out of both peoples one united family together with Jesus Christ, the master who laid the cornerstone. All of which was like saying to those who were present: "This is the moment when Zacchaeus' faith, his obedience to God's orders, his fairness, his selflessness and his charity, have made him a true son of Abraham. He is also one of those by whom the Son of Man has come to instruct and teach in person and to exercise his ministry on earth. For the firstborn son of the sons of men has been sent to all the places of Palestine, to go and search for himself, to gather and save the lost sheep of the house of Israel." The Son of Man who has come to seek us and save us is Jesus Christ, the light of our darkness, the medicine of our evils, the way of our exile, the protection, security, progress, perfection, beginning and end of our life. So that, however advanced we are on the path of perfection, if we want not to detract from curing grace and final perseverance, we ought to always believe being numbered among those who have perished. The Venerable Bede comments on this passage: "This is the foolishness which the tax collector converts into wisdom by taking it from the sycamore, as one who bears fruit from the tree of life, since he later appears as wise as he was previously foolish. Wisdom means returning with high interest those things which have been taken by fraud, returning them to their lawful owner; wisdom means renouncing one's own things and despising those which can be seen in order to obtain those which cannot be seen; renouncing oneself and desiring to die in order to live in the thereafter and reign with Jesus Christ; and wisdom finally means to constantly follow in the footsteps of him who tells us that *If you want to be perfect, sell all your possessions and give it to the poor, and if you want to reach the kingdom of heaven, take up your cross and follow me*; for this I came, says God, from heaven to earth, taking flesh and becoming man, to seek with doctrine and to save by grace what was lost by guilt. Having lost his innocence, man acquired his natural innocence, which is the likeness of grace and the adoption of glory. As to the first it is compared to the lost sheep; as to the second, to the drachma which was also lost; the third, to the prodigal son. Jesus Christ came to put these three things right; and so this is what he said to us through Saint Luke: *He does not come to call the righteous, but sinners to penance*. Saint John Chrysostom tells us the same thing on this as the Saviour said to the murmuring mobs and Pharisees: "Why do you reproach me if I come to excuse sinners? So that far from hating them, I have come into the world owing to the love I have for them. I have come as a doctor to heal them, and not as a judge to condemn them; for this reason I become a guest of the sick, suffering and enduring the intolerable stench they exhale;

all to give them the remedy they need." In truth it is kind and pious for Jesus Christ to silence the mob's murmuring by explaining the mysteries which they did not understand, teaching them that looking for sinners and bringing them on the right path was the important business which his Father had entrusted to him.

After all this Jesus Christ left Jericho, again accompanied by several mobs who wished to hear his doctrines for far longer. He started his march along the desert way, to be able to spread with more relief the loving affections of his heart for the good of that immense multitude, and desiring to nourish their spirit with an overfill of consoling doctrines which he uttered. It is worth hearing the important reflection made on this occasion by Saint Chrysostom: "Nothing can be greater witness to the anxious request of a farmer as an abundant harvest which he takes from his fields; similarly nothing justifies more a doctor's jealous resolve as a numerous clientele attending his practice frequently. None of those who followed Christ were stopped by the arduous way, because spiritual and true love never feels any tiredness or fatigue. No one loses the mindfulness or care of the goods possessed on earth, having entered through the door by means of which he possessed the heavenly kingdom. For indeed no one considers anything to be good on earth after having started to like heavenly goods truly related to Christ; for just as a man who once tasted delicious food and fed on it for a long time would then find common food tasteless and coarse, so also would anyone who tasted the sweetness of Christ's delicacies, then be irritated and does not find pleasant flavour to his spiritual palate in any earthly delicacy. Truly, Jesus Christ was on this occasion the beautiful rose that dawned in the lush fields of Jericho, such as is celebrated by Solomon in his Book of Wisdom: a white rose owing to the holiness of his righteousness, and incarnated by the blood of his passion. And just as the fragrance of the rose is smelt from afar and, before the rose is found or seen it is already felt to exist by its fragrance, so also while the Lord was passing through the streets of Jericho did two blind men smell the fragrance of his divinity before experiencing the full effects of his power."

It was a happy murmur which the two blind men heard caused by the great multitude following Jesus Christ. Many kings and prophets desired to hear him, and could not. However they, who had the joy of encountering him, started crying out, *Lord, Son of David, have mercy on us*. They were not disappointed in their hopes, and the Lord bid that they be presented to him. One of them, who was more known than the other, was called *Bartimaeus*, which means, *son of Timaeus*, and many passers-by wanted to silence him because he shouted more than his companion, with a repeated and clear cry for mercy. But hearing that Jesus Christ had commanded them to be brought before him, some of the same mob came to Bartimaeus and said: Get up and have great hope, for that man calls you." When he heard this the blind man jumped for joy, let go of his mantle and ran with his companion to the Saviour who, before granting them what they wanted, asked them *what was it they were asking for?* They answered without ceasing: *Lord, open our eyes, give us sight*. The sovereign physician, who did not ask many questions when those who begged him were driven by true faith, knowing that those two hapless persons truly acknowledged him, was moved to compassion. So, touching their eyes with his all-powerful hand, he said to them: *You can already see; your faith has given you salvation, and at the same time you have regained your sight*. They had cried out loud and prayed at the appropriate time, for they had cried out and prayed to the source of light, and for this they were instantly enlightened. The Lord touched them as a man, and healed them as God. When they called him Son of David, it was as if his healing power was suspended; but when they called him Lord, he granted them salvation, that they might know that they were not saved by the Son of David, but by the Son of God. Whoever runs to the Lord and invokes him with faith like the blind men, experiences in his heart what they tasted in their body. Whoever calls upon the Lord hears his voice fruitfully, and experiences the touch of grace in himself, being illuminated by the praises of holy doctrine; he is inwardly comforted by the charisms of grace and strengthened by the sacraments of the Church; by means of which he remains proficient and unobstructed to follow Christ and speak out publicly his mercies as those blind men.

Origen assures us that these two blind men represent the two peoples, the Gentiles and the Jews. The Gentiles were blinded by idolatry, and the Jews by the perversity of evil doctrines taught to them by the scribes and Pharisees, and breaching God's precepts by human traditions. Just as the blind were seated on the opposite side of the road, so were these two peoples also seated, because although they apparently had heard the news of the Law, they were ignorant of Christ, the true way. The Lord first healed a blind man before entering Jericho, and then two when leaving that city. By this, according to the Venerable Bede, he wanted to instruct us how he called a people before his passion, and two peoples after his resurrection and ascension to heaven; and how he manifested with all clarity through the apostles to both Jews and Gentiles, the inviolable mystery of the union of divinity with humanity, and of his most sacred passion and death.

CHAPTER 61
JESUS IS RECEIVED BY MARTHA AND MARY IN THE FORTRESS TOWN OF BETHANY; AND BEING INVITED TO EAT AT THE HOUSE OF LAZARUS, THEIR BROTHER, MARY POURS OINTMENT OVER HIS HEAD (*JN 12:1-12*)

HE time of Jesus Christ's passion and death was instantly approaching, and Jesus Christ desired to have it fully known as foretold by the prophets in fulfilment of their prophecies. On Monday the Lord had left Ephraim and turned towards the plain, city and deserts of Jericho, returning to Bethany on Friday evening. Along this journey Jesus Christ's designs did not match the apostles' ideas: they were convinced that the Saviour then wanted to go to Jerusalem, if only to the house of Lazarus, whom he had raised from the dead. But the Lord arranged matters in such manner that as he approached the village of Bethany night was falling, and the Sabbath began at sunset. He respected the Law of holy rest and did not leave the place where he was caught up; but the following day in the afternoon when the Sabbath obligation came to an end, he reached Bethany as night fell. Jesus Christ's stay so close to that place was a way to spread the news of his arrival and the Jews, eager to see both the Saviour and Lazarus whom he had raised from the dead, ran in droves to the place where Lazarus dwelt. It was indeed a spectacle worthy of the greatest admiration to see in the same house such a powerful man who had been raised from the dead after laying in the tomb for four days and had become corrupted. He was so happy, not only for having received from Jesus Christ this singular grace, but also for having the joy of hosting in his house the beloved Benefactor who had restored him to life.

If one considers Jesus Christ's most ardent love for Lazarus, it would be easy to understand the reason why, as one believes, he laid for his Benefactor a sumptuous supper which the Gospel itself calls *great*. For if gratitude, for a small favour, is the daughter of a noble bosom and goes well with all people, it fares much better with the magnanimous and the noble who received that which is most extraordinarily and here specifically indicated. However, a difficulty arises from this, and seemingly not a little one, which has to be clarified. Saint John, whom we follow in this chapter, implies, although he does not say it clearly, that this lodging and supper were in Lazarus' house, as he states that Jesus Christ went to Bethany six days before the Passover. This must be counted in full from the Sabbath, which that year coincided with the eighth day of the month of *Nisan*, equivalent to our 28th March, until the sixth day or Friday, when the Passover began in the evening. And naming the persons who appeared on this occasion, he only mentions Martha, Mary and Lazarus. This circumstance and others, as conveniently noted and sketched by the Evangelist, prove that this historical passage is not identical, nor should it be confused, with that referred to by Saint Matthew and Saint Mark about the lodging and banquet laid for the Lord also in Bethany and in the house of *Simon the leper*, which took place two days before the days of unleavened bread and the Passover, namely on Wednesday or the following fourth day.

Furthermore Saint John adds that *Mary, having taken a pound of precious balm, anointed Jesus' feet with this ointment and wiped them with her hair*. Saint Mark says that Jesus Christ was residing in Bethany, in the house of Simon the leper, and while sitting at the table, *a woman came with an alabaster pot* (supposedly a vessel or flask), full of ointment or perfume made from the spike of the tuberose, which was very expensive; and breaking the pot, she poured the balsam on Jesus Christ's head (Mk 14:3); and Saint Matthew says the same thing almost with identical words (Mt 26:6-7). Then, according to the Evangelists' narrative it is shown that Jesus Christ was at two dinners or invited to them in Bethany in the space of six days: the first was at Lazarus's house and the second at Simon the leper's house, since that was six days before the Passover and these being only two, it might very well have happened that in one and the other Mary repeated doing the affectionate gift to her beloved Master, since being the more of a contemplative disposition and given to prayer, it might perhaps have been better revealed and understood by her more clearly that Jesus Christ was ever drawing closer to his death; and for this reason she would no doubt have better wished to lavish him with much more solace. Without contradicting or repelling this explanation, the disciple who was a traitor burst on one occasion or another into bitter and violent censure against Mary's charitable action, trying to disguise his greed with a mask of zeal and charity; since he was always unfaithful, perfidious, greedy and, like all hypocrites and wicked people, constantly abusing of piety and religion to hide his vices.

Jesus Christ came to Bethany, that is to say *to the house of obedience*, as relating to the cause of the passion, for he became obedient to his Eternal Father until death, and death on the cross; and as relating to the fruit of passion, which is obtained only by those who obey Him, as Saint Paul said (Heb 5:9): "Although he was the Son of God, as a man he learned to obey; and so being accomplished or *sacrificed* on the cross, he came to be a cause of eternal salvation *for all those who obey him.*" And Saint Jerome also provided a similar commentary in Saint Mark's text, saying: "The Lord, having suffered for the whole world and washed all nations with his blood, came and dwelt in Bethany in the house of obedience, for the deer's kid always returns to the kennel bed or to the burrow from which he came out, and the Son obedient to his Father unto his death demands obedience from us." By going to the house where Lazarus had died and where he was resurrected, was also to show that those who are dead of guilt in that same house, are also raised to walk along the path of justice. And it was right there that a great supper was prepared for Jesus Christ; certainly not devoid of any mystery, because the Lord receives great strength when he rejoices in our obedience. A caring Martha served the Lord, Lazarus ate at the table and Mary poured the balm at his feet; for obedience shows itself in action and concern; it is at the same time calm, frugal and modest and, above all, ardent and contemplative; and its lovely conditions were perfectly portrayed in the two sisters and a brother who dwelt in the house of obedience.

Yet these are not the only mysteries that are enclosed and discovered when Jesus Christ departs to Bethany six days before the Passover. Six days before the works of redemption were consummated, it was in the house of obedience that he spent six days in the works of creation. It is on the sixth day that he created man, and redeemed him in the sixth era of the world, on the sixth day and in the sixth hour. That supper that was celebrated six days before, was the work of the love shown by Lazarus, Martha and Mary, and stood for the faith of the new Church, which is the work of love. And it was celebrated very opportunely, in Bethany, house of obedience, because the Church is the true house, office and asylum of obedience, and includes within it only those who are truly obedient and obey out of love. Those who obey by force or by fear, resist with their will and obey only in appearance. This is why Wisdom says that *Only obedient holy man would sing the victory*. He who truly obeys, walks joyfully to martyrdom, obeys God and triumphs over the tyrant, torment and death; but he who denies God by obeying the tyrant obeys Him out of fear and strength, and loses merit, salvation and life.

There resided two sisters and a brother in the castle of Bethany, and each prepared gifts their own way to receive the divine guest. Lazarus procured the provisions, Martha seasoned them and served them at table, and Mary prepared a pound of tuberose spike ointment, which was the most precious and valuable ever known. After the Saviour sat down at table, Mary approached Jesus Christ, threw herself at his feet, sprinkled them with the balm, and wiped them with her hair. What a most excellent example worthy of being brought to the attention of all beings! This anointing is the living image of the zeal to worship God, and also of how far we should go to come to the aid of the poor and to love our brothers and sisters! There is no doubt that so many showy expenses made on some occasions to honour Christ would be very well spent on feeding his members; but there are extraordinary throwaways whose excess in cult is much commended, and whose scarcity would be very deplorable. In such a case it would be a short walk with Christ, under the pretext of helping his members. Only the author of charity can let us know when, how and to what extent we are allowed this excess; but it will always show very little love to his religion, whoever treats what is spent on external worship as lost. Those who at this point walk tight-fisted and mean-spirited with Christ, set their eyes on value and authority which he gave to this external worship, accepting him and taking him for good only when he tried to establish the inner adoration of the spirit. Today, it is said, let Christ and his Church, the cult and his ministers, be cut off from all that can make the dignified mysteries of the religion of the Crucified appear great, and give to his ministers, prestige, reputation and authority; so that the great are clothed with so much prestige, decoration and pomp, that they only need to receive on earth the incense and honours which are only due to the Divine.

Yet to what extent would their pride be subdued were they to consider Mary's humble and tender action as they should? She poured the balsam on Christ's feet; yet to pour it out she broke the alabaster pot, and afterwards cleaned his feet with her hair. Why do you not pour out your heart's intentions at the feet of the Redeemer? Why do you not have the courage to break your pot? Why do you not resolve to break the hard and vile chains which imprison you? Why do you not show up to weep at his feet with the greatest sorrow, and then wipe away your tears with the affections of love and the most ardent charity? Has it even occurred to you to think of the mysterious significance Mary's beautiful hair? Take a good look at what hairs are on the head. They are nothing but the body's leftovers, dead cells and overabundance. The poor are the feet of Christ, and your leftover goods are your hair; in leading a good life you anoint Jesus Christ's feet and follow in his footsteps, with alms you clean them. Hear what Saint Augustine says: *Do not ask what to make of your overabundances;* your leftovers are needed for the feet of Christ. This may be why the Lord made his Evangelist write, *As you did it to one of the least of these my brethren, you did it to me;* you poured out solace on the heads of the poor, you filled their bosom with bread crusts, you covered their nakedness with your superfluous garments; but you must know that you rewarded me with it, and that it was myself who received the reward. Mary approached Jesus Christ as she was required to do before the source of mercy to wash away her faults; meeting her he poured out abundant torrents upon her. She broke the alabaster pot, for she had already broken the hardness of her heart, and the house was filled with the fragrance of ointment, the same as the heart is filled with the fragrance of grace when the Lord pours his mercy upon us. A creature, in pursuing holy customs, spreads a good odour all over the place; it is modest in its actions, prudent in its words and presents itself everywhere as an edifying model. So it is that Saint Paul could very well say about himself, spreading everywhere Christ's good fragrance (2 Cor 2:14-15), for by his preaching and example the fragrance of God's news spread throughout the world. Mary could never use the precious balm she held in store any better; her action, however, was not approved by all those present, for they approved even more the criticism coming from where it should have been least expected, that is from Judas Iscariot, the disciple who had to deliver Jesus Christ into the hands of his enemies. He asked, *Why has this ointment not been sold for three hundred denarii, and this amount distributed among the poor?* Note that the value of the denarius amounted to little more than that of a silver *real* or two *vellon reals* of today's currency, and consequently the total sum of just over two ounces of gold. He spoke this way, however, not because he cared for the poor, nor due to any affection of love and mercy towards the needy, *but because he was a thief and was in charge of the money bag*; for he was the keeper of the alms he received for the upkeep of the Lord and his disciples, and he stole and cheated of the money that was kept in it. It looked like he was doing charity for the poor, he who would within a few days hand over God to men in the hands of his enemies. He who was still numbered among the apostles, was the same one who dared criticise the generous liberality of this fervent and loving disciple. Oh, how many Christians today still imitate the sacrilegious murmuring of the traitorous disciple! The liberality with which some pious people seek to maintain the magnificence of divine worship is generally attributed to a secret hostility to religion, by hidden greed and the hypocrisy of ungodliness, covering itself with the affections of sincere charity and compassion for the poor. No one complains or rebukes in support of the needy about the Asian luxury of the kings' palaces, the superfluous pomp of big-heads, excess in vestments, the superabundance and luxury of distinctive livery, the magnificent horse trains taken out for strolls, the sumptuousness and frequency of the invitations and the excessive bounty of food and drinks; but a sad look is cast, justifying one's love for the poor, when a Christian shows interest in the decency of the altars.

Creatures surround themselves with this luxury and external show to make their authority and person assume greater importance; were an inspection and search to be made of their rooms, cabinets, rostrums, and perhaps also of their sheds and horse stables, not only will mere lavishness be seen all around, but also a wasteful extravagance in gold and precious stones, with no account of compassion for the wretched. And is it possible that we have precisely within us this mercy in being attentive to keeping decency in the Lord's house, to whom we owe everything, and to whom we frequently also see indecency lodged in the narrow enclosure of a small tabernacle? Is it possible that so much splendour is sought, so much magnificence is spent and so much gold is dispensed to give prestige to a vile maggot of the earth, and little care is taken to give it to Him who fills everything with his majesty and greatness, who disposes everything with His adorable providence, who adorns everything and embellishes it with his immense wisdom and who, finally, bought back and redeemed all with his blood? That which spoke in Judas was perfidious ungodliness, indeed, and his covetous greed gave vent to his speech. It takes only a single mumbler to disturb the peace of a family, the repose of a nation, and to hinder within the fruit of good example. There is no work, however good it may be, which is not exposed to cursing and slander; a thousand times does disgusting envy cover itself with the most precious mantle of charity. The world, as summed up in Judas, easily barters the names of things; fervour is called indiscretion, zeal is called bad temper, and the tears of penance and the sighs of repentance are called the whispers of hypocrisy. What does the world understand of God's doings? What does your spirit have to do with the spirit of God? There is no connection between light and darkness, between truth and lies. God is the light and the truth; the world is darkness and lies. Only He can condemn those who do not follow His teachings and award those who use their strength, health and good deeds to serve and follow Christ.

It is clear from what has been said so far that Judas was an evil man and that his heart was full of sinfulness; and although he followed Christ, he did not do so with his whole heart; but only with the body, as Saint Augustine warns. He counted among the number of twelve apostles, but had no apostolic bliss within him; it was only apparently that he seemed to be the twelfth. As he fell and another succeeded him, the apostolic truth was supplemented and the number was still whole. A very important consideration, however, stands out in all this and it goes with an admirable example that should not remain unnoticed. What does Christ want us to understand, in enduring among his apostles a man who is lost like Judas? Nothing else but that we have to tolerate the wicked that we might not suffer seeing the body of Christ slashed or divided. Look at Judas among the apostles, and the good thief among the saints; the murmuring disciple was with the saints too. Peter and Judas ate from the same bread; Peter ate the bread of life and Judas ate it to his condemnation. So it is verified that what is a reason for joy and an occasion of eternal salvation for one who is faithful to God, can be a reason for misfortune and eternal damnation for the one who is unfaithful. However, to justify Mary's innocence, Jesus Christ did not reveal Judas' hidden offence; he publicly praised the accused woman and silenced the bad disposition of the guilty one. "Let it be so," he said of this fervent Israelite woman, "that she anoint my feet today with that precious and exquisite balm. Yet she can still lavish it with economy and save what is left of it to honour my burial tomorrow." So that Jesus Christ was looking at the poor showing interest to reach their heart, loving them and not wanting them to stop being looked after. Yet you will never cease having poor people to help with your almsgiving, and you will not always have me in a position to receive such showing of affection and respect.

Christ taught and clearly showed in these doctrines how dangerous it is for the creature to manage temporal riches; for he saw how Judas, who was destined for this task and lived among the apostles, was losing his head most miserably. It is also for our solace if we discover that Christ will always be the defender of slandered virtue; it is up to him to defend his own and to suffer in silence the wicked judgment of the world in imitation of God, as long as the interest of the truth and the debt of charity does not force them to defend themselves. In truth, it is very flattering to fall in love with the heart of the creature, with that tender affection with which Christ celebrates Mary's gift, for she honoured within herself in anticipation the mystery of his burial. His last words were a clear announcement that his death was ever drawing closer, being such that they could not help but grieve and cause distress to the hearts of those present. However, it seems that none of them took seriously enough ample notice of this frank manifestation; so that the Jews who heard him, having returned to Jerusalem full of faith and trust, could not conceal the affections and feelings brimming in their hearts. And judging by the consequences of some disputes against unbelievers, by means of which some of the school of the Pharisees separated from them and believed that Jesus Christ was the promised Messiah, and had the glory of being counted in the number of his disciples, it can be concluded without fear of error, that they greatly impelled this stimulating prophecy to be fulfilled in the shortest time possible.

CHAPTER 62
JESUS ENTERS TRIUMPHANTLY INTO JERUSALEM SITTING ON A DONKEY, AND ALTHOUGH WELL RECEIVED, HE THEN WEEPS OVER THE CITY, FOREBODING ITS RUIN (MT 21:1-9; LK 21:41-44)

NEVER have the centuries seen such a grand and impressive spectacle as that of Jesus Christ's glorious entry into the Holy City of Jerusalem; it was an entry worthy of attention since it had to be a clear sign of the victory Jesus Christ was about to achieve against the world's vanity and hell's tyranny. The city prefigured the spiritual lordship it exercises in his Church and in the souls of righteous persons; it was the school of those who seek glory in humiliation, because it was an affront to those who only want to be exalted by the ways of human pride; let all the great and powerful men of the earth be so confused in the midst of the extravagant strategies with which they seek to cover up the miseries which equate them with other men. The King of kings and lord of lords, the Dispenser of sceptres and empires, the One who throws down rulers from their throne and confounds them with the dust of the earth, the One who raises the poor and humble and seats them on the thrones of his eternal empire, the King ultimately of heaven and earth, not vested with the diadem and sceptre of his almightiness, but with the mysterious veil of simplicity and poverty, shows that he comes into the world as the prince of the humble, to destroy the kingdom of pride and to condemn all laws of vanity and pride that govern the children of those times. He prepares to enter Jerusalem in a novel and unaccustomed manner, but prophesied and foretold by the prophets. He had a great urge for the Passover in which the lamb was immolated, so that being himself the true Lamb who was to be sacrificed for the sins of the world, he willingly approached the place of his passion, thereby confirming that he was very willing to humble himself and obey his Father up to the most harsh and bitter death to be ever seen.

The Law bid that from the tenth day of the first month all the sons of Israel were to take a lamb and keep it in their house until the fourteenth day of the same month, on the eve of which they were to kill it. And so it was that the true unblemished Lamb, which was chosen first among thousands and firstborn among all flocks, had to be sacrificed to render the people holy. A few days before the sacrifice, that is on the tenth day, Jesus Christ went up to Jerusalem so that the meaning of the number would correspond to the truth; for which reason Bethany also came to be known as a place *of ailment, of hearing and of response*. Yet by whom? By Christ, and by us. It was a place of afflictions for Christ as the Saviour perceived them to be very great with the anointing he had received from Mary in her own house and in Simon the leper's house, by means of which his death and burial were clearly expressed. For this reason we must also grieve in our hearts, not only in recalling Christ's passion but also in remembering our own offences, for which the Lord suffered. We should infer from this that we ought to implore Christ's mercy, being assured that we will be heard by him who suffered and died for us even before we came to be. Such a kind Lord will answer us by anointing us with his mercy, his grace and his gifts, and by making us worthy to perceive the fruit of his mysteries, that we may imitate with all promptness and perfect obedience the dispositions of his eternal goodness. By this simple sign we get to know very clearly the reason why Jesus Christ had journeyed from Ephraim to Bethany. By staying there he did not spurn from receiving the reverential welcomes which Lazarus and Simon the leper had prepared for him in both of their houses. He sent from Simon's house two of his disciples to Bethphage, at the foot of the Mount of Olives, so that the dispositions of his Eternal Father's will may start to be fulfilled.

Jesus Christ was not unaware that after the raising of Lazarus, the chief priests had lost all hope about growth in the people's faith, and they were determined to cut off all roots in one stroke. Lazarus, who was resurrected at the gates of Jerusalem as all could see, was well known by all and spoke with everyone, and the more so was the subject of claiming everyone's attention and of convincing them of the truth. Seeing him people could become more convinced, and the issue unresolvable; so the Pharisees, who were already resolved to put Christ to death, also thought and agreed of taking the life of Lazarus, and to bury him again in the tomb from which Jesus Christ had taken him out. Once the plan to kill God was hatched, they were not daunted from committing a new sin of murder. Making the situation even more difficult, the members of the Sanhedrin said unhesitatingly that they were preparing a decisive event, and contemplating the violent measures they would take in Jerusalem, all knew of the determination of the Pharisees to put an end to the Saviour's life. David's sad prophecy was about to be fulfilled, and the scribes, Pharisees, doctors of the Law, princes of the people, any big shot in Jerusalem, and all those who could be called the court at that time, it is worth knowing two envious chief priests and a council which was as ambitious as it was violent, all worked in harmony with each other and moved on headlong to their end. To achieve their ends, they personally inflamed the spirits of the inhabitants of Jerusalem, and their emissaries were like burning torches that roamed around that province and others where Jesus Christ's news made headway, stirring them up and fomenting against him. Everywhere they went they sowed slanderous rumours against his person and his doctrine; and since his ongoing miracles were a discomfort of which they could not get rid, they attributed them to a pact with hell. To alarm the people against their God and Lord, they threatened them with the weapons used by the Romans, and with the wrath of heaven, without despising some of the few means of wickedness suggested to them by their cunning hypocrisy and refined malice. Such was what was arranged for Jerusalem and the interwoven plan they had adopted, that only a miracle of his almightiness could have derailed it; which was far from what Jesus Christ wanted to do, for the hour of his death and triumph was approaching, as had been determined by his Eternal Father from eternity.

In fulfilment of the prophecy, then, he sent two disciples of his to the village which he had in his sight, and as Lord and prophet said to them: *Go there, and at the entrance of the* place you will find a she-donkey with her colt that no one has ever mounted till now; untie them and bring them here to me; and if anyone tells you anything, about what you intend doing and what right do you have to move around those animals, you will only answer: *The Lord needs them.* Saying this to them would not allow any other disagreement, and they will let you execute my orders.

Everything happened as Jesus Christ had said, and that was when the oracle of the prophet Zechariah was fulfilled, in writing of the Messiah making his entrance into the capital of the kingdom to the tune of acclamations and applause by the daughters of Zion, who set themselves before this Lord as a king who wins hearts with sweetness and humility; for he comes to them with a poor man's baggage, being led in a borrowed and common cavalry in the country, saying: *Say to the daughter of Zion: See here your King who comes to you in a spirit of meekness, sitting on a colt, and on whose son he has borne the yoke,* which is the same in reality, *do not want to fear, daughter of Zion; look at your King who comes sitting on the donkey, son of the young ass.* The apostles and the other of the Lord's disciples had not until then applied these prophetic words to the person of the Messiah; but when Jesus Christ was in his glorified state, which was a time reserved for the communication of his spirit and the perfect understanding of the Scriptures, they knew perfectly well that this oracle prefigured their Master's person, and that in obeying his orders they were then working in fulfilment of the prophecies.

After the apostles had diligently fulfilled the orders of their Lord and God, without encountering any kind of resistance or opposition from any person, seeing that the Lord was preparing to enter into the Holy City with pomp and magnificence, they adorned the donkey as best as they could, forming with their cloaks a sort of horse blanket or tack, making him ride on it. It was no surprise in the country that Jesus Christ on this occasion used that small donkey, since both great and small in the city used it without distinction, so that no one held back, *neither low, nor proud.* Yet what was most extraordinary was that, until then, Jesus Christ had made all his journeys on foot in the company of his apostles. On this day, however, he wanted his people to recognise him as a peaceful King, who entered the capital like its former judges and leaders.

He proceeded thus and was followed by a large crowd of faithful Jews, many of whom had accompanied him from Jericho. Others were inhabitants of Jerusalem and bordering villages, who had witnessed with their own eyes the resurrection of Lazarus. Yet others were God-fearing Gentiles, who came to Jerusalem on days of solemnity to worship the Lord; and others lastly were those who had been told of his journey and had gone out to meet him, showing their veneration and love for their King and Messiah, having no part in the worries of the scribes and Pharisees. And they all laid their garments along the road through which he was to pass, while others, cutting tree branches, laid out carpets for him with their greenery; still many others came from the city carrying palms in their hands to receive him; and they all cried with enthusiasm and joy: *Hosanna to the Son of David. Blessed is he who comes in the name of the Lord.* Never before has a spectacle more worthy of attention been seen on earth. This was undoubtedly the most amazing miracle, and perhaps the least noticed one, that had been reserved to be wrought unshielded among many other more common ones which seemed to have been performed rashly and in the course of events. Let the Lord be acclaimed as the victor over death, who kills by dying, and slays the sin he overcomes, suffering like an evildoer. Surrounded by the applause of a huge crowd he triumphantly enters the city, where the moguls and the powerful hate and loathe him, and plot his death. And yet in the midst of such fury and conspiracies he holds fast to his freedom, independence and pervading authority to act and speak, and he stops the tempest and keeps it suspended over his head until the precise instant when his Father will deliver him to the power of darkness. Meanwhile he will allow this triumph to annoy his enemies, so that hell's rage may help in the redemption of the human line of descent. The cries of praise and glory are repeated everywhere and the crowd, of men, women and children, preceding and following the procession, do not cease repeating: "Honour, glory and blessing to the Son of

David. Blessed be him from God who comes to us in the name of the Lord. Today we have been afforded salvation by our King, who comes to us in the name of God who dwells in heaven. The Lord has been reconciled with us for peace has been established between heaven and earth. We are already going to see our people's innocence and the glory of the kingdom of our Father David rise with splendour. May it be a reign of blessing, honour, glory and praise to the Most High." Oh, with what meekness and tenderness the Almighty presents himself to those who are scheming a thousand ways of taking away his honour and life! Never have Jesus Christ's disciples and the number of faithful who believed in him had more hope of their approaching freedom. Never have the apostles flattered themselves as to their wild guesses about what they thought with great certainty of their Master's forthcoming greatness. The scribes and Pharisees themselves shuddered and trembled and began to distrust the fitting outcome of their scheming. They accounted all on the people, and seeing the gifts lavished on Jesus Christ they feared being left behind in disappointment. Not being in the limelight, and being hidden, they thought of triumph; but now despair and anger had once again taken hold of their heart. So coming together in a new Sanhedrin, they said to each other: "*Do you not see that we have not achieved anything? The whole world goes after that man;* the backing this person gets is publicly shown, and they follow him as the Messiah, as Christ and as the king of Israel."

While the scribes and Pharisees were taken over by despair and filled with even more courage and rage plotted new projects to take revenge on the meekest and most peaceful of all men, God inspired the descendants of that enlightened patriarch Abraham new songs of praise and glory in honour of his Only Son. In so doing news might come to all that he was the desired One of the eternal hills, the sigh of the ancient fathers, the hope of all nations, and the Son of God who came to work the redemption in the midst of the Holy City. All these said to him: "*You are the king of kings* from all eternity; your kingdom is eternal, and not of this world. It is through you that your kingdom comes to me; with your power you reconcile the world to

God and endow peace in heaven and on earth. All creatures sing hosanna to the Son of David, and this cry reaches the far ends of the earth and rises to the top of the highest heaven. Trees honour you by lending their branches; forests should acquire tongues; the works of your hands should be obedient; animals and soulless things surrender to you. What is invisible and that which is visible, bending their knee, should adore you. Being able to see the man for his Creator and comforter, man calls his guilt blissful because he deserved that you enter today to wash it with your precious blood. You bring praise out of the mouths of children; the humble divulge your glory while trying to crush those who are proud. Blessed are the grateful, the ungrateful curse you. Go along with simple persons, flee away from those who are vain. For you are the poor and humble King, your garments are the poverty of heart, your splendour is found in meekness, your plans lie in worldly contempt, your cross is the aim and end of your path. Blessed are you, Oh King of Israel! Hosanna to the Son of David. Blessed is he who comes in the name of the Lord."

Nothing could have been more disastrous for the scribes and Pharisees; no setback could be more awkward and tedious; no other circumstances any less for the purpose of inciting violence. So they forced some of their own to mingle with the crowd, while they had the audacity to come forward to Jesus Christ and say to him: "Master, rebuke your disciples and order them to restrain themselves." As if they were saying: "You see better than us the consequences which these popular movements can have; those who accompany you cannot restrain themselves, they cannot foresee anything; they say that you are Christ and openly proclaim you as their King. What misgivings will the Romans not entertain against us and to what are you exposing us?" And Jesus Christ replied to them: "It would be in vain to impose silence on my disciples. Were I to silence them, the stones themselves would speak out in their place and cry louder than them." With his answer the Pharisees were forced into a corner to be soothed and to shut their mouths, because it was a very unfavourable occasion for them to carry out their plans. So everything went on as before; the cheers grew louder, and the envious could not help but sense all the shame arising out of such great platitudes as were being publicly made to him whom they so truly hated.

What Saint Augustine very appropriately said cannot be denied, namely that in many of the places mentioned in the Gospel, there were as many sacraments as mysteries that were hidden under the most trivial and simple words, and under which they were apparently very insignificant, as confirmed in the text of this Gospel. And indeed, who can properly ponder on the prompt obedience to Jesus Christ's voice as expressed by the two apostles whom the Lord sent in search of the donkey and the colt? They were weak and stuttering; but their obedience on this occasion was like a lightning bolt of heroism. In the words and proceedings of some of them they at once saw themselves as signs of envy, ambition and even of recklessness, although they were constant and perfect in obedience and submissiveness. The voice of the Lord always found submissive reason and an open heart in them, and it was no small test to venture into human abusive remarks and insults, and perhaps to be regarded as thieves for obeying Jesus Christ. What will those say who, with frivolous pretexts, resist obeying the precepts of the Lord's holy law, and appearing to be fearless as Christians refuse to comply with the precepts of the Church in the sight of others? And what shall those lukewarm ministers say above all, and those successors of the apostles who by means of temporary persecutions and not to incur the indignation of temporal powers, neglect to fulfil their most sacred duties?

Another no less important and worthy consideration lies in the instruction Jesus Christ gives to his apostles. The donkey and the colt were tied. That was a symbol of the Jewish people who had long carried upon themselves the heavy yoke of the Law, and the colt denoted the Gentile peoples who themselves carried no yoke, apparently shed their self-control and let off themselves to the whims of a restless and unbridled freedom. Yet Jesus Christ commands them to untie both donkey and colt and to bring them before him; like he did with his death, unleashing all from the bonds of sin. The apostles, by their preaching of the

Gospel, absolved the Jews from the Law of Moses which was entirely abolished; the Saviour signed with his blood consent for the New Testament, and announced to the Gentiles the freedom which he as Christ had bought them. The creature embodies the figure of those two living beings in the two parts of which it consists; the spirit, which serves the Law of God, and the flesh, which desires none else but the law of sin; being passionate about this and bound to the passions that dominate it, the creature must acquire its confidence. This has to be provided by the successors and heirs of the apostles' holy ministry, who take special care to seek these creatures, untie them and present them to the Lord. These three important and mysterious words should never be forgotten: *You will find a tied donkey and colt; untie them and bring them to me.*

To this awful command Jesus Christ added another expression which is no less mysterious but worthy of our attention, which was like telling them: *If anyone says anything to you, say that the Lord needs them, and then depart.* For in truth, it points towards the almighty and irresistible power of the Lord, the universal dominion he exercises and which he has over all things, for it is only him who can say, *Mine are all*; and above all, it shows how futile it is for all of earth's creatures to resist by opposing the Lord's will. The promptness with which those seemingly poor people gave the Lord what he had asked of them, condemns the harshness of some rich people who resist giving what is over and above for them, even when Jesus Christ's poor say they need it.

In addition to the mysterious meanings expressed so far, those that indicate the misery in which the whole world was found before the coming of Christ ought to be noted in the first place. Both Jews and Gentiles were bound; but neither knew of their captivity. The Jew believed himself free since he was the son of Abraham; the Gentile also considered himself as such, for no one recognised the Lord in the world, being, as Saint Paul says, without Christ and without God (Eph 2:12). The proud Jew spurned true justice with his false justice. The Gentile, being deceived with false wisdom, despised true wisdom as foolishness, and both were tied on the outer side of the door, breathless, without shelter, or anyone having pity for their moral poverty. They had masters, who were however unmoved and selfish, caring for their own honour and not about the good of others who dominated them, and they did not feed them; if they ever spoke about them it was only to oppose their freedom and to take away from them the glory of being brought to Christ by the apostles. But neither the priests among the Jews, nor the rulers among the Gentiles, were entitled to oppose the spiritual freedom which Jesus Christ came to give to the whole world; but in this way, one as the other, abusing their authority, used it to delay their preaching of the Gospel and to hinder the apostles, in the name of Christ and with the power of his grace, from setting free those who were bound and tyrannised by the prince of this world.

Also extremely mysterious is the laying of the apostles' garments on the donkey which the Lord was about to ride, because it was the symbol of his doctrine, of his faith and of the purity and holiness of his life; these are precious jewels which successors keep, like Elisha kept the mantle of Elijah, to prepare and adorn with them those souls where Jesus Christ was to make his throne, as co-workers of their sanctification and to cause the yoke of the Gospel to be loved by them. The apostles' disinterest and ardent charity is also evidence shown in the promptness with which they stripped themselves of their clothes to prepare a place where their Saviour can be seated. From this arises the obligation for each and everyone of us who is faithful, each in one's own respective state, to strip and detach ourselves of everything to prepare the way for souls to receive Christ, to cover their sins with secrecy, their weaknesses with meekness and their humiliation with the charity expected of us. Only in this manner does Jesus Christ take his throne in the hearts of creatures. Yet one should also consider the ease with which the wild donkey, together with the colt, subjected themselves to Christ, since they discovered in him the tenderness and promptness with which grace takes possession of man and dominates him, which was also demonstrated every time the Lord addressed himself in some particular way to the Gentiles. The Magi of the East obeyed and followed promptly the star that led them to Bethlehem; and the eunuch of the queen of Candace, having been instructed by Philip, accepted the explanation of the Scripture passage which he did not understand, and immediately received from the apostle the life-giving baptism, recognizing God as his Lord and promptly and submissively subjecting himself to the soft yoke of the Gospel.

The Lord walked, and the people shouted Hosanna to the Son of David; these praises would have been of great comfort to Jesus Christ if he did not recall the shame into which they would fall within a few days, and the other terrible consequences of which he knew the source well. With Jerusalem in sight, he set his eyes on the thankless city, which he loved as the main portion of the field entrusted to him by the great Family Father, and gave free rein to his divine tears; for he did not let himself to be blinded by the splendour of his triumph or to behave with joy by such magnificent pomp. By his example he taught us what he had already told us through the Book of Wisdom, that *in joyful days we may we not forget the sad days*, that we are always to keep before our eyes the image of death, of the vanity of the world and of the inconstancy of creatures. For the same reason, he wanted us to learn that for the Christian there is no affection of which he can take better advantage than sadness and crying. Christ did cry, not as men usually do, out of weakness, out of fear, out of selfishness or in hypocrisy; he wept over his people's blindness and ingratitude, the ease with which they would be casting upon themselves the fullness of divine wrath and the punishment which was already within reach. Those tears which bathed his cheeks, being heaven's delight and joy, were none else but zeal for the glory of God and perfect charity for the salvation of souls.

He wept, and as if he did not want to cry alone, because he wept over the ingratitude of his beloved city, he turned around to those who could hear his voice and exclaimed saying: If you had recognised, unfortunate city, namely, if in your prophets, or at least in these that are peaceful and quiet days for you, you would like to learn what you do not know and of which I am aware, what other things were prepared for you! Which was like saying: "You would definitely do penance with ashes and in silence like the Ninevites; but you are blinded and hardened and do not want to believe that you are threatened with a very great and imminent disaster and devastation."

How different, contradictory and opposed to each other are Jesus Christ's thoughts to those of men! Nothing is more pleasing to an enemy than the pleasure of revenge. The scribes and Pharisees were against Jesus Christ and desired to avenge him; and yet, the most loving Saviour wept over the thankless city and shivered when he foresaw the punishments which his divine Father was about to inflict upon them for having persecuted him to death. Sinners rejoiced in their sin, traitors in their stubbornness and harshness, and executioners in the torments and death they were about to inflict on the world's Redeemer; and he, who desired the cross, torments and death to save men, shed abundant tears, knowing of the monstrous ingratitude with which they were filled. How many are lost because they do not know the health-endowing times or paths! How many for choosing to neglect the effective means of their sanctification! How many for abusing God's gifts or for not taking advantage of the happy instants when the Lord invites them with his protection and grace! What does it matter about the false peace that the sinner thinks he enjoys because he has peace of mind and apparent happiness, if he lacks God's grace in his inner self? What can he expect but that after this day of peace of mind, which in his opinion he enjoys, the great and terrible day of God arrives when the Most High puts his revenge to work? Wrath comes from God and that false peace which the evil one finds in delight, in the forgetfulness of his own hardness and in contempt of others' needs, is a terrible song. What does this deceptive peace of the passions have to do with the solid and true cross with which God visits, comforts and nourishes his servants? Oh heart of Jesus Christ! How tender and compassionate! Truly, he cannot see the evils of his children without desiring for them and providing them with a proper remedy.

The bowels of the Saviour's mercy for the benefit and in favour of his people apparently opened up, and he could not help but tell them that the mysteries of his Father's justice were hidden from his sight. God waged war with those people who, being far from true peace, did not know Him. Jerusalem is a figure of a rebellious soul which resists God, refuses his graces, stifles his inspirations, despises his commandments, make a mockery of his promises, mocks his threats, does not think of mourning past sins, nor of making amends of present ones, or of preventing future ones. Neither does he care about the mercy of God who extends his arms to him, or of His divine justice which prepares punishments for him, or of the present life that ends and flees, not even of approaching death, or of the judgment in which he will appear; all these are hidden from his eyes. He is not aware of the visits God makes him, plunging himself in scarcity while swimming in abundance, enveloping himself in a harsh and horrible war believing himself to be enjoying peace. What will become of whoever sets out to examine himself carefully about all that which happens to him, would he even be able to carry on with the continuous visits God makes to him? And whoever is it that searches deep into his soul and ignores the voices God sends him to attract him by them and to awaken gratitude in his heart, living faith, confidence in his goodness and the salutary fear of His judgments to detach us from the world and unite us with him just for love? But we, ignorant, blind and stupid, who not only let God pass in front of our doors, but when he desires to take us into His house, we hinder Him with a thousand excuses and with the coarsest impoliteness? What will become of us unless we do prompt and fervent penance?

Saint Gregory says: "What the Lord once did over the thankless city, he does every day in the Church over those whom he called to the last dignity of his children, because they are unaware of the most dire position in which they find themselves. He weeps over the wicked, those who are unaware of the reason for their evildoing, and thus rejoice and persevere along their path to perdition, even when eternal damnation threatens them, since the torments awaiting them are hidden from their eyes. Bad days will come upon them when that of eternal vengeance arrives, for they knew the time of their visitation, which is the day when

God visited them. God visits a perverse soul every day with His precepts, sometimes even with punishments, but very often with miracles, so that hearing what he did not know, or repenting through the conjunction of events, or being overcome with benefits, he may be ashamed of the bad relationship he affords to the Lord. But being fully endowed with wisdom he despises both punishment and miracle, he does not know the time of the visitation, and at the end of his life he gives in to those enemies of his, with whom he was joined in constant union during his life. Days will come upon you, the Lord said to Jerusalem, when your enemies will surround you with trenches, encircle and squeeze you tight on each side. Surrounded and encircled is the sinner in all places by the perfidious suggestions of the enemy, by the inner incitement of the flesh and by the burning and concern of all delights and passions. He is surrounded by the weakness and debility of his own nature. He is distressed and afflicted by the fear of his conscience. And what can whoever fails to take advantage of piety expect but justice? This dreadful ruin of the material Jerusalem is a slight blur of the horrible havoc which guilt and sin wreak on the spiritual Jerusalem of our soul, and of the punishment which God has kept for the afterlife. And so Jesus Christ said to the earthly Jerusalem: "They will destroy you and your children who are within you, and they will not leave in you stone upon stone, for you did not know the time of your visit." The spiritual Jerusalem is thrown to the ground when it gives its inner consent to the perpetration of the crime. Their children, which are its good works, are entirely mortified by that and there is no stone upon stone left in it when because of their distrust they give in to intense irritation. It is then fenced and always surrounded by demons, constrained and oppressed by sins, and entirely prostrated to be destroyed, leaving no stone unturned within it, when it is delivered to unquenchable flames. There is nothing more than deserves to be destroyed as promptly and terribly as the one who rises up against God and destroys with a sacrilegious and daring hand the material temple where he is worshipped by his faithful children, or the spiritual temple where he receives the incense and adorations of the most selfless and fervent charity. Graces and virtues are the stones with which God lifts up and carves out the building of our heart. What is there for whoever desecrates the temple of the Holy Spirit himself and does not repair this desecration with penance; what can he be promised or expect, other than to be forever the temple of the devil? God destroyed the temple and the Holy City, not only to punish the sin of the Jews, but also to take away from them their cause of keeping on embracing Judaism; and also mysteriously to denote that the ancient sacrifices had been abolished, and the Judaic cult had disappeared.

It is not strange, then, that the Lord wept over the ungrateful city bearing in mind the terrible punishments of his justice which were inevitably to come upon it because of its obstinacy and harshness. Four times did the Lord weep in his lifetime, covering himself with the mantle of our fragile and sickly flesh, without ever reading that he laughed. Four times he wept, for in those mortal tears we received four springs and inexhaustible sources of his mercy; and although he cried four times he felt, while living this mortal life, the motives causing him to shed those tears. He wept on being born over the common mercy and universal misfortune of all who are born. He wept over the tomb of Lazarus, though he knew that he was to be resurrected, because he was aware of the difficult resurrection of all sinners who died of guilt to the life of grace. He wept at the sight of Jerusalem, for he had in mind its evildoing and the immense accumulation of its ingratitude; the sins of the children of the new Church and those of the old, together with that of all ages and centuries. And he finally wept on the cross over each and every human, because he could foresee how fruitless his passion would be for many. However, his tears were heard by the Father to reconcile his mercy and for all to merit the antecedent and exciting grace; to heal the miseries of mortals, to blot out the sins of all and to deserve everlasting grace and glory.

Another effect of all that was said, and something much more useful reported to us, are the tears of our beloved Jesus Christ; and it was because of them that a very vivid pain was aroused in our hearts for our sins and those of our neighbours, also shedding for them the gift of tears we need to repent from our own faults and weaknesses. And since it is not that these should be inner or visible tears, they are at least those which are indispensable to bear witness of our contrition and confirm our act of true penance. Let us therefore look well at our beloved Jesus Christ weeping over Jerusalem and apply his tears to the spiritual Jerusalem of our soul; let us also weep for a long time, heartily and abundantly, for only so can our weeping correspond to that of the Son of God. Jesus Christ wept with bitterness in his heart contemplating the temporal and eternal danger of the miserable sons of Judah, for they did not know the time of his visitation, that is when he would visit them coming from on high through the mystery of his incarnation, and so they ignored him, not only decrying his preaching, but also persecuting him to death, which was a disgraceful death on the cross.

This clear prophecy was fulfilled in all its parts, and Jerusalem was isolated and destroyed some thirty-seven years after Jesus Christ's death, or very close to the seventieth year of the first Christian century. Emperor Titus was the executor of this sentence pronounced by divine justice against the city which killed God. The calamities, however, which the Jews experienced in the ruin of Jerusalem and before and after that, were such and of so great extent and consequence that were the chief chronicler of these horrific events not a person of such authority, wisdom and respectability, and a great direct witness who was present and saw everything, then he would not be believed. This historian was Josephus, a Jew by race and faith; one of the rarest men of his age in eloquence, prudence, knowledge of Scripture, and above all, in generosity and courage. Being governor of the province of Galilee, he defended the city of Jotapata (*Yodfat*) against Roman power for forty-seven days; and all men of courage being dead, it seems that Providence wanted to keep him alive to write about this Jewish war, as he did. Because no one could write it with greater truth, or more eloquently, or with less suspicion of partiality; for he says at the beginning of his writing, that he was the son of Matthias, a citizen and priest of Jerusalem, and that in the first and second conquests he fought against the Romans. Very hard then, wicked and exceedingly ungodly is the heart that remains insensitive and obstinate regardless of Jesus Christ's tears and what causes them to be shed. Doomed is the man who, being overwhelmed with misery and sin, rejoices and laughs when the wisdom of the Father weeps over him. Wild is a person, perhaps even a furious one, if he remains undaunted seeing the doctor cry on coming to know of the full gravity and extent of the fever that devours him; he cries for you with bitter tears, as if you were crying over the death of your only begotten son. The tears of your eyes come out in torrents day and night, without letting you catch some sleep or allowing the eye's pupil to close. Also look at Jesus Christ's disciples who follow him with very great restraint and reverence without being able to contain the tears falling from their eyes when seeing those that flowed from those of Jesus Christ, and while in the same manner you weep over your faults and sins you still hope to have the abundant fruit deserved by all those who belong to the divine Saviour.

CHAPTER 63
JESUS HITS HARD FOR A SECOND TIME THOSE WHO BUY AND SELL IN THE TEMPLE ATRIUM: THE WIDOW THROWS TWO COPPER COINS INTO THE TEMPLE COLLECTION BOX, AND HE EXPLAINS THE PARABLE OF THE PHARISEE AND THE PUBLICAN (LK 19:45-47; LK 18:9-14; MT 21:10-17)

WALKING at a steady pace along his journey, Jesus Christ came to the Holy City, showing in his tears the pain he had for the loss suffered by his nation. He entered the city triumphantly through the golden gate that stood at the foot of the temple and at the side of the Josaphat valley; but as he was entering to save one and all, he was moved and marvelled at the city saying, "Who is this?" as if to say that when the Redeemer of the world entered Jerusalem, heavenly, triumphant over the underworld and death, the angels in heaven had to ask themselves: "Who is this King of glory?" Origen says about this: "When the Lord entered the true Jerusalem of heaven, the heavenly powers were marvelled, they wondered and said: 'Who is this King of glory?' And as he entered the earthly Jerusalem, the earthly powers were overcome with terror and dread. They also wondered and said, 'Who is this?' as if they wanted to say, 'He is neither well known nor a great person to deserve the honour and reception being given to him.'" Being full of spite and sorrow they saw the great throng of people who had gone out to welcome him, certainly ignoring the great dignity and divinity of him whom they accepted with so many praises and songs, which had never been chanted before, so that Saint Chrysostom said: "Very reasonably, the big heads of Jerusalem were moved and amazed for, while abhorring Christ, they saw him exalted and praised, calling him with his proper name, without themselves knowing the meaning of what they were uttering, since it was he who directed them and impelled the hand of the Eternal Father who directs all things in good time and successfully. The anguish of the princes was passed on to a large part of the city, and sprouting from the same fear, they directed to the mobs hailing Jesus Christ's victory the same question which pointed to their fear; 'Who is this?' The simple, faithful people answered in all truth that they did not want to hear, and they repeated their chant without really knowing what they were saying, stating, 'This is Jesus, the prophet from Nazareth of Galilee, and even so he is Lord of the prophets, for which reason he must receive greater honour than all of them.'" This confession of truth came from the mouths of the simple, and the praises of God from the little ones or children, so that more grown up persons and adults may later learn it and utter it themselves. So that Saint Jerome says about this: "The princes and elders of Judea, doubting their faith, seek to satisfy their wilful doubts while the little ones, and those who were held in less esteem among the people, confess the Catholic truth."

As Jesus Christ arrived at the temple door, he entered at once and noticing the abuses tolerated by the priests and leaders, he condemned them with his full authority in conformity with his personal dignity and the extent of his mission. Yet it is now appropriate to know more about this place where Jesus Christ suddenly entered before referring to the events which happened there.

Let us divide the temple into two parts. One part was called the Holy Place, where there was the gold-covered altar of the incense or *Thimiama*, and the table where the loaves of proposition and the chandelier were placed. The other was the Holy of Holies, where the Ark of the Testament and the two Cherubim rested. In the Holy Place, priests entered daily to offer incense, while other people were definitely not allowed to enter. It is in the Holy of Holies that the high priest entered alone, and then only once a year. Before entering these two parts of the temple, there was a square space surrounded with a wall, which was called the priests' atrium; there, under a beautiful cupola, was sited the altar of burnt offerings, completely covered with bronze. Not only was it priests that entered inside this court or atrium, but also the Levites and all those having to do with the slaughtering, flaying and washing of the victim animals;

but other persons could not enter the atrium, but offered the living animals to the priests at the door of that court. Christ did not enter any of these two places, for he was not known to be a priest or a Levite. It was additionally said that there were two other parts where men stood in prayer in one section, and women in the other. These two atria, or main courts, were commonly known as the temple, so that we must understand that when Jesus Christ entered the temple he entered one of them.

The Venerable Bede says Jesus Christ suddenly entered the temple for three main reasons. The first was to teach us the religious way we must follow, so that we may know that before undertaking any business, whatever that may be, and more particularly some hard task, we must first visit the house of prayer, so that committing ourselves to God from there, all our things are directed to our soul's greatest glory and spiritual benefit. Secondly, since it was a public place, it could be found more easily, thus showing that no one would be forced to do anything, except by one's own will. And thirdly, to show that the city's ruin and the lost cause of the people, over which he had wept so much, came largely from the bad faith of the priests, as was also from there that the essential root of the prediction was born.

The Lord wanted to make these motives known to some extent by suddenly entering the temple after having announced the great evils and calamities which threatened Jerusalem, and throwing out from that place those who were buying and selling. He also wanted to show that unworthy priests should exercise their highest dignity and office, otherwise one day they too would be thrown out of the temple. And this would come about when the city was entirely destroyed, and when the people also perished with the temple because of the bad priests' abominable example and doctrine; so that their ambition and greed was cause of the Jews' loss and destruction. Nourished as they were by their greed, the priests sold on their own account, in the porches and vestibules of the temple, all kinds of offertory bread, victims and oblations; so that it might not happen that when the people came to offer the Lord one thing or another, they would not fail finding it promptly and its sellers at hand, and leave without presenting their offering to God; and they did this by reselling over and over again what had been bought and offered to the Lord. To the end that the poor would have no excuse not to buy their desired offering, they also had money changers' tables in place; the changers lent them against a receipt the amount they needed to buy the offertory victims, all in the hope of some prize or for usury. Yet they did not consider that this was expressly forbidden by God to the children of Judah through the prophet Ezekiel's mouth when he said: "You will not receive usury or any profit for what you have lent to your brothers." The interpreters of holy Scripture warn us that both at the first and the last time the Saviour entered the temple after his baptism, he showed great anger against the irreverence with which the Jews desecrated it. If only this example would stoke the zeal of those who not only can, but must banish from our temples the immodesty and irreverence which are ever present in constant struggle to seize the very house of prayer! This desecration cannot be regarded with indifference by anyone who is truly called by God to the church ministry, whose purpose is to sanctify the name of God and to save souls, for as Saint Chrysostom says, "nothing destroys the Church of the Lord so much as the fact that the clergy are worse than the laymen".

So when Jesus Christ saw his Father's house converted into a house of business, usury and robbery, this aroused his spirit and inflamed him with the fire of holy zeal eating away at him and devouring him. He made a whip with some cords and started tossing the temple buyers and sellers; he rolled over all things and animals used as an offertory, and the money changers' tables, breaking the pigeon sellers' cages. Nor did he let the vessels and any other utensil which had not been offered and consecrated to the Lord cross from one part of the temple to the other, and finally, he threw out anything which did not serve for divine worship and had not been previously consecrated or offered to God, not letting it to be taken back again inside. Jesus Christ's outrage appears in all its fullness in the words he then says: "It is written, he says to the merchants and temple desecrators, *my house is a house of prayer, but you have made it a den of thieves.*" If it was thieves in the eyes of God who did those common and ordinary actions, in that temple which bore only a glimpse of our mysteries, what name do those people deserve who with profane, useless and sinful entertainment, with immodest actions and words, with scandalous nudity and with vain and irreverent gestures, desecrate the churches where the Saviour himself resides and where sacrifice is offered? God is mocked by those who go to sin where instead they should go to mourn, those who turn the house of prayer into a theatre of prostitution, and who seek anger in the treasury of mercy. What terrible punishment awaits such desecrators! Saint Chrysostom knew what this meant and made it known with these meaningful words: "In the temple Christ patiently suffered the insults addressed to his person, but he punished terribly those addressed against his Father."

The flogging dealt by Jesus Christ himself on this occasion against those whom he called thieves in his Father's house, and the manner in which he threw them out of the temple, were formerly prefigured in the very terrible and dreadful event which happened against Heliodorus, who entered armed in the temple to steal all its riches. There are however, circumstances which are worth noting much more. Heliodorus was scourged by the angels; on this occasion the temple desecrators were flogged by Jesus Christ. Heliodorus was scourged for sacking the temple; the Jews were flogged for contaminating it with their usury; and they were called thieves, because they did not care for anything but their temporary gain, without regard to the condemnable way they procured it. And yet Jesus Christ remained calm and peaceful, teaching not only on that day, but on all others, within the enclosure of the same temple; Jesus Christ spoke on this occasion too and acted with an air of authority and grandeur which gave a good idea of him being much more than a man; for being alone and unarmed in the midst of his enemies, they feared him so much that no one dared resist him or be so severe with him.

On this occasion they came and approached the Lord in the temple; they were blind, lame and several others suffering various ailments; and he healed them all. These mercies of the Lord produced diverse and very well-founded effects on the spirits of all those present. The leaders of the priests and scribes lost their patience and were even more irritated, as simple credulous persons and children lavished thousands of blessings and praises upon Jesus Christ, singing full of gratification and joy: *Hosanna to the Son of David.* Hearing this, the priests' leaders and the people's judges who were called elders, went to meet the Saviour along with a horde of scribes and Pharisees to rebuke him for allowing that commotion to happen. And they said to him very angrily and in great outrage: "Do you hear what they are saying?" "Yes," Jesus Christ answered. "How come, have you never heard what the prophet chanted? *From the mouth of infants and sucklings, you have obtained, O Lord, full and perfect praise* (Ps 8:3-4)." Having given them this answer, he did not wait any further, closing their mouths and forcing them to silence. Despite so many miracles as the Lord had done before them, they did not believe in him, in line with what the prophet Isaiah had uttered before: "Lord, who will believe our words, what we preach (Is 53:1)? *To whom will the arm and strength of God be made bare and shown? In vain have I stretched out my hands to the unbelieving and rebellious people, who walk in ungodly ways, in pursuit of their senses and their sins* (Is 65:2)." They could not believe the motive which the prophet himself had previously shown when the Lord said to him: "Go, and tell this people, prophesy unto them: *You will hear and you will not understand; you will see and you will not look, you will fail to be aware. The heart of this people is blind and dull; it hardens and hinders their ears from hearing with them; blind their eyes so that they may not see with them, nor hear with their ears, nor their hearts understand, nor will they be converted, nor will I heal them, nor will they receive health from me* (Is 6:9-10)."

Isaiah uttered these happenings when he saw Christ's glory with prophetic eyes and spoke of it. In effect, God gave the Jews a spirit of emotions and stupor, eyes with which they do not see and ears with which they do not hear; a blindness and an obstinacy which they still hold to this day. And David also said: *Turn your table into a snare and a net, and into a stumble and cause of ruin, to punish those* who deserve it. Their eyes are darkened that they might not see. Overwhelm them for ever, forcing them to carry heavy weight on their backs, and move about with their heads bowed to the ground like beasts of burden (Ps 69:23-24). Yet in spite of everything, the priests and elders, and the scribes and Pharisees, dared to ask Jesus Christ: "With what power do you perform those things, assuming an authority which you say you do not have?" Being unable to answer the Lord directly or to justify the carelessness they showed in performing the priestly ministry by their criminal tolerance in all the irreverence and unseemly acts which they allowed in the sanctuary and House of God, they believed they could avoid all difficulties by rebuking the way Jesus Christ reacted about the temple desecrators. The conduct of the priests and leaders was undoubtedly foolish on this occasion, and also equally daring and reckless; for they could not ignore that on several previous occasions Jesus Christ had proved before them his divine mission through the fulfilment of prophecies, by his heroic virtues and by his miracles, which they could never deny. They knew that the Lord had shown that all the qualities and attributes of the Messiah were embodied in his person, and that he should delight in the authority of king, prophet and lawgiver, like Moses; and so it is not strange that seeing themselves being directly attacked, they attended with an aim of rebuking Jesus Christ for not confessing his criminal behaviour.

Nor can it be deduced from the actions which the Saviour of mankind manifested this time and on other occasions; for his character was not extremely meek, sweet, kind, prudent and tolerant, given that the severity he used against those dealers was neither an act of harshness, nor of anger or of violence, but one stemming from his zeal and legitimate and divine authority. It is undeniable that Jesus Christ always kept his dignity together with a grave and majestic attitude suiting God who became man, descending from heaven to instruct and correct, and not to flatter, seduce, or tolerate abuse. Merchants could trade outside the temple; but keeping their exchange tables, selling animals and making loud noises and racketing within, was a criminal desecration of the sanctuary, which could not be allowed without seriously contravening the Law. It was pointless that the priests and leaders allowed such bargaining to take place under the pretext of sacrificial convenience. The same God to whom they offered themselves and to whom the temple belonged, could undoubtedly bring this desecration to ruins, though still clothed with humanity.

After this Jesus Christ sat facing the collection box in the Temple treasury, and watched attentively those who drew close to it to make their offerings. Having first seen some rich people who put in it several silver coins, he then saw a poor widow who threw in it two copper coins; she had gained these by shedding sweat and with hard labour. So Jesus Christ said to his disciples: "That poor woman has offered more than all the rich men, because she gave not only what she required for her needs, as she would surely need it for her food, while others made their offering from what they had to spare and would not otherwise need. It is worth noting, however, that he did not say that *they gave what was left over, but what they had left over*, to show that they did not give all that was unnecessary, but a very small part of what was unnecessary. The priests, full of greed as they were, taught that whoever made a greater offering in absolute terms in the temple, was the one who had the greatest merit. But this was false reasoning, for the amount of merit gained is not at all measured according to the size of the gift, but by the promptness with which one gives, by the unhesitant manner shown by the giver, and by the will and devotion with which he offers it to God. It is thus inferred that according to the priestly doctrine, most of the rich made many and big offerings; but according to Christ's doctrine, it was this poor widow who gave most, considering her potential and good will. Saint Jerome says about this: "God does not consider *how much*, but *from how much*, and the will and affection with which you give; he does not look at how much the coin is worth, but with what affection it is given; not the quantity, but the charity, so that it can be said that the gift that was given with greater desire and fervour is more generous and greater. The widow gave what she could, and she wished to give more than she could; for this her gift was more acceptable to God and won Christ's approval. And just as the two copper coins that she put into the treasury box pleased God more than all other gifts, so also the love of God and neighbour, who is a creature which ought to be always kept in the treasury of his heart, please God more than all the gifts and offerings made to Him in public, in ostentatious display of an outward and apparent affection."

Keeping this in mind and with the desire to impartially adopt Jesus Christ's doctrine, Saint Gregory said: "What God our Lord mainly seeks is the heart with which you offer him the gift; and he does not keep tab so much on how valuable or precious the gift is, nor does he consider how great a thing is offered to him in sacrifice: and what he looks at most is the will with which it is given. This poor widow is the soul of man, who already being free from the enemy with whom she was united, puts in the temple's treasure box two coins, which are her flesh and her spirit; the flesh through abstinence and the spirit through humility; and so can the Lord say, that by her service she gave all she had to maintain herself, leaving nothing to the world from her estate." And Venerable Bede says: "This morally teaches us how very acceptable to God are those gifts, however small, we offer Him with a good heart. The rich who threw their offerings into the treasury box, represented the haughty and presumptuous Jews, those who according to what they thought, considered the Law as a matter justice; and this poor widow stands for the simplicity and purity of the Church, which is called a poor girl since it keeps itself far from the spirit of pride and greed for temporal goods. She calls herself a widow since her spouse, Our Lord Jesus Christ, suffered death for her; and she puts two small copper coins in the collection box of the Temple treasury, so that it may be understood that in deferential respect to the Divine Majesty, with love for God and neighbour, she brings and offers gifts of true faith and persevering prayer, which she keeps for trivial little things by virtue of her own humility; so that these are more pleasing to God than all the works of the ancient Jews."

To declare this moral and necessary meaning with more propriety and even more extensively, the Lord decided to tell this parable to all those present, being aware that some of them boasted they were righteous while despising others. Two men went up to the temple to pray, one was a Pharisee and the other a publican. By simply saying this he already showed his way of thinking, and that the Pharisees were very much aware of the Saviour's relationship with them, so that knowing their spirit and knowing from experience that all his doctrines were intended to discover and condemn the hypocrisy of the Pharisees, one could not but on this occasion expect a formidable reprimand. After Jesus Christ had established one of the main conditions of prayer, which was perseverance, he wanted to teach the other no less necessary condition, which is humility and distrust of our own merits; since he wanted to heal the pride of some and avenge others for the scorn they had received from the hypocrite Pharisees. It is very noteworthy that Jesus Christ said that those two characters go up to the temple to pray, because since prayer is the elevation of one's mind and heart to God, it is necessary to do things as they should be done, and the creature rises with heart, spirit and all the powers of his soul, to ask with humility for the gifts and graces which he needs, while looking with contempt at the earth and all that belongs to it. It is futile for a man to pray unless he is intimately persuaded of his fickleness and poverty; for he would then only see in himself merit and not sin, and so he will not believe himself in need of Christ's grace and mercy. On the other hand, the same pride that blinds him from seeing his misery, arouses recklessness and injustice in him to denigrate the works of others known for their sins, hypocrisy or superstition. So that while the proud are seen to grow great presumption for themselves, they show at the same time great contempt for others.

With Jesus Christ saying that the one was a Pharisee and the other a publican, he already denoted the differing self-respect both in turn had for themselves, letting their supplications to be revealed at the same time as their beliefs and positions which were also different. The Pharisee, instead of praying and humbling himself in the presence of the Lord, stood with raised head to reach up to God, showing in his posture and gestures, and even in the place where he chose to pray, all of his heart's haughtiness and pride. His plea was one of self-praise and so said within himself: "I thank you, Lord, for I am not like other men, and in particular like this tax collector; for he and the others are thieves, unjust, adulterers; but I have a blameless life. I fast twice a week and pay all the due tithes for what I earn." The publican, however, regarding himself as a public sinner, stayed at the far end of the temple; and without daring to lift his eyes to heaven, beat his breast and just said: "Oh God forgive this wretched sinner." In the words of the Pharisee, his inordinate pride stands out in the first place, preferring himself to all men, condemning everyone with recklessness and, in particular, as a person who built his outward countenance but did not know his inner self. The publican's words laid emphasis on his humility while pronouncing his own judgment, accusing and condemning himself, yet still imploring with confidence God's mercy. The Pharisee forgot that the righteous man ought to accuse himself when starting his prayer, and this is why his prayer was neglected. So that the publican, who was accusing himself, was heard and well attended to, and the Venerable Bede says about this: "As to the words of the haughty Pharisee, which he deserved being humiliated and dejected for them, it is our duty to warn that in order to be exalted, just as he considered his brothers' vices while being in love with his own virtues was proud of his fall, so must we spare no expense in acting the opposite way, not only in our indifference, but also as to the virtues of others, so that in swallowing our pride while bearing this in mind, glory sprouts from our humility." The publican who was standing at the back did not dare raise his eyes, but beat his breast. There corresponded to the wound the love rising out of them, begging for pity and mercy; and for this reason, also striking his heart, which was the source and origin of his evil, he desired and asked that from that place where his vices were born all virtues would now be born. Saint Augustine also struck this same note, namely that when the publican was crying out he was aware of his crime and confessed it saying to God: "My God, show mercy to this sinner, and do not look at the defects of this evil heart; but forgive me my sins and be lenient with me, for there is nothing in me that can please You nor anything which deserves and obtains Your forgiveness. For I have always sinned against You with my heart, with my body, with my thoughts and with my words and deeds: I am worse than everyone and I cannot save myself but by Your leniency and mercy alone."

If anyone wanted to ask the reason why the tax collector was accusing himself with such humility, and disclosing his defects so loudly, and what fruit he was expecting from this very public accusation, he could be told that the publican was not expecting anything but to be absolved and justified; and he was not only granted this, but also had his repentance and justification made public by Jesus Christ himself, when he said, *This publican came out justified*; which means that from an evil creature he came out righteous and in grace, while the Pharisee returned to his house with his sins. Undoubtedly, it was the publican who was justified and not the Pharisee who only held within him an apparent justice because of his presumption, while the publican held it true by virtue of his humility. The Pharisee justified himself by his works, and the Lord justified the publican by the merit of his faith. One boasted with pride, and the other confessed his guilt in all humility. Saint Augustine says of this: "It is better to make humble confession after committing evil, than assuming presumptuous glorification in good works. For which reason it is said that the humble sinner is better than a proud just person; for after a righteous person becomes proud, he ceases to be just and starts being proud; with which human pride is confused, so that men must never boast of their merit."

What great confidence of forgiveness of one's faults and sins is given by this penitent publican to those who really abide by true penance, by being aware, weeping and confessing them. Saint Ambrose made us understand this with these words: "The Lord told this parable to explain to us how the tax collector and the Pharisee prayed in the temple; so that if the proud one had all the other virtues but not humility, he offends Him more with them than the humble sinner who has no presumptions about himself; before the Pharisee becomes aware of his miseries because the devil always tries to deceive with shows of presumption those who with all diligence were given to performing good customs." That Pharisee did his very best not to be unjust, not to commit adultery and not to sin as the publican did; but though he paid tithes on all he had and gained, and though he fasted twice a week, he was deceived by the enemy; he wounded him with a deep and grave wound, so that being self-presumptuous, in what he believed to be most praiseworthy, he was judged by Christ to be worthy of greater rebuke. No one, then, ought to boast about one's good works, but only of the grace of God, trusting in him with all humility. For what the mentioned Church Father says: "When you come to the presence of the Lord to beg him mercy, throw yourself on the ground as a humble servant in his divine presence, and do not ask him anything on the score of the grace of your merits; if you are aware in your heart of hearts that you have done some good work, cover it up, so that keeping silent about it, the Lord will pay you in many ways and with the greatest abundance, recalling the tax collector that you might find forgiveness the same way he found it." So that you can be saved, discard from you the presumption of your own merits, because it could bring you down from the highest heavens, and embrace humility, which can rise to heaven even if you are placed in the deep abyss of your sins. This humility gave eternal life to the publican, while the Pharisee was condemned for not possessing it. It led the good thief to paradise before the apostles, and the pride of the bad angels threw them into the depth of eternal doom. Let us therefore try to be extremely humble and to cast pride away from us, knowing very clearly the opposite effects that each of these two things brings to man.

CHAPTER 64
THE LORD CURSES A FIG TREE IN WHICH HE DOES NOT FIND ANY FRUIT; PARABLE OF THE GRAIN OF WHEAT, AND OF THE DETHRONING OF THE PRINCE OF THIS WORLD (JN 12:10-36)

OON evening came of the day the Lord had spent giving holy and wholesome advice, not only to his apostles and disciples, but also to all those attending at the temple; he did so most particularly to the scribes and Pharisees who, burning with envy, were unceasingly hatching plans on how to get rid of Jesus Christ's person. Having carefully searched the temple and watched over all places to see whether anything disorderly was being committed, Jesus Christ, seeing that night was approaching and that no one had opened his house for him in all Jerusalem, he resolved to punish the city by turning away from it; for indeed, it is a lasting punishment to separate oneself from Jesus Christ, even if only instantly and for a short time. So he promptly returned to Bethany with his disciples, where he ate very little, but without allowing himself any rest or staying in that place for a long time; so that very early in the morning of the next day he left the town and set out again, accompanied by his disciples, on his way to Jerusalem. As this was the last day intended for the instruction of his followers, he took advantage of all instants and occasions to give the utmost of interesting witness to them.

Shortly after his departure from Bethany, he saw from afar a fig tree planted on the side of the road, copiously covered with leaves, but not bearing any fruit; so he went towards it. He apparently wanted to pick some fruit from it, even though it certainly was not the right time for it to bear any. So seeing that it did not bear any, he felt very upset and angry against this fruitless tree; and turning to it, he said in a harsh tone heard by his disciples and followers: *Never will you bear fruit from now and evermore; no one will ever eat of your fruit again.* And at that very instant the tree dried up, although the ravage was not known at the time, having been left leafless up to the morning of the next day. The fig tree, on which the Lord had cast this terrible curse, stood for the Synagogue, which even in its last times kept the outer skin of piety and of religious ceremonies; for these were the leaves with which the tree was adorned, yet bore no fruit. And so, the Lord's preaching had no effect, even if it was done in full view of the scribes, Pharisees, doctors, and priests; and with his heart being eaten away out of zeal for the salvation of the sons of Israel, Jesus Christ cursed the fruitless tree, being devoid of the fruits of righteousness and of every kind of virtue, which with its shadow also prevented others from believing in the Lord and giving fruit at the right time.

Also, under this mysterious symbol Jesus Christ declared to his apostles that the Synagogue not only had impaired and was still abusing the care entrusted to it, but also their zeal and all their apostolic endeavours; by becoming a fruitless inheritance for heaven, this would henceforth deprive it of becoming aware of the evangelical truths, and would no longer produce good works meriting eternal happiness. The Lord's disciples were well aware of the meaning and significance of this symbolism when they carefully reflected upon and collected all events in Jesus Christ's story. When they saw, however, all these things passing before their very eyes, they did not get that far in their intelligence, nor did they understand then the main designs of the Saviour's adorable providence. Saint Chrysostom says: "The Lord cursed the fig tree not because he did not find fruit in it since it was not the time for figs, but to teach his disciples and inspire them with confidence and faith, so that by that miracle they would also know that, if he so desired, he could dry up and exterminate the Jews who persecuted him in an instant." And Saint Jerome adds: "Jesus Christ, having suffered for the salvation of all peoples, and carried on his own shoulders the scandal of the cross to the top of the mountain of sacrifice, wanted to strengthen the faith in his disciples' heart with that early marvel which assured them of his power and authority, and that however great the Synagogue was, it would have always been very insignificant and useless to oppose God."

After this event Jesus Christ went to the temple, where a portion of Gentiles who had gone up to Jerusalem had gathered to worship the Lord on the feast day. These Gentiles, who had heard of the fame of Jesus Christ's doctrine and the recount of the many miracles he worked, judging themselves unworthy to present themselves to a man so holy, powerful and worthy of respect, approached Philip and told him: *We wish to see Jesus*. It may be no mystery that they first approached Philip, for later he was the first to announce the Saviour to the Gentiles, namely the Samaritans. These Gentiles stood for the conversion of all of them, which had to take place within a short time, and which through their ministry and work were to be inflamed in ardent desires to see Jesus Christ glorified in the homeland. Philip gave the news to Andrew, who as first among the called and apparently more familiar with the Lord; and also because having been converted by the news given to him by Andrew, he wished to act this time around after seeking his opinion and advice. Having conferred with each other, in common agreement and in each other's company, the two disciples went to give the news to the Saviour. Jesus Christ graciously heard the devout supplication of the Gentiles who were already prepared to believe, and seeing that they had come to receive the faith, and that the conversion of the Gentiles had to start with them, he not only granted them their request, but started announcing clearly to them that the time of his passion was very close, after which the Gentiles were to be immediately received in the knowledge of the truth. Lifting up his heart, burning and inflamed with the fire of love and eternal charity with which he loved men within his Eternal Father's bosom, Jesus Christ said: *The time has come for the Son of Man to be glorified*, as if to say: "The Jews do not want to believe that I have come to preach to them so that they would be the first called; but since they despise the most unique benefit I came to do for them, the core of the people whose first fruits are already being presented to me will believe in me, and the Son of Man will be glorified in the presence of them all."

In fact, the Son of Man was glorified in his passion and made known by his own Father, as being God, Redeemer and Saviour of mankind, by the great wonders and signs that were seen in the heavens, in the sun, moon, stars and all over earth; he was glorified in his glorious resurrection and in his majestic ascension to heaven; and finally, he was glorified in the conversion of the Gentiles for now his grandeur and glory, his holiness and virtue, his infinite wisdom and endless almightiness, are preached and announced all over the world. Then finally, when the Gentiles made him a plea and he responded to it, after having said that the time had come for him to be glorified, with his glory springing from his disgraceful death, he proposed to them this comparison to confirm this truth: *Unless a grain of wheat falls to the earth and dies, it remains alone.*

The Lord contrasts with the glory of his good reputation the rebukes and pains which he would then be seen suffering; with divine eloquence he compares himself to the grain of wheat which, after being sown until it is reaped, passes through countless pains as we see things. First it is buried, then it rots, and so it would be ready to sprout cane and leaves; in seeing the light of day, it is subject to another thousand insults, the ice burns it, the air fights it, the sun hits it, the strider steps on it and cattle graze on it; but its torments will not stop here. For when the reaping season arrives, new suffering comes its way too; it is mowed, threshed, winnowed, sifted, grinded to flour, and even then it is thickened in water, kneaded and burnt in the oven with fire. So that in this sole comparison it is seen how Jesus Christ embodied the great and cruel martyrdoms which he went through from birth to death, being so many that what the Evangelists wrote about them, caused Saint Jerome to question the amount of events which actually occurred. For similarly to the grain of wheat, if it does not die on being sown would bear no fruit, remains alone and does not multiply, so too, Christ says, "Unless I die, I will be left alone, just like a grain of wheat, but the human race will still be unredeemed, given that it has been determined that it should be rescued in this manner."

After this simple and thorough explanation of this Gospel passage, it is also necessary to warn that the righteous ones who would like to reach Christ's glory must above all try to be the grains of wheat of their time, and not straw destined for hellfire; so that, if the grain of wheat dies, it will bear fruit. Who is that Jew who was not promised that once Christ died his new school would come to an end as would the congregation he had formed? And who did not believe that after the Shepherd is struck to death, his sheep would not disperse in such manner that they would never return to the flock? This was promised to the Jews, whose plan was no less than to erase the name of the Saviour from among the living, so that no trace or memory would remain of him. But just as when Joseph died, the children of Israel multiplied greatly and grew in wealth and prosperity, so that all the land was filled with their offspring, so also the Church would grow once Christ died, not only in the number of the faithful, but also in the riches of holiness. These prayers are a beautiful commentary on the earnest words uttered by Jesus Christ, in which the vocation of the Gentiles, the world's conversion and the sanctification of men appear with all glory, men having given so much glory to their Redeemer, who was the subject of so many beautiful prophecies which could not, however, be accomplished but by Christ's passion. It was necessary that the Saviour should die in order to acquire the new people and the numerous posterity that had been promised, and so that his passion might bear many other most ample and abundant fruits; for he had given the fruits of the remission of all sins, of the conversion of all Gentiles, and of the most fulfilled joy in the kingdom of heaven.

It is also since Jesus Christ compared himself to the grain of wheat, and he was pure and perfect, that the custom was held within the Church to make bread of pure wheat, without any other kind of mixture, for it to be then converted into the Body of Christ, through the sacramental words; and since it is not enough that the grain of wheat should fall into the ground for it to bear fruit, but that the farmer should bury it, he foretold in his symbolism not only his passion and death, but his burial and resurrection, leaving us all with sublime examples of humility, resignation, conformity and obedience to the will of his Eternal Father which we ought to imitate, that in everything and for everything we might constantly follow in his footsteps. To this end Jesus Christ further added: *He who loves his life will lose it*, where losing one's life here means *the one who loves his life inordinately*. For he who loves his soul more than the glory of God, than virtue and justice, is the one who will lose it; but he who hates it in this world, is the one who watches over it and preserves it for eternal life.

Saying this the Lord amplified his first doctrine, further extending to all the faithful what he had said of himself under the likeness of the grain of wheat. He wanted them to understand very clearly, that if he was to bear fruit, he had to offer himself to the harshness and bad treatment of his flesh, and if necessary, to death itself, for to gain enjoyment of a blessed and endless life. This sublime sentence can also have another very similar meaning, though an entirely different one, being that whoever loves his life, its joys and delights more than God, whoever wants to satisfy all his tastes, even if he does it by running over the Law of the Lord, is so far from loving his own soul and life that, on the contrary, he hates it and loses it. Whereby it is seen that there is no greater revulsion causing more harm than the false love which many have for their ego and for others. Many love others for in their worldly goods or personalities they find fodder for their damned passions; so that what they truly love is vice; and it is the one whom they keep as a friend, whom they so lose with that love. Saint Augustine said about this: "If you loved badly, then you have hated; if you have hated well, then you have even hated more; happy are those who have hated by keeping the Lord's precepts, because then they are certain they will not be lost because of love."

This is the most excellent and most perfect rule of love and revulsion man must have for himself; detest your belief in what you love; forget believing that you are winning, and win by judging that you are losing, and that you love yourself much more when you hate yourself even more. Saint Chrysostom says: "No other saying states these words so well, *He who loves his soul will lose it*, than those of Saint Matthew, *Deny yourself and follow me*. What a man does in denying another, namely ignoring him, leaving him on his own, doing little about him, is what he must do to deny oneself, to say no to all one's evil desires, to ignore and abandon those things which pull him apart from God, not to take notice of the world's mockery and vanity, and to keep for himself only that which gives strength and vigour to the spirit." So let us detest little pleasures, those things of the earth which perish, and may we love to the utmost, as is done in heaven itself, those things which last for ever. We are invited to this and Jesus Christ toasts each one of us every day saying: *If anyone serves me, that is, whoever aspires to be my servant, let him follow me, and where I am, there will my servant also be: whoever serves me, my Father will honour him.* It is like him saying: "Whoever wants to be my servant must begin his service by following me; any steps he takes off this path are lost, for no one comes to the Father except through me." He then further added: "Where I am, there will my servant also be, giving proof of his soul's glory, supposing it to possess already the bliss promised to my servants and the great mercy they will receive on being admitted into his Eternal Father's grand chamber." This is the honour which prepares them, much greater than every human desire; it was enough for men to pursue their endeavour in search of virtue, since they would cause their Father to be honoured also on earth. The Apostle disentangled this sort of evangelical enigma, and developed this fruitful core idea in a reflection of his.

"Man will reap," he said, "whatever he sows. Whoever sows in the flesh will reap corruption from it; but whoever sows in the spirit shall reap eternal life from it" (Gal 6:8). "Prudence, carnal and worldly wisdom spell death, but prudence of the spirit spells life and peace" (Rom 8:6). So that carnal persons cannot please God. "Know ye, then, brethren, that we are not debtors, we are not obliged to live according to the disordered affections and desires of the flesh, for living in that manner, only leads to death; but if with the power of the spirit you mortify the works of the flesh, you will live" (Rom 6:12-13). "Those who are of Christ crucified the flesh with their vices, bad habits and affections; because carnal lust, temptation and the desires of the flesh fight against the spirit, and this is in conflict with the flesh. The fruits of the flesh are well known, and I have preached to you about them, for those who do such things should not inherit the kingdom of God" (Gal 9:17-25). "So, mortify the members of your earthly body, die to sensuality by stripping yourselves of the old man with his acts, and putting on the new one, who by the knowledge, faith and grace of the Holy Spirit, is renewed and restored to his primitive dignity, and made according to the image of Him who raised him" (Col 3:5-10). "So let us run with constancy and patience to the prize which is being offered to us, fixing our eyes on the author and end of our faith, Jesus Christ, whose glory was the fruit of his humiliation until death, and at that death on the cross" (Heb 12:1-2).

After this, it looks as if wanting on this occasion to comfort his servants, the Lord wanted that he too would pass through the natural compassion anyone would feel at the sight of an imminent danger and the horrors of an impending death. So he continued telling his disciples, *My soul is troubled now*, really meaning that he wanted to make them understand that he knew of all the sorrowful horrors awaiting him; they were those which had been put at that instant before his spirit in such a lively manner, that he started trembling and was overcome with great fright; to which, he added as a consequence, *And what will I say?* as if saying to them: "Whom shall my voice address? It is to you, oh my Father, to whom I turn in the midst of the horror and dread that have overwhelmed me. Save me, if possible, from the hour which is now ever drawing closer to me. But no, I have not come into the world to avoid the horrors of this hour, but to sacrifice myself to your commands. Accept my perfect submission to your will, and glorify your holy name. Make yourselves known to your creatures, oh my Father; manifest to all peoples of the earth the greatness of your name, for you desire that my life's works and the ignominy of my death serve your greatest glory." So that, in order to comfort him and sustain him against his fears, it was only his Eternal Father who answered him about his absolute request, and when Jesus Christ finished uttering those last words, *My Father glorify mine to your name*, a voice was heard coming out of a cloud, saying: *I have already glorified my name and I will glorify it again* (Jn 12:28). Which was like saying: "My son, I have heard you and I will always hear you. God has been glorified and worshipped among the Jews, and from now on He will be glorified among the nations. I have already been glorified under the rule of the Law, and I will be glorified in a worthier manner under the Gospel. I have already been honoured by you through the obedience which you render me, and I will be even more honoured for the obedience I will render you."

The attending crowd had heard the loud and frightening voice and thought it could be thunder; others said that some angel had spoken to him; for such was the bystanders' bewilderment. It was not strange that the Gentiles did not understand the meaning of some words spoken by the Jews in their language, but this being strange to them, they hastily judged that it had thundered, while the Jews who perceived clearly and distinctly the articulated words, attributed them to some heavenly angel. But Jesus Christ immediately put himself in the midst of the discussion and said to them, *It is not for me that this voice has come down from heaven, but it is for you*; which is like saying to them, it was done for your instruction and edification, that you may see in me the Son of God, whose pleas are heard by my Heavenly Father. *Know ye, however, that the judgment of the world is coming, and that the prince of this world will be cast out.* Now men will be avenged, reintegrated in their rights and restored to their true freedom. Now the prince of this world will lose all his lordship and reign." It seems very plausible that by these words he understood and wanted to demonstrate the Saviour to the Synagogue in a very particular manner, and to all its leaders who from that time onwards did not use their dominance except to give scandal to their subjects. This is how the apostles explain themselves many times in their writings, following Jesus Christ's model. It could then be clearly seen that Jesus Christ did not speak on this occasion of the final judgment at which the living and the dead will be judged, and the good will be separated from the wicked so that each will receive the reward or punishment due to his works, but of the Father's judgment in favour of men, against the devil who overwhelmed and wounded them with chains in wretched servitude. In this judgment Jesus Christ is the intermediary of men and not a judge; here the sentence is given according to the judge's mercy and not according to the prisoner's conscience; here the defender wins over the oppressor, his accuser; and the tyrant is defeated by the legitimate King and Lord. The time has come to do justice to the oppressed, to dry the face of the helpless, to wipe away the tears of the afflicted. God makes a show by breaking the pride of the world's high and powerful who use their power and authority to increase misery and poverty, and possibly the vices of the downtrodden; for which earthly misfortune will the worldly princes and the powerful call on God about it, as also those who have command and authority over it, and those charged with meting out justice?

It must also be understood that from the time of Jesus Christ's passion there was a true judgment and separation of those faithful who believed and those who were unfaithful, being the ones who were obstinate against the faith. Yet a time will come when the sentence of condemnation against the unfaithful will be pronounced, as will the sentence of prize and reward in favour of the faithful. So that expounding and clarifying what he had first said, he added that *Now the prince of this world*, or the devil, who is the prince of those who love the world and of evil men who dwell in the world, who from Adam until now was lord and still dominates within those who are evil and given to the world, since leading a worldly life they willingly subject themselves to sin, *will be cast out*, meaning that in this judgment the devil will lose the power and the freedom he had to snatch men and take them for himself to enslave and oppress them; for by Christ and the virtue of his passion the door of glory was opened and the devil can no longer prevent anyone as he had done before, from the attainment of this bliss; for by Christ and his passion man was given the virtue to resist his enemy and the strength to overcome him; so that Christ casts out this worldly prince the same way as he was banished from heaven for his pride. Having been cast down from heaven, the devil seized with tyranny and cruelty the court of paradise, which is this world, and destroyed the cult of the true God by inspiring idolatry to the peoples; and not only idolatry, but also passions and vices, like an impetuous whirlwind which had razed the earth. This is how the world was the devil's dwelling place and kingdom, until he who was the Father's arm and strength snatched it from his grip, steadfastly holding the evil one who does not want to be dominated by charity, while teaching us all at the same time how we could detach ourselves from the harmful love towards worldly exaltation and greatness, by virtue of the great mystery of his annihilation in his passion and death on the cross.

In Christ, true God and true man, there is a wonderful mixture which has and will always astonish us on earth if we have faith in this high mystery, as well as the blessed spirits who enjoy its clarity of vision in heaven. Flesh, with conditions of God, is discovered in him, as is God with conditions of flesh; divinity and humanity together, God made man of father and mother, and without father and mother, without either mother in heaven or father here on earth; the Eternal born in time, and the Son in whom the whole edifice of the world was born, born among those of the world as a son. In him the truth triumphed, humility was honoured, charity reigned, mercy shone and humanity was sanctified. Christ banished from the world its prince by disarming him of his power, and by overcoming man's lust in which he had put hope of his victory. The devil is weak unless man gives up himself to him through his evil affections; and so Jesus Christ cast out the prince of this world, he who made wicked men become good, and turned the tyranny of concupiscence into the soft and sweet yoke of charity. The stockade of this victory was the holy cross; in it ignominy and weakness were brought together, with the most painstaking work and torments, with the infamous death which the vile and lawless people condemned him; and on it the Redeemer won, as a leader and prince over all that which grows out of pride. Two are judged by this judgment, Christ and the world. The world judges Christ by treating him as a madman and deceiver, persecuting him, putting him to death, even desiring to erase his memory. Christ judges the world by overcoming its prince, condemning the works of darkness, punishing those who flee from the light of truth and the fire of charity, with the scourge of eternal justice. The world judges Christ, and he triumphs over the world. In being humiliated Christ overcomes pride; in being tormented he condemns pleasure; in being affronted he recovers honour; and when he is dead he restores life. Christ in the eyes of the world is men's scum of the earth; in the eyes of faith, he is the redeemer of all mankind. From the wood to which he is nailed he reigns as Prince, Lord and Saviour of the world; thus he immediately stated, *And if I am lifted up above the earth, I will attract all things to me*. So will the Son of Man be glorified, since he allows himself to be raised above the earth in the same way as he had often prophesied.

These last words uttered by the Saviour, *If I am lifted up above the earth*, need a particular explanation. There is no doubt that what he has come to fulfil must inevitably happen; *exalted* means nailed to the cross; *I will attract all things to me*, all these being the men chosen and predestined for healing, from which the devil is excluded, "and I will be the head of those members, stripping the one who unjustly deceived the first man stripping him of his beauty and grace." Saying these words he also gave the most timely signs of his triumph, denoting the death with which he had to die and showing that to defeat the devil he would not show off the weapons of his power, but only humiliation and the cross. He calls his crucifixion an exaltation, not because the Crucified One was raised up high, but because the cross was in the eyes of God the beginning of our true glory and exaltation. With Christ exalted and honoured on the cross, the sinner man is saved through the cross, such being mysteries as could not be understood by the flesh, Worship them in faith, being aware of the charity with which the crucified head thus attracts and unites the members to it. Christ hanging on the cross spiritually united all his own with him in a tight embrace; as if to say, "He was fruitful of all and sealed them all in himself so that in the death which he suffered in his enduring flesh, their flesh would die to evil doings and sin, for which this flesh is condemned to death; and since he is afterwards gloriously reborn, they may also be reborn in him to the life of righteousness and glory." Finally, the Lord was exalted in the air and raised on the cross, to teach us that just as the air is freely available for all, so were his passion and death also common to all. For the passions, torments and martyrdoms of the other saints were proper to each one of them; but the passion of Christ was common and universal, since with it he wanted to merit the salvation of all; and just as air is the medium between heaven and earth, so also Christ in dying lifted in the air showed that he was the mediator between God and man.

The Jews understood somewhat clearly some of what the Saviour had just told them; and harbouring incessant wicked thoughts against him and attempting to convince him in a way of untruthfulness, they said to him: "Through the Law we know that Christ and his reign will last eternally. How then, claiming to be Christ, do you dare say that the Son of Man will be lifted above the earth? Does it not mean, in your language, that he will be crucified? And being so, is it not clear that he will not stay here forever? Does not the title of the Son of Man or the firstborn of the sons of men apply to Christ? When you speak of the Son of Man, would you not be speaking to us of Christ? And will not Christ remain forever? Tell us, then, who is the Son of Man who will not remain forever?"

If the less carnal Jews had absorbed the Scriptures well, that is the Law and the Prophets, they would have observed that if it was true that Christ and his reign were to last forever; yet it was no less true that Christ, the Son of Man par excellence, would be lifted high above the earth and die on a cross. After this shameful death, it was also written that he was to rise again and live eternally in heaven, and reign in the Church to the end of the centuries which he had bought with the price of his life and acquired with his blood. But the doctors of the Synagogue did not understand it that way, and full of ambition they explained all that the Scriptures contained, which was great and magnificent about the Messiah, and separated from his person all that which was foretold to relate to humility, pain and sadness. The mobs to whom Jesus Christ had to answer were not ready for such great teaching as they needed, and so he said to them: "*There is still very little light in you*; yet walk along with it as it enlightens you that you may not be overwhelmed by darkness." Which was like telling them: "For a little time the light will still be with you. I am this light, and with it you will even know that the Christ will be with you eternally. Hurry up, draw near, take a good look at what could only be seen with the glow of this torch. Understand the mystery of the Saviour, not half-heartedly but in its fullness, that his death is not incompatible with his victory; that with it he will establish his kingdom forever; that his blood will be the captives' ransom, his cross the exaltation of those of you who suffer outrage, his death the coming together of the scattered ones. Darkness will overwhelm you, if it so happens that you believe in the eternity of Christ but deny in him the humiliation of death. You well know what the proverb says, that the one who walks at night does not know where he is going or where he puts his foot."

The Saviour had already said that he was the Light of the world; now he advises them that while they hold on to that Light, they would believe in it; that is, while he speaks to them and instructs them to have the joy of becoming children of the Light. Among the Jews, with whom Jesus Christ explained himself in such a kind manner, there were some faithful persons, but this was not the case with all of them. There was a large number of scheming Pharisees who were ready to riot and spark seditions and tumults, despite the solemnity of such a glorious day for Jesus Christ, as they could no longer conceal their intentions or hide the treacherous plots they had laid against him; and it is for this reason that the most beloved Saviour turned away from them and went into hiding.

CHAPTER 65
DESCRIPTION OF JERUSALEM

ITH the sole exception of Lamartine, whose imagination is so poetic and his heart so compassionate that man and nature are always presented to him under the most beautiful outlook, all travellers and writers consistently call Jerusalem a place of desolation. Stones, ashes and some thorny shrubs is what both ancient and modern men have seen in that place.

The streets of Jerusalem are regular, straight, well cobbled, sometimes even with sidewalks; but they are also melancholy, narrow and almost all on an inclined plane. Houses are usually two or three floors high, with very few windows; the doors are very low, the facades adjoined, and simply built of stone without the slightest ornamentation. Walking along the streets seems like entering the corridors or galleries of an immense prison, so that in a word, we are aware that the depiction Jeremiah has left us of the Holy City is completely true. What a contrast with the streets of Mecca, so well adorned and cheerful! But the queen of the nations is today a widow, as Scripture says.

We should however still know how this city assumes an entirely peculiar character of desolation which would only be sought in vain in the solitude of other ruined cities.

Jerusalem is melancholic, says Chateaubriand, but its sadness has an undecidedly mysterious and poetic aura, like the prophets' songs. The solitude of Zion, covered in mourning, has that feeling which attracts us, because it is twinned with our cradle memories, our middle-age reflections and our graveyard thoughts: for you cannot take a step on that sacred ground without feeling your heart beat. The peoples' crimes and calamities are blended with images of mercy and salvation, a crowd dragged by fury, the just condemned, self-punishing betrayal, repentance, compassion, the most steadfast backing, human weakness adjoining the most sublime virtues, hell devouring its prey, a risen God who ascends to heaven and the spirit of hope that He will descend from there. This is what lies in the midst of the ruins of Jerusalem; we see our destinies on earth, the goods and evils of humanity, and it seems to us that we are walking all the paths of existence. In these places where God died through our life, dying as we die, everything seems to explain the human condition. This is what we really feel when leaving the Holy City, like we were abandoning our existence which, despite being buried in a valley of tears, finds itself attracted to the same pain.

When Michaud speaks of spring in Jerusalem, he says: "In this city you do not see, as in our spring in Europe, flowering forests, meadows and streams that murmur in the midst of green grass. The nightingales are not heard singing the harmonious hymn of the year's dawn. Only a few turtledoves sigh on the palm trees of Caiaphas' house and on the tall trees fencing the gate of Zion.... There is nothing joyful about spring in Jerusalem."

We now see how the affectionate Lamartine describes the Holy City to us in October.

"To the left of our horizon view, coming from the desert where Saint John the Baptist abode, a league away, the sun shone on an almost square tower, a tall minaret and the walls of some buildings crowning the summit of a small hill. From behind could be seen the peak of a city forming a slope along both sides of the hill; to be precise it must have been Jerusalem. We thought we were very far away from the city and all of us, without daring to ask anything of the guide and fearing to see our illusion destroyed, enjoyed this view in silence with all that stood around us telling us of Jerusalem. Indeed, that was it rising in the midst of a gloomy yellow background against the sky and the dark background of the Mount of Olives. We stopped our horses to contemplate the city in this mysterious apparition. One more step that we took and going down to the deep and gloomy valleys, which we saw below us, would certainly make us lose sight of it.

The general appearance of the surroundings of Jerusalem can be described in a few words: exposed mountains, dry valleys, fallow fields, fearless rocks with no grandeur about them, some brown boulders and from one stretch to the other, maybe a fig tree, some vineyards or pale olive trees affording a weak shade on the steep fields on the hill. Then we saw the walls and brown towers of the city's fortifications, appearing in the distance on Zion's summit: these are the features the land offers. The sky is clear and deep, without either morning or evening taking a purple hue. On the side of Arabia you can see a sort of abyss descending from among black mountains, opening the way to a view taking up to the Dead Sea and the summits of the mountains of Moab. Not a whiff of wind murmurs among the battlements or the dry branches of olive trees; no bird makes its trills heard on the road or in the fields.... This is Jerusalem."

In spite of the brilliant colour splashed by Lamartine on these ruins consecrated by religion, and despite the fact that he gilded those mountains and barren fields with the rays of the sun to give them some dignity, the silence and solitude of the population, those high deserted walls, those gates through which hardly anyone enters, those old trees which hardly bear any fruit, all present a melancholic combination, while at the same time making us realise that nothing could be more appropriate to open out a field view for us to deep thoughts and religious reflections.

Yet on finding oneself inside, another sixty-year-old traveller says, that appearance of grandeur seen from a distance, that illusion which momentarily produces an imposing spectacle of domes, mosques and minarets domineering over the remaining buildings, will completely vanish; and that Jerusalem does not seem more than it really is, a city of rubble and ruins. Its square houses, usually small, low and without windows on the inside, are covered with a flat ceiling for a rooftop over which there sometimes rises a small rotunda which, more than a room, resembles a stack of stones piled together in some kind of construction; and to say the truth all this produces the saddest of effects.

The population of Jerusalem consists of Muslims, Greeks, Armenians, Catholics, Copts and Abyssinians. Industry and trade are of little recourse to the city; surrounding rocks and mountains never witness any harvest. All live according to their belief. There is no sect or tribe in the East that does not send alms to Jerusalem; the Armenian and Greek pilgrims take with them considerable amounts, so that the gifts and devotional offerings sustain both Christian and Jewish peoples. Muslims make the most of all these treasures sent out of piety, so that each sect lives on the faith it professes, while it can be said that unbelievers live and enrich themselves at the expense of everyone's faith.

To study Jerusalem's features, each community of peoples has to be particularly observed. The Jews of the Holy City inhabit the dirtiest quarters, sited near the Dung Gate leading to the *dumping site*, now called the Gate of the Moors, or Mughrabi Gate. They are separated from other sects and they are even divided into two enemy factions, sadly gathered in their Synagogues and with their eyes turned towards the Valley of Josaphat, eating their bread in affliction and drinking their water in fear. Seeing them in their small and dirty dwellings, let it be known that they have not come to Jerusalem to live blissfully, and not even to live, but only to be able to rest in the funereal valley, waiting for the time of the final judgment. Jews come to Jerusalem from all countries of the world, and none depart; most of them are old persons whose existence has written off time and no longer think about what matters in life. Jerusalem is home to many Jews who are over a hundred, and a hundred and twenty, years old.

The Armenians and the Greeks are in Jerusalem what they also are in all places. Although both peoples know their trade ropes in all their branches, they could not sustain themselves in the Holy City unless aided by pilgrims showing their dedication. The Armenians' quarters, located on Mount Zion, are the most beautiful in Jerusalem. This nation, which has neither territory nor a homeland, and which lives wandering and scattered around the sons of Israel, does not show its power and worth, and each day seems to prosper even more in the midst of the ruins and miseries of the East. Along the way to Jerusalem, you would only come across caravans of Armenians arriving from all parts of the Ottoman Empire and even from Persia, carrying their riches along with them.

The Greeks live around the Church of the Holy Sepulchre, which comforts them when they think of their homeland's calamities. Being persecuted in all Muslim counties, they do not crave to make any offering to Jerusalem, and their pilgrims had forgotten the way of Zion. It was only under Eastern Byzantine protection that many pilgrims visited the Holy Land arriving in large numbers from Asia Minor, from the banks of the Hellespont (Dardanelles), and even from Constantinople (Istanbul). They have retained their former character, and if any joy were to be found in a sad Jerusalem, it will be necessary to look for it among the Greeks, for although being more superstitious than other sects, they nevertheless have educated persons among their high clergy.

In the midst of this contest of opposite and rival beliefs, there is one that dominates all the others, and it is certainly the most jealous and intolerant. Muslims take upon themselves a whole air of masters; the Muslim population is turbulent and restless, and can neither suffer themselves being tied in chains nor giving freedom to others. Each of these unbelievers holds the right to insult Christians and Jews in the street and even in their homes, without allowing them to complain or seek reparation. And what is most unique is that these Muslims pray together with Christians and Jews, very much venerating the same sacred places, for both the Bible and the Gospel list a few names which are respected by Mohammedan followers. All these hostile peoples are governed by a Mutzelim, a Qadi, a Sub-Qadi, in charge of the police, and a Mufti in charge of the mosques and the observance of religious precepts. But they all toe the same line and treat the sectarians of different religions by extracting their money. The city is under the patronage Saint John of Acre.

The Mount of Olives has at all times been a promontory that has greatly struck the imagination of Christians. In the first centuries of the Church miraculous fires were discovered on the mountain, and ninth and tenth century pilgrims believed seeing the glorious scene of the Saviour's Ascension happening again. Some, on reaching the mountain top, fell to their knees with outstretched arms, their prostrated bodies in the form of a cross; shedding tears they asked heaven to deliver them from bodily imprisonment in the same place where Jesus Christ rose to heaven. Claber the chronicler speaks of a pilgrim from Autun, whom God called to the dwelling place of the elect on the very day he had prayed on the Mount of Olives. That is where the crusaders' processional march stopped before their final assault on Jerusalem, and certainly that facet of the Holy City must have inflamed the heroic enthusiasm of Godfrey's crusaders, more than the clerics' and bishops' speeches. Jerusalem preserves the Mount of Olives as its ultimate glory, as a radiant headband crowning the daughter of Zion.

Every time you ascend there, you discover some new quarters and some new building of Jerusalem, so that without exaggeration you can move around counting all the houses. The entire Holy City stretches out beyond the two mosques and the site from which the temple rose, without missing from seeing a roof or a stone, as if it were a city plan in relief that an artist laid out for us on a table. This city, adds Lamartine, is not how we would have wanted to see it, a jumble and confusing set of ruins and ashes, on which some Arab huts have been tossed or some Bedouin shops planted; they are not like Athens, a chaos of dust and toppled walls, where a traveller seeks in vain the shadow of buildings, the paved pathway of the street and a population's particular aspect. But it is an outstanding city which still nobly presents its intact and tooth-like walls, its blue mosque with white colonnades, and its thousands of resplendent domes over which the light of the autumn sun is reflected. Finally, in the middle of that ocean of houses and that cloud of small domes that cover them, another black dome rises, much wider than all the others, dominated in turn by a white one. It is that of the holy Sepulchre and Calvary, muddled together and as if floating in the immense labyrinth of buildings and houses surrounding them. Such is the city seen from that mountain top, appearing like the New Jerusalem being brilliantly reborn from the bosom of the desert. It is the most excellent panorama that could be seen of a city which no longer exists, but which still seems to exist as if full of life and the prime of youth; and yet, if you look at it carefully, you know that all this is really nothing more than a beautiful vision of the city of David and Salomon. No noise comes out of its squares and streets; no road leads to its eastern and western, southern and northern gates; only a few pathways wind randomly through the rocks, showing up a few almost nude Arabs, some camel-driving Damascus inhabitants, or some women from Bethlehem or from Jericho who bring a basketful of Engaddi grapes to be sold in the morning at the city gates. On the left hand side of the temple and the walls of Jerusalem, the hill forms a decline, so extending with a gentle slope, and about a hundred steps from the city we find ourselves before a mosque and a group of Turkish buildings. It is the mountain of Zion! It is David's palace and tomb!

A viewer standing on the Mount of Olives, who entertains purely religious considerations, cannot help but recall fearfully that this is the place where Jesus Christ, seated in view of the temple, spoke to his disciples of the terrible signs that must precede the destruction of this sacred building while casting his eyes on that city of grace and weeping for the calamities which threatened it. He could surely not have chosen a more imposing place to cast this anathema against Jerusalem.

After having taken a bird's eye view of a city interior which nonetheless seems like any other city from a political and religious spectrum, it would be useful and interesting to see the meld presented by the surrounding walls. We cannot judge it as if it were a stronghold; we only have to look at it as a kind of fortified field for many centuries, in the middle of a barren plain, and a barrier against the voracious greed of desert Arabs. Above all, it is very strange to think that within a short distance we face the same line of walls which, under different forms, with principles of different architecture and in very distant times, has seen so many enemies and has been attacked so many times that, despite the passage of time, it is still so invaluably treasured in the eyes of Christians. The Turks regularly preserve these fortifications to be able to call themselves masters of Jerusalem, collect some mean-spirited taxes and rip off those who go to visit its ruins.

The current precinct of Jerusalem, enclosed within a boundary of about a league, is almost a square. Yet the walls do not present a perfectly straight line any more than

CHAPTER 65 ✤ 375

in its eastern part, since the other facades are irregular. Its height is about one hundred and twenty feet, its width over thirty feet, with square towers from one section to the other, with seven main gates. The *Gate of Mercy* leads to Bethlehem; the others bear the name of the *Prophet David*, the *Golden Gate*, with a wall now built around it, the Gate of the *Holy Virgin*, that of *Dawn*, the one of Damascus and that of the *Berbers*. To the west a castle can be seen with some towers surrounded by an open court, or rather a deep ditch; from one place to another stones supporting Herod's ancient abode are discovered there; it bears the name of Castle of the Pisans. It is known that these were very distinguished at the time of the Crusades and they now serve as quarters for the Aga and his troops. To the north the wall extends to the Valley of Josaphat.

Recalling the eighteen sieges and pillages suffered by Jerusalem, one can form an idea of the frequent reconstruction of its fortifications; they had already been built more or less high and magnificent, even more or less solid and on a more extensive level. Yet the most complete destruction of the walls of the city which had condemned the prophets to death and was unknown to the Messiah, occurred in the seventieth year of the Christian era, during Vespasian's reign. Their triple lines of fortification collapsed in the space of five months that the siege lasted, and opened the way to the conqueror on mounds of corpses and dying men. The flames set fire to what the war machines had left standing, and the plough passed over the temple foundations. The prophecies were then fulfilled: "Your enemies will hem you on all sides, and dash you to the ground, you and your children, and they will not leave stone upon stone in you, because you did not know the time of your visitation". This foreboding was made some six hundred years before its appalling fulfilment.

The present walls, around which Chateaubriand has gone three times on foot like Jonah went around Nineveh, have four sides facing the four winds, and form a quadrilateral, with a main stretch running from east to west. Daville proves with local measurements and positions that the ancient city of the Jews could not have been much larger than the modern one, since it occupied the same site with the only difference that he included the whole mountain of Zion and omitted Calvary. The present walls were erected by Suleiman, as evidenced by the Turkish inscriptions discovered within them. It has been said that Suleiman's idea was to include Mount Zion within a circle encompassing Jerusalem, later condemning the architect to death for not having executed his orders. But nothing proves this barbarism, because the city is almost dominated over from all sides, so that in order to resist a regular army it would be necessary to build many bulwarks to its west and north, as well as a citadel over the Mount of Olives.

On the whole, this incomplete state of fortifications around the Holy City brings about countless evils, as every year daring troops attempt seizing the city with impunity. They are prodded on with the bait of treasures they believe to be considerable but which are actually not; and animated by the pride of reigning on rubble and stones whose name still resonates all over the world and are visited with respect by all peoples.

Surrounding Jerusalem are some monuments which recall great events. You can see the Virgin's tomb open in the bosom of a rock, to which you can climb through a staircase of fifty steps; on the same mountain the graves of Anne, Joachim and Joseph were also opened with a chisel; had these monuments not been actually built for the people whose names they bear, it does not mean they would cease being remarkable. On the other hand, it would be difficult to date them to a particular century. At the foot of the sanctuary of the Virgin you can see the Garden of Olives, so well known in the history of the passion. It fields eight olive trees; according to tradition, they were already in place when Christ gave his last breath on the cross. Some of the oil extracted from the fruit of these venerable trees fed one of the lamps of the Holy Sepulchre, and the other lamp was sent as a precious gift to the benefactor monarchs of the Holy Land. Now, the friars of the Latin convent share the olives and make rosaries from their bones, which are of great value for pious souls. In the same valley are the rock-hewn tombs of the kings; but their architecture, which is of Ionic order, belies the antiquity attributed to them. The cemetery of the Jews is located in the Valley of Josaphat, where Jews coming as refugees from all nations aspire to rest when they die. The nature of this valley is most distressing, as Chateaubriand says: the western side features a chalky cliff, supporting the city's Gothic ramparts, above which Jerusalem is seen. The Mount of Olives and the Mount of Scandal lie on the eastern side. These two mountains are almost bare and of a dark red hue; on their deserted slopes you can see here and there some vineyards, some forests of olive trees, vacant hyssop covered lots, chapels, oratories and ruined mosques. At the bottom of the valley you can discover a single-arched bridge built over the valley of the Torrent Valley of Cedron. The stones of the Jewish cemetery located at the foot of the Mount of Scandal, named after Solomon's idolatry, die out in a pile of rubble, and under the Arab village of Silwan it is hard to pick out village shacks from surrounding tombs. Witnessing Jerusalem's grief or contemplating the solitude of the mountains, in which hardly any living being is seen, and witnessing the disorder of all fallen, shattered, half-open tombs, it only seems like the trumpet of judgment has already sounded and that the dead are about to be resurrected in the Valley of Josaphat. The pool or fountain of Siloam lies at the farther end of the Valley of Josaphat; the water springs from a rock, but flows gently dropping into a twenty-foot long pond, ten feet deep, where one can descend by a multi-step stairwell. Near Siloe and towards the east, there rises Mount Zion, part of which sits within the precinct of Jerusalem; the top of this little mountain is the site of the ruins of three monuments which are supposed to have been the Holy Cenacle, the house of Caiaphas and David's tomb; but there is nothing to assure us of the certainty of these traditions.

CHAPTER 66
JESUS CONFOUNDS THE SCRIBES AND PHARISEES ON ALL QUESTIONS THEY ASK HIM, AND TELLS THEM THE PARABLE OF THE LANDOWNER WHO PLANTED HIS VINE AND RENTED IT TO TENANT FARMERS WHO THEN KILLED THE LEGITIMATE HEIR (MT 21:33–46)

S we have just seen in the previous chapter, Jesus Christ hid from the presence of his persecutors, the scribes and Pharisees, to deceive them completely and tear away the obstinacy and hardness of their hearts after that he had given them the important witness to which we had formerly referred. When he returned to the Holy City very early in the morning, taking the same road as the previous day, Peter, who usually meticulously examined the events occurring before him, noticed that the fig tree Jesus Christ had cursed the day before was completely dry. Turning to Jesus Christ, he said to him: "Master, look at the fig tree which you have cursed. See how the curse has fallen upon it, for now it is dry." On seeing all his apostles equally astounded, Jesus Christ replied to Peter, giving him and all a common answer, the same as he had already given them elsewhere. So he said to them: "Truly, I say to you, if you have perfect trust in God, if you are unhesitatingly convinced that you will obtain from my Father all that which you ask of Him in my name, if you pray incessantly, without any doubt and concerns about the result, you will not only do to a fig tree what I have just done before you, but if you say to this mountain to move from that place and be thrown into the sea, your desire will be fulfilled. Believe, then, that by prayer you will obtain what you wish to achieve; believe that God will not deny you anything of what you request through me to benefit your apostolic work or for your progress in virtue; for nothing is impossible for God and all is granted if a plea is made with faith and with that same charity which teaches to forgive insults before asking God to forgive our own offences."

As they were approaching the last times of Jesus Christ's life, it seemed that he was growing in the ardour of his zeal, in the same manner that a torch is further fanned when it is closer to exhaling its flame. That is why he was so concerned about inspiring his apostles and disciples with the thought of holding on to the torches of faith and charity. And after having given them these holy instructions along the way, on entering Jerusalem he walked straight up to the House of God. There he walked around for some time, until he found himself soon enough surrounded by a crowd of people to whom he resumed explaining the mysteries of spiritual well being. Yet he had barely started that the leaders of the Priests, scribes and elders of the people, came forward to openly oppose him in the exercise of his ministry. They sought to convince the Lord that he was usurping their rights and abrogating functions pertaining to them, showing contempt to the legitimate court. Saint Chrysostom says about this: "They drew near to him when he was teaching, that is, when they could in no way prevent him. Those who drew near to him were the Priests' leaders, who could not be excused for their ignorance. And there were also the people's elders who were arousing their restlessness rather than giving them good example and enlightenment. Contriving among themselves they colluded saying: We are the columns of the temple, and see that the whole Church rests upon these columns: we are the visible language of the Scriptures which are silent, while he resonates harmoniously in the midst of the temple, so that we are forced to the silence of discordant zithers; we were the fathers, and he now begets children making us entirely sterile. Oh, how much we are degraded in our people's sight!" So in order to excite some tumult in the holy place against him, who had declared himself its defender and custodian, they drew close to him and told him: "In whose name do you have the audacity to perform these things before us in this holy place? Preaching publicly, teaching the people, reforming abuses and settling scores with the temple police, all these and many other acts fall within our jurisdiction, for which you must ask for power from us, and have it from us, and which you have not received. So tell us, who has given you power to act in this manner, and with what authority do you carry it out?"

Badly warned against Christ and becoming extremely furious, they understood and wanted to persuade the people that all he did was with the help of the devil, as they had already assured them on another occasion when they said he cast out demons in the name of Beelzebub, prince of them all. Jesus Christ, however, being aware of all their malice, held back from answering them, other than pitting an objection against another and one argument against another, as one wanting to pull out a nail with another, vehemently refuting all their slanders, for theirs were no more than evil questions. It was necessary to be very blind and hardened not to recognise the great power and authority with which Jesus Christ was clothed in the splendour of his miracles, in the sanctity of his life, in the sublimeness of his doctrine, in the public testimonies of his Heavenly Father, and in the fulfilment of the prophetic oracles which announced the Messiah. So that, not doubting that those surrounding him were passionate men, since they forgot or seemed to be unaware of what was known by all, he wanted to close fully their mouths by making a contrast between his ambitious audacity and a respectful docility of unconcerned persons, besides other facts of which he had become aware recently.

"You ask me," the Lord answered them, "with what authority I work in your sight as keeper of my Father's house decorum and as this people's doctor and teacher. I do not refuse nor will I refuse to answer you; but first I must reply to you in the manner of your teachers and doctors of the Law, with a question I want to ask you. If you answer sincerely and frankly, I will also tell you, for my part, the authority with which I exercise my mission. So tell me wherefrom was John's baptism, was it from heaven or did it come from men?" This was like telling them: "The Baptist preached in the midst of these people and established a baptism of penance which you saw him administer to all those who asked for it. Did John perform and practise this new institution by the authority of God or out of the impulse and action of his own spirit? Yet, what is really undoubted is that he did not act under your orders or with your permission since, far from having your approval, you pursued him with fury and your persecutions forced him to retreat to Galilee, and there caused him his imprisonment and death. Of course, then, in his preaching and baptism he did not work except by the authority of God rather than his own, so which of these two will you accept?"

They did not expect this retort from Jesus Christ, and so found themselves running, confused and ashamed before their people, whom they wanted to confuse and terrify with their presumed wisdom and authority, So, being aware of the fatal consequences to which they had been exposed, they withdrew silently from the midst of the crowd to deliberate among themselves and agree on a standard reply. "If we answer," they said to each other, "that John's ministry came from heaven and was authorised by God, this man of our faith would take advantage of it and overcome us in this contest, because he would not stop asking us why we did not believe him, after having actually declared to us more than once that he was the Christ and Son of God And if we tell him that the Baptist had not received his mission from on high, that he was a man without character, and that those who followed him were nothing more than fickle men, simpletons or gullible persons, even though there is no need to applaud the praise he gave him, we would be exposing ourselves to the people's rage, and things might go so far as to stone us as blasphemers. Fact is that he still retains many supporters and admirers among the crowd who venerate him, at least as a great prophet raised by God, and they would not take it well that he is hurt or that the reputation of such a great and eminent man is undermined." The Venerable Bede says: "So they knew that Jesus Christ's infinite wisdom had laid a snare for them from which they could not escape and go anywhere they wanted; they had either to confess the truth, or they had to suffer the people's contempt and threats. They chose the lie, the mock and the treachery, and with a gesture of contempt they answered the Lord they neither knew from where John's baptism or his ministry came, nor were they obliged to answer these questions. It was him who should answer theirs, and so for the same reason they were asking him to account for his conduct and the authority he was usurping."

They responded mysteriously to Jesus Christ so that the Lord, who did not think himself obliged to reply any further, said to them: "For if you do not know with what authority John preached and baptised among us, and by saying this you believe you are not obliged to give a satisfying reply to my question, I will not answer yours by telling you the power with which I perform whatever you see. Nor will I fail to ask you another question which will not be any less embarrassing for you." Jesus Christ found this manner of getting along, by which the questioner must be answered and the tempter confused. He sought to teach, while the scribes tempted him with their questions wanting to mislead him, so he confused them with his silence and destroyed them with his new question. "There was a certain man who had two sons," he said to them. He called the first and eldest of the two and sent him to work in his vineyard; however, refusing to obey and not caring about his father's behest, he answered him dryly that he did not want to go. Yet after a very short while, his inner self became aware of his doing, recognised his mistake, and ashamed of his lack of care and obedience, ran to his father to beg forgiveness, and went off to work hastily. A short time after the father called the second son, gave him the same order as the first, and appearing submissive and obedient, the son feigned to his father he was going, while what he thought about least was ever going to work. Which of these two sons, do you think, fulfilled his father's will?" Jesus Christ concluded.

The answer which the Pharisees had to give him does not seem doubtful, and much less could they foresee how Our Saviour would interpret this parable. "Undoubtedly," they told him, "his first son was more obedient, but the second was a cheat and a hypocrite." This was precisely what Jesus Christ was expecting to confuse them and to interpret justly his doctrine. "Truly, I say to you," he instantly replied to them, "that tax collectors and harlots will precede you in the kingdom of God," namely in the Christian Church, in the militant Church, "by faith and penance; and in triumph for glory, leaving you out due to your infidelity. Although not obeying at once, the first son later did his father's will, and is worthy of mercy. The second, who snubbed him and did not, is worthy of reproach and punishment." This was just as telling them: "Not only are the Gentiles much better than you Jews, according to the judgment you have brought on yourselves, but the worst among the Gentiles such as tax collectors and harlots who openly lead a most hopeless life among you, will in the presence of God enjoy a much greater merit than you, for it is without comparison better not to promise but actually fulfil God's righteousness, which is fulfilling one's duties in God's presence, than to promise and to lie."

Saint Augustine teaches that fairness or feigned justice is much of a double immorality; and this vice is the one that shines mostly in priests and scribes; being by this like the second son of the Family Father. They made a show of being perfect and observant of the Law, but after never fulfilled it, following the traditions that they and their parents, who were perverse just like them, had established, taking little care to truly observe it. Whoever hears them will think that they were always ready to obey; but their true character was that of pride and disobedience to the most important precepts. This portrait made them see clearly that they might be confused; but knowing that instead of convincing themselves they would be more irritated against his person, Jesus Christ also wanted to let them know that none of the immoral thoughts they had formed to take his life were hidden from him, and that he was well aware he was already on the eve of falling into their hands. He blamed them for their ingratitude since they had not betrayed their ministry, and did not flee from them as he did on other occasions, because the time had come to fulfil his Father's will; for which reason he proposed to them an awful parable with the charitable design that they should take advantage of his final teachings.

"There was a careful and vigilant Family Father," he told them, "who planted a vineyard, surrounded it with a strong fence and built in it a winery and a tower." This vineyard, planted by God, was the Synagogue with respect to the Jews, just like the Church with respect to Christians, and figuratively it is our own soul. To speak in this manner to the priests of Jerusalem, knowing that in two days they had to be the judges who would judge him, was not only to admit death, but also going out to seek it, without wanting to adopt any action or to prevent it or by any human means to avoid it. So that, indeed, Jesus Christ was willing, and every day prepared himself even more, to fulfil his Father's will, and while warning good souls against the scandals of the cross, he evidently showed in many ways the easy manner with which he walked toward it for our love. Thus he also made known to us not only God's adorable providence, but his long-suffering and endurance in waiting so long, to see if he could soften the treachery of the Jewish race. This, being enclosed and protected under the walls of Jerusalem, made for a perfect image of the vineyard which was defended by a good fence. The press placed in the middle of the vineyard stood for a symbol of holy doctrine and perfect knowledge of God's law. The tower for its defence was the Lord's holy temple itself sited in the middle of the city, and the thieves or the winemakers who were farmed out to cultivate the vineyard, were the sanctuary priests, entrusted to instruct the peoples and obliged to watch over their conduct.

If by the vineyard we want to understand our soul, planted by creation and sanctification, we will also see that however it may be known, it belongs to God and not to us: we receive it from His hand as landlords to cultivate it and return to Him the fruits of the good works it yields, helped by His grace. For it the best fence is the Lord's law and his holy word; the winery being Christ's sacrifice and the sacraments through which the merit of his blood is communicated to us. The tower is the church, which is the house of prayer, where man raised in spirit lives detached from the world, united with God and protected by Him against his enemies of eternal healing. The vineyard is thus made available with all that is necessary for it to profit, rented out to some farmers who would care to cultivate it; and after agreeing with them, he proceeds to a strange country where he intends staying for a long time. By this he wanted to tell them that although God is always pouring out healthy graces on his people and protecting them with visible prudence, He no longer manifests Himself to them through the senses but seems to abandon them to the righteousness of their conscience and to the direction of those guiding them. So in the old time He gave His people Moses and the prophets, and in the new era He gave us His apostles and all their successors.

On his arrival, he sent his servants to reap the fruit which had grown in his vineyard; but those miserable ones received a most unworthy treatment from the rustic and brutal farmers; the first servant received many blows, the second was covered with insults and head wounds, and the third lost his life. The owner of the vineyard sent his house and farm servants three times over to receive the fruits due to him from the farmhands. In three former times, during which He found His chosen people, when they were already flourishing under the rule of His kings, when they were already groaning in the chains of slavery and when they were already re-established under his chieftains, God sent his prophets to ask the priests and leaders to count scrupulously the souls entrusted to their care and conduct. The unfaithful farmers and cultivators insulted them, mistreated them and killed them, some with stones, others with the sword, for no other crime than that of the great Family Father's being servants. Priests, leaders and kings had become tyrants and persecutors of the prophets; so Jesus Christ could say very well to the blood-strewn city: *Jerusalem, Jerusalem, you kill the prophets and stone those sent to you by God; how many times have I wanted to gather around me your children as the hen collects and gathers its chicks under its wings, and you were not willing: in truth, Jerusalem, do I tell you, that your house will be deserted, and your enemies will breach your walls and not leave no stone unturned.*

His landlords' insolence could not sit well with the Family Father; he concealed it, however, without taking any revenge, and was content to send other servants; but although these were in greater numbers than the first, they did not receive any better treatment. When the landlords were determined not to pay anything, they verbally mistreated them with great shame; some were beaten with the utmost harshness, others were wounded and persecuted with stones, and others were killed at the same place; and although the owner of the vineyard after so many attempts, which did not bring about any effect, tried new means to move the hearts of those landlords, and after some hard thinking, he resolved to put at risk the person he loved most, sending them his own son, in whom he had placed all his hopes, thinking that they would have more respect and esteem for him, and that if they still had some vestige of humanity within them, they would undoubtedly view him as the image of the Family Father; yet he was deceived in his judgment.

God's tenderness towards men is very vividly shown in this image of the owner of the vineyard, only chastising men with pain because His punishments are eternal. For their sake He sacrifices his beloved Son, because although He knows that for a great number of them this sacrifice will not bear any fruit due to their lack of remorse, it will bring blessings to many and it will render the victim glorious. Maybe, the Good Father says, that they respect my Son. This expression, although doubtful, does not denote that God is unaware of future events, but it implies the freedom of man's will and the indifference he retains in all his considerations, so that it can never be said that man's will has been subjected to violence.

The Family Father sent His Son, to make us understand the great effort of love with which God the Father gave His only begotten Son to regain possession of our soul: but with everything, like those ungrateful farmers, we cast him out of our hearts as they threw him out of the vineyard's precincts, making with our passions such a horrific covenant, as they did to each other to take his life and to be owners and possessors of his estate; but the same way they erred, we also very often err, and falling under the formidable weight of the almighty anger of the great Family Father, we perish, the same as he made the father-killers perish. When the owner and lord of the vineyard later comes to punish these murderers, what punishment do you think he will give them? The scribes and Pharisees, who prided themselves on being righteous, could not contain themselves when they heard of the imagery Jesus Christ had used in their regard, and so they all instantly raised their voices and said, that there was no punishment great enough for such horrible attacks. They knew they should not expect anything but death, and that their ordeal must have been so extraordinary that it corresponded to the horrible nature of their crime; and that the master would not keep back from replacing them with other winemakers who would not miss from bringing him the fruits of his vineyard and paying him his dues in the right time.

This was the great prophecy which was already so close to being fulfilled. It was verified to the letter when Jesus Christ, being condemned to death by the leaders and priests, was led out of the walls of Jerusalem and crucified on the hill destined for his sacrifice. For which reason the Eternal Father, having then been irritated, avenged the death of His Only Son upon the rebellious city with the death of all its inhabitants; He passed faith in the Messiah and the religion founded on the God who was made man from the Jews to the Gentiles; He formed His Church from them and entrusted it to the care of his apostles who, by cultivating it with the cares and sweats and watering it even with their own blood in the same manner as its founder and Divine Master, reaped from it abundant fruits. This is the last effort of love made by God the Father towards His only begotten Son to take possession of our soul and demand from it the fruits due to Him, since it was He who planted it by creating it and bought it by redeeming it. And who can have the courage to rebel against an almighty and eternal Father and a Son so worthy of being loved that he gives himself up totally and surrenders himself to the hands of his enemies, subjecting himself to the pains of a passion soon to be accomplished and of a most affronting death to redeem and save us? This seems like a horrible thing, and human affection lacks the courage even to think about it. But this is so hard to believe, namely how easily and for what slight causes the creature acts upon it! What respect does he have for the Son of God when he casts him out of his soul and crucifies him by sinning? What will the Lord of the vineyard do with these men when he comes searching?

This coming of the Lord will come about when each one of us dies. What then will the sinner answer to the unyielding Judge? A huge crime it is, for certain; how can man distort the charge laid against him by his own conscience? How can man deceive him who is the peak of wisdom? How can man distort or pervert him who is righteousness itself? How can man resist the Almighty? Alas! how forgetful we are of this coming of the Lord! No matter how much we forget it willingly, we will not get rid of it, nor will our deafness and insensitivity appease the anger of the upset Judge. The more we now disregard God's judgment, the worse shall we find ourselves in it. So that Jerome says about this: "We were rented the vineyard, but on condition that we render to God, Lord of our soul, the fruit of good deeds and of all vineyards at the time when He asks us for them; that is, on the day of His coming and of our judgment, and so that knowing that we owe everything to Him, we would never forget what we should talk about or what we should do."

The leaders of the priests and Pharisees, the scribes and elders knew that this strong and frightening parable was not only intended for them, but also for their parents; and this made their bravery for affront and rage grow to extreme fury. In fact, their fathers were singled out as persecutors and murderers of the ancient prophets, while being portrayed with the same shades for having caused the death of the holy precursor; for they were already being prepared to dye their sacrilegious hands with the blood of Jesus Christ, the true Son of God, against whom they were about to lodge a horrible attack and throw the last straw to the ungodliness of their lives; which would cause, hasten and witness the complete desolation and ruin of their homeland. They availed of all their schemes to experience this, and although the most loving Jesus Christ saw that this was the greatest chance they had to accept the holy plan of attracting them to repentance, they never wanted to convert or get to know anything of his doctrines, virtues and miracles which the people admired and knew; as they did know that he was the *cornerstone* which had been foretold and announced and which they rejected; and that they were about to stumble upon it, or it would fall upon them, crushing and breaking them to pieces.

Steeped in disgrace in the presence of the people they tried to seduce, they breathed nothing but revenge and treated the Saviour in their great despair as a liar and impostor. Had they not been restrained by the fear of being stoned to pieces by the same people, they would right then have tried to seize Jesus Christ's person; but this fear was an insurmountable dam which did not dare strike off the hatred which they harboured against him. Whenever they came to know he was around in Jerusalem and that he was about to go up to the temple, they went after him determined to seize him, yet always turning back without even daring to threaten him. Malice inflamed them, but cunning held them back, for by it they became aware that he was very exposed to be persecuted and seized, being a person who had won the will of the people by the great amount of benefits he had bestowed upon them; so that they could not even afford casting a shadow on his character, being for the same reason held and respected at least as a great prophet. For which reasons they resolved to return to their old conduct of hatching concealed plots against the Saviour, flattering themselves that he would lose the confidence of the same people who looked up to him for their own support.

The scribes and Pharisees were condemned by what Jesus Christ had said and stated before the people who afforded him great respect. This was because they could not help but answer to the question put to them that when the Family Father himself requested an account from his tenant farmers, he would punish them severely and lease his vineyard to other farmers who would pay him and give him the fruit in due time. Such is the understanding men have of God's justice, however evil they may be and do not show it to continue along the sinful path they were treading. When the soul is separated from the body, God will open their eyes, so that they may see with all clarity the unreasonableness of their guilt and the righteousness of divine justice. They will then take out that very sad but vain and sterile consequence: *then it is true that we erred along the way.* What might have helped him before as a correction, will then make their despair more furious. However Jesus Christ, who wished to pursue his doctrine and rather seek the conversion of those miserable persons who added to their despair, continued his address saying to them: "Have you never read in Scripture that the stone which the builders set aside became the building's cornerstone?" This stone is Jesus Christ, head of his Church by his authority, founded by his word, and his union and connection to it by his spirit. In his body he binds and unites the Jews who cast him out from among them, and the Gentiles who did not know him. He despised the world, and the Jews wanted to erase his name from human memory with the most atrocious death to which they condemned him; but all this only served to bring to the fore God's great work in the redemption of the human race. These truths foretold by the prophets, and most particularly by his father David, were read many times by the priests who, however, did not understand them. For this reason Jesus Christ further told them: *The kingdom of God will be taken away from you and will be given to an emissary to yield its fruits.*

If what Jesus Christ had until now told the scribes was dreadful, these words were no less scary. Indeed, if only they had understood what it meant to wrest the kingdom of God from their midst! This is one of the clearest and most terrible proofs of God's hatred of sin. Who can take it for granted and be able to say, I will not be visited by this punishment? Sometimes the hidden sins of one kingdom are enough for God to snatch away the faith from it and transfer it to another, when not even the prayers and public virtues of righteous persons would be able to calm his anger. And what shall we say and hope for when they are public sins which flow from the head to the members, and when scandal and corruption are the general mood? Whoever falls on that stone, despising the Saviour's mysteries, abusing his gifts, conspiring against the Gospel, or holding back from taking him as his rule of life, will be torn to pieces, since human efforts to achieve these ends are always futile. Despite his spitefulness and rage, the truth will always be there, because the Gospel could not be distorted, twisted or corrupted: *it can be disobeyed and fought, but not destroyed.* Truth is always truth, and this truth is Christ. Whoever contradicts it in word or deed, will crash into it and tear himself to pieces; but on whoever it falls, he will be crushed; because it is almighty and there is no one who can resist the weight of its almightiness.

It would have been a great fortune for the priests and other individuals of the Synagogue had they, knowing that Jesus Christ's words were directed against them, taken advantage of the truths that were in them. It is by God's mercy that we know the truth, and even a greater one than that we have applied to run our own life. The truth is for us: this is what the Saviour came for, that we may walk towards him, who is truth and life. Woe to those who although they understand how to apply truth according to their customs, do not take advantage of it! It was not respect for the truth that held back the anger of the Pharisees, but their fear of the people. Yet of what benefit can this fear be if in their hearts they were already sacrilegious murderers? Even if it only takes the creature a little or nothing not to commit an offence out of respect for the world, if he holds fast to his thought and consents to it, he would so commit it in his heart. *The law of the Lord is without blemish, and it converts souls; he is faithful to his word which gives wisdom to little ones;* for which reason Saint Paul said to the Ephesians: "*So, be imitators of God as beloved children and walk in love, just as Christ loved us and gave Himself up for us as a fragrant sacrificial offering to God.... Let no one deceive you with empty words, for because of these things the wrath of God comes upon the children of disobedience.* Have nothing to do with them. Because in a former time you were darkness, but now you are light in the Lord. Walk as children of light. And know that the fruit of light consists in every kind of kindness, and of justice and of truth" (Eph 5:1,7-9).

CHAPTER 67

A RICH MAN INVITES SEVERAL PERSONS TO HIS SON'S WEDDING; SOME EXCUSE THEMSELVES AND MANY OTHERS REFUSE GOING TO THE WEDDING FEAST; A PERSON WHO SHOWS UP WITHOUT A WEDDING DRESS IS THROWN OUT; JESUS THEN SATISFACTORILY ANSWERS THE QUESTION PUT TO HIM ABOUT PAYING TAXES, AND ABOUT THE WOMAN WHO HAD SEVEN HUSBANDS, AND REPLIES TO THE PHARISEE WHO WISHED TO KNOW WHICH WAS THE FIRST AND GREATEST COMMANDMENT OF THE LAW (LK 14:16-24; MT 22:1-21; 35-46)

THE lovers of things of the world have certainly always shown being annoyed by the things of God, even those who are most holy and revered among them. They hate not only God the Father and Jesus Christ his Only Son, Our Redeemer and Saviour, but the servants of this God made man, the richest ever seen during the ages, who came into the world to fill us all with the gifts of His grace, mercy and love. For in them the exact opposite effects can be seen from what God's love produces in their hearts, their motive power being love of the world. They always look at him as the only witness to their unwinding, while likewise seeking how to destroy him. What world is this which entirely abhors good souls? They are the heirs of Cain's spirit and imitators of his grudge and envy. They are the Jews who persecuted Christ and those Christians who are practical enemies of his Gospel. For this reason they want to rejoice in all this, in their riches, in their vain and sinful curiosities, in their luxury and pride, and they flee from God even when he invites them with other more delicate, pure and permanent joys and delights. In order to convince the scribes and Pharisees, and draw them out of their error, and to teach them and all their followers and listeners, the

Saviour told them a parable in which he manifested the sovereign greatness of his divine piety, while contesting and contradicting the Jews' ingratitude who, more particularly than all other peoples, had been invited to eternal bliss.

A man, he told them, held a sumptuous dinner and many were those invited for it. There is no doubt that the Jews were first called, and they were called by God Himself, by Moses and by the prophets. Then they were called out by Jesus Christ himself and by his apostles; but having despised everything and refusing to come forward to meet Christ, it was necessary to call the Gentiles, those who had responded at once to God's call of love and grace. This man was Jesus Christ our Redeemer, true God and man, who is called man by truth of human nature, and God by divine truth. For he is One by the uniqueness of his person and has laid out the banquet of heavenly and eternal life; he is also the perpetual bliss of holy souls in heavenly and eternal glory. It should be called a supper, because it is the last banquet; and just as supper is prepared for the time when the day is over and sunset, and after which there is no other meal, so does the everlasting life begin at the end of the present life, after which none follows but that life. It is a great and sovereign meal, as its immensity cannot fit into this life, nor can man's heart comprehend it. To this end do I call the Lord great, because Jesus Christ wants all honours to be for our healing and blessed. Some he calls through angel emissaries, others through the patriarchs, others through the prophets, and still others through the apostles. This supper also denotes the vocation of all peoples to faith in the incarnation, in which Jesus Christ became one with human nature with an indissoluble bond, and married with the whole Church. This was the narrowest, most tender and rich of all praises the world had seen, so that we understand the advantage enjoyed by the Christian soul in the intimate union desired by God in uniting with it in His own Son by faith and love.

There was reason to suppose that the sons of Abraham, Isaac and Jacob, preferentially called sons of the kingdom, would look upon the great number of guests as being to their glory. Yet those who were negligent, obstinate and rebellious refused to attend the banquet at which the children of light, free from the darkness of ignorance and error, were to sit at the table of great invitation to the Eucharist which the Saviour had laid for them all; for while it is true that if on many occasions men invite each other to meals out of necessity or delight, in many other cases they invite each other out of interest and these would form the greatest group of invited persons. Jesus Christ, however, invites one and all to his table without harbouring any need of his own, and gives himself as food out of pure truth with a desire to communicate to all and make his guests take part in his eternal happiness. Indeed, why do not men unfortunately understand the Lord's immense goodness and hurry to attend at the great supper, to which they are invited!

At the time of the invitation the Lord sent his servants to let the guests know that it was all laid. And he says, *at supper time*, so as to mean that it was the last age, in which he had begun to proclaim to all the grace of the Gospel. Properly speaking, this is what the last hour means, in which the power of hell must be chained forever, the righteous would very soon enter into everlasting glory, namely those who were counted among the dead up to that time had descended to Abraham's bosom. Before the coming of the Redeemer, this beatific supper had not yet been prepared, for no one could enter eternal life through the observance of the Old Testament; but after the Son of God, the most innocent Lamb, was crucified the door of the heavenly kingdom was also opened, and then the apostles were sent as faithful and prudent servants to invite all men to come to the great supper; and it had to be that in the same manner as Jesus Christ was sent by his Father, through their preaching and miracles all would hasten to appear at the feast. But what monstrous ingratitude of men! All would excuse themselves, some by words, others by thoughts and yet others by deeds. It is said that they all excused themselves, to imply that most were excused, so that it may be understood that there are few who are saved compared to most who condemn themselves; for according to Saint Gregory, many are called to the supper, but few are those who come with good works. But woe to us! For as the same holy doctor affirms, when in the world a rich man send out an invite, the poor man hurries, and rushes to the invitation, and we are invited to what God our Lord prepares for us, and we excuse ourselves from going to him like lost sons. This excuse shows an unwillingness of the power of ill will of those not wanting to be saved, some because of pride and others of carnal vices.

Those who excused themselves from going to the supper fall under three classes. The first, who said that they had bought a field and wanted to go and see it, represent all those who, full of ambition and pride, believe that they were only born to accumulate treasures on earth, forgetting the heavenly riches that will last forever. The second class represent those who dedicate themselves only to profit and worldly trade, who despise God's affairs and being with God; they can give rise to unique and solid advantages, because His greatest and most important interest is in providing the creature with true and permanent riches in heaven. And the third class is of those who wounded, mistreated and finally killed the Family Father's servants who had gone out to call them; these represent the heretics and unbelievers who in all times have persecuted, wounded and mistreated the sinners and ministers of the Gospel; these, being pushed to fulfil their duties and like Jesus Christ enflamed with fiery zeal, have travelled to the ends of the earth, seeking to lead to Jesus Christ's flock the scattered and wayward sheep to take part in the land of the delights of the Eucharistic meal, and in an unfathomable and eternal paradise, were wounded, mistreated and killed by those very ones to whom they had sought to do so much good.

The resistance and excuses of the guests clearly show the tolerance of God and that of His Church, and that no one can be obliged or taken by force to resist this great invitation; for it is a union of one will to another, from one heart to another, and only by desiring and consenting can the creature go to God and closely unite with Him. In frivolous excuses we see the most frequent obstacles which we are used to put up against salvation, like society, pleasure and pride, which are all brought about by riches. Curiosity, the senses and perception, work, occupations and worldly business, all suffocate thoughts and steal the time that must be devoted to the important task of salvation.

Soon enough that great Family Father received news of his own vassals' conduct which was so little expected of them, at a time when he thought of bestowing honours upon them. Flamed up with a righteous rage, he sent armed men against the murderers ordering that they were all to perish, setting fire to the city and reducing it to ashes. Notice, however, that the righteous anger shown by God on this occasion is not the same as man's anger; it is not an ardent or vengeful passion, nor is it the inflammation of the blood drawn back from the heart, but it is the effect of executing justice regarding anything He desires to correct and punish. From that which is inferred, that which is called God's wrath is, as Saint Augustine says, righteousness done against the sinner owing to his sin. It shows God punishing him justly for his contempt of not attending the supper of eternal life which was prepared for him, discarding it for the vile and rude pleasures which the world offers him.

Avenging himself in this manner from his enemies, that man still thought of honouring his son's wedding and filling the banquet hall. "You see," he said to his servants, "that the food is ready, but those I had invited have become unworthy of my having set them apart. So now go out on the streets and at the gates of the city, and invite to my supper anyone you might find on the way." The streets and gates of the city, which for the greater part were enclosed with fences, mean the vocation the Jews had; they were fenced in the observances and ceremonies of the Law and they were almost like the sole citizens of God, because they held to His ancient law. That some of them were in the squares means the very broad race of prosperity and the life of vice; others were in the neighbourhoods or narrow and enclosed streets, which is the narrowness of adversity and tribulation, as the suburb and silence are always narrower than the square. Obeying the prince, the servants branched out along various streets and roads, and having assembled many, still not all places were filled. And when the servant went back to his master to recount all that had happened, the master was angry and said to him again: "Go out then to the crossroads and bring here as many poor, crippled, lame and blind as you find, so that the table I have laid may be filled," which is like saying, call those who are poor for not being virtuous, and the weaklings who are poor for lack of good works, and the lame and the blind who are in that state because they lack true knowledge; bring along all these since they are humble and consider themselves unworthy of the divine favour, and yet desire to enter the sacramental supper. And so it was that he left out the leaders of the Synagogue, the priests and the expert lawmakers and the sages of the Jews, owing to their ingratitude and pride; while only God's helpless and simple ones, and the people's publicans were called, as it is written in the Gospel. On this Saint Gregory further says: "As those who are proud despised coming to the King's supper, the poor are called to enjoy it, because God chooses the humble to confuse those who think themselves to be wise and strong."

From suburbs and squares the Lord wanted his servants to go out to the crossroads; thus the vocation of the Gentiles might be better understood as these were rural and savage men who went about on the roads of worldly prosperity and walked along the forests and wastelands of dangerous adversity. "Give them the strength to enter," he said, "so that my house may be filled with guests with anxious fervour and the persistence of preaching; so that all are called to be saved; at times with fervent exhortations and at others with harsh threats."

The way in which the Lord wants the Jews and the Gentiles to be called to his supper is undoubtedly mysterious and worthy of attention. The Jews were invitees and guests, and the Gentiles were compelled and forced persons. A more gentle calling would have sufficed for the Jews, disciplined as they were by the doctrine of the Law and Prophets they kept among them; but this would not have been enough for the Gentiles, who were buried in the darkness of ignorance, idolatry and the most lewd error. And he added: *That my house may be filled with guests;* to show that by the house is meant the heavenly church, where the eternal invitation of the predestined is celebrated by a number which will be perfectly complete. We can also say that heretics are compelled and rewarded to enter the supper when. on being punished and corrected by the Church, they reject their heresies; or when any other sinners turn away from their sins and mistakes, and tired out by the shattered state of their life and being disillusioned and repentant, return to the love of God they had abandoned. Oh blessed need which requires man to leave the crooked path and re-enter the right way from which they had set themselves apart! Many are those who believe they live in the security of enjoying prosperity in the world; but when tables turn on them and everything goes against them, then they renounce modern life, hate it forever, and truly convert to the Lord. For this reason Saint John Chrysostom says: "It takes much more to win over greed in safe times than to scorn riches in times of danger; because that same fear of danger which causes the heart's displeasure and disgust, gives a man strength to overcome all those affections which had previously more easily dominated his life."

In this manner it is very easy to understand the reason why many were lost in times of prosperity and bounty, while others were won over in times of adversity and labour, giving up their goods and also their lives for God's sake. As nothing is hidden from the Lord's knowledge and infinite understanding, he very often allows some to be stripped of their riches, so that free from the cares of the earth, they can more certainly rest in God. It is thus seen clearly that some are called and do not deem it fit to come; so that although they have received from God the gift of intelligence, they did not act the same way as Jesus Christ had given them to understand; others were called and they came, because they acted according to the grace of prudence they had received; and others were regaled to enter as invitees, since they wished to flee from the many labours with which they were punished and afflicted.

With a full house and all seats being occupied, the King entered and saw there was a man who was not dressed up in the ceremonial gown; that is, there was one who had faith in Christ but did not work as a son of Christ, because the wedding dress, according to Saint Jerome, are the Lord's precepts and those works which are supplemented by the fullness of the Law and of the Gospel. A man might have faith without works; he carries along material ideas to the weddings of the Church, but fails to adapt the harmony of his life and customs to the faith's key principles. To say the same thing, he has faith but not love; this faith is the true wedding dress which covers a multitude of sins, since it protects against the cold dryness of temptations and adorns one with very rich jewels of gifts and virtues. As Saint Augustine says, it makes for the difference between the sons of the kingdom and those of perdition. "In truth, love is called the wedding dress, because this was undoubtedly Our Saviour's precious hallmark," Saint Gregory says, "when he came to celebrate the wedding with his new Church. He who, then, wore the wings of charity, came to men; he could well show that this was his wedding dress. It is necessary to warn, however, that just as a dress has two faces, namely, an interior and an exterior one, so does love have two precepts, being the love of God and of neighbour, both of which must be perfectly kept by anyone wishing to wear the bridal dress, so that not even out of pity for his neighbour will he abandon the contemplation of God, nor will he attend so exclusively to it, that because of it he completely forgets his neighbour."

The King told this man, who was not wearing the wedding dress, namely the precious mantle of charity: "My friend, it is worth knowing by participation in faith, but not by the works of faith; my friend, for the obligation of the debt you contracted with me, but not for the resolution or payment of this debt; my friend by name, but not by works; and finally my friend by nature, because you have been formed in the image and likeness of God; how did you enter this place without wearing the wedding dress?" That is, if faith is kept alive by love, for without this dress no one should approach the sacred table of the Eucharist, it being the great supper, for it is not becoming for guests not to wear the same dress as the bridegroom, and there are many seen wearing the revolting sack of greed, others dressed in the purple of pride, others adorned with the mantle of vainglory, others vested in the sheepskin of hypocrisy and feigned justice, others wielding the weapons of wrath, others wearing the stinking garment of lust, others weak and haggard, torn apart by envy; others who are very upset and negligent, mastered by laziness, others lukewarm and slack owing to their pleasures, and others extremely voracious due to their gluttonous greed; about all of whom God said through Zephaniah (1:9-10): "On that day I will punish the officials of Jerusalem and the king's sons, and all those who array themselves in foreign attire, and all those who enter through the temple's thresholds full of pride and arrogance, filling the house of the Lord their God with injustice and fraud." This He had already said through Ezekiel (23:12), when under the allegory of the two harlots He made him describe the clumsy idolatry of Jerusalem and Samaria, owing to which they were to be delivered into the hands of the Gentiles for their total ruin.

The ill-starred person could not but be struck dumb and keep quiet, either because of the great fear instilled in him by the charge, or because of the shame that inspired his own baseness in full view of the other guests, and finally because not knowing what he had to say, he was confused whether he had to answer in his own defence, for no one can answer back God. And if man were to argue with his own conscience, he would be suddenly convinced and fall silent, which shows that in the last judgment there can be no excuses of any kind. So that in view of his silence, which was just as much as confessing to the offence, the King said to the administrators of his justice: *Bind his feet and hands and throw him out in the darkness*; that is, "Leave him powerless to do any good, to turn back on the path of healing and to regain grace; throw him to the place where he is forever deprived of God's vision and out of the realm of divine mercy. While he was still alive, he had an opportunity to free himself from inner and outer darkness, but he was unwilling." The inner darkness, which causes a mental fogginess or the vagueness of ignorance, leads to the darkness of guilt, and to gloom of sorrow; about which Saint Gregory said: "Inner darkness gives rise to the blindness of understanding: but external darkness causes an eternal night of damnation. Those who by their own will bind themselves over here with inner darkness, will on the other side be forcefully bound with exterior darkness, and there sorrow will bind itself with those who in this place did not want to be bound by good works." In that place *where there will be none else but weeping, crunching and gnashing of teeth*; that is, mental and bodily pain, to which all diabolical sorrow is reduced, about which Job said: "He will pass from the drought of the snow waters to a most intense and excessive heat" (Job 24:19-20), because sin will accompany him to hell. Divine mercy will forget him; worms will be his food; he will not be remembered, but will be reduced to splinter wood like a sterile tree. It is here where you can find the crying and gnashing of teeth.

Finally, the Saviour concluded this mysterious parable by saying: "Indeed, I say unto you, that none of those who are called to my banquet and refuse to come, shall enjoy my supper, nor even see it with their own eyes; only the saints will partake of it and see it in the present and future life." As David said in the Book of Psalms: 'Taste and see that the Lord is good: blessed is the man who trusts in Him.' The house of the Lord shall be filled with the number of the predestined and the sons of salvation; but the proud sinners who were called but did not want to come and excused themselves, would be banished forever from that heavenly gathering: there is much to fear in this sentence of the Lord!" No one should despise the invitation nor fail coming to him, because if when he was called he excused himself from attending, when he later wanted to enter of his accord he would find the door closed and will be thrown out. Whoever fails to enter must certainly be devoured by an eternal hunger, without being able to do anything about it, nor ever enjoy the nourishment of glory, and the eternal balsam and vision of God.

The scribes and Pharisees were very confused, not helping to do otherwise after hearing the terrible threats made to them by the Saviour in the preceding parables. Instead of taking advantage of such wholesome and healthy advice, and being severely moved by the devilish malice that engulfed them and regretfully forced by their fear of the people then to abandon the idea of seizing him, they went along with their narrative and plan to further tighten and stir up hate against him among the Jews, and to get strangers ready and to arm them against him. But it was useless that they laboured so hard and greatly increased their guilt when these could not serve them to achieve their depraved attempts, for Jesus Christ could not be surprised and the hour was no longer far from when he had willingly to surrender at his discretion.

In ignoring him they were unknowingly following his plan, without sparing any efforts to achieve their attempts; the Pharisees contrived with the Herodians and agreed to hatch an ambush against him; so they sought whether they could lay a snare for him by asking him misleading questions about whether they should pay taxes to Caesar or not.

The Pharisees, according to Saint Chrysostom, knew that the Lord looked upon them as suspicious and cautious enemies; and since they thought that they could not deceive him, however covert their malice might be, they agreed to send him their disciples. They chose from among them those whom they knew to be the most cunning, those who together with Herod's servants intended to accuse him as a criminal; howsoever he would answer them, either in favour of Caesar, or in favour of Israel's freedom. This prince had come to Jerusalem for the feast of the Passover, bringing with him not only servants, but also some of his courtiers and friends. His aim was to be a close friend of the Roman emperor, to justify his friendship even more; and to give him public witness of it, he inserted in all his deeds, and mainly in his coins, the name of a friend of the Claudian family; so that, Herod's servants were to be believed in whatever they claimed that Jesus Christ had said against Caesar's rights or privileges. The Pharisees formed part of God's people and believed they were exempt from paying taxes to man; the Herodians were tax collectors of the tributes levied by the Romans in Judea and believed themselves like bearing some authority over others. So that in this case, clubbing and bonding together, they would use force against Jesus Christ about anything he said and asserted and, although belonging to diametrically opposed bands, they went along together to the detriment of innocence and justice. It is so seen that the world and hell often bring together two parties which are entirely opposed to each other in their doctrines, to make them act with common interest in persecuting Christianity. Only truth opposes the father of error, and those who commit it, even though appearing to go against each other, find themselves on the devil's side.

United and colluding with this object in mind the Herodians and Pharisees, went up to the temple, where they believed they would find, and actually found, the Saviour busy instructing the people who did not depart from him, and having found him they said to him: *Master, we know that you are truthful and that you teach with truth God's way without regard or consideration for human respect.* It is with this flattery that they praise him whom they never wanted to believe. Master they call him while despising his doctrine. A wretched contradiction which by their very words, those who meshed nets from them to entrap Jesus Christ were themselves snared. This is how they appear to be those who flatter good persons in their presence, while completely tearing apart their good opinion and reputation behind their backs, bringing discredit to their name. Oh, how full is the world of these evil men, whom we must ask our God to keep far away from us! Speaking about them Saint Augustine says: "There are two descent lines of men's persecutors: one line is that of those who utter their insults in public, the other is that of deceptive flatterers: be aware, however, that the flattering tongue causes greater damage than the bullfighter's hand." And so, those treacherous men, wanting to deceive the Saviour, ask him with all meekness and sweetness, flattering him about his truth and his justice, while really wanting to slander him. He was also praised for being altruistic, so that he would answer on behalf of the Jews and chide the Herodians' conduct. The answer given by Jesus Christ confused the proud foolishness of the disciples of the Synagogue and the haughty pride of the Herodians, for to both one and the other he suddenly showed them terrible harshness, bearing in mind not the words they had spoken to him but the falsehood of their perverse consciences, thus teaching us the harshness with which we should hate flatterers.

How is it, he told them, that you come to tempt me as a daring hypocrite? They called him Master, and Jesus Christ treated them as deceptive persons, since they assumed being what they were not, some by talk and others by deed. Whoever chides in this manner those who flatter him, is truth itself and teaches God's way without regard or respect for people. Whoever is governed by Jesus Christ's spirit, closes his ears to the deadly hiss of flattery, lest it compels him to stray from the truth and fail to do what he owes doing to God.

Show me, Jesus Christ told them, the *Ten-nummi coin*, that is, the money that was paid by way of tax by one and all. This silver-minted coin was commonly with this name because it was worth ten *nummi* and was the currency used at the time; on one face of the coin was Caesar's bust or image, while his imperial name was shown on its reverse side. Jesus Christ taking the coin in his hand to utterly confuse them, made them aware that he was God, thus showing them clearly their treacherous inner thoughts, and so asked them: *Whose image and inscription are these?* He did not ask out of ignorance, but because he wanted them to utter by their very mouth and accept their obligation, and to be aware that with their spurious hypocrisy they had caused the remarkable answer which he was about to give them and leave them confused. "Caesar's," they said to him, and he immediately replied to them: *Give then to Caesar those things that belong to Caesar, and those belonging to God, give them to God.* It was like telling them: "Give to Caesar the tribute which you confess being bound to give him as his subjects; that which must be given to him because it is not contrary to the precepts of the Law. For if anything that is thus given were to cause damage to the faith, it would not be an asset to belong to Caesar, but a tribute paid to the devil." And Jesus Christ added: And those things pertaining to God, do give them to God, for as supreme overlord, tithes and first fruits, offerings and sacrifices, are due to Him. As Saint Jerome says: "With what the Saviour himself practised, when he sent Saint Peter to pay for himself and for him the tax to the same emperor in the city of Caesarea, and to give to God those things that belonged to Him accomplishing in everything the will of his Father, Jesus Christ's answer may also have another explanation. Saying to the Jews, give to God what is God's and to Caesar what is Caesar's, it seems like wanting to say to them: 'Then this is not the tax imposed by Moses. Pay Caesar with the currency issued by Caesar; and since God allows you to be subject to Him in punishment for the manner how you abused your independence, live with him as faithful vassals. You did the same thing under the domination of the Greeks and under the rule of the Persians. But do not stop paying God what belongs to Him; that is, the *half a shekel* that you owe Him according to the Law and which keeps on being minted by you by order of God, according to the measure preserved in the temple. The fulfilment of this obligation does not dispense you from the other, for they could not be compared.'"

Tribute has nothing to do with divine law. Saint Paul sends one to pay it to whoever it is due. And since it is God who raised Caesar to his position, whoever pays Caesar his due ought to give to God that which is due to Him. There is no vassal who is more faithful in paying taxes than the true Christian. But as philosophers neither want to be vassals nor faithful, no one openly denies the sovereign Leader the tribute which Jesus Christ here commands to be paid. Just as Caesar's image was reason enough for Jesus Christ to send the Jews to pay him the tax, so we must pay God the tribute of our soul, for there the image of God is etched in it. This image is a continuous memory of our due and a disperser of our indifference. If we belong to God, if we do not entertain any other existential principle, if this work of His hands was sealed by God with His image so that no one would be unaware that it was His, if after being erased by sin He came to renew it with His own blood, of course we must wholly give ourselves to God, for all we have is His. And just as Caesar does not take the tribute for granted with a false and adulterated coin, so God is not content that we return to Him distorted and counterfeited with guilt the work that came out of His beautiful and perfect hands. It is to God that we must return our soul when we die: if we are Jesus Christ's lawful currency, we will be worthy of him putting us in his treasury and public funds; but if by sinning we have blotted out his image in us, we will be cast into the flames destined to consume the dross of the world, as sinners are known to be.

The Jews had no reason to be offended by the wise and prudent answer Jesus Christ had so cautiously given them, as they were subject to having a foreign currency being minted in their land; nor could Caesar's ministers be offended in the slightest manner. And they were primarily those who ought to have been served, because their enemies were determined to abandon Jesus Christ to the vengeance of foreigners if by flattering the hypocritical zeal of the Pharisees the Lord had declared himself in favour of his nation's freedom. But since it was not convenient owing to his Father's glory or to the honour of his sacrifice for the Gentiles, who were only to be executors of the death sentence given against him by the Synagogue in abhorrence of his doctrine, it seemed that they sacrificed him as a seditious person against the interests of Caesar's empire. With his infinite wisdom Jesus Christ wanted to avoid this disastrous obstacle, and so he chose the middle course which left his holiness as authentic as his righteousness.

This was not the one and only conflict in which the Pharisees now wanted to implicate him; after coming out so badly with their hypocritical moves and being left full of confusion while, despite their envy, still admiring the Saviour's awe-inspiring prudence. The Sadducees came after the Herodians as new envoys of the school of the Pharisees; they wanted to see whether they could at least discredit Jesus Christ by putting him a very difficult question; they hoped he would not answer them and gain greater advantage than they had managed to get from previous questions. It was a wretched subterfuge of a hatred which can only achieve just a little, but such that a stubborn blind man never thinks of himself being unarmed no matter how often he is defeated!

The Sadducees were a sect of pitiless persons who denied the resurrection of bodies, because they neither believed in the spirituality nor in the immortality of souls. So as soon as the Jesus Christ had satisfactorily answered the question put to him by the Pharisees, the Sadducees came back couching their supposed difficulty in these terms: "Master," they said to him presenting a hypothetical case, "*Moses gave us a law which says: If a man of the blood of Jacob dies without leaving children, the brother of the deceased will marry the widow to give heirs to his brother; and the first child born of this marriage, will be considered as the deceased's son, and will at least enter into all his rights and take over the succession.* Now seven brothers lived here among us; the first married and died without children, and the second in obedience to the Law, married his elder brother's widow and also died without any. So that all brothers went on marrying her in this manner, with none having any children. Our difficulty is that we would like to know, what will happen in the afterlife, after the resurrection since during her lifetime she had them all as her lawful husbands?" It seems clear that posing this question they wanted to teach there was no resurrection, or that if there was, will marriages still be celebrated the same way as they are now when we are all resurrected? There is no doubt that if this were to happen in this manner, it would be a great problem as to whose wife the woman would truly be; for all having been husbands here in this life and not being able to be the same in the other, but for only one of them, anyone of them would claim the same right to possess her. So that by this they assumed and wished to conclude that the resurrection, which we are expecting according to Catholic faith, is somewhat of a fantasy. Yet although they desired to embarrass the Lord, he not only confused them, but demolished their error and heresy telling them:

"*You are deceived and in error for you know not the Scriptures, neither do you know how far the power of God extends: listen and you will learn.* Those who live on earth and spend a short life which will soon pass, contract obligations here. Men marry women and women take a husband: in this manner our life carries on and men succeed each other. Yet it is not so after death. Those who die out of God's favour will not be resurrected in body and soul, but will be punished in hell; and those who are worthy of glory would be resurrected to enjoy a blissful immortality, and would no longer be subject to the impulses of flesh and blood. There will no longer be wives for men, nor husbands for wives. They will be forever exempt from the rule of death, and this continuous succession of those who are born to replace those who disappear will not take place in heaven. In the resurrection there will be no marriages, but men will be like God's angels in heaven. They will call themselves His sons and not sons of men, because they will rise to live eternally by virtue of God's own almightiness."

According to the Venerable Bede, the woman's seven husbands condense within them the universality of the wicked, whose wife is a worldly life and talk; and to destroy all the doctrine of the Sadducees, who represented the lovers of a sterile world which keeps man away from doing good works, because they would undoubtedly be snatched away by a miserable death before their presumed time. Then he further said to them: "Men will live in heaven like God's angels; not because they are angels by nature, but because they will be like them in the realm of purity; for they shall be immortal and incorruptible, and since none shall be begotten ever again." So that Jesus Christ did not say this that we may believe that after their resurrection men would become angelic spirits, but to teach us that men ought to be spiritual, and that their life and talk should be endowed with a serene purity which sees and enjoys God; for it is certain that by cutting off the cause, its usual effect ceases too; and since marriages were ordained for the begetting of children, that they might be raised in God's honour and service, this effect will only last until the number of the elect in the universal resurrection is completed.

After the Saviour had answered this deceitful question of the Sadducees, by refuting and confusing their heretical error, He spoke to them about the resurrection, confirming the parts underpinning it by authority of Holy Scripture. So that he achieved for his purpose a bliss of infallible authority, as authentically recorded in Deuteronomy, saying to them: "Have you not read what God Himself said about the resurrection of the dead? I am God of Abraham, Isaac, and Jacob. For you should know that He is not God of the dead, but of the living." By this authority the Lord proved the immortality of the souls which was denied by the Sadducees, and thus the resurrection of bodies, by which all good and evil works were performed. God does not call Himself Lord of non-existent things and which lack being, or of things that mean nothing, because the creature's respect and relationship with God his creator is very true and certain; as this relationship cannot be founded on nothingness. And since God is called God of Abraham, God of Isaac, and God of Jacob, who have already passed away, it follows that they still abide, live, and exist; for God did not say: *I was their God*, but *I am*; as if these patriarchs were still present and bodily alive, from which it may be inferred that they are also as to their soul, so that we conclude that it never dies.

It is by this same authority that God also proves the resurrection of bodies by the truth of His righteousness; for to say that He is God of Abraham and of the others who served Him in their bodies, it is only right that they are remunerated and fulfilled with the same bodies which they worthily merited; and according to this principle it is true that everyone's bodies and souls will receive the good or evil which they deserved in their lifetime when these were joined together; for it suited man and it also unsuited him to have soul and body joined together; and so it is reasoned that in the afterlife both one and the other will be punished or rewarded; and this could not happen unless the general revival of all bodies were to be expected with the firmness of an infallible faith.

The Lord's logic shown in a few words, definitely closed the Sadducees' mouth, so that from this instant they did not dare attack Jesus Christ or involve themselves again in any dispute with him. All the people admired the Sovereign Master's doctrine, and what is more, it also merited the approval of the scribes and Pharisees who were well in the know about the dispute. Since they were extremely opposed to the Sadducees, both as for the interest of their sect and for the principles of their religion, and believed in the resurrection, they could not hold themselves back from going in droves to Jesus Christ to show their satisfaction with the effective and wise manner in which he had confounded his opponents' error.

And so they said to him, *Master, you have spoken admirably*. It was as if to say that there could not have been any better way how to fight or confound these daredevils' lack of faith as you have done with Scripture testimony. However, although they apparently expressed great pleasure at seeing his enemies humiliated, their joy was not complete, for a man whom they abhorred more than any contemporary faithless man had been made triumphant. They envied Jesus Christ because of the honour this triumph had given him with the people due to his eternal wisdom; and fearing the consequences which might result from all this against them, they soon returned to their attacks. They gathered in council with an aim of having one over him or to catch him in some word, so that one of them was sent to him, accompanied by a great multitude of proselytes and teachers of the Law, to see whether they could intimidate him. Saint Chrysostom says of this: "They gathered around together, thinking of confounding or intimidating him with a crowd of people whom they could not win over with refined logic. So that it appears that what they lacked in truth and logic, they wanted to supplant and confound with the presence of a great crowd; but human plans are always vain and fully sterile and fruitless when these are directed against God's faithful ones."

It should be noted that Jesus Christ was first attacked by the Pharisees and Herodians who, being confounded, gave up their arms and let the Sadducees take their place. Being beaten and confounded they fled in shameful defeat, and the Pharisees returned to the attack; one of them who was sent was a doctor of the Law, not because he desired to learn what was unknown to him but to see whether the all-knowing Jesus Christ would err in answering him. So covering himself under the cloak of discipleship, he assumed the office of a tempter, and calling him Master said to him: *What is the great commandment in the Law?* A dispute about this immediately erupted among the Jews. The greedy Pharisees preferred sacrifices rather than the honour owed to the poor; they tended to their comfort rather than to the good of others. There were those who opposed them in this; and since both sides made their arguments, they hoped that the answer Jesus Christ gave them would provide them with some reason to rebuke and accuse him, either as a dabbler of the Law or as a scorner of traditions. But the Saviour, as servant of Church teachers, did not scorn teaching his enemies, though he saw the evil intent out of which the question arose. So that in his response he hinted to them and to all of us a most important precept, which is the very soul of religion. He called him *Master*, as Saint Chrysostom notes, not wanting to be his disciple; and here he who does not even keep the least one, is dealing with the great commandment; it being so that it was like only him who could ask about greater perfection and justice as if he had already fulfilled and carried out the lesser ones. Jesus Christ, however, disregarding all precedents and as if ignoring all that had previously happened between them, replied: "The highest and greatest of all precepts is that invoked by the Lawgiver, in saying: 'Hear, oh people of Israel: The Lord your God is the one God. You shall therefore love the Lord your God with all your heart, with all your soul, with all your mind and with all your strength.' This is the first and greatest commandment; but there is a second one similar to the first, which says: *You shall love your neighbour as yourself.*"

The Law does not say, *you shall fear*, but *you shall love*; for fear pertains to servants, and love belongs to children. Nor does he say, *you shall know*, but *shall love*, for to know God our Lord pertains to human nature, but to love him certainly belongs to the faithful and perfect heart. *You will love with your whole heart*, which means, of your full will, without going wrong, so that no error abides in you in professing the Divine Person; and *you will love Him with all your soul*, that is, without any contradiction, so that you love nothing which goes contrary to Him. *You will love Him with all your mind*, that is, with all your intellect, without any forgetfulness and not recalling anything which might separate you from His love. And *you will love Him with all your righteousness and all your strength*, so that all your strength and all your willpower shall serve Him, and be spent and employed in serving Him.

The great Saint Augustine expresses his opinion on this precept of God's love saying: "You are commanded to love God with all your will and with all your soul, and with all your heart, so that you may put all your thoughts, all your life and all your mind in Him from whom you have received and have all things you give Him. According to this commandment, nothing should be idle in us, nor should we love anything we possess more than God, and we must love all others for Him; so that any other good thing which presents itself to the heart to be loved, if you love it with the love preordained for its purpose, which is God Himself, then arise and run towards Him alone with all the force of love, for it is only so that the good man acts, when all his life is directed and ordered to the service and love of the supreme bounty which is God. To love God with all your heart is not to split up love with other creatures, but to love God for who He is, and creatures only for God's sake." And Saint Bernard says: "To love God Our Lord with one's whole heart is to go wisely against all evil thoughts and against all the amusements with which the enemy presents us so that we will not be deceived; and to love God with all our soul is to conduct a manly fight against the false pleasures of the flesh, so that we may not be seduced by his whispering; and to love God with all our mind, is to walk with determined courage against the adversities of the world, so that we may not be mistreated or faint on tasting the favour of virtue, for these are the three main things that mostly separate man from the love of God: the world, the devil and the flesh."

Jesus Christ did not only say that this is the greatest commandment, but also the main and first one, for it is both a sovereign commandment and the main and first one because it is placed first among all commandments, even before that of loving one's neighbour. It is called great, because it contains the greatest and most excellent thing a creature can do; and it is called the greatest or supreme, because it is confirmed by the evangelical law ordained and given by the Son of God, Christ our Lord, himself.

After this the Lord added: "The second commandment is similar to this one. Note well that I do not say the same, but similar; for it speaks of love and of who resembles God, Our Lord, namely man made in the image of God; and so that is why he said to love your neighbour as yourself. It is like saying: "Love your neighbour in all that which you love in yourself, that is, in all righteousness, virtue, and salvation, wishing him grace in the present life and glory in the age to come, as you would desire it for yourself. And when the Lord says that the second commandment is similar to the first, it must be understood that the love of neighbour comes from the love of God." Saint Paul says about this that whoever loves his neighbour fulfils the Law, because the love of one's neighbour is born of that which the creature has for God (Rom 13). For this reason Saint Gregory said: "From the love of God is born that towards one's neighbour, and by that same love it is increased and strengthened." And Saint Augustine adds: "See first whether you know how to love yourself, and having done this, seek to love your neighbour as you love yourself; but if you do not know how to love yourself, do not deceive your neighbour as you deceive yourself."

The doctor to whose question Jesus Christ had answered seems like being one of those men who, without envy or passion, become enemies by pure commitment and loyalty to their country, and detest more out of a spirit of comradeship rather than owing to hatred or loathing; owing to this they sometimes show signs of sincerity and frankness. Likewise in this instance, being convinced of the answer Jesus Christ gave him, the doctor said to him: "*Master, you have answered well.* Nothing is more true than what I have just heard from your mouth, and I profess having your same belief, that our God is the only One, and that there is no other but Him; that we must love Him with our hearts, with our minds and with all our strength; and that we must also love our neighbour as ourselves. To fully accomplish this precept is to render one thing more pleasant in God's eyes, than all burnt offerings and sacrifices can ever be."

The Saviour could not look with indifference at the sincere naivety of that doctor and so, treating him with due kindness and praising the wisdom of his answer, and his submissiveness, he said to him: *Seeing your disposition, you are not far from the kingdom of God.* Which was like saying to him: "You are well prepared to embrace the Gospel and its doctrine, which would make you, if you ever want to be, one of God's servants and subjects and of His Christ." His friends' attitude was however different; returning in droves, they did not have the intention of being instructed, but to draw out him whom they wanted to have condemned, taking him by surprise in some word. Nevertheless, as nothing went well for them, they lost their spirits and hope, and when the Lord saw them dejected, foolish and disorderly, he asked them the last question, with which he finished off confusing them: *What do you think,* he told them, *of Christ? Whose Son is he?* Now that the Saviour silenced the Pharisees by showing them that he is eternal wisdom, he asked them about the Messiah. He did not ask whether they believed that he was to come or to be born of David's family, because they knew this from Scripture; but whether they believed that he was only human, or Son of God, and true God and man. They, who did not let themselves be carried away by the spirit of God to fly over the shell of the letter, said that he was the Son of David, that is, human and not God. Then Jesus Christ said to them, *How is it that David, whom you hold as His son, in spirit calls him Lord?* Is not parental authority greater than that of children? He who comes after us may be our son; but not lord, because lordship only belongs to those who are with us or came before us.

Jesus Christ knew well that they all shared this reasoning, and he did not stop to approve their consent on this article of tradition, and on the faith about him which they acquired from their fathers' prophecies. So he proceeded by strengthening his last reflection saying to them: *If Christ is the Son of David,* as if speaking of him, he says: *The Lord said to my Lord, sit at my right hand until I put your enemies as a platform under your feet?* This is how Jesus Christ argues, not to prove that Christ is not the Son of David, but to correct the error they entertained of not considering him as true God, but as purely human. He so wanted to show them that when David called the Messiah *Lord* before he was born, and *his Lord*, he saw in him with the light of the spirit a being superior to human nature, and his dignity he held of an earthly king. The Pharisees did not give any answer because they did not know much about it; but being as they were in the source of light, it depended on them if they were not perfectly enlightened, and their ignorance could not be excused. They did not answer him since they could not deny Scripture, and because the argument was such that nothing could even bring them about to answer; and from that day on no one dared to ask him more questions, and this was because with the testimony of Scripture and by using their own logic they were still convinced of their beliefs and remained confused. About which Saint Jerome says: "Since they were confounded by the reasons given by the Redeemer in his defence, his adversaries did not ask him any more or present him with other sophisticated doubts; but they still sought and tried to catch him, so that when he was so caught they would hand him over to the Roman judge. We might understand from them that the venom and poison of envy can be hidden once in a while, but sooner or later, with great difficulty, it can find its way back and soon enough start burning again.

CHAPTER 68
JESUS CHRIST SAYS THAT ALTHOUGH THE DOCTRINE TEACHINGS OF THE SCRIBES AND PHARISEES MUST BE ADHERED TO, THEIR WORKS SHOULD NOT BE IMITATED, AND WHO WILL RECEIVE JUDGMENT OF ETERNAL DAMNATION (MT 23:1-12; 34-39)

HE truth always leaves strong and equally bitter impressions in a heart consumed with arrogance and pride which wants to deceive, like the rudeness shown by the scribes and Pharisees who withdrew from Jesus Christ's presence. But one confusion followed another, and one distress was even followed by a greater one. They believed that the people would follow him even if it were for no other reason than the fear that their injustices could inspire in him; but people with good sense were in love with Jesus Christ's wisdom and admired the seriousness of his speeches, the modesty of his manners, and the dignity of his person. They were never tired of hearing him, which caused the Pharisees to become exceedingly furious when they saw themselves abandoned by the same people to whom they would give the Law. Finding himself alone with his disciples, and being already with the docile people who loved him, Jesus Christ took advantage of his resolve and the flight of his enemies to warn the faithful against the foul teachers by whom they were surrounded. The time of his life was very short and it was convenient for him to exploit all instants to give his last instructions. Unfurling the banner of his love and ardent zeal which animated him, he said to them: *The scribes and Pharisees sat on the chair of Moses; do all that they tell you, but do not act like they do.*

On this introduction to Jesus Christ's speech Saint Chrysostom says: "After the Lord had confounded all his enemies with his response, he proved beyond doubt to all his followers the incorrigible and rebellious condition of those hypocrites who never wanted to admit their defeat, for a speech condemning a person is of no use unless it serves as a bidding to another." So it was the same as if he had told them: "The scribes and Pharisees have received the power to teach you and put you on the right path as to how to observe the precepts, rites, and ceremonies of the Law. The leaders lording it over you pass on the burden of teaching on these doctors; follow their lessons on all that which pertains to their ministry, for the day has not yet come to repeal the practice, and it should be respected; and while the Synagogue and the temple survive, they must still be followed. Listen to them with all due prudence and practice what they teach you, and with this you will honour the chair on which they sit; but be careful not to do what they do and to imitate their appearance and conduct. If they are your doctors, in not acting they way they should, they cannot be of an example to you and your models. They speak from their chair about what should be done, but they do not do what they should do nor that which is appropriate. There is only one truth, unchanging and principled, and it loses nothing no matter how mean the minister announcing it might be; tell it in whatever manner you want, for it always comes from God. For it is given to us by God and we must receive it with respect owing to the source from which it derives, without looking at the channel through which it passes, because however flawed it may be, it can bear no rupture or damage. It is up to man to follow truth, but not evil; therefore hear and follow in good time the holy doctrine preached to you by God's minister, but do not imitate his life if it were bad. And if it is not lawful to despise his authority, owing to the customs with which he disdains it, nor is it licit to imitate his bad customs out of respect for his dignity."

"They," Jesus Christ continued, "want to acquire merit for you, imposing hard, unbearable and grievous burdens on others' shoulders; yet they do not even want to touch them with their finger in relief from their discomfort. Otherwise, do not be deceived; they are only engaged in show-off works and an extravagance which are devious and pleasing to men, but which neither do nor can they even penetrate the inner self; but what they think least about is how to be pleasing to God who examines and probes hearts." These are the bad ministers mentioned in the Gospel, about whom Chrysostom said that with their lives they deny the exercise of their ministry; that they give others the peace which they do not have; who preach the faith and themselves live as unfaithful, who praise the truth and love vanity; who recommend generosity but walk along the ways of greed, and who condemn themselves, according to Saint Paul in the very exercise of their ministry. However no way did the Saviour here want to rebuke the evangelical strictness of good ministers, but the pharisaic harshness of false teachers; and the faithful must be particularly aware that they should neither consider as heavy burdens the observance of precepts which tone down love, nor the penances imposed by confessors in recompense for the penalty due for sins. For it is a great danger for them, and for the souls they lead, to widen the path which Jesus Christ narrowed and to remove or to add something capriciously to the unalterable law which he made, burdening life with useless practices, which rather contribute to weaken the same spirit they always ought to lead along the path of virtue, and to strengthen and fortify them in it.

These are not the only observations which the Saviour wanted to make to his disciples so that they would learn in advance what is highly recommended by holiness itself. Beauty and kindness recommend themselves and each other, and it is only an atrocious conscience which is terrified at the sight of virtuous beauty which abhors it. Yet even if only a few really embrace the virtue preached and practised by the saints, what will happen if all its advice is reduced to words which later belie the works and doings of whoever utters them? Good ministers discipline themselves and treat others with utmost tender and affectionate sweetness. They pity each other for the others' misery; they promote seeds of conversion in penitents, agreeing with them as much as possible about the laws of penance, for if the minister errs in imposing an easy or simple manner, is it not much better to answer for having used mercy than for having been extremely cruel? Where the Father of families is a delivering and beneficial donor, his steward must not be stingy and hapless. If God is good-natured, how can His ministry be austere? Do you want to appear holy? Be austere to yourself and kind to others. Listen to the men who command you little things, and see how you practise the great ones. Hypocrites, on the other hand, seek honour in treating weaklings with excessive harshness, and nothing is given to them that might enhance the principles of holiness in a weak soul, that they may be regarded as demanding and zealous ministers. Fools! They will believe they are not known! The Saviour himself made them known when he said: *They do all their works to be seen by men.*

Because the Pharisees affected to the extreme a virtue they did not have, they abused the Law's very precepts to appear virtuous. God had commanded the people *to love him with all their heart, with all their soul and with all their strength*; and when Moses exhorted them to observe this commandment, he said to them: "This and the other commandments I have given you will be stamped in your heart, you will teach them to your children, and in them you will meditate sitting in your house and walking around, and when you lie down in bed and rise in the morning, and you shall bind them as a sign upon your hand, and they shall be as frontlets between your eyes" (Dt 6:6-8); which means that *you will always remember them, as if you had them in front of your eyes or in your hands.* The Jews however took these words materially, carrying the commandments written on parchment slips tied to their arms and foreheads which in the time of the Pharisees they came to be a kind of ornament that received the Greek name of *Philateria*; it is this adornment which the Saviour was precisely rebuking on this occasion.

At the same time the Jews also widened broadly the tussles they were commanded to put at the corners of their garments with blue ribbons or cords (Nm 15:38); this hallmark in their dress was also ordained as a continuous reminder of the extraordinary benefits they had received from God, since they were His chosen people. Referring to these tussles Jesus Christ said to his disciples and to the faithful mobs who were listening to him: "Take good note of the cloaks and garment layers they wear, and you will see in them all their vanity and hypocrisy clearly portrayed; they have an extraordinary length and amplitude, they also have wider and more dilate stripes or gallons than usual; and this is the refined vanity, and an ensemble that only tends to excite public admiration, with which you should not let yourselves be seduced or deluded. If seeing all this you are still not aware of their vanity, observe them in their banquets, gatherings and church meetings; they always take the front places of honour, wanting to be given the first place wherever they go. If they let themselves be seen by people anywhere and in public and frequented places, you will understand what they aspire for because over there they are greeted and paid respect, and since all call them masters and teachers."

Surely these were not the lessons that the Lord had given to his apostles and to those who were after them to preach his Gospel. Called to a ministry far superior to that of Moses, he wanted them to distinguish themselves in humility, because it is a horrible vice in persons consecrated to God to seek preference even in the doings of civil life. Saint Chrysostom says that men usually come together for three things: either to deal with matters of the flesh, as happens in feasts and banquets; or to confer on spiritual matters, as in the Synagogues; or else to resolve day to day affairs as when they meet in squares. And it is shameful that everywhere the Lord's ministers seek to occupy place of preference, seeking glory in public, and where only their voice may be heeded. "Be warned though," says the Venerable Bede, "that those to whom the supreme honours pertain should not be rebuked, because of their dignity and office; but those who always aspire for the honours of the prelature, although not being entitled to them, so that it is often convenient to yield to the respect given to secular persons, for the honour of one's own dignity." Public esteem desired out of vanity degrades dignity in priests, just as love of humility adorns and uplifts them.

"I do not want," he added to them, "that among you and in your internal affairs to which you tend mutually, you address each other with honourable names that breathe vanity or outright pride. You will not deal with each other as teachers, for you all have the same Lord and Master who is Jesus Christ. There is no vice in meriting this name, but there is in desiring it. Worthy of it is that doctrine which is acquired through study and prayer; let the former be proud. Whoever is not a teacher of humility and love does not deserve to be called a teacher in the Church. Without these two virtues all the world's science is but a whiff of wind, nor could anything build a fellow man; you can teach vanity and you can be called a master of vanity, which is by the way quite awful praise. It is only in Jesus Christ that there is the great and true *magisterium*. In the Jordan and on the Tabor the Eternal Father declared him our Master and commanded us to hear him; He taught us the truth and practice of all virtues. He alone deserves the name of Master, because he governs everything by his knowledge, and enlightens the heart by opening its doors and introducing into it the truth, and with it the love with which it must be embraced."

Nor is it fitting," he resumed, "that any person is addressed by the name of father on earth. All those following me have left those who have generated them, and all have the same Father in heaven; this is the only One whom you should recognise and to whom the name of Father belongs." From Jesus Christ we learned and through him we confess that our heavenly Father is One whom we invoke as children and whom we greet as Father, saying *Our Father who art in heaven*. Since we so confess to have this Father calling God with this name, it is most awful that we invoke an earthly father, confessing that we consider our father to be the one on earth. For this reason, the Lord does not want us to ignore and dishonour those who begot us, but He wants us to put Him before them. He who created us and inscribed us among the number of His children, for we are His children by creation, and by the adoption of grace called to the possession of His only inheritance, which is the kingdom of heaven. It is an endearing consolation for priests and spiritual directors to be able to pray for themselves and for them to the Eternal Father, who is the first and best of all fathers, and from whom derives the name, authority, love and paternal providence; them being not only fathers according to the flesh and superiors and civil leaders, but also for spiritual shepherds, as well as for Jesus Christ's mission and that of his ministers. Saint Jerome said about this: "All Christians are in a special way called brothers, and so do they commonly call themselves before all men, as if born of one God, their Father. And the Lord not only forbids desiring pre-eminence and the first place among all, but induces all His children to the contrary telling them: 'He who among you was the greatest, will serve others and will be a servant of the servants of God.' If anyone prefers himself and tries to exalt himself, God will not stop humiliating him; and on the contrary, he who humbles himself will be exalted."

There was no need for Jesus Christ to see on some occasions what the apostles were really thinking, to give them current rules founded clearly on humility. Even though they were imperfect and rough, they were very much inclined to abrogate all distinctions arising out of the greatness of their vocation, and from that time onwards they reserved their dignity as the first Gospel ministers. Nothing would have been more capable of scandalizing the new faithful, especially the circumcised ones, than to see the Messiah's apostles acting on this point like the doctors of the Synagogue. It is thus very appropriate that the Gospel doctors greatly restrain themselves and attend with special care to the fragility of the little ones. Do you want to be before others in authority and leadership? Be so in conferring rewards and in serving others. Charity favours the highness of dignity according to the service given in aiding others' needs. What Church ministers should allow themselves to desire most is to live as a great sacrifice to God by true humility, yet still dedicated to the good of the faith and to the salvation of souls, by an untiring charity which is never again idle. What shepherd will look upon himself as lord of his sheep, after the Lord of the world became a servant for them? The minister of the Most High must be a companion of all those who work good deeds through humility, and he must rise up against miscreants out of zeal for justice. He who exalts himself in the present life by pride and arrogance will be humiliated in future life by being damned and punished; and whoever humbles himself in the present life, not with hypocrisy but with truth, will be exalted wonderfully in glory in future life.

The way the scribes and Pharisees behaved went totally against Jesus Christ's doctrines; so that when his Divine Majesty saw that they abused their position by assuming authority to oppress and deceive simple persons, he could not help but tear off the mask they wore, so that knowing themselves thoroughly they would not ignore the voices of the Author of Life who spoke to them and instructed them. On other occasions the Lord had struck hypocrites and declared enemies of his Gospel with a thousand anathemas; but this time it seems that he clothed himself with new strength and greater authority to discover all the wickedness and refined hypocrisy of his people's seducers. "And just as in the Old Testament," Origen says, "blessings are bestowed on those who observe it and curses against those who break it, so also in the Gospel are blessings showered to encourage the righteous, and curses thrown against hypocrites and treacherous cheats of justice." So that Jesus Christ said to them: "Woe to you, hypocrite scribes and Pharisees, for you keep men apart from the kingdom of God! You will not enter into it nor do you want others to enter, for you are not loyal to Christ, nor do you allow those who are well disposed to be his subjects. You scandalise little ones with your evil examples, and with your twisted explanations you let them down as to what they know of the truth contained in the Holy Scriptures; and so neither you will enter into God's Kingdom nor let others enter whom the Son of Man has come to seek for them to enter it and abide there for ever.

"Woe to you, hypocrite scribes and Pharisees! You eat and devour the substance of lives, consuming their houses under the pretext that you offer up long prayers for them. Know ye that you will be judged for this with the harshest severity; that the most exacting judgment will fall on you, and that you will suffer the most appalling punishment." For which reason Saint Chrysostom says: "Whoever does evil is worthy of being shamed; but he who works it under the cloak of religion, is worthy of a much more terrible punishment."

Jesus Christ continued with his anathemas: "Woe to you, hypocrite scribes and Pharisees! You go around by land and sea to win a convert, believing this to be the greatest conquest you can ever make, drawing in a follower to the Law of Moses, and straight away making this law hateful and its yoke unbearable with your superstitions and false traditions, and rendering all your work useless, you lose all your glory and cause the naïve person an evil much worse than the good you thought you did him. Which is that tremendous responsibility which you would not fall into? When either native or Gentile whom you initiated as your new believer kept to his law, he simply erred and simply deserved a punishment; but if on seeing your vices and corrupt customs, he returned to paganism because of what you had done to him, shirked his duties and became an apostate, he will receive double punishment in hell, suffering there the greatest torments, for at least you were not idolaters like him.

"Woe to you, blind guides and overseers! You who say: If one swears by the temple it does not amount to anything, he is not bound by oath; but if one swears by the gold of the temple, he is a debtor; he is bound to abide by his promise or to pay the gold to the temple because he swore. Crazy and blind, say, what is the greatest, the gold, or the temple which makes the gold holy? And you also say that swearing by the altar does not mean anything at all; but anyone who swears by the offering or gift lying on the alter, is a debtor and therefore bound by the Law: say, what is greater, the gift and offering, or the altar which makes the offering holy? He who swears by the altar, swears by it and all things laid on it; and he who swears by the temple, swears by it and Him who dwells in it. And he who swears by heaven, swears by the throne of God and by Him who is seated on it.

"Woe to you, hypocrite scribes and Pharisees! You pay tithes on mint, dill and all kinds of pulse, but abandon what is most important in the Law, good judgment, mercy and faith; righteousness and justice; charity, truth and loyalty. This is what ought to be done without omitting the others, as he has already commanded you. God through the mouth of his prophet when he said to you: *Oh man! I will show you what should be done and what the Lord asks of you, to do justice and to love kindness, and to walk humbly with your God* (Mi 6:8). Woe to you blind guides and overseers, who strain your drink not to swallow a mosquito, and without scruple swallow a camel! That is, you keep even the most frivolous human traditions, and despise the divine precepts which much more surpass those legal trifles, which you interpret in your own way, as much as a camel is much bigger than a mosquito."

Saint Chrysostom says that those prelates and priests who are always seeking their own honours, and little or none of those pertaining to God, are like these; they take great care to obtain what belongs to them, and exceedingly strong in defending their rights; while careless to the extreme in watching over and defending those of the Church; they murmur against persons who fail to offer or cheat on their tithes, while they remain silent and mute like ungrateful dogs when they see most sinning against God. These are the ones who by their example teach the people to suck or swallow a camel, and to cast aside or lunge at a mosquito.

"Woe to you, hypocrite scribes and Pharisees!" Jesus Christ went on to say. "You cleanse the outside of cup and plate, but are full within of greed and filth, avarice and wickedness. Oh fools! Do you not know that whoever wrought what is outside, also did what is inside? Blind Pharisee, clean first what is inside cup and plate, so that even that which is outside will be cleansed and purified." It is worth noting here that whenever the Pharisees had to go up to the temple, they made a show of cleanliness by washing the utensils of their house casa, dresses and other similar things, but took little care of the inner cleanliness of their soul. On the outside they made a show before men of their holiness and of modesty in their dress, of their fringes and ornaments, words and long-winded details of their prayers; but within their inner-self and conscience, in their heart and soul, they were full of ravaging affections for their ambition; they overflowed with filth out of carnal sensuality, and with sordid greed from the disgusting stains of their vices; for those who ate and drank took it away from others. Origen says about which: "Telling us this the Saviour wanted to let us know that we must make haste to being righteous, not to look like being so; for whoever wants to appear as if being righteous which he is not, takes great care of what is on the outside, but is very negligent in that which is of greater interest to him, namely the inner-self."

So that Jesus Christ added: "Woe to you, hypocrite scribes and Pharisees! You are like whitewashed tombs, which appear beautiful outwardly, seeming elegant and beautiful to men, yet are within them full of bones, corpses, rot and filth. You too show yourselves to be righteous on the outside, appear to be righteous before men, but inwardly you are full of falsehood, hypocrisy and sinfulness." With reference to which Saint Paul said to Ananias, the high priest: "God shall strike you, you whitewashed wall! Are you sitting to judge me according to the Law, and against the Law you order that I be struck?" (Acts 23:3). Call yourselves sepulchres, that is, *half-clean*, because on the outside, that is, in the dress and humility of words they show whiteness, feigning a goodness they do not have, and inwardly they are full of hypocrisy, vainglory, wickedness and hatred of the truth.

At that instant a lawyer or doctor of the Law, not being able to bear so strong reprimands, tried cutting off the Saviour's speech, saying: "Master, are you not aware that speaking in this manner you are also discrediting and affronting us?" Yet Jesus Christ, without interrupting his speech, went on saying: "Woe to you, hypocrite scribes and Pharisees! You build monumental graves to the prophets and adorn the tombs of the righteous whose lives was taken by your fathers. You foresee that the saints and God's messengers will be delivered to death for your nation, while not wanting their bodies to be left unburied; this notwithstanding, you say: 'Had we lived in our fathers' time, we would not have been complicit with them in the death of the prophets.' As you also fill with the measure of your fathers; make the most of their wrongdoings, by committing the huge crime you have already hatched, taking the life of the Just One, your King and Messiah. Poisonous snakes, race of vipers, how will you avoid fire if you do not do penance? I send you prophets, priests and interpreters of the Law that you may try to seek and embrace your conversion, and you will kill and crucify some of them, and scourge others in your Synagogues, and you will persecute them from city to city, and you will seek them even in the darkest and most hidden corners. In this manner you will be responsible and if they demand of you all the blood of all the righteous and all prophets that has been shed since the beginning of the world on earth, as if it had been shed by your own hands, from the blood of Abel, the just one, to that of the priest Zechariah, son of

Barachias, whom you killed between the vestibule and the altar when he went to seek a hiding place against your fury. Truly, I tell you that punishment for so many offences will fall on the ungrateful and unfaithful generation which abuses the means of healing offered to them." Which was all like saying to his apostles: "This people whom I now instruct with so much love after which it will be your task to teach them, will also be ungrateful with you as it is with me, and for this reason the final and most terrible retribution from heaven will fall on them."

As Jesus Christ knew and was aware of all things, even those which would not happen before the end of all times, his loving heart was greatly moved by the coming misfortunes which were to rain upon the unfaithful city, and so exclaimed with bitterness: "Jerusalem, Jerusalem, you who kill the prophets and stone those who are sent to you from God, how many times did I want to gather your children as the hen gathers her brood under her and you refused it? Soon your house, your temple and your city will be deserted, and this country will be completely abandoned: those walls and places which are today covered with flowers and so frequented will be demolished, everything will be deserted and reduced to solitude. I tell you that from now on you will not see me any more until the time comes when you say: 'Blessed is he who comes in the name of the Lord.'" The scribes and Pharisees were very irritated with this way of thinking, they started resisting him with full resolve and tried to impose silence on him in many ways, laying snares for him to make him fall into some blunder or say some word about which they could accuse him; but the Lord decided to set out for Bethany. Yet before leaving he still paused for a while in the temple and sat in front of the offertory box, an alms casket or chest, about which the Scripture says (2 Kgs 12:9): "The high priest Jehoiada took a chest, and bore a hole in its lid, and set it on the right-hand side of the altar at the entrance to the temple of the Lord." It was there that Jesus Christ observed, among those throwing money into it, the poor widow who tossed her two copper coins, about whom we already spoke in chapter sixty-three of this volume.

CHAPTER 69

THE LORD FORETELLS THE SIGNS THAT WILL PRECEDE HIS LAST COMING AND THE PERSECUTION OF THE CENTURY: HE DECLARES THE COMING INTO THE WORLD AND THE PERSECUTION OF THE ANTI-CHRIST BY TELLING SEVERAL PARABLES: HE WARNS HIS APOSTLES TO BE FOREWARNED, AND THEN ANNOUNCES TO THEM HIS APPEARANCE AS A JUDGE OF THE LIVING AND THE DEAD, AND WHAT WILL HAPPEN NEXT (MT 24:15-35; 3-13; 42-47; 1-13; MT 25:14-23; 31-46; LK 21:9-19; 25-33)

AFTER that Jesus Christ had given to his apostles the great and most important lessons we have just seen, he left the temple, and as he went out of the city, his disciples begged him to turn his eyes on that dignified sanctuary, which could be seen as one of the wonders of the world. And as one of them approached Jesus Christ, he said to him: "Master, look and consider that magnificent and splendid edifice; what stonework, what well-built joints and what solidity in them, what greatness, what magnificence in its architecture, and what of the riches and treasures enclosed within it!" No doubt they wanted to mean that that work, the most beautiful structure in the universe, deserved to be preserved, because it could undoubtedly serve them well when the new kingdom was established. It is not strange that his disciples thought so, for they had not yet been solidly instructed about the nature of Christ's reign, nor were they yet much advanced in being spiritual, nor had their ideas been perfectly retuned. The Lord looked at them, and opening his divine mouth, made them promptly understand the anomaly in which they lived. "You look at these buildings and admire their magnificence and grandeur," he said. "Yet how greatly you are deceiving yourselves! Behold them at your pleasure; but truly I say unto you, that the day shall come, and it is not far away, in which all that you now admire will be undone, and no stone shall be left standing on stone; everything will be reduced to ruins and its foundations will be destroyed too. It is in this place that the desolation foretold by the prophets will take place." It was like telling them that it was in that place that the terrible threats foreboded in another time would actually occur, such being the threats which had to fall on the cities and peoples who were unaware of it and ignored it.

It was in this manner that the Lord manifested the revenge he was about to take on the abominable cities; the curses written in the book of God's righteousness were to fall upon them, and the Lord would blot out his name from under the heavens and exterminate them forever from all the tribes of Israel. "So that all nations would say: 'Why has the Lord treated this land in this manner? What malice and great fury is this?' And they will answer: 'For they broke the Lord's covenant which He made with their fathers when He took them out of the land of Egypt, and they served and worshiped other gods, those they did not know and to whom they did not belong.' I will uproot Israel from the face of the land that I gave it, and from this house that I have sanctified and consecrated to my name; I will throw it out of my presence and Israel will only be known as a proverb and a tale by all peoples." (Dt 29:24-28) And this house that was the summit of glory, anyone who passed through it was astounded and gasped, and all people will say: "Why did the Lord conduct himself in this manner with this land and with this house? What is the cause of such great rage? Hear ye now, princes of the house of Jacob and judges of the house of Israel, that you abhor the Law and justice and pervert the righteousness of the precepts; that you erect buildings in Zion and in Jerusalem with injustices and blood at the expense of the sweat of the wickedly oppressed poor man; for your sake Zion will be ploughed up like a field and Jerusalem transformed into piles of rubble, and the mountain where the house and the temple are will be changed into summits thriving with weeds, and everything will remain uncultivated and uninhabitable." (Mi 3:9-12)

The apostles were hurt with these terrible forebodings, although at first they could only respond to the Master with a sad silence which clearly pointed to the terror engulfing them. Soon reaching the Mount of Olives they saw Jesus Christ sitting in a place from where he could see the whole temple façade. Peter, John, James and Andrew who, being most familiar and beloved by Jesus Christ, enjoyed greater confidence with him, approached him and asked him in a low voice: "Master, tell us, when will these things happen and what sign will be given before the time when it will happen and be fulfilled? What are the signs which will announce your last coming, the desolation of the world and the end of times?" The Saviour satisfied them and taught men what they should believe about these articles. He proposed many things to them which could be certain omens of those evils, all of which were distressing and dire. "Keep yourselves well," he said. "and take care that no one deceives you; do not be seduced. Many will come in my name saying 'I am the Christ'; and they will deceive many. The time is coming; do not go after them or follow them. The other signs will be wars and rumours of moving armies. The spirit of farsightedness will reign everywhere, and one would only hear of destruction and death. Seek preparing yourself with resolve and perseverance in the face of such great turmoil, for these will be the first tests of your patience, while the toughest blow and greater evils will await later times. From the beginning of this uproar, streams of blood will run all over many places. Men, who should love each other as brothers, will forget all the feelings of humility that nature inspires even in the greatest barbarians; they will be treated as strangers and enemies, with all animosities which had apparently been overcome raising their heads again, and complaints being stoked with greater passion than ever before. Life will then turn to old claims to have grounds for disputes, and cities will rise against cities, towns against towns and kingdoms against kingdoms; and there will be plagues, famines and earth tremors in different places."

"During this time horrible phenomena and immense signs will appear in the air. But these will not be but a few drops which will leap out from the cup of anger, that your unhappy homeland will fully drain: all this will be but as a trial and the beginning of misfortunes, because before the incursion of Roman armies in the land of Judah, God will fight against it with contagious diseases and with earth's sterility, so that while running blindly over its own ruin, men and forces will be drained by internecine wars and by the domestic uprisings," Jesus Christ forebode. Saint Gregory has this to say about this: "It is by the great evils that are said to precede, that the greatest and perpetual ones that will necessarily have to follow are shown; for many great evils must come before, so that these can be real forebodings of others which will last for ever." "Yet you, dear disciples," Jesus Christ continued saying, "will take a good part of these miseries and general evils; they will persecute you until they make you die by force of torments. But do not be afraid, that I will make you carry victory over all your enemies, and I will suggest to you whatever is necessary to challenge them; I will put answers in your mouth which no one can oppose or answer; and when they take your life in my name, do not fear or grieve, for it is short and miserable; I will give you another one of great happiness and which is eternal."

Moreover, it is also worth knowing that, since there were false prophets among the Jews in past times, so will there be among you, false doctors, who will covertly introduce sects, leading to perdition, and deny the Lord who rescued them and bought them with his blood. Many simple ones will follow their arrogant and ruinous doctrines, by which the way of truth will be cursed; and hauled by greed with false and feigned words, they will reduce you to traffic and merchandise. So be aware that no one might seduce you with some useless and false philosophy, and with vain subtleness founded on human tradition, according to the world's empty deceit and doctrines not being those of Christ (Col 2:8). There will be no shortage of apostates, preachers of deceit and demons' doctrines, who with a corroded and hole-ridden conscience, will discharge pus and decay all around; and in those dreadful times sown with dangers, men will love men, they will be covetous, miserly, proud, arrogant, blasphemous, cursing, disobedient to parental authority, ungrateful, evil, cruel, insensitive, unsettled, slanderous, incontinent, untempered, fierce, inhuman, traitors, wicked, conceited, pleasure seekers rather than searching for God, making a show, indeed, of an appearance of piety and faith, yet estranged from their spirit. From which one must flee, since their doctrine spreads like a cancer. These particular wars, caused by the ambition of governments and opposing interests, between neighbours and peoples are born of the same blood and will be the prelude to the final disasters, just like the history of prophets during the last years of the Jewish republic and of all the events which will occur before the end of times.

Without going into explaining why these wars and battles occur, the Lord further said to his apostles: "There will also be others who will turn against you, whose attacks will be more furious as the end approaches; see how they will happen. The Jews, irreconcilable enemies of the New Testament, to whom you preach with the greatest zeal, shall persecute you without rest or truce, and will make you die for yourselves; and when they judge that they cannot take your life with their hands, they will drag you to the Synagogues and frighten you with sending you to prison, they will hand you over to the governors and kings because they loathe my name, whose memory they will seek to erase. Wherever you go they will regard as seditious and criminal, for nothing will prevent you or stop you from publicly professing your faith and bearing witness to me. Be suspicious, however, when these sad moments come, of all those who are most united with you with the bonds of blood, for it is from among them that your most horrible persecutors will arise. Brother shall deliver his brother, father his son, and children shall rise up against their parents and murder them. You will be given away even by your parents. brethren, relatives and friends, and they will take the life of some of you, and you will be hated by all for the sake of my name. Those disciples of yours who will escape this last ordeal, will not cease being treated badly and they will live in constant fear."

The kingdoms and nations mentioned in the latter paragraphs are the various portions into which the ancient kingdom of Israel was divided, such as Galilee, Judea, Samaria,

Syria, and others. In this way, though in a slightly different manner, an ancient prophet forebode the disasters which would afflict the Holy Land during Asa's reign. These ordeals started increasing shortly after the death Jesus Christ's owing to the ambition and greed of the procurators and governors of the Roman Empire; mainly due to greatly opposite interests between peoples and their neighbours, and above all, due to the restless and troubled spirit of the Jews. Procurators Pilate, Cumanus, Felix, Albinus, Gessius Florus, treated many cruelly, such cruelty giving rise to public revolts and to people rising up against the empire's leaders, and to insurrections, civil wars and scenes bloodier than those enacted by the said Romans. From here followed uprisings of people against people, cruelties over cruelties, robberies, deaths, plagues, fires and so many other misfortunes, that if the Jewish historian recording them were not so cultured and impartial an eyewitness and contemporary author, they would all seem unbelievable.

And who could calculate or reduce to simple figures the Jews killed under molten iron in these rebellions which kept going on for thirty-five years? In Caesarea alone, where a horrible storm was raised against the Jewish inhabitants of this city, over twenty thousand men were sacrificed. In Scythopolis, the town's citizens surely killed over three thousand Jews while they were sleeping. It is not easy to fix the number of those who were torn to pieces and killed in Ashkelon, Ptolemais and Tyre. In Alexandria, when the procurator commanded his troops to attack the Jews, they made such a horrible slaughter, that more than fifty thousand men were found dead in the field, without condoning either the elderly or children, putting them all to the sword. In Damascus, Zebulun, Jaffa and other cities, they underwent the same carnage. And what shall we say of the rivers of blood shed in the conquest of Galilee, the Jewish governor of this province being the renowned historian Josephus who wrote about the event, and which conquest led by Titus, son of emperor Vespasian? What about the disasters experienced by the Jews, when Gadara was captured by the Romans, the siege of Yodphat defended by the said historian, and the siege of Jaffa and Masada from where women and children were thrown out, are these ever forgiven? In order to give a detailed idea of the evils suffered by the unfortunate nation, one must collate all the events narrated by Josephus. No doubt that Divine Providence would keep it to refer to the facts that illustrate, unfold and confirm Jesus Christ's prophecy.

But just as what Jesus Christ had foretold was fulfilled to the letter against the Jews, so did it also occur against the apostles, as we can read in their Acts. Peter and John preached to the people, and when the temple priests and leaders rose together along with the Sadducees, they took it very badly that they were teaching the people and spreading the word about the resurrection of the dead in the name of Jesus Christ; so they arrested them and kept them in custody till the next morning (Acts 4:1-3). It was by the hand of the apostles that many miracles and wonders were wrought among the people. So that the chief priest and all those accompanying him rose, seized them and put them in jail (Acts 5:12-18). King Herod sent out companies of soldiers to afflict and mistreat some faithful of the Church, and James, John's brother, was killed with a sword. And seeing that in doing this he had pleased the Jews, he moved on to seize Peter; and having seized him, he cast him in prison, delivering him to four pickets of four soldiers each to guard over him, with the intention of taking him out and killing him before the people, after the Passover (Acts 12:1-4). And finally, as recorded in the Acts of the Apostles, instances will be seen confirming this same prophecy.

The Saviour did not want to hide anything from his apostles about what they would have to suffer in the course of time when the Synagogue would declare itself against Jesus Christ, so he even supported and gave them a sign that those persecutions were a harbinger of the foundation of his kingdom. "So see from right now," he further said, "what you have to do. When you are taken to be delivered, resolve that you do not think of defending yourself, nor of making your apology, nor of deliberating as to how to speak or answer; for I will put words in your mouth and wisdom which all your opponents will not be able to resist or contradict. Whatever is given to you to say at that time, speak out, for it will not be you who will speak, but the Holy Spirit who will speak for you. And although you will be hated by all, yet not a hair of your head shall perish. Through your patience and perseverance you will have mastery over your souls and attain eternal healing. Do not fear anything you will have to suffer. These great persecutions, calamities and misfortunes will not hold back the faith from spreading, for it is necessary that before all these things happen the Gospel is proclaimed to all peoples. This Gospel of the kingdom of God will so be preached in every inhabited land, as witness to all nations; so that none can claim being unaware of it." This had already partly occurred in the early days of the Church. It has so happened that Saint Paul said: "Have not all heard the apostles' preaching? Yes, indeed, their voice has gone out throughout the whole earth and their words have echoed to the ends of the world" (Rom 10:18). To the Colossians he wrote: "The Gospel which you heard has been preached throughout the world, and it will bear fruit and grow as it did in you from the day you heard and knew the grace of God with truth. The Gospel is preached to every creature existing under heaven, and of which I, Paul, became a minister" (Col 1:23).

This was the last sign that Jesus Christ gave to his disciples, showing them that when it was accomplished it would be very close to the day of completion and the end. And so he told them further: "When you see the abomination of the desolation foretold by the prophet Daniel, placed in the holy place, then those who read the prophecy must do their best to understand it." Although these words allude to the destruction of Jerusalem, Saint Hilary sees in them a clear prophecy of the Antichrist, whose coming will disturb and confound the regions of the world. It seems like we are preparing for this dreadful calamity with weak virtue and our increasing malice. Men are already beginning to hate each other with ever more fury, to persecute and betray each other. How strange will it be that when the deceiver of the world, the enemy of the truth, comes he will find the door open and the bed made to introduce into the hearts of men all his poison? The hatred which the faithful harbour for each other is the Antichrist's precursor and settler. For that the devil sows enmity and discord; for he preserves resentments, with which the spirits become spellbound, the truth, justice and life in faith are forsaken, as will the pursuit which lifting its head it will resolve to keep on doing in those days. Who will not tremble seeing this horrible tribulation hastened by divine wrath which will punish the scandals which plague the Church, and especially the desecration of sacred things?

Jesus Christ was telling them "See the abomination of desolation as foretold in Daniel's prophecy and conceived in these terms (Dan 9:24): 'Seventy weeks are decreed concerning your people and your holy city to bring to an end the perversion of justice, to put an end to sin, and to atone for gross immorality, and to bring in everlasting righteousness and seal both vision and prophecy, and to anoint the most holy of holies;' so that when you see Jerusalem surrounded by Roman armies, know ye that its destruction is at hand. Then those who are in Judea will flee to the mountains, and he who is on the rooftop of his house should not come down or enter it to take anything from it, and he who has been in the field should not return to pick his clothes, and those who are about in Jerusalem let them move on, and those who are in other regions let them not enter the city, for these are days of revenge in which all the things which are written will be fulfilled. Escape is very useful and necessary to placate the wrath of God to flee from sin, to move away from the perversion of the age, not to let their customs and principles stick to us. In calamities people mostly seek to save their estate, healing or life; few try to save their souls by doing penance.

Jesus Christ admonishes and teaches first of all those who are in Judea to flee and go to the mountains; for when the Antichrist comes, he will first be received in Judea than in any other part of the world, and owing to his physical presence persecution will be greater in that place than in all others: and he says that they should flee to the mountains, as they should go to secret and desert places, where they could hide; for by mingling with those people who are bound to believe in that man of sin or son of perdition, let the Christians not put up to them with force or beat around their infidelity. And those who stand on the rooftop, namely in the peak and height of perfection, let them not descend to take anything from their house out of greed for worldly things, by which the faultless are often torn down from the cusp of perfection at the time of temptation and persecution.

Jesus Christ quite rightly added in this very important address that neither should those who were working in the fields return home to pick their robe; for those who work in the good works of active life must not leave them to return to worldly occupations, which can hardly be unaffected by sin; and he symbolised these in the robe, which he forbade them to go and take again. But according to a proper literal meaning the Lord wanted to show in these words, that due to the occurrence and haste of the tribulations and the present evils, and for the fear and uncertainty there would be at the time of the judgment and of the coming evils, there will be no place where one can attend to temporal affairs, and that it would suit better one and all to think as to how he will present himself before the supreme Judge to obtain eternal life, than how to preserve his estate.

But *woe to pregnant women and breastfeeding daughters in those days!* This sentence corresponds to the other one where the Lord calls blessed in those days the barren ones who never bore children and the breast that never gave suck (Lk 23:29). A wretched fruitfulness is that which only gives birth to children worthy of God's wrath! Woe to the fathers who fall into the hands of the living God, for not averting their children from the pitfalls of harmful or indiscreet love with which they love and spoil them! What does it pay us to increase or strengthen the world's affections and passions, if in the end we have to break them before dying so as not to perish eternally? Oh holy prudence of those who in due time detach themselves from worldly love and respect, to be unburdened and work without hindrance in their only calling! The Lord makes comparisons with pregnant women to show how difficult it is for those who always worked to pile treasures and riches on earth, to renounce to worldly cares; for the great difficulty which women have in being able to flee, taking into account the seriousness of the pregnancy, and also those who have children, because of the duties and care small children expect. Mystically, pregnant women mean those who conceived in their hearts thoughts of evil purpose, and those who raise children being those who support the evil deeds found in the evil acts which are executed. Saint Augustine says: "Pregnant women mean those misers who covet others' goods and hope to gain riches in an evil manner, like the pregnant woman who hopes to raise a generation. And those who err mean those who possess what they covet and take great care to increase the wealth they possess, always safeguarding and enlarging it." So are the greedy hearts for worldly goods like pregnant women who are seeking, and like those mothers raising children who believe in possessing.

Other expressions pronounced by Jesus Christ are no less significant and terrible as to clarify what is apparent and give greater importance to what he had said so far. *Pray*, he added, *that your flight will not take place in winter, nor on a Sabbath feast day, for there will be great anguish and predicament on earth, and so dreadful a tribulation that there has not been since the beginning of the world until now, nor will there ever be.* Just as the winter rains and cold, and the discomforts of journeys in this season, slow down and hinder walking, and during the Sabbath the Law forbids the Jews from undertaking long journeys, so did the Saviour also desire to prevent the apostles from taking all holy resolutions in advance, so that his awful coming would not take them by surprise in such a time when they would no longer be able to prepare. So that this was the same as if he had told them, and in his person to all of us: "Where can you flee to in winter? To the mountains? They are covered with snow, and frigidity does not allow them to make them a dwelling place. In wintertime days are short, roads are bad, it rains a lot, night cover falls early, and some kind of bother raises its head at every step. On the other hand, the short trip allowed according to the Law and tradition on Saturday will be enough to keep the risk afar." These words, which if taken literally were addressed only to the Jews, since the keeping of the Sabbath did not last but until the ruin of the temple, but if taken mystically are addressed to all creatures, so that with continuous prayer we may all face up to great temptations and avoid the surprises of the flesh with zeal and the mortification of the senses, that we may always flee from spiritual apathy and tiredness, for there is no time when we are not exposed to great fights; and so although all times are good for us to flee the world and the snares which the devil lays for us, there are certain more timely spears for this escape, which we ought not to despise; for it is not a matter of where the difficulties grow or where we find insurmountable obstacles to our weakness at the time of fleeing. Winter is the image of old age; gloomy for the most part, idle and accompanied by a thousand ailments. Who will ponder on the impediments which conversion finds in man at the end of his life? God earnestly asks us not to leave up to that time to renounce the world and to flee its deceitful pleasures; for one should fear that what he did not desire previously may not be possible to achieve at a later time; and that if it is done, it would bear no fruit and be without merit, only through sorrow, namely, out of self-love and not out of true desire to serve God.

The reason that there will be great tribulation, as there never was since the beginning of the world, is because then all the persecutions caused by infidels and heretics, and by tyrants and false Christians, will come together like a furious wind which ignites the most appalling persecution. These four force lines of wickedness are the four winds and the four beasts which the prophet Daniel (Dn 7) saw fighting in the sea, so that then Jesus Christ's faithful will be tormented throughout all the parts of the world, with torments no less cruel in pain than diversity in amount. And Christians will be much more tormented and afflicted in those countries and lands where Jesus Christ preached and was crucified, for then all demons which are now chained will be unleashed; and just as the Antichrist will be more cruel than all the persecutors found in the world, so will the saints living in those days be stronger than all past martyrs.

And if those days had not been shortened, no man would be saved; but for the sake of the elect those days will be shortened. This shortening will be wrought by the Lord out of love for the elect, for He knows well the frailness of human steadfastness. And He has to hasten it, according to the restrain shown by his eternal wisdom and merciful intentions; for by delaying those cruel times the faith of believers is neither altered nor endangered, and also since the persecutor's malice does not change a Catholic person's perception; for which reason this cruel conflict will not last any longer than three and a half years. This is what the prophet Daniel expressly says about the Antichrist's reign (Dn 12.): *It shall last for time, two times, and half a time;* which means that the persecution in that horrible form will last three and a half years. The prophet mentions a time of one year, and times of two years, and a half time of one half year, during which that son of perdition will reign, for this was the same the time during which our most sweet Redeemer preached his new Gospel of mercy and love. The said prophet Daniel speaks of this time more clearly: The days during which the reign of the deformed and very fierce beast will last, will be one thousand two hundred and ninety, which are three and a half years. And when he says that if those days were not shortened, all flesh would not be saved, this must be taken to mean that *There would be no man who could be saved.* So, if at that time the Lord does not shorten the days of persecution, very few would remain who could suffer those excruciating woes and cruel tribulations; and although it says that those days will be shortened, it is not understood whether they would be less in terms of hours or in terms of the presence of the sun, but only because they will be few in number. Then the same Saviour adds that *If anyone says to you, see that Christ is here, or there, do not believe it,* nor should you seek to arrive there by stages of reasoning, believing the doctrine of those who tell you such evil things, nor should you want to follow them by walking towards them affectionately, conforming your lives with their customs, for many disciples of the Antichrist will come to deceive people saying that he is the true Christ promised by the Law and Prophets. *For false Christs and false prophets will then rise to do great miracles and wonders, until the very chosen ones would possibly be deceived.*

The Lord here warns carefully, for all of them will lie, each of them claiming to be Christ; but in truth they will be but Antichrists, false Christians, destroyers of the doctrine of the true Christ and sowers of lies. They will destroy the doctrine of the Law and Prophets, taking it out of its true context, usurping divine revelations and claiming to be the enlightened ones. And these will be the Antichrist and his disciples. They will work signs or wonders well worthy of admiration in the eyes of men to see whether they can mislead the elect themselves, for just as the Lord allowed the true miracles of Moses to be counterbalanced by other false ones by the Egyptian magi, the same will be allowed to happen in the end of times to purify the faith of good servants and give them new merit for being steadfast. Yet even if they seem like miracles, they will not be as remarkable as the lie they tell; about which Saint Gregory says: "We must think that inasmuch as great will be the temptation suffered by the human heart at the time, so much greater will be the steadfastness of the pious martyr, who will surrender his body to the tyrant's torments the more the tormentor insists on doing miracles in the presence of the tormented." And Saint Chrysostom adds: "As in Jesus Christ's advent the prophets worked miracles before he showed himself to the world, and as after his ascent into heaven the apostles worked them by virtue of the Holy Spirit, so also when the Antichrist comes, false Christians will work wonders in evil virtue."

"I wanted to tell you all these things," Jesus Christ further said, "before they come, so that you may provide what is necessary, foreseeing what is to come, that you might be well forewarned." The Lord then declared these truths to all of us, so that his doing may make us humble, vigilant and persevering in the living faith. Unless we take advantage of these warnings a terrible judgment awaits us, engraving in our hearts the risks which the Lord foretells, and guarding against them with the arms of prayer. All has been already said, all has been announced; we can neither claim ignorance nor excuse; it is the fault of our apathy if we are deluded or surprised by some seducer or false prophet. So, if they tell you: *Behold, he is here in the desert, do not go out, it is here where he dwells in the most hidden part of the house,* do not believe it. Repeating this shows the importance of the message, showing the risk which God fears that it will make little dent in us. The impression suddenly caused by eternal truths can be easily weakened and erased. It is miserable not to take into account this horrible frigidity at which the world has stopped, let alone to place against it the fire of meditation and prayer. *For like the flash of lightning rises in the East and shines to the West, so will it be with the coming of the Son of Man.* Just as the sun shows itself in the eyes of all, and does not shine only in one part, but in all, nor does it need a harbinger or crier, but in an instant and brief moment of time appears on earth's horizon, so will the coming of the Son of Man in the general judgment, be sudden, very clear and manifest to all, making it impossible for anyone to doubt it. He will not appear here or there, but in all places by the common outpouring of his brightness and glory. It will shine on that last day with the light of the great victor, whose brightness will never cease, so that in that night of sadness and bitterness we may see the glory of the resurrection.

Wherever the dead body is, there will the eagles gather. Which means that wherever Christ our Redeemer is present, as for his humanity, according to which he will judge the world in a human and glorious manner, there will also gather all the saints who shall go out to receive Christ our Redeemer, when he comes to do judgment, where all their young people will be renewed in the likeness of the regeneration which eagles undergo. About which it is very noteworthy that Jesus Christ is here called *body*, to signify the truth of the flesh and to present his bodily form, in which every creature will see it. The elect are here called *eagles* because of the renewal the resurrection will perform in them, and because of the perfection and gentleness of the sight with which we will see Christ our Redeemer, sun of righteousness; without the eyes losing sight in a fainting fit from the terrible throbbing of the rays of eternal light that will come out from Jesus Christ's face.

But after these days of tribulation pass, the sun darkens, and the moon will not give off its light, and the stars will fall from the sky, and the virtues of the heavens will be moved. He finally announces the complete ruin and desolation of the Jewish people. The sun, the moon, the stars and the heavenly virtues, according to some interpreters, stand for the temple, Jerusalem, the cities of Palestine, and the countless and fruitful Jewish nation. Some Fathers have very opportunely applied this part of the prophecy to events affecting the Church. For them the solar and lunar eclipses, the falling of the stars, the heavenly movements and those of their virtues, all refer to the evils which the Saviour has indicated, and they will afflict the Church during the same life of the apostles, and even much later, when knowing Christ and knowledge of his doctrine start weakening, some principles of evangelical morality are overshadowed with the challenges poised by the passions, thus cooling down their compassion, and the faithful become worldly and some masters of religion perverted. Then due to lack of faith, anxiety will spread to all peoples of the earth; the sea being swollen with its furious waves, as in the very midst of a violent storm, it will fill hearts with fear and fright, and men will be arid and pale fearing the final blow which will threaten the whole world. The heavenly virtues, namely the angels of God, will be set in motion and will want to have a part in the destruction of the Lord's enemies.

Although the history of the Jewish and Christian Churches is an ongoing commentary on this prophecy, when speaking in this manner Christ nevertheless depicts more vividly the universal ruin of the world than that of Judea. However, with the same ideas and almost in same terms, Isaiah prophesied to the Assyrians the fall of Babylon (Is 13:9-10), Ezekiel prophesied to the Egyptians the ruin of their capital (Ez 22:7-8), and Joel foretold to a sad Jerusalem, Sennacherib's campaigns and Nebuchadnezzar's events (Jl 2:10,30). It is not seen in all their texts, other than that they are cruel days of anger, outrage and fury; the sun will darken, there will be eclipses of the moon, stars will fall and horror and darkness will spread over the whole surface of the earth. The stars of heaven shall weep and be in distress, and the Lord will make His voice heard in front of the armies, enemy of his people; and finally, the blood, fire and smoke which will cover the countryside. Such are the acclaimed but most distressful images with which the Lord foretells the world's destruction and ruin before his last and dreadful coming.

Then the sign, the banner of the Son of Man, will appear and will be high in heaven, and all the tribes of the earth will cry out and moan, when they see the Son of Man coming upon the clouds of heaven with great power, majesty and glory. This is what the Apocalypse itself reveals to us (Apoc. 1:7): "Behold, he is coming with the clouds with millions of his saints, and every eye will see him, everyone who pierced him, and all tribes of the earth will wail on account of him." At the same time he will send his angels with trumpet and with a great voice, and gather his chosen ones from the four winds or angles of the earth, from the remotest ends of it to the highest peaks of heaven. Then all, with their eyes looking up, will see the holy and terrible sceptre of the great King discovered, and they will remember that Christ had announced this very thing, saying that before his coming the sign of the Son of Man shall appear in heaven, and they will understand that after this the King will come. Majestic coming! Terrible judgment! The same as on the cross Christ made the first judgment of the world and of the prince who kept it under his tyranny, so would he in the second and final judgment through this same cross, complete it all by overcoming and making his enemies his footstool.

But when these things start happening, look up and lift your heads, as your redemption, your freedom, and the fulfilment of Gospel promises are approaching and are nearby. You already know what will happen to this superb city which proudly raises its head to heaven; so heed ye as from right now the signs I give you to bring about my revenge, lest you will be wrapped in universal misfortune. Learn from the fig tree this parable; once its branch is tender and the leaves are sprouting, you know that summer is near. So also when you see all these things happening, understand that it is well nigh, that its revenge will suddenly burst in with a roar, that your freedom is near, and that my kingdom is already being established. Heaven and earth will pass, but the words I tell you will not pass away. Truly I assure you that this generation will not end; namely, that all presently living Jews would not have yet died, and that many of you would still be living when it will be seen that the great events which I have just told you about will happen. Leave aside all worry and mistrust when that day arrives. You know that I always spoke the truth, and that I say nothing without knowing that it is my Father's will; no one knows the time of that day and of that hour, not even the angels in heaven, nor the Son himself, but the Father alone. Which was the same like telling them: "What you wish to know is the effect of pure curiosity, which is neither appropriate nor profitable to satisfy. You well know that I do not say anything out of my own will, nor do I teach but what I have heard from my Father. Being appointed by Him doctor, teacher and judge of men, I do not ignore anything which might be of advantage to their healing. But I must not reveal anything which my Father wants to remain hidden. This means that I do not know everything."

Be very careful, watch and ask God, do not think of this time when you are relaxed, Do often recall these warnings, meditate on them and reflect on them seriously. Take great care, above all that your hearts are not burdened with drunkenness, with too much delight or with a superfluous care of worldly matters. Think carefully that this will be the fatal hour which will decide your happiness or eternal despair, which will befall you suddenly; that all men living in it would be surprised and be like being caught in a net. So that even if this hour is unexpected, let it not catch you off guard. Continuous vigilance and prayer are the means to save you from all those evils with which heaven has determined to punish the world. In this manner you will be in a state of utter trust when you appear before the Son of Man seated on Jesus Christ's throne as sovereign judge.

The coming of the Son of Man in the days of his vengeance will be as in a former time, in the days of Noah's flood. In those times that preceded the flood, men celebrated feasts and weddings, feeling secure and enjoying all pleasures. The wise warnings of that holy patriarch did not perturb their joy or made them take any greater care. But the terrible day arrived; Noah entered the ark God had commanded him to build, together with his family, and Noah and his daughters were saved in that refuge, along with all other animals that were given shelter in it; the flood came, but none of the others was saved. See me there as an image of sudden appearance when I will come to judge men and take revenge on my enemies. It happened in Lot's time; they ate, drank, bought, sold, planted and built. But on that day when Lot left Sodom, God instantly sent a burning rain of sulphur and bitumen. All the inhabitants were burned and reduced to ashes, and the earth became desert land. The same thing is now naturally happening with Jerusalem's misfortunes and the shock of its inhabitants. And so will it be for all men on judgment day, when the Son of Man will manifest himself. I say to you that on that night of which I speak to you and whose horrors I prophesy, two persons will sleep in a bed, travel together, or work in the same field; and one shall be taken carrying his provisions, and the other shall escape retaining his freedom; that is, one will be elected and chosen and the other will be condemned. Two women will be grinding together at the same mill; one will be taken captive and the other will be let completely free. So keep watch, I repeat over and over again: think of your lives and pray, for you neither know the day nor the hour.

As the zeal which Jesus Christ had for good of souls was always most forceful and perfect, he did not omit any occasion to warn all of the evil that threatened them, for nothing hurt him more than their loss. But he wanted it to be known that he expected from all men what a master expects from his servants when going on a long journey, leaving them the care of his house to do all that which they judge to be in his service. He orders them to be vigilant so that they can open the door for him on his return. Yet off he goes without saying anything about the time he would be back, all like saying to them: "My apostles, be you forewarned and ready to render me an account of your doings. Warn your disciples not to forget themselves, so that each one may do the same on his part and give an account of how he has performed his obligations." About which I say to you all, and in particular to you, to watch and pray, for you do not know the hour when your Lord will be coming, whether it will be in the evening, at midnight, when the rooster crows or when the sun sets. Watch, then, that it does not come unexpectedly and finds you asleep; I who love you more than any other person, I wish to see you very wakeful and ready to depart when your Lord calls you, like those good servants who have their loins girded and torches lit in their hands, like those men waiting for their master to come. In a few words the Lord commanded them to do three things. The first, that they had their loins girded to do something difficult or dangerous; the second, that they kept their torches lit; and the third, that they waited for the Lord vigilantly. As for the first, it is known that ancient easterners ordinarily wore long clothes; but when they offered to serve or to do something requiring great diligence, they turned up their girdles with great care not to have them in the way. So did the angel command Saint Peter to be girded to get out of prison; Saint Raphael appeared to Tobias girded his clothing and gestured him to walk; and Elijah ran girded before Ahab. The Saviour wanted his terms to have a spiritual and sublime sense in telling his disciples to gird their loins, meaning that they should get rid of all earthly matters that could hinder them on their way to heaven, and that with this girdle they would be ready to enter into the struggle they had to fight with their enemies. With this he also wanted to explain to all how careful we ought to be in restraining our passions, and not to put our hope in the sons of men who cannot save, but in God who is the only One who can and wants to save us.

In the second request the Lord makes to his disciples together with the first, Saint Gregory feels that he shows the two elements of Christian justice, namely to cease doing evil and to do good, because the flesh, always much heavier than the spirit, not only prevents it on many occasions from flying to heaven, but oftentimes kills it down and causes it to roll around in the bosom of passions. And notice that the Lord did not say in your hand, but in your hands, like a person who passes, as Saint Bernard says, through a windy place, carrying a candle in one hand and with the other trying to shade it so that the wind will not blown it off. And in the third request the Lord indicated the confidence with which Christians should await death as a day of rejoicing and wedding, comparing it to the hour when he called us to himself. Look at this in a good light, and it will be seen that we leave nothing behind us when we die, which does not deserve being abhorred and belittled, considering that what is promised to us in the coming age consists fully of extreme kindness and is very much worth achieving. We leave affairs, diseases, deceit, misery and a false security, and we are promised life without death, healing without disease, a safe condition, a perpetual reward, undecaying glory, a heaping of all possessions at the end, without either a blend or shadow of evil. The Lord does not want us to expect him to be angry and vengeful, harsh and distressful, but cheerful, benign and open-hearted, as one who comes from weddings; he does not want his arrival to cause us terror and dread like his evil servants fearing the very abode where they live, but comfort and joy as good children who look forward to their Father to receive tender and affectionate embraces from him, and so keep a continuous vigil; they know it is Him when he knocks at the door and hastily open it for him. Happy are those whom the Lord will meet keeping this vigil and taking great care to wait for the instant of his arrival. I assure you, indeed, that he will make them sit at the table, girdle around him his clothes and serve them in person, taking great care that they do not lack anything.

The Lord so expressly commands that we wait for him and watch very carefully, since he can come at all hours and catch us by surprise. You know well enough, Jude says in verse 14 of his letter, that the Lord's day will come as a thief at night. That when men say peace and safety, and when they believe themselves to be safer and calmer, destruction will come upon them, disaster will strike them suddenly as pains come to a pregnant woman, and they will not escape. But you, brethren, are not in darkness, that such day might take you by surprise as a thief. You are all children of the light and day; we are not night people; nor sons of darkness; so that we do not sleep like all others do, but rather try to keep watch and live with sobriety and temperance. If you do not watch, I will come to you like a thief, says the Lord (Apoc 3:3), and you will not know at what hour. Behold, I come as a thief; blessed is he who watches and guards his clothing that he might not walk naked and fail to see his ugliness. And Saint Peter also says: "The day of the Lord will come like a thief at night, and then the heavens will pass away, will be ruined echoing a loud noise, and the elements will be burnt with fire, and the earth and the works that are upon it, will be scorched" (2 Pt 3:10). Since all these things are so to be dissolved, what kind of persons ought we to be for the advent of the Day of the Lord, when the heavens will be burnt and the scorched elements will be molten with fire? But, according to his promises, we hope for a new heaven and a new earth, in which righteousness dwells. So, oh beloved ones, in hoping for these things to occur, take care to live diligently so that the Lord will find you pure, without blemish and faultless, awaiting his coming in peace. And if the master came at the second vigil, or well during the third, and found his servants ready and willing to serve, there is no doubt that they will be blessed forever.

After the Lord had set the prize as a caring patron for whoever keeps watch, he could not but tell us about the penalty a sleeper deserves, thus encouraging us to keep watch continually and this being the whole object of his parable. So that he further said: "Keep in mind what I say to you, and always remember it, for it is a pity if you are less careful about what happens to your souls, than worldly beings think about the security and care of their homes. If a family father knows or gets to understand the time when the thief would come, he would undoubtedly remain awake so as not to be taken by surprise, and he would not allow anyone to drill a hole or scale his house; but not knowing the time the thief would come, he would keep watch all night. You must not therefore be any less careful as to that concerning the hour of your death and the coming of the Son of Man, who is your Lord and your Judge. You must always keep your last hour before your eyes, and it is a matter of infinite importance to be prepared well with extreme vigilance, assuming that none is either more uncertain or less known."

Saint Peter had heard very attentively what Jesus Christ had said, and noting a short pause in his speech, he asked him: "Have you said this parable, Lord, specifically for us or for all in general?" In his answer the Saviour showed well that his instructions were generally addressed to all men, but that he wished them to particularly serve those who were much pleased to be close to his person, and that if these seemed difficult to perform, in practising them they would have more merit and have their faithfulness abundantly rewarded. So that he answered him with great familiarity and pleasure, seeming more like a friend conversing with his friends than a teacher teaching his disciples, saying to them: "Who, in your opinion, is the faithful and prudent servant to whom the Lord, at the time of his departure, leaves to supervise his house so that he might, during his absence, provide all his servants with the wherewithals needed for their upkeep? Blessed is the steward whom on his return the master finds busily performing his duties. I really tell you that he will shower him with trust and let him administer all his goods. But if a servant who is given this task by his master becomes unfaithful and negligent; if he says in his heart my master will not be returning so soon and so thinking starts chasing and mistreating the other servants, and wastes his time eating and drinking excessively with drunkards; when his master will turn up one day without warning and at the least expected hour, he would in outrage remove this evil administrator and steward from the property and running of his house, and put these in someone else's hands; and he would count him among cheats and hypocrites." What a miserable state and wretched fate, in which he would find himself and have none else to do but to weep, groan and gnash his teeth. For that servant, who knew his master's will but did not dispose of things or prepare them, nor did he conduct himself according to his will, received many scourges; but whoever not knowing of his will but did things worthy of punishment, received less. For much will be demanded from whoever has been given much, and more will be asked of him who has been entrusted with many things.

The Lord was adamant with this example, to prepare those who serve him with blind, prompt and demanding obedience, and to this end he repeated to them in other terms what he had already told them. "God," he told them, "is like a family father who asks some servants for the estate he has entrusted to them. Some would have increased it with their industry and good diligence; he bestowed on these the fullness of new rewards making them participants of the joy that he himself enjoyed, saying to them: 'Enter into your lord's happiness and joy.' Others fled from work and lazed in a shameful and inexcusable idleness, for they knew well how much their lord wanted them to manage and trade with his money; but after stripping these vile servants of the administration of his property, he sentenced them to life imprisonment, with which he had before threatened them many times. He sought here that they would be punished in proportion to the talents they had received and how much they knew of what their lord really wished."

There is no doubt that these parables all seek to instruct us and that we may so live in the most exact observance of our obligations, without tending towards vice and keeping ourselves in continuous vigilance, waiting for the hour of the Lord, who will come as our judge when least expected, to take account of our conduct and stewardship; namely, of the use we have made of the treasures of his grace and benefits which he has poured out upon us. Considering all this and taking into account the circumstances in which Jesus Christ spoke to his apostles, the meaning we have just given them seems to be very accurate, taking into account the doctrine of the Fathers and of the Holy Scriptures, the more so when he accompanies them with another figure who uninterruptedly follows the latter and seems to have the same purpose, continuing with the same parallel between Galileans and Jews. Then, the Lord said to his disciples, namely about when God will suddenly come: "As I have prophesied to you, to put an end to the age of the Law, a distinction will be made in the kingdom of the Messiah, whose figure I will expose to you; but it must be noted that this first distinction is at the same time the image and the figure of what will happen in my kingdom and in my Church, from it being established among the Gentiles to the end of time."

The kingdom of heaven, he told them, *will be similar to ten virgins who, taking their lamps, went out to receive Bridegroom and Bride.* These ten virgins generally stand for all Christians, in the sense in which the prophets called the ancient people of the Lord *virgin of Israel, virgin of Judah,* and God as the *guide of their virginity*, owing to the immutable faith they received from Him. Similarly, Christians are called virgins, since they hold the virginity of the true faith and because in baptism they married the One heavenly Spouse, Jesus Christ, turning their backs on Satan and all his works; so that in him we received the white vestment and the lit candle, and we are told to keep our baptism, so that when Jesus Christ comes we can go out to meet him. The Apostle made use of this similarity to tell the Corinthians, that through baptism he had incorporated them with Christ Jesus Christ, saying: "I betrothed you to Christ to present you as a pure bride to her one husband" (2 Cor 11:2).

According to Jewish custom and also that of the Gentiles, the virgins took their lamps and went out to receive the spouses. The young men who went out to this feast were called the husband's sons, and when the wife was taken to the husband's house, her virgin companions carried lit lamps, as David shad chanted: "The virgins will be led to the king to escort her, with joy and great celebration, they will be taken to the king's palace" (Ps 44:16-18). It is clear that when Jesus Christ bases his parable on this custom, the husband was Christ; the virgins' lamps signify the faith professed by every Christian and their self-giving to the Spouse to serve him. The oil here means the penance and works which need be done to worthily receive the Spouse, without which the lamp is extinguished, because faith without works is dead. But of the ten who were there in all, there were five fools who forgot to take oil along with them to fill up their lamps. The other five, who were much more prudent, took care to fill a few extra vessels with oil and take them along with them. Yet as it took long for the Spouse to arrive, they had time to take some rest. We can call prudent those maidens who, knowing what they were born for, and what to do to seek life and their role in the Church, try to behave in everything they do according to these principles, adopting with God's help the necessary means to save their souls. Fools are those who either do not care about salvation, or who do not figure out the necessary means to achieve it; they hold their conscience as a broken vessel, which neither warns them as to desires nor good thought, and live like runaway horses, rushing into an unfathomable abyss of vices.

With the foolish virgins being unprepared, in contrast to the obedience shown by the wise ones, the Lord wanted to state that in due time, in his very day, the things now hidden in darkness and the secrets of the heart would be revealed (1 Cor 4:5). While still pilgrims, the outward profession of faith confuses true Christians with that of false and adulterous ones. But this confusion will end on the same new day when the righteous will shine like the sun, and sinners would be left as coal soot in perpetual darkness. All virgins fell asleep while the Spouse delayed; but at midnight a call to order was given: *Watch out for the spouse who is coming; rise up and go out to meet him.* That lateness of the spouse and his delay in coming is the period of penance granted to the sinner. At this time the Lord, not wishing anyone of us to perish but that all should reach repentance (2 Pt 3:9), shows great forbearance towards us to bring us safely on the path of penance. But this same forbearance must cause us great terror, because it also reminds us of how great his wrath can be; for even though he may take time to wield the sword of revenge, he rewards this delay exorbitantly with the heaviness and frightfulness of punishment.

All the virgins fell asleep, this being death's dream, common to both good and bad, wise and foolish, for all understand the sorrow of dying once, to be followed by judgment. At midnight the spouse came, with a cry hailing his arrival, and from the midst of the call a voice arose saying: "Go out to receive him." What distressing and terrible thoughts did the Lord present to the miserable sinner with these few words! The silence of the night and the helplessness in which man finds himself in the midst of his darkness, are a vivid image of what is to happen to us at the hour of our death. We will not have our relatives, friends and supporters around, and we will also be left without any strength at that sad hour, and we shall be surprised with the sudden and unexpected coming of the Lord. It would be worthy both of admiration and pity that men, being warned as they are of the terrible coming of the Judge, are uncertain as to when it will happen but certain of the severity with which he will judge them; so that as the same Lord says, he will take them by surprise like a bow striking a bird when it hits it, how and when the bird thinks least about being hit. So do sinners, indeed, who are always deaf and without feeling to calls of God's mercy and grace.

All the virgins arose when they heard the cry, and began to adorn their lamps with flowers, as was then the custom. Then seeing that the lamps of the foolish ones were put out, they became aware of their carelessness; and not having a single drop of oil to light them again, nor even knowing where to buy some, they started saying to the prudent virgins: "Give us some of your oil, because our lamps have snuffed out." The Lord here drew a very lively picture of what would happened at the hour of death to whoever led a careless life and did not think of linking it in good time to the oil of good works, so as to make the lamp of his faith shine ceaselessly, sustained by the zeal of his charity and love. The righteous, who as time goes by, provide themselves with good works and hold tightly to Christ's cross with the light of charity burning within them, prepare to receive the spouse. Evil persons, on the other hand, seeing the time of their lives wasted, are terrified at the sight of the danger that threatens them and do not know what to do or where to go. It is a weird idea and great insanity that such a serious affair as this, and the depth of our involvement in it, is left for the time of life's greater affliction and turmoil; when we fail to be attentive, our intellect is perturbed, and our inner and exterior forces decay to the utmost, and as we extend our hands to the world it rejects us. So let us lift up our eyes to heaven, about what is upsetting us, and let us seek in the poverty of men that which we need most. It will then be in vain that we cry out that God hears us, even though during our lives we do not listen to Him.

It is easy that those to whom we cry out either ignore us or excuse themselves, and stop giving us help, as the wise virgins did with the foolish ones, rather saying to them: "Go to the sellers and make your own purchases." When the prudent virgins did not give any of their oil to the foolish one, this denotes that no one takes advantage of the merits of others to attain eternal life, other than one's own works by which each one is to be judged. In this life we can help each other with prayers, fasts, almsgiving, sacrifices and all kinds of good works; but coming before the judgment seat of God, it will only be our good works which will be considered valid. No one can bend the rod of divine justice that the Lord may save anyone deserving to be condemned. If a righteous person who in his time provided himself with good works is barely saved, where will the evil person, who mocks virtue and despises all that is of merit to heaven, put his trust?

The foolish virgins actually took the prudent virgins' council; they went to buy oil, but while doing this business the spouse arrived, and finding only the prudent ones he entered with them in the wedding room and immediately closed the door. It was no longer the time when they could mend what they had lost before, nor could they stock up any longer by exercising virtue; and so the door of mercy for forgiveness, of grace to be deserving, and that of glory, which had been open for so long to enter in the rest of the kingdom of God, was closed for them. It was in vain that they cried out and said: *Lord, Lord, open for us*; for the Lord whom they called ignored them and told them in clear terms: *I do not know who you are*. They were already counted among the condemned, and for this reason he did not know them. Which is like what the Lord will say to all the condemned ones in his terrible day: "I do not recognise you as my disciples, because you are not marked with the seal of charity which distinguishes my followers. I do not recognise you as sons, because I do not see in you works that take after me; nor as soldiers in my field, for you have stripped yourselves of my weapons, which are those of righteousness, and soiled and torn the vestment of grace with which I clothed you in holy baptism."

See here, the Lord concluded, a figure of what will happen when the Spouse of holy souls makes his wedding banquet. He will not admit to it anyone but the worthy; seek you, therefore, to deserve this grace, do not be negligent, watch over how your heart is disposed given that you do not know at what time this heavenly Spouse will arrive, whose coming will be no less terrible to those who are not in a state of receiving him, than it is joyful for those whom he will find duly prepared. Yet to understand well what these parables really mean, it helps looking at them as a continuation of the long conversation which Jesus Christ had with his apostles on the occasion of the temple and the city of Jerusalem, about his second coming and about the destruction and censure of the Jewish people. There is no doubt that these divine parables in which future events were declared in a sensitive way, although not giving away the specific day when they would happen, would arouse the attention of the apostles and make them more vigilant. With this plan, Jesus Christ abiding by the same lesson and addressing it always towards the same subject of what will precede his second coming to punish an unfaithful Jerusalem, went on making his initial speech explaining of other new signs that were to precede the universal judgment.

He now spoke to them about the general resurrection and universal judgment, that the Son of Man to whom every right was given to judge in heaven and on earth, will show himself visibly and in person, with Jesus Christ's splendour. All his angels will accompany him as subjects and ministers of his will and executors of his orders. He will sit on the throne of his glory, from where he will summon to his court each and every one of the men who have successively occupied the world's different states and conditions, from its creation to its final and total destruction. He will divide them into two large parts, just as the shepherd sets aside and divides his flock, separating the sheep from the goats. The righteous, represented by the meek and obedient sheep, will be placed on the right hand, and the bad, represented by the goats as dirty and unclean animals, will be cast onto the left side. Who might not be frightened by the Lord's imagery of his second coming? How could a person gain anything by sinning, if he believes in standing before Christ to give an account of his works, including his most hidden desires and thoughts?

"The Lord will not come alone, nor accompanied only by Moses and Elijah," Chrysostom says, "as when he was transfigured on the mountain, but with an innumerable army of heavenly powers. Not among beasts as when he came down on earth, but with the pomp and highness with which he ascended to the Father. Not standing as a prisoner, but sitting as a judge; not between thieves on the cross, but among angels on the throne of his glory." "There was a time I was a sheep," says the Lord; "as a lamb they took me to the sacrifice and I did not open my mouth; I suffered, I hid my feelings, I went through everything they wanted to make of me. Will I always be silent, perhaps? Oh, no. The day will come when I will raise my voice; I will scream like a woman going about in labour pains; and as the fierce sea usually swallows the ship with all those sailing on it, so I will ruin and I will drink and swallow in a lump the world and those who belong to it." Both good and bad, everyone will appear before the Judge. There will be the bitter sobbing of the world's lovers, of those people who are now so prosperous and flattered. Those who now step on His laws would then like to hide from the angry Lamb, but they will not succeed (Apoc. 6:16). Those who now hide in Christ's wounds will not have then to hide in caves and rock fissures. Oh, how frightful and terrible will that day be! How distressing and heartbreaking will the separation of the good from the bad be! Those who now terrify the world will be the same who will tremble at the sight of those whom they persecuted and killed, and seeing their bliss will be the greatest torment they will suffer in their eternal misfortune.

But since one of the most influential causes on the perverse bent and customs of man is inequality, not only of fortunes, but of learning, because there are very few who want to learn that we are nothing before God but very small beings. Those who dedicate themselves to act according to this idea of salvation, although they have learnt it, if God's good will blows favourably upon them and death and justice come to teach them, albeit belatedly, know that true inequality in the Lord's presence consists in the merit of their works. One might well be poor in this life, yet if his works are rich in merit, he would be rich before God; just as on the contrary, he might well be rich before men; yet if his works are poor in merit, he will indeed be poor in the sight of God from whom nothing is hidden, and poor will he be forever. Whatever man's works as he leaves the world might be, such will be his fate in eternity: either wheat in the barn of glory, or straw in hellfire. He does not say that he will separate poor from rich, commoners from nobles, or wise from foolish, but sheep from goats, that is, the good from the bad; and he will place the good on his right hand and the bad on his left. One trembles and one's most daring heart shivers when one comes to think of this with faith. What will my fate be on that terrible day? Where shall I go to? Proud and conceited, lewd and greedy, I will not be among the small and humble, or among the abstinent and poor; I will be placed right in the midst of the goats, for I never knew how to slow down with moderation and virtue.

The dreadful cry of the gathering will be followed by a deep silence, a certain indication that Jesus Christ's voice will soon be heard. The Son of God, King of heaven and earth, mediator and sovereign Judge of all men, will return his consoling and joyful sight to the righteous standing at his right hand, and he will call them to share his glory saying to them: "Come unto me, my Father's blessed ones; come and possess the kingdom where He reigns; that which is prepared for you from the creation of the world; Him who conquered you with the pains of my passion and death, and acquired you with the price of my blood, and which you have finally deserved with your good works; for I was hungry and you gave me food, I was thirsty and you gave me drink, I had no place where to lodge in the world and you hosted me, I was naked and you covered me, I was sick and you visited me, and being captive and imprisoned you came to console me." Oh, what words of such glory and comfort! Who will be able to ponder the joy that the good ones will feel when they hear them? How surprised and admired would they be to hear such words from the mouth of their sovereign Judge that would afford them such a sweet and appreciable treat? "What then, Lord," the righteous will answer, "when have we seen you so poor and hungry, and were so happy as to serve you with food? When were you thirsty and we have provided you with drink? When have we met you on a journey and not having where to lodge, and have been honoured with lodging you at our house? When did we see you naked and were comforted in dressing you, and finally, when sick or in prison and we had the great fortune of visiting and helping you?" "Ah!" the Lord shall answer. "You have made me more good than you think: I was receiving your gifts and comforts, and your eyes did not see me. Truly, I tell you, every time you have made these good works with any little one who believes in me, you have made them with me." What is given to the poor is being lent to God, and He returns it with great benefit and inestimable gain. "It is a gift," Saint Basil says, "because you give it out of your wealth, without expecting anything back from the poor who receive it; but it is also a loan because of the Lord great generosity who wants to pay for the poor. He cannot pay it to you, yet the poor man's guarantor will pay it to you, saying that what the poor man received from your hand was given to him." And John of Damascus adds that: "The poor man is the mask which God wears and hides; so, inasmuch as we help and comfort the poor, that much shall we be paying honour and favour to Christ."

The supreme and most upright Judge would have barely uttered the sentence in favour of the good ones, when he will turn his dreadful sight upon the wicked, and utter against them using the same words, although in an opposite sense as to condemnation and eternal damnation. "Turn away from me," he will say to them, "you cursed ones: go into eternal fire prepared for the devil and the rebellious angels who followed him; for I was hungry and you did not give me food, I was thirsty and you did not give me to drink, I was a pilgrim and you did not host me, naked and you did not clothe me, and I was sick and in prison and you did not visit me." "When was it, Lord," the wretched condemned ones will answer, "that we ran away from you, hated and despised you, and denied you all these comforts?" "When you denied them to one of my disciples, to the poorest of all my little ones, then you denied them to me." Harsh, terrible, dreadful and frightening words, more unbearable than hell itself! God will cast out and move away from him forever those who cut off themselves from him and do not know him. This is that perpetual banishment, that sudden fatal excommunication separating the condemned from the eternal companionship of the elect. What will become of the creature visited by such an ill-fated destiny? What end will it lead to? To eternal fire, to the tears of fruitless penance, to perpetual despair, to the torment of the gnawing worm which torments the heart without making it any better, and tears it apart without destroying or killing it. Merely thinking of this definitive sentence is terrifying, from which there can be neither a plea for mercy nor an appeal. What would it be like then to see the earth open with horrible shattering, sink into that chasm curled up into a fireball of men and demons, with hell opening its mouth wide to swallow such a wretched mouthful? Ah! The Lord then closes the door of the bottomless pit with the padlock of his unyielding justice, so that it may never be opened again. There will be the gnashing and grinding of teeth; there will be howling like that of rabid dogs in the land of oblivion, in the death chamber; the agonizing without dying, the tearing to pieces without fruit, and the eternal crying and shouting: *So it was we who strayed from the way of the truth*...

The righteous will go to eternal life. To the realm of light, to the bosom of joy, to the mansion of tranquillity and peace. To be citizens of heaven, companions of the angels and eternally happy with all the saints and the righteous. To enjoy God, in the end, and to take pleasure forever in his kind company, in that of his Holy Mother and that of all the blessed spirits. What a fool will he be whoever says I do not want to go to heaven, nor do I want eternal joy or rest? If the joy of happiness is inborn in man's heart, how can we flee from the path which leads to it? This way is Jesus Christ: it cannot be for one first to live a worldly life and then to reign with Jesus Christ; he lived humiliated and died crucified; in order to reign it has to be said with Saint Paul: "By the cross the world has been crucified to me, and I to the world" (Gal 6:14).

THE PASSION OF JESUS CHRIST BEGINS
CHAPTER 70
A COUNCIL IS HELD IN JERUSALEM AGAINST JESUS CHRIST, AND IT IS DECIDED TO SEIZE HIM AND KILL HIM

HAT year the Passover was already drawing very near. It was the solemnity known as that of the Unleavened Bread, in which the Jews had the precise obligation to comply with their Law's precept of consuming the ordinary bread in the house, since during the festivity they could not eat but unleavened bread, not containing any yeast. And as the time was already pressing when the Father's plans of justice and mercy should be accomplished, which was being awaited eagerly by His Son, he could not fail also to fulfil His plans of mercy and love, as described and foretold by the prophets. He had to live the qualities of a Doctor and Master who was sent with the sole purpose to prepare God's kingdom for people walking in the shadows of darkness and death. This had already been sufficiently fulfilled during the three years when he travelled throughout Samaria, Galilee and the length and breadth of Judea, which formed the ancient domain of God's chosen people. But Jesus Christ was more than this, for he was the great victim who was to offer himself to the Eternal Father for the healing of the whole world on the mountains of Israel; and being Messiah, Doctor, Shepherd, Teacher and Saviour of all men, he had to die by this title to earn for them the full merits of his divine blood's outpouring and, together with his passion and most painful death, the graces of salvation and the glory of adoption. Never had either more severe justice or more tender mercy been seen on earth than that which was seen to shine in the passion and death of the blessed Son of the Eternal Father; being as he was, holy, innocent,

without blemish, cut off from sinners, and far superior to the angels in all that could constitute him infinitely kind in the Father's presence. His soul was the most beautiful, most perfect, most complete and absolute thing that had ever come out of the hands of the Most High, and so he was the most beloved among all the creatures of heaven and earth; his most precious life was the life of all that lives, and his death was to be the agony of all nature, the horror of heaven and the sorrow of angels. It was said in the Scriptures, however, that he was to be sacrificed for the glory of God, for the healing of men and for the foundation of a new cult founded on the divinity of his person and on the merit of his sacrifice; it was this victim and this host which were to be offered on the solemnity of the Passover.

The Saviour then, being faithful and most precise in fulfilling his Father's will who for more than four thousand years had been waiting for this host whom He had offered since entering into the world, seeing that all had already been prepared and that nothing was left to do but to carry out the sacrifice, gave permission to hell to unleash all its powers against his sacred person. The hour had come and Jerusalem was the place where the heavily armed one had gathered all his forces; for at the same time as the docile and simple people had turned out to give Jesus Christ evidence of respect and witness of trust, the leaders, priests and religious leaders, burnt by the fire of their envy, were on the contrary busy plotting his loss. This caused Jesus Christ to leave the city and walked to Bethany; and it was there that, giving free rein to the fondness of his heart as he had done several times before, he spoke frankly to his disciples about how his time was drawing near, saying to them: "Know ye that within two days the Jews will be celebrating their Passover; but know ye also that not being content with sacrificing their lambs, they will also sacrifice the Son of Man who will be given to non-Jews, and they will crucify him." And it was actually at this same time that his greatest bloodthirsty enemies, who held leading religious and secular offices and occupied the front seats in public schools, gathered at high priest Caiaphas' house to deliberate among themselves on how to get hold of him and kill him. They did not want to use violence, nor did they dare trying to do this during the Paschal solemnity, fearing an uproar from the people who thought very highly of Jesus Christ. This was not the first time they had resolved about the matter, but it was now agreed during this meeting that there was no time left to be wasted, and that it was necessary that this wicked plan should be carried out before the Passover, as this was fully opportune for the people's healing. So the high priest pronounced: *It is fitting that a man should die for the people and that not all people perish.*

No man could ever utter such an important truth as Caiaphas had spoken in the great council of Zion, for it was but repeating what had been resolved in eternity in the grand council of the Divine Persons. The Evangelist refers to the fact, makes the words public, and does not censure them as blasphemy but passes them on to the Church as a prophecy pronounced by the Holy Spirit to the presiding head of the council, saying: *This he did not say out of his own wits, but being chief priest that year, he prophesied.* However, it is worth knowing that Caiaphas kept in his heart the fury of a basilisk, keeping it infested with asps' poison and dragons' bile, and yet though he then prophesied, he was no prophet at all; he was ungodly, he was evil, he was an apostate; he was a declared enemy of Christ and wanted him dead; and the people's healing of which he appeared to be so jealous, was only a pretext to cover up the fierce and unforgiving hatred by which he was possessed against Jesus Christ, and which he sought to conceal under the pretext of the people's wellness. As the famous historian Josephus says: "The scribes and Pharisees were a class of cunning arrogant men who abrogated for themselves a very great faithfulness in observing the Law, never separating themselves from it in anything towards which they were inclined with the hard-headedness of their befogged reasoning, following it with tenacity, even if it went against the said Law, reason and justice, so long as they believed it to suit them in achieving their plans and designs."

The Evangelist very opportunely says that he *prophesied*; for had he known how mistaken his blasphemy was, he would surely not have uttered the prophecy, thinking weirdly as he thought of Christ. It was in this manner that he covered the full appearance of his ill-famed vice with the honours of virtue, but really so to speak of abuse, with the most important of all resolutions, seemingly doing the greatest good to the whole world for so was it decreed in heavenly councils. There was only one very notable difference in this, and it was that neither he nor his companions wanted the sacrifice to take place on the day of the Passover, whereas Jesus Christ, prefigured so many centuries before by the Paschal Lamb, wanted to die on the day of the Passover. So Jesus Christ allowed the devil, the invisible head of the plot made against the Lord himself, to offer to the Jews a timely occasion to seize him, which they accepted with great joy, putting in action on the same day in which in terms of their resolve nothing could be executed against the person of the Saviour.

CHAPTER 71
HE EATS IN BETHANY AT SIMON THE LEPER'S HOUSE, AND A WOMAN SPILLS OVER HIS HEAD A MOST FRAGRANT BALM

THE Lord passed all night in prayer as he was used to do, and the disciples each withdrew to the house where they also had to spend the night; when the Lord caught up with them he dealt with his Father about the completion of the work with which he had been entrusted. The Evangelists say nothing of the place where the Lord stayed on that terrible night, and it seems very likely that it was some site at a distance from the Mount of Olives. The day came, and Jesus Christ letting it be known he was there, was immediately sought by Bethany's inhabitants who, remembering the wonderful miracle of Lazarus' resurrection, always ran after him since wherever he went he made them feel the health-giving effects of his goodness. One of them called Simon, who also bore the name of *the leper*, and whom the Saviour had also healed his illness, invited him to supper. Jesus Christ accepted the invitation, and after having spent the day in his ordinary occupations, preaching to the mobs and healing the sick, he went in the afternoon with his apostles to Simon's house, where the main events of the banquet in which he had found himself a few days earlier in the house of Lazarus, the brother of Martha and Mary, recurred. They had hardly sat down to supper according to the custom of the Jews, when a woman showing zeal for Christ's glory and having deep reverence for his person, entered the banquet room. No need to repeat that this was Mary Magdalene who so loved Jesus Christ that she could not depart from his company, being ever so eager to be instructed more and more in the doctrines which he constantly taught, and to show him the steadfast gratitude of her loving heart for the personal mercies she had received from him. She carried in her hands an alabaster jar full of an exquisite balm of spikenard, a very costly ointment which gave off a very soft and most pleasant

smell. She approached him with great respect blended with confidence, broke the jar, and poured the ointment on the Saviour's head. Such ceremony was not unknown among Jews, and its use and practice is well expressed in various parts of Scripture.

On another similar occasion Judas had given a bad example, which was followed by some other apostles, although his objection did not arise from the depths of the greed filling the traitor's heart. This woman's pious liberality seemed to them an excess deserving to be condemned; they felt anger against her and murmured against the generosity with which she so splendidly manifested her gratitude and love towards Jesus Christ. The thoughts harboured by some of those present were not hidden from the Saviour and he kept a respectful silence, showing that he was approving what some of his disciples disapproved. And feeling in their opinion that the Saviour's silence meant consent, they dared to utter publicly their disapproval, saying in a fairly loud and intelligible voice: "What is the point in wasting such precious ointment fruitlessly? This balm could have been sold for more than three hundred denarii, and this hefty amount could undoubtedly be much better spent to relieve the poor." As they knew well, the manner in which Jesus Christ held them in great esteem, they figured out that their intentions were in perfect agreement and harmony with those of Jesus Christ. Undoubtedly, the Saviour loved them with a very great tenderness, and on every occasion he had declared himself to be their Father and protector; but in spite of this, he did not want the obligations of charity to serve as a pretext to condemn those of religion, nor those of gratitude and of loving. For this reason instead of approving the apostles' conduct he rebuked it severely, saying: "*Do not upset or disturb this woman for what she has just done to me.* This is a labour whose value and merit you do not know. It has great merit right now, and it has nothing to do gloriously with future times. It is a sign of what is about to happen soon. As long as you keep your sight on the poor for whom you care, your compassion is praiseworthy, but you will always have the poor with you, but you will not always have me; you will always have a chance of doing them well, but it will not always be my destiny to receive such evidence of your love." Which was like telling them: "In order for you to understand the true mystery of this woman's particular action, I ask you, 'What is customarily done with the bodies of the deceased when they are laid in the tomb?' You know well that they embalm them with exquisite ointments; then see here the true meaning of what this woman did. She has anticipated the instant of my death; and if I was quite well informed by her closeness, she has prepared my body for burial. *Truly, I say to you, in a short time you will be telling the story of what she did; you will make it public and proclaim it throughout the world as a glorious act of piety when you go to preach the Gospel, and the memory of this action will last as long as my Church.*" This prediction has been fulfilled out and out, so that no one in the world reads or hears of the passion of Jesus Christ, without at the same time knowing and learning of the prodigious extravagance of the woman of Bethany in Simon the leper's house.

CHAPTER 72
JUDAS AGREES WITH THE SCRIBES AND PHARISEES ON A SET PRICE WITH WHICH TO SELL HIS MASTER

NE of the apostles attending this banquet in Jesus Christ's company was Judas, a native of Kerioth, and for this reason called Iscariot; his heart had been seized by the evil spirit in such manner that it possessed him as it liked. This spirit so took him out of Jesus Christ's company and that of the other disciples as to lead him like a willing slave to the meeting or assembly of the priests' leaders who had gathered in Caiaphas' house, while the Lord remained in Simon's house, instructing his apostles in the manner we have just seen. And this evil disciple, having been presented there, began his betrayal saying to the leaders: *What would you give me, and I will hand him over to you?* The burning greed he had in his heart knew no peace: every day he watched with grief his hopes of tracking his Master fade, missing all chances of gain for which he eagerly sighed. Believing he must take advantage of circumstances, knowing the ardour with which the Synagogue leaders sought to seize Jesus Christ in person, he worked out things in such manner for them to be the shortest way how he could enrich himself; and for this reason he did not hesitate to present himself before them.

No proposal could be made to the scribes in a better taste, and so they decided to give him thirty silver pieces; these he was to receive after executing his abominable plan. This was the price of the life of my God, and this was enough to move this timid and despicable soul to the most abominable of all plans. David, the king and psalmist, contemplated him in spirit, and possessed with bitterness and emotion he could not help but cry out in the person of Jesus Christ, and say: "If my enemy had cursed me, I would have suffered it with patience. If those who hated me had spoken ill of me, mocked me and sold me, I would have tried to hide from their presence; but that it was done by a man who was one with me, who was one of my relatives, and whom I had chosen to be one of the first captains and chieftains of my army, this is what has filled me with sadness and bitterness." And who might not have been filled with holy outrage for such a horrible and appalling betrayal? For thirty pieces of silver Judas sells his Master; but according to his own expression, it still seems like he would have sold him for less. He is seen as if not asking for a certain price and is only saying: *How much do you want to give me?* And they offered him thirty pieces of silver. A very small amount indeed for doing a service which they felt was so important. It was surely not as much that the sentinels who guarded the tomb after the death of Jesus Christ earned, and yet, so that they would say that his disciples had come and stolen his body while they slept, they offered, as Saint Matthew says, a large sum of money (Mt 28:12). Yet as the Scriptures were to be fulfilled, they offered him only thirty coins to sell Jesus Christ to them.

Had Judas been able to penetrate Jesus Christ's heart and understand the full intensity of his love, and know of the most forceful desire with which he was animated, he would have surely given up on his sacrilegious and devilish plan; yet blind and hardened as he was, he accepted the deal and the offer, and soon he was not thinking of anything but how to find the right time to put his plan into action, without being hindered by the people in any way. Having given his word and agreed to his commitment, he returned to Bethany possessed by the devil, waiting for the right time to carry out his plan; and he was apparently calm and self-satisfied, as if he found nothing for which he had to be chided. In the morning he joined again Jesus Christ and the other apostles, without showing himself troubled in any way or upset. Then, Jesus Christ did not reveal even the slightest suspicion about his abhorrent betrayal, wanting to keep the traitor away from the embarrassment he would surely find himself were Jesus Christ, whose penetrating gaze he could not miss and whose justice he had to fear, to show him either by his countenance or by his words that he had received news of his treachery, and of the vile price for which he was about to sell him.

Saint John the Evangelist brings a circumstance to the fore which he considers as being of divine force: he tells us that when Judas did this, it was night (Jn 13:30). In a blind night Judas lost all heavenly lights; he did not see or consider the horrible abyss towards which he was rushing in separating himself from Jesus Christ and the apostles to join the political leaders. Origen says of this: "It was night; but it was not a deep night, for its darkness troubled Judas' soul. That an apostle cuts off himself from his brotherhood, passes over to the secular bloc, deals with those trying to harm Christ's cause, gives way to his pacts, writes his decrees and does whatever enemies want, is all so impossible to believe it could happen at the first flash of temptation; for it cannot happen unless the divine ministry is abused, and until the heart has been opened to the devil and he has been given complete possession of the soul, by the intense desire to steal; that is when the fierce enemy enchants the soul at its pleasure and drags it to all extremes of evil, so that it will no longer be possible for it to unite with the disciples of Christ, but precisely with his enemies, to sell him and deliver him." It must be that self-interest, ambition and evil extinguish in his intellect and in his heart all the lights of eternal truth, and the darkness of the most horrible night is diffused upon his soul, in consequence of which he neither sees his downgraded honour nor the desecration of his order, or the violation of his oaths, or the deformity of the sin he commits; neither does he see the beauty of the grace he loses, nor heaven which is now closed for him, or hell which instead opens its doors; or Christ delivered to his enemies, or his soul being sold; but let him throw himself into the midst of this horrendous darkness and dread, to all the dangers and misfortunes into which the devil, now the absolute owner of his soul, wants to cast him. But in order to prevent so much ruin in the Church, in the apostolate and in souls, Saint Paul warns us: *Do not give the devil the chance to enter your heart* (Eph 4:27). About which the Venerable Bede says: "There are many who are horrified to contemplate Judas' wickedness, but very few who hasten to avoid falling into it. For whoever despises the rights and duties of charity, sells and gives himself to Christ, who is the fullness of charity."

CHAPTER 73
JESUS CHRIST SENDS TWO OF HIS DISCIPLES TO JERUSALEM TO PREPARE ALL THAT IS NECESSARY TO CELEBRATE THE PASSOVER

OWEVER vivid Judas' eagerness was to deliver Jesus Christ into the hands of his enemies, he could not fail from remaining in his company up to when the expected right time arrived. He was still in Jesus Christ's company when he called two of his disciples, Peter and John, and sent them to Jerusalem to prepare everything necessary for the celebration of the Passover; he wanted to celebrate it with them on that day as it was to be the last in his life. The time of mercies was pressing on and the Lord of them all was willing to save his people; not with gold and silver which can decay though being precious metals, but with the invaluable treasure of his most precious blood. He wanted to celebrate with his disciples a very significant supper before being separated from them by death; it was to be an immemorial and perennial sign of his love, in which to contemplate the mysteries that were about to be fulfilled. This supper was foreshadowed in the loaves of proposition which Abimelech offered to David; but it was on a much larger scale and much more magnificent, for what happened in it was incomparably much greater. To understand it well, it is necessary to note that the Passover began in Jerusalem for the Galileans at three o'clock in the afternoon, and the day on which the Pasch began was called the first day of fasting; on this day and from the mentioned hour until sunset the priests were busy killing and flaying within the enclosure of God's house the lambs which each family grabbed to that place, to eat, according to the rituals prescribed by the Law. This day was the fourteenth day of the first month, that is a Thursday and the vigil of the Passover, when the lamb was eaten.

Jesus Christ, who by his family name and place of birth was a member of the tribe of Judah, and who also by virtue of his abode, family and choice of domicile was considered to be a Galilean, could himself choose either the day appointed for foreigners, or the next day when the inhabitants of Judea and Jerusalem had to fulfil their solemnity. But Jesus Christ, who knew that on the very day when the Jews were to eat the Paschal Lamb he had to breathe his last breath on the cross and substitute in his person the figure with reality, opted for the day of the Galileans. And so did his apostles, who all resided or had their origins in Galilee, and had no doubt about their Master in whom they saw their Family Father, desired him to preside over the celebration of the feast. Saint Matthew wants us to notice that the apostles invited Jesus Christ and asked him where he wanted them to prepare for him to eat the Passover (Mt 26:17; and Saint Luke is the one who tells us that Peter and John were the disciples who had been sent (Lk 22:8). The Lord heard his disciples' remark, and as master of all things and as the One who indeed had perfect knowledge of all that was about to happen, ordained them to go to Jerusalem, and assured them that at the city gate they would find a man carrying a pitcher of water. They were then to follow him, entering the house to which he went; there they would meet its owner, to whom they had on their part to say: "The Master, whose disciples we are, knowing that his hour is drawing near, has sent us to ask for your room where he could celebrate the Passover with us today. There he will actually show you a very large room adorned with all that is required to furnish a table, and in it you will prepare all that is necessary to eat the Paschal Lamb." The two disciples set off without delay, and having found everything as they had been told, prepared and arranged all that was necessary for them all to celebrate that feast.

The Venerable Bede says of this place: "Since the disciples had prepared the room for the celebration of the Passover, a man carrying a pitcher of water came to meet them, to show that on that Passover day the sins of the world were going to be blotted away. Water means washing by grace, and the pitcher means the fragility of those for whom grace itself was one day to be delivered to the world." Jesus Christ came to them telling them, *the Master says*, to show that the man who had to provide them with the place, was also one of Christ's disciples, although a hidden one, and for this reason he was not only providing them with a room, but also with a lamb and all that was necessary; which shows Christ's extreme poverty, he who had no abode, no room, nor anywhere from where to buy what was necessary for the celebration of the Passover. for which reason he concludes that he was asked by the disciples *where was the place to eat at the Passover to be prepared for him*. Only a God made man, for whom nothing is hidden and who knew future things as clearly as if occurring right, now could have given such orders so assuredly. The two apostles whom the Lord had ordered, who knew him well and had placed their full trust in him, set out at once not querying anything they had been told by their Master. They walked hastily to the city and found everything as Jesus Christ had told them. Having prepared the room they went to the temple, had the ordained victims sacrificed in it, brought up the Paschal Lamb, bought the wide lettuce, provided themselves with unleavened bread, and finally gave orders to have the lamb roasted, so that everything was ready by the time Jesus Christ entered the room with the other apostles.

CHAPTER 74
HE SITS FOR THE CUSTOMARY DINNER WITH HIS APOSTLES, AND DECLARES THAT ONE OF THEM WAS ABOUT TO SELL HIM AND HAND HIM OVER

IT was at about seven in the evening when the Lord arrived with his apostles at the prepared room, namely, on the holy and sublime Mount Zion where he had to eat the Passover. The meaning given by many Church Fathers and Doctors to the Cenacle is that it is a place where high and grand mysteries occur. It was the place where Jesus Christ's disciples hid after his resurrection because of their fear of the Jews; and also the place where they received the Holy Spirit promised by the Saviour on the holy day of Pentecost. This Mount Zion is a mountain full of justice and holiness, a mountain of abundance, a pleasant mountain, a mountain on which the Lord was pleased to dwell and where he worked the greatest of all miracles; it is also known as a mountain distilling sweet honeycombs, and a flower which pours out a most comforting and pleasant scent, filling the soul when recalled to memory with many sweet consolations, which are impossible to be all remembered and counted unless man has the most religious respect, the most forceful fear and the most vivid love. And so it was on this mountain, or in this cenacle, that Jesus Christ sat at table together with his disciples, in the same order they always kept between them.

Although the rite of eating the Paschal Lamb. according to what God prescribed in the Exodus, was that it should be eaten standing, with staff in hand, girded with belts and wearing outer garments, it is really believed that this was not the case except in the first Passover celebrated in Egypt, when the Jews were to set out to conquer the Holy Land during forty years of tarrying through the desert. So that at the present time being in Jerusalem, which was subject to the Roman Empire, the Jews would have adopted Roman customs and would eat lying on a kind of couch, according to their custom. However, it must be confessed that the *supper according to the Law* in which the Lamb was to be eaten, took place with all the regularity prescribed by the Law, which was proper to the Divine Head presiding over it, since from its very first celebration in the world it was confined to the observance of the Law with utmost and punctual accuracy.

It did not seem regular that at this supper further events took place other than ordinary and customary ones on such occasions; but the last Passover of God made man, before his death, was to be accompanied by truly divine circumstances. Soon after having sat down at table and begun their supper, while conversing together with the freedom which the loving Master gave to his disciples, he cast upon them a look full of goodness and said to them: "In a great way and with a forceful desire I wished to eat this Paschal Lamb with you before suffering, for I assure you that I will not eat any more of it until it is accomplished in the kingdom of God." Which was the same as telling them: "I eat the Paschal Lamb for the last time; the Passover according to the Law is over for me; the time has come when with my death the foundations of my Church are laid, and when with my blood the kingdom of God may be established and strengthened among men. The supper of the Lamb ordained by Moses will be substituted by that of the true Lamb of God who shall be slain for the world's salvation. From now on prefiguring ceases, and the true Passover represented in the old one will be effectively fulfilled by the sacrifice of my life. These are my yearnings from now on in this world, those that have made me sigh for this day as we celebrate this solemnity together."

Having said these words, Jesus Christ filled a cup with wine, gave thanks as was the custom to his Father, and handing it to his disciples, after blessing it he said: "Take it and share it among you, let all partake of it; for truly I say unto you, that from now on I shall drink no more of this wine, nor eat from the fruit of the vine, until that day when I shall drink it again with you in my Father's kingdom." And so it was that he only drank it triumphantly and gloriously in his Church with his disciples; with us who ate and drank with him after he rose from the dead. This is what made him say to Saint John in the mysterious book of the Apocalypse: "Behold, I stand at the door and knock. If anyone hears my voice and opens the door for me, I will come in to him and eat with him, and he with me" (Apoc 3:20). These words uttered by Jesus Christ have another no less mysterious and prophetic meaning: "*I will not drink any more with you of the fruit of the vine as I do in this supper, until the kingdom of God has come;* that is, in this time that is already drawing near, being raised from among the dead, and being declared King by my Father in his heavenly kingdom, which is His Son's Church, even I will drink of the wine in your company, with new joy on my part and renewed happiness on your part; so then the faith of the new life will be still more strengthened in your hearts." At their Master's order they all drank from the cup, with the purpose and awe which his words had suggested to them. Judas had no fear to drink from the cup like all others. They were all extremely moved. Judas also claimed feeling the same emotions as all others; but the traitor was distracted by very different thoughts.

The Lord had said that he had come to set fire to the world, as Saint Luke refers to us (Lk 12:49), and that what he desired was that all would be inflamed with the fire of love which consumed his entrails; and so, not being able to look with indifference at the treacherous under-handedness, blind obstinacy and unprecedented hardness with which the evil Judas had been possessed, grief-stricken as he was he burst out in a loud voice and said: *One of you is the traitor who will hand me over to my enemies: his hand is here with me on this table, and he is here eating with me.* As if he wanted to say: "I am going to be sacrificed; but seeing myself nearing death is not what haunts me most. There is another torment, another bitter remorse which is causing me torture and affliction: were I not to tell you about it, you would not believe it." This warning caused so much horror and pain to the apostles, that not daring to trust themselves or to count on their own faithfulness, they started asking: *Is it me, Lord, perhaps?* But the Saviour only told them that the one was there eating from the same plate with him. He was also assuring them that he was resolved to die, and that this would be fulfilled to the least detail as had been prophesied about the Son of Man in Holy Scripture; but he added: "Wretched is the one who put the detestable act of delivering the Son of Man into effect; *it was better had he not been born.*"

On hearing this they all shuddered, but not the traitor he was addressing who, fearing to be discovered if he did not do like all others, conceitedly and arrogantly asked him: *Is it me by chance, Master?* To which the Lord answered him, not holding back as he did with the others, but clearly: *You have said it.* With all that, he spoke to him in a low voice and with such serene countenance, that not even anyone who was nearest to him could understand, nor did they show any emotion having been overtaken by the fear and horror caused by the offence of which they had just been told, without knowing who the offender was. He wanted to win over this treacherous man this way by freeing him from the dishonour he deserved, and to perform with him, as he later did, one of the most praiseworthy acts of charity and humility ever seen. Although Jesus Christ's answer was final, the apostles did not harbour any suspicion about who the culprit might really be; so that they stopped inquiring any more about something which only Jesus Christ could tell, and always refused to do so.

The most beloved Saviour looked with merciful eyes at this false and hapless disciple, whose soul had been seized by the devil, while at the same time considering that the hour had come in which it was important to reach the peak of the most important event of redemption entrusted to him by his Father. Jesus Christ could not help but see whether he would be able to captivate the heart of him who was so close to being lost for ever, and this forced him to make new efforts to see if he could win him back.

CHAPTER 75
HE WASHES THE FEET OF HIS APOSTLES

AT the end of the supper ordained by Law, he stood and proceeded to the table, took off his cloak or upper clothes, and girded himself with a linen cloth or towel. Pouring water into a washbasin, and prostrating himself at the feet of his apostles, he began washing their feet. It was indeed an accepted custom among the Jews to wash themselves once before sitting at table; and when they celebrated the Passover, they practised this act a few times, but they never washed their feet, and certainly not by such holy hands as those now used in this ministry. He washed them and wiped them with the linen or towel with which he had girded himself, for he wanted his own to be perfectly clean since he was preparing them for a new banquet, all so heavenly and divine and requiring extraordinary purity like that of the angels. And he prepared them briefly to preach the Gospel of peace, humility and love. So it was that the Lord was seen at the feet of the servants, the King at those of his vassals, the Master at those of the disciples, and the Creator at the feet of his creatures, including those of the most vile and contemptible of them all. He who is seated above the cherubim and has the heavens themselves as his own carpet, was seen blended with earth's dust; and the God of majesty, greatness and holiness was seen prostrated before the most unclean and lowly feet which ever trod on earth.

The first one towards whom the Lord walked to pay this compliment was Simon Peter, the chosen one to lead the holy apostolic college and his vicar on earth; and it was right for him to show the distinction he made for the first of his disciples. Yet being taken over by fear and brimming with confusion, the apostle drew himself back and exclaimed, "What now indeed, Lord, that you want to wash my feet! How would you do this to me, Jesus Christ to Peter, the Son of God to a sinful man!" Jesus Christ did not condemn such righteous great affections and feelings;

yet he was bound to carry out that mystery even if at that time none of those present understood its meaning. And so he said to him: "You can neither know nor understand what I am doing now; yet you will know soon enough; this is nothing more than preparing for a higher purpose which you also have later to fulfil; then I will explain the mystery to you." Peter was not convinced by his Master's prudent excuses, and resisted with greater tenacity, so much so that Jesus Christ had to urge him with new fervour; and so, clothed with his almighty authority, he now not only ordained, but also had to threaten for, as the Venerable Bede says: "On another occasion Peter had already shown his pettiness and misery before Jesus Christ telling him, *Leave me, Lord, for I am a sinful man*; and in another he had confessed and recognised him *as the Christ son of the living God*; and he knew that he was the God of gods, the King of angels, the Son of the Most High, the spotless mirror of God's majesty, and the true image of his Father's goodness; that it was him whom angels and all heavenly powers worship, before whom bow all those who by his order sustain the weight of the whole world, and before whom all the creatures of heaven, earth, and the underworld bend their knees." For which reason it was even necessary at a certain point for Jesus Christ to threaten him, telling him: *If you resist and do not allow me to wash your feet, you will have nothing to do with me;* that is, "I exonerate you from the dignity of my discipleship, and you will not partake of the grace to which I destine you."

Peter knew well the profound example of humility which his Master gave him on this occasion; but he could not understand the main reason for this dejection and mysterious ceremony, which was not only a lesson of spiritual humility, but more particularly one of sincerity and purity of heart. It was portrayed in the symbol of the washing and cleaning of the feet, as a required preparation for the great Sacrament for which he was to make the apostles co-participants, a perpetual sacrifice in his Church, the heavenly bread of his children, and a source of purity, healing, and grace. And though he did not go deep into so many secrets, Peter yielded to Jesus Christ's will to avert his warning, and said: "Oh Lord! as this involves the loss of your grace, which is the only benefit I esteem, I yield to you and wholly subject myself in all to your will; do to me whatever you will, and wash me, *not only my feet, but hands, head and my whole body*." He was thus clearly stating that he was ready to undergo anything so long as he did not incur any adversity or be deprived of any blessing. To all this the Saviour could not but reply that what he was offering to do was not required; since having washed before supper, according to custom, they should all be considered as having come out of a bath, but those who had already washed face and body, had only to fulfil this same requirement as to their feet, which was what they only lacked to be perfectly clean. This was the same as if it had been said to them: "Having been purified by the graces you have received from me, your conscience is clear; but it is necessary to use this precaution and remedy against imperfections and faults which human weakness almost cannot avoid." He thus showed them what purity was expected of those who wished to share the heavenly table, of which they could not become worthy if they did not first purify their soul of the slightest stains, as symbolised by the dust sticking to their feet.

It was awful for Peter to hear Jesus Christ's answer, and he feared losing his Master's grace and friendship, of being excluded from the apostolate, and of becoming unworthy of deserving new favours; so he immediately submitted himself to all of Jesus Christ's designs as to his will, without showing any resistance to him at all. There was one thing, however, which Jesus Christ further said to them, and this must have greatly dismayed Judas. He told them: *You are quite clean, but not all*; thus implying that he knew the plans and secret hatchings of that evil disciple, to whom he gave these reflections and warnings from time to time, to compel him to be aware of his offence and to detest it.

Jesus Christ washed everyone's feet, most especially those of Judas who would very soon run along the paths of wickedness and perdition and cause his precious blood to be shed; those were the feet which, as several exponents say with regret, the Lord washed with tearful eyes rather than with the water he had in the washbasin; he pressed them hard against his heart, so that hearing the beats of his love Judas might desist from his criminal venture. After having done with the washing of the feet he put on his garments, and sitting once more at the table he said to them: "*You have already seen what I have just done with you. You call me Master and Lord, and you say well, for I really am. Learn, then, from me, you who are my servants and disciples: learn how to practise humility, for if I am your Lord and Master, I have knelt down and humbled myself to the point of washing your feet; much more so you must perform this with one another, for the servant is not greater than the master, nor the apostle greater than the One who sent him. This is a truth which I have repeated to you over and over again, because it is very important that you believe it. Happy are those who put it into practice.*"

CHAPTER 76
EUCHARISTIC SUPPER, OR INSTITUTION OF THE BLESSED SACRAMENT OF THE EUCHARIST

HESE words, inspiring an ardent expression of true love, uttered by Jesus Christ just after his anointing, could not but enflame the apostles' heart. They were looking at Jesus Christ's lips with their sight fixed on him to observe most scrupulously even his tiniest and most unimportant actions, eagerly desiring that Jesus Christ would continue with his speech to see if they could understand the great mysteries which he was humbly announcing to them. So, seeing that they were eager to satisfy their cravings, he said to them: "Not all of you, my disciples, will be faithful and blessed. I know you intimately; I know well who are those I have chosen to be my apostles, and none of them is hidden from me. I also know that you will soon see the Prophet's prediction fulfilled, when he said, *He who eats with me, that friend with whom I share my bread, has raised his foot against me to make me fall, he has laid snares for me and superseded me.* It is in me that David's words are fulfilled." Which was like saying: "The betrayals made against this King of Israel by his sons or by his subjects, were only a symbol of what one of my disciples is hatching against me. So that in a strict literal sense, this would fulfil a prediction that personally characterises the Messiah. I warn you of this so that when you see my prediction being fulfilled, you may believe in me and start recognising me for who I am. Confirm yourselves in the faith in which I have instructed you, and do not ever let the hope in your heart waver; for of the state of pain through which you will very soon see me going through must precisely confirm what I have told you, as it cannot be hidden from you that I have foreseen all, accepted all and prophesied all."

"Do not grieve over this or believe that despite the rage of my enemies and a traitor's fierceness which would put me in their hands, I will desist from protecting you; for I will always be with you, repeating now what I have already previously promised you. Be assured of my Father's and my assistance, and that we will receive as our own the respectfulness men will show you. For whosoever receives whom I send, would also be receiving me, and whoever receives me receives my Father who sent me." These divine lessons of profound humility, of a perfect purity of heart and of a respectful charity towards his brethren, prepared the apostles admirably for the heavenly banquet which Christ wanted to institute. The time during which the institution of the sacrament of love was delayed looked like taking ages; but given the sacred text in Saint John's Gospel (Jn 13:21), it looks like Jesus Christ wanted to act with some caution. Judas's presence was important to him, although he was joyfully abandoning himself to be gladly delivered to his enemies and to redeem the world. Yet he feared exchanging his body and blood in the sacrament of his love to an unfaithful disciple, and of giving him the power to consecrate him. And it seems that there was no reason why the divine mysteries and the priesthood of the New Testament should enter the Church with the desecration made by a sacrilegious apostle whom, although Jesus Christ had sought to convert was unable to satisfy his most loving heart's desires.

Nor was Jesus Christ unaware that the time had come when he was to pass from this world to the Father; for as a unique victim worthy of God, the Lamb of God was running to his sacrifice, without intending either to stop or to hinder this event from happening. He looked around him, at those he had chosen to be preachers of his Gospel and founders of the kingdom of God on earth. He had always loved them tenderly but in the end, at the instant when he was preparing to be separated from them, he wanted to give them proof of a greater and more tender love. He recorded the immense secrets of his power and wisdom and found in them very effective means to reconcile his absence, which was equally necessary and glorious, when his disciples became orphaned; a small flock, which seemed to be abandoned and exposed to all the dangers of the world and the persecutions of its enemies. So in order to encourage, console and comfort them, he said to them: *Do not be afraid, I am with you until the end of times: I will not leave you orphaned, neither unprotected nor without reward. I have prepared for you a kingdom the same as my Father has prepared for me, so that in it you may eat and drink at my table and be seated on thrones to judge the twelve tribes of Israel.* Indeed, words so replete with consolation could not but flatter the apostles' hearts, seeing that they were to be admitted not only to the new and mysterious banquet that was prepared for the Church, but in that which he promised in the new kingdom. It was also because under the symbol of the thrones they were about to be vested with a spiritual authority to govern and instruct, to condemn and to absolve, to retain and forgive sins, and to consecrate and offer eternally to God the pure and excellent sacrifice of the New Testament, of which they and their successors in the priesthood were to be sole ministers until the end of times.

Such great thoughts could not be born other than in a soul as unique and generous as that of a Man-God, nor could they take flesh except with the greatest of miracles of his infinite power. When all were seated at table, Jesus Christ, who performed the role of Father of families, took a loaf of unleavened bread, which was free of the yeast which according to Jewish custom should be in it, during the supper of the Lamb and, holding it in his hands, gave thanks to his Father for the immense power He had entrusted to him over all nature. Such power which was useless without thinking of leaving to his Church a symbol and figure of his body and blood, the appearance of a sacrifice and the shadow of a priesthood. He blessed the bread, broke it, and gave it to his disciples, saying: *"Take and eat; this is my body. The same one I will be delivering unto death, and which from this instant onwards is offered in sacrifice as it will be offered throughout all ages."*

On the night of great suffering the bread of the strong is prepared; on the eve of the passion its perpetual memory is instituted; in both one and the other Christ's infinite charity shines out. The Saviour catches sight of the joys and delights of the world's banquets with the sadness of this supper in which he sees his ordeal to be so close. God is dishonoured by those excessive vents of passion that are so frequent at the tables of friends. Here at this table is a small picture of the Catholic Church, an intermingling of the good, the faltering and the bad, united in the outward profession of the same faith, and in the participation of the same Sacraments. In what is outwardly seen, there has not and apparently never been in the world a gathering more equal or more united than that of those who ate at this table. Yet what a difference exists in God's eyes between the author of life who takes bread to bequeath to all a living memory of his death, and the traitor who had already sold him to hell's ministers! Before distributing it, he gives thanks to his Father and teaches us to prepare ourselves to receive God's gifts, and to use them well; and being so prepared, *he institutes the Sacrifice, the Priesthood and most adorable Sacrament of the Altar of the New Testament.* What should we do, knowing that these so special benefits have been ordained to make us holy? The heart, spirit and mind do indeed pass out as they contemplate them.

This is my body, Jesus Christ says, *which will be delivered for you.* Oh, what tender words! Oh, what sweet words! Oh holy words, worthy of being heard with utmost love and appreciation! Oh most effective words like those that came out of the mouth of God Himself in the days of creation! *The Lord spoke and all he said was done; he ordered it and all was created. This is my body,* Jesus Christ said, and the substance of the bread immediately transformed itself into the real and true substance of the body of Jesus Christ. These healthy, dignified, awful words justify the faith of the Catholic Church about Jesus Christ's real presence in the Eucharist; they encapsulate within them the foundation of Christian worship, the institution of the New Testament, the pact of the true covenant, the testament of a Father who dies that his children may live. By this new institution the sacrifices of the Old Testament cease, the shadows clear away and the truth takes hold of the figures. Since he was God, Jesus Christ created bread to feed our bodies, and now transubstantiates it into his own body to nourish our souls and to transform us into himself. Let us admire and revere this darkness and humiliation with which Christ worked the greatest of all miracles. There is nothing more plain and simple in appearance than what the Lord does here; but there is also no higher and more wonderful work in the eyes of faith. By instituting the Eucharist in the Cenacle, the Lord anticipated the sacrifice of his death, only that he was to consummate it on Calvary; by allowing himself to be killed on the cross to give life to the world, he wanted that gruesome sacrifice to continue all over the earth through the bloodless one that is celebrated on our altars, and that is why he said: *Do this in memory of me.*

What Jesus Christ did in transforming the bread into his body, he repeated doing in transmuting the substance of the wine into his blood. Everything is new, remarkable and prodigious in these mysterious operations, although performed under common and perceptive elements and symbols. He then took the cup or chalice in his hand and, saying his blessing as he had done before with the bread, he passed it in the hands of the apostles, saying to them: *Drink ye from it all: this is the chalice of the New Testament in my blood, for which I make a New Testament with men, and it will be poured out for you and for many others, that it may be in remission of all sins.* Here we have a summary of our most holy religion, man's covenant with God confirmed with the blood of the Man-God. As long as religion remains on earth, which will be until the end of the world, and as long as this covenant, which has only just begun, is being fulfilled over the ages, it is inevitable that this blood also remains on earth, really present for those entering into the covenant. May it be offered to God, and may its sprinkling become a means of communion in the hearts of Christians, wherever this pact is celebrated. This is the perpetual remembrance which Christ commanded us to perform of his sacred passion and death, announcing it up to the day of his coming. So that we are certain that the Church will never lack a sacrifice with which to placate God, and that the Eucharist will subsist until the second coming of Christ, in which the whole Church will be renewed by participation in his glory; and united to him as to its head, it will offer for him, with him and in him this sacrifice; and it will partake in him feeding itself on uncreated truth, which is the bread and the life of the elect.

Ancient sacrifices authorised by the Law of Moses, while useful in the situation and circumstances in which the Jewish people found themselves, were not instituted to last eternally. They were very imperfect and ineffective elements to sanctify men and purify souls and spirits, so that Saint Paul said about them: "What matters above all is to strengthen the heart with grace, not by those foods which have been of no benefit to those who took them in trust. We have an altar or a victim that is Jesus Christ's same body, which those who serve at the tabernacle cannot eat" (Heb 13:9-10). These were the men who believed themselves bound to observe the Old Testament, which forbade eating of the victim in the sacrifice of atonement; so that, all of the Jews' victims, sacrifices and offerings should cease before this new sacrifice, and darkness disappears with the presence of light, as announced by the prophets. It was through one of them that the Lord expressly said to his people: "I have no pleasure in you, nor can you please me, and I will not accept an offering from your hand. Your sacrifices are not acceptable to me. For from the east to the west my name is great among the peoples and nations; and in every place incense and a clean and pure offering shall be offered to my name" (Mal 1:10-11). So that what was announced so long before the coming of Christ was verified in the institution of this most dignified and adorable Sacrament which is to subsist, according to Christ's promise, until the end of times; his flesh being true food and his blood being true drink, so that whoever eats of his flesh and drinks of his blood may be united to Christ, and this ineffable Lord may be also truly united to him. This is the great and mysterious significance of those words with which Jesus Christ announced in advance this so admirable transubstantiation, saying: *The bread that I will give you is my flesh, which will be given for the life of the world.* So it was that the disciples, apostles, the first faithful, pastors, ministers, sages and doctors of Christianity, and finally so many men eminent in wisdom and virtue, all enlightened by God and flourishing in the Church since its foundation, have understood what the Saviour said; it is the same way as the Roman Catholic Church understands it today, witnessing to Jesus Christ's real presence in the adorable sacrament of the Eucharist. From all of which it is inferred that the dogma of transubstantiation is not a new dogma or a mere invention of some gullible doctors, but that it draws its origin and institution from the same author of the Sacraments; it is a perpetually and constantly believed article of faith in the universal Church, and is a main and fundamental article which if a man fails to believe in it he cannot attain eternal salvation.

CHAPTER 77
CHRIST MAKES SEVERAL IMPORTANT THINGS CLEAR, AND MAKES FERVENT SUPPLICATIONS TO HIS ETERNAL FATHER

N the one hand the apostles were sad, afflicted and dismayed, hearing Jesus Christ announce his nearing death to them, and on the other they appeared to be somewhat comforted with the pleasing promises he had made to them. At the same time the divine Saviour had his heart full of bitterness and he could not see, without bearing excessive pain and inexplicable sorrow, his most holy body being received in the hands of a traitor who had already sold him. The sight of such horrible sacrilege forced him to sigh once more against the treachery that was about to be carried out on him, and he spoke again about it to his apostles with much more heartfelt words than those he had previously uttered; and although it is true that no passion could cause the slightest disturbance in his spirit, he was nevertheless so seized by the sadness of his heart that he was totally moved and perturbed; and the One who makes heaven tremble, the earth shake and disturb hell, shuddered with horror, either to show us the gravity of the crime, or to let us know the revulsion he felt by sighing against the infidelity of one of his own, and perhaps he also wanted to teach us how careful we ought to be not to talking about others' faults when we can hide them, inasmuch as these were likewise acted out by those who so much condemned them. So leaving all the unease of his soul show on his countenance, and possessed by great sadness, he said to his disciples: *Truly I tell you and I assure you again and again, that one of you will be giving me up.* This was a second warning for Judas, bit still it was not understood. The others looked at each other, seeking an answer by looking in each other's eyes, but also examining themselves while doing so. If their mind thought of suspecting anyone, they dismissed it to the point of rashness. Judas remained blind in his obstinacy without anything making him change his intent, which was that of

reaching the peak of his misery. Peter was tired of finding himself in such a cruel state of uncertainty. All knew what he loved about his Master; this was already the third time he heard him speak of a coward who wanted to become a traitor, and that he was numbered among the twelve apostles; so nothing was enough to silence him and hold him back; however, he was restrained because he observed that Jesus Christ never named the traitor, although he so bitterly sighed about his betrayal.

Jesus Christ's discretion held back Peter's boldness, and although he did not yield his love for his sovereign Master to anyone else, he dared not directly ask him a question to satisfy his curious anxiety. He had before him the beloved disciple reclining over Jesus Christ's left side with such great familiarity that only Jesus Christ's kindness and his dignified state could allow this to happen. So Peter and John reclining next to each other, Peter signalled him to secretly inquire who was the one about to deliver him. Since John was within hearing distance of his Master and had his heart, he took the liberty of asking him who that wicked man might be; and the Saviour answered that it was him to whom he would give a morsel of bread dipped in his plate. After this Jesus Christ took without fuss a morsel of bread, dipped it and gave it to Judas; and Judas received it and ate it. After taking this morsel the devil began to shake him and move him with hellish fury; he had no other concern but that of finding some pretext to leave the table and go to complete his betrayal. He might have hoped that the night darkness would cover him well in his escape, or that when the supper was over Jesus Christ would retire to pray. But Jesus Christ, who had designs to fulfil, in which he did not want to have an apostate for a witness, offered him the occasion he was expecting, saying: *What you have to do, go and so do it.* Only the beloved disciple could understood the meaning of these words; but none of those present grasped their meaning; and the most some could make out of it was that, since Judas kept the money offered out of charity by the faithful for their provisions, the Lord commanded him to go to make some purchase for the Passover, or to give some alms to the poor. The wicked one then departed from

Jesus Christ's company, without the favours or caresses of such a kind Master having been able to soften his heart. Jesus Christ let him go as a condemned and sick sheep which could only serve to infect others.

After Judas had departed from the Cenacle, Jesus Christ said to his disciples: "Now the Son of Man will be illuminated and exalted, and God will be glorified by him. And since God will be glorified in him, he will also glorify him in Himself, raising him from the dead, and will then exalt him by seating him on his right hand in heaven. My little children, for a short time I will still be with you. This same night my enemies will take me away from you to lead me to death. You will look for me; but as I said on another occasion to the Jews, *where I go you cannot come*; I repeat it now to you." These words which Jesus Christ uttered were brief, yet forceful and affectionate. One discovers the great dignity of the person who utters them and the character of a God made man, superior to all men; in them one admires the heroic strength and tranquillity of his soul being sure that very soon he would have to be delivered into the hands of his enemies, and to a most cruel and disgraceful death. It reveals how he foretells to his disciples, with the greatest peace of mind and cold blood, the events of his passion and all that he foresees happening, and the weakness and faintheartedness of the apostles in their shameful flight and in abandonment at the time of his greatest anguish. But at the same time the tenderness he shows them also shines out in instructing and promising them comforts with the coming of the Holy Spirit, and by the affectionate way in which he entrusts them to his Father. And to encourage them even more and spur them on in the midst of the persecutions which awaited them, he said to them: "I give you a new commandment, which is to mutually love one another as I have loved you. By this all will know that you are my disciples, if they see that after I go from among you, brotherly harmony prevails among you which distinguishes your fellowship as a great family, with an already glorified head awaiting the rest of its body members in glory's dwelling place." In these, the children of God and the children of the devil are and will be manifest, for anyone who does not do justice and does not love his brother, is not of God; for this is a summary of the preaching, the doctrine I have heard from the beginning, that we love each other. And since we have known the love of the Son of God who laid down his life for us, so too must we lay down our lives for our brothers and sisters" (1 Jn 3:11-16).

Jesus Christ had told his apostles that he was leaving, and this sad thought was of great worry to them, but he had further told them that where he was going they could not go. Peter, conceiving that there was not in the world so difficult a pathway along which he could walk and follow him, so replied to him and said: "Lord, why can I not follow you now? I am resolved I am ready to die; I will risk my life for you." Jesus Christ answered him: "Will you risk your life for me? Truly, truly, I tell you, the rooster shall not crow before you have denied me three times, as if I were someone you had never met." If Peter had understood his Master's words well and regarded them as a most certain prediction of a very close event, there is no doubt that he would have died suddenly, but he heard them as a threat of precaution made in order to keep him careful and vigilant. It was to no avail that Peter was no less confident of his heart's alleged fearlessness; and being assured by the conceited testimony which he himself gave in his current temper, he did not want to fear the future. Jesus Christ had sufficiently forewarned him; so letting him praise himself for his zeal, he continued with his speech.

"Do not be afraid," he said to them. "Let not your heart be troubled. If you believe and trust in God, you must also believe and trust in me. In my Father's house there are many mansions and dwellings. If it was not so, I would not have told you I am going, and that I anticipate preparing the seat and place suiting each one of you. You must believe that I am not only the Messiah and God's envoy, but also God made man, the mediator of the New Testament, the chief and prince of all relations and religion between God and men. I shall not delve any further into this matter of your belief, for I have already given you the necessary instructions on other occasions. If I now depart, it is not to leave you forever. I will walk away and I will return; it would do you well to know, at your life's last instant, that you prosper with me, so that you may be where I am. Anyone who dedicates himself to my service, does not tire in following me, for wherever I am there must also be whoever serves me. So be faithful in fulfilling your obligation, so that I will be faithful in keeping my word. Now you must know where I am going, and know the path which leads to the end."

The apostles should have no doubt about what the sovereign Master had just announced to them. A hundred times did he preach to them that he was returning to his Father; that heaven was the aim of their passing lives on earth; that faith in his divinity, partaking in his merits and abiding by his laws, would be the way which would henceforth lead to his divine dwelling and to the exclusion of ancient ceremonies and Moses' imperfect cult. The Lord had the right to speak to his disciples in the manner they would understand him, so that being instructed as they were, they would not change anything or with all that they would even alter them, but they were not to understand them well until they received the Holy Spirit. It is at this point that Thomas immediately said to Jesus Christ: "Lord, if we do not know where you are going, how can we know the path we should follow? Then Jesus Christ gave him this remarkable answer: *I am the way, the truth and the life.* The path that leads straight to the truth, and the truth that infallibly leads to eternal life. The path you must take, the truth you must believe, and the life you must live. Walk after me, follow my councils and doctrines, and you will so come straight to my Father, *for no one goes to the Father unless it is through me.* That is, through a living faith which is a gift and which cannot be attained except through me; which is yet achieved by anyone seeking it, as it is not denied to any person. The difficulty you have of knowing my Father arises from the fact that you have never known me well; for had you known the Son well, you would likewise have known the Father, for the Son is intimately united with the Father, and he is perfectly like Him in everything and for all. But from now on you will soon know him, you will see Him and you will know who He is, by virtue of the lights and wisdom which the Holy Spirit will pour out upon you."

Jesus Christ's words caused new difficulties for the apostles. They had still not risen to the height of that faith, in which they were to believe and preach the idea of God subsisting in three persons truly distinct from each other, of whom One became man. For this reason Philip, who could not understand what Jesus Christ was thinking, took the liberty of saying to him: "*Lord, do that we see the Father; this grace we ask of you will be enough for us to be fully comforted.*" "Well indeed, Philip," the Saviour replied, "after having been with you for so long, have you not known me? Where is your faith? Do you not know that those who are enlightened with supernatural and divine lights, and see me with the eyes of faith, cannot see me without seeing my Father in me? So why do you tell me to show Him to you? Are not my deeds and my words enough to convince you of this truth? More than the human nature subsisting in a divine person who speaks, who works and converses with you, I also have the same divine nature as my Father, which is however invisible to your mortal eyes other than when it is shown in my workings and miracles. *The Father, who dwells in me, is the One who works the wonders which you see me doing*; namely that it is not by my purely human power by which I perform miracles; I am the Son, and the much beloved Son; I ask Him, and my Father performs them with his almightiness, even though this almightiness is common to both of us as the divine nature. *And if my words are not enough for you to believe fully in me, my works confirm them, for them you must believe me. Truly indeed, I tell you, that whoever believes in me, the works which I do he will also do, and even greater ones than these and more extraordinary ones.* So the faithful disciple will hold within him this comfort, enjoy this privilege, and in my name make use of it. This is actually promising a great amount to faithful servants but I do not promise anything which one day the whole world will not see with admiration. I go to my Father, from whom as Man-God and as the Only Son of God, I will receive all power in heaven and on earth. *I go to the Father, and whatever you ask in my name* with living faith and firm trust, *I will give unto you*, that the Father may be glorified in the Son; likewise *what you ask of the Father in my name*, for my merits, do not have the slightest doubt, *I will grant it to you.*

"Yet you, my disciples, have to prove that you return my love and that you truly love me; in no way can you justify this any better, than by putting into practice the principles which I have taught you, no matter how great the difficulties you would have to overcome: do not let yourselves to be overcome by work or fear, nor should you grieve for my absence: *I will pray to my Father, and He will give you another Comforter and Master so that he may remain with you for ever*; namely, the Holy Spirit; the Spirit of truth who cannot be received by those who are guided by the spirit of the world, for they are not disposed to see and know him. This divine Spirit is so good that in truth he also communicates his true wisdom. Those people among whom you live, that rebellious Judaism which persecutes me, that infidel Synagogue which represses me, does not know or want it, and is prepared to cast it away. Earthly matters occupy and alienate them, and so they do not walk among those belonging to heaven; but you will be acquainted with this divine Spirit and taste his sweetness, because he will be poured into your souls, dwell in them as in his temple, as in his paradise and as on his throne, and fill them with so many delights, graces and intelligence, that you will come to have a very clear knowledge of my attributes and perfections.

"I do not feel like leaving you alone in the world, orphaned and abandoned. I will come again to you and I will be in your company for a little while, and the world will not see me; but you will see me, for I will be alive and you will live. I have a real fatherly love for you, and I will not abandon you. It is true that the world which does not take me into account but under this external appearance which is subject to the senses, will very soon lose me from its sight; but you who have this more penetrating sight and who look at me more with the eyes of the soul than with those of the body, will always have me present in your spirit. The world, immersed in temporal goods. leads an animal life that can be called true death; but those like you who seek a life superior to the senses, a fully spiritual life, which death cannot snatch away, you and them will live for ever. I have the power to leave life; and in spite of those who think they have taken it from me, I will recover it. I want to deliver myself to the fury of my enemies; but I know how to defend you from their abuse. I will not let them do to you what I myself will be suffering. I will keep your life that I may return to see you and talk to you again after I will triumph over death. Then you will know three essential truths which I have preached to you today, and which you do not understand, not even imperfectly. You will understand that I am in the Father by communication of the same nature; that you are in me by communication of the same nature; that you are in me by communication of my merits, and that I am in you by impression of my spirit. *He who has my commandments and keeps them, he is the one who loves me; and he who loves me will be loved by my Father: I will also love him and I will manifest myself to him*, communicating to him the treasures of divine wisdom."

Jesus Christ's speech so admirably inflamed the apostles' hearts, that they all humbled themselves and were confounded seeing him give such a correct answer as to strike them with every word he said. Judas, bearing the familiar name Thaddeus and who was brother of James, was so amazed with what he had just heard, that he could not help but say to his Master: "Why, Lord, do you hide yourselves from worldly beings, and deign to manifest yourself to us?" And the Lord answered him: "*It is since for those who love me and keep my commandments, my Father will love them, and we will come to them, and we will establish our abode and dwelling in them*. On the contrary, those who do not love me, despise what I tell them and do not care about what I command them. This will not happen to you: I have hidden nothing from you from what I learned within my Father's bosom to communicate to you, from which you will receive perfect wisdom. When I have told you, I said it to you as my Father's envoy to be your doctor and Master. These are the things, and this is the doctrine that I have spoken to you while I was with you. Take care to keep them in your memory, so that when you are enlightened from high above, you will see that I have not concealed anything from you. The Holy Spirit, whom the Father will send in my name, will teach you all; he will remind you what I have said to you, and he will instruct you to discover the meaning of all the truths and mysteries which I have preached to you. He will come for this purpose, and you will admire within yourselves his perfect works; your conviction and joy will lie in seeing his teachings conform with my doctrine; nothing can then disturb you or hold you back on the path you have started walking; wait for these blissful moments and console yourselves in my absence, for your sorrow must not last for long.

"The time of my departure is near; for which reason, as a most precious legacy, I leave you peace, my peace I give unto you, not as the world gives it do I give it to you." That which I leave to you and give unto you is the basis of the happiness that man can enjoy on earth; it is the fruit of the Holy Spirit and also of justice; it is very much the kingdom of God which abides within us, which, according to the Apostle, consists in justice, peaceful living and joy, in the Holy Spirit, and is like a consequence of the quietude, order and calmness of vehement passions, this being a supreme good which the world cannot give. "Let not your heart be troubled, intimidated or frightened. You have heard how I have told you that I shall be departing and leaving you; I have also further said that I will return to you; yet it seems to me that it is in vain I promise you to return, for I know that you grieve quietly thinking that you are without me on earth. If the love you have for me makes you desire what you deem as most convenient, you have no cause but to rejoice that I depart and go to my Father, with regard to whom I am, as a man, inferior in dignity and perfection; but who wants to give me so much more honour, of which I have received very little from the world. I tell you before it happens, so that when it would have happened, you may believe and understand that nothing happens to me which I do not foresee, and that I am the Son of God from whom my heavenly Father does not hold back any news or knowledge. I will no longer speak much to you in this mortal flesh; for the prince of this world is coming, that is, the devil, the prince of darkness, stirring up the rabble of the Synagogue to seize me and sentence me to death. He has got nothing to do with me, for I have no sin; and if I want to, it would be easy for me to avoid death. This is for the world to know that I love the Father, and that whatever my Father has commanded me, I do." Which was like telling them: "Were the leaders of the Synagogue to notice well how everything will happen, they would understand that if I am sacrificed and die, this is due to my obedience and not to my power. So see what I had to tell you before separating from you; let us get up now and follow me, for the time has come for me to prepare for the great conflict which awaits me."

Some very serious Gospel scholars believed that Jesus Christ said what still remains of this important speech in another more hidden part of the same house, where the apostles were less disturbed with fear. Others think that they left after the speech, and that the Lord continued with his speech along the way until reaching Gethsemane. However, it seems more plausible that everything happened in the same Cenacle referred to by Saint John where he says: *When Jesus Christ had spoken these words, he went forth with all his disciples to the other part of the torrent valley of Cedron* (Jn 18:1). For it is not normal that such a long and tender sermon, and such a fervent prayer to the Father, are said while walking. As it is very natural that the farewell of the Lord with such beloved disciples was quite detailed, and that even when Jesus Christ says *Let us get up and go*, everyone got up from the table, still, the rest of the sermon would be given or would occur in the same Upper Room while they were about to leave. Be that as it may, it is well worth noting that the Lord himself who has hitherto given them so many reasons to console themselves and rejoice in his death, is now going to exhort them to be constant in their faith and in their love, despite all persecutions and labours. To let them know how necessary it is for them to remain united with him, he makes use of the comparison of the branch, which does not bear fruit or live unless it is united with the vine. The prophets had already called him *the rod of Israel or of the root of Jesse, the bud of righteousness, a famous bud;* and depicted his disciples *as seedlings of the Lord's garden, and as a vineyard planted by the right hand of God.* Thus Jesus Christ, now alluding to these metaphors and to many others relating to farming, says to them: "I am the true vine which feeds its shoots with food and life; that is, the vine which produces the most generous and proper wine to gladden man's heart; a spiritual vine producing the same effects in souls as the sap does to the branches, but in a much nobler way. My Father is the farmer or vintner; as a wise and experienced farmer, he will cut off and separate every branch which does not bear any fruit in me; that is, who belonging to me even by his belief does not bear the fruit of good works; but to those disciples whose life corresponds to faith, he will every day enlighten them with new lights, and he will open for them a more excellent way to perfection, so that their fruit may be more seasoned and abundant."

Further encouraging them he then says: "You are, my disciples, all pure and clean; my Word has sanctified you, and you only need to give yourselves ripe fruits of virtues; and to do this you must understand that you need me as much as the branches need the trunk or vine from which they receive the sap. Keep being united with me, be constant in my love, that on my part I will remain with you by communicating to you my grace and my spirit. Just as the branch cannot bear fruit by itself unless it is assimilated with the trunk or the grapevine, so you cannot do any good or any work of merit worthy of the prize of heaven, if you cease to be united with me. I was worthy of the prize of heaven, but I saw that you ceased being united with me. I am the vine that gives food and life to its offshoots. You are the branches; he who is in me and I in him, bears copious and abundant fruit. If it does not remain in me, it will be a useless and fruitless branch. Without me, and being separated from me, you cannot do anything to give you the advantage of eternal life for its merit, and nothing that by way of justice prepares you to be sanctified. But since you cannot do anything which is good without me, be very careful not to separate yourselves from this principle, that the same does not happen to you as what happens to the branch when it is cut from the vine and becomes dry, and will only be good to be thrown into the fire; since by the same destiny you will, due to this separation, also become dry wood for a fire which will never be extinguished. If you persevere in your union with me, and if my words remain deeply engraved in your souls, you will ask for whatever you want and all will be given to you." Saint John said about this: "Beloved, if our conscience does not rebuke us, let us trust in God, that whatever we will ask of Him we will receive from Him, because we keep His commandments and do what pleases Him" (1 Jn 3:21-22), to which Jesus Christ further added: "My Father is honoured and glorified in this, that you produce much fruit of holy works, and show yourselves worthy disciples of his Son, your Master. I assure you that you will not have much work to do on it; for the Holy Spirit which we will send you will make you capable of being my disciples and will help you to imitate my virtues. To make it easy for you to practise them, he will inspire within you a great love for me. You will undoubtedly be harder and more insensitive than the stones, unless you love Him more tenderly who has loved you with such a tender and affectionate love. As the Father loves me, so also have I loved you. Keep deserving my love; knowing that if you keep my precepts, I will always love you, as my Father does not cease loving me, because I never depart from his most holy will."

Saint John said: "He who keeps Jesus Christ's word and doctrine, love for God is truly perfected in him. He who says that he abides in him, ought to walk and live in the same way in which he walked" (1 Jn 2:5-6). And Jesus Christ further said to his disciples: "All these things I have said to you and I repeat them to you, to find within you the fullness of my joy, and that you may enjoy perfect comfort. Be most attentive to observe the precept of charity and love. Love one another with this pure and spiritual love, of which I have given you such a good example, loving each other until you end up consumed with concern for your salvation. This is my precept and strictly speaking a law which I have made, founded on the intimate union which I have contracted with men. I want perfect charity, and there is no greater love than to give oneself to death for those who love one other. This is the perfection of love, and you will soon know if I love perfectly." On this precept Saint John also tells us: "If anyone says I love God and hates his brother, he is a liar.

Because he who does not love his brother, whom he has seen and with whom he lives in company, how can he love God whom he has not seen?" (1 Jn 4:21-22). And he went on: "You are my friends, and you will always be if you do the things I have commanded you. You well know that I am your Lord and Master; however, I do not want to deal with you as a master deals with his servants; he never tells them of his plans, nor does he reveal family secrets to them, nor does he admit them to his inner thoughts and preferences. I will call you my friends, because I have told you of all the things I hear from my Father, the profound mysteries, and the hidden secrets and councils of His Providence for the foundation and government of the Church, and made them known to you. You did not choose me, but I chose you, and I have planted and formed you to go and bear lasting fruit. Be aware then of this most particular favour which you could not acquire by your labours, nor have it by your merit, nor possess it by your choice."

"Nor should you forget that after having chosen you in this manner and distinguished you from common men, I have given you the first places and seats in my kingdom, I have entrusted to you the direction and conduct of the souls that I have come to rescue with the price of my blood, and I have formed you as teachers and shepherds of peoples, that filled with my doctrine you may spread this heavenly seed throughout the world in the hearts of mortals, that they might bear abundant fruit which may always remain, in spite of the perversion of the age. With this you deserve that my Father grant you all that you ask of Him in my name and for His glory. Do not forget what I command you yet again to know; that you love one another. If the world hates you, know ye that it has hated me, the first and most worthy among you. If you were of the world, if you had followed its core ideas, the world would have loved what is its own. But because you are not of the world, as I had chosen you and separated you from it beforehand, that is why the world detests you." No doubt this was what compelled Saint John himself to say: "My brothers, do not marvel if the world hates you. Consider what great love the Father has shown us in calling ourselves children of God and so we are: this is why the world does not acknowledge us, because it does not know Him. Little children, you are of God; sinners, heretics, fakers, false prophets are of the world; that is why they partake of the world and the world hears them" (1 Jn 4:1-6). "So remember what I told you a short while ago, that the servant is not greater than his master; and so having persecuted me I should not believe they will let you go. If mundane society had followed my council, you could expect them to also follow yours, and if they had heard my word, you could also believe that they would not despise yours; but you know very well that they have done the opposite and that they have abandoned my doctrine. Therefore, do not think that you will find in their hearts greater righteousness, nor in their discernment any greater submissiveness than I found. That notwithstanding, do not fear them, because all the bad things they will do you, the contempt, insults, outrages and all the violence you will undergo, will be done in hatred to my name. They do not want to acknowledge Him who has sent me, so see here why their enmity against me will pass on to you. The cause of your sorrows and labours must comfort you, for merit and glory will result from them."

These lessons which the Saviour gave are all intended to inspire the Apostles and his successors, and to encourage them with his examples, protection and rewards, to fulfil their ministry faithfully, and to abide correctly with their vocation and to prepare them to face up to their enemies' persecutions. "I have chosen you and raised you to the dignity of apostles and co-operators in the foundation of my kingdom. Although relieved of all human help, you will lack nothing so that the seed of the word carefully shed by you, watered with your sweat, and if so necessary with your blood, produces fruitful, abundant and permanent fruits. But you must rely, not on being loved by the world, but on the contrary, on being hated and fought all over the world and everywhere. If you had had a part in my enemies conspiracies and evil plans, and followed the devious principles of worldly politics, and disguised the truth, which is always bitter to mortals, and paid compliments to the powerful, and flattered the ears of wicked men, and sanctioned disordered passions, and preached a lax morality which is accommodating to incite vices, you would be loved by the world and achieve credit, reputation and renown. But the stern truth and evangelical doctrine announced by you with as much freedom as conviction, would put to the forefront your reputation and your life, and there will be a time when anyone who gives you up to death, thinks he would be doing God a pleasure which would raise his very cruelty to great merits. The Jews' blindness will sink so deep that they will not want to recognise in the most sensitive signs neither my Father's testimony, nor respect for me, or confess that I am the Son of God sent for their salvation." All this was like telling them: "They will know their injustices and will boast of their violence; for what is it that you should not expect from a furious people, whose hatred will be armed under the pretext of religion? Masters of deceit and gullible subjects, envious priests and corrupt disciples, all will all be unleashed against you in their own way; but in order not to fear them it will suffice that you agree that your Lord and Master, from whom nothing is hidden, foretold all these things to you one by one, and did not call you in his service without making evident to you all the sorrows which he had to undergo; and that if he could foretell them, so would he also have the power to reward them."

"Do not believe, my disciples, that all this has been previously hidden from you to draw you close to me and to mislead you while in my company, for it was not so; I was with you, and in the meantime you should not fear dangers or persecutions, for I could calm all the storms that might arise against you; for much as well as I knew, I was only a subject to the attention, hatred and animosity of my enemies: they persecuted the Master and were content to hate the disciples. But now that I return to Him who sent me, that they can no longer do anything against me, because they will not even see me, they will unleash all their fury against those who believe in me, follow me and preach my doctrines, and commit themselves to my defence and that of my Gospel. Yet there is one thing I notice among you which I admire. I speak of leaving you, and this warning does not make that effect on you which it ought to be making. I go to Him who sent me and return to heaven where I came from; and instead of wishing me well for it, either for the honour that I will receive, or for the benefit that serve for my exaltation, you grieve, you look thoughtful and melancholy, and none of you ask me where I am going, nor what are the riches and delights of that place for which I leave the earth; but because I tell you about my departure and the consequent events you will undergo, your hearts are very sad, so much so that it seems that you have lost your sense of direction and speech.

"However," he further said, "I tell you the truth, that it is inevitable for you and in your interest that I go to the Father; for were it not so and I remain with you, the Holy Spirit will not be sent to you, the Comforter who will fortify you and instruct you will not come to you; but when I leave, after the sacrifice has been consummated, I will send him to you myself, and he will not delay pouring out upon you his lights and consolations. And when he comes, he will convince the world of sin, righteousness and judgment; he will convince it through your preaching and ministry, casting these in the face of its unbelief, with which it has denied me and disowned me; a horrible sin, indeed, which cannot fail to be punished with awful harshness. Of justice; that is, of the divine justice that shines and radiates in the reward given to the good, and the punishment given to the bad; and in my exaltation to glory, for I go to the Father, and you will no longer see me in this state of dejection and humiliation, but triumphant and glorious. And owing to all your rebukes which will be strengthened with the grace of the divine Spirit, the Jews will be convinced of the condemnation which is reserved for them. Already hearing this you are being instructed as to what evil the prince of this world will be judged and condemned. The unbelieving Jews will be cast out from among the number of the children of God; their city, their cult, their temple and its ceremonies will no longer survive. Strengthened by my spirit you will throw these threats in their face and, this generation will not pass away before this event happens.

"As I do not yet consider you quite capable of understanding many other things I have to tell you, I shall not be telling them to you; for it is not yet convenient to overload your spirit too much; however, you will understand them when the Spirit of truth I have promised you descends upon you. This divine Spirit will not speak to you out of his knowledge, but he will tell you all the things that he will have heard in heaven, and will announce them to you so clearly, that he will show you those things which will occur in coming ages as if happening right now, so that knowing about them you will become the new prophets which I will be sending into the world. He will glorify me on earth, because he will receive from what is mine, and it is from me that he will receive the doctrine which he will be entrusted with instructing you. All that my Father has is mine; for this reason I have told you that he will say nothing that does not come from me; as to his beginning and which he has not received from me; and he shall dwell with you in my absence, for in a short time you shall see me no more; and if this first absence is not for ever, as indeed it will not be, for you will see me from time to time, know that these visits will last only until I return to my Father and go up to heaven, where I will establish my dwelling place forever, and which place you will not see until you go up to Him by the same path which I regained and earned for all."

Some of his disciples, who could not understand what he meant by these expressions, said to each other: "What does he want to imply with all this, soon you will not see me, and soon after you will see me, because I am going to the Father?" It is true that he kept this conclusion both concise and mysterious, so that the apostles could understand it but also need some explanation. The short time after which they would no longer see him was that which was to pass from the instant he was speaking to that of his burial; and that after which they were to see him again, was the time in which he would be in the tomb until his glorious resurrection. And as Jesus Christ knew that they wished to ask him about this, he foresaw their desires, as he usually did, and said to them: "I know well that the words I have just told you concern you, and that you have not understood their meaning: wait for them to be fulfilled, and you will see that there is nothing of what I have told you that is not true So hear what I am going to tell you, that you may better understand it. The time has come when you will weep and the world will rejoice; but your sorrow will not last long, and a more abundant joy will follow. Just like the woman who goes into labour cries out and grieves when the hour of her travail draws near, she will however no longer remember her anguish when the fruit of her womb happily comes to light, owing to the joy with which she is filled for having given a man to the world, so too, my disciples, will your sorrows be as short as these pains. The time has come, and I must absent myself from you; this will bear you sorrow and grief: but you must console yourselves with the hope that you would hardly have lost sight of me, when I will return to visit you, risen and glorious. This will soothe your tears and anxieties and fill you with such a solid joy that it cannot be taken away from you by all the creatures of the world. Then, on that day, you will no longer ask me any questions about my departure. Truly, truly, I say to you, that whatever you ask of the Father in my name, He will grant it to you, and the Holy Spirit will enrich and adorn you in such manner with his gifts, that you will not need to have me near you to consult me about your doubts. Until now you have asked nothing in my name; ask and you shall receive, that your joy may be complete."

Although it was not difficult to delve and know the literal meaning of this speech, yet as much easy as it might have been, it was not within the reach of the apostles, although it is also true that it was not long before discerning it. They did not doubt that the Master, who was pleased to give such important witness to them in the last moments of his life, knew perfectly well all they needed, and while not denying them or being scarce with them in providing them with all the comforts they needed, he further said to them: "Until now I have spoken to you in a figurative and proverbial style which you have been unable to decipher; from now on I will no longer either use figures of speech or parables. I will speak to you clearly of my Father, and I will reveal to you the most secret and sublime mysteries, and you will have a great place with this Father, who is infinitely generous and merciful, and will manifest to you His will about the founding of His kingdom. Ask Him in my name what you desire, as it would be just and convenient, and I need not tell you that my supplications will accompany yours, and that you will have no need to remind me about them, for even if I could forget about them, my Father's love for you would suffice to have them attended to promptly. He loves you tenderly, because you have loved me, and because you have believed me when I told you that I have come out of my Father, and that it is from there that I came to earth. This will suffice, so that seeing the firmness of your faith in my words, your union with my person and my merits which you will always keep in mind, and knowing all your needs, I may listen to you with kindness and grant you whatever you ask of Him. Remember that just as I came out of my Father's bosom to come into this world, so now I am about to leave the earth and return to His own bosom to live there eternally. For all eternity I am the Word of God; the Word is personally united to my humanity from the first instant of my conception. This is how I have descended from heaven, which is the throne of Divinity; this is how I came to fulfil my ministry among the Jews, to whom I was primarily sent as their preacher and Master, and I will consummate the redemption of all men, to leave this world and return to my Father." Brief but forceful words, basically condensing the whole essence of the Saviour's adorable religion, insofar as it is for the dignity of its head, Jesus Christ himself, Son of the living God, Redeemer and Saviour of mankind.

There could be no less a clear explanation given by Jesus Christ to leave an agreeable impression on the apostles; and so it was that, being possessed with the greatest glory, they said to him: "See then, Lord, that now you are speaking to us clearly, not with riddles or proverbs. Now we know that you know all things and you do not need anyone to ask you if we know it; you see everything clearly, and with your superhuman wisdom you penetrate even the most hidden secrets of hearts; this is why we believe that you have come out of God. You have discerned our thoughts, come out to meet our doubts and calmed all our fears. No one who is simply mere man can do so, for this is one of the most beautiful features of Divinity; we know you then, and we confess you as Man-God, the Only Son of God, whose holy humanity is destined to lead and judge all men, and who receives at every instant of his life the lights of the Divinity, to which he is personally united." Then Jesus Christ replied to them: "By chance, is it true that you now believe? For know ye that the hour is drawing near and it has already arrived, when you will be scattered, and each one of you will go along his way and you will leave me alone, although I am not alone, because the Father is with me. You will abandon me, yet in truth I pity you, I more pity you than myself; and you will feel it much less deeply to see me without consolation, than for me to see you in such turmoil and anguish. Do not be perturbed or saddened by this prediction of mine, for I know that you will briefly be ashamed of your cowardice, and you will erase the shame and dishonour it with faithfulness for the rest of your days. But know ye that I have told you these things and I have foretold them to you so that you may have and keep your peace in me; but I do not promise you that you will have this without struggles or battles, for I want it to be a glorious peace and the fruit of your victories. For as long as you are in the world, it will not stop persecuting you; but do not fear it, for I have won a complete victory against it; and if your trust in me remains firm, you would not be won over. I have overcome it with patience, and I will triumph over it with death. So I will deserve the glory of reigning over all peoples and the faculty to leave to all those who will fight for me, the strength to overcome and triumph like me over hell and all the fierce pride of its legions."

It seems that in giving such a forceful speech, the heart of the most beloved Jesus Christ was inflamed with a new fire, and after having paused a little in all this reasoning also to give his disciples time to breathe, raising his eyes to heaven, he said: "My father, the time has come to make my glory seen. You want your dying Son to impress the world with his miracles; may his death be followed by a glorious resurrection, his sorrows by a sweet rest, and his humiliations by an eternal triumph; and since You have chosen this time for such a great plan to be carried out, start by glorifying Your Son, that the Son may glorify You;

let all nations know him and the world know who he is. For this so holy, noble and glorious end is the reason why You have given him power, so as to attract all men to make for them the best thing of all, namely to give them eternal life. The path leading to such a blissful end is to know and adore You, oh my Father, and that they recognise and worship Your Only Son Jesus Christ, whom You have sent. I ask You nothing which has not been well deserved. You have commanded me to work in this world and to seek Your glory, and I have done so. Is anything missing now for You not to reward my obedience? As Your Only Son, before all ages, I had in You the glory which is essential for Divinity. Yet after taking this mortal flesh, and the likeness and form of a servant, I have always lived in contempt, and the shameful death which I am going to suffer will be the peak of my opprobrium. What I desire and now ask from You has to do with my humanity after death, humiliated and as up till now astounded by Your love.

"Oh my Father, I have manifested your name to those whom You have completely separated from the world and made them living members of my flock. Creator and absolute master of them all, You chose and predestined those whom You wanted to follow me faithfully, as sheep follow their shepherd. It is for these disciples whom You have placed under my care, and whom I entrust to lead others, that I ask and beg You. I entrust them to You and put them under Your protection. I taught them the doctrine which You have conveyed to me and having received it, they came to know that it came from You, and they believed that You sent me. I beg You for them; I do not expect anything from You for the world, but for those You gave me, because they are Yours. Which means that I say nothing to You on behalf of the Jewish people and for the Synagogue which corrupts them; I do not ask and beg You to forgive them the temporary punishments and the ruin threatening them; I know what their fate is; You have revealed to me the eternal decrees founded on their future stubbornness and their obstinacy which You foresaw. I adore Your sovereign justice, and I now limit my desires to these men whom You have given me to form with my lessons, and whom you have chosen as ministers of mine and of my Gospel. They were Yours before You put them in my charge, and they are always Yours even though You have given them to me, and they worship You and Your Son. All my works, everything I own, are Yours: the same as all that is Yours is mine and I have been glorified in them. You are well aware, oh my Father, of the reasons why I make this reverent plea to You: these disciples You gave me have particular love for me, and it is now their duty to spread the glory of my name throughout the world; and as I am about to leave this world and return to You, I feel compelled having to leave them alone in the midst of the enemies of virtue and truth; so save them and protect them. I beg You for this flock which is being relieved from its shepherd, that You may deign to take care of it and defend it from the wolves with the virtue of Your holy and mighty name, so that those whom You have placed under my protection may be closely united with me and among themselves, and that loving one another, as we love each other, they may be one, as we are One; namely, that they be so by charity, as we are by nature.

"I conserved and affirmed in Your name those You gave me when I was with them in the world. I watched over them, and none of them perished, other than the son of perdition, the treacherous Judas, whose ill-fated destiny and just punishment will ensure that the Scripture saying, pronounced by the Holy Spirit by the mouth of David, is verified and accomplished; for it is written in the book of Psalms: 'May their camp be a desolation, let no one dwell in their tents. May his days be few; may another seize his ministry and office' (Ps 69:25; 109:8). Now that I come to You and that I have only a few hours left to leave this world, I return them to You and put them in Your hands; and I do it in their presence, that by sensing the favours with which you fill them following my pleas, they may take comfort in seeing me leaving them and may receive from me, though absent and set apart from them, the fullness of joy and the peak of consolation. I entrusted them with Your word, I taught them Your doctrine, and the world hated them because they are not of the world, as not even I am. I do not beg you to take them out of it, but I ask you to preserve them from the evils with which you threaten the sons of iniquity. I know Your plans for them; I want them to fulfil them, that the generosity of their zeal corresponds to their great vocation. Sustain them, oh my Father, in Your fervour, so that the persecution of the wicked will not cause them to waver in the faith they have promised me. They are not of the world, therefore they do not pertain to those whom You hate; they are like their Master, who also does not belong to the world. So do sanctify them and confirm them in the truth of the heavenly doctrine I have taught them. You know well that I took it out of your bosom, and that it is the foundation of the true cult of justice due to You and which is to be established in my name among all peoples of the earth. Your word is true and infallible. Your eternal righteousness and Your commandments and Your law are truth itself, enlightening souls and sanctifying them. You well know how inevitable this grace is for those for whom I ask it from You. It is for them that I offer myself as a sacrifice, and You already see me ready to shed my blood to merit them a true and perfect sanctification. Come to their help, oh my Father, and shower upon them with Your mercy the unique graces which I ought to merit for them and for all by sacrificing my life.

"I do not only pray for them, but also for those who in the all future ages will believe in me by their preaching and teaching, honouring the Father through the Son. Let it be so as to all of them, that they live together united by partaking of the same spirit like You and I are One and the same; as You, oh my Father, are in me, and I who am the Son am in You by the union of the same nature which I receive from You; and by this intimate brotherly union and due holiness, the world will believe that You have sent me and that it is from You that the doctrine which I have taught, my mission, my dignity and my power proceed. I have given them the lucidity, glory, grace of adopted children and supernatural gifts which You have communicated to me, and of which I will make all my members participants. The world therefore, as witnéss to our intimate union and which all creatures have with You through me, will know that I am in them as You are in me; that they are my members, and I am their head; and that in this manner they reach the most perfect union which can be achieved between creatures and their Creator. These signs of an accomplished holiness between me and my disciples, by which the world will be astounded, will force it to believe that I send them as You have sent me, and that I love them as You love me. And since You have given them to me, I desire that You place them near me in heaven, that they may see the glory which You have prepared for me from eternity, and by that they may know how much You have loved me before all ages. Oh my Father, whose ways are all straight and whose judgments are all just! The world to which You have sent me did not want to know You as I have declared you to be by Your order. Yet you are aware that I have known You intimately, and that my disciples have also known You and know that it is You who has sent me. I have taught them to revere Your name and to observe Your sovereign plans. I have manifested Your greatness to them, and the Holy Spirit who proceeds from You and me will very soon teach them with the greatest clearness, so that the love with which You love me is in them and, in a special and new way, makes them Your children by adoption and, commensurate with them, dwell within them as it does in me by the infused practice of charity and by the most full and perfect knowledge."

CHAPTER 78
HE DEPARTS FROM THE CENACLE AND GOES TO THE GARDEN OF GETHSEMANE OR OF OLIVES

ESUS Christ concluded his prayer and left the Cenacle with his apostles to go to the Mount of Olives; but at the time of leaving and along the way, he returned to deliver to them the two most essential and interesting things which they had to remember mostly. One was that being so close to the hour of battle, it was strictly required of them to be prepared to face the common enemy; and the other to know that whether at some time or occasion they had felt cause for complaint or mistrust against him. And so he said to them: "When I sent you to preach the Gospel without sack, saddlebag, footwear and purse, did you miss anything by chance?" And when they answered him that they did not, he availed himself of this occasion to tell them that, if until then he had been careful to provide them with all their needs for their living, and had been their father, protector and defender, the time and the hour had now come for them to fight, for he could no longer afford them any visible help, so that they needed to provide for themselves certain items. And so he further told them: "He who has a purse let him take it, as well as a saddlebag; and he who does not carry a sword, let him sell his tunic and buy one. For I truly tell you, that it is necessary that all that is written is fulfilled in me; for as Isaiah already said: *He was numbered and sentenced among the evildoers* (Is 53:12). This will happen later, as all prophecies are about to be fulfilled." But the apostles, who reasoned out everything, did not understand about what the Lord wanted to warn them in telling them to arm themselves with the shield of faith and the sword of the word of God since they were going to enter into great tribulations; and taking everything literally, believing that it would be necessary for them to use a sword to defend their person, they answered him naively and said to him, "Lord, we have two swords here," and they delivered them

to him, as if wanting to ask him if those weapons would be enough to defend himself in the fray which he had just referred to them. But Jesus Christ, eager to bring to an end that conversation and to diverge from what he really meant, just said to them, "Enough."

After this he thought it necessary to tell them that within a very short time all of them would be defeated and take to a cowardly flight on seeing his enemies. So he said to them: "Look here, this is a disastrous night for you; no matter how resolute you imagine yourselves to be, you will lack the courage; for after the many warnings I have given you, you will reduce my passion to a motive for your fall and scandal. The cruelty which I will be shown, will amaze you: and if you will not forget me entirely, you will hardly keep any mild relic of a half-hearted faith and hope. This is what Zechariah said: *Strike the shepherd that the flock may be scattered* (Zec 13:7); but since I know that although I give my life, I will take it up again, I will come back very soon to help you. And after my resurrection I will wait for you in Galilee, where you will take refuge to avoid the Jews' fury: there you will see me risen from the dead, full of glory and victorious over death."

It is in this manner that the spirit of foresight and the most beloved character of Jesus Christ are revealed in these admonitions which he made to his disciples, considering that, warning them of the cowardice they would show by abandoning him within a short time, he did not want in any way to throw them into despair. He judged it to be much better to console them with the certainty he gave them that in a short time they would see him again in a very different way from how they were then seeing him; and then in a more praiseworthy, brilliant and glorious state. Yet Saint Peter, who ardently loved Jesus Christ, and did not believe that he would become so cowardly that he would abandon him on seeing him in the hands of his enemies, clothed himself with zeal and told him that although all his companions would fail in their duty, and being shocked and horrified at the thought of his master's imprisonment, he would always and faithfully fulfil his duty and would never abandon him. But Jesus Christ answered him, that on that very night, before the rooster crowed for a second time, he would have denied him three times. Yet in spite of all, Peter did not cease to moan and assert that whatever happened, he would never deny or abandon his Master; so that the same protestation as was made by Peter was repeated by Jesus Christ's other apostles and disciples. But since the Lord wanted penance to make them more humble, faithful, and holy after their fall, which they might not have been able to accomplish unless they had fallen, he let them speak out; but without stopping further for a single moment, he cut off the dispute over the imaginary constancy they were promising. Seeing that the hour had come, he recited the Psalms with them and chanted a song of thanksgiving with which the children of Israel, who were truly religious, usually finished their meals, and the more so the Passover supper. He then left Jerusalem and went to the Garden of Olives, where he was accustomed to pray during the night; and having crossed the Torrent Valley of Cedron with his eleven apostles, he left them at the foot of the hill next to the place of Gethsemane, ordering them to remain there while he proceeded to pray to his Eternal Father.

It was a long time since the world was founded: fifty centuries had passed, when the great leader whom God had sent into the world to win it over in personal triumph from the full power of hell and death, was due to come out of hiding of darkness to fight his Father's battles and defeat the infernal dragon in a terrain resembling in all and equal to that on which the first man had been beaten. He thus chose an orchard for the fight since it was on another one that man had declared war on God. This orchard, enclosed on that beautiful mountain and sited on one side of God's house, looked over a great part of Jerusalem. It is the place where the holy soul, desiring to unite itself closely through prayer with the Lord, must withdraw when the right time comes, separating itself from the world which is a valley of desolation and a torrent of misery. There, from that orchard, the soul will share separately the astounding comforts with which the Lord, in the midst of tribulations, gladdens the heart of all those who turn to him and hope in him. The distance from the city to the hill was barely a thousand steps, and this makes us aware that the Lord never moves far from those whom he saves, although he leaves them apparently exposed to the most serious and awful trials. And although Jesus Christ walked to the garden with his disciples, he nevertheless commanded them on entering it to keep somewhat separate from him and at a safe distance; which also teaches us that we ought to seek God in solitude, where we must call Him and where we will undoubtedly find Him. And there He will deign to speak to our heart, as He said through His Prophet, *I will bring the soul to the wilderness and speak tenderly to it* (Hos 2:14), so that we may know that God is not found in the midst of the boisterous unrest of a deceiving and corrupted world; from this we must certainly flee if we want to be intimate with God and deserve his consolations. Yet we must be warned that although Jesus Christ commanded his apostles to keep somewhat apart from him, he called his three dear ones, Peter, James and John to draw nearer to him, that they might not lose sight of him, warning them of the need they had to pray to obtain the heaven's help against the temptations which threatened them.

CHAPTER 79
JESUS CHRIST IS CAUGHT IN THE GARDEN AND TAKEN TO PRISON

AFTER this Jesus Christ took some steps forward, followed by his three apostles who were the only witnesses of their Master's intense sorrow. The Lord entered a more secluded place with them, and there uttered some words which they understood very clearly; as he was overwhelmed with an extraordinary fear of death, with an excessive sadness, and with a fainting spirit brought about by a vivid and painful awareness of the insults which those to whom he was greatly bound would make him suffer; as well as by the horror of the ungodly and bloodthirsty plans which were about to be put into action against him, and by the certainty of the countless evils which he saw at hand. Yet he set himself apart from them, a stone's throw away, and walking away he said to them: *My soul is sad unto death; wait here and watch over me.* Feeling in advance the wounds of his passion's pains, his face was troubled and his countenance restless, his pale features being more mute than his own words. Falling on his knees, he let his face drop down to the ground and started praying; this was the posture in which he worshipped God more deeply than he cared for his own extreme affliction. The most conflicting affections and esteem mortified and hurt him. He was innocence itself, the immortal King of ages, the firstborn of men, the Man-God and the Only Son of God; and considering the outrages he had to suffer, the pains he was about to feel and the death he had to suffer on a dreadful cross, all shattered his soul, made his spirit tremble and the dread of death to take hold of him. Yet he had done this through his obedient will to the Father, to which he had submitted, not out of any need but moved by charity, and then also because he was concerned with the thought of saving men, of opening the door for them to God's justice. And yet although he was aware of the benefit of men being saved and God's justice being accomplished, recalling that in order to achieve these opposing

ends he had to fall into the hands of external justice, he still shivered and was overtaken by an even more terrible fear. So that it was necessary for him to acclaim and say: *"My Father, if it is possible, take away this cup from me without having to drink of it; but it is not as I want it to be done, but as You want.* You well know, that I subscribed to the decree of Your righteousness to save man and gratify You; and so let not my will be done, but Yours."

In the midst of this conflict, knowing that his Father loved him, Jesus Christ adopted the council and the voices of love; and offering to his Father even the most ardent affections of his heart, he awaited the comfort which he knew He would bestow upon him. While heaven's will differed from his own, he rose and went to seek his disciples, wanting to tell them of his sorrows and to console himself in talking to them about them. But he found all three asleep, and he had to wake them up. It was such a sad consolation for an afflicted man who needs relief which he seeks from his friends! True to say that his sadness was mainly brought about by the anguish caused by that dream. Yet Jesus Christ could not stop rebuking them for not being watchful; and addressing Peter he said to him: *Simon, are you sleeping? You have not been able to watch with me for at least an hour? Watch and pray that you will not be overcome by temptation. The spirit is willing and deemed ready for all that may come; but the flesh frequently drags the spirit, and it yields to the flesh.* So take care as for yourselves, be wary of your strength, and do not cease imploring help from heaven.

After Jesus Christ had thus encouraged his apostles, he left them returning to pray for a second time, repeating the same prayer and saying: *My Father, if you cannot pass this cup from me unless I drink it, your will be done.* As if to say, "If it is necessary that I subject myself to such a cruel and disgraceful death, let the eternal decrees of Your righteousness, oh my Father, be fulfilled." The Lord no longer asks for the cup to be taken away from him, though it is still full of bitterness. He knows that God does not want to stop him from drinking it, and so he surely accepts it, desiring that the Father is given the full and perfect gratification demanded by His justice; for as a submissive and obedient

Son, he also wants His entire will to be accomplished. So being resolved to fulfil His Father's will by doing all on his part, he rises again, though still tormented with sorrow, walks to his disciples and finds them sleeping. He woke them, as their eyes were heavy and laden with sleep, but he did not want to rebuke them again; his presence alone was enough to confuse them, and they would not know how to answer him. So he left them and went back to his place, repeating the same prayer for a third time, saying: *Father, if you will, remove this cup from me; but let not my will be done, but yours.* In the midst of this union of wills, Jesus Christ, desiring to fulfil that of his Father, only sought the occasion of suffering. He knew that only by suffering could the sins of man be recompensed; by refusing all the sensitive sweetness of which he could deprive himself, and by arousing against himself the most angry passions, as they only serve to afflict nature with a thousand reasons for pain. And so remaining in holy prayer and denying to his soul all the consolations which the divinity of his blessed spirit could offer him, his Father sent him an angel from heaven to comfort him, who let himself be seen in human form. Drawing near him respectfully, he worshiped him as he would to his Lord, comforting and strengthening him. He presented to him his Father's will, showing him the infinite merit of his obedience, the man's salvation in his embracing of the cross, the fruits and rewards of his passion in reparation for the insults done to his Father, the destruction of sin and how men were to replace the seats emptied by the loss of the proud angels by filling them. With all these thoughts making him once more desire death rather than flee from it, he armed himself with the will of resistance against distressed nature; and it was this sustained combat which made him sweat profusely from his body and drip blood droplets which ran to the ground.

The blood which was thrust out from the heart, where it had collected in fear, gushed out quickly and opened a thousand pores. Here, indeed, the Lord could cry out with the Psalmist, and say: *Save me, O God! for the waters of distress have reached my soul, and I sunk to my neck. I sink in deep mire, where there is no foothold; I have come into deep waters, and the flood sweeps over me, raging storms have plunged me into the depths. I am weary with my crying; my throat is parched, and my eyes grow dim with lifting them to heaven waiting for my living God who saves* (Ps 68:2-4). Yet little by little that dreadful agony of Jesus Christ was attenuated, and the blood reverted to taking its course, for owing to his reverence the Son had been heard.

From this instant on, Jesus Christ once more accepted the Father's confirmation of the sentence, and was filled with fearlessness and encouragement. He again rose from prayer, went to his disciples and found them sleeping, saddened; and then, as if sarcastically, he said to them: "Go on sleeping, and rest, and continue dreaming. You could not have chosen a more favourable occasion to rest from the work of this painful day. The time has come when the Son of Man will be delivered into the hands of sinners. So shame on your laziness; rise up without delaying any further unless you want to be taken by surprise by temptation without having the occasion to implore God's help." It was like saying to them: "Oh Father, my spirit rejoices in this hour, for your only begotten Son which You have given to the world, that it may not perish but have eternal life, will give his body to his enemies and his own spirit to You, for the world's life and salvation! Oh world, rest now, eat, drink and indulge yourself, because the time has come for me to suffer hunger and thirst for you, and you give me to drink gall and vinegar! Oh men, crown yourselves with roses, be filled with precious wines and ointments, spend your days in pleasures, because the hour is drawing near when I will be slapped and wounded for you, spit upon with saliva, torn to pieces with spanking, crucified with nails! Oh angels, the time has come when you will weep bitterly while I suffer the most resentful sorrows and terrible pains! The time has come, and he who will deliver me is not far away; let's go out to meet him."

The Saviour had not yet finished talking to his disciples, when Judas, one of the twelve, arrived; he knew the place well, and all its approaches, entrances and exits, because Jesus Christ had gone there many times and met with his disciples. The false apostle was leading a company of soldiers, masters or bailiffs given to him by the Pharisees' high priests, carrying lanterns and torches, together with a mob of people armed with swords, sticks and clubs, accompanied by officers of the governor's guard. Judas had given them a signal by which they might know who the Lord was in the darkness of the night. He told them that the man who he would kiss was the One they were seeking. As he also knew that Jesus Christ worked wonders, and surely could not have forgotten all the wonders he had witnessed; and as he knew that having been forced to surrender to the scribes he had more than once freed himself from their fury and disappeared from their sight at the very instant when they were armed to catch or stone him; being fearful that also this time their hopes would be thwarted; he warned them of the caution they should adopt in seizing him, by guarding and well securing his person. Having thus worked out all ploys to his satisfaction, he entered the orchard leaving his crowd at a distance. He came to see his companions, recognised Jesus Christ, his Saviour and Master, ran to him and saying *May God protect you, Master*, he threw himself on his neck and gave him a kiss of false peace. It was easy to foresee all the consequences of such an act of perfidy and although these were not hidden from Jesus Christ, he yet received the treacherous disciple with all due kindness. Speaking to him in the most eloquent language of his love, Jesus Christ addressed him clearly, saying in very few words: *Friend, Jesus Christ said to Judas, what have you come for? Is it with a kiss of false peace that you dare give in the hands of men the Master who loves you so much?* This sweet complaint was a great sign of the tenderness and compassion which the Lord had for this evil man, even offering him his grace had he been willing to abhor his crime. The betrayer, however, withdrew from him who had called him to repent, and hastily returned to his Master's enemies to receive from them what he was eagerly awaiting, namely thirty pieces for which he had sold him. He wanted to collect them on the spot, as the scribes believed that now that they had captured the Saviour, Judas was already entitled to receive what they had promised him. Yet Jesus Christ, seeing his council go fruitless, and his laments being despised, thought of nothing else but to submit himself entirely to his Father's will, so that the prophets' utterances might be duly fulfilled.

Jesus Christ followed Judas, and behind them followed his apostles, walking towards the enemy troop which awaited him. Judas joined them while the Lord went ahead of them, asking them, *Whom do you seek?* What greatness of soul, what fearlessness, what encouragement were shown by Jesus Christ before his enemies! "Who are you looking for?" he asks them. And answering him that it was Jesus Christ of Nazareth, he answered them with a voice of majesty and almightiness, *I am*, and hearing these only two words, the officials, soldiers, servants and masters, the chief plotter of the betrayal and all those who accompanied him, fell back to the ground on each other. This voice *I am*, is an abridgement of all the perfections which shine in God. *I am*, that is, *I am* of myself, depending on no one and everything depending on me: *I am* the beginning and the end; *I am* the first and the last; all is done through me, and without me nothing was done; no one can say it either in heaven or on earth, but the one to whom all power is given on earth and in heaven. *I am*, no one can say it but God; and if anyone else says so, he is a liar and there is no truth in him. So that by saying *I am*, Jesus Christ confessed that he was God, and his sight and his sovereign and almighty voice could not do no less than terrify his wretched persecutors; for which reason they fell on their backs to the ground. Had this fall inspired penance and repentance in them, they would have risen with magnificence and glory; but the horrible crime they were about to commit had blinded them and they had no courage either to reflect or contrive matters; and so they could not get up nor would they have ever gotten up, were it not that the voice of Almightiness which had thrown them to the ground not revived them again. To this effect the sovereign Master asked them once more: *Who are you looking for?* And replying Jesus Nazareth as they did before, Jesus Christ answered them with the same air of greatness and majesty as he did the first time: "*I have already told you that I am: if it is me you seek, do not disturb these disciples of mine; let them go.* I will allow you to do me whatever is required to fulfil the designs of my Father's will; these other ones, however, let them go their way; so that the word I said a short while before would be fulfilled: *I did not lose any of those You gave me."*

The Jews, having already recovered from their confusion, instead of worshipping the almightiness of this God made man and allowing themselves to be won over by his sweetness, rather treated him as an evildoer; so they laid their hands upon Jesus Christ, bound him and secured him tightly for fear that he might escape from them. The apostles, already startled and not doubting that they were seeking to seize their sweet and beloved Master, believed that the time had come to defend him; but notwithstanding all, they did not act without first asking him for some sort of permission, saying: "Lord, shall we use the sword?" Yet Peter, without waiting for his Master's reply, laid his hand on his weapon and hurled himself on the first man he could reach. This was a servant of a certain priest called Malchus, and slashing at his face with a knife Peter cut off his right ear. Jesus Christ disapproved of this forceful act committed by his disciple, even if he was clothed with a spirit of zeal to defend his person; on the contrary, he rebuked him and forbade his own from using any armed force and violence to avenge the insult that was inflicted upon him. But since it was not his plan that his enemies should suffer from his apostle's indiscreet zeal, he caused the wounded person to be brought to him, touched his ear and healed him. Not even so was the ardent charity of Jesus Christ satisfied, but in the presence of the mentioned high priest's servant and of all those attending with him, he wanted to instruct the assailant and with him the other disciples, of the tolerance, meekness and suffering they were bound to keep. Addressing Peter and the others, he said to them: *"Put back your sword in its place; put it in the sheath, for all those who use it unjustly or against public authority, will die by the blade of the sword. Whoever sheds the blood of another man will see his own shed by the hand of man. Do you think that if I wanted to defend myself from my enemies, I could not ask for help from the Father, who would immediately send more than twelve legions of angels,* of whom only one would suffice to destroy all men? What else do you intend doing but to oppose God's designs, and to prevent me from drinking the cup my Father is offering me? Do you not know that his will is to drink it all, so that the Scriptures expressly declaring it might be fulfilled? Let that troop come to me, and stop opposing its violence." The Saviour was however compelled to express his grievances to them; he gave them all a severe rebuke, and in particular to the civil leaders, priests, chief officers of the temple and elders who led that despicable troop of soldiers and warriors, censuring them for having come armed with swords and sticks to seize him, like an evildoer, whereas he had been with them every day in the temple, without them ever daring to do him any violence against his freedom or life. "But this is your hour," Jesus Christ added, "and this is the time when all is allowed to the spirits of darkness and to the princes of hell; this is a fateful hour for you, granted to your freedom and malice, so use it to its utmost limits; do against me whatever the spirit of darkness can prompt you to do, for obstinate as you are in the wickedness and unjust abhorrence you have for me, you wish my death with such great desire."

With unspeakable sorrow the apostles heard the Saviour, for from what he had said they knew that arming themselves to defend him would be in vain, being resolved not to use his power and was fully resigned to letting himself to be seized. And fearing lest some disaster would befall them, they left him on his own and all fled away like cowards. The rude troop, believing it had achieved its most glorious triumph, threw itself into all the excess of a fierce joy, hurling themselves upon the meek Lamb with a force and rage which only hell could unleash like them. Now was the time for beatings, wounds and bad treatment; now was the time for the dangling sound of chains, the noisy sound of arms, the racket of armed men, the shouting of the leaders, and the joy, contentment and hellish laughter of the Synagogue members; and still the Lamb of God did not resist to anything. In the midst of insults and outrages, he let himself to be led away, without complaining or anyone expressing condolences or showing any interest in his mishaps. Some soldiers who had gone in pursuit of the apostles, took a young man who went about covered in a sheet, someone likely from the hamlet of Gethsemane who, having been awakened by the din, knew he would run into trouble; but being caught by armed men, he threw off the sheet and ran away naked. This detailed event referred to by Saint Mark, makes us believe that the young man was not one of Jesus Christ's disciples, as some have thought; but that the Saviour himself did not allow him to be held, so that no one would suffer for his sake when he began to suffer for all humanity and for the salvation of us all (Mk 14:51).

CHAPTER 80
JESUS CHRIST IS PRESENTED TO ANNAS

WITH the greatness and majesty that innocence and virtue always inspire in the heart of man, the Man-God, most holy by essence and by nature, walked to his torture in full resignation as a victim who sacrificed himself from the origin of the world. He did so not inasmuch as owing to his people's fury as to the glory of God and the salvation of the universe. Those who led him bound like an evildoer shouted great cries of joy, repeating and sharing thousands of congratulations for the mob's doing; which although this was a reason for triumph for them, it was a deed worthy of full compassion for the fearful and faithful who believed in Jesus Christ as the Son of God, both owing to his sonship and the beneficence of all those who revered and loved him with the greatest tenderness. And so it was that with the noise made by one part and the sighs, tears, sobs and yells of the others, the whole city was shaken in such a silent and sad hour; in such manner that walking in captivity, fulfilling the prophets' oracles and considering with self-mastery all that through which he passed, the Son of God began to manifest himself in the ignominy of his passion; and yet he was still as almighty, great and sovereign as when he raised the dead, calmed the storms and showed his power against the fury of hell.

From this instant onwards, which was instantly followed by all that which can be imagined as being utmost unjust and frightful, Jesus Christ would not speak a word, take a step or do anything which would not entice us to tears and praise; for we will always see united in his person the painful extremes of a righteous man who sacrifices himself for the salvation of his brothers and the adorable greatness of a Man-God who suffers and dies in such a great and admirable manner which he could not undergo were he purely human. Jesus Christ's capture was spoken of publicly in Jerusalem, as it was now certain and all necessary measures had been taken to proceed with the case and sacrifice the innocent man; for certainly, it had to appear all so lawful. Caiaphas, who that year performed the functions of high priest, held the office of high priest in partnership with his father-in-law Annas who was a very old man. On account of his old age it was agreed that, as soon as Jesus Christ was taken captive, he was to be led to Anna's house, to be questioned. So, without the possibility of this being interpreted in any other way than light-hearted attention and disdain towards his person, they took him to Anna's house. There, he asked Jesus Christ about his disciples and his doctrine, to which the Saviour answered with the modesty and fortitude which characterised his life's holiness and the divinity with which he was clothed: *I, he said to him, have always spoken publicly in the world; I have taught in the Synagogue and in the temple, where all Jews gather, and I have said nothing mysterious or secret.* And this is precisely what David had said: "Oh Lord! I will tell of your name to my brethren, and in the midst of the assembly I shall praise you" (Ps 22:23). And further: "I proclaim your saving acts in the great assembly; I do not seal my lips, Lord, as you know it well. I did not conceal or keep hidden in my heart your righteousness and justice; I preached your truth and your salvation, as well as your faithfulness and mercy amidst the assembly" (Ps 40:9-10). So that Jesus Christ continued: *Why do you ask me? Ask those who have heard what I told them and taught them; for they know well what I have said.*

Having been installed in the dignity of high priest, Annas was entitled to question Jesus Christ and to make as many observations as he thought conducive to ascertaining the truth and of knowing it from his own mouth. But while the Saviour was aware that his confession would not be believed, he put his fate in the hands of his very critics and enemies, namely those of the Pharisees, priests, scribes and doctors who had so often heard him with admiration preach in the Synagogue and in the temple; for having witnessed his miracles, with which he confirmed his own doctrine, they could not but recognise his divinity. Jesus Christ could not have given a more satisfactory answer, or a more effective proof of his innocence, ever keeping himself prudent and impartial and without failing from the respect due to a public leader. Yet he had scarcely finished his answer, when one of the present ministers raised his daring hand and gave the meek Jesus Christ a most terrible slap; this made not only those present go into a shiver, but as the Blessed Albert the Great assures us: "It was the whole Cenacle which trembled, and the Most Holy Mary who was locked inside, felt her most pure heart tremble and she almost entirely fainted at the violent blow, for he wore on his hand an iron glove, which left an imprint on that beautiful and adorable face of the bruise caused by that horrible slap". And it was given with such violence, that Christ's face which was turned to the querying judge, bent to the opposite side with the violence of the blow; and as Saint Vincent Ferrer further says that with it the Lord fell down flat on the ground. It should also be noted that this was an exceedingly humiliating punishment for Jesus Christ, and one bearing the greatest shame; because it was given before the most noble and prominent assembly of Jerusalem, by a despicable minister of the people's scum, only for the purpose of flattering the master whom he served. That horrifying slap had been given to the most worthy person in heaven, on earth and in all the universe, and in such a most holy and venerable part as the face, which was formed by the Holy Spirit and was the spotless mirror of the kindness of God the Father, on whom all the blessed angels and spirits constantly set their gaze, from whose eyes come those rays and torrents of light and eternal clarity with which the immense spaces of glory are illuminated. And finally, it should be noted that it was given with plenty of verve by that most dejected and despicable servant, a monster of fierce ingratitude; for it was the same one to whom a few moments before the Lord had miraculously healed him of his wound in the garden putting back his ear in its right place, that returned haughtiness and pride for the humble restraint with which Jesus Christ had healed him, saying to him on hitting him: "Do you answer the chief priest in this manner?"

In the midst of such a great affront, Jesus Christ's meekness shone brighter in his simple, but precise and appropriate answer: *If I speak badly,* he said to the servant, *show me in what; And if I speak well, tell me, why do you strike me?*

Nothing else could be said in a more effective, eloquent and persuasive manner; and giving this answer he not only silenced the thrust of badly repressed and tamed revenge, but held on to his innocence without losing any of his constancy or ceasing to be respectful to judge and court before whom he was standing. To publicly condemn an injustice is neither forbidden by religion nor by justice; rather, it is often a sacred duty religion and justice impose on the person suffering an injustice, taking into account his own dignity; and as there has never been, and never will be, on earth such an authoritative, venerable and holy person as Jesus Christ, it seems that only he could then answer the ungrateful and unknown servant with such justice. Truly, no one better than Jesus Christ could say to the servant: *Why do you smite me?* For no one can ask creatures more justly than the supreme Creator: *Why do you smite me?* Perhaps because he raised you from the ground when you should not have been raised? Perhaps because he preserved you from being lost? Perhaps because after losing him through your fault, he descended from heaven to redeem you? Or for having so many times given you proof of his love as the many instants of your life? "*Why do you smite me?*" Jesus Christ might have asked. "Perhaps because of the excessive charity with which I loved you? Or perhaps because of the loving care I always had for you? Or for the immense benefits with which I esteem you?" The high priest's minister deserved to be severely punished for the insult with which he had treated Jesus Christ by breaking the lawful order, showing great lack of respect for the laws and for the council members who were present; they should have shown ardent zeal on such occasion, both to punish so horrible a crime, and to give proof that at least in appearance they sought proper law and order. Yet it was necessary that the prophets' sayings were to be fulfilled, and that the Lord's Anointed One was to be mistreated very horribly; so that altogether exchanging their dutiful roles, those who should have condemned and punished the whole affair instead applauded it. And the Saviour, without receiving any other answer to his righteous question, was transferred from Annas' house to that of the high priest Caiaphas, and there he was further questioned.

CHAPTER 81
JESUS CHRIST AT THE HOUSE OF CAIAPHAS, AND BEFORE THE COUNCIL OF THE ELDERS, SAINT PETER'S DENIAL

AVING been told that Jesus Christ was being sent to him, Caiaphas gathered the priests, scribes and the people's elders in his house; they were those who, being possessed of a petty vengeful passion, strongly desired to see the Saviour taken prisoner. In the house of this chief priest and supreme judge of the council, the Angel of great guidance and God of justice and truth here appears to be falsely accused, wickedly judged and sacrilegiously condemned. These three things the two evangelists Matthew and Mark noted with these words: *Then seizing Jesus Christ, they led him to Caiaphas, the leader of priests, where the scribes, elders and Pharisees had gathered. And the leaders of the priests sought some false testimony against Jesus Christ to deliver him to death.*

At this same time, some of the Lord's apostles who had abandoned him when he was taken captive, came to themselves after the first instants of fright, and being ashamed of their cowardice they wanted to follow their Master. Seeing that from Annas' house he was led to that of Caiaphas, they followed him there too. Peter and John were the two who had more courage and constancy; and because they loved the Lord in a more extraordinary manner, they arrived at about the same time as Jesus Christ had entered the house. John was an acquaintance of the chief priest and his family, and there was no difficulty in letting him in. While they led the Lord to the council hall, they left him in the courtyard of the house. John did not doubt that Peter was following him; but having sought him out among the crowd in vain, he felt downcast that he did not care about his movements, and he did not want him to remain outside. He went out, and having spoken to the doorkeeper, he made things easy for him to enter. Peter was very impatient wishing to know where this whole event, which had begun so sadly, would end. He drew strength from his own weakness and timidity, and proceeding to the place where the officers and servants of the house were sitting, he sat among them as if to warm himself, but with an aim of observing attentively all that was going on.

Actually, this was the time when the scribes' and priests' cunning malice was making every imaginable effort to bring the Saviour to ruin. They received him disdainfully, looking at him with haughty eyes and a menacing countenance, treating him in all as a most despicable man. This council was held and respected as the most serious authority, of most famed repute, of most dignified majesty and of the most holy religion in the whole world. Their decisions were regarded as little less than infallible, and their answers were regarded as oracles; however, that was the council of the wicked, the council of iniquity, and those who had gathered in it were those of whom David had said: *The leaders gathered together, agreed among themselves, and condemned to death their God and Lord.* For this reason they sought false testimonies to cover up their iniquity and to make their judgment appear to be done with a justice they did not hold. With this attitude nothing good could be expected from the judges. The chief priest asked him some questions in all much like those Annas had asked him, digressing on how he gathered his disciples, and even more about the holiness and truth of his doctrine. All pointed to the fact that the thoughts they had conceived were those they always had: to lay a snare for Jesus Christ and make him fall into the deceptive net which was being laid for him. Yet it was all in vain. The eternal wisdom could not be taken by surprise, and so his replies were all in all concepts with the same meaning as those he had given to the chief priest's father-in-law of. With the malice of the Pharisees, being shrewd in their advice, they did not think of abiding by the ordinary laws and methods usually adopted in court proceedings, but of disposing in appearance and forming some criminal offence on which to base a death sentence. In Jesus Christ's answers his innocence shone through, and therefore they could not condemn him for them. They were looking for false testimony against the accused person, to have a plausible motive on which to base the sentence. They heard all those who came forward, and although they had a great number of false witnesses, they corroborated so badly that it was impossible to make use of their evidence, neither on the points required by law, nor as to the order of justice. At last, two more skilful and cunning witnesses showed up, apparently giving evidence that they had heard Jesus Christ say in a speech, by which he wanted to stir up the people, that he would destroy the temple of God built by the hands of men, and rebuild another one within a period of three days without seeing anyone's hand working on it.

These two witnesses did not corroborate fully in their assertion, for the other only affirmed having heard him say, "I can destroy the temple of God and rebuild it in three days"; but none of them made faithful reference to Jesus Christ's words. He had then only spoken of his body: *Destroy this temple, and I will restore it in three days*. For this reason Jesus Christ showed himself to be making little of the evidence given against him, and he kept constant silence. The chief priest forgot the dignity with which he was vested and the gravity and moderation he was bound to keep; and standing up furiously and manifestly beside himself, he faced Jesus Christ and as if to compel him to answer, he said to him: "Do you answer nothing to what they testify against you?" Jesus Christ's silence was profound, and was not interrupted by the chief priest's sudden utterance. They could not hide from him, who was infinitely wise, either their nefarious plans or men's injustices; so that, knowing that he could not be condemned by interjected feelings, and that as he saw things the chief priest had to resort to other tricks to make him answer about eternal truths, Jesus Christ retained his impassive silence which repeatedly put the chief priest in even more pressing conflicts. Seeking new witnesses was like bringing to light a conscientious person who feared God and knew of Jesus Christ's virtues, of his doctrine's holiness and of his bountiful merciful love; declaring these in public would even further embarrass the Pharisees' wicked and vengeful thoughts. Becoming then very spiteful and ablaze with courage, Caiaphas went into a violent fit which he thought would intimidate the meek

Lamb and force him to answer, telling him: "I conjure you, and in the name of the living God I command you, to answer me and say before all whether you are Christ, the blessed Son of God, as you say publicly, and in whose honour we sing all days songs of praise and glory."

The supreme veneration which the Son of God had towards God his Father, the honour and glory which he was resolved to give Him, the desire to establish with his solemn profession the foundation of his hallowed religion, and the manner how he ought to have revered the high priest no matter how much he hated his malice, compelled him at last to answer him and say: *Yes, I am the One you have just mentioned. And soon you will see the Son of Man seated at the right hand of God coming upon the clouds of heaven.* As this was the answer which Caiaphas expected to have, at least as an apparent reason to condemn Jesus Christ, he rejoiced greatly having received it, He nevertheless concealed his great joy and outwardly manifested nothing but outrage and hostility. In order to show off a zeal which he did not really have, he tore his garments, which among the Jews was a sign of reprobation; and renouncing the office of judge for that of a prosecutor, he turned to his comrades and said to them: "He has blasphemed, so what further need do we have for witnesses? You have now heard his blasphemy. What do you think?" And they all instantly retorted: "What further testimony do we want? We have all heard it from his mouth. He deserves to die." Here too the Scriptures had to be fulfilled when David said about the person of Christ: "Oh Lord! Do not give me up to the will of my adversaries, for false witnesses have risen against me, and they breathe out violence, and are ready to sacrifice truth by slander and deceit" (Ps 27:12); "Those who hate me without cause or motive are more in number than the hairs of my head; my enemies have been strengthened, and mighty are those who would unjustly seek to destroy and ruin me" (Ps 69:4). But just as the chief priests and teachers of the Law forgot these testimonies which marked them and revealed all their scheming, so also they did not know all those who recognised Jesus Christ as the true Son of God. *You have said it,* Jesus Christ answered Caiaphas, knowing that he could have very well repeated to him what David had said to his Father: "I am the One of whom the Lord said: 'I anointed my king and gave him the endowment on Zion, my holy mountain. You are my Son today, eternally. I begot you. Ask anything of me, and I will give you nations for your heritage, and the ends of the earth for your possession.' So now, be wise, oh kings and leaders; be warned, oh rulers of the earth! Serve the Lord with fear, with trembling kiss his feet, lest he be angry, and you perish in the way; for his fury is kindled little by little. Blessed are all who take refuge in him, obey him and worship him with purity and simplicity" (Ps 2:6-11).

From then on the despicable tormentors guarding the captive Jesus Christ mocked him, began spitting in his face and hitting him with slaps and punches. Covering his face, they beat him and wounded him with rods, telling him: "Prophesy unto us, oh Christ, who is it that hurt you." They also made several other offensive utterances, all in fulfilment of what Isaiah had said: "The Lord God has opened my ear to His word, and I was not rebellious, I turned not backward, nor did I keep away from his commandment. I gave my back to the smiters, and my cheeks to those who pulled out my beard. I did not turn away my face from those who reviled and spat on me, for the Lord God helps me, and I will not be ashamed or confounded." (Is 50:5-7)

While all this was taking place and happening to Jesus Christ, Peter remained seated amidst the house ministers and servants, warming himself with them by the fire. Soon one of the chief priest's maids came along, and fixing her eyes on him, looking as if she knew him, said to him: "Were you not also one of this man's disciples? You cannot deny it. You are from Galilee like him." But Peter denied this in the presence of all, saying: "I am not, nor do I know what you are saying. I do not know him." It seems plausible that while Peter was sitting at the fire with the ministers he had heard them speak ill of his Master, and that not wanting to make himself known, he would not only not have been interested to speak in his favour, but would rather have tolerated very indifferently their conversation; so that it was very easy for Peter to refuse what was first said about him. Confounded within himself as he was, he rose up, and as he was going out to the atrium or hallway, the cock crowed. There, at the entrance, another maid came across him, and seeing him shy, sorrowful and as if beside himself, she turned to those next to her and said to them: "Do you not see this man? He is undoubtedly one of Jesus Christ's disciples. Undoubtedly; this one was with him." One of the horde, who heard what the maid said, ran to Peter, stopped him, looked at him, and began asking him with the same tone. Undoubtedly the attack was terrible, and Peter was already too weak to resist him; so that hesitatingly and the best he could, he answered him: "Certainly not, I am not one of those of that captive's company, nor do I know him, nor do I belong to him," and he affirmed all this with an oath. As blame kept on heaping on him, the more vulgar these men became. Silence was followed by indifference, then by falsehood, and after by lies bolstered with a false oath. As Peter was used to speaking confidently on his own strength to the point of obstinacy, God allowed his weakness to reach external signs of apostasy; but all these were none else than the forerunners of the great combat which was awaiting him, and for which he was given an hour of truce.

After a short while, and when the council session was over, the ministers led Jesus Christ to the hallway to deliver him to the soldiers, much of the mob moved away and went to the wretched apostle who hardly had any peace. Noticing his embarrassment they started saying to him: "You are a disciple of this man, you cannot deny it." Others added: "You speak well the Galilean dialect and you know its tone. All this reveals whom you are and reveals also you." And one of the servants of the chief priest, a relative of the man whom Peter had cut off his ear, said to him: "By chance have I not seen you in the garden with him?" This was the last assault which an already dejected and weakened man could suffer without again giving in to a cruel denial. The temptation was much greater than the little good spirit he had left for his Master; and since one sin commonly evokes another, and a lesser fault often starts off a greater one, he was so frightened of the danger of death that he found no means, however unjust they might be, which he could soon employ to save his life. "I have not deceived you," he repeated, casting the most vehement curses and uttering the most terrible oaths. "Let me be excommunicated and considered unworthy should I know the man about whom you are speaking to me, and if I have ever had anything to do with him." Peter knew only too well his most benign Master whom he was renouncing with so great indignity. He touched him very intimately, and he was loved by him very tenderly. He himself adored him and groaned about his misfortune at the very instant he was ashamed of knowing him. But he did not any longer feel the truth which he had formerly felt with that deceiving fervour he had shown more than once for Jesus Christ. He had even told him: "I will follow you to prison and to death." Yet he was not unfaithful in his heart; he still believed that Jesus Christ was the Son of the living God even though his tongue belied his faith. He still spoke, even cursed and swore when the cock crowed the second time. Peter heard it and became aware of his sin with all its ugliness; he clearly also saw all his ingratitude. As he who owns all hearts cast a fiery gaze of love upon Peter's heart, faith, hope and the most fervent charity were instantly rekindled in him. Peter suddenly moved, and left the chief priest's house in tears mourning his sins, weeping for them with such bitterness that, even if he could have become an example of unfaithfulness, he became a distinctive model of penance and true repentance.

CHAPTER 82
JESUS CHRIST IS TAKEN TO PILATE, AND PILATE SENDS HIM TO HEROD. JUDAS REPENTS HIS ACTION AND HANGS HIMSELF

HE King of Israel, the Only Son of the living God, the much beloved One of the Eternal Father, the Saviour of mankind, and the adorable subject of the veneration of angels, stood bound with strong ropes and thrown into a corner of the hall, while Peter went outside to weep bitterly his guilt. All that which had been done by the chief priests and elders in the council was none else than a well thought out sham, intended to deceive people and pass off Jesus Christ's doctrine as an abuse of the Law. His apparent miracles, his quality and his title of Messiah were misused sacrilegiously with the perverse design that if these accusations did not at least make a great impression on the mood of a Gentile leader, to whose ministry they had to resort to take his life, they expected the people to riot against Jesus Christ and ask for his crucifixion and death. They also cleverly plotted the new offence with which they would accuse him; and all being forewarned in terms of their plans, they led the captive Saviour through the streets of Jerusalem, which were full of people owing to the great Passover festivity. They led him to the praetorium, or the civil leader's audience hall, and there handed him over to Pontius Pilate who presided; they still did not dare enter the praetorium lest they would be contaminated and stained with a legal blemish. The people, blind and ungrateful as they were, thrived on the bewilderment it saw its true King go through and madly applauded a few resolutions and steps which foretold his ruin; they far from believed that Judas, the author of such an accumulation of evils, saw the pathetic spectacle presented to him with the same eyes of Jerusalem.

Seeing all this Judas came to know of the gravity of what he had done and of all of the Synagogue's and the people's ferocious malice. He now understood that in presenting Jesus Christ to their leader they intended nothing less than to obtain confirmation of the death sentence which had been passed on him by the council of elders, and so he was not bold enough to behold the dread brought about by his betrayal without trembling. It might have been with the aim of doing penance that he took his thirty pieces of silver but, overwhelmed with a dark remorse, he ran with the coins to the temple where the people's elders and the priests' leaders were gathered. With sadness and despair showing on his countenance, yet with a melancholic but strong voice, he said to them, "I have sinned in delivering the blood of the righteous One." All the answer that those denatured beings gave to the treacherous disciple was a sardonic and insulting laugh, a disgusting mockery, a hellish contempt and an apathy more fearful than death itself. "What do we have to do with it," they told him, "whether you have sinned or not? It is your business, see to that yourself. Our conscience is not stirred at all; it is up to you to examine your heart and search deeply your intentions; but we do not regret the money it cost us." He surely did not expect this answer and it whipped up desperate anger within him and inflamed him to the extreme. He might have harboured the idea that in his most excessive remorse his very important statement might have served as justification for his Master; but all his hopes soon vanished. So he threw the money into the temple and ran out. This is one of the greatest testimonies of Jesus Christ's holiness and divinity. *He sinned, in delivering the blood of the righteous One*, and he threw back the money. The remorse of the betrayal which devours him, his repayment of the price of his treachery, and the despair into which he falls, are a naïve confession of the Saviour's innocence, and a more complete apology than if he had been acquitted by the courts themselves; it also showed that which had until now been done against Jesus Christ, and all that which was still to be done, was blatantly unjust, abominable and sacrilegious to the full.

Had he, who had so openly admitted to his crime and his pain, been sustained by a more courageous trust in the Lord, he would certainly have obtained his forgiveness. But the devil, to whom he had surrendered himself, portrayed his crime out of all proportion for him, as he could not have seen until then. He persuaded him that he had nothing to expect from divine mercy and so, accusing himself with this wretched prompting, he allowed himself to be cowardly overwhelmed by it. Falling into a new and most pitiful apostasy, a most horrible despair entered him and taking a rope, he tied it round his neck and dishonourably hung himself, so that with his body bursting through and his intestines gushing out, he died surrendering himself to utmost despair.

For this reason the priests' leaders took the money and said: "It is not licit to throw them into the treasury or money chest, because it is the price of blood." So that, having taken advice, they bought with them the Potter's estate or field for the burial of pilgrims or foreigners, for which reason that field was called to this day, *Haceldama*, meaning the Field of Blood. In this way was fulfilled that which had been predicted by the prophet Jeremiah, when he said: "And they took the thirty silver coins, its evaluated sum, as estimated by the sons of Israel, and gave them for the Potter's estate or field, as the Lord ordered me to do and showed me" (Jer 32:7; Zec 11:12).

Pontius Pilate, who in the name of the Roman emperor Tiberius, exercised authority in Judea, was apparently a naturally just and upright man, but timid and a politician. The Jews wanted on that day to bring this most important affair to an end, but Pilate was little if at all disturbed by their ongoing disputes as long as his master's imperial interest did not get in the way. He knew well of all their different opinions concerning Jesus Christ's person and doctrines, and it was not unknown to him that such noisy restlessness was incited by envy clothed with the mantle of religion. So he did not fear its ensuing consequences before the case came before him, hoping to put the unruly spirits on the path of just moderation. After Jesus Christ was presented by the Jews in Pilate's court, he went outside where they were gathered, and said to them: "What accusation do you bring against this man?" To this question the Jews answered with a dry and spiteful answer, saying: "If he were not an evildoer, we would not have delivered him to you." The governor's response quite clearly shows that he was offended by such a proud reply as that of the scribes, because he naturally tried not to have anything to do with the matter. "If you know so well," he told them, "what this man did, and of his offences or crimes, I will revert him to you for yourselves to take him, and it would be up to you to judge him according to your Law." They would have undoubtedly accepted being permitted to conduct his trial had they only wanted to punish him as a blasphemer, since with the province governor's approval they could sentence those whom they prosecuted on matters concerning religion. But they absolutely wanted Jesus Christ to be condemned as a prisoner of the state, and this forced them to answer him: "It is not lawful for us to carry out a death sentence against anyone." By this they were confirming the word Jesus Christ had spoken earlier about the kind of death with which he would die. The torture of the cross was not in use among the Jews; and Jesus Christ had always said that his angry people would deliver him to the Gentiles to be condemned to death. This had to be accomplished, and it was his own enemies who worked to bring about the fulfilment of eternal prophecies; so they accused him of being seditious, that he upset the people by preaching and teaching new doctrines, starting from Galilee all the way to Jerusalem; that he forbade the payment of tribute to Caesar; and that he took upon himself the attributes of Messiah, and so those of king.

So on hearing these accusations Pilate sat still in suspense before passing any comment. Knowing how sensitive and vicious the scribes and Pharisees were, and not trusting them, he entered his chambers seeking that the accused was also brought in as he wanted to hear him before condemning him. He specifically queried him about these radical views, and said to him: "Are you king of the Jews?" This single question fully condensed the other points; and to defend himself from all charges, it would have sufficed for Jesus Christ to have made him understand the nature of his reign. But the silence he had kept when the Jews were accusing him told plenty and meant a great deal, so that it awakened the curiosity of any least informed person. Pilate felt himself in good spirits with Jesus Christ, and the more so when he did not see his countenance change at all; and despite the nervousness shown by Pilate, who asked him whether he had heard of the charges being laid against him, Jesus Christ still abided by a most imposing carefulness. But now, to this question which Pilate again asks him alone, the Lord answers him in an edifying and instructive manner. "Are you asking me this," he tells him, "because you want to know the truth, or because you have been led to believe that I want to usurp the crown of Judea?" The Saviour said this with such a resolute, majestic and modest tone that Pilate, far from being offended by it, answered with the greatest frankness, and said: "Do you by chance think that I am a Jew? I neither know nor understand the meaning of the Messiah's kingdom which the Jews await. The leaders of your nation, the priests and the rest of your people, are the ones who have brought you to my court. What have you done? Why should they believe that you aspire to reign? Or what have you done to make these people deject you so badly?" And to this Jesus Christ replied: *"My kingdom, is not of this world; if my kingdom were of this world, my subjects and ministers would fight and struggle forcefully so that I would not be handed over to the Jews.* So you need not fear anything: my kingdom does not belong to this place, for it is a spiritual, universal and eternal kingdom, and it is not a temporal and political state like that of earthly kings."

In each of the passages of Jesus Christ's life, in all his doctrines and in each and every one of his answers, he radiated that universal and absolute sovereignty which shone brightly in him and with which he was clothed. If the leaders and priests who were so versed in the Holy Scriptures had been less concerned and forewarned against him, they could not fail but to admire him clothed in that eternal crown with which Daniel portrayed him, when he said: "In the days of these kings, the God of heaven will raise up a kingdom which will last for ever and shall never be destroyed, a kingdom whose sovereignty shall not be left to another people; and it shall break to pieces and consume all these other kingdoms, and it shall stand forever. Behold, I saw in the night visions one like a Son of Man coming in the clouds of heaven; and coming to the Ancient of Days, he was given dominion, and glory, and kingdom, and all peoples, nations and tongues, will serve him; his lordship, being an everlasting lordship, shall not pass away, and his kingdom one that shall not pass away" (Dn 2:44; 7:13-14).

"So you are a king," Pilate replied. "Yes," Jesus Christ answered him. "You are saying it, and for this I was born. I came to this world to reign, yet to reign over souls and hearts, not to dispute with earthly kings about their sceptres and crowns. I have come to it and let myself to be definitely seen in Judea, to bear witness to the truth, from which the Jews should be less far apart than the other peoples of the earth, since their Law prepares them for it. Whoever hears the truth, for which alone I have come to reign, hears my voice and recognises me as his king." Jesus Christ's words were pure and simple, as the truth itself; if Pilate, as supreme minister of righteousness, had loved the truth and was seeking it, he would have availed himself of the most important lesson he had just received from him who was uncreated and Master of eternal and infallible truth. He would then have shown himself more upright in the failures he had to commit in the thorny and most interesting cause that had been submitted to him. Had he done so he would have supported Jesus Christ's purposes, contributed to the shaking off of hypocrisy, made virtue and justice to be loved, and strengthened the true faith he came to establish among men; yet being unable or unwilling to grasp it, in spite of the flashes of light he had, he urged the Lord to tell him the meaning of truth. With his exceeding liveliness and timidity, he hurried up matters and did not wait patiently for the time needed to meditate on Jesus Christ's reply, who was little by little preparing his spirit for the moment of grace; the Lord withdrew it and never went back to it again.

After having spoken these last words Pilate, was even more convinced of Jesus Christ's innocence, and that he was being persecuted due to the hatred of a furious and misguided people; so that he returned to the Jews, and said to the priests' leaders and to the mobs: "I do not find any crime in this man; and so no cause to convict him." Such a clear and public testimony given by the judge himself in favour of the accused, brought about anger and fury in the minds of the accusers who, for lack of crimes and evidence, had to strive to crush him and to intimidate the judge's spirit with noise and commotion. Consequently, they increased their uproar, furiously repeating and yelling that he was a seditious disturber, that he excited the people throughout Judea, that he taught a new doctrine contrary to God's law and that finally he had roused uprisings in Galilee without ceasing or desisting until these were introduced into Jerusalem. The furious restlessness of the scribes augmented Pilate's peaceful desires, so that he became ever less willing to believe these false accusations. Jesus Christ meanwhile showed a very impassive peacefulness without answering in the least to so many calumnies and murderous cries which Pilate attributed to cowardice or fear; so that he put an end to the disturbance to give time to the accused to recover his courage and reply. Yet he who had kept himself mute amid those yells, persevered in keeping silent, not answering a single word as he was urged to do by Pilate, who becoming increasingly troubled as to whether silence was to be interpreted as generosity in favour of treating the captive as guilty, or as indifference in view of the greatest danger he was facing, and choosing a way out of the difficult situation in which he had found himself, on hearing Galilee being mentioned he asked whether this man was a native of this province. Knowing that if this was so, he would be very happy; not only for having found a favourable opportunity to shed off discomfort, but to win a friend at the expense of an innocent man; for he considered this to be a good purpose to send him to Herod, the tetrarch of Galilee, who like many other Jews had come to Jerusalem on the occasion to celebrate the Passover.

Jesus Christ was not unknown to Herod; after he had sacrificed the life of the Baptist to his sensual passions, he had heard of Jesus Christ as a unique and extraordinary man; so that he held a great desire to see him, know him, and possibly also witness some of the miracles which he constantly worked. So that he was very happy of the gift Pilate had sent him, the same as Pilate could rejoice in disengaging from Jesus Christ. Pilate refused to follow and conclude such an unpleasant case in order not to upset the Jews, who had almost raised a tumult, and demanded stubbornly and threateningly the death of the righteous One; on the other hand he wanted to flee the occasion of tarnishing his name, discrediting himself and compromising himself with the high government of Rome, should Caesar hear that he had pronounced a notoriously unjust sentence and become complicit in the death of an innocent man. He so took into account more of his personal interests than the duties of his office, making clearly known the scheming of his intrigue. Herod, whom the Saviour compared to a vixen, had a cunning disposition, was a man devoted to his pleasures, raised from his youth in unruly ideas, and a godless politician whose hands were even stained with the blood of the righteous. Having Jesus Christ in his presence, he started questioning him with vain curiosity in many different ways; but the Saviour did not deign to answer even a single word to all his pointless questions, although the priests' leaders and scribes accused him of serious offences with such rage, roughness and stubbornness, as could only befit Satan's ministers.

Pilate's conduct in returning the case of Jesus Christ to the foreign leader is as deplorable as Herod's in accepting it. It was devious politics in both one and the other. Personal interest, as we have said, indifference and flattery, forced the former's actions; pride and a vain and prying curiosity held mastery over the latter's actions. Pilate was negligent in acting in line with the powers of his office, and did not live up to the integrity expected of Caesar's minister. Herod, who held no jurisdiction in Jerusalem or Judea, could not intervene in this affair without blowing up the empire's rights. Jesus Christ's case, the criminal trial, the compilation of evidence and the sentence, corresponded in the first instance to the Sanhedrin, or the Jewish nation's great council, which effectively pronounced a death sentence. But it was necessary for it to be valid to return the case to the governor presiding over Judea, since he was the leader in whom the empire's supreme authority was deposited; and he could either revoke or confirm that sentence. Pilate could not preside, nor should he have presided, over this judicial precedent. So sending back Jesus Christ to the tetrarch of Galilee, the new interrogation and charges laid against him, and all that Herod did was impertinent, illegal, and forceful. Without doubt, this was the reason why Jesus Christ did not recognise the foreign leader as his competent judge, and did not answer anything to his questions.

Herod was very far from seeing a miracle from him whom he could not get out a single word; and so he resented him regarding him as the peak of contempt. Those having this leader's temperament, while getting easily irritated, dare not make decisions making them look like being gullible. To get out of this conflict with honour, he thought saying that Pilate had sent him a madman and a fool, and saying this he dared to insult God's wisdom, which is ever unknown by human reason in all ages. He therefore commanded that he be dressed, in a white garment, with the aim of making him appear in public, either as a self-conceited man who thought he was someone great, or as a purely comic king. In this manner he sent him to Pilate, and this was a means of reconciliation between the two, as from this day onwards these two wicked judges made friends, and from enemies they became friends, joined together with the bond of a common injustice.

CHAPTER 83

HEROD SENDS BACK THE SAVIOUR TO PILATE, WHO MAKES SOME EFFORTS, EVEN IF WEAK ONES, TO SAVE HIM. HE UNDERGOES A NEW INTERROGATION; IS WHIPPED, CROWNED WITH THORNS, DRESSED IN A PURPLE CLOAK AND RIDICULED, CONFRONTED WITH BARABBAS, AND FINALLY CONDEMNED TO A DISGRACEFUL DEATH ON THE CROSS

HIS short walk was for Jesus Christ as much of an annoyance as an affront, all resulting from the middle course which Pilate had chosen with such delight to get out of the conflict in which he found himself; although he could have reconciled with his enemy, he nevertheless did not free himself from a danger he did not know how to avert. Being however resolved not to yield to his enemies' violence, he convened the priests' leaders, chieftains and people's elders and said to them: "You see this man whom you have brought before me as a seditious person who keeps the people away from obedience and tries to take them away from Caesar's authority. I have examined him carefully as to all details, I have questioned him before you and I find that he neither admits nor could be convicted of any of the crimes of which you accuse him. To satisfy your desires, I have referred him to Herod, who must know of Jesus of Nazareth as well as you do, and better than I do, for he has spent the best part of his life in the towns falling under his jurisdiction. Although despising him, Herod did not judge him worthy of death; so neither can I condemn him without committing an injustice. So, I will have my attendants execute punishment upon him, and then I will let him free." No greater injustice could be delivered, nor a more hopeless and reckless contradiction could be awarded. Pilate had already declared three times that Jesus Christ was innocent, and yet he still offers to treat him as a criminal. Would it not have been better to make the unjust slanderers tremble by threatening them with the severe punishment which Roman laws imposed on such crimes, than to yield to the atrocious demands of slander and malignity? Is it possible that there should be such an unjust leader as to sacrifice to the vile and low passion of interest the good desires of his heart, the remorse of his conscience and the interests of justice and public vengeance?

Pilate thought that punishing Jesus Christ in this way would suffice to appease his enemies' infuriated spirits; but considering that he was dealing with headstrong and obstinate spirits, unable to listen to reason, he hoped winning them over in a manner about which he thought there and then and which seemed to him to be the most fitting. Indeed, since the very first years of the Jews' subjection to the Romans, the emperors had conceded to them that in memory of the freedom of the sons of Israel from Egyptian captivity, the governor sent to them by Caesar would let them select at the time of Passover a Jew imprisoned for a capital offence; the chosen prisoner would then not only be granted his freedom, but an irrevocable abolition of his crime. On this occasion Pilate believed that he would put them in a position of consenting to letting Jesus Christ go free, also because he was persuaded of his innocence, as well as of the envy with which the priests' leaders looked upon him. So that being aware that the people knew they had received none but benefits and favours from Jesus Christ, he limited their choice to only between two persons about whom they had to deliberate. One was the holiest of holies, the other was a famous criminal called Barabbas, whom they had captured with arms in hand in a revolt during which he had murdered another person; more than that he was a thief by profession, discredited by his thefts and robberies. So bringing the people before him, Pilate said to them: "Today is the day when you should enjoy the graces customarily granted to you. I intend letting a prisoner go free on the occasion of the Passover solemnity; but I want you to choose one from the two I will name to you. You have presented Jesus Christ of Nazareth to me to judge him; and having examined him in your presence, and in detail, I find nothing in him worthy of death. So now see whom of these two you want to let go free, Jesus Christ, or Barabbas." Undoubtedly, this was a very humiliating choice for the Saviour; but Jesus Christ consumed all the bitterness in the depths of his heart solely for the love of us.

Pilate reckoned that in proposing these two persons there would be no doubt as to who was to be chosen, and that the people would cry out for the freedom of him who was considered as the Messiah, rather than for that of a public evildoer. But the priests' leaders and the elders had already given advice to the people and made them ask for Barabbas' freedom and the death of Jesus Christ. The people's response asking for the murderer's freedom and the death of the just, could not fail to surprise the governor, who in view of so much fierceness and inhuman cruelty, could not but fervently ask the people and say to them: "So what do you want to do with the One whom you call king of the Jews, or of Jesus who calls himself Christ?" Yet the people, upset as they were and moved by the priests' fury, cried out saying, "Crucify him." Pilate was still dazed by this thought of Christ and his kingdom, so hoping to inspire some restraint in them; but nothing went well for him, nor did anything suffice to soften their hardened heart. Yet he replied to the people: "What evil has Jesus Christ done to you? What crime did he commit for which I may condemn him?" "Crucify him, crucify him," the mob urged, with renewed noise and uproar. "We ask for his death, he deserves it and only you can deny it." "I cannot grant it," the governor replied, "because I find no cause or pretext to make him die. I will punish him and set him free." Hearing these words the fire within them was rekindled, the shouting increased and the tumult grew; and amidst the angry echoes of the revolt, only these voices were heard, growing ever stronger: "Crucify him, crucify him."

Pilate, shivering to see the revolt grow and become even more threatening, raised his voice and said to the people: "Your desires will be satisfied; but I want you to be aware of my temperament right now." So believing that he was in some way appeasing or softening the rage of Jesus Christ's enemies, he caused him to be tied and whipped cruelly with a kind of whip used only to punish slaves. The King of kings suffered this torment without complaint; for being

God, he not only wanted to make himself man for us, but a slave in the midst of men. So that Pilate, greatly fearing a tumult would break out, was a tool of divine justice, preferring to violate justice to the detriment of innocence rather than to defend innocence at the expense and risk to his own life. However, Jesus Christ's words and Holy Scripture sayings had to be fulfilled. The Saviour had told his disciples that he would be handed over to the people to be mocked and scourged; as he had already been mocked around, this now had to be followed by whipping. He is taken to the praetorium and he, who would soon attract all things towards him, follows those dragging him along. The tormentors loosen the ties and strip off his clothes. They put Jesus Christ before the column, and drawing near to it he embraces it, so implying with this magnanimous act that in being bound to it, it is not because man could bind him but because he wanted to be bound; and he was tied by his feet, hands and neck, so that he, who had come to seek those who fled from him, would not flee from the punishment of being wounded, mistreated and scourged. This mystery of God being scourged in his human form is so great that it cannot in itself be understood or explained. As referred to by Saint Jerome: "Six tormentors draw near to him; two of them carry thorny rods, two with knotty straps, two with iron chains. The first cause injuries with all their strength, adding wounds one upon the other, with blood flowing. Tiring out, the first two men were replaced by a second couple; they too heaped new wounds on the old ones. They were then followed by the third pair who used sticks to tear off his flesh and skin. So that with utmost fury they hurled themselves on the flesh of the Incarnate Word, the scope then being to see human flesh surrender not being able to hold out against such great torments. By whipping him, hitting him with straps and repeated blows one upon the other as on a hard anvil, they tore off forcefully and atrociously the skin from the flesh, the flesh off the bones and destroyed as much as they could the physique and constitution of the human body. They wanted to leave nothing in him, neither blood in the veins, liveliness in the nerves, strength in the limbs, unity in the joints, flesh on the bones, agility in the hands, firmness in the feet, hair on his head, beauty on his face, or spirit in the body, rather not even a semblance of a man in humanity. The words he uttered by David could have never been any more true: "I am a worm and not a man. I was once the most beautiful of the sons of men; but now for you I am a worm and not a man" (Ps 21:7).

Pilate apparently did not want to leave anything undone to free Jesus Christ from death, the same as the Jews did not omit anything to put him to death. Thus, while one against all attempts to exempt Christ from death, all but one do their best to exterminate him by death; so that in the midst of all this rivalry in whatever he did, Pilate saw that he was working uselessly. From this it results that in being divided within himself, partly in favour of Christ and partly against although not daring to take his life unjustly, he still wanted to punish him against all human mercifulness and justice. Alphonse and Adolph estimate that the number of lashes they gave him amounted to fifteen thousand three hundred and seventy; and Lanspergius writes that by divine revelation it was known that the drops of blood which were shed from Christ's body exceeded two hundred and thirty thousand. But so many blows, so many sores, so many wounds, so much blood, are all so little compared to the love with which he suffers and to the desire to suffer even more and more; for being so excessive, it cannot be calculated, it does not match any number, it being infinite. So great was Christ's love, that he was all set, for the salvation of a single creature, to receive as many blows as there is sand in the sea, as many wounds as there are stars in the sky, and to shed as many drops of blood as there are atoms in the sky region. He was very much willing to be scourged, not for an hour, but from the beginning to the end of the world. Briefly, he was resolved to die, and for this reason he obeyed Pilate without saying anything. And though he knew well what the result of his inhuman ploy would be, he submitted himself silently to it, not to appease the people's fury but that the prophecies might be fulfilled, that he might obey his Father, and that all heavenly vengeance for our sins might be consumed on his innocent flesh.

Although Pilate knew that all his attempts were in vain, he gave in to being inhumane to the extreme rather than to be compassionate uselessly. He left Jesus Christ in the hands of his Roman soldiers to do deal with him; these soldiers, being advised by those who had treated him so unworthily in the chief priests' houses, were not content to imitate their fierceness but went even further, exceeding their doings to such an extent, that their brutal debauchery could only suit the Synagogue's harshness and cruelty which no sensitive soul could interpret or contemplate without shedding torrents of tears. The Roman soldiers had heard it being said that Jesus Christ was to be greeted as king of the Jews, and they thought of really making Jesus Christ a king of mockery, however adding to mockery the harshest pains, so that the confusion would be more shameful. Around Jesus Christ, who is surrounded on the throne of his glory by nine thrones of never tiring or resting angels who assist, serve, worship and praise him, there gathered the praetorian guard. They clothed his bloodied and almost lifeless body with an old purple mantle or cloak, wove a crown of thorns which they laid and pressed tight on his head and forced him to hold in his hand a broken reed instead of a sceptre. Kneeling before him they scorned him, mocked him and said, "Hail, king of the Jews." And spitting upon him, they took the reed from his hand and hit his head with it.

Meanwhile the sacred veins open all over his body, with ample blood streams gushing from them to wash away the stains of our sins. So that those things which were tortures for Jesus Christ serve as our instruments of glory. When the ungrateful people deliver him, and an unbridled troop of soldiers pierces his head with thorns, the Redeemer uses them as loving arrows to pierce his Father's heart and incline Him towards mercy. Here pain overwhelms faith, and it would be a horrendous crime just doubting this faith. In this contempt and torment Jesus Christ is the object of the angels' veneration and of God's triumph. And what do Christians do in his presence who pride themselves in being his disciples, frail and gifted, friends of their convenience or slaves of their ambition? Pilate, being a gentleman, sees him, pities him and does not console himself except with the hope he has left to soften with this pitiful spectacle the hardest and most merciless hearts; so that having seen Jesus Christ in such a pitiful state, he could not but be moved and concerned. So, believing that the sight of that sorrowful spectacle would produce in the minds of the people the same effects as it did in his, he went out of the room onto the balcony and summoned the attention of the people who were waiting very impatiently, saying: "Wait a little, because I am going to bring you this man. I have asked and examined him in every manner, and I find in him no cause or crime making him deserve death."

There was a large crowd and an immense multitude of Jews outside the praetorium as Jesus Christ appeared holding the reed in his hand, the crown of thorns on his head, the torn and shattered purple cloak on his shoulders, causing his body to be seen well bound and darkened with his blood; in his disfigured countenance they could see the features of a modest pain, of a deep humility and of a most generous subservience. "*Ecce homo*: See this man! I bring him to you, that you may know that I can find nothing in him worthy of death. Look at him well, and see if you can recognise him. He hardly has the figure of a man. Why then do you want to take away from him that part of his life which he still holds, which he will certainly lose due to his great pains? See if this is that fantastic king whom you accuse of wanting to usurp the empire's rights. Do you think he will want to be king, or that people will go to great lengths to become his subjects? I hope that after so great a beating your desire will be satisfied; for in such a way I have corrected him, that now he is more worthy of pity than envy."

If the princes of that barbaric, blind and fanatical people were not so perverse and evil, surely the people would have had pity on Jesus Christ; but the chief priests and priests carried out their treacherous plans, and being deprived of all feelings of humanity they snatched it from timid souls as not a single hint of pity would come from them. So that these people, who were drunk with the blood of the Just One and possessed with furious vengeance, could only answer Pilate's pitiful exhortation: "Crucify him, crucify him." The priests' leaders and their ministers tried shouting most, although by their position and allegiance to the sacred ministers they were those who ought to have most abhorred the shedding of such innocent and most pure blood. Against such a tumultuous background of sedition, horrors and death, Pilate seems to have been somewhat enraged, and could not but answer them: "Take him and crucify him. Insofar as I am concerned, I find him innocent and I cannot condemn him to die." This meant abandoning the Just One to the hands of justice and to be themselves who would crucify him; for in publicly confessing Jesus Christ's innocence he was doing none else than openly confessing his injustice, delivering into the hands of the tormentors the man who, according to his own testimony and as it resulted from his inquiries, did not deserve the death penalty.

The Jews believed that the answer they gave Pilate did not even suffice to bring him about to pronounce a sentence against Jesus Christ, according to the reply he had given them, so they added: "We have a law, and according to our Law he must die, because he made himself Son of God." When Pilate heard these arguments, he found himself fighting divergent feelings. On the one hand he thought it was necessary to persevere in his opinion, considering that the One whom he had treated as a prisoner, was in all respects a great, exceptional and extraordinary man, or better still, a God who could not even be ignored by a pagan raised in idolatry; and on the other, he feared a popular commotion if he resisted deigning to the exaggerated pretensions of the Synagogue, who were accusing him of two capital crimes. With regard to the first, which was the sin of blasphemy they were imputing to him, they had already said to Pilate: "We have fulfilled our obligation by condemning him to death as a blasphemer, and now we come to ask our sentence to be confirmed. But as to the second offence, which is the crime of rebellion against Caesar, that falls only under your competence, and it is up to you to condemn him to death on the cross: and so, you have to crucify him, as you are the only one competent to do so."

The Jews' rebuke evoked great fear in Pilate, so that he again entered the hall commanding Jesus Christ to follow him. Being alone with him he said to him: "Where do you come from?" This was like telling him: "After hearing all these things being said, I perceive I do not know enough about your origins." Until then Pilate's admiration had also grown by witnessing the Redeemer's composed serenity which, together with the efficacy of his words, had not only greatly impressed him as to what he heard but also penetrated his heart in such manner that he was firmly convinced of his innocence. However, there was another new affair which pressed upon and disturbed Pilate's mood on this occasion. A man was sent to him by his wife bringing him an order from her; going to his side he told him what she said. "Hear what is obsessing me and let your own wife tell you to beware of failing in the cause of the righteous man whose cause you are judging. He is innocent, and you are bound to protect and safeguard him, for I have been terribly tormented this past night for his sake with visions which have frightened me greatly, and so look carefully to what you do. No doubt the God of the Jews has wanted to let me know that he loves this man very much, and wants me to give you this warning that you may acquit him.

It could be easily understood what terrible impression such message would bear on Pilate's mind who was already afflicted and afraid; and although he knew that Jesus Christ was a Galilean, it seems that he wanted to delve deeply into his origin and that of his ancestors so as to impose fear on the ferocity of the ministers of the Synagogue and so obtain freedom for that miserable man. The Saviour, however, did not answer a word to this question as he had resolved not to say anything in his defence. Also because he knew on the other hand that he should not explain the mystery of his origin to a man who had shown great curiosity on the matter of his reign without showing any desire to learn that which was of greater importance and went ahead with his determination, so he kept absolute silence on this point. Above all, because the Messiah's death on a cross and his glorious resurrection had to precede the teaching to be imparted to the people and prepare among the Gentiles the paths leading to the true religion. Pilate was offended by Jesus Christ's silence and, as if angrily, he said to him: "Do you not speak to me? Do you not know that I have enough power and authority to crucify you or to release you?" Jesus Christ, however, who did not answer as to anything when it came to his defence, did not want to keep silent when the time came to defend his Father's honour; and so to allay the pride of his judge who was so conceited about his own authority and power, he said to him: "You would hold no power over me except that it were given to you from on high." It was like telling him: "Every man is subject to the rule of law, and not to the whims and free will of judges, who receive public authority from sovereign princes; not to abuse it, but to keep order and provide security to the citizens; to restrain the impunity of the wicked, and to ensure that justice reigns and no one's rights are breached. By heavenly disposition go and serve the power given to you to perform God's designs and to cause the sacrifice which I seek to make of my life for the salvation of the whole world. My death is decreed by my Father; but not so that you will cease being seen as a violent oppressor of an innocence which you should protect, by taking advantage of the strength and authority which have been entrusted to you. Your fickleness, weakness and cowardice, your self-interest and vile kindness, are unforgivable; and how much more will that of the chief priest be who, in front of the people he has seduced, delivers me in your hands and with that popular commotion violates your equity and justice?"

From then on Pilate sought to try again and finally conclude by all possible means how to let free Jesus Christ, fearing he would receive some blow of divine justice; but as he was seeking these means very cautiously and timidly, he caused justice to belch out its last breaths in his own hands, and abandon this precious virtue at the very instant in which he should have shown greater strength to preserve it. He let himself be seen by the people, and all his concerns about him were exposed. He spoke in favour of Jesus Christ in the most effective and strongest manner possible, asking for his freedom; and since he could not command and order them as their master, they refused it crying out in tumult, that if he granted freedom to a man who was such a criminal, he would neither be a good minister nor

Caesar's friend. "It is your duty," they told him, "to uphold the rights of the empire, as it is our duty to defend the integrity of our laws. And how can you believe that a man who declares himself king of the Jews not to be Caesar's enemy? All those who make themselves king goes against Caesar." On hearing Caesar's name resound in his ears, Pilate feared a conspiracy, and the more so being compromised in the emperor's court, he forgot all about his good intentions. Fearing much more as to his prince's outrage than heaven's vengeance, he fell silent, shivered and in a cowardly and treacherous manner gave in to them, resolving to condemn the Holy and Just One by essence and by nature. So that he led out Jesus Christ; and about the sixth hour of the day, which was a Friday and the eve and preparation day of the Passover, sitting in the court which was sited in front of the courtyard, that which the Greeks called *Lithostrotos* since it was embellished with beautiful stones very artfully laid together with mosaic, and which was in Hebrew called Gabbatha, meaning a high place, he ordered his ministers to bring him water in a basin. He told them to pour it on his hands which he washed in the presence of all the people, saying in a loud voice: "I call heaven as my witness that I am innocent of the death of this righteous man. If you are determined to take upon yourselves the terrible responsibility which must pass on to your consciences, there you see it: your God's wrath will be felt over the heads of those who are really guilty." And then turning to Jesus Christ who was at his side, he made him come forward a little to stand before him, and he spoke loudly to the Jews: "You see your king here." And as it was, a loud yell was heard all over the place: "Take him away, remove him from our presence, make him die, crucify him." Then Pilate was content to answer coldly and indifferently to the troubled people saying: "Shall I crucify your king? The chief priests replied: "We have no king but Caesar." Whenever Caesar's name was repeated, Pilate shivered and his heart trembled, seeing that the tumult was raging and that nothing could now be done to contain the people's fury. Hearing how they answered him back, repeating with fury: "Let his blood fall upon us and upon our children," that is, "We consent to the imputation of this death upon us, and we are responsible for all its consequences," he finally consented to pleasing the people; and giving them the sentence for which they asked, he condemned to death the Son of the living God, Redeemer and Saviour of mankind, Jesus Christ God and true man, delivering him to the will of the executioners to be crucified.

Here is a transcript of the sentence by which Jesus Christ, our Redeemer, was condemned to a shameful death on the cross.

SENTENCE

E, Pontius Pilate, governor of the whole province of Judea within the sacred Roman empire, here present in our court and audience hall, having heard the criminal charges brought by the Priests, Scribes and Pharisees, the disturbance and cry of the people against Jesus of Nazareth, all being in agreement and saying as to how he has agitated and stirred up the whole city and towns, teaching new doctrines against the Law of Moses, making himself author of a new law, pretending to rise as a king, and as such having had the audacity to enter triumphantly into the city with branches and palms, and for having despised the jurisdiction and authority of Caesar, the great emperor, forbidding vassals to pay him tribute; but even greater scandal being caused by his presumptuous and blasphemous self-glorifying and repeated claim that he was Son of God, though being a man of low condition, the son of a poor craftsman and a poor woman named Mary, while pretending to be very holy, being a great deceiver, a restless man, a conspirator and a destroyer of the common good. Having committed many other colossal crimes, which are more worthy of being punished than made public.

So then, having considered very well and examined the truth of the aforesaid charges and finding his crimes to be most grievous, we determine that he must be convicted and sentenced, as we actually condemn and sentence him to be led through the customary streets of the holy city of Jerusalem, in such manner that he is crowned with thorns, with a chain and noose around his neck, himself carrying the cross, accompanied by two thieves for greater humiliation, and to mount the hill of Calvary where *villainous men are executed by convention, there to be crucified on his cross, where he will remain hanging until after his death, without anyone daring to remove him from it without our authority and permission. The two thieves will be equally hung on their crosses, one on the right and one on the left, while he hangs in the middle like a king for greater derision and indignity, so that he may set an example and give a lesson to all evildoers. We order this sentence to be published at the sound of the trumpet and uttered in a loud voice by the crier, so that the news of this reaches all and no one can allege not knowing about it.*

— PONTIUS PILATE.

CHAPTER 84

JESUS CHRIST IS LED OUT OF JERUSALEM CARRYING THE CROSS ON HIS BACK: WHILE CLIMBING TO CALVARY HE PROPHESIES THE RUIN OF THE UNGRATEFUL CITY, AND AFTER HE ARRIVES AT THE PLACE OF SUFFERING HE IS CRUCIFIED BETWEEN TWO THIEVES WHO ACCOMPANIED HIM

HE prophets' sayings had to be fulfilled, and in particular what Jesus Christ had said: The Son of Man will be delivered to the priests' leaders, those who will deliver him to the people to be mocked, scourged and crucified. David had foreseen these great events; and being possessed with utmost sadness he asked the Son of God himself: "For what reason, Lord, did they roar with courage and rage, and people and nations plotted and rioted unjustly and in vain? Earth's princes rose up, and by common accord consulted secretly against God and His Christ and Anointed One" (Ps 2:1-4). Certainly, Herod and Pontius Pilate met in this ungrateful city with the nations and people of Israel, to do what had been decreed in the eternal councils. They broke the strap of justice as they wished, shaking off the Lord's light and sweet yoke. Yet he who dwells in heaven shall withdraw from all His decisions; the Lord will mock them, speak to them in the midst of his fury, and trouble them with their viciousness; and then they shall be delivered to the power of the invisible enemies, whom they will now obey and deliver the Lamb of God to the most voracious wolves to be devoured, to rabid dogs to be bitten and to the most cruel lions to be torn to pieces. And it so happened that when the sentence was pronounced, the soldiers took him and with barbarous inhumanity and unspeakable fierceness they stripped off him the purple cape with which they had mockingly dressed him. And as it was stuck to the body with congealed blood, most of his wounds were fully reopened, causing him new and very intense pain. They dressed him his own clothes that all might recognise him; they loaded

upon his shoulders the heavy cross on which he was to be nailed; and laden as he was with this shameful and heavy burden, they made him set out on the long walk to Golgotha or Calvary. The word Golgotha, in its derivation taken from the Syriac, means the skull of a man, since many men had seen execution for their crimes in that place. Saint Paul gave the reason why Jesus Christ suffered death outside the city when he said (Heb 13:11-12): "For the bodies of those animals, whose blood is brought into the sanctuary by the chief priest as a sacrifice for sins, are burned outside the royal camp, and so also Jesus Christ, to sanctify the people with his own blood, suffered outside the gate."

The bad treatment he had received during the night, and especially the deluge of whipping and the crowning of thorns in which he had just lost so much blood, reduced his body to such great weakness that on leaving the city he fell under the weight of the cross. Letting himself to be crushed by it he groaned and stood still, not being able to move any farther. One can judge for oneself how the executioners would look at his faintness, and the inhumanity with which they would insult his frailty and weakness. The mobs which came out to touch him, as in other times, and regain their salvation, hoped for none else other than to crucify him; and the people who were crying out earlier to have him taken away from before them and to be crucified, were already glad to see their wishes fulfilled. The trumpet bearer walked at the front, and with the trumpet's hoarse and resounding noise called the whole city to the gates; he was followed by the administrators of justice, the executioners and soldiers, and then by the two notorious thieves, as much or even more depraved than Barabbas himself; and finally, stained with unblemished blood, came the great destroyer of hell, the great conqueror of death, the restrainer of sin and Redeemer of the world, Jesus Christ, bearing his triumphant cross. The people, who six days earlier had received him within the city walls, had then sung joyfully, "Blessed is he who comes in the name of the Lord," now cursed him as he passed by them; and as he carried the cross, they crucified him with their voices being unable to do it with their hands. Jesus Christ was going to work, through them and in the midst of the earth, for the salvation of the whole universe, as mediator between God and men. In this manner, those who had been sick and distraught had no regard for themselves and threw out the doctor who effused virtue to heal all. It was so that the children of wrath condemned the Father of mercy; it was so that wicked servants cast the Lord of the family away from his house; it was so that the cruel labourers drove the heir out of the vineyard. With this melancholy pomp, bearing the infamous bulk of that tree and the disgraceful weight of the cross, the Son of God trod his way through the squares of Jerusalem, murmuring to himself many times: Jerusalem, Jerusalem, how many times I wanted to gather your children together, as a hen gathers her chicks under her wings, but you were not willing!

Although the Lord preserved his life with his divine virtue for a few hours, according to the time allotted by his infinite wisdom, and in spite of all human power, he was not to die other than when it was with his own most holy will. As this was ignored by the Jews they yet feared that, crushed under the weight of the cross, he would take his last breath in their hands and would not entertain their pleasure of seeing him die under the torture intended for murderers and thieves. Owing to this well-founded fear they decided to stop a countryman, originally from Cyrene in Libya, who confessed the Jewish religion; he was named Simon and was the father of Alexander and Rufus. He was coming from the countryside and they detailed him to walk behind Jesus Christ and carry his heavy cross which the Son of God could not carry since he was very weak. Oh Simon, how we envy you and how all of Jesus Christ's Church admires you! In other circumstances it would have been a shameful affront to a free man to be called to perform this ministry; but what an honour and joy to be chosen by God on this occasion to relieve the labours of His precious Son! It may be that the surely Cyrenean did not know the price of the favour being made to him; undoubtedly, having as from now been received in the number of conquests of the crucified God, he has not been dealt a hundred thousand blessings to his bliss; for he may be happy indeed having been able to relieve, albeit for a few instants, the One who willingly bore upon himself all the sins of the world. As Saint Peter says, that we might die to sin and live to righteousness by his wounds with which we have been healed (1 Pt 2:24). Yet although this pious Jew was able to somewhat relieve the Lord of his heavy burden, that does not mean that he also delivered him from all torments. Jesus Christ lived only to suffer, and so he sought new sorrows which greatly increased his inner sorrows while outwardly expressing some relief.

A great crowd of faithful people and pious women followed the Lord, showing with their tears and sighs how intensely they felt his torments, and so giving public witness to the sacrificed Innocent One of the tender and respectful adherence they had towards his person. But Jesus Christ, who had refused to answer the great ones of this world, did not want to depart without a tender and affectionate answer to the fervent tears of those truly Jewish women, and so he only said to them: Daughters of Jerusalem, do not weep over me, but weep over yourselves and over your children, for soon days will come when they will say: Blessed are those who cannot bear children, and the wombs that did not conceive, and the breasts that did not give suck. In those days men will seek death and will not find it; they will long to die and death will flee them (Apoc. 9:6). Then they will enter the caves of the rocks and the holes in the ground, fleeing from before the frightful presence of the Lord and Jesus Christ's radiance (Is 2:19). And they shall say to the mountains, Cover us; and to the rocks, Fall upon us; and to the hills, Enfold us under your ruins (Hos 10:8). Hide us from the face of him who is seated on the throne, and from the wrath of the Lamb (Apoc. 6:16). For if they do this with the fertile and green tree, what will they do to the dry wood, and with the barren and fruitless tree? Surely, the righteous will be put to trial and be troubled on earth; then, how much more the wicked and sinful man (Prv 9:31)? And the time having come when affliction, trial, and judgment are about to begin in the house of God, if it first begins with us, what will become of those who do not believe the Gospel and where will they go? If the righteous can hardly be saved, even with work, where will the unfaithful and the sinner go, where will they show up? In this way, forgetting himself and grieving for his people's misfortunes, the Lord proceeded to put himself in the hands of his executioners and take up and bear his cross.

As the Saviour had come into the world to teach and to draw it to himself, not even a limp walk towards torture could contain the fiery advance of his charity, and not give to those who followed him very important lessons; and going forward as a brave and valiant captain to the combat site, he was followed by the two thieves who were to be executed with him. It had to be that nothing in the passion of the Son of God, which was so painful in itself, should be lacking in any detail which could shatter the summit of his disgraceful treatment; and in the midst of so many sorrows the only relief granted him was a little wine mixed with myrrh which was no more bitter than the unpleasantness of gall and vinegar. This ought to have calmed him and was customarily given to condemned persons to numb their sense of pain. Jesus Christ wanted to experience all of sorrow's bitterness and harshness, and he cast aside this small relief since he destined that severity to the glory of his Father; and he wanted to reserve for himself all this unpleasantness, to achieve his merit. At once the executioners stripped Jesus Christ of his proper garments to crucify him. But in doing this, it was necessary to refresh all the wounds of his most sacred body; for since the blood had dried, the tunic was stuck to his body; so that in tearing it away, part of his flesh and skin were torn off, and a copious amount of blood spouted once more from his body. It was also necessary to tear off the crown of thorns and so renew all the wounds on his most sacred head, opening new ones to put the crown back in place. Thus Jesus Christ, exposed on all sides to the cold air with his whole naked body, covered with the blood that flowed from it, torn to pieces, wounded and pressed down with fatigue and comforted with sorrow, looked out far and wide to either side with his bloodied eyes to see whether there was anyone around to console him, yet he did not find anyone. Looking over his shoulder he saw his Mother, fully depressed with pain, and fixing his sight on her, this sovereign Lady naturally sensed her Son's feelings and most bitter sorrow seeing him naked in the sight of so many people. And although she herself was only a little less than worn out, she ran to her soul's beloved and removing a veil from her head she girded and covered her son's loins with them. This was what she herself showed in a revelation to her dear Saint Anselm, saying to him: Hear, Anselm, as I shall tell you of a fact, a most pitiful and sad one, and which none of the Evangelists has described: Having arrived at the ignominious place called Calvary, where dogs and other dead bodies were thrown, they completely stripped my only son Jesus Christ of all his garments; and although I was almost lifeless, I nevertheless removed a veil from my head, ran towards him and covered his loins.

After Jesus Christ had been given to taste the mixture prepared for him to make him feel its bitterness, he did not want to drink it, as we said, or feel the relief it might bring him. He also wanted to let it be publicly known that he was only asking for their good will and love, so that then obeying the executioners' voice, he lay down on the wood of the cross to be nailed to it, as he actually was, suffering everything with the greatest humility, resignation and patience. With how many nails Jesus Christ was crucified, is the reason for another very strong and hard-fought controversy among writers.

CHAPTER 85
THE SAVIOUR IS NAILED TO THE CROSS, MOCKED AND INSULTED BY HIS ENEMIES; FROM THERE HE UTTERS SEVEN MYSTERIOUS WORDS, AFTER WHICH HE GIVES UP HIS SPIRIT INTO THE HANDS OF HIS ETERNAL FATHER

T was the third hour, when Jesus Christ was crucified by the Jews; and the two thieves with him, one on the right and one on the left, and Jesus Christ was in the middle as Pilate had order. He who in heaven is surrounded by *angels*, served by *dominations* and *thrones*, assisted by *principalities and powers*, magnified and ennobled by *archangels* and *virtues*, feasted and applauded by *cherubim* and *seraphim*; who is worshipped and revered by an immense multitude of saints who praise and bless him forever and ever; who works for our salvation among us on earth, was nailed between two thieves. Who can behold the Son of God in heaven, and the Son of God on earth, without trembling and dying! God from eternity, without either beginning or end, is for all eternity seated at the right hand of his Father; and God made man in time, is born in a stable, laid to rest in a manger and placed between two beasts, dies on a rubbish heap nailed to a tree and flanked by two thieves. Yet between Bethlehem and Calvary there is a very noticeable difference. In Bethlehem he is feasted on by blessed spirits with melodious hymns and heavenly music; he is announced to the shepherds and wise magi of the East, with new lights and stars appearing in the sky; and he is sought after by all those who eagerly adored and regaled him. And here on Calvary he is cursed, blasphemed and mocked by the Jews, Roman soldiers and executioners; and while the sky, sun, moon and stars dress in mourning and deny their lights to the earth, they bury all in darkness to hide as much as they can the blood soaked tragedy which the passion represents; and the inhuman and fierce executioners do not offer to God the Creator and preserver of the whole universe, anything

but gall and vinegar, torments and pains, thorns, scourges, nails and the cross. At birth, the whole earth is clothed with beauty and joy, and the angels of peace fly around the heavens, rejoicing and singing; and at death the whole earth groans and trembles, and the angels of peace, standing at the eternal gates of glory, weep with the greatest bitterness. What a frightful contradiction!

Yet to reconcile the apparently conflicting opinions of the Evangelists, about the hour when Jesus Christ was crucified and lifted up on the cross, it is convenient that we should know of the division the Jews made of the day into four periods, which they called, *first, third, sixth and ninth*, but which could not be as exact as our hours. Like each one of the other periods the first took up three hours or so, and extended from the beginning of the day until nine; the third was from nine o'clock to noon; the sixth from noon to three o'clock, and the ninth until six o'clock; yet there always were some short differences of time due to the greater or lesser extension of days. Therefore, it is none other than an apparent discrepancy which seems to result in the way Saint John and Saint Mark refer to the crucifixion event. John says that it was about the sixth hour, and Mark says that it was the third; and as this period of time ran from nine to twelve, John could very well say it was about the sixth hour, and Mark that it was at the third hour. For this purpose, Cardinal Baronius finally added that it means that the time *started running after the third, to the sixth hour.*

At the top of the cross Pilate commanded these words to be written on a board: JESUS OF NAZARETH KING OF THE JEWS; as this was the underlying basis of his condemnation, and at the same time a glorious title, a public testimony of his reign, even if the world looked upon him as a trickster and a fool. This inscription was read by many Jews, because the place where they crucified the Lord was not far from Jerusalem; and to even those foreigners who had gone up to the holy city to celebrate the Passover, could understand it because it was written in three most common and spoken languages of that time, namely Hebrew, Greek and Latin. This did not please the chief priests and scribes, for more than a title of ignominy and affront, it was one denoting glory containing eternal truths which the Synagogue had so fiercely persecuted the Redeemer for having announced them. So Pilate had written them to justify Jesus Christ's innocence, about which he had spoken the truth by repeatedly assuring all that he found no cause in him to condemn him. Ultimately too, it was an inscription which announced to the whole universe, that the one who was nailed to the cross was true God and man; for he was seen to suffer as a man, he was announced as the Messiah promised in the Law, true Saviour of mankind, Son of God, the promised Christ, awaited and desired by them all. Then the chief priests roared out with full verve and courage; the scribes gnashed their teeth and were enraged; the Pharisees raged and burst with wrath. Understanding the glory of this title, they promised themselves to outshine it, but they could not; for having gone to Pilate to have these words erased, and to have instead written that it was Jesus Christ himself who had said: *I am King of the Jews*, this time Pilate did not want to accede to their request. Tired of their customary pestering, he dismissed them saying: WHAT I HAVE WRITTEN, I HAVE WRITTEN; without any need of waiting for him to change a single letter. Pilate on this occasion said, without him knowing it, that the Jews were truly criminals in Jesus Christ's death for having asked for it, and that he was as much of a criminal as they were, for having granted it to them. Jesus Christ was Saviour, and so he should not die. The word *Nazarene*, meaning *flowery* and *beautiful*, was a clear indication of his sincerity and innocence; so he should not have been condemned. If he was king, who had the power to judge him? And if he was a Jew, should they not have great respect and veneration for him? These were the great considerations which preoccupied the spirits of the Synagogue leaders, and it was for this reason that they asked Pilate to wipe out the title; but he could not set it right, for it had been written.

The victim of the world, the peaceful host that ought to have placated divine justice, was already on the altar of the cross. There was no doubt who he was, the title declared him, and he had to confirm that he indeed wanted to be the Saviour of mankind, and of his own enemies and executioners too. To this end he carves a pulpit, or majestic and holy chair, out of torture, and starts giving from it the most important and sublime lessons. There he sees the decrees of his Father's justice, beholds His almighty and vengeful right hand as being armed, and hears the terrible voice of vengeance, saying to Him: "For how long, righteous and holy Lord, would you not take revenge on sinners of the blood and grievances done to your innocent Son?" And on hearing this, he sees the justice of the lightning bolt of His wrath being armed, and then, showing His infinite love to the Redeemer of the world, he lifts up his half-closed eyes to the Eternal Father, and presenting him with his obedience and merits, says to Him: "My Father and Lord, withhold the arm of Your righteousness, and for the sake of this cross on which I die and the blood I am shedding on it, I ask and beg you, that you forgive sinners the sins with which they have laid me on the cross. FORGIVE THEM, FATHER; FORGIVE THEM, FOR THEY DO NOT KNOW WHAT THEY ARE DOING. They are killing YOUR ONLY SON, because they do not know him; and despite their ignorance is voluntary, it still makes them guilty, since they deserve compassion for all they are doing." The Lord could no longer move his body or his eyes, for some thorns had been driven deep into his pupils, but he still used his tongue contentedly for the salvation of his enemies. On the bed of pain, he conceived peaceful thoughts rather than distressful ones. Oh infinite charity of our most loving Jesus Christ, whose burning fire could not quench the tempestuous waters of so much cruelty and tribulation! What such high doctrine you teach us! Oh how well does the most merciful Jesus Christ fulfil the same precept he taught us to forgive our debtors! That we may love our enemies, and pray for our persecutors and slanderers, and prove ourselves children of our celestial Father who is in heaven! He taught it by living it, and practised it by dying. Who can refuse following such a noble example? So that it is necessary to forgive if we want God to forgive us.

While the Saviour strove to ask his Father for this very wide and universal pardon, the chief priests, other priests, elders and scribes were busy infuriating the corrupt mob of those requesting his death, while not ceasing to outrage him while he lived and helping and encouraging them by their example. The profane rabble passed by the cross shaking their heads; and insulting the Lord, saying to him: "Shame, you miserable One who boasted that you could destroy the temple of God and rebuild it in three days. Give us now proof of such almighty power with which you pride yourself. If you are truly the Son of God, come down from the cross and we shall believe you." The priests' leaders and scribes also mistreated and insulted him with the most dire mockery; and looking at each other, they directed their ridiculous and farcical gestures to the Lord, saying: "This man has delivered others from death, but he cannot spare himself on his own. If he is the chosen Messiah of God, if he is the King of Israel, let him come down from the cross, let him make us see his power, and we will believe in him. He says that he hopes in God, that he is the Son of God; so let God deliver him. If He loves him as much as he said, He can presently manifest it by freeing him from death."

The princes and doctors of the Law should not have admired such excesses in an ignorant and seduced people; but being vilified to this extent, and little satisfied seeing on the cross him whom they hated as an enemy, they would still fill their eyes with his affliction and insult his pains, acting in an unexpected manner, and something which people of their character never performed without bearing dishonour. There is nothing that ever leads to this excess, but it is reached when man fosters great hate within himself, and above all, when man hates with great envy. This abominable scandal played out its full effect. One of the two thieves who were crucified on each side of the Saviour, also opened his filthy and sacrilegious mouth to insult and blaspheme Jesus Christ, saying to him: *If you are the Christ, save yourself and us.* Wretched thief! Why do you doubt? If you doubt, you deny; and if you deny, what hope of forgiveness can there be left for you! Are you not moved to confess that it can only be Christ who with such unique humility in the midst of so many insults, with such profound silence among so many obstacles, with such undefeated patience among so many sorrows, with such well proven innocence among so many harangues, and with such a voice of mercy and love can ask the Father for forgiveness for his own tormentors?

The other thief could not remain unconcerned to his comrade's excess of cruelty; and being more faithful to the grace of the Saviour with whom he was dying, while searching deep within him and detesting his earlier crimes, he took liberty to put right the other thief as to his ill-doings and murder, so saying to him: "Is it possible that being so wretched in the state in which you see yourself, and being so close to death, you do not fear God? You imitate the angry people who harangue this holy man with insults and blasphemies. It is true that he bears the same torment as we do; but his cause is not the same as ours. We have no reason to complain, since we suffer for what we deserve; but this man has done nothing wrong, he has committed no crime." Let heaven and earth hear this; let Jews and Gentiles hear it; let the chief priests and scribes hear it; Caiaphas and Pilate and the leaders who accused him asking for his death, even blasphemed him after crucifying him. Finally, let the apostles who fled him, the disciples who went into hiding, the friends who fell silent, the Jews who mocked him, the Romans who crucified him and all the world waiting with bated breath for his condemnation, hear him. It is only a thief who absolves him, a thief who accuses the injustice of it all, a thief who testifies to the innocence of the One who is condemned as a criminal. Although two Evangelists say that before he too had insulted him (Mt 27:44; Mk 15:32), now he already acknowledges him, confesses him, worships him as his true God. Oh Lord, how fruitful your light is! Who is there to resist your help? Wounded by them this happy thief turns to Jesus Christ and with a tender but ardent and loving voice, says to him: "In you I trust, Lord, and in you I hope; you are my Father, you are my God and Lord, you are my King; and although you are the immortal King of the ages, and your kingdom is an everlasting kingdom, you have said that your kingdom is not of this world; *so remember me, Lord, when you are in your kingdom*. You are going to die, but I believe that your death will be the beginning of your eternal and true triumph. Then you will freely exercise your infinite power, for you will not fear the unjust persecutions of the Synagogue, in a much wider manner than you have exercised it during your lifetime: so I beseech you to remember me when you enter your kingdom.

"Oh Lord! Look at me and have mercy on me, for I am poor and helpless. Forgive me that I implore your patronage not out of boldness, but out of trust. *Remember me*, since you created me. *Remember me*, since you redeemed me. *Remember me*, for you have enlightened me and made me aware that I depend on you; I believe in you, in you I trust, in no one but in you I hope. Oh author of life! Oh my life! O life of my soul! Remember me, so that I die with you. May I share with you that precious blood which you have shed for me and for the salvation of the whole world, to compel you to use mercy with me, rather than all my wickedness to strive to make you abandon me. We are both condemned as thieves, both crucified as malefactors, both executed as criminals, so *remember me*, now that we are going out of the world together, so that we go to heaven together; now that I already accompany you in sorrow, that I may also accompany you in glory, and since I know you as King and Lord on the trunk, may I see you, rejoice in you and possess you as Lord and God in your kingdom. Look at me now, Lord, encompassed by death's yearnings and agonies; with pale countenance, tied tongue, soaking in a cold sweat, throbbing heart and dying in a hurry; hearken unto me, Lord, do not forsake me: *Remember me when you are in your kingdom*. Inasmuch as I beg of you, so much do I hope."

Such a beautiful attitude, such sincere repentance, such generous faith, such solid hope, such ardent love, such a frank, innocent, public and candid confession, could not but be promptly rewarded. Christ, then, to whom a single word in death suffices to forget the bad deeds committed in life, even of all, seeing him confess in this manner, grants him full forgiveness, not only of all guilt, but also of all sorrow, saying to him these tender and loving words: *Truly, I say to you, today you will be with me in paradise*; that is, "Today you will come to join me in the mansion destined for the friends of God, while I take possession of my inheritance and admit you into it after me. Before the sun sets on the world, you will see me face to face in the other. Today you will go out to the sheltering and calm harbour, from the midst of this gulf full of great bitterness and torments; today you will move on from battle to triumph, from aridity to the drinking fountain, from darkness to light, from scarcity to abundance, from vanity to truth, from what is temporal to eternal happiness. *Today you will be with me in paradise.* There will be joy without affliction, salvation without pain, light without darkness, rest without work, honour without humiliation, abundance without fault, life without death, glory without end." Oh happy sinner! Oh blessed and repentant one! You arrived on a great day; you arrived when the Redeemer had the key in his hands, and when the door was wide open. Blessed is the thief who succeeded in arriving at such a favourable time! Blessed was also him who had the great fortune to imitate him.

During the entreaty made by Jesus Christ to his Eternal Father to forgive his enemies, and in making the promise to the thief, he kept his eyes fixed on heaven, still praying to his Father for all that was agreeable to the salvation of mankind. Then, all at once, lowering his eyes to earth and looking from the high place where he was, he spotted in the distance a group of timid and virtuous people, who were weeping, sad and in great distress, all pitying him; there mingled among them his apostles, friends and some other ones very close to him, whose faith was shaky and whose hope was furiously embattled and frightened. A few steps away he saw the soldiers charged with watching over Jesus Christ up to when he breathed out his last breath; at the foot of the cross he sighted his Most Holy Mother, tenderly loved and infinitely respected, by one of his disciples, who was the most beloved and inseparable companion of his dear Mother; Mary, wife of Cleophas, Mary Salome, and Mary Magdalene, the most faithful and most generous of his chaste admirers, were also there; and above his head the Saviour beheld a sky which, though up to that time had seemed like bronze and not at all interested in his glory, was already beginning to be covered with clouds and a sudden fading of sunlight. Black and dense darkness spread over Jerusalem and over the whole of Judea; an ungrateful land, worthy of being buried in eternal darkness; it lasted for three hours and did not disperse other than when Jesus Christ expired his last breath.

God speaks of honouring the sacrifice of his Son, and heaven and earth, and even the insensitive and inanimate creatures, were to weep and wear mourning clothes on the death of God the Creator and preserver of them all. This was the beginning of wonders with which God wanted to show His beloved Son's divinity in front of all nations gathered on that day in Jerusalem, so that they would witness the sacrifice of the HIS VICTIM, of the GREAT VICTIM, who was to be sacrificed to Him on the mountains of Israel (Ez 39:17); and although in the sight of this first prodigy, which the furious mob did not seek to ascertain or delve into its cause, the majority of those present were not moved, nor did the soldiers withdraw, or the Jews show repentance or tremble; and friends and enemies, stood still together on Calvary. Nevertheless, the heart of the Most Holy Mary was impressed with so great fear that, had she not been sustained by the grace of God, she would have died there suddenly; but knowing her Son well and being perfectly aware of his greatness, she expected to see him, though penetrated with utmost intense pain, manifest his glory; and this glory was to receive greater splendour with the humiliations and torment of the cross. The hour was already near when he speaks of consummating the sacrifice, so Jesus Christ, wishing to close his testament, then turned again to his blessed Mother and to his beloved disciple, and saying just three words to each one of them, he closed his love's most admirable chapter. WOMAN, BEHOLD YOUR SON, he says to his Mother; and then looking at John, he said, BEHOLD YOUR MOTHER. Saying this, he looked at both of them, looking at everyone even farther and casting his sight and thought to the consummation of all ages.

He looks and calls his Mother, at his tender Mother, at his most loving Mother, at his afflicted Mother, to whom while still living in this mortal life he will no longer address with the most sweet name of Mother. He does not call her but woman, fearing that calling her with the name of mother might increase her pain; he also wanted to contrast the name of woman in the moments of redemption to the idea and name of another woman in the moments of perdition. First, it was a woman and mother who, at the foot of a tree and with the fruit of the tree, gave us death and opened the doors of hell for us; then it was another woman and second Mother who, at the foot of a tree and with the fruit of the tree, gave us life, closed hell and opened heaven for us. Truly, that if for man these words were of great consolation, for Mary they were a two-edged sword which touched as far as where soul and spirit are divided (Heb 4:11). How great must her pain have been, she who was easily known the great love she had for her Son. It was only the Mother of God who could have so much love for her Son, surpassing that of all men and angels together. And as Saint Augustine says, if the measure of pain is in proportion to love, there can be no pain which can be compared to that which Mary felt. Saint Anselm further says that: "No matter how many cruelties were dealt on the bodies of martyrs, they were slight or of not much import in comparison with the pains that the Mother of Jesus Christ felt on this occasion in the innermost part of her heart." And Saint Bernard concludes saying: "Such was the Virgin's pain on this occasion, that if it were shared among all creatures, all would die suddenly. But see here that while this queen of martyrs suffers at the foot of her Son's cross in the most atrocious of all martyrdoms without shedding a drop of blood, while this comforter of the afflicted is being most brutally afflicted and flooded with frightening waves of sorrow, there appears before us a most abundant field of joy and consolation. For it was not only to John, but to each one of us and to the whole Church, that he said as a dying man: *Behold your Mother*. The Mother obeyed, surrendering herself to the will of Jesus Christ and taking John for a son, and in his person each and everyone of mankind. What an incomparable bliss! And John, submissively obeying what Jesus Christ said, accepted Mary for Mother. What happiness! Mary is our Mother, Jesus Christ is our brother. The Eternal Father so loved the world that He gave His own only begotten Son. The Son so loved the world that he gave it his own Mother; and the Mother loved us so much, that she gave us to her own Son. For our sake, the Father did not pardon him and delivered him into the hands of his enemies; for our sake he did not pardon the Mother and pierced her most loving heart calling her woman; and for us, Mary did not pardon herself, making herself a shining light on the top of Calvary with the pains of her heart, accepting us as children instead of Jesus Christ. Oh kindness of the Father! Oh charity of the Son! Oh most ardent love of Mary! When would men know how to acknowledge him and thank him!"

From that hour John received Mary for his Mother, and had the heart of a true son for her; from that hour he consecrated himself to the service of such a good and affectionate Mother with all of his soul's affections; from that hour he took her home with him, and did not want his Mother to find another home other than his own. He was happy indeed to have hosted in this world that Lady who carried the Only Son of God in her womb, with all the gifts and riches of heaven.

After this loving testament made by Jesus Christ, in which he so explicitly showed his will and love for John and for all men, and in which he lavished the last cares of his mortal life to the most worthy and afflicted of all mothers, he did not seem to lack anything other than to deliver his spirit into his Father's hands. As darkness spread all over the earth, an underground rumbling sound was heard crossing from east to west, and from north to south, giving rise to a frightening earthquake and to universal shaking. They soon became aware of crushing rocks moving to break off from mountains, and of all nature being disturbed as had already become evident. In this state of human powerlessness it seemed that the Eternal Father did not want to produce any other form of evidence to prove the glory of a Son whom He had made obedient to Him until death on the cross to prove his glory. So then Jesus Christ lifted up his eyes again from earth towards heaven as if to tell Him: "Oh Father! You see that there is nothing else I can do that all men may be saved: put the work to an end and close it with your sovereign decree." But seeing his Father's effective decree that only the elect were to be saved, and that his blood and death were to be thwarted in innumerable souls which were to be lost, he began with this greater torment to agonise in his soul, further increasing this deep feeling when he saw that his Father resolutely closed the decree, letting him suffer without consolation so many torments in the body with so many pains in the soul; and seeing himself defenceless even without help from his Eternal Father, because so much did the sins deserve for which he had been made guarantor, he felt such anguish and so extremely sad, that breaking into a distressing and painful groan, he complained lovingly to his Father of his utmost sorrows. His greatest desire then was to teach man what he suffered for mankind, so that seeking some relief in his heart, he said: "ELI, ELI, LAMMA SABACTHANI, which is to say, MY GOD, MY GOD, WHY HAVE YOU FORSAKEN ME? Why from the instant when, as You willed, You gave me into the hands of my enemies, have You not made one of those sensational signs which would have made my innocence known to the world, while I still breathed and confessed to this unbelieving people, that the One whom they have nailed to the cross is Your Only Son whom you have sent to the world?"

Some of those present, hearing Jesus Christ's prayer and neither sensing its feeling nor the forcefulness of the words *Eli, Eli*, said: "He is calling out to Elijah," while others yet repeated "Let us see if Elijah will come to deliver him and take him down from the cross," uttering further insults and swear words against Jesus Christ. Yet what his words really meant was but a proof of the natural effects and innocent desires of a spirit troubled by the weaknesses of a patient humanity, and an excess of its sorrows and torments. It was also the desire to instruct us about what he cared so much about wanting us to know, namely that he was truly human, with feelings about miseries, sorrows and death, like all humans. If Jesus Christ did not show signs of feeling and of how much the cross weighed on him, and had retained a stoic apathy or serenity of spirit, and the silence which he observed throughout his life and even during his passion, it might be suspected that his body came from out of this world or that the Divinity had made him impassive; and so men would not properly appreciate what he suffered for them. For this reason he cries out, moans and says: "Why have You forsaken me? Why do You turn away from saving me, and from hearing the voices with which I cry unto You and the words of my groaning? Do not withdraw or run away from me when suffering and anguish threaten me so harshly, without anyone being present to help me and defend me. I was surrounded by many bulls, and the forts of Basan encircle me. Like a ravaging and roaring lion, they opened their mouths over me to devour me. Like water I poured out, I lost my stability and solidity, and all my bones were disjointed. My heart has been melted like wax and dissolved in the midst of my bowels. They pierced my hands and my feet, and my bones can be counted. They see it, look upon me and underrate me. But You, our Lord, do not walk away but be my strength; hasten to help me (Ps 21:2-13). Oh Father, hear Your Son at this very sad time in which he finds himself; remember that this is the same as teaching his disciples and the mobs that followed him, vaunting to fulfil Your will with utmost precision, and so that all may fulfil it I also said to them: *My food is to do the will of Him who sent me* (Jn 4:3-4). *I always do what is pleasing to Him* (Jn 8:20); and that to prove that I was your Son and that You had sent me, I kept on telling them that *I have glorified You on earth; I have accomplished the work which You gave me* (Jn 17:4), and which You have Yourself twice spoken out about Your Son, saying, *This is my beloved Son, with whom I am well pleased and delighted; listen to him* (Mt 3:17). Listen to him now, and do not abandon him or forsake him."

After this, being already aware that all things had been fulfilled and so that Scripture might be accomplished, namely that only one prophecy was still missing from his passion during his lifetime, Jesus Christ said: *I thirst*. His thirst was not the least agony caused either by those who condemned him to the torment of the cross, for whom he commonly held great compassion, or by the charitable women who brought him a drink purposely made for this occasion, in which they mixed some vinegar to give it added effect, and to fortify the hearts of those being executed and lessen their torture, possibly by also shortening their pains and hastening their death. The soldiers had, according to their custom, a glass full of this liquor, which they used while they wagered and had to stand guard for a long time; and as it also had some cooling effect on the body, reapers drank of it in their arduous labours. So then it was that when a soldier heard Jesus Christ's voice, he ran at once and taking a sponge he soaked it in that vinegar, tied it on a reed with a branch of hyssop and put it up to the Saviour's mouth to drink, without providing him with any other balm than the heavy mockery with which they insulted him at the same time. Who can describe the motives and reasons for this terrible and mysterious thirst which Jesus Christ now suffered?

That blessed tongue, an instrument of so many wonders, was stuck to the roof of his mouth: those loving lips, suffering the bitterness of so many torments, were dry; being exhausted with blood and sweat, he was afflicted anew and more sorrowfully with unspeakable thirst; and for this reason he said with a hoarse and tender voice, *I thirst*. It is not strange that this true Samson, nailed to the wood of the cross, closed with his death the gates of hell and opened those of heaven, and that in dying he triumphed, not over a thousand Philistines, but over all the power of hell and death. So that like Samson he said after the battle: "You gave to the hand of your servant this great triumph and victory, and now I die of thirst" (Jgs 15:18), for as always a terrible weariness produces a frightful thirst. Yet it is him who is thirsty, he who once called to all who are thirsty saying, "Come to the waters" (Is 55:3); and "If anyone is thirsty, let him come to me and drink" (Jn 8:4). And it is even the more so that in the excess of bitter thirst he should be helped with gall and vinegar; but it was necessary to fulfil what had been sung so many centuries before by David: "They gave me and mixed gall in my food, and to quench my thirst they gave me vinegar to drink" (Ps 68:21). Oh Jesus Christ! If you are the eternal source of living waters, what is that thirst which causes so much strenuousness and torture? It is an insatiable thirst to undergo more torment for our salvation; it is an inflaming and burning thirst for souls and tears; it is a thirst for even more love for created beings. This is why when they present vinegar which he tastes but does not drink of it; and knowing that heaven's designs were to be fulfilled, that divine justice is fully satisfied, that the prophets' sayings actually occurred, that the work of our redemption is concluded, that man's debts are already settled and repaid, and that they have nothing left to do but to join their labours to the merit of his sorrows, he shouts out and says: IT IS FINISHED, IT HAS ALL BEEN ACCOMPLISHED. I have nothing left to do; there is none else I can do for man's benefit and favour, other than what I have done. Oh most sweet Redeemer of souls! Truly, there is nothing left for you to do, for you have reached the summit of charity and the last line of love; you have now reached the fullness of your love, having done and suffered so much. Blessed are you, adorable Redeemer, for such an immense benefit, for such intense and adorable love. Let all the heavens and earth bless him; let all creatures bless him; and in due thanksgiving of such an unforgivable benefit, let them not ever offend you, but love you unceasingly, and bless you eternally.

With this mysterious and significant word the Saviour declared that he had finished what he had come to do and that he had faithfully fulfilled his Father's commandments. So, throwing himself entirely into His arms, he raised his voice, and taking the tone of a man full of strength and vigour, as a master of retaining his life and of giving it up, he cried out: MY FATHER, INTO YOUR HANDS I ENTRUST MY SPIRIT. This was not a supplication he made to the Eternal Father asking for His protection, as we sinners who live and die in the uncertainty of our salvation do, but it was the consummation of the sacrifice he made of his life, a voluntary acceptance of the death which seemed to be so near, and to which he offered himself generously. He so placed his soul in his Father's hands, and at that point he was the One who breathed, for whom they were breathing, for whom they sigh and breathe and for whom all the blessed spirits, both of men and of angels, breathe. Christ gave his body to the power of the Jews, so that using all their cruelty, they might, at their discretion, destroy him, injure him, martyr him; but they had no power to ill-treat his spirit. Only then he reserved his spirit to give it to the Father, that the Father might return it to him after three days and restore it to his body. The eternal lover of men bowed his head and died of love. He died, and the whole universe was filled with terror.

CHAPTER 86
EXTRAORDINARY EVENTS WHICH OCCURRED ON THE DEATH OF JESUS CHRIST; JOSEPH ASKS PILATE FOR THE SAVIOUR'S BODY, WHICH LOWERED FROM THE CROSS IS DEPOSITED IN THE ARMS OF HIS MOST BLESSED MOTHER, AND THEN BURIED

ESUS Christ died, and if anything before had been lacking to prove that he was true God, the occurrences and events happening at his death would have justified what he claimed. It seems that heaven suddenly gave a sign, and heaven and earth began to suffer, leaving him to suffer, him whom all power was given in heaven and earth. The sun reached its noon position when all light-giving bodies in the sky were put out, and a dense, dark and gloomy night, like that of Egypt, covered the world. All the sky was covered with a dreadful darkness, and the day only showed the horrible aspect of the darkest and stormiest night; so much so, that an amazed great Dionysius Areopagite, who was not more than twenty-five years old and was in Heliopolis, a city in Egypt, studying astrology with Apollophanes his companion, could not help but exclaim: *It is either that earth's motive power is dying, or that it is the God of nature who is suffering*; of course meaning that such long and frightful darkness could not be seen nor happen in that hour of the day, unless a clear and evident miracle was being wrought. The Athenian philosophers who were in the Areopagus, understood the same thing as their countryman Dionysius. So they erected an altar to the god of nature who outwardly suffered so much, even though they did not know him at all; for which reason they consecrated the altar *To the unknown god*, IGNOTO DEO, as we read in the Acts of the Apostles. The earth shook from its deepest foundations, trembling with tremors, quivering and wavering on all its axes, the graves moving and tombs being raised, the temple veil being torn from top to bottom and shred in two parts; as the elements rise in mutiny, nature seems to return to its

primordial chaos, and all things created look like perishing with the Creator. Even if it is true that when the tombs were opened, the bodies of many saints came out of them who, without waiting for the general resurrection, arose with the Saviour, as if death had not been but a dream for them. They proceeded to Jerusalem, and allowed themselves to be seen in this holy city, appearing to many people after Jesus Christ was resurrected. They were the firstborn of the resurrection, as Saint Jerome says, and the first among the living and among the dead, so that it may be understood that they did not arise immediately after Christ's death, but after his resurrection, and that it was later when they let themselves to be seen.

Had the hearts of the Jews not have been overpowered with such petty and ferocious passions, there is no doubt that so many great prodigies would have made them more tender. But being dominated with such a fury, which was rather hellish than frenzied, they were infuriated with divine signs, and no wonder was enough to cure them. The Man-God who, when asked, had claimed to have power over the living and the dead, and even over hell itself, had already died and no longer seemed to frighten them. They could no longer deny the wonders, but they described them blasphemously, making use of all their malice and superior influence they held over the people to discredit them; so that they were only rushing even faster into the unfathomable abyss of eternal perdition. When the centurion, or chieftain of the praetorian guard, who was near the cross, heard the words Jesus Christ had spoken from it in which he saw that man's agony, and sensed the earth quaking under his feet, and such extraordinary and horrendous wonders in heaven, on earth and in all nature, he was overwhelmed with fear and troubled in spirit; so that he adored God's wisdom who permitted the righteous to be humiliated, bearing witness to the truth and, without fearing the contempt to which the Jews might subject him, he exclaimed in the presence of the whole world: TRULY, THIS WAS THE SON OF GOD. It is heaven itself that declares this. He had said it himself; he had been persecuted without cause; he was innocent. The soldiers close to the centurion thought likewise; they shouted together with him and repeated his words. This was the first anathema that the Gentile world uttered against the Synagogue. It was already written in heaven; and those on earth indignantly repeated it. The sons of light were left in darkness and the children of darkness came to the light. The Synagogue remained outlawed for ever: and in spite of all its tricks, persecutions and cunning, it could not prevent a large section of the people from detesting its errors and condemning its proceedings, passing over to the party of the Crucified.

So many and such great upheavals forced the mobs to leave Calvary at once, some coming down the hill even more hardened, and others blissfully seeing things for what they are and being converted. Those persons closest to Jesus Christ, either owing to friendship, or by reason of kinship, among whom were those three holy women who had assisted and followed him, both in Galilee and on his last journey to Jerusalem, among whom were Mary Magdalene, Mary Salome mother of James the Lesser and of Joseph, wife of Zebedee and mother of the two specially dear disciples of their Master, all had for this reason greater freedom and occasion to approach the cross and meet the Saviour's loving Mother, even now with the holy and pious aim of consoling her and weeping in sympathy with her, or with that of presenting to Jesus Christ the honours and gifts which go with the burial. Some apostles and disciples of Jesus Christ, who had attended the scene from afar, also approached the heartbroken Mother who was now surrounded, without even being aware, by loving and faithful children. These, in fulfilment of her Son's will, came to pay tribute between them as homage to a most compassionate and tender love, and their respects of sincere faithfulness.

While Golgotha's peak, hitherto a theatre of fierceness, horrors and sacrileges, was being converted into an asylum and sanctuary of piety, Jerusalem, dominated by the fury of the scribes who had no concern for the horror of their deicide, and being occupied in seeing that the feast's requirements were set in place, only cared about seeing that the work of their wickedness was carried out, if anything still had to be done. It was necessary, according to the Law, to remove the bodies of the executed from the cross, and as the Sabbath happened to coincide with the Passover celebration, they believed it to be more convenient than ever to abide by this practice and remove those objects of terror from the people's sight. They begged Pilate, for this reason, that the bones of those who had been executed be broken and the bodies taken down from the crosses. Yet hidden in this shadow of lawfulness and with a show of piety, the true object was to lessen, or at least to mitigate as much as possible, the atrocious remorse of their conscience for the death they had given to the Saviour. Pilate granted them what they had asked for, and so they broke the thieves legs. But coming to Jesus Christ and noticing that he had died, they did not break his legs, but a soldier took a spear and opened his side; he did this either to assure his enemies of his death, or being impelled by an inner force unknown to him, in fulfilment of what was written, *Let not the bones of the Lamb be broken* (Is 12:16; Num 9:12). From the wound there instantly gushed out blood and water, either to show that the Son of God had a real body just like ours, or indeed to point out the main outcome of his passion, which was to blot out our sins and wash away all our stains, as it was written by Zechariah (Zec 13:1); or finally, to instil in all of earth's inhabitants a feeling of admiration and sobbing, the greatest which had ever been seen, as he himself had said: "I will pour out upon the house of David and upon the inhabitants of Jerusalem the spirit of compassion and prayer, *because I will teach them to pray from the cross, and nailed to it I will merit them with grace*, and they will fix their eyes on me, whom they have pierced, and mourn for *the One they have wounded*, just as one mourns for an Only Son, and they will weep over him bitterly as one grieves over a firstborn child. On that day the mourning will be great in Jerusalem, and the whole earth will be in great grief" (Zec 12:10).

When the chief priests and scribes went on plotting how to bring their wretched designs to an end, a righteous leader called Joseph, who in spite of his position had never intervened in their hellish schemes and was a hidden disciple of the Saviour, originally from Arimathea, formerly known as Ramathaim, a city of Judah, who had already shed all fright and fear since he awaited faithfully the establishment of the new kingdom of Israel, approached Pilate with holy boldness and confidence, and asked for permission to pull out the nails holding the Redeemer's corpse hanging on the cross. This was the time he chose to show up, for he knew that the time of the true call made by Jesus Christ to all people on earth had come, and so to respond to him as soon as possible, he lay aside all earthly respects and fears. Pilate was astonished when he got to know that Jesus Christ had already died, and wanting to be more sure of himself of what really happened, he summoned the centurion who had witnessed the execution, to know from him what was in all this; and being ascertained that Jesus Christ had indeed died, he commanded that the body be given to Joseph. Saint Jerome retains that in order to praise the integrity of this righteous man, David wrote at the very beginning of his Psalms: "Blessed is the man who walks not in the council of the wicked, nor walks along the path of sinners, nor sits in the seat of scoffers where fetid and deadly resolutions were decided." Being a senator and a councillor, he did not enter to deliberate with the wicked; yet owing to his faith in Jesus Christ he used to attend at night to hear his doctrines. For this reason, he was more in line with Nicodemus who, though being an authority on the Law like him, also attended at night to hear Jesus Christ. These two holy men went together to the mount of Calvary, and having also obtained permission from the Saviour's sorrowful and loving Mother, they went about the tender and sad ceremony of lowering Him from the cross. According to an ancient and constant tradition, Jerusalem is said to be the place where the Mother sat to receive her Son's body in her arms, thirteen steps away from the place where the cross stood. She counted each and every one of his most sacred sores, which she adored and wiped with the tears of her eyes, then flowing over the whole body, and this was the saddest and most tender spectacle which could ever be seen throughout the ages. All those standing around wept with the Mother; Magdalene, his ardent follower, did not depart from her Master's feet; the beloved disciple, now a son, stood near his head, holding both Mother and Master; and the weeping was so passionate and aloud, that its echoes resounded not only on mountain rocks, but also throughout the city streets and squares. All wept in unison, and all worshipped the body and most sacred wounds of Jesus Christ.

The day had come to its end, and the sun's last rays were soon to leave men immersed in darkness. Joseph and Nicodemus, who stood responsible before Pilate for Jesus Christ's corpse, dealt with paying him the last honours of burial. Nicodemus had brought with him about one hundred pounds of myrrh and aloe to anoint and embalm his holy body, according to Jewish custom, and Joseph prepared a new and very tidy sheet in which to wrap him. He had a garden near mount Calvary, where he had hewn a tomb for himself in a rock cave, and wherein no one had ever been buried before. Such close neighbourhood of the tomb, together with the short time available for the Saviour's burial, caused them not to carry Jesus Christ's body farther away; for the Jews began the feast in the evening, and on the Sabbath no one was allowed to carry a dead person from one place to another. So it was God's will that time was so curtailed, that there should be no more time than was needed to carry Jesus Christ's body to that nearby tomb, desiring that the piety of Joseph and Nicodemus should rise to the greater glory of His Son, without either being aware of the designs of His providence. So they led the funeral procession, the sole mourners being the pious persons who had been as if hidden on Calvary during the cruel event, Jesus Christ's relatives and next of kin, and some apostles and hidden disciples; the most loving Mother, the beloved disciple and the holy women who had remained with her at the foot of the Cross, closed the funeral cortège. When the Mother arrived at the tomb, she respectfully approached her Son's sacred corpse, and imprinting for the last time on his majestic and divine forehead, bathed with his blood, the sweet seal of love, she gave her consent for him to be covered with the shroud, that the body wrapped in the sheet be tied with linen sashes, according to Jewish custom, and that it be deposited in the tomb; there he was to be left alone and tightly sealed, so that when he came out of it, there would be no doubt about his resurrection. Even so, she undoubtedly inspired Joseph that on leaving the tomb he was to close its entrance with a thick and enormous boulder; and having concluded the charitable and honourable task for which angels envied them, they returned to Jerusalem, to which place they were hailed by the Sabbath and the celebration of the Passover.

It would be much easier to conceive than to explain the anxiety and unease dominating the minds of all of Jerusalem's inhabitants, in consequence of the great spectacle which had just been presented to them. The Gentiles knew from the sequence of events and from what the Jews themselves recounted, that the priests' envy, the scribes' malice, the Pharisees' hypocrisy and the leaders' horrible injustice, had sacrificed the Son of David and heir to his throne, making die as painfully and as shamefully as they could the greatest and most exalted among all men ever seen on earth, even were the least learned and attentive persons to catch sight of the great revolution which that death was to cause throughout the universe, giving rise to the beginning and fundamental cause of the complete destruction of the kingdom of Judah. The opinions and beliefs of the Jews were even more divided on this occasion. Judea's inhabitants, mostly those of Jerusalem, although not being unaware of Jesus Christ's foretellings about his passion and the consequences of his death, pretended not to believe anything and tried to soothe themselves with the shadow of the victory they thought they had achieved against him whom they did not want to confess as the true Messiah; but the Galileans, among whom were counted all the apostles and almost all of Jesus Christ's disciples, still retained some hopes, although still struggling with their great grief. While they feared and waited, the others who seemed secure owing to their triumph, were the ones most troubled and scared. They could not be disillusioned that Jesus Christ was a true prophet, and this conviction did not allow them to doubt that Jesus Christ's further predictions would be precisely fulfilled; but as it was demeaning for them to show they were believers, or feared the almighty power shown by the Saviour on other occasions, they seemed wanting to be cautious about anything his disciples attempted doing.

The spirit of fear, anxiety, and uneasiness with which they were possessed, compelled them to meet together again as in council, and they resolved to seek Pilate and tell him: "We remember that this impostor some time said while alive, *I will rise again on the third day after my death.* So command his tomb to be guarded well until after the third day, lest his disciples come and steal his body, and then tell the people that he is risen from the dead, and a fallacy happens worse than the first, and causing the State a more pitiful turmoil than it ever saw during his life." Pilate, who from his last secret discourses with Jesus Christ was ever attentive to the constant hearsay of what had happened in his passion and death, was not far from giving full faith to what his oracles said. The malice with which the Synagogue ministers spoke was not hidden from him, so that he mocked their vain precautions; answering them dryly, he told them: "You are permitted to have guards for the security of the temple: take from them those you wish, and place them around the tomb to defend its entrance." Receiving this order, which seemed to them very broad and satisfactory, they withdrew at once; and not being content with merely keeping the tomb under guard, they sealed the huge stone that covered it, that no one would dare enter inside. Saint Ambrose has this to say: "Consider the great treachery and malice of the scribes and chief priests, who not only dare slandering the Saviour after death, but also to drag in the apostles and disciples in calumny. The Master is accused of seduction and the disciples of being thieves, capable of causing a new flare-up among the people, disseminating a mistake even worse than the first. By ignoring him they utter a great truth, as Rabano says, for the Jews' contempt of penance was worse than the error caused by ignorance. Even worse was their infidelity in the resurrection than their cruelty during the passion; consequently, they would be plainly confessing having committed an error in the Lord's death."

With usual mastery Saint Chrysostom paints a beautiful brush stroke on this interesting picture, saying: "See how even the scribes themselves could not agree to prove the truth; for by what they pretended having done, the resurrection turned out to be indisputably demonstrated. As the tomb was kept under guard, it is evident no fraud was committed; and if there was none, it is without doubt that the Lord had been resurrected. The tomb was hewn out of a hard rock, and it was closed with another huge boulder; and it was surrounded by a sentry of soldiers, so that inasmuch as with great caution it was guarded, so would the virtue of the Most High shine forth when he arises. The scribes' holy concern worked out to the benefit of our faith. Guard him, you Pharisees, guard over him: God cannot be held in captivity; God cannot be kept in the grave. He who made heaven and earth, who holds them with the tip of his finger, and with palm of his hand embraces the whole universe, could not be held in the bosom of the earth." And finally it is Saint Jerome who says: "It was not enough for the priests' leaders, the scribes and the Pharisees, to have crucified the Saviour; they had to guard the tomb and seal the stone that covered it. When he was on their side, they did so to oppose the resurrection, but all their precautions only served to affirm our faith."

As all these memorable events, and many others which are not generally annotated, took place on the sixth weekday, or on a Friday, we close this chapter with some Latin verses which recall some of them.

Hail oh festive day, which heals our wounds;
An angel was sent, Christ suffered on the cross.
Adam was made, and he at the same time fell.
On account of the tithe, Abel fell by his brother's sword,
Melchisedek made an offering, Isaac was laid on the altar,
John, Christ's Baptist, was beheaded.
Peter was rescued, James was killed under Herod.
Many of the Saints' bodies will rise again with Christ.
Yet the good thief will receives his through Christ. *Amen.*

CHAPTER 87
THE SOUL JESUS CHRIST'S DESCENDS INTO THE DEPTHS TO COMFORT THAT OF THE RIGHTEOUS WHO AWAITED HIS HOLY ARRIVAL

HEN Jesus Christ died, his most blessed soul united to divinity, descended to the lower world to visit those of the holy fathers who were held captive there. He kept these illuminated with his divine presence, making them rejoice and comforted with the pleasure of his divine vision, filling them to such an extent that they were then truly in Paradise, not as to the place itself, but as to the joy of eternal happiness, being delighted by the divine presence which they saw clearly at that instant. The promise which Jesus Christ made to the thief a few hours before, saying to him, *Today you will be with me in Paradise*, had been fulfilled. Yet although Christ's flesh was by death separated from the soul, which was united with divinity, this notwithstanding, it remained whole after the death of the Son of God, since the grace of wholeness is by reason and nature a greater and more permanent gift than the grace of adoption which is never lost in saints without feeling guilt. Therefore, since never did sin abide in Christ, it was impossible for the union of divinity with the flesh to be broken, but it always remained whole, so that the same hypostatic union of the Word with the flesh of Christ still existed after death, even though it did not enliven it with the soul's presence, for this is how the body is made. And just as it is spoken about the Son of God in a manner suiting the body separated from the soul, namely that he was buried, so it is also said of his soul in a manner which is proper and specific to him, namely that he descended to the lower world, always retaining the hypostatic union of the Word with body and soul. Saint John Damascene clearly teaches this, saying: "Although Jesus Christ died as a man and his most holy soul was separated from his body without blemish, yet divinity was inseparable from one and the other." Christ's flesh rested in the tomb,

his soul descended to the lower world, and eternal wisdom remained united to one and the other, as Saint Ambrose assures us, disseminating in the midst of those places the true light of eternal life. That true light of wisdom shone; it illuminated the lower world, but it could not be locked up in the underworld. Job asks in amazement where can his place be, or where does he reside, and answering his own question, he says: "Earth's abyss says: 'It is not within me; and the sea affirms: Nor with me.' It is hidden from the view of all those living on earth, and it is also hidden from the birds of the air. Perdition and death said: 'We have heard of her fame.' God knows how to find it, and He alone knows where it dwells" (Job 28:14-23).

After this it is also worth noting that the term *lower world*, meaning a lower, below ground and deep place, which is hidden and invisible, is used by sacred writers in different senses, and it represents various ideas, such as the primitive words *Sheol* and *Hades*. The first is Hebrew and the second Greek, from which it derives, so that sometimes they mean the grave, and at others the state of the dead and the dissolution of bodies after death; sometimes the place of sorrows and torments that sinners will suffer for their offences and crimes after this life; at others the abode in which the righteous who had died before the coming Jesus Christ's remained waiting for the fulfilment of the Redeemer's promises. The existence, then, of a place reserved as an abode for souls separated from their bodies, was an article of the symbol of faith of ancient patriarchs and of the whole Jewish nation, and a necessary appendix or consequence of the belief in the immortality of souls and the future bliss they hoped to achieve by the merits of the Messiah. Before the coming of the Redeemer all the righteous died with this faith, waiting for the fulfilment of the promise in the *Sheol*, which they also called *Paradise, House of the Fathers* and *Bosom of Abraham*. This belief was not only specific to the Jews, but common to philosophers, to pagan moralists, and to all peoples who professed belief in the immortality of souls. All of them recognised *Hades*, a delightful place reserved for virtuous persons, or a place of punishment for criminals which they expressed with several and different names, according to the different concepts for which it was applied; as a place of prize, it was called *Elysian Fields, Happy Islands, Abode of the gods*; and as a place of punishment it was called *Orcus, Tartarus* and *Pluto's Kingdom*. Yet while not taking any notice of the faith and opinions of the pagans, it is necessary to know the belief of the patriarchs, Jews and Christians, or in the same manner, that of the Synagogue and that of the Church.

The lower world lying under the earth is thus of three kinds, or there lie three lower worlds beneath it. The first is eternal and very dark, in whose prison damned souls are tormented by unclean spirits, with an everlasting and undying fire, and it is called the *lower underworld, eternal fire, inextinguishable fire, burning furnace, place of eternal torture,* and *lake of fire and brimstone*. Job says about this place: "Let me so lament my sorrow for a moment, before I go where I will not return, to that dark land covered with the shadows of death; a land of misery and darkness, where the shadow of death has its seat, and where everything is without order and in everlasting chaos and horror" (Job 10:20-22).

The second lower world, which is also called Purgatory, is a place where with the same fire of the lower underworld souls are tormented for a time determined by divine justice, so that when their time is over, and they have been purified of the stain of guilt, they can freely enter the eternal homeland, in which no one enters unless having been perfectly purified. It seems that David was speaking expressly of this place when he said: "You made us pass through fire and water; but at last you took us to a place of restoration and rest" (Ps 66:12). So did Saint Paul when he taught the Philippians that on hearing the name of Jesus Christ being uttered, every knee shall be bowed in heaven; on earth and in the lower world (Phil 2:10). It is clear and evident that the creatures of both heaven and earth praise God and bend their knee on hearing the name of Jesus Christ being pronounced; but we must also know what those who dwell in the lower underworld do when his name is uttered. They are not those that exist in eternal and perpetual fire, for those blaspheme his goodness, curse his righteousness; and it was about them that David spoke when he said: "Turn to me, Lord, and deliver my soul: save me by your mercy. Because in dying there is no one who remembers you, and in the lower underworld who will pay you praise?" (Ps 6:5-6) "Oh Lord! You will not be praised by the dead or by those who go down to the underworld" (Ps 115:17). So, then, the souls who under the earth bend their knees on hearing the most sweet name of Jesus Christ being pronounced, are those who in purgatory await his mercy. And the third lower world is *Sheol* or *Hades* which we mentioned earlier. It is in this place that the greedy rich man was seen rushing from Tartarus to Lazarus in Abraham's bosom, and it was here to which place Jesus Christ descended after death.

If foolish and daring unbelief should in reply say that the story of the greedy rich man is not a true story, but only a parable, even conceding this truth we would still say that it is a parable which is intended to recall or represent edifying and instructive truths; that it evidently teaches the great difference in fortune which awaits the righteous and the wicked in the afterlife; and speaks of the existence of a space or place of rewards and recompense for the righteous, and punishments for offending persons. This is a truth which was announced by the greater part of ancient prophets, among whom there stand out David, Hosea, Zechariah and others, and which was afterwards constantly taught by the apostles as a dogma. It was a truth which Saint Paul instilled in the faithful of Corinth, which he repeated to the Colossians, Ephesians, Hebrews, in various chapters of his Epistles, and which lately Saint Peter spelt out in his Letters addressed to the whole Church. Only by knowing and confessing this truth can one reconcile several thousands of different passages of Holy Scripture: tell us, if not so, what would Holy Scripture wants to tell us, that when Abraham died he went to join his people, and that his two sons Isaac and Ishmael buried him in a grotto located in the fields of Efron (Gen 25:8-10). To say that these expressions mean that Abraham was placed in the same tomb as his fathers makes no sense and is a revolting commentary on historical truth; for the elders and fathers of this patriarch died in Chaldea, and Abraham was buried with Sarah his wife in the country of Canaan. The same applies to Isaac, Abraham's son, and to Jacob, who was Isaac's son (Gen 35:29; 49:12). But the place where this doctrine is discovered as clearly as possible is in the death of Moses. This great man climbs by express order of God to the hill of *Abarim*, to mount *Nebo*, located in the country of Moab, opposite Jericho, and from there God himself says to him: Behold and acknowledge the land of Canaan which I will give to the people of Israel that they may possess it, and then you will die on the same mountain you have climbed, and you will be added to your people and reunited with your people; in order that this does not apply under any circumstances to the gathering together of ancestry and posterity in a common tomb, since his parents died in Egypt and his ancestors in Chaldea (Nm 27:12-13; Dt 32:49-50). Thus, it is clear that these gatherings of the holy patriarchs together with their families, point towards the existence of this *Sheol* or *Hades*, where the righteous gathered from the beginning of the world, there waiting for the coming of the Messiah, Redeemer and Saviour of mankind; there where Jesus Christ the true Messiah, Redeemer and Saviour descended after death to rejoice and comfort them.

As a victorious captain over the lower world and death, he would make his triumphant entry preceded by celestial music. Its resounding but consoling echo would cast down to the ground the bronze doors locking up the lower world, and their gloomy abodes would be illuminated by the brightness of the eternal sun, inflamed with the brilliance of that new light which had been awaited for so many centuries. So that then they would say to the Saviour: "You have come at last, you have arrived, our sweet Saviour, and having mercy on us you came to break the chains that have bound us to this place for so long. Our sighs were addressed to you, our long and heavy laments were directed to you, and you came to fill us with glory, consoling us with your divine presence, because in seeing you, Lord, we see true glory. Blessed are you, most beloved Redeemer, and bless all creatures of heaven and earth, for you are holy and merciful, and you have been bountiful with all." Jesus Christ's Church professed this doctrine of the symbol of the apostles from when it was first established: and although it is not read in some symbols used by the Greek Church, nor in the Nicene Creed, or in that of Constantinople chanted every day by the Latin Creed, it is found in that of Aquileia as interpreted by Rufinus, and in several others whose ancient origins date back to apostolic times. This should be enough for us to believe and confess it as a dogma of our faith deposited in all the Churches of the Christian world, in terms of the Apostles' declaration and promulgation. All the bishops, fathers and doctors of the Eastern and Western Church, Greek and Latin, have taught and preached it uniformly and constantly; and that of Spain has published and taught it in several Spanish Councils, most particularly in that of Toledo IV and XVI, and for the same reason this was also the belief and doctrine of our elders, fathers and saints. And if all that has been said were not sufficient to dispel any doubt which impiety might arouse about belief in this dogma, let there be borne in mind the famous profession of faith of the Lateran General Council, celebrated during the pontificate of the great Innocent III. So this is not a debatable and controversial point from which no Catholic is allowed to waver, for only an unbeliever and an infidel are those who dare deny what the Catholic Church believes and confesses, and which it holds to be definite and approved.

CHAPTER 88
JESUS CHRIST RISES FROM THE DEAD, AND THE GUARDS OF THE TOMB FLEE FULL OF FEAR AND DREAD: HE APPEARS THE SAME DAY, FIRST TO HIS MOTHER, THEN TO MARY MAGDALENE, THEN TO THE PIOUS WOMEN, AND FINALLY TO THE DISCIPLES WHO WALKED ALL THE WAY FROM JERUSALEM TO EMMAUS (MT 28:1-7; MK 16:1-7; LK 24:13-35; JN 20:1-9; 11-18)

FROM six o'clock in the evening of Friday, that is, a short time before the beginning of the Sabbath and the Passover, until the dawn of the first day, that is of our Sunday, the body of Jesus Christ remained in the tomb, when it then rose out of it victorious and triumphant over death. The soldiers posted by the Synagogue watched beside him, and the Eternal Father, into whose hands his beloved Son had put his soul, reunited it to his divine body. Jesus Christ, who in the midst of the insults and pains of his passion, and the anxieties and agonies of his death, had not ceased for a single moment to be the Son of God, who gave up his spirit because he wanted to, who took it again at his pleasure, and because by doing so he suited the majesty and glory of the Only Son of God, already enjoying a new life, he neither bothered nor did he remove, in order to leave the tomb, the large stone that closed its entrance, penetrating it with the virtue belonging to glorious bodies, and leaving the clothes in which his body had been wrapped, he moved away from his burial place. If there were nothing left but to meditate on this mystery, we could certainly adopt Saint Jerome's thought, perfuming ourselves with exquisite scents and filling our hearts with soft and fragrant ointments like the Holy Bride, to go out to receive the heavenly and triumphant King, and crown him with the diadem of honour and glory, with which his own Mother was crowned on the day of the main joy of her heart. For indeed the winter of the blackest and fiercest storm has already passed, and the clear and peaceful day of true bliss, of fortune and peace, which the Lord made that we might all be glad and rejoice in him, has already started to dawn.

But following this mysterious allegory, we must agree that it is not only the tender cooing of the turtledove or the gentle caress of the dove that is heard on earth, and although the vines had already bloomed and spread their pleasant smell, although the flower of life sprouted and gave redemption's copious fruit, though after a black and stormy night the beautiful sun which had been eclipsed on the cross reappeared, and although the Spouse appeared resurrected already in his glory and he who for about three days had slept under his shadow to awaken those who slept the sleep of death, a great earthquake shook in the surroundings. The angels of the Lord who had so bitterly wept over the horrors of the death of the God-Man, hastened to prepare the way for the manifestation of his glory, and for it to be as terrible and frightful as the manifestation of his triumph had been; Saint Augustine said about this: "After the mockery and the scourging, after the thorns and the cross, after the nails and the mixtures of gall and vinegar, and finally after death and the descent into the lower world, came the glorious and magnificent resurrection. How embarrassing was that event!" The same insensitive creatures who had been moved in his misfortune, were equally moved when they saw his magnificence and glory; and when the thick boulder at the entrance to the tomb was turned, when the eyes of the heavenly minister who sat on it sparkled, and when they saw that their gazes gave off rays that illuminated the dark rooms and terrified all of them, some fell as if dead, and others fled possessed of dread and fear to give to the members of the Synagogue the new mortal news no one expected. Nothing worse could ever happen. The angel's appearance was as terrifying and dazzling as that of lightning, and his garments were as white as snow and with their radiance troubled their eyes.

While the Jews fled in terror from the tomb and gave the ministers of the Synagogue the news they did not expect; while the women bearing the name of Mary were preparing the fragrance mixtures to go very early in the morning to visit the place where all their affections were directed to once more anoint their Master, then, when the hour comes, Jesus Christ leaves the company of the righteous ones whom he had gladdened, and goes to console and rejoice with his most beloved and afflicted Mother before doing so with any other creature of earthly beings. The Evangelists do not speak about this event; yet all conceivable reflections support such occurrence. Saint Bernard says that: "Mary, being the Mother of Jesus Christ, deserved more than all other creatures; for never did she lack faith in his divinity, and consequently neither in the sure hope of his resurrection; and so while the other women called Mary prepared to go to the tomb, she was left alone, not so much because she was weakened and almost entirely fainted by grief, but because she did not want to go looking for the living among the dead. He appeared to her before all others, because as she was the one who had suffered the most, the first and the greatest comforts were due to her, according to the order of love and justice. Mary prayed, resigning more and more the affections of her will to the Father's hands, unceasingly uniting them to those of her Son, shedding tears of compassion and tenderness, when suddenly the triumphant and glorious Son appears to her, clothed in the most beautiful garments of his glory, the most beautiful and graceful among all the sons of humans; in an instant all his sorrow is transformed into contentment, all his weeping into joy, all his sadness into joy, and the tears he sheds are already those of satisfaction and comfort. Bow to the sight of your Son and worship him with as much as you ever can. She embraces him tenderly, carefully searching his body as if to see if all cause for pain had already disappeared. Oh for the special joy which occupies your soul when you clothe the body of your Son with those intensities of glory, *agility, impassiveness, subtlety and clarity,* which belong to blessed spirits? Oh, what so complete satisfaction on hearing from her Son's mouth how he had delivered the whole world from the power of the lower world, how he had chained its rage, and the sweet talks and conversations he had with the Fathers' souls in Abraham's bosom? Oh! What an inexplicable joy to hear from Jesus Christ news of her spouse the patriarch Saint

Joseph, of her parents Saint Joachim and Saint Anne, and of their relatives and next of kin!"

Although the Evangelists tell us none of this, the Church does not condemn this pious belief; on the contrary, it seems to approve it with the processions it authorises to be held on this day and on the occasion of this first apparition of Jesus Christ to his Mother, the first of which is made to the church of Saint Mary Major in Rome. If we were not to believe it because no Evangelist mentioned it, nor could it be believed that the Mother would have gone to the risen Son, for it is not said that he appeared to her even later. This would be a very remarkable oversight in such a Son with respect to such a Mother, even more so when the Son has placed in the first line of his law's commandments that after the honour and glory due to God we owe them to our parents. Moreover, it was not expedient for the Mother to be the first to witness her Son's resurrection, for if what the other women said seemed to be a delusion to unbelievers, how much more would the Mother, who was so interested in her Son's honour, have been slandered? Saint Ambrose asserts with the grave weight of his authority, and says: "Mary saw her Son's resurrection; she was the first to see it and she believed. The Evangelists did not want to write about this, but took it for granted and true." And Saint Anselm concludes saying: "If anyone asks how is it that the Evangelists do not say that the pious Lord first appeared to his Mother after his resurrection to relieve the pains suffered in her heart because of his passion, I will say that having asked this same question to pious and wise men, they have answered me that: These holy writers did not write anything superfluous in their Gospel, and it would undoubtedly have been written that the Son of such a Mother, Queen and Lady of the world, Empress of heaven and of angels, would have appeared to her when he rose from the dead, teaching her the mystery of his resurrection. This would have been to equate the Mother with other creatures, of which it is said that sooner or later he appeared them."

Wisely and opportunely the Lord had permitted that on seeing the angel, the guards standing by his grave were full of fear and fright, and they fled; so that the news of such a magnificent and most glorious event would spread everywhere with the greatest speed. The flight of the sentries enabled the pious women, who had bought aromatic mixtures once more to anoint and embalm the body of Jesus Christ, to go to that place free of all misgivings. It also made it possible for the apostles to safely assess what had happened. The woman who loved him most, ran very fast and was the first to reach the place of the grave; but still hoping to see her beloved before her companions, who were also making their way to the grave, and to have the courage to weep and vent alone to him the tender affections of her hearts, both she and the others were thinking and asking each other: "Who will lift the slab closing the entrance to the grave?" Mary Magdalene arrived, carried on love's wings, although it was still dark or before it was clear day, and she was astonished to see the boulder removed. She still did not retreat, but love emboldened her and she entered the burial place; but not seeing Jesus Christ's body, she ran off and came to Simon Peter and the other beloved disciple of the Saviour, and said to them: "They have taken the Lord from the grave, and we do not know where they have laid him." The angel who terrified the soldiers was not seen by Mary on this occasion; that is why she spoke to Peter and John of what she only knew and could tell them namely that *They have taken the Lord.*

The unconvincing nature of the news did not give any rest to the apostles: they both rose and ran, although the other disciple ran faster than Peter; but when the former arrived, he dared not enter, and going down a little, he saw the linen cloths laid and tucked aside. Simon Peter came and entered, and saw the linen laid aside and the shroud which had been placed on his head, not with the linen cloths, but wrapped and placed in a separate place. On this occasion John watched over his emotions of love, so that it would be him whom Jesus Christ had chosen as head of the College of Apostles who would first learn of all that had happened and find things in the position in which the Saviour had left them, so that he might compare facts with foreboding predictions, and so decide with authority what could be properly concluded from it all. With proper prudence of one who was to bear clear and authentic witness of the truth of a greatly interesting and glorious event, Peter examined what he saw and made John observe with him, and they were both convinced that from the manner in which the sheet and the shroud were placed, these did not show there was any rush as in a secretive and planned theft, but rather a fully evolved pattern of well thought strength of will and the realisation of an admirable design of Providence to show such a great miracle. So that without even seeing the angels or Jesus Christ himself, he must surely have had such a pure and certain faith in the mystery of the resurrection, that he was already in a state of being able to gather his companions and assure them, not only that the promises they had heard from Jesus Christ's mouth had been fulfilled, but also that his body had not been stolen and he had truly risen from among the dead, by which he wanted to encourage them to wait for the time when his divine presence would confirm this truth to them.

On this occasion Peter's faith is all the more praiseworthy, since it is true that neither he nor his companion John had as yet perfectly understood what the Scriptures said, and so not even the manner in which Jesus Christ would be resurrected. But it is undeniable that they returned fully comforted to Jerusalem, departing with strong feelings the graveyard where they would have otherwise remained for much longer, also because very soon it would have been dawn; for it was not convenient for them to make the truth of the mysteries public, even for the safety of the disciples themselves, that two of the Saviour's most faithful and close followers should be found by the ministers of the Jews in that place. Magdalene, the woman who loved him, dared not follow them, but kept on weeping bitterly, in the conviction that someone had taken away her Master from there: she was very sorrowful, as it should have been, and bowing her head she cast her eyes at two figures at the far end of the tomb. She did not see the sweet person of her love, but she saw two young men dressed in white and seated with majestic tranquillity, one at the end where Jesus Christ's head had been, and the other at where his feet had rested.

One of them was looking at her all in tears, when someone said to her with a kindness which she did not understand: "Woman! Why are you crying?" And she answered him, *Because they took away my Lord, and I do not know where they put him.* But when she spoke these words, she turned her eyes to the place from where the voice was coming, and she saw Jesus Christ; little did she even recognise him at all, but made him out to be the gardener who tended that place. And asking her why she was crying and whom was she looking for, she gave him the same answer as she had given to the angels: *If it is you who have taken it away, tell me where you have put it and I will take it.* Jesus Christ loved Mary tenderly; and as if to comfort her he called her by her own name, saying *Mary!* No more was needed; she could not move and fixed her tearful eyes on him, for if the sight of his presence might have deceived her his voice certainly did not, nor was she disappointed altogether. She knew him, so she threw herself at his feet to kiss and hug them as she used to do, exclaiming RABBONI or Master! But Jesus Christ, turning away a little from her, said to her: "Do not touch me, for I have not yet ascended to my Father. But go to my brethren and tell them I go up to my Father, to my God, and to your God." Having said this, he disappeared from her sight.

Some Fathers and other writers may cite several reasons why Jesus Christ appeared to Magdalene after his Mother and before the apostles, making this woman the first harbinger of his resurrection. It was a woman who first ran towards sin, and now too it is a woman who first runs towards the source of forgiveness. She who first made way for treachery in the depths of her heart when she was in paradise, is now the first to run to be clothed with faith in the tomb. She who greedily snatched death from the bosom of life, runs to the tomb of death to seek the first fruits of life. She who was then a rebel, now shows herself to be such a faithful servant, who apparently forgets her companions and friends, and obeying her Master's order abandons them to run to give the apostles the news of what had just happened to her. Let her then hasten to Jerusalem, as much beside herself for joy as she formerly was out of sorrow; as much overcome with joy as she was before with weeping; as much inflamed by triumph as she formerly was dejected by the offence; and finally as proud for utter victory as she was formerly humbled by frightful defeat. She then finds the same two apostles who had shortly before run weeping with her to the grave, and others who were still crying, saying to them: "*Jesus Christ is risen as he had told us.* Do not doubt; I have had the joy of seeing him, he called me by name and ordered me to come and give you these glad tidings. Hear the very words I have been instructed to tell you in his name and by his order: *Go to my brethren,* he said, *and assure them that I will ascend to my Father and your Father, to my God and your God.*" Peter and John did not doubt for a single instant; they knew this to be the Saviour's language; and recalling that they had heard him repeat these very same words on some other occasion, they instantly believed. Others, however, being more shy and timid, no matter how much they heard her affirm and repeat *I have seen him*, did not believe her (Mk 16:11), saying it was all due to the hallucinating imagination of a woman who was surely behaving like having been deceived by the force of her love.

It is not possible to pass on silently about what the Fathers and Doctors of the Church say on this occasion. Mary, full of bitterness, scorched with love, and not knowing what she should do, for she was not able to live without her Master, wept because she could not find him and did not know where to look for him. She was standing outside the grave, that is in the garden, since the force of love did not allow her to sit or lie down; and as she was standing, she wept and lamented for her Lord. Such was the fire of love which motivated her, so much the force of piety which drove her, so much the efficacy of the will that dragged her along, so strong the bonds of love that imprisoned her, that forgetful of the natural frailty of women, or of the fear darkness should cause her, or of the idea of the persecutors' barbaric fierceness, that all were enough to keep her from visiting the tomb very early in the morning, or to force her to turn away from it when the disciples departed. Being scorched with love's fire, as the fire grew more and more in her heart, nothing relieved her but weeping, nothing comforted or strengthened her but groaning and weeping; so that she could truly say: *My tears have been my food day and night, while men keep on saying to me day and night, 'Where is your God?'* (Ps 41:4). For by crying Mary achieved all she wanted; by weeping she had obtained forgiveness of her sins; by weeping she obtained the raising from the dead of her brother; and by weeping she deserved the consolation of knowing of the Saviour's resurrection. The eyes which had attentively sought him and not found him, now called out to him with tears, crying much more because they had removed him from the grave than when they wept seeing him hung on a tree; for she had no hope of ever seeing again such a Master so worthy of being loved.

No less remarkable and noteworthy are the words with which the great Origen praises Mary Magdalene's zeal, firmness, love and constancy on the occasion of her early departure to the tomb. "We have heard, brethren," he says, "that Mary remained standing outside the tomb, and that she was weeping. Love took her there, love made her stay, love forced her to cry. She was standing, and she looked around to see if she could see the One she loved and so she eagerly sought. Her pain came back to her completely, and she who had formerly mourned the deceased, now wept the One who had been stolen. This pain was more terrible than the first, because now she had no hope of consolation. If she had lost him alive, she now hoped seeing and possessing him after death; but stolen, she was also robbed of hope and consolation: for this reason she could not console herself with the sorrow of not finding him. Worry did not make grow cold within her bosom the love she had for the Master, becoming even more inflamed just by looking at him later as a dead man; as a result she wept bitterly, because one pain had been added to another. She carried both of them in her heart, wanting to relieve them with tears, but she could not. She lacked bodily and spiritual strength and did not know what to do. Peter and John feared, so they fled. Mary, however, did not worry, because she did not fear anything might happen to her, so why should she be afraid. She had lost her Master, whom she revered so lovingly, besides whom she could neither love nor hope for anything. She had lost the life of her soul, and she believed it would be much better for her to die than to live, since she thought that only by dying could she find him whom she could no longer rejoice while living. Here it was truly seen that love is stronger than death itself. What else could happen to Mary? She had become like a lifeless person, she had lost her feelings. Feeling she did not feel, seeing she did not see, hearing she did not hear: she was not present wherever she found herself, for her mind was at the place where her Master was, and she did not know where he was. She knew nothing but to love and cry for her dear One. She had forgotten how to be afraid, because she had forgotten herself, and everything in the world except her beloved One."

Saint Gregory says it is not enough for anyone who loves to look just once, since the power of love forces one to greatly increase one's efforts of inquiry. Mary Magdalene at first searched once and found nothing, but she persevered in her search and succeeded in finding him. While seeking her desires grew, and in growing she reaped the desired fruit. She bent down to search, and saw two angels who came to comfort her: her sight was the beginning of our bliss, and the outward showing of her sorrow was the beginning of new glories. Jesus Christ hears her crying, talking to the angels, groaning and sighing, and tells his Mother, with whom he was speaking, of Mary's zeal, and he takes leave of her to go and comfort her, she who was his disciple, for Jesus Christ is the consolation of those who mourn, and sees this pious woman shedding tears. Being moved by love, she looks away from the angels present to seek her beloved One, and that is when he deigns to appear to her, because it is only those who convert to God by love that see Him. She turned round and saw him, but did not recognise him, because she saw him less glorious; and so her first concern was to ask about the sweetest subject of her love, while the beloved One asked her why she was weeping. Jesus Christ loved her, and not wanting to cause her any more delay from reaching the happy instant, he calls her by her own name. Mary, he calls her; and Mary recognises him. Oh happy moment! Only the authority of the sovereign loving

One could restrain the outbursts of Magdalene's love. Love alone is enough for love, and nothing else fulfils it.

While the Saviour was preparing these events according to the order of his providence, to give his still mostly unbelieving disciples other lessons of no less importance, the pious women, who had left Jerusalem before sunrise accompanied by Mary Magdalene, headed towards the tomb. Having stopped along the way, they now approached the garden and, almost as if forgetful of their good friend and companion and being unaware of all that happened that early morning, they were saying among themselves who would remove the stone placed at the entrance of the tomb, as it was large and heavy. And while they were struggling with this thought, they did not know that Providence had already removed the boulder and even a greater obstacle by making the guards watching over the tomb to flee away. So looking from afar attentively, they could see clearly, since the sun had already risen, that the boulder had been removed from the door of the grave, and they rejoiced greatly about this precisely because they believed that thus they could enjoy more thoroughly the fondness of their piety. With this unexpected advantage they approached the garden with a certain joy, although mixed with some fear; but their surprise came at most when on entering the tomb they saw the angel of the Lord seated on the right hand in the image of a beautiful young man covered with long white clothing; and being overcome with fear, not knowing what to do, they were comforted at once by the same heavenly messenger, who said to them: "*Do not be afraid or fear anything; I know well for what you have come. You seek Jesus Christ of Nazareth who was crucified: he is risen as he has foretold. Come, see, and look well at the place where they had lain him.* Come, indeed, lower your gaze, and you will see the place where your God and my God, the God and Lord of angels and men, rested. Make sure for yourselves, and since you vaunt belonging to the number of his faithful disciples, fulfil such office of yours by carrying to the apostles, particularly to Peter, the joyful news of his resurrection. Yes, go and tell them; Our Lord and Master is risen: he goes before you to wait for you in Galilee, there you will see him as he has promised you."

There is much to be said about this event, but she cannot say everything. She feared, and an angel appears to her, but a good angel, who although at first terrifies her with his radiance, he later encourages them with his conversation and finally makes them happy with the glad tidings he gives them and with the important task he sends her to perform. It is here that the good angel acts differently from the bad one who first frightens with his horrible voice, then he deceives with false promises and makes man finally sad since when the deception is discovered he leads him into despair. The good angel, however, commands them not to fear, as one who says: "Let those fear who do not love the company of heavenly citizens, who being oppressed by the desires of the flesh despair of ever being able to obtain it. Nevertheless you who seek the servants of the Lord, and in them find your fellow citizens and friends, why should you fear? You who seek Jesus Christ crucified and dead, you have already been very fearful in his passion and death: the time has passed to fear any longer and the time has come for true satisfaction and for that of complete joy. You, who do not seek him in his triumph, but being dejected, you should know that he has triumphed and has been exalted magnificently and gloriously. He is resurrected, he is not here. But so only insofar as the presence of body and flesh are concerned, otherwise he is here by his Divinity and Majesty. He is risen insofar as to his humanity, for he could not be harmed as to his divinity." And he added, *as he said*, to bring to mind all that he had told the Lord beforehand as to his passion, death and resurrection, wanting to say to them by this that if they did not want to fully believe him, they should at least believe their Master's prophecies, showing them the place where he had been laid, to confirm the truth he had announced to them.

He commanded them to go and announce it to his apostles and to Peter to teach them that she did not bear them such happy tidings to keep the joy for themselves locked in the depths of their hearts, but so that they would pass it on to those who, like them, loved and believed. Note, however, that he did not send them to those who loved the world, but to the apostles and disciples, because it was up to them to proclaim these great mysteries to all peoples and nations of the universe. And finally, he told them to announce to them to go before him to Galilee, for the Lord wanted that the place where the splendour of grace started, should also be the place where the splendour of glory begins. It is women whom the angel commands to bear the news to the apostles of the resurrection of the author of life, for it was a woman who, having been persuaded by the devil, announced to the first man the entry of death into the world; and just as death made its way into the world by the devil's suggestion to a woman and by her to a man, so also were the good tidings of life confirmed through an angel to women, and by them to men.

Peter was especially mentioned either owing to the primacy among the apostles promised to him by the Lord, or since, though having committed the sin of apostasy, he did not despair of reconciliation and did not shy away from appearing together with the other apostles before the Saviour. For he had felt himself unworthy of being a disciple after having denied the Master three times; so that it was essential that he should be expressly called. *There you will see him*, the angel said to them, a short sentence indeed in terms of syllables, but great as to how much it promised. It is *there* that the source of our joy and eternal salvation is prepared. It is *there* that all the scattered gather together, and where the timid and humble of heart receive their strength. It is *there* that you will see him; but not as you were used to seeing him before, but triumphant and glorious, risen from the dead, yet never again to die.

Even in the remaining part of this narrative there is some very small difference between the Evangelists; they all agree that, obedient to the angel's voice, they entered the tomb where the Lord had been buried, and as they did not find the Holy Body of Jesus Christ which they were seeking, their fear grew to such an extent that they left that place without daring to lift their eyes to view two other angels who appeared to them in human form, until being dazzled by the radiance of their clothes, which shone with an extremely white, beautiful and resplendent brilliance, they had to fix their attention on them. They then said to them:

"Why do you seek among the dead he who is alive and is life itself? He is not here, he is risen. Remember what he said to you one day when he was still with you in Galilee, that it had to be that the Son of Man was to be delivered into the hands of his enemies, be crucified and on the third day rise again." This admonition reminded them of the Saviour's foreboding, but it was not enough to dispel entirely their fear. They left the tomb hastily, but at the same time bearing great joy, to go and give the news to the disciples; but the speed with which they walked, and the fear and joy with which they were filled, did not allow them to talk to anyone. While still on the move with this admonition in mind, behold, Jesus Christ came to meet them and greeted them, saying *May God preserve you*. But drawing near to him, they hugged his feet and worshipped him. In the meantime Jesus Christ said them: "Do not be afraid, go and tell my brethren to go to Galilee where they will see me." So they walked on and gave news of all these things to the eleven and to the others who were with them. Some considered this to be a raving relationship, unbelieving of what they were told. The women bringing the news were Mary Magdalene, and Mary, wife of Cleophas; Joanna, wife of Chuza, one of Herod's household managers; Salome, mother of John and James; and others who usually followed the Saviour and had walked up with them to Jerusalem from Galilee. And all, by common accord, testified that Jesus Christ had risen, and that they had the joy of seeing him and speaking to him.

While with these and other no less admirable wonders Jesus Christ wanted to divulge and give witness to the mystery of his holy resurrection, his furious and relentless enemies were committed into looking for means, no matter how detestable, to fade him out of sight, destroy him and make him incredible. In spite of the fact that the sentinels had simply and plainly told them that they had seen a young man full of majesty coming down from heaven to the place where they stood; that on arriving he caused the ground to shake under their feet; that the tremor folded and blew off the stone closing the tomb, from where the corpse of the Man who had been crucified disappeared; that this frightful noise and the sight of the young man, whose face was resplendent and more terrible than lightning, had knocked them down, making them roll on the ground senseless and as if dead; yet, the evil men were still unconvinced at the sight of such marvellous wonders. Instead of worshipping and revering the power that triumphed over their own strength and death, they were with even more hardened hearts bent on doing an offence to prevent the mystery of the resurrection from being believed. They gave the soldiers a large sum of money to say that while sleeping at night his disciples came and took away his body; and to allay the fear which should enter them in confessing the crime which they had recommended to them, they assured them that should this fact come to the governor's attention, they would stand in the way with their authority to exempt them from all liability and punishment. The soldiers believed what they were told and, having received the money, they began to spread everywhere the coarse and criminal deception, to which the treachery of some gave witness and insolent stubbornness would not refuse to believe.

For this reason Saint Chrysostom says: "The soldiers narrated what had happened to them, so that the truth announced by the opponents themselves might shine even more, and for that purpose the earthquake and the angel's wonderful appearance took place in their sight. They made public, against their own will and intention, the designs of Providence which they wished to impede, only for what they wanted to hide to be disclosed even faster. Oh what a truly stupid and coarse foolishness! Those present were sleeping witnesses! If they slept, how could they see the theft? If they failed to see it, how can they be witnesses? If they were guards, why did they not do their duty and stop the thieves? Ah! They lied grossly, for they would not have been so acquiescent that if they had seen the thieves they would not have stopped them. Indeed, what they said appeared to be nothing else but a lie. If the disciples were poor simpletons, and hated in being disciples of Christ, how dare they steal their Master's body? If even while he was still living they fled from him fearing the soldiers, how would you expect them to go after his death to the place guarded by such a great number of soldiers? It follows that the Jews were plotting more than just Christ's death. They were also plotting how to get the apostles out of the way, wanting to involve them in the crime of theft. Having left the Synagogue, the negligent and criminal soldiers gave in to their own mockery and contempt. The disciples had recovered their Master, not by theft but out of faith; not by fraud, but owing to hope; not by committing a crime, but out of love. This is why they recovered him alive and not dead."

The malice and treachery of priests and scribes spread even further; they wanted to buy, and effectively bought with money, the soldiers' silence; but let it not be believed that it was anyone's money, but money from the temple treasury; money offered by the poor, and that which should have served for the greater glory of the Lord, was used so that he might be crowned with humiliation. They bought his blood with money, they also bought the lie which obscured his glory with money. About which Saint Jerome says: "The soldiers confess the miracle. Those who in his sight ought to convert and do penance seeking the Risen One, instead persevere in their malice, and turn to redeeming themselves with a lie out of the money given for the benefit of the temple, just as they had previously invested the thirty pieces of silver to purchase a traitor." And so Saint Chrysostom continues: "Let us not marvel then, that money could be found so much in the soldiers' hearts inasmuch they were in that of Judas, who as one of Christ's apostles and disciples they made him a traitor. There is nothing that is closed or hidden which with money cannot be opened, revealed and manifested."

So that in order to assure us of the reality of this glorious and important event, to completely shut the mouth to the scribes' deceptive malice, Jesus Christ after his passion showed himself alive to his apostles for forty days, giving them ample proof of his resurrection, eating and talking with them about the kingdom of God and the setting up and governing of his Church. He was seen in the course of those days by many who had gone up with him from Galilee to Jerusalem. He appeared to Cephas, and after to the eleven, and another time he showed himself to more than five hundred brethren at one time. Of these Saint Paul wrote to the Corinthians, that many of them were still alive and the others had died. Then he showed himself to James, then to all the apostles. And last of all, as of one born out of due time, he was also seen by me. All of whom are now his witness to the people, that is to all his heralds and tiding bearers of his resurrection, of which we are witnesses (Acts 1:3-4; 13:1-31; 1 Cor 15:5-8).

One of these great and most important appearances to heal his disciples' unbelief, took place on the very day of his resurrection, and it happened together with very interesting events. Two of his disciples, apparently wanting to distract themselves from the great melancholy which took over their spirits, proceeded in the afternoon to the village of *Emmaus*, some two leagues away from Jerusalem. One of them is called by name, and as it is believed, according to Saint Ambrose, the other's name is of this event's history teller himself, Saint Luke, which is kept hidden out of humility. They were regularly discussing the events which had taken place those days in the great city, when at best an unknown man joined them on the road and asked them what they were talking about, where they were coming from, and why were they so sad as to show it on their faces. No doubt that this sadness showed their love for their Master, for they really loved Him. They saw him, but as they doubted they failed to recognise him, and so the Lord had occasion to speak to them without being recognised. The questions Jesus Christ asked rather served more to increase his apostles' sorrow, since they believed it impossible that anyone visiting the city those days could not know what had happened in it. So, one of the two named Cleophas, answered him in a mournful and distressed tone, telling him: "How come that among so many foreigners who these days were in Jerusalem, only you are unaware of what happened there?

Jesus Christ continued with his plan, and as if he was unaware of everything, he told him: "Well, what happened?" So that Cleophas started telling him the reason why he was sorrowful, explaining to him all the events of the passion and death of Jesus Christ, saying: "We spoke of what happened to Jesus Christ of Nazareth, who was an exceptional man, a great prophet, powerful in deeds and words, approved by God and loved by all people." The Venerable

Bede says: "They thought he was a pilgrim, since they did not recognise him; and indeed he was already a pilgrim before them, full as he was full of the glory of the resurrection, he showed none of the fragility of human nature; and with their faith being extraneous to the mystery of the resurrection, he presented himself to them as a stranger. And he noticed that they only called him by the name of prophet and not mentioning that of Son of God, either because they did not perfectly believe, or not to fall into the hands of the Jews; since they did not know to whom they were speaking, they concealed the truth of their belief and kept it hidden in the depths of their hearts." Yet, in spite of everything, they went on saying: "Our chief priests, other priests and leaders treated him unworthily, and after having handed him over to Pilate, they brought him about to be condemned unjustly to die on a cross between two thieves. His death has filled us with terror and dismay, for we lived in the hope that he was the one who would redeem Israel; but we already see our hopes lost, for today is the third day following these events. True to say that some women of ours have made us express great admiration today, since they went before dawn to the tomb, and not finding his body in it they came back saying they had seen there a vision of angels, who said that Jesus Christ had risen and was alive, and some of us went to the grave and found that what the women had said was true, and they did not see him. Yet who will believe such a great wonder which rests on such weak testimony?"

The distrust of these two disciples had reached the extreme, and could not be cured except with strong and somewhat violent remedies. So the Lord took advantage of this occasion to rebuke their unbelief and instruct them in a timely manner, so saying to them: "Oh fools and slow minded to believe the prophets' sayings! *Fools*, because of the blindness of your understanding; *slow minded*, owing to the coldness of your affections; and both, because you still do not understand well what is written about the mysteries of the passion, death and resurrection of Jesus Christ. By chance, was it not necessary for Christ to suffer all this and thus enter into his glory? It may be that you cannot match the humiliations of the Messiah with his greatness, and the shame of his death with the glories of his resurrection." And so he started stating and interpreting all those Scripture passages which spoke of him, starting from Moses and concluding with the prophets.

Saying these things, he kept on walking with them until they reached near the village to which they were going: then he made as if he wanted to leave them and go farther, which was but only a pretence. It was a very important lesson, however, to teach the disciples through this as to what he wishes to be asked for when one desires the joy of possessing him and having him with him; at the same time he wanted to give them occasion to practise the hospitality so recommended by the Jews, and so prepare them and make them worthy of the grace he wanted to grant them. They then tried with great effort to stop him, begging him most effectively to stay in their company, because it was already late and night was well nigh, and the Lord agreed with this request. He entered with them in the same house and even was so kind hearted as to eat in their company; so much so that while seated at table, he at once took one of the unleavened loaves from the table, for the Jews were forbidden from taking anything else during the Passover, and blessing it, he broke it among them; and with this action it seemed to them that their eyes were opened, and they knew the Lord at once, but he vanished and disappeared from their sight.

All these things which Jesus Christ did with his two apostles on this admirable day, are all so great and significantly important. That door was already narrow and exceedingly small so that he could enter through it into an earth's castle, he who by the most strait and narrow gate, which was that of his passion and death, had entered the eternal palaces of glory. So those who, without suffering tribulations, desire to enter into other people's glory must be deranged and reputed by people as being of little judgment, when Christ did not enter his own without sufferings. He agreed that he should suffer much to enter his natural kingdom; therefore we too must suffer much to enter the same kingdom of God given to us by grace. We have an example of this in all the friends and beloved ones of Christ who by way of voluntary passion arrived in God's kingdom; for it would have indeed been very strange were the members to resist entering through where the head entered, or if the vassals were to have no desire to enter through the door through which their King entered. And Saint Bernard adds: "Christ our head entered heaven through the pathway of passion; it would so be much like in a dream to believe that we could get there by any other way."

Christ disappeared from the sight of the two apostles, and they were left only with the confusion of their unbelief and the grief of no longer being able to enjoy his amiable company; so that in their astonishment they thought of their blindness. "Were we not feeling within us a burning but secret fire which uplifted our spirit and burned our heart while he spoke with us on the road? How could we not cease from not recognising him when he so masterfully explained to us and unfolded before us the meaning of the Scriptures? Listening to him talk inflamed our souls, diverted the coldness of our ineptness, and our soul was each time enlivened with holy desires." Far from earthly advice, desirous of hearing more freely heavenly precepts and councils, which like scorching axes, continually clean out the soul with fire, this was the reason why, at this very instant and prodded by an internal fire, they rose from the table and returned to Jerusalem. There they found the others gathered together, along with some other faithful who had gathered with them, and the joyfully said to them: "Truly is the Lord risen and has let himself be seen by Simon Peter." The two added their testimony opportunely, telling what had happened to them on the way, and how they had come to recognise him in the manner he broke the bread. Still, not even this way did some of them believe the mystery that was announced to them.

CHAPTER 89
ON THE SAME DAY OF HIS TRIUMPHANT RESURRECTION THE SAVIOUR APPEARS TO HIS APOSTLES AFTER DUSK AS THEY WERE LOCKED IN THE CENACLE, BUT THOMAS WAS ABSENT: THE SAME THING HAPPENED EIGHT DAYS LATER AT THE SAME PLACE WHEN AGAIN THE DOORS WERE CLOSED, AS THOMAS WAS THERE WITH THEM (LK 24:36–47; JN 20:19–31)

OR some writers, who are more timid than prudent and reflective, the difficulties that arise from the simple reading of the latter passages of the Evangelists after Jesus Christ's resurrection, appear to be quite significant and weighty. They believe it to be contradictory that Saint Matthew tells us that Jesus Christ appeared to the eleven disciples on the mountain to which he had called them, without referring to the appearance of the fortress or hamlet of Emmaus about which Saint Luke recounts. They hold that this omits what Saint John tells us, which took place on the same day and late at night, when most of the apostles were locked in the Upper Room, with the other Evangelists passing in silence this so remarkable and marked event on all accounts. However to resolve these issues, clarify them and get out of all of them in one stroke, it must be known that the style of the Evangelists is fast and concise, and that on several occasions they omit many circumstances, be it the chronology or the time and occurrence of events to which they refer. In the present matter we see that Saint Matthew and Saint Mark relate in a brief chapter the events happening in the forty days which passed from the Jesus Christ's resurrection to his glorious ascension into heaven. Some have recorded in their history several facts while omitting others, or did nothing more than point to them; and there is no one who cannot easily be convinced of this truth by simply reading the Gospel. All this was done without distracting us from our purpose of narrating the Lord's different appearances

to his disciples in this intermediate time between his resurrection and ascension into heaven; so that we will follow the order which seems most plausible, considering the truth of the facts to which the Evangelists refer.

In the evening or at nightfall of that same day, the first of the week, the disciples being gathered with closed doors for fear of the Jews, as soon as those who arrived from Emmaus had just told the others what had happened to them, Jesus Christ came in at once, appeared to them, stood in their midst and said to them: "Peace be with you, it is me, fear not." But they were overwhelmed with terror and fright and imagined they were seeing a spirit or a ghost. This was the first time when the apostles, but for Thomas, were all together and they saw the risen Saviour. If you examine their situation well, there is no doubt that it was very sad for them. They knew they were guilty in the eyes of Christ, because they had abandoned him, and those of the people, having been made fanatics by the scribes who regarded them as suspects of sedition. So that they kept themselves hidden after the Master's shameful ordeal and did not let themselves to be seen together as they used to do, because they believed they could not do so without being punished for it, and so they locked up themselves behind closed doors with all diligence and precaution. Jesus Christ, in order to make himself known to his disciples and convince them that his body was endowed with all the qualities of a glorious body, having gone through the doors without opening them, found himself suddenly and unexpectedly in their midst. Saint Augustine says that: "Just as he who was born into the world, leaving his Virgin Mother and rising from the tomb did not find the slab enclosing it of any hindrance, so could he enter that lodging without opening its doors. Raised upon the wings of love, he entered before the apostles to heal them of their unbelief and take them out of the predicament in which they found themselves, wavering between hope and fear, between turmoil and joy, between anxiety and peace. To free them of all their trouble, he gives them peace and breathes it out, because his will is almighty. He does not give them the deceitful peace of the world, but heavenly peace, which is the first gift of the Holy

Spirit and the first fruit of Christ's resurrection; and when he considers them to have been sufficiently strengthened, he commits himself more to setting them free from any reasonable doubt or mistrust."

"Why are you in distress," he asks them as if he is unaware of everything. "From where do these thoughts come that stir your hearts? Look at my hands, my feet and my side, and there will be no doubt at all that it is me, the same One with whom you used to discuss, the same One you saw dying on the cross." The Lord still had the wounds to heal those which unbelief had opened in the disciples' breast. "Touch and see that the spirit has neither flesh nor bones as you see that I have." It is true that this warning soothed their troubled spirits; but their joy was not yet fulfilled, because their faith was imperfect. Seeing him caused them deep admiration, but they hardly dared to rejoice, because what they saw seemed so incredible. He showed them his hands, as if challenging them to a fight, which was just like telling them: "See the hands with which I fight faithfully for you; I show them to you that you might know that you must always be ready to struggle, for unless you do so you will never win. So fight courageously, for only he who fights and wins will sit with me on my throne." He showed them his side to arouse their love, as if to say to them: "See my open side, my pierced heart, that you may know how much I love you, and how much you must love me in a just relationship." And he showed them his feet to teach them how to walk on the path of virtue, to confirm them in perseverance, and to show them that they should not turn back from the path on which they had started to walk.

Jesus Christ's resurrection was a great miracle, but it was not a small thing such as to let himself be touched and seen; for the immortal and incorruptible body of Jesus Christ could not be seen or touched through corruptible and mortal eyes and hands without a very great miracle. So that this is what Saint Gregory says: "He allowed his body to be touched to confirm us in the faith and so that, being incorruptible, it could be seen to affirm us in the hope of the prize." With this trial the disciples got carried away with joy, and were troubled and beside themselves as if they had not got through believing what they were seeing; then Jesus Christ, in order to convince them even more and present them with evidence, said to them: "Do you have anything to eat here?" And having brought to him a piece of fish which was at hand and a honeycomb, he ate, not just in appearance but really and truly, regardless of his state which did not need any food, and then shared with his disciples the remaining food.

To confirm them in the faith which had already inspired them, he said to them: "Remember the words which I spoke to you when I was even one with you, that it had to pass that all that was written about me in the Law of Moses, in the Prophets and in the Psalms, should be fulfilled." For after Ezra's division of the holy books, after the sons of Israel had returned from Babylonian captivity, only those books included in this classification were considered to be canonical in the Synagogue, and so it was for this reason that the Lord spoke to them in this manner. At the same time he dispelled the darkness hovering over his mastery, and opened their minds so that they might understand the true meaning of the Scriptures, saying to them: "So it is written, and so it had to be that Christ should suffer and rise from the dead on the third day, and that penance and the remission of sins should be preached in his name in all peoples and to all nations starting from Jerusalem."

The harsh criticism of those who want to satirise everything, and try doing all to take advantage in discrediting the apostles' faith, besides Jesus Christ's charitable conduct towards them and towards us, has led their audacity to the point of criticizing the loving Saviour's attitude as being utterly superior. Yet this was so because they undoubtedly misunderstood that the Lord was not merely trying to secure faith in the resurrection in those hearts, but to dispose them to become its martyrs and to render faith in an authentic mystery, without which our belief would be vain and our hope deceptive. To this end, and for the purpose that what was said by Isaiah may be fulfilled, namely that *Out of Zion shall the Law come forth* (Is 2:3), as referring to the preaching of the Gospel; and also to the end that the word of God might resound majestically in Jerusalem; he was preparing them so that, knowing well the full force, sweetness and effectiveness of the same charity he had shown them, they would also be ready to love others, whom he would promptly send to them.

He immediately gave them his peace once more, granting it to them as its author, as its deliverer and sharer; and greeting them in this manner all over again, he thus assured them that with it he forgave and forgot their lack of faith, thus preparing them for the mission with which he would honour them, assuring them that they would be as much authorised to preach the Gospel as he was when he came into the world to proclaim it. *"As my Father has sent me,"* he said to them, *"so also do I send you.* My Father sent me to teach the truth to Judea. I am sending you to announce it to the whole world. I appoint you to be my vicars and helpers. I give you my place, and I charge you with this new office of teaching, preaching and baptising, so that my Father's name and mine may be glorified. Since I love you with that charity with which my Father loves me, I send you as he sent me. I send you to be glorified among the scandals of persecution, as I was in the midst of the rebuke of passion." But since Jesus Christ knew that in order to carry out properly this great ministry, with which he had just honoured them, they needed the grace of the Holy Spirit, he embraced them so as to confirm the peace he had just given them; and blowing his breath upon them, he further said to them, *Receive ye the Holy Spirit; those whom you shall forgive their sins, they shall be forgiven; and those whose sins you shall retain, they shall be retained.* Whose words taken together with preceding events, are a full authorisation for them to perform the mission that he had given them, just like saying: "When you forgive the faults of those whom you judge which are worthy of absolution, or when you retain the faults of those who seem to you to be unworthy of it, you will be doing it as administrators assisting the sovereign Judge; He will confirm your sentence, and ratify in heaven all that is done by you on earth." The Church teaches that these words contain the power to forgive sins through baptism and penance. Oh what a high dignity belongs to him who receives the Holy Spirit to communicate it to the members of Christ! It is worth hearing Saint Augustine speak about this: "To demonstrate more clearly that sins were forgiven by the virtue of the Holy Spirit which he communicated to his faithful, and not by human merits, he immediately added: 'If you forgive anyone, *they are forgiven him*'; that is, the Spirit forgives them, not you. For the Spirit is God, and God is the one who forgives, not you. The ministry is yours, but not the authority; that comes from God. And God who dwells in his temple, in the hearts of faithful saints, forgives for them the sins in His Church, because they are living temples."

Thomas who was called *Didymus*, the Twin, was not present when all this happened, and there was no way he wanted to believe that Jesus Christ had risen, even though the other disciples assured him that they had seen him, and that they were very certain of his resurrection. They recounted to him all the circumstances of his appearance and the conversation they had with him; yet he did not give in to any proof, nor did he bend his overwhelming unbelief, and kept on answering his companions: "Unless I see the holes which the nails made in his hands and feet, and I put my finger in them and in his side wound, I will not believe what you are telling me." Thomas teaches us how fearful it is to lose God's promised graces by those who live united in love as members of the mysterious Head to whom they must remain united; how powerful is the force of common prayer; and how influential is the grace of good example. Outside the Church neither faith nor the salutary practice of truths are acknowledged. All this apostle's resistance started since he was not in the company of others when the Saviour appeared to them, standing in their midst and giving them peace; he was with them at the time of the scandal, when he was seized and all abandoned him, but was not found when he came to confirm them in the faith and give them grace. He shared in the pain caused by fleeing, but not in the benefit obtained when he came to them; and this is what was wrong with him. For this reason he wanted to give the Law to the Master and bind his faith to a condition which he had no right to choose, in contempt of the Master's authority and that of the apostles whom he had already authorised to reveal such an important mystery. This obstinacy was apparently worthy of severe punishment, but the Lord, who can discern both aptitude and inner hearts, and who can weigh and knows well all his tendencies, was not offended by the freedom sought by his apostle, so much so that he abandoned him to his blindness; on the contrary, he allowed this to tear off the seed of disbelief from the others' hearts.

To this end, eight days later, all the apostles were again gathered together, and Thomas was with them, even behind closed doors, when the Saviour appeared again. Standing in their midst as he had done before, he repeated to them his earlier special greeting: *Peace be with you*. Very often Jesus Christ announced peace to his disciples, recommending and commanding it, because without it, it would be absolutely impossible to serve and please God, who dwells only in those hearts which love harmony and peace; for the place of His rest is the place of peace. He came into the world to bring us peace, and he went out of it leaving us peace. In conversation with men, he constantly preached peace to them, and taught them that the whole perfection of Christian and religious life consisted in charity and peace. So we must look for it very diligently and preserve it with utmost care. To this end Gregory of Nazianzus tells us: "We should be ashamed to belittle the mission of peace, since at the time the world failed to understand what Jesus Christ said to us: *Peace is a good mission for all, yet sought after and coveted by few*. And why is it so? Owing to the ambition of being in command, for the love of riches, for being preferred in one's opinion, for ill will, for hatred, for contempt or for any of those things into which those living a life forgetful of God fall into very often."

Jesus Christ directly confronted his apostle, and showing him his pierced hands and his open side, with all kindness said to him: "Approach your Master, put your finger here, see these wounds for yourself, then explore the one on my side, and be no longer unbelieving, but have faith." Such great kindness shown by Jesus Christ must have been a very sensitive rebuke and severe correction for his disciple. It is hard to believe that Thomas had the audacity to take the liberty his Master gave him; and if he really did, it could not be except by way of obedience, to give us this invincible proof of the Lord's resurrection; for undoubtedly the apostle was already confused, contrite and persuaded. The sight of Jesus Christ, the imposing tone of his voice, the examination of his wounds, the awareness shown by him from the depths of his heart, were very effective reasons to cease resisting; and this mostly in the heart of an apostle who wanted no more than to be convinced. Thomas could not fail to be perfectly enlightened in the sight of that unfathomable ocean of charity and light, so that he burst into a most sincere and perfect, though belated, confession of faith, exclaiming instantly: *My Lord and my God*. See there the unbeliever now become faithful, the brittle and broken cane transformed into a bronze column. Only Jesus Christ could turn this disciple's scandal into victorious proof of his divinity. Saint Augustine says: "He saw and touched the man, and confessed to God, Him whom he neither saw nor touched; but because of what he saw and touched, he believed the other without any doubt." And Saint Gregory adds: "He who, considering the true man, exclaimed that he was true God, Him whom he could not see; there is not the slightest doubt that looking he believed, and that believing he tore the doubt from our heart. He owed it neither to flesh nor to blood, but to the heavenly Father, giver of knowledge and love for the Son."

In spite that Jesus Christ knew this much better than his disciple, although he accepted well his frank and public confession, he manifested the manner how he accepted it by showing how much greater and more praiseworthy was the conduct of the other apostles. *Because you saw me, Thomas, you have believed: blessed are those who did not see and yet believe.* Which was like telling him: "What would have become of you, and what would you have done if I had denied you this sensitive testimony of my resurrection? Your faith was reluctant, and you abided more with your senses than by my word. I do not rebuke your confession, but the lateness of your heart. Blessed are those who being more obedient and unassuming than yourself, blotted out their doubt with their prompt faith, though having formerly abandoned me." Thomas had been absent eight days before the visit in which his colleagues had received their mission, authority and powers from Jesus Christ: it was very much expected that the most conscientious Master would now also confer them on him since, as he here also granted peace to the others and being so deigning and merciful, he must have acted again in the same manner, then disappearing from before them as usual.

Many other wonders which the Lord then worked in the presence of his apostles are not mentioned here, because those referred to are sufficient for all who read this Gospel to believe, that Jesus Christ is the Messiah and Son of God; and so believing him to be, they may attain eternal life, which could not be obtained except in his name and by his infinite merits. Saint John says of this: "My children, I write these things to you, so that you may not sin; but if sadly anyone sins, let him not despair, for we have an advocate with the Father, Jesus Christ the just and holy One; and he himself is the victim of propitiation for our sins who offered himself on the cross and not only for ours, but also for the sins of the whole world" (1 Jn 2:1-2). He is offered every day on the altar, and with him God's righteousness is satisfied and appeased; for he offered himself not only for our sins, but for those of the whole world, he who prays to the Father for all sinners, standing before Him with his obedience and the manner of death he suffered to redeem them and save them all. This is undoubtedly what Isaiah had announced long before, when he said: "Oh heavens. sing hymns, and you, oh land, rejoice: resound in praise, oh mountains, for the Lord has comforted his people and had pity on his poor. Just as a woman cannot forget her child or cease having compassion for the child of her womb, so neither will I ever forget you. See how I remember you engraved on the palm of my hands" (Is 49:13-16). Nor how was it possible that he would forget us being so horribly wounded to redeem and save us? This is how Saint Augustine concludes: "Look now to the Lord, and contemplate his great and habitual kindness, his humility, and his fervent love, See how he shows his wounds to Thomas and to the other disciples to uproot all doubt from their hearts, for their own and our usefulness; he is with them speaking to them of the kingdom of God that they may be comforted, and to confirm them in the faith he works many miracles before them for forty days."

CHAPTER 90

THE DISCIPLES GATHERED ON THE MOUNT DOING AS COMMANDED BY JESUS CHRIST, AND THERE HE APPEARS TO THEM; AND THEN HE APPEARS AGAIN BEFORE THEM ON THE SHORES OF THE SEA OF TIBERIAS OR LAKE GENEZARETH (MT 28:16–20; JN 21:1–24)

ON the terrible and stormy night of his passion Jesus Christ had said to his disciples: You will all fall away because of me tonight; for it is written: I will strike the Shepherd, and the sheep will go astray. But after I have risen, I will go before you to Galilee (Mt 26:32). And he had scarcely risen, when he spoke through his angel to the holy women who had gone to seek him at the tomb saying: Make haste: Go tell the disciples of Jesus Christ: Your Master is risen. He is going before you to Galilee; there you will see him, as he told you (Mk 16:7). And as if everything seemed little to him, he himself appeared shortly afterwards to his devout handmaids, allowed them to embrace his feet and adore him, after which he renewed the command the angels had given them, saying to them: Go and tell my brethren to go to Galilee; that is where they will see me (Mt 28:16).

It is from here that a dispute arose as to when it was first that Jesus Christ appeared to his disciples; whether it was the one we just mentioned, or the one that took place on the mountain where the eleven were gathered, as Saint Matthew says. The question, however, seems to be resolved by Saint John, for he tells us that this apparition took place on the evening of the first day of the week, that is, on the very day of the resurrection; and Saint Matthew says nothing about the day and time of that other apparition. The Eagle of the Gospel assures us that Thomas was not present; and as to the other one Saint Matthew affirms that the eleven were assembled; and this being so, the doubt which Didymus had would have no longer been retained, since he had already seen Jesus Christ on the mountain; so that everything leads us to believe that Jesus Christ appeared on the mountain after his previous appearance in the Upper Room. They therefore obeyed the apostles and went towards Galilee, to the mountain where Jesus Christ had so expressly told them where to go. But it seems that it was not in the province called Galilee where Jesus Christ manifested himself to the apostles on this occasion. It is not only probable, but most plausible and certain, that they did not depart from the capital during the Passover solemnity, and that it was there that they saw Jesus Christ, not only on the first day of the week, but eight days later, as the Evangelists assure us, since the two disciples, who had left Emmaus, were going to that place at nightfall on Sunday, and where they had informed the others who were assembled that they had the consolation of seeing and carefully contemplating the Divine One who had been risen; all from which it was inferred that this mountain would be some place or mountain in the capital's surroundings, or on one of the peaks of the Mount of Olives, belonging to Galileans as to their property, where they would lodge together when they came to celebrate their feasts in the temple; and that this peak or hill was the same where Jesus Christ was accustomed to retire whenever he went to Jerusalem to preach. It would be for this reason that he commanded them to meet there again, for one could not possibly understand this command as referring to Galilee, having regard to what has been said, and that this province was sited twelve leagues from the capital of Judea.

Although in the previous appearances Jesus Christ had opened his apostles' mind to understand the Scriptures, and had given them, together with the Holy Spirit, the power to forgive sins or to retain them, yet there were still some unbelievers among those present who kept on doubting; and to take away all their doubts and confirm them in the faith, he newly invested and entrusted them with a more specific, greater and much more important mission. "Let all power in heaven and on earth be given to me," he told them, "by virtue of the infinite dignity of my person and of the hypostatic union of the Word of God with humanity: a power which I possess from eternity as the Son of God, and as was given to me as God and man also from the first moment of my conception. Now that by my resurrection from among the dead I have recovered this state of glory from which I voluntarily deprived myself during my mortal life, by using and exercising this public and supreme power, which belongs to me under many titles, I communicate it to you and I institute more definitely the first ministers and envoys to establish my Church. GO, THEN, AND TEACH ALL NATIONS, BAPTISING THEM IN THE NAME OF THE FATHER, AND OF THE SON, AND OF THE HOLY SPIRIT."

"Go, and with your diligence condemn those who are lazy and negligent, who although seeing the need do not want to go, because they would rather be idle, preferring idleness to the work which ought to be done by all those whom it would be good to send to cultivate my vineyard. Teach, and know that this is to be your continuous and unceasing work; for this you will be taught by the Holy Spirit, with whom you are to speak in prayer; and just as in prayer he will teach you continually, so also with the fruit you will pluck from it, which you will communicate to others. To all nations, because in the presence of God there is no personal distinction. So you must not make preference with the rich and powerful, and those who may not be worth anything in the world, but you must care for all; and if there may be any preference in this, it must be in favour of the poor, the helpless, and the needy; for I was sent by my Father to proclaim the Gospel to the poor (Lk 4:18)." Note however that it does not say convert, but preach. Since attributing the sanctification of listeners to the preaching minister's efforts is like robbing the infinite merits of Christ's passion and the world's saintliness from his grace. Baptising them, because whosoever was not reborn with water and the Holy Spirit will not enter God's kingdom. In the name of the Father, and of the Son, and of the Holy Spirit, so that the unity of the essence and trinity of Persons may be understood. The unity of divinity, and the greatness and efficacy of grace. In such cleansing the stains of our sins are washed away, the Father adopts us as children, the Son adds us to the mystical body of his Church, and the Holy Spirit inspires us to live consecrated to him in holiness and righteousness. From what Saint Augustine says: "Give Jesus Christ all the power in heaven and on earth, because as for his divinity he has an immense and infinite power from eternity, and as man he has, from the very first instant of his conception, equal power in heaven and on earth; he did not, however, have this implementing authority before his resurrection, but wanted to make it possible for our redemption. Jesus Christ therefore spoke about his humanity, in which he is less than the Father; not as to divinity, in which he is entirely equal to Him."

According to divinity, so much is the Father, or the Son, or the Holy Spirit, as much as the Father, and the Son, and the Holy Spirit. So much is the whole Trinity in the Father alone, or in the Son alone, or in the Holy Spirit alone, as much as it is together in the Father, and in the Son, and in the Holy Spirit. And as this is the sound and holy doctrine, one and true, beginning and foundation of our belief, by which and through which all men are saved, and which unless confessed, it is impossible for anyone to obtain eternal salvation; as this is the Christian life represented in Jesus Christ's death, burial and resurrection. He cleansed us with his blood so that we might serve him in spirit and truth, according to the spirit of charity, which is the summit of the Law and Prophets; so he further said to them: Teaching them to keep all things which I have commanded you to keep, practise, and fulfil to be eternally happy; and be assured that I will remain in your company up to the end of all times. A great, ineffable and consoling promise, that just as it has been inviolably fulfilled within a period of several centuries, it would still be fulfilled with utmost faithfulness until the consummation and end of the world.

In prophetic spirit David sang the perpetuity of this Church and its stability until the consummation of all times, for the consolation of all his children, more than a thousand years before it was founded, and said: "Great is the Lord and worthy of praise in the city of our God, on his holy mountain; with the joy of all the earth, the sanctuary has been built on Mount Zion, in the city of the great King, sited in the far north. God will be known within its citadels where He will surely defend it. For behold, the kings of the earth have assembled and conjured together. As soon as they themselves saw it they were astounded, panic stricken and as trembling took hold of them they took to flight. Anguish seized them as that of a woman in childbirth. Yet you with an impetuous wind did shatter apart the ships of Tarshish. As we have heard, so have we seen in the city of the Lord of hosts, in the city of our God, WHICH GOD HAS FOUNDED FOR EVER" (Ps 48:1-8). Will this city or Church, however, which has spread over and dominated the whole world, by chance ever be destroyed? "Ah! No, never, it will never be destroyed," Saint Augustine says, "because God founded it that it might survive forever, without fearing that its foundation will ever falter. The foundations of this holy Jerusalem stand upon the holy mountains, and the Lord loves without comparison the gates of this illustrious Zion more than all of Jacob's dwelling places (Ps 86:2). For this reason, in order to enlarge, protect and defend it visibly on earth, he constituted and appointed some to be apostles, other prophets, and other evangelists, and other pastors and doctors, with an aim to work for God's holy people, in their ministry's functions and services, in the building up of Jesus Christ's mystical body (Eph 4:11-12).

Seeming to the Apostle as if he had not explained well enough his thought to declare the existence of this same Church until the end of the world, and the protection which visibly ought to be given to it, he added: "Until we all attain to the unity of this same faith and of the same knowledge of the Son of God to mature manhood, to the measure of Christ's perfect fullness, according to which Christ is to be mystically formed in us" (Eph 4:13); but according to the Fathers' testimony this will not occur until the end of the world and on the day of the universal resurrection. Listen, if anything at all, to the famous Grotius' testimony: "As this promise has for its scope the consummation of all ages, and the apostles were not due to live up to that time, it is undeniable that Jesus Christ assured the Church, and the successors of those entrusted with administering, of his protection and assistance which will last until the end of the world." And finally, if there were no testimonies in Scripture and in the Fathers who would fully justify this truth, these would be abundantly provided to us by heretics and apologists themselves; so let us at least hear one for all of them: "I do not deny that for some centuries the purity of faith has remained in the bosom of the Roman Church, and that it has been the true Church of Christ; but then the true Church cut off itself from Rome, becoming obscured in the course of time with lots of darkness; so that the true Church embattled with so many errors, could hardly be known; indeed, this is how it is. For truly, what else did they do other than produce so many copies of new doctrines, whether on the primacy of the Roman Pontiff, or on his infallibility, and also on justification for the satisfaction and merits of good works, as well as on transubstantiation, purgatory, the worship of saints, images and relics and other superstitious matters, only to attract thick darkness upon the purity of the true Church...? But you ask me now whether the true Church always existed. Without any doubt or hesitation I say it did. But where did it hide, where did it moan and cry for so long? My answer is that it remained hidden right in the bosom of the popes; and indeed, if this true Church had not remained enclosed right in the bosom of the papacy, how would so many witnesses of Gospel truth have been found in the space of so many centuries to come out of the bosom of the pontifical Church and defend its doctrine with utmost loyalty, faith and worship which it professes and teaches, even at the cost of its own life, against the fierceness of so many newly aborted monsters wanting to destroy it? Although it was then the Roman Seat," the heretic concludes, "which contaminated, overwhelmed and filled the true Church with errors, it could never destroy it at its roots."

With the testimony of the same apologists and heretics, this has thus remained perfectly shown through Jesus Christ; he promised his protection and assistance to the Church up to the consummation of all ages, and it has till now faithfully fulfilled his word. So that being as it is, faithful, and truthful, and most precise in the fulfilment of his promises, we must utterly and wholly believe that he will also fulfil all until the end of the world, so that we can never tell him what Chrysostom says, that so great were the labours and tribulations which surrounded us, that we could not overcome them, for the Lord will say to us: "You should have known that with me you would always triumph and consume your enemies till they are no more," (Ps 59:14) as I have announced through David; and that in all times and forever my Church was to be as unfailing in its teaching as it was to be infallible in all its pronouncements, because I would never fail it, having founded it on Peter, the most solid stone laid upon me, who I am the true cornerstone on which I was able to build this immense building, against whose firmness all of hell's power will always crash."

Jesus Christ had just given these sublime instructions and magnificent faculties to his apostles, when he suddenly disappeared from their sight, leaving them on the one hand full of ineffable joy, beholding they had been vested, not only with the sublime power to forgive or retain the sins of men, but also with that of being preachers of the New Law, authorised to carry this precious seed to the ends of the world. But they were also sad and heartbroken not knowing, among other things, how long it would be before ever again enjoying Jesus Christ's gracious presence. Convinced of the indefinite extension of their ministry, they believed that they would not abuse confidence if, by going to their native lands, they would give to their relatives and countrymen, even with the greatest reserve, the glad tidings which they had received and held within them.

When the apostles returned to Galilee, where they lived with some greater freedom and latitude, since there they were neither stalked with the perfidy of the scribes nor with the Pharisees' unjust persecution, Peter said one day to his fellow fishers: I am going fishing. Those who were then gathered were Thomas or Didymus, Nathanael, by some called Bartholomew, originally from Cana of Galilee, James and John, sons of Zebedee, and two other of Jesus Christ's disciples. They all answered Peter: "We too will go with you"; since being animated with the same spirit and truly wanting to make sure about Jesus Christ's resurrection, they hoped with sincere faith he would fulfil in their sight the promise he had repeatedly made to them that he would go before them in Galilee; so that thus, with this amount of unchallengeable proofs and authentic testimonies, the truth of his resurrection might be even more established; and so they did not dare being separated for one instant. Having taken their tack aboard they made out to the open sea, working hard all night but not catching any fish. Although being unaware of the happy ending to which such an apparently useless work was to lead them, they nevertheless continued with their innocent task until drawing very near to the shore in the morning, when they happened to see a man who they did not recognise as the Saviour; neither did he make himself known to them, but he said to them: "Mates, do you have anything to eat?" And they answered him they did not. Saint Gregory says that they had caught nothing after the seven disciples had struggled and rowed all night, since they worked in darkness and were bereft of divine help which, for lacking or being deprived of it, they had passed a hard night. This passed and the light came; and though they had him in their sight who is the true light, they did not know him as he wanted to make himself known to them through a miracle; and so, as if seeking to buy food, he spoke to them in everyday human speech.

The Lord did not ask them for the sake of knowing, for he was not unaware of how they felt, but so that by merit of their obedience they might attain the fruit of their labour, he told them to cast the net on the right side of the boat where they would find fish in abundance. Although the man commanding them was unknown to them, they still obeyed him; and soon enough pulling back the net on board, they could no longer drag it ashore owing to the great quantity of fish they had caught. This marvel could be seen and felt, and this miraculous catch looked more like another quite similar one which Jesus Christ had again wrought for them, seeming that it should suffice to open the eyes of some of his disciples. This was a true prophecy which was later to occur to them in the other spiritual fishing to which they were destined. Their docility and apostolic obedience were rewarded with good success. The marvel was seen by all, and the disciple whom Jesus Christ loved said to Peter: "It is the Lord." As soon as Peter heard that it was the Lord, he put on his robe, because he was naked, and jumped into the sea. John had the joy of first meeting Jesus Christ as a reward for his purity and love; and vigorous as he was, Peter crossed the waves and went to throw himself at his

Master's feet. In these two apostles the various effects of love are seen clearly: John is discerning, Peter fearless; John shows his love in understanding, Peter in activity; John becomes the eyes to know Christ, Peter the hands to imitate him. God's love encourages us to enter into his ways and to probe humbly the depth of his mercy. In a most certain manner John affirms that this stranger is the Saviour: do not deceive yourself, love enlightens you; whoever is possessed by God's spirit does not doubt His truth. He greatly helps whoever has a living faith rather than those who are still shrouded in the darkness of ages. Church Fathers and Doctors say of this: "John represents contemplative and silent life, while Peter represents that which is active and arduous; nevertheless those who by day dedicate themselves to it, if during the night of contemplation they hear the voice of the Lord calling, they must promptly abandon the apparent sweetness of rest and go to search their God."

The other disciples, not leaving the coast other than for some two hundred cubits. came to the boat arduously dragging the net full of fish. As Saint Chrysostom says, the state of the apostles is very well explained here: John was the first to recognise Jesus Christ, yet Peter ranked before him; the sea represents the tribulations of the present age, so that those who wish to reach Christ throw themselves into the sea, not shying away from the world's doings; they know that it is through them that one can enter the kingdom of God, and that the true and faithful disciple of Christ remains bound to him and emerges clear of them, just as Peter came out of the sea safely to Christ. The boat represents the Church, and so did those who sailed and arrived safely on land; they represent Christians who, having embarked on the boat, which is the Church, arrive safely at the port of eternal salvation, as no one can be saved outside it.

When they disembarked, they saw a charcoal fire, with fish lying over it, and a piece of bread. The Saviour had, in his almightiness and being always attentive to his disciples' needs, prepared this little breakfast for them. Peter had arrived before, and Saint John does not tell us that it was only him who saw that miracle; but soon they all arrived, then even discovering fire, fish and bread. Saint Augustine reveals this hidden event to us: "The roasted fish was the figure of the dead Christ, and the bread also represented the living bread coming down from heaven, with which the Church is incorporated to have a share in his glory." And Saint Chrysostom says: "See yet another miracle, not as on other occasions, of anything specific or subject matter, but of already existing loaves and fishes which he now multiplied; but rather that out of nothing he again created, by his divine virtue, burning coals, fish and bread, to enlarge and confirm his disciples' hearts in the faith of his resurrection. Sited a league away, to the east of Bethsaida, is the place where Jesus Christ stood on the seashore, where his footmarks can be seen printed on a hard rock, and where about half a stone's throw away was the place where the fire was lit, the fish lay over the charcoal and the bread was found; it was there that the Saviour had commanded them to bring some of the fish which they had caught.

The seven apostles had scarcely disembarked that Jesus Christ said to them: "Now bring here some of the fish you have caught." And Simon Peter instantly went to the boat and dragged the net full of big fish, one hundred and fifty-three, and yet the net was not broken with such a great number. Saint Isidore says: "All the kinds of fishes in the sea are represented in this number of one hundred and fifty-three, because the apostles should be fishermen of all men. It is for this reason that they ceased fishing, and in spite of such a big catch the net was not broken." The number of fish and the large catch are mentioned to show the miracle that the net had not been broken. And by calling his disciples to eat, and eating with them, his resurrection is even more justified, for he was making it known to them that he was not a ghost, but had a physical and true body. None of those present dared ask him whom he was, because they were full of reverence and fear contemplating his majestic and imposing face, and since being certainly aware it was him, it was superfluous to ask him. Yet, to remove from them all grief or suspicion, he took the bread in his hands with his accustomed humility, blessed it and distributed it to them as he used to do, and did the same with the fish, and ate together with them as he had done before his passion;

and so all believed again that it was him, and also in the mystery of his holy resurrection.

This is the third time, says Saint John, that Jesus Christ let himself be seen by his disciples, that is, according to the order of his sequencing, and not including in them that of the journey to Emmaus, to which Saint Luke refers. But this shows clearly that Christ's apparition to the disciples in the province of Galilee was in fulfilment of the promise which he had repeatedly made to them, and it could not be the first or most solemn apparition which he then made. There can therefore be no doubt that after appearing to the two who were on their way to Emmaus, the first and second apparitions took place in Jerusalem where, as we saw, they were gathered in the upper room behind closed doors; it was in that building that their reunions and meetings were still held after the Sovereign Master's ascension into heaven, while waiting for his divine promises to be fulfilled. Little does Saint John seem to take into account the appearance or manifestation on the mountain to the eleven disciples as referred to by Saint Matthew, and in his recount he so only hints at to the sequence of apparitions to which he refers. But as this was to be a memorable apparition, not only for the miracles of an abundant catch and the newly created fire, fish and bread, but also for the results it produced, Saint John mentions it in a very distinguished manner.

In fact, after the meal Jesus Christ began to converse familiarly with his apostles. Addressing his speech to Simon Peter, he said to him: "Simon, son of John, do you love me more than these who are here present?" "Yes, Lord, Peter answered; you know that I love you." "If is so be it," the Saviour replied, "feed my flock." Then he asked him again the same question and the apostle gave him the same answer, and the Lord recommended to him as before to care for his lambs; but when for the third time he forced him to tell him whether it was true that he loved him and whether he was saying this from his heart, then Peter, sad and confused remembering his past infidelity, answered him: "Ah, Lord, why are you asking me this question? Nothing is hidden from you: you know better than myself whether it is true that I love you." "Then feed my sheep," Jesus Christ said to him.

Saint Augustine says: "This apostle, being ever more fervent to love Christ and who, being afraid to deny him, followed the Lord when he went to suffer, could not then attain the crown. He followed him with his feet, and he did not do it just for the purpose of following customs. He allowed him to die for him, although he could not do so with him. The Lord had then to die for the servant, and not the servant for the Lord. He who dared to promise more than he could, loved disorderly, and so feared and denied." The risen Christ teaches Peter how he should love; loving in a disorderly manner, he collapsed under the weight of passion; loving in an orderly manner, the passion is promised to him. Peter sees risen him whom he had feared dead; but he does not see the Lord dead, but death itself is dead in him. With the example of Jesus Christ's flesh he learned how vain is the fear of death: this is the school where one learns how to love. The Master knows what he is asking of the disciple; but he wants the mouth to be united with the heart, and he wants to know from him how much he loves him.

"He asks him for three times how much he loves him," Saint Augustine says, "not ignoring how he had to confess his love for him, but because the threefold confession of love erased the threefold denial of fear; so that the tongue would not serve love any less than that which served fear, and it seems that he gave more voices to escape from imminent death than to appreciate present life. He asked, not because he wanted to learn, but to teach him who he left as vicar of his love when he ascended to heaven, since he did not want to entrust his lambs or his sheep, for all of whom he had deigned to die, other than to him whom he knew that he loved him. For this reason he first asks the Shepherd whether he loves him before entrusting him with feeding his flock, so that as fear was shown in denying the Shepherd, so would it also be a positive sign of love to feed the flock. 'If you love me, walk before your brethren, and that ardent love which you have formerly shown me, prove it now by giving your soul for my sheep, as you have said that you would give it for me; for this is the greatest proof you can give me of your love.' If, then, the Shepherd's care is a true sign of love, little would anyone be committed to loving him if, although having virtue and knowledge, refuses to feed them."

Besides love, self-denial and obedience were also needed; and to show it and explain it to Peter, Jesus Christ further said: "When you were younger, not in age but in virtue, strength and resolve owing to which you were weak enough to deny me, you used to gird yourself, and walked and went wherever you desired. But when you grew older, not as much by age as by being aware of your duties, among which is that of the good example you ought to give to your sheep and by firmness and stability in virtue, as you have already proved in your confession, then you will stretch out your hands on a cross and someone else will gird you and take you where you do not want to go; that is to death, which always shuns sensuality and what is willed by nature." It was so that Jesus Christ announced to Peter the kind of death with which he would one day glorify God, suffering it for him and after his example. Saint Augustine says of this: "This situation related to him who had denied and loved, who by boasting had exalted himself, in denying he had fallen, by weeping he had cleansed himself, by confessing he was accepted back, and by suffering he was crowned. With perfect love he died for him for whom he offered to die in a false hurry. It was appropriate that Christ should die before for Peter's salvation, so that Peter should die later owing to his preaching about Christ. Now Peter, you will not fear death, for he whom you wept for as dead, whom by worldly love you hindered from dying for us, now lives. Daring to precede the master, you were afraid of the pursuer; having shed for you the price of your ransom, you will now follow him who has bought you, and you will follow him perfectly until death on a cross. You have already heard the words of him whom you know from experience to have always spoken the truth. He prophesied your denial now prophesies your passion."

Peter was not upset by this preaching. Having greater feelings for the honour of dying on the cross, like the Lord, than for the glory of governing his Church under his orders, he never forgot this important prophecy. So that when he knew that the time of its fulfilment was drawing near, he wrote to the whole Church two Letters full of very important and salutary directions, telling all faithful in the second letter: "My children, it is advisable that I should hasten to exhort and instruct you while I am in this mortal flesh. I am already old, and very soon I will be shedding off the tabernacle of my body, even as Jesus Christ our Lord did for the sake of showing me (2 Pt 1:14)." Jesus Christ had indeed called his apostle apart to speak to him confidentially about this very difficult and interesting matter, that he might be well forewarned; and Peter turning around, he saw that they were being followed by that disciple whom Jesus Christ loved; and so he became curious to know what would be the fate of John, his dear companion. He had not forgotten that during the dinner he had seen him rest his head familiarly on his Master's breast, and that only he among all the apostles had dared to ask him who the traitor was; and not doubting that he would keep his old predilection, he said to him: "What have ye ordained and arranged that should become of him? Do you not also give him the charge of following you?" But just as cloaked as this curiosity seemed to be, he received an answer that shut his mouth completely. "Of what concern is it to you," answered the Lord, "to inquire into what does not involve the exercise of your ministry? I want this beloved disciple to remain as he is until I come? If I have been kind enough to instruct you about what will become of you, you have no right to ask me about what will happen to others. Be content to follow me, and do not seek to know more."

These words of Jesus Christ were insensitively spread among all the brethren: I want this disciple to remain like this until I come; and concluded that the beloved disciple, far from giving his blood for the preaching of the Gospel, would never die. Yet Jesus Christ did not say that he would not die, but that he would not die like Peter. But then, all the interpretations they then gave to the Master's words were dispelled when the heavenly light communicated to the apostles by the Holy Spirit made them infallible interpreters of divine prophecies. And the same one about whom they then spoke is he who has given authentic and written testimony of all these things, and we cannot doubt them because we know that his testimony is true.

CHAPTER 91
JESUS CHRIST ALLOWS ALL HIS APOSTLES AND DISCIPLES TO SEE HIM FOR THE LAST TIME IN JERUSALEM, AND AFTER HAVING CONVERSED AND EATEN WITH THEM HE LEADS THEM TO BETHANY, WHERE BLESSING THEM HE ROSE MAJESTICALLY IN THEIR SIGHT AND WENT UP TO THE HEAVENS WITH HIS OWN VIRTUE AND POWER (MT 16:14-20)

HE day was not far off when the ancient prophets' sayings were to be completely fulfilled, and when all the promises which the divine Saviour had made to his apostles and disciples were to be confirmed. He had explained the mysteries of religion, which they had to preach, more clearly during several times when he appeared to them, yet only within the terms he could use; so that when, as disposed by eternal councils, Jesus Christ had brought it to the necessary degree of perfection, in such manner that none else was needed other than the anointing of the Holy Spirit, he resolved to ascend to heaven; which was from where he had promised to send it to them.

When he last appeared to his disciples in Galilee, he sent them back to Jerusalem. not fearing the violence, outrage and unjust persecutions of the Jews, as help would be always coming from high. He indicated to them the place and the day when he wanted to find them gathered in that place; it was the fortieth after his resurrection; yet he did not hint anything to them about the great event which was about to happen. "It is very plausible," Saint Augustine says, "that in these forty days the Lord appeared more frequently to his Mother, to Mary Magdalene and to the pious women, for the grief and sorrow caused by his passion and death had been so forcefully impressed on them, that they were much more in need of being consoled. And many holy Patriarchs might have accompanied Jesus Christ on these visits, the more so Abraham and David, to whom a special promise had been made of his coming into the world. Many were those who would go to see his most excellent daughter and Mother of the Saviour who for them and for all others had found grace and conceived the Redeemer, although not being seen by the people whom they visited. Oh! with what joy they would look upon that most pure creature, and with what reverence they would bow before her, seeing her to be so dear and beloved by God! Oh, with how much veneration would the knowledge of Jesus Christ's immense love be infused in them; for after so many years of labours and afflictions, after such a cruel, ignominious and harsh death, he was able to return instantly triumphant to the throne of his glory, and from there console and comfort his apostles through his angels' ministry; he wanted to converse familiarly with them for a period of forty days, and to prove to them in many ways and by various methods his resurrection!" About which the Venerable Bede says: "It is well worth that the Lord felt dignified to persuade all of the certainty and truth of such an important mystery by means of many miracles, in order to edify the faith and to uproot the treachery of all hearts. It was for the purpose of making it known that he was present everywhere by his divinity that, wanting to satisfy the desires of all good persons, he appeared so frequently in his body form after he had risen from the dead." And Saint Jerome adds: "He showed immortality to mortals that we may all duly render him thanks, understanding what we were and knowing who we shall be."

Being persuaded and even convinced of Jesus Christ's true resurrection, the apostles returned to Jerusalem according to his instructions, firmly persuaded of his promise being further fulfilled. At about noon on the appointed day, the Lord entered the house in Jerusalem, where the eleven were seated at table awaiting his arrival. Greeting them with his natural and eternal kindness and gentleness, he wished them and gave them peace; and even though some disciples worshipped him only for as long as they saw him, they persisted in their doubts. Although the disciples' delay in believing in Jesus Christ's resurrection greatly benefited and was useful for the whole Church, it always dented them with a very reprehensible and inexcusable fault, considering the repeated promises of his resurrection he had made to them and further confirming them with innumerable miracles. For this reason the Saviour formerly reproved, rebuked and condemned them, but with great prudence he turned their hearts to him, converting them into apostles of faith capable of bringing the light of faith to the ends of the world; and into preachers of the doctrine of salvation and of the holy principles of the Gospel before all tyrants of the universe.

The Lord treated his disciples with the tenderness of a true Father and with all the outpourings of his immense love; so that during the meal he spoke to them familiarly and recalled all the truths he had announced to them, of all the wonders which they had seen, and of all the orders which he had given them. And that they might not forget the great and important mission for which he had chosen them and to which he had destined them, he told them once more: "*Go unto the whole world and preach the Gospel to every creature.* I who am the Almighty King, on whom all the kings of the earth depend and to whom they are subject, I who am the Creator of heaven and earth, so that in this manner all things are mine and I can dispose of them all, I who overcame the armed strong one , and who with one of my ministers destroyed the power of all the tyrants of the universe, and buried horsemen and horses in the hollows of the deep seas; I am the one who tells you to walk along the paths of the world; the mountains will be levelled in your sight, the hills will open your way, the towers and battlements will bow before you, ramparts will be vanquished, and city gates will be rent open for you. Do not fear anything: the universe is mine, go over all of it, this I command you. *Preach the Gospel*: that is, the truth, the holy doctrine in which I have instructed you. Destroy wicked customs, curse lies, condemn unbelief and error. Teach men that the path which leads to life is narrow, but ample and wide that leading to ruin; that the kingdom of heaven is achieved only by self-denial and the cross, not by idle tranquillity and delight. And finally, that the doctrine of Christ crucified goes entirely against that of the world which crucified him. *Preach this to every creature.* To Jew and Gentile, pagan and idol worshipper, and to every nation under the cloak of heaven. Your duty and the ministry with which I entrust you apply to all; so you will serve me as witnesses, as I will narrate with the fidelity of your testimony, and you will experience the faithfulness of my promises."

Whoever believes and is baptised will be saved, and whoever does not believe will be condemned. Salvation is promised to those who believe, damnation to those who fail to believe; for the Lord who forgives wickedness and covers up the opposition of his rebel people, did not retain his anger forever, because he loves mercy. He will go back to having pity on us, destroying our iniquities and casting all our sins into the depths of the sea (Mic 7:18-20). For it is written: "From Zion will he come as Redeemer to those in Jacob who turn away from wickedness" (Is 59:20). "To him all prophets bear witness, that all who believe in him will receive forgiveness of sins through his name" (Acts 10:43). He who confesses the Lord with his mouth, and believes in his heart, that God raised him from the dead, will be saved; for Scripture says: "Whoever believes in him will not be confounded, and whoever calls on the name of the Lord will be saved" (Is 28:16). But how can they invoke him in whom they have not believed? And how could they believe in him, of whom they never heard anything; and how will they hear if there is no one to preach to them? And how would they preach if they were not sent? (Rom 10:14-15) See why the Lord said to his apostles: *Go into all the universe, preach the Gospel to every creature; whoever believes and is baptised will be saved, and whoever does not believe will be condemned.* "Yet it should be advised," Saint Gregory says, "that perhaps someone will say within himself that as he already believes, so he will be saved. He is saying something true, but the works should be according to his faith; for faith is that which does not contradict with deeds what words affirm, and practises with deeds that same thing in which it believes. That is why James said: "What does it profit, my brethren, for a person to say he has faith but does not have works? Could by chance faith save this person? Just as the body is dead without the spirit, so also is faith dead without good works" (Jas 2:14-17).

So that then it might be known who were those who had a living and true faith, the Saviour added: "I will grant these men the power to perform miracles, with which they will cast out in my name demons from bodies; speak tongues they never knew; kill the most poisonous serpents and dragons; any poison they give them to drink will not harm them, however deadly it might be, and by only laying their hands on the sick all diseases will be healed. These miracles are promised to those having a living faith." The Lord deposits his almightiness in the hands of whoever possesses this most precious virtue and trusts in the word of God, and he will confirm to him all that he asks of him through the virtue and efficacy of his holy name. "Understanding these miracles in a spiritual sense. they are no less admirable than when they are played on the lyre," Saint Gregory says. Every day the Church performs spiritually what it then did physically, these miracles being so much greater than those, as they move from the spirit to the body. Physical miracles usually show holiness, but they do not cause it. Spiritual miracles do not denote the virtue of life, but they cause grace. All the miracles that Jesus Christ foretold, were wrought in the primitive Church by the apostles and by other enlightened men who believed with lively and ardent faith, not only to convert unbelievers, but to cast deeper roots in the faith for those who already believed, conforming them in it with new miracles; for that faith would have already taken root and grown, so that there was no more need for these miracles to be now done as often as they used to be wrought; for it would be enough only to read and hear what had happened, and to receive it with full and true faith. If you ask, however, why do not contemporary preachers and the faithful now work miracles as they were then wrought, the answer is, as Saint Gregory himself says, that since the Catholic faith has already been sufficiently proven by the miracles of Christ and of his apostles, there is no need for further miracles or wonders to be repeated after those. For just as plants are often watered after they have been planted to take root, but after sprouting they no longer need so much watering, so also after Christian faith was planted throughout the world and it took deep root being watered with the blood of the apostles, who confirmed their faith and the preaching of their doctrine by the miracles they worked, new ones need not now be repeated. However, it cannot be denied that in all times God has worked them to console the true faithful; for the unbelievers always find specious and apparent motives to contradict or deny them, and to seek the sting of death and eternal damnation, wherefrom others draw hope for their salvation and for their life.

Jesus Christ was still eating with his apostles when, like the prudent master he was, knowing he will be absent from his house for a long time, arranged and ordered his servants even as to the smallest and most insignificant details. He wanted all to keep going on, while he is away. with the greatest accord and harmony between them. So he commanded them not to depart from Jerusalem, but to wait there for the Father's promise to be fulfilled: "You have heard of it from my mouth," he told them, "for indeed, John baptised with water, but you will be baptised in the Holy Spirit within a few days." The Lord was definitively and clearly showing the apostles the designs of his will; for just as he had spent his whole life in the great work entrusted to him by his Father, so he also sought that in that of his apostles and disciples there should neither be an empty instant, nor a vain word, neither a useless step, nor anything that should disregard the highness, importance, and dignity of their ministry, after they had received the Holy Spirit; for they had already seen perfectly formed the indestructible chain which was to serve as their reinforcement to raise the magnificent building of the Church, which was to last until the consummation of all times. They had, in the same manner, seen the prophecies fulfilled, the Scriptures explained, the apparitions repeated and the great mysteries, which had been hitherto secret and hidden, announced; their public revelation had to deserve the persecution, torments and death with which they would be martyred and crowned. Yet when the Holy Spirit comes they would receive from him the strength necessary to carry on their task, in spite of the fierce obstinacy of their adversaries, and likewise the spirit of wisdom to confound the spirit of those who were wise and cautious in the ways of the world; for trusting in their cunning and subtleties, they disregarded the humble credulity of the little ones. And finally he showed them that John's baptism was none else but a preparatory sacrament and that a public profession was made through its penance; yet still a purely significant profession of faith in the Messiah who was still hidden; and the sanctity of Christian baptism, which was a sanctifying sacrament by faith, obliging us to follow the Gospel wholeheartedly, and which by representing the death and resurrection Jesus Christ's, applies its virtue and merits to us.

Some of those who were present there, animated even by coarse and earthly hopes, dared to ask him: "Lord, you speak of going up into heaven and leaving us, yet o console us you make great promises to us. Could this be the time when you will restore the glory of the kingdom of Israel, and the independence and freedom of your nation?" Jesus Christ knew well that in a few days his disciples would not be speaking this language; and he was content to tell them: "It is not for you to know the time and events, the knowledge of which my Father has kept reserved to Himself, and of which He will make use according to His power." It was like telling them: "You have no right to know future events whose purpose is the restoration of that kingdom you are asking about. God precisely keeps these things for Himself to dispose of them as He wills. You ask for a worldly, temporary and earthly restitution, but only my Father knows whether it will take place in this manner, or whether it will be a spiritual restitution, when near the end of the ages the Jews will believe in Christ, who was their King, yet they crucified Him. So that it is not up to you to investigate these secrets, but you should only try asking about what really concerns you, as it is a very punishable boldness wanting to scrutinise God's doings to satisfy human curiosity. You will receive the virtue of the Holy Spirit who will come upon you, and with it you will be purified and strengthened, that you may utter my words and spread my doctrines throughout the whole world. This almighty virtue, manifesting the emanation of God, will move you towards other men, and you will be able to serve me as witnesses in Jerusalem, Judea and Samaria, and to the far ends of the world."

Oh! And how wonderful are God's mercies! How great and incomprehensible the designs of His Providence! Jerusalem, Jerusalem, a fateful theatre of so many atrocities, outrages and sacrilegious excesses, was also to become within a few days a place of God's majesty and greatness; although owing to the stoning of Stephen and the death of James, the apostles had to leave it abruptly to go to preach to the outer limits of Judea, then to Samaria, and then to the very end of the world. Who would believe it! Will Peter be the first harbinger of the glory of his resurrection before those same ones who crucified him? Ought not Peter to tremble now being the same apostle who, at the sight of an ill-favoured woman, trembled and denied Jesus Christ? Thomas! Should that same Thomas, who did not want to believe in him until he touched him with his own hand, be one of Peter's companions and preach Christ's greatness and glory before the Synagogue? Will it be the apostles, who all ran away and hid on the night of Jesus Christ' passion, who will go out together on the same day and hour of their exiting the Upper Room and passing through Jerusalem's most public streets and squares announce the splendour of the Crucified One? Is it them who will travel through distant provinces and kingdoms to spread the fruits of this same passion, happy to be mocked and punished in the world's courts for having borne witness to the truth? Truly, this is the work of God's finger; this is the change which produced the virtue of the right hand of the Most Sublime.

The beautiful and elegant pictures that the prophet Isaiah portrayed so early and with such precision in chapter 53 were now fully fulfilled. Who has believed or will believe our news? And to whom has this Messiah, the Lord's arm or virtue, been revealed? He will grow in the eyes of the people like a humble plant, and sprout like a root in the arid earth. We saw him; and though he was neither handsome nor beautiful, but disfigured, he nevertheless stole our feelings. Let us see him despised, a man of sorrows and as if having a face covered with shame and distress, reputed as a leper, wounded by the hand of God and humiliated; bruised by our iniquities and torn to pieces by our wickedness; offered in sacrifice, for he willed it to be so himself, he did not open his mouth to complain; he was led to death without putting up any resistance; like a sheep being taken to the slaughter, he kept silent in the presence of his executioners like a mute tender lamb is before a farmhand wanting to shear it; and who after being oppressed was lifted on high. But as to your generation, who can explain it? He has been uprooted from the land of the living: "I have wounded him for the atonement of my people," says the Lord. And in reward for descending into the grave God will grant him the conversion of the wicked: he will have the rich man for the price of his death, because he did not commit sin, nor did he ever utter any deception in his words. After he offers his life as a host for sin, he will see long and lasting offspring, and through them the will of the Lord will be accomplished. He will see the fruit of the cares of his soul and he will be appeased: this same *Righteous One*, my servant, will justify many with his doctrine, and will bear their sins upon himself. Wherefore, I will give him as his portion or inheritance a great multitude of nations; and he will distribute the spoils of the strong, because he gave his life to death, and was mistaken as being wicked, and took upon himself all of man's sins, beseeching for his transgressors.

Compare this chapter of Isaiah with all the sacred life, passion and death of Jesus Christ. Let us compare the last words spoken by the Saviour to his apostles, *And you shall be witnesses to me in Jerusalem, and in all Judea and Samaria, and even to the farthest reaches of the earth*, with those uttered by the prophet about eight hundred years before Jesus Christ came into the world, *the Just One will justify many with his doctrine, and I will give it, make as its portion and inheritance a great multitude of nations, and divide the spoils of the strong*. Then let us compare with one prophecy and the other the far reaches and dominion of the Church, the object of both, throughout the whole universe; the irresistible power which it exercises in the hearts of true believers; the rapid progress it has made in its beginning and that made in the succession of times, in spite of the horrendous persecutions of tyrants, of the heretics' abominable blasphemies, and of the war without rest or truce which hell has made on it; and we shall see whether these prophecies have from their beginning, or have to this day, or shall until the end of the world, be duly fulfilled. By what misfortune should unbelievers not read the holy books? By what destiny should they not take the work of confronting predictions with occurring events, and those happening right now, to justify the holiness of the Church and the divinity of the adorable religion of the Crucified One? What a fall! What shame and humiliation to the strong spirited men, to the world's wise and conceited ones, not to be able to destroy the work which the heavenly Master entrusted to such poor fishermen, always sustaining the small and the weak against the desperate rage of the powerful and the strong? See things as they really are, even for once and for the peace and salvation of peoples and nations; they so often say they wish to lay down their foolish disbelief, and enter in good faith on the straight and sure path which religion designs for them, wanting to ensure unfading happiness.

As soon as the Lord finished speaking those words which were so consoling for his apostles and for the whole Church, he arose and led his beloved company to the whereabouts of Bethania, to a certain place on the Mount of Olives, a mountain of the saddest and most glorious memories. Then, stretching out his hand over them to bless them, he was gently lifted up before their eyes, until they imperceptibly lost sight of him, and as a cloud hid him he ascended to the highest of the heavens; and with acclamations from all the heavenly hosts he went to take a seat at the right hand of the Father. Never has such a great and admirable spectacle been seen in the world. The King of glory had brought to an end the great quest for which he had been sent by his Eternal Father. By dying in a very tough fight, he conquered the infernal prince who had abrogated the power of the world. He not only snatched away the sceptre from his hand, but also those righteous souls who groan as if in harsh captivity; he took them out of Hades and carried them as trophies of his triumph to his Father's kingdom; and the heavenly princes, the sublime powers, the most high dominations and all the virtues of heaven went forth to receive him. Seeing such majesty and greatness, they could not but cry out and say: "Lift up, oh princes, your gates, and raise yourselves high, oh gates of eternity, that the king of glory may enter, the Lord who is strong and mighty in battles, the Lord of hosts, he who is the King of Glory" (Ps 24:9-10).

The apostles, who neither had the wisdom, nor the purity or nobility of that spirit, but whom the spirit of God wanted to inspire with the greatest and utmost sublimeness which any creature ever had on earth and who, having been left in a state of holy contemplation, were unable to prepare themselves to receive it, saw beside them two angels. They appeared like humans, wearing white robes, and they said to them: "Men of Galilee, what are you doing here looking towards heaven? This Jesus Christ, your Saviour and our God, who has just ascended in your presence, will return some day, as he has prophesied to you." Oh, if only we kept in mind this precious moment when Christ ascended to take possession of all prerogatives at the right hand of His Eternal Father! He rose to fulfil with his own faithfulness all the prophecies, to fill our hearts with his Spirit, the whole Church with his gifts, earth with the greatness of his name and heaven with his glory and presence; for hell was already confounded and subdued with his power, and the world with the testimony of his words and preaching, of his miracles and mysteries. Once speaking with Nicodemus, he had so surely declared the mystery of his glorious ascension into heaven that he depicted it as an event which had already occurred, saying: "No one has ascended into heaven except he who descended from heaven, namely the Son of Man who is in heaven" (Jn 3:13). When, after multiplying the loaves and fishes, he taught his disciples the adorable mystery of transubstantiation in the Holy Eucharist, and some of them were scandalised, did he not say to them: "Does this offend you or scandalise you? For what will you do when you see the Son of Man ascend to where he once was" (Jn 6:62-63)? And on the night of his trial on being asked by the high priest to say whether he was Christ, the Son of the living God, did he not answer him: "I still tell you, that in a short time you will see the Son of Man seated at the right hand of God the Almighty and coming upon the clouds of heaven" (Mt 26:64)?

And above all, did he not say to his apostles very clearly and precisely: "I have departed from the Father and come into the world; now I leave the world and return again to the Father. Because I have told you these things, your heart has been filled with sorrow; but I tell you the truth: It would be better for you that I should go, for if I do not go the Comforter will not come to you; but if I go, I will send him to you. That Comforter, the Holy Spirit, whom the Father will send in my name, will teach you all that which I have said to you. When the Spirit of truth, who proceeds from the Father, comes, he will bear witness to me and teach you all truth" (Jn 14–16)?

As the angels appeared again, as in almost all mysteries of the Son of God, and as they will also appear at his second coming, they reminded the apostles that they had to comply with their duties, those who had worshipped Jesus Christ with utmost humility for the second time, then left the mountain very joyfully and locked themselves in the house where they were staying since arriving in the city. Saint Luke carefully refers to the names of the eleven who gathered, and we are told that they were: Peter, head of all, John, James, Andrew, Philip, Thomas, Bartholomew, Matthew, James, son of Alphaeus, Simon, also known as the Zealot, and Judas, son of James (Acts 1:13; they retired to that house only going out to the temple, preparing themselves as observant Jews for the celebration of the Pentecost Festivity; so that neither their being together nor their very presence would cause any misgivings to the Synagogue members and to the unbelieving Jews. They prayed continuously and with exceeding earnestness beseeching the Lord, in a single and conforming voice, to fulfil his promises. The Mother of Jesus presided over and authorised these acts of adoration and love of the Church in its infancy which, with no less fervent hope, were attended by the holy and pious women and those who called themselves Jesus' relatives. It would be much easier to know, and even understand, than to explain the consolations and interior sweetness with which the Lord would encourage them in that retreat, placed under the protection and tutelage of his most holy and pure Mother. And the Lord knowing too well that most of those persons were still weak, timid and also little enlightened as to what was being said about them being the founders of the new Church and the first heroes of Christianity, it must accordingly be confessed that it was only with the Lord's help, who knew all needs and distributed all consolations, knowing them well and being the only One who could come to their aid and fill them with all they needed to remain calm and firm until the Spirit of strength and love would descend upon them, that they later came out of the Upper Room announcing to Jerusalem, Judea and the whole world, the glorious triumph of him who had been crucified, confirming their preaching and doctrine with wonders and miracles.

If the children of Israel, Moses and his sister Mary, after passing through the desert of Shur, sang a song of praise to the Lord to enliven people's hearts and excite them to a most sincere gratitude and a most fervent thanksgiving to the great God who had redeemed and saved them from the harsh slavery of Egypt; how could the Christian and faithful people, having been redeemed and saved by Jesus Christ from the most harsh slavery of hell and condemnation to eternal death, to which he had come and crossed over the Red Sea by his passion and death, having seen him ascend triumphant and victorious into heaven taking with him the captive masses held by the prince of darkness, now not hear in heaven anything but the most sonorous and harmonious song of praise being unceasingly repeated? *"Worthy is the Lamb who was sacrificed to receive power, and divinity, and wisdom, and strength, and honour, and glory, and blessing.* And all creatures which are in heaven, on earth and under the earth, and those abiding the sea, and as many as there are in all places, all together repeated: *To him who sits on the throne and to the Lamb, blessing, and honour, and glory, and power forever and ever"* (Apoc. 5:12-13). *The kingdom of this world has become the kingdom of our Lord and of his Christ; and sin having now been destroyed, he will reign for ever and ever. Amen* (Apoc. 11:15). It is right, truly meet and just, that all of us, who were redeemed with the blood of this same Lamb, all of us who have been called by baptism to the high dignity of his children and heirs of his kingdom; and so all members of this Holy Church, keepers of his precious body and blood, and of the infinite merits of his sacrificial passion and death, which are communicated to us through the Sacraments; let us also call upon this Church by conclusion of this our little and insignificant work, in profession of our most sincere gratitude and recognition, and in thanksgiving of the great and immense mercies which he has used with us out of his kindness; with the same song with which the King Psalmist described his admirable ascension into heaven, prophesied the vocation of the Gentiles and desired to inflame the hearts of all creatures with the most sublime and enthusiastic affections of joy and gratitude.

All peoples of the universe, all nations of the earth, clap and applaud the Lord's triumph; sing joyfully to God hymns of joy, worship and praise with joyful voices. For the Lord is exalted and terrible, he is seated above the Cherubim and makes all his ministers like flames of blazing fire. He is the great King over all the earth; he is the King of kings, the immortal King of the ages, and whose supreme will cannot be countered. Being bound to enlarge and give dominion to his Church, he fulfilled his promise faithfully, and subdued peoples to it, setting nations at its feet. He chose the apostles to be his heirs; a beautiful portion of Jacob, whom he had loved, and all who came after them in belief unto the ends of the world and until the end of all times. God ascended to heaven, from where he came to redeem us, accompanied by thousands of saints, among voices of happiness and joy and to the sound of sonorous trumpets. Sing praise to our King, peoples of the earth! Since God is King of all earth, sing psalms wisely to Him. God, seated on his holy throne, must reign over all nations. Oh, indeed, the happy day will come; the desired and auspicious day will come when the princes of the Gentile and idolatrous peoples will lay down their errors, and the unbelievers and heretics their blindness and obstinacy; they will be reunited with the God of Abraham; they will enter into the bosom of the Holy Church, peace will be made throughout the earth by the irresistible force of His grace, there will only be one flock and one shepherd, for our God is the God who protects the earth, and who has been greatly exalted. Hasten remarkably, oh Lord, this time, banish from among us the spirit of turbulence and error, and grant to this faithful nation, and to all those who were reborn and regenerated with the salutary waters of baptism, the spirit of faith, love and peace, so that united together with these holy bonds we may come to form your true people on earth, and on departing, let us ascend to enjoy your most loved company with that of your Holy Mother and all the angels and saints which are in your happy and eternal kingdom. Amen.

ABOUT THE TRANSLATOR

DESCRIBING HIMSELF AS A CARTHUSIAN AT heart and a Jesuit in spirit and action, Victor Cauchi was born in 1950 on the island where St Paul was shipwrecked some two thousand years ago. Malta has always been seen as a bastion of the Catholic faith and a cultural crossroad between Byzantine and Latin Christianity after a short brush with Islam.

After receiving a Jesuit education for eight years, the translator was for a time a postulant with the Carthusians at the Order's novitiate at the Farneta Charterhouse in Lucca, Italy. Trained as a lawyer he has worked as a solicitor in private practice since 1974, joining government service at Malta's Attorney General's Office in 1983 where he served until retirement in 2011. His verve for translation was mainly induced in 1985 with the translation of local legislation from English to Maltese and vice-versa.

As the need for a well organised team of permanent translators grew in view of Malta's accession to the European Union, he was entrusted with supervising the translation into Maltese of the voluminous EU *acquis communautaire* and the Union's case-law. He attended various conferences at the time in EU countries on the subject.

His flair for translations into English from Italian and Spanish, as well as Latin and Middle English, started about his reaching pension age and he has to date translated further works of a spiritual nature, like the *Discourses of Isaiah of Schetis*, into Maltese. He has also had a brush with writing a novel and playwriting. Steeped in Catholic church movements, he has been married for over forty years to Marie Therese and they have one daughter, Rebekah.

www.ingramcontent.com/pod-product-compliance
Lightning Source LLC
Chambersburg PA
CBHW030243010526
44107CB00030B/1319/J